The Russian Context

The Culture behind the Language

To Ken Nalibow –
who was there at
the very beginning.

Eliot Jr. Bagle

10 February 2003

THE RUSSIAN CONTEXT

THE CULTURE BEHIND THE LANGUAGE

EDITED BY

ELOISE M. BOYLE &
GENEVRA GERHART

Bloomington, Indiana, 2002

SLAVICA

Technical Editors: Jennifer J. Day, Andrea Rossing McDowell, Yvonne
                    Wittman, Michael Yadroff

Library of Congress Cataloging-in-Publication Data

The Russian context : the culture behind the language / edited by Eloise M. Boyle and
Genevra Gerhart.
        p. cm.
Includes bibliographical references and index.
ISBN 0-89357-287-X (pbk./CD ROM)
1. Language and culture—Russia (Federation) 2. Russia (Federation)—Civilization. I.
Boyle, Eloise M. II. Gerhart, Genevra.
P35.5.R9 R87 2002
306.44'0947—dc21

Library of Congress Control Number: 2002002613
ISBN: 0-89357-287-X

Slavica Publishers   [Tel.] 1-812-856-4186
Indiana University   [Toll-free] 1-877-SLAVICA
2611 E. 10th St.   [Fax] 1-812-856-4187
Bloomington, IN 47408-2603   [Email] slavica@indiana.edu
USA   [www] http://www.slavica.com/

Table of Contents   Содержа́ние

Foreword   Предисло́вие

Barry P. Scherr

While there are obvious differences between the two, it is impossible to read
The Russian Context without thinking of its predecessor, Genevra Gerhart's
The Russian's World—one of those rare books that are both so original in concept that they seem to create their own genre and so remarkably useful that it
soon becomes difficult to imagine how one ever got along without them.The
book has become a favorite among those who have used it over the years in
large part because it simply filled a huge need by bringing together widely scat-
tered and often hard-to-obtain information in a manner that is clear, concise,
and lively. In no other single source could students find out the interior layout
of peasant huts, how to read a mathematical formula out loud, what Russians
call playing cards, the names of common insects, how a Russian samovar works,
and the social significance of specific names in the years before the Bolshevik
revolution.

And, I must confess, it is not just students who have benefited from *The
Russian's World*. As a person for whom a sturgeon is a sturgeon is a sturgeon,
and who does not like rushing to an encyclopedia while engrossed in a story or
a novel, it was only after perusing this book that I understood the difference between *beluga* and *osёtr*. The picture of a *drozhki* gave me a much better sense
than I had before as to how it differed from the enclosed *kareta*. The revelations did not just apply to Russian realia; sad to say, it was not until I came
across the informative chart that concludes Chapter 1 (Chapter 2 in the second
edition) that I finally realized just how a person is related to a "second cousin
once removed."

In *The Russian Context* Eloise Boyle and Genevra Gerhart continue the
tasks of the earlier work, but they have shifted the emphasis somewhat, from a
focus on daily life to exploring the realms of society and culture. The authors of
the various chapters all attempt to provide the kind of "general knowledge"
that informs the use of language and the perception of the outside world on the
part of any native speaker. James West's chapter on "Art and the Language of
Russian Culture," where he shows how cartoons in the popular press regularly
rely upon images from famous Russian works of art, effectively illustrates just
why it is necessary to possess such knowledge. Early in that chapter he discusses
several cartoons which refer to Repin's painting of Ivan the Terrible, in which
the horror-stricken tsar clutches the head of his son, whom he has just
murdered. In the first of the cartoons a museum visitor rushes by that very
painting, afraid that "Next thing you know, you'll be involved as a witness." It

would enrich a person's understanding of the cartoon to know that it is making use of an extremely famous by painting by one of the best-known Russian artists of all time; in this case, though, the basic humor is probably accessible even to someone who had never heard of Repin, since the bloody scene shown on the canvas and the widespread fear of getting involved already get the point across. However, what would one make of the next cartoon, showing one hockey player cradling the head of another after (apparently) striking him with a stick? Ivan the Terrible is mentioned in the cartoon as the culprit about to receive all of a two-minute penalty, and that would only be all the more confusing to the poor non-Russian who might be quite familiar with hockey fights and could even be aware that Ivan the Terrible was a Russian tsar, but who knows nothing about Repin's painting. Such a reader would remain mystified by the cartoon. Why this strange pose? Did Ivan the Terrible really play hockey? It is easy to imagine a non-native figuring out the precise linguistic meaning of the Russian caption and still missing the entire cultural resonance that is responsible for nearly all of the effect.

Thus the ability to comprehend what one reads or hears requires a knowledge not just of the language, but of cultural referents called forth by various words and phrases, The "Russian context," like that for any language or society, is infinitely rich and varied; in a way, it may be even more difficult to become "fluent" in a language's context than in the language itself, but this volume will provide readers with an excellent start.

Part of that context consists simply of factual knowledge, of knowing the geography, the history, and the political structure of the country. These days, following the breakup of the Soviet Union, much has changed in terms of both the administrative units within Russia and the political structure, and the reader will find up-to-date information on both topics. History is presumably a more stable element, though as William Comer reminds us in the political joke that he quotes, in Russia even the past, particularly during the Soviet era, has been subject to change, depending on just who is writing about it. Still, historical references abound in newspapers, in films, in literature, and for that matter in everyday exchanges. The opening chapter, "Russia's History," contains just what its title promises—information which is absorbed by Russians simply from having grown up in the country. It offers, in a no-nonsense, almost outline form, the historical background that provides an essential part of the context within which the language is used.

But the requisite knowledge extends beyond the major historical events and figures to cultural history as well—to the artists, writers, composers, performers and film directors who have shaped the sensibilities of the nation, and as well to their more notable creative efforts. The historical overview that forms a part of each of the chapters on the arts turns out to be important not just for providing the names of artists and their works, but also for providing another essential part of the context: a sense of the chronology and of the varying influences that helped determine the directions of Russian culture.

Also important is an awareness of specific places that are a part of every educated person's vocabulary, and in this regard certain sections of *The Russian Context* can serve as a useful guide to those visiting Russia. Thus the chapter "Geography" includes information about the major sites in Moscow and St. Petersburg, and discusses a number of areas throughout the country that are well-known to every Russian. The chapter on "Theater in Language" contains comments about the major theaters in Moscow and St. Petersburg, rekindling memories of my own first trip to Russia, when a Moscow teacher took a couple of hours to offer a brief synopsis of the city's drama scene. I suddenly realized that in Moscow one did not just choose which play to see but gave equally (or more) serious consideration to the theater and the director. And that too turns out to be part of the Russian context.

But this volume is ultimately concerned with a language and its mutual interactions with culture. I have said that *The Russian's World* is not a language primer, and the same is true of *The Russian Context*. And yet in many vital ways it is truly *about* language. On the most basic level, in every chapter and virtually on every page, one will find useful vocabulary. Those with a serious interest in music can quickly learn the basic terminology they will need to discuss musical notation or to talk about instruments. Scientists will find an enormously valuable introduction to the scientific lexicon and how it is constructed. The chapter on science also offers a historical perspective, with insights into the manner that scientific language has evolved over the years, discussions of how scientific imagery spread among the intelligentsia in late nineteenth-century Russia and found its way into literary discourse, and observations on the manner in which after the Bolshevik revolution technical terms came to be employed with far greater frequency in both ideological and cultural contexts.

Thus the interest here is not just in vocabulary, but in the way that language itself has become part of the cultural fabric, and nowhere is this phenomenon more in evidence than in the sayings and phrases that have entered the language. As the chapter on proverbs illustrates, the differences between the clusters of sayings found in two languages can say much about broader cultural distinctions; while many Russian proverbs will be readily understandable to speakers of English (and may even read like direct translations from one language into the other), others require a familiarity with Russian customs, often from the distant past. And, since Russian sayings, like those in English, are often only partially quoted or are modified to fit a particular situation, understanding the point a speaker is trying to make often requires the ability to recognize the underlying proverb. Toward this end the chapter's appendix, which lists over 200 of the more widely used proverbs sorted by difficulty, will prove especially valuable for many.

The sayings that have their origins in literary allusions tend to be still more culture-specific and more difficult for the non-native speaker to recognize. Even (especially) children's literature is important in this regard, since nearly everyone of a particular generation will share similar experiences in terms of the fairy tales, songs, poems and literary works that were part of their youthful years. References to these items appear frequently in newspapers and in spoken conversation, but the non-native is likely to be less familiar with them than with works of "high" literature. If virtually every adult Russian today knows the children's poetry of Chukovskii and Marshak, the same can hardly be said of those who have learned Russian as a second language. To deal with this lacuna, Robert Rothstein and Halina Weiss, in their chapter on children's literature, provide a generous selection of Russian children's songs and rhymes, describe the best known folk tales, and mention or quote from the most significant works of children's literature.

Two other chapters offer a wealth of literary quotations and references, items that, again, will be familiar to most Russians. The sheer number of phrases from Pushkin show the degree to which entire lines from his works have simply become a part of the language, almost as readily usable (and recognizable) as the individual words that comprise the quotations. Similarly, among prose writers it is the very titles of Gogol's works or the names of his characters that have entered into the lexicon. It is not necessarily the greatest of the writers, though, who have most enriched the language; the fables of Krylov are quoted nearly as often as the works of Pushkin, and the mere mention of "a swan, a crayfish and a pike" is immediately evocative to any Russian. Arguably the most amazing work of all in this regard turns out to be a play by an author virtually unknown to general audiences outside Russia: Griboedov's *Woe from Wit*. In addition to the names of the characters, several dozen quotations from the play (listed in the chapter on theater) are readily recognizable to Russians. The student of the language who comes across the concluding words of that play ("What will Princess Maria Alekseevna say!") in another context and who is not aware of the source (or of the fact that they imply adherence to a hypocritical morality) will be just as much at a loss as the person who looks at the cartoon based on Repin's painting without knowing the original work.

Like its predecessor, *The Russian Context* offers delightful browsing. Such readers may find themselves learning about political administrative units in post-Soviet Russia at one moment, finding out who have been the leading performers of modern popular music at the next, and at a third gaining familiarity with some of the language's most significant literary quotations. At the same time, it more than repays intensive study, and offers an unduplicated collection of valuable information for the serious student of Russian. In either case, whether examined casually or studied intensively, *The Russian Context* will guide each person toward a deeper understanding of the language and the culture.

Editors' Preface

Eloise M. Boyle and Genevra Gerhart

These are essays on how Russian culture finds its life in the language, and how the Russian language finds its life in the culture. To know another country's culture, one has to know the language of that culture, or serious misunderstandings can arise. A famous example of this occurred in the 1950's, when the American public, already suspicious of the Soviet Union, was whipped into an anti-Soviet frenzy by a remark made by Nikita Khrushchev. Khrushchev said, **«Мы вас похороним»**, which was translated in the United States as "We will bury you," and this led to even more dire Cold War tension. The actual translation of the sentence is something like, "We will say funeral rites over you," in other words, we Soviet Communists will be around long after you capitalists have lived out your time. One sentence, one mistranslation, years of misunderstanding.

If language is more than words, is in fact a symbolic process wherein the speaker and listener are each engaged in sharing both that which is spoken and that which is simply assumed as in evidence by both, then a non-native, in order to truly participate in conversation, must learn the basic symbols (assumptions) that are the givens of communication For there *is* a body of information that "everyone knows" and refers to, even if it is a little fuzzy on the edges.

In 1996 nine people agreed to take a particular part in a major project. The aim was to write down Russian common knowledge in Arts and Letters very broadly conceived, and specifically as evidenced in the language. It must be emphasized that the knowledge of a specialist is not the information presented here. We looked for the information most educated Russians have about their world, and their attitudes toward it. What emerged is common knowledge, that is, the knowledge about the world expected of an educated Russian – a linguistic definition that applies both to the people and the culture in which they live. If the American must know "Play it again, Sam" and "Frankly, my dear, I don't give a damn," in addition to "To be, or not to be," what must the standard literate Russian know? What proverbs are regularly used? Which fables are referred to? What takes the place of Jack and the Beanstalk? We in the United States have definite mental (and sound) pictures of the Middle West, the Southwest, the Northeast, the South. How does the Russian divide Russia, and how are the divisions characterized? The intent is not to show the full range of possible information on a topic, but rather the limits of *expected* knowledge, what one must know to understand the culture. This project was too large to be accomplished by one or two human beings, and so this group was formed to try a major attempt at the impossible. The authors included in this volume used research, personal insight, conversation, cajoling, argument, in short all the tools at their disposal to come up with the impressive amount of information you now hold in your hands. The editors of this work are eternally indebted to all our fine writers for their efforts on your behalf.

The method of research varied from author to author, but one approach was supposed to be common to all: numerous Russians of various generations were interviewed, and the authors solicited Russian opinion about what is generally familiar to most people. Sasha Prokhorov (Science) took his efforts to (among other places) both a beach in Russia and a train station in Moscow, where he asked people from all walks of life about their knowledge of scientific facts and myths. But to discover what is obvious, or accepted, or understood by another group of people is not so easy as it might seem, therefore this book is an approximation: sometimes more information than is necessary is presented, sometimes less. All but four of the authors are not native speakers of Russian, and there exists an obvious gap in our knowledge. We need not apologize. This is a first attempt. There will be omissions of truth and commissions of error.

The Accompanying CD-ROM

A CD-ROM accompanies the book. It contains entire quotations read in Russian by Russians, as well as innumerable pictures to render the visual context of the language, and music that reveals something of the Russian psyche. Used together, the book and the CD-ROM arm the reader with the background necessary to follow Russian conversations. When you finally laugh at the same jokes the Russians find amusing, when a painting recalls to your mind a fact of history or passage of literature, when a song stirs up melancholy in your soul, you will know you have absorbed Russian common knowledge. The CD also incorporates the list of sources for both the book and the CD.

Before trying out the CD-ROM for the first time, the reader is advised to read Appendix 5 on using the CD. In order to get started on the book, however, it is enough to note that illustrations and sound clips included on the CD are labeled in the margins of the books, with the icons ▓ and ◀)) or ♪, respectively, and a number such as "12-41" which corresponds to the CD file.

On Transliteration from the Russian

We tried diligently to follow what seemed a reasonable plan: the basic system for transliterating would be the Library of Congress (LC) system (see Appendixes) since the major use of this book would be at universities. However, the chapter on Geography would use the Board of Geographic Names (BGN) system, partly because its use is more logical there, and partly as a demonstration of how the two differ. And finally, we agreed that famous names that have become part of English would remain there, for example, Tolstoy, not Tolstoi, and the like.

Acknowledgments

The editors have many people to thank. This was an enormous effort, and we truly needed help. Eloise Boyle is indebted to Tatiana Smorodinskaya, Middlebury College, Galya Diment and Zoya Polack, University of Washington, Hugh D. Hudson, Jr., Georgia State University, and The Russian and East European Center at the University of Illinois, Urbana-Champaign, and especially the Slavic Librarians there. A very special thank you to my husband and sons, who supported me mightily in this project.

Genevra Gerhart thanks her long-suffering husband, James, for the huge gift of time, and quantities of money that made her contribution possible. And many thanks to Diane Camber for patiently dealing with a computer, two alphabets and an old lady, all at the same time. Special thanks to friends at the English School No. 1239 in downtown Moscow, Natalia and Vladimir Bagramyants in Moscow, and Lyudmila and Vladimir Leontyev in St. Petersburg. I am richer for knowing them.

Both editors wish to thank the many Russians who acted both as sources and reviewers: especially the professors Vera Khokhlova and Oleg Sapozhnikov from Moscow State University, and Tatiana Zolotareva, a professional copy editor, now of Seattle. Others helped with particular chapters and include Vera Brekhovskikh from Moscow; and Julia Tolmacheva and Andrei Yusov of Seattle. We are grateful to the many who read chapters early on, including: Nancy Condee, University of Pittsburgh; William Derbyshire; Gerard Ervin; Ben Rifkin, University of Wisconsin; Sandra Rosengrant, Portland State University; Barry Scherr, Dartmouth College; and Marina Tolmacheva, Washington State University. Alina Israeli, American University, and Olga Kagan, UCLA, plowed through the entire manuscript and provided much valuable advice and many helpful suggestions. Lindsay Johnston (MLIS University of Alberta) aided us by finding and annotating all those web sites relating to Geography. Larry Lesage of the University of Washington's Language Learning Center engineered the recording of some of the materials heard on the CD. Professor Dmitri Khokhlov of Moscow University aided in the acquisition of music. Thanks to Professor Yuri Tolmachev of St. Petersburg University for supplying the fine voice in the military commands. The recordings for History, Children's Literature, and Science were read by Tatiana Zolotareva. Valentina Zaitseva recorded the passages in Poetry and Prose. Proverbs and parts of Theater were read by Valentina Troufanova. Elizabeth Ginzburg of the University of Chicago helped us with some music, Vladimir Padunov of the University of Pittsburgh helped with some entertainment, Henry Hale of Harvard University helped with political parties, and Paula Sapienza supplied the picture of the clock that decorates the Puppet Theater in Moscow.

Words are not sufficient to express our deep gratitude to Jennifer Day at Slavica Publishers without whom quite literally this book would not have seen the light of day. Her Herculean efforts on our behalf produced the volume you hold in your hands right now. We also thank George Fowler at Slavica for his advice, comments and technical help along the way, not to mention his willingness to assemble a CD.

The authors, too, have people they wish to thank. William Comer acknowledges David Shengold, Maria Kipp, Yaroslava Tsiovkh, Galina Griffiths, Tatiana Spektor, and Irina Prokhorova for reading the manuscript and consulting on the content.

Thomas Garza wishes to thank Elena Lifschitz (University of Texas, Austin), Tatiana Tsivjan (Institute of Balkan and Slavic Studies, Moscow), Natalja Tokareva (Moscow State Linguistic University), Igor' Garanin and Yurij Gariyev (Moscow State Linguistic University).

Material for Lawrence Mansour's chapter was collected from extensive interviews with Natalia and Sasha Ivanov; and with Maria Keahon. Henry Hale of Harvard kindly supplied information on political parties.

Ludmila Pruner would like to thank the Research Institute of Film in Moscow for allowing her to use their archives, the Cinema Center, Kinotsent, and Iskusstvo kino, Lev Karakhan in particular, for suggesting the article "Paremii kino" in *Kinovedcheskie zapiski* 19 (1993). She adds,"My deepest appreciation goes to all those who helped me with this chapter."

Valentina Zaitseva writes: Apart from tapping my own memory and scanning periodicals, this work is the result of my interviews with the Russian friends and colleagues both in US and in Russia and of street interviews in Moscow, Petersburg, and Sochi. It was fun asking a teenager on the street or a militia man on the train to continue a quotation. I am deeply grateful to Scott Scullion, Masha Gitin, Bill Yokoyama and the editors of this volume for their help with editing my English text and translations; Masha Gitin also translated Gogol's "lyrical digressions," Lermontov's and Nekrasov's poems. Special thanks to Dr. Elena Andreevna Zemskaia of the Institute of Russian Language for her materials and advice on sources of quotations; to the librarians of Sochi Public library on Iasnogoraskaia Street, Larisa Shalovna Vartanova and Nikolai Stepanovich Vartanov, for their generous help with periodicals. My heartfelt thanks to all my colleagues and friends in Russia and US who helped me to verify the "collective memory," especially to I. Belodedova, A. Greenlee, S. Grigoriev, M. Kokovkina, S. Kokovkin, L. Kolossimo, L. Pan, A. Rodionova, N. Savitskaia, L. Sikorskaia, M. Solov'eva, L. Suniaikina, G. Zharkova and N. Zharkova.

Other writers acknowledged assistance within their chapters.

Part 1. A Framework for the Russian Context

All the meaning is in the context.
Ilya Kabakov, Russian artist

Russia's History　1　История

William J. Comer

INTRODUCTION　　　　　　　　　　　　　　　　**ВВЕДЕ́НИЕ**

The average Russian has a greater interest in his country's past than his American counterpart, although his version of actual events may be as romanticized as an American's. What the average Russian knows about his history comes only in part from what was drilled into his head in 10 (now 11) years of schooling. Russia has a long-standing tradition of depicting historical events in all its arts—literature, film, painting, architecture, music, opera, and ballet—as well as in political humor. Indeed, when the average Russian is asked to conjure a mental image of Ivan the Terrible **Ива́н Гро́зный**, his imagination can draw on Repin's famous painting *Ivan the Terrible and his Son Ivan on November 16, 1581* **«Ива́н Гро́зный и сын его́ Ива́н 16 ноября́ 1581 го́да»**, V. Vasnetsov's painting *Tsar Ivan the Terrible* **«Царь Ива́н Гро́зный»** where Ivan descends an ornate Kremlin staircase, or Eisenstein's movie *Ivan the Terrible*.

Fig. 1-1.　　Il'ia Repin, *Ivan the Terrible and his Son Ivan on November 16, 1581*
«Ива́н Гро́зный и сын его́ Ива́н 16 ноября́ 1581 го́да» (1885)

Fig. 1-2.   Victor Vasnetsov, *Tsar
Ivan the Terrible* **«Царь
Ивáн Грóзный»** (1897)

Fig. 1-3.   Close-up of Nikolai
Cherkasov in the title role
of Sergei Eisenstein's film
Ivan the Terrible **Ивáн
Грóзный** (1944)

This chapter, then, will try to describe not so much Russia's actual history
or even the interpretations of that history, but the myths, images and verbal
icons that Russians associate with their history, the origins of these myths, and
the ways in which historical events, phenomena and myths are referred to in
everyday discourse. Although omissions are unavoidable in a work of this kind,
I have tried to make this chapter as complete as possible, so that the reader,
who begins the chapter with no previous knowledge of Russian history, will
come away with a coherent overview of the country's past and the vocabulary
that Russians use to describe it.

A warning—the changes that occurred in Soviet society with the coming of
Gorbachev in 1985 have touched Russia's past as much as its present. The
Soviet regime guarded the nation's history and molded its interpretations as

closely as it guarded nuclear secrets, since the correct interpretation of history was the foundation upon which all Marxist-Leninist ideology was built. To question key concepts, such as the development of class struggle **кла́ссовая борьба́** in Russia's history, was to threaten the country's whole political and economic system at its very core, and authorities dealt swiftly and decisively to limit or eliminate such questioning. Furthermore, history was often subject to the whim of Soviet leaders and could be re-interpreted to suit changing ideological goals and needs. Only with the liberalization of the press in the late 1980s, under Gorbachev's banner of glasnost' **гла́сность**, did the general population start to learn of the gaps **бе́лые пя́тна** (*lit.* white spots) of Russia's history, particularly in the 20th century.[1] At first the interpretation of these "gaps" took as their point of departure "If Lenin had not died in 1924 ..." «**Вот если бы Ле́нин не у́мер в 24-м году́...**», since this assumed the fundamental correctness of the country's political system and assured the leading role of the Communist Party **руководя́щая роль Коммунисти́ческой Па́ртии Сове́тского Сою́за (КПСС)** in the country.

The collapse of the Party's hegemony in 1991 has allowed Russians to re-evaluate, re-discover, and even re-invent their past. Soviet heros have been discredited, their statues removed from public places, their names detached from streets and cities. Some Russians are casting about for historical models who embody the new ideas of a capitalist, democratic Russia. For the new entrepreneurial class such models are the entrepreneurs and industrialists of the late nineteenth and early twentieth centuries, such as Savva Morozov, Mamontov, the Riabushinskys, Stroganovs and Brodskys. Finally, the change of political systems and the end of censorship complicate the task of documenting "what every Russian knows about Russian history" since a sixty-year-old Russian was taught a very different version of Russian history than today's twenty-year-old.

Periods of Russian History   Пери́оды ру́сской исто́рии

While much of Russian history is simply categorized and characterized by century names, usually written in Roman numerals (for example, 17th Century — **семна́дцатый (XVII) век**, 18th Century — **восемна́дцатый (XVIII) век** or by the name of a decade within a century (for example, the 60s — **шестидеся́тые го́ды**), certain time periods are known by special descriptive names.

---

[1] A political joke **анекдо́т** from the Gorbachev years illustrates this point very clearly. A Japanese and a Russian team are trying to negotiate the terms of a treaty. They seemed to have worked out all the details, but then the following day the Japanese team comes back, and refuses to sign the agreement. The head of the Japanese team explains: **С вами договори́ться нельзя́. Росси́я — страна́ непредсказу́емого про́шлого!** "It's impossible to make an agreement with you. Russia is a country with an unpredictable past."

Time periods	Descriptive names
862–1237	**Ки́евская Русь** Kievan Rus' **Домонго́льская Русь** Pre-Mongol Russia
1240–1480	**Монго́ло-тата́рское и́го** Tatar-Mongol Yoke
1240–15th century	**Уде́льный пери́од** Appanage Period **Феода́льная Росси́я** Feudal Russia **Феода́льная раздро́бленность** Feudal Fragmentation
14th–16th century	**Собира́ние ру́сских земе́ль** Uniting of the Russian lands
1598–1612	**Сму́та/Сму́тное вре́мя** Time of Troubles
1861–1917	**Порефо́рменная Росси́я** Post-reform Russia **Капиталисти́ческая Росси́я** Capitalist Russia
1917–21	**Револю́ция и Гражда́нская война́** Revolution and Civil War
1922–29	**НЭП (Но́вая экономи́ческая поли́тика)** NEP (New Economic Policy)
1939–45	**Втора́я Мирова́я война́** Second World War
1941–45	**Вели́кая Оте́чественная война́** The Great Patriotic War
1953–64	**Хрущёвская о́ттепель** Khrushchev's Thaw **Хрущёвское десятиле́тие** The Khrushchev Decade
1970s and 1980s	**Бре́жневский засто́й** Brezhnev's Stagnation **Засто́йное вре́мя** The Time of Stagnation

Before the Beginning   До нача́ла

One ancient people who inhabited the lands of modern-day Ukraine and southern Russia has significance for contemporary Russians' self definition. They are the Scythians **ски́фы** who inhabited the northern shore of the Black Sea between 700–200 BC. Nomadic, but possessing considerable military prowess, they developed a rich culture, whose remnants include intricate gold jewelry. The cultural image of the Scythians for the modern Russian has much more to do with a poem **«Ски́фы»** by Alexander Blok whose first two verses, written in 1918, read:

1-3

1-4   Мильо́ны — вас. Нас — тьмы, и тьмы, и тьмы.
             Попро́буйте, срази́тесь с на́ми!
         Да, ски́фы — мы! Да, азиа́ты — мы,
             С раско́сыми и жа́дными оча́ми!

Для вас—века́, для нас—еди́ный час.
    Мы, как послу́шные холо́пы,
Держа́ли щит меж двух вражде́бных рас
    Монго́лов и Евро́пы!

There are millions of you, but there are hordes, and hordes, and
    hordes of Us.
    Just try to do battle with us!
We are Scythians! We're Asiatics,
    With slanted and greedy eyes!

You've had centuries, but for us there's a single hour.
    We, like faithful servants,
Have held the shield between two warring races
    Of Mongols and of Europe!

KIEVAN RUS'   КИ́ЕВСКАЯ РУСЬ

The earliest name for the loose political organization, which the Russians claim as their first state, is Rus' **Русь**, which has lent itself to the Russians' name for their nationality Russian **ру́сский**. The central city of Rus' was Kiev **Ки́ев**, traditionally called the "mother of Russian cities" **мать городо́в ру́сских**.

Archeological evidence suggests that Kiev was first settled in fifth century AD, and the most ancient chronicle **ле́топись** documenting this period, *The Tale of Bygone Years* **«По́весть временны́х лет»**, compiled by the monk Nestor **Не́стор** in the 12th century, ascribes the founding of the city to Kii **Кий** who had two brothers Shchek **Щек** and Khoriv **Хорів** and a sister Lybed' **Лíбидь**. (The last two names are given in Ukrainian spelling.)

Political Development   Полити́ческое разви́тие
First Princes   *Пе́рвые князья́*

Traditionally, the rise of **Русь** in the 9th century has been ascribed to its importance on the trade routes from the Scandinavian Norsemen (Varangians **варя́ги**) to Byzantium. The path from the Varangians to the Greeks **путь из варя́г в гре́ки** was accomplished by travel on a series of rivers (Volkhov **Во́лхов**, the Western Dvina **За́падная Двина́**, Dnieper **Днепр**) and with portage of the ships over rapids and between rivers. In 862 the people of the northern city Novgorod invited a Scandinavian prince Riurik **Рю́рик** to rule over them since they had come to an impasse in selecting a new leader. Thus Riurik founded a lineage of princes (known as the "Sons of Riurik" **Рю́риковичи**) that would rule over the East Slavic lands of Rus' until 1598.

In the early period one descendant of Riurik who deserves mention is Oleg the Seer **Ве́щий Оле́г**, well known from the "Ballad of Oleg the Seer" **«Песнь о ве́щем Оле́ге»**, Alexander Pushkin's (1799–1837) poetic reworking of historical legends. Oleg was warned by a sooth-sayer that his death would come from his favorite horse. To avoid death he had the horse sent away. Years later, after a battle, Oleg found his horse lying dead on the field. He recalled the words of the sooth-sayer and regretted that he had believed him. As the Prince was examining his fallen steed, a snake, slithering out of the horse's head, bit the Prince and killed him.

Christianization of Rus'   *Крещéние Русú*

In the middle of the ninth century, Rostislav, one of the princes of the Slavic tribes living in Central Europe, sent to the Byzantine Emperor for missionaries who would come to convert his people to Christianity in their own language. The Emperor chose the academic Cyril **Кирúлл** and monk Methodius **Мефóдий**, since they were brothers and of Slavic heritage. To carry out their mission, Cyril devised an alphabet for translating the sacred texts into a common Slavic language. While experts today question that he created the Cyrillic alphabet (**кирúллица**) that is named in his honor, Cyril is still honored for bringing literacy to the Slavic peoples. The many sacred texts that he, his brother, and their followers translated into Church Slavic **церкóвно-славя́нский язы́к** provided a rich store of literature for the people of Rus' when they later converted to Christianity.

In Rus' Princess Olga **Óльга** (ruled 945–62) was the first among the princely family to convert to Orthodoxy **правослáвие** or Byzantine Christianity. *The Tale of Bygone Years* shows her as a strong and able ruler, who cunningly took revenge on the tribe of Drevliane **древля́не** for the murder of her husband Prince Igor **князь Úгорь**.

Fig. 1-4.   Pre-revolutionary postcard showing the statue of Prince Vladimir erected in Kiev on the banks of the Dnieper in 1888 to mark 900 years of Christianity in Russia

Olga's grandson Prince Vladimir **Влади́мир** (ruled 980–1015) was responsible for the Christianization of Rus' (**креще́ние Руси́**). In 988 he was baptized and made Byzantine Christianity the official state religion, for which he was canonized. Statues of the pagan gods of the Slavic pantheon were hurled down the Dnieper's steep banks into the water.[2] Historians continue to dispute the precise motives for this change, but clearly Rus' found great benefits in political, economic and cultural ties with the Byzantine Empire. According to the *Tale of Bygone Years*, Vladimir sent representatives to neighboring peoples of different religions to learn about their faiths. Islam, Judaism and Latin-rite Christianity were all rejected: the first because it required circumcision and spurned alcohol (**Руси́ есть весе́лье пи́тье, не мо́жем без того́ бы́ти**; roughly "For Rus' festivity means drinking; we cannot exist without it."); the second because the Jews lacked a homeland, since God in his anger had deprived them of it; the third because previous generations had rejected it. Byzantine-rite Christianity was accepted because, as Vladimir's representatives reported, Byzantine churches (particularly Constantinople's Holy Wisdom [St. Sophia] Cathedral) and services were so beautiful that during them they could no longer tell whether they were on earth or in heaven.

Later Princes   *Князья́ XI–XII веко́в*

Yaroslav the Wise **Яросла́в Му́дрый** (who ruled 1019–54) extended the territory of the Kievan State to its broadest and left behind an impressive legacy of internal developments in Kiev's cultural life—building the city's Golden Gates **Золоты́е воро́та** as well as its main cathedral dedicated to the Holy Wisdom **Софи́йский собо́р**, and producing for Kievan Rus' the first code of laws, the famous *Russian Justice* **Ру́сская пра́вда**. During his reign he made numerous dynastic alliances with Western European rulers, including marrying his *literate* daughter Anna to *illiterate* Henry I Capet of France. This fact is often cited as evidence that the level of cultural and educational achievement in the Kievan State was higher at this time than in Western Europe. It has even given some Russian nationalists in recent years cause to claim that medieval Russia actually educated Western Europe.

The last famous prince who managed to rule over Kievan Rus' as a single unit was Vladimir Monomakh **Влади́мир Монома́х** (ruled 1113–25), an energetic, wise and capable politician and military leader. Grandson of Yaroslav the

---

[2] Relatively little is known about Slavic paganism. Throwing statues into the Dnieper clearly accomplished very little in removing the pagan concepts, values and practices from the average citizen of Kievan Rus'. Indeed, it has often been stated that Russians developed a "dual faith"—**двоеве́рие**, that is, aspects of Russian paganism were blended into Christian belief and practice. For example, Perun **Перу́н**, god of thunder and lightning, was associated with Elijah the Prophet (**Илья́ проро́к** who ascended to heaven in the fiery chariot), and Veles **Веле́с**, the god of cattle, was transformed into **Свято́й Вла́сий**, Saint Vlasii, the Christian protector of cattle.

Wise, on one side, and the Byzantine Emperor, Constantine Monomachus, on the other, he came to represent an important link in later Russian princes' attempts to establish the prestige of their blood line. The cap of Monomakh **шáпка Монома́ха**, a fur-rimmed crown topped by a gold cross, purportedly belonging to Vladimir, became the royal crown of the later Muscovite princes. In Pushkin's play *Boris Godunov* **«Бори́с Годуно́в»** the cap **шáпка Монома́ха** becomes an emblem of the responsibility of royal power, as Boris Godunov exclaims: Oh, how heavy you are, crown of Monomakh! **Ох, тяжела́ ты, шáпка Монома́ха**.

Despite these distinguished rulers, almost every transfer of power in Kiev occasioned internal fighting **междоусо́бица** between brothers and uncles for the position of Grand Prince **Вели́кий князь** of the city of Kiev. Two victims of such conflict were the martyred princes Boris **Бори́с** and Gleb **Глеб**, immediately recognized as saints and always depicted on icons together.

The Oral Tradition   Ýстная тради́ция

Most of what we know about early Russian history comes from the stories compiled in the chronicles. Another (although vastly less reliable) source is the Russian oral tradition, particularly the epic songs **были́ны** (singular—**были́на** from **быль**, literally, a song about what truly "was"). Three of the most common heroes of these songs are the warriors **богатыри́** Il'ia of Murom **Илья́ Мýромец**, Dobrynia Nikitich **Добры́ня Ники́тич** and Alesha Popovich **Алёша Попо́вич**, all adventurers constantly involved in struggles against the enemies living in the south Russian plains or steppe **степь**. These heroes are well known today since the stories of these bylinas have been turned into children's stories. Another famous work, which seems to have started out as an oral tale, is the *Igor Tale* **«Слóво о полкý Ѝгореве»**—about the unsuccessful campaign of Prince Igor' against the Polovtsians in 1185.

Society and Social Organization   О́бщество и обще́ственный стро́й

Each major city and its surrounding lands in early medieval Russia formed a princedom **кня́жество** ruled by a prince **князь** (*pl.* **князья́**) who maintained a bodyguard/retinue **дружи́на** which would accompany him on campaigns. The main prince of the East Slavs (first situated in Kiev and later in Vladimir and Moscow) would receive the title of Grand Prince **вели́кий князь**. The male head of the most influential families was known as grandee **вельмо́жа** or boyar **боя́рин** (*pl.* **боя́ре**), while other male members of the upper class were collectively called **мужи́**.

Merchants, usually foreigners, dealing with long distance trade were known as **гóсти**, a fact preserved in the name of the famous shopping stalls of St. Petersburg, **Гости́ный двор** Merchant Court. Free peasants and tradespeople were collectively called **лю́ди**. They practiced many trades **ремёсла** whose names much later became incorporated in Russian surnames. As in English, these trade names are known today mostly from being preserved as common surnames and place names.

Name of Trade/Occupation	Last Name
гонча́р—potter	Гончаро́в
ме́льник—miller	Ме́льников
кузне́ц—smith	Кузнецо́в (and Кузне́цкий мост)
сапо́жник—boot-maker	Сапо́жников
стреле́ц—archer	Стрельцо́в
мясни́к—butcher	Мяснико́в/Мясни́цкая у́лица

In the Kievan period, the nobility found limited representation in their city's affairs through a council ду́ма, while ordinary citizens from the trading classes could voice their opinions in another council ве́че. These "democratic" traditions are especially associated with the ancient city of Novgorod Но́вгород, formally called Lord Novgorod the Great Господи́н Вели́кий Но́вгород. In that city the citizens' council was summoned by the ringing of a bell ве́чный (вечево́й) ко́локол located in the city's center. A symbol of Novgorod's tradition of self-rule, this bell was removed by order of Ivan the Terrible when the city was finally subdued by Moscow in the fifteenth century.

Pagan Rus' knew of sorcerers and soothsayers куде́сники and волхвы́, while the Christianization brought parish priests свяще́нники (known popularly as попы́) and monks мона́хи and nuns мона́хини. The Church was administered by bishops епи́скоп (also архиере́й), who resided in major cities. One main bishop received the additional title metropolitan митрополи́т and was responsible for the Russian Church to the patriarch патриа́рх of the Orthodox Church in Constantinople. The administration of the Russian Church remained technically subordinate to Constantinople until 1589, when the metropolitan of Moscow was elevated to the status of patriarch. The official acceptance of Orthodox Chrisitianity in Rus' is closely connected with the spread of literacy and the beginning of Old Russian literature.

Those who worked the land and could be called upon for military service were known as сме́рды (from the verb смерде́ть—to stink). At the bottom of Kievan society there were slaves холо́пы and a class of outcasts изго́и.

THIRTEENTH CENTURY   ТРИНА́ДЦАТЫЙ ВЕК

The Mongols   Монго́лы

Two events from the 13th century played major roles in the development of national history and national mythology. The Mongol-Tatar invasions монго́ло-тата́рское наше́ствие of 1237 to 1240 devastated all the major centers of Kievan Rus' except Novgorod.[3] Having sacked and pillaged Rus' (and many Eastern European cities as well), khan Baty **хан Баты́й** withdrew and set up a government in the lower Volga valley, known as the Golden Horde **Золота́я Орда́**. From there he and his descendants extracted tribute **дань** from the Russian lands. They also forced Russian princes to come to the Horde for the yarlyk **ярлы́к**, a document which recognized their rights to rule. The Mongol-Tatar Yoke **монго́ло-тата́рское и́го** continued for approximately 240 years and left many traces in the Russian language and in Russians' interpretation of their history. Many Russian words (for example, **де́ньги**—money, **сунду́к**—trunk, **ямщи́к**—driver of a horse-drawn vehicle) have Tatar roots; and comments about Tatars have become fixed in proverbs like: "An uninvited guest is worse than a Tatar" **Незва́ный гость ху́же тата́рина**. Some Russians even attribute the obscene expression "**Ёб твою мать**" as an artifact of the Mongol yoke since one horrible thing that the Mongols did was to make a Russian witness the rape of his mother.[4] The negative influence of the Tatar Yoke on Russia has often been cited as the reason for Russia's supposed backwardness **отста́лость Росси́и** and for its failure to keep up with Europe. Paradoxically, at other times Russians stress that the West needs to be grateful to Russia since the former's superior development was bought at the cost of latter's bearing the brunt of the Tatar invasions.

Teutonic Knights   Неме́цкие ры́цари

Alexander **Алекса́ндр** (1219–63), Grand Prince of Novgorod, chose to make peace with the Mongols and pay tribute to them so that he could oppose the Swedes and Teutonic Knights **неме́цкие ры́цари/крестоно́сцы**, who were encroaching on Russian lands from the west. After his victory over the Swedes in 1240 on the Neva River, he received the name Nevsky **Не́вский**. Two years later on April 5, 1242 he completely defeated the Teutonic Knights in the Battle on the Ice **Ледо́вое побо́ище** on Lake Chud **Чудско́е о́зеро**. When the ice broke up under the weight of the Germans' heavy armor, the knights could not even retreat, and many were drowned. This episode is well known to Russians from Sergei Eisenstein's film *Alexander Nevsky* with Prokofiev's musical score. The film, produced in the 1930s, leaves little doubt about the interpretation of Nevsky's importance as a strong leader who united the simple Russian people (exemplified in Prokofiev's chorus: Rise up, o Russian people

---

[3] In Russian folklore another city was spared destruction as well. Divine Providence made the city of Great Kitezh **Вели́кий Ки́теж** invisible to human eyes by covering it with earth and thus it became the Invisible City of Kitezh **неви́димый град Ки́теж**. According to legend (and Rimsky-Korsakov's opera), the righteous who come on a pilgrimage to the Bright Sea **Све́тлое о́зеро** will see a reflection of Kitezh on the water and hear the pealing bells of Kitezh's churches.

[4] This is only one of the many possible explanations for this expression, which should not be used by foreigners.

Встава́йте, лю́ди ру́сские) for a battle with the cruel German forces. Nevsky's promise "Whoever comes at us with a sword shall be killed with the sword" **Кто с мечо́м к нам войдёт, от меча́ и поги́бнет** became a frequently repeated line during World War II.

## THE GATHERING OF THE RUSSIAN LANDS	СОБИРА́НИЕ РУ́ССКИХ ЗЕМЕ́ЛЬ
### Moscow	Москва́

From the beginning of the 14th century the princes of Moscow actively promoted their city and pushed it into the center of East Slavic politics. Turning Moscow into the capital of the Russian lands was a lengthy process, both politically and architecturally, and this fact is reflected in the Russian equivalent for the English proverb: Rome wasn't built in a day—**Москва́ не сра́зу стро́илась**.

Tradition has established that Prince Yuri Dolgorukii **Ю́рий Долгору́кий** founded the future capital in 1147. Actually, 1147 is the year when a settlement, concentrated in the area currently occupied by the present day Kremlin, was first mentioned in the chronicles. By 1156 around this site Prince Dolgorukii had established a wooden fortress, **кремль** in Old Russian, **кре́пость** in modern speech. Thus the Kremlin, the name for the center of Russia's modern government, derives from a common noun, meaning "fortress," which is why modern tourists can visit kremlins in Russian cities other than Moscow. The patron saint of the city is Saint George the Victorious **Гео́ргий Победоно́сец**, also **1-6** known as the Dragon Slayer **Змеебо́рец**. The emblem of Saint George on a white horse stabbing a winged dragon is part of the city's crest, and can now be seen even on the city's police patrol cars.

Fig. 1-5.   Contemporary view of the Moscow Kremlin

Moscow's Grand Princes   *Велúкие князья́ моско́вские*

Ivan Kalita   *Ивáн Калитá*

Moscow's rise to prominence can be traced to Prince Ivan Daniilovich (ruled 1328–41), nicknamed "The Moneybag" **Калитá**. Ivan Kalita convinced the Mongol khan **хан** to install him as the chief collector of tribute from the Russian princedoms, and for this he and his descendants earned the title Grand Prince. Ivan acquired land around Moscow in every way he could, including trickery and buying out penniless princes. Ivan also enticed the head of the Russian Church Metropolitan Petr **митрополи́т Пётр** to visit Moscow often, and in 1326 Peter's successor moved the administrative center of the Russian Church from the city of Vladimir to Moscow. Thus began the close working relations between the Moscow princes and the heads of the Russian Church, which played an important role in establishing the city's prominence.

Fig. 1-6.   Simon Ushakov, *The Tree of the Moscow State* «**Дре́во госудáрства моско́вского**» (1668)

Dmitri Donskoi   *Дми́трий Донско́й*

Ivan Kalita's grandson Dmitri Ivanovich (ruled 1359–89) completed the construction of white limestone defense walls around Moscow in 1367, and thus the
expression White-stoned Moscow **Москва́ белока́менная** entered the language. Of far greater importance, however, is Dmitri Ivanovich's victory over
the Golden Horde **Золота́я Орда́** at the battle of Kulikovo field **Кулико́во
по́ле**, where he defeated the Mongol commander Mamai **Мама́й** and his troops
on September 8, 1380. Since the battlefield was located beyond the Don River,
Dmitri became known as Donskoi **Донско́й** "of the Don." The Muscovite victory, often embellished in Soviet histories as the Russians' united victory, was
the first against the Horde, and it gave an enormous boost to Moscow's position as leader of the Russian lands, and showed that the Horde was vulnerable
and could be defeated.

Fig. 1-7.   Dmitri Donskoi in battle at Kulikovo field (manuscript miniature,
late 16th century)

The final end of Mongol control came only 100 years later in 1480 when Ivan III refused to pay tribute to the Mongols, and the forces of khan Akhmat **Ахма́т** (from whom the 20th century poet Anna Gorenko took her pseudonym Akhmatova) proved too weak to cross the Ugra River to exact payment by military force. This stalemate, known as the **стоя́ние на Угре́**, was interpreted as Moscow's victory over the Mongols. The victories over the Golden Horde, which by that time had converted to Islam, were reflected in the new design of crosses on Orthodox churches. The new cross was placed on top of a crescent shape whose ends point skyward, symbolizing the triumph of Christianity over **1-7** Islam, whose traditional symbol is the crescent moon.

Ivan III   *Иван Тре́тий*

Ivan III (ruled 1462–1505) increased the prestige of the Moscow grand princes by marrying Sofia Paleolog **Со́фья Палео́лог**, the niece of the last emperor of Constantinople in 1472. Through this dynastic tie Ivan claimed the Byzantine **1-8** two-headed eagle **двугла́вый орёл** for his crest and the titles "tsar" **царь** (from the Latin *Caesar*) and "autocrat" **самоде́ржец** (originally meaning that he had no overlord). Court life during his reign became vastly more elaborate, importing many rituals from Byzantine royal life.

Furthermore, Ivan III continued to increase the size of Moscow's territory, adding vast tracts of lands, principalities and cities—Yaroslavl′, Rostov, Dmitrov, Perm′, Viatka, Uglich, Ryazan′, Novgorod and Tver′. By 1493 this allowed him to lay claim to the title: Sovereign of all Rus′ **Госуда́рь всея́ Руси́**.[5] Ivan III, who is also known as "the Great" **Вели́кий**, left his mark on the appearance of the Moscow Kremlin, overseeing the construction of its main cathedrals, as well as the massive multi-tiered bell-tower which now bears his **1-9** name **колоко́льня Ива́на Вели́кого**. The square at the base of the belltower was known as Ivan Square **Ива́новская пло́щадь** and was the site where the tsar's heralds **глаша́таи** proclaimed royal edicts. The booming voice that was needed to make proclamations heard produced the idiom "to shout to all Ivanovskaia Square" **крича́ть во всю ива́новскую**, meaning to yell as loud as one can.

The rise of Moscow was assisted by the network of fortress-monasteries **монастыри́-сто́рожи** that grew up around the city and were linked to more distant areas. One figure who stands out in particular in the revival and spread of monastic traditions is Saint Sergii of Radonezh **Свято́й Се́ргий Ра́донежский** (1322?–92). The monastery that he founded in the fourteenth century has become the spiritual hub of Russian Orthodoxy; and, granted the honorary status of Lavra **ла́вра** in the 18th century, it is currently called the

---

[5] This title and others like it (Patriarch of Moscow and All Russia **Патриа́рх Моско́вский и всея́ Руси́**) preserve the archaic feminine genitive singular form **всея́** from **весь**, meaning "all."

Holy Trinity-St. Sergii Lavra **Тро́ице-Се́ргиевская ла́вра**. It is located to the 🔲 **1-10** northeast of Moscow in the town "Sergii's Settlement" **Се́ргиев Поса́д** and formerly known in Soviet times as Zagorsk **Заго́рск**.

Moscow the Third Rome   *Москва́—Тре́тий Рим*

The idea of Moscow's role as political heir to Byzantium and its vital place in the world as the last free Orthodox Christian kingdom was formulated at the beginning of the 16th century by the monk Philotheus **Филофе́й** in an *Epistle to Grand Prince Vasilii* «**Посла́ние вели́кому кня́зю Васи́лию**». According to him, Moscow was the Third Rome **Москва́—тре́тий Рим**, the natural successor both to the first Rome which lapsed into heresy and the second Rome (that is, Constantinople) which fell to the Ottomans in 1453. Thus, as leader of the only remaining Orthodox state, the Muscovite tsar had a duty to protect the Orthodox Church throughout the whole world and maintain the purity of the Christian faith since there will be no Fourth Rome. Philotheus' succinct formulation is: "Two Romes have fallen, the third now stands, and a fourth one is not to be" **Два Ри́ма па́ли, тре́тий стои́т, а четвёртому не быва́ть**.[6]

Late Medieval Society   **О́бщество в по́зднем средневеко́вье**

The Nobility   *Дворя́нство*

As Moscow's grand princes fought to bring Russian lands together, they increasingly relied upon retainers or servitors **служи́лые лю́ди** to perform work at their court **двор** and to make up the ranks of their army and its leadership. These servitors became known as **дворя́не** and later formed the core of the gentry **дворя́нство** in tsarist Russia. As payment or reward for service, the grand prince could bestow an estate **поме́стье** which the grand prince could theoretically take back upon the death of the servitor.

The elite of the army, however, was drawn from the nobility, who performed its service for the grand prince voluntarily. These nobles held independent economic and political power bases in the form of their hereditary land holdings, the votchina **во́тчина**. Over the course of centuries the **поме́стье** became indistinguishable from the **во́тчина**, both remaining in families from one generation to the next.

---

[6] There are some variations in how Russians remember this formula. Purists might want to know that Philotheus wrote: "**Блюди и внемли, благочести́вый царю́, я́ко вся христиа́нская црьства снидоша́с в твое́ еди́но, я́ко два Ри́ма падоша́, а тре́тий стои́т, а четвёртому не бы́ти.**" Listen and pay heed, o pious tsar, since all Christian kingdoms have fallen to yours alone, since two Romes have fallen, the third one stands, and a fourth one is not to be. (*Pamiatniki literatury drevnei Rusi: Konets XV-pervaia polovina XVI veka* [Moscow: Khudozhestvennaia literatura, 1984], 440).

The Peasantry   *Крестья́нство*

From medieval times onward the estate, either **во́тчина** or **поме́стье**, consisted not only of land, buildings and natural resources, but also of peasants **крестья́не** who lived on the land and worked it for themselves and the noble. As sources of labor became more difficult to find and keep from the sixteenth century onward, nobles pressed the tsars to impose tighter restrictions on the movement of peasants from one noble to another. In 1649 the mobility of the Russian peasantry was legally ended and their former privilege of being able to leave their masters at St. George's Day **Ю́рьев день** (provided that their debts were all paid off) was revoked. The bitter memory and effect of this event has encoded itself in the expression **Вот тебе́, ба́бушка, и Ю́рьев день** (literally, "Well, that's Saint George's day for you, grandma!"), said on occasions when expectations are suddenly dashed. From 1649 to 1861 a peasant who worked for a noble was a serf **крепостно́й** and lived in the condition of serfdom **крепостно́е пра́во**. In exchange for his small plot of land **наде́л**, the serf made payments to his master either in the form of corvée **ба́рщина**, where he worked directly for the master a fixed number of days a year, or quit-rent **обро́к**, where he paid a portion of the land's produce or manufacture in kind or in cash to the master.

Serfdom is often cited as the reason for the passivity of the Russian peasant **мужи́к**, a person who resorts to activity only under duress. As the saying goes: Unless the thunder rumbles, the peasant won't cross himself. **Гром не гря́нет, мужи́к не перекре́стится**. (See Chapter 5.)

Fig. 1-8.   Grigorii Miasoedov, *The Mowers* «Косцы́» (1887)

The Cossacks   *Казáчество*

In the fifteenth and sixteenth centuries, some peasants fled from their masters and resettled in the free southern borderlands of Muscovy, mainly along the Dnieper, Don and Iaik **Яи́к** (commonly pronounced "Ik" **«Ик»**) Rivers. The descendants of these runaway peasants formed distinct groups known as free people **вóльные лю́ди** or Cossacks **казáки** (these terms are combined in the well-known expression **казáцкая вóльница** freemen). Having escaped the limitations of serfdom, the Cossacks valued their freedom highly and in times of peace they governed themselves by democratic processes. They became celebrated for their military daring and their raucous drinking and carousing. As free frontiersmen, the Cossacks become a significant military force in the southern areas of Moscow's territories fighting their many neighbors, the Crimean Tatars, Turkish settlements along the Black Sea coast, and the semi-nomadic indigenous population.

In the 16th century the allegiance of the Cossacks clustered at the rapids of the Dnieper River, the Zaporozhian Cossacks **запорóжцы**, was actively courted by the Polish-Lithuanian kingdom. However, attempts to polonize the Cossacks and their culture pushed them to rebellion in 1648 under their hetman Bogdan Khmel'nitskii **гéтман Богдáн Хмельни́цкий**. In 1654 at Pereiaslavl', after a short-lived period of autonomy, the Zaporozhian Cossacks swore allegiance to the Moscovite tsar.

Fig. 1-9.   Il'ia Repin, *The Zaporozhian Cossacks Write a Reply to the Turkish Sultan* **«Запорóжцы пи́шут письмó турéцкому султáну»** (1880–91)

The process of incorporating the Cossacks into Russian society, however, was very slow. Throughout the 17th and 18th centuries, Cossacks in some areas remained intimately involved with popular rebellions, sometimes initiating them, other times just supporting them. Only at the beginning of the 19th century were the Cossacks finally made part of Russia's regular military organization. From that time onwards the Cossacks become known for their fierce personal loyalty to the tsar and the tsarist system. In revolutionary situations in the late 19th century the tsars relied heavily on the Cossacks' loyalty to quell rebellions.

In addition to these aspects of Cossack military traditions, Russians have a variety of associations when they hear the word "Cossacks" since the Cossacks in different regions of the Russian Empire held different customs. Thus, L.N. Tolstoy's story, *The Cossacks* **«Каза́ки»** romanticized the Cossacks of the Northern Caucusus **гребенски́е каза́ки** portraying them as "natural men"/ "noble savages" living in harmony with nature. Repin's painting *The Zaporozhian Cossacks Write a Reply to the Turkish Sultan* **«Запоро́жцы пи́шут письмо́ туре́цкому султа́ну»** depicts the Cossacks of the Dnieper River Rapids as colorful warriors; Sholokhov's *Quiet Flows the Don* **«Ти́хий Дон»** depicts the patriarchal life of industrious Don Cossacks **донски́е каза́ки**.

MUSCOVITE KINGDOM   МОСКО́ВСКОЕ ЦА́РСТВО

Ivan the Terrible   Ива́н Гро́зный

The sixteenth century was dominated by Ivan IV **Ива́н Васи́льевич**, whose personal reign began in 1547 when he was awarded the title tsar **царь** at his coronation (his father and grandfather used the title tsar in many of their dealings, but were never granted it at their coronations; each was crowned grand prince **вели́кий князь**). Shortly thereafter he summoned the first Assembly of All the Lands **Зе́мский собо́р**, where representatives from all social classes **сосло́вия** convened to solve the nation's problems. Ivan undertook military campaigns against the Tatars, capturing the Tatar cities of Kazan **Каза́нь** and Astrakhan **А́страхань** in 1552 and 1556 respectively. The ruthlessness of his victory in Kazan earned him the epithet Groznyi **Гро́зный** (literally, "awe-inspiring, awesome," but usually rendered into English as "the Terrible"). In thanksgiving for this victory he had built on Moscow's Red Square **Кра́сная пло́щадь** the Cathedral of the Virgin's Veil **Покро́вский собо́р**, better known by its popular name Saint Basil's Cathedral **Храм Васи́лия Блаже́нного**.

Legends say that Ivan had the architect blinded upon completion of the project so that he could never construct anything more beautiful. Uncharacteristic of earlier Russian church architecture, this structure, with its network of small chapels surrounding a large central chapel, symbolically represents the unification of smaller Russian princedoms around Moscow's powerful centralized leadership.

Fig. 1-10. Contemporary view of St. Basil's Cathedral, formally titled "The Cathedral of the Virgin's Veil on the Moat" **Собо́р Васи́лия Блаже́нного/Собо́р Покрова́ Богоро́дицы, что на Рву** (1555–61)

The capture of Kazan and Astrakhan had important consequences for the territorial growth of the Muscovite state since it opened up the whole of the Volga River Valley for Muscovite expansion. This, in turn, paved the way for conquest of Eastern Siberia by the Cossack chieftain Yermak Timofeevich **атама́н Ерма́к Тимофе́евич** (cf. Surikov's vivid canvas *The Conquest of Siberia by Yermak* **«Покоре́ние Сиби́ри Ермако́м»**) at the end of the 16th century.

In the 1560s Ivan instituted the oprichnina **опри́чнина**, a new system of royal management whose administrators would be personally responsible to the tsar alone. Ivan's main goal in this change was to consolidate power in his position as autocrat **самоде́ржец** while undermining the rights and privileges of the aristocracy, the princes **князья́** and the boyars **боя́ре**. The enforcers of this system were known as oprichniki **опри́чники**, and they spent their time uncovering alleged plots against the tsar and ferreting out supposed enemies. An **опри́чник** was easily identified by his black monastic-like garb, a dog's skull attached to his horse's neck and a wisp of dog fur attached to the handle of his whip **кнут**. These emblems were meant to suggest that they were the tsar's guard dogs, who could sniff out enemies. The most notorious oprichnik was Maliuta Skuratov **Малю́та Скура́тов**, whose name is now associated with the torture and executions of the time.

Books and Literary Culture   **Кни́ги и литерату́рная культу́ра**

The sixteenth century witnessed several important developments in Russian letters. An important book of the age was the *Domostroi* **«Домостро́й»**, a manuscript attributed to the monk Silvester, which prescribes in astounding detail all aspects of running a household: how to cultivate fruits and vegetables; how to serve meals and act at table; how to treat children and spouses. The text recommends that men frequently beat their wives, children and servants in order to inspire obedience. This has made the word **домострой** in modern Russian a synonym for severe, backward, and patriarchal values and views.

The 16th century witnessed the production of the first printed book in Muscovite lands—a fact emphasized with national pride in virtually all Soviet history textbooks. In 1564 Ivan Fedorov **Иван Фёдоров** (often remembered as the "first printer," or **первопечатник**) produced the first printed book *The Acts of the Apostles with the Epistles* «**Апостол**». Although printed, this text attempted to preserve all of the visual peculiarities of manuscript books.

THE TIME OF TROUBLES	СМУ́ТНОЕ ВРЕ́МЯ, СМУ́ТА

The period of instability stretching from 1598 to 1613 is known as the "Time of Troubles" **Смутное время** or **Смута**; and its memory is strikingly clear even to contemporary Russians mostly because the period has provided such rich material for historical fiction and drama. The term **Смутное время** is sometimes used today about the possibility of political instability or civil war resulting from the economic hardships brought about by the breakup of the Soviet Union. The fact that the country was led in the 1990s by another Boris (that is, Yeltsin) has only fueled the tendency to see a parallel here.

Boris Godunov	Борис Годунов

Fig. 1-11. Mikhail Nesterov, *The Murdered Tsarevich Dmitri* «**Царевич Дмитрий убиенный**» (1899)

In 1584 Ivan the Terrible died, leaving the throne to his weak and sickly son Fedor **Фёдор**, who managed to rule for 14 years only with the guidance of his brother-in-law Boris Godunov, a former oprichnik who had risen from the lower ranks of the service gentry. When Fedor died without heirs in 1598, the dynasty of the "sons of Riurik" came to an end since Ivan's other son Dmitri **царевич Дмитрий** had died seven years earlier in Uglich, under mysterious circumstances.

Boris Godunov was elected tsar in 1598 and ruled until 1605. While there is little historical evidence that he was involved even indirectly in Dmitri's murder, Pushkin's play *Boris*

Godunov (1825) finds the character of Boris wracked with guilt for having ordered the murder of the innocent child. In the play Boris must prepare for an invasion of Polish-Lithuanian forces nominally lead by the impostor Grishka Otrep'ev **самозва́нец Гри́шка Отре́пьев** who claims to be Dmitri, miraculously saved from death and grown to adulthood. The name Grishka Otrep'ev has entered Russian as a catch phrase to describe anyone masquerading under a false identity.

1605–12   **1605–12 гг.**

The reign of the first false Dmitri **Лжедми́трий** was brief. Within a year of his arrival in Moscow in 1605, several Russian boyars successfully staged a coup and killed him and all his Polish supporters. In the seven years following this, Moscow witnessed incredible political instability and a number of attempts by the Polish Commonwealth to assert control over its eastern neighbor. The instability and threat of Polish intervention were ended by a national revival originating in Nizhni Novgorod with the burger Kuz'ma Minin **мещани́н Кузьма́ Ми́нин** and Prince Dmitri Pozharskii **князь Дми́трий Пожа́рский**, and supported by the Church, especially in the person of Patriarch Germogen **Патриа́рх Гермоге́н**. The national military force **наро́дное ополче́ние** that Minin and Pozharskii pulled together succeeded in forcing the Poles out of Moscow towards the end of 1612. A statue representing the two patriots, ready to sacrifice themselves for their country in an hour of foreign invasion, was erected in the 19th century and now stands on Red Square in front of St. Basil's Cathedral.

Fig. 1-12.   Martos, *Monument to Minin and Pozharskii* (1804–18)

Another hero of this time is the Kostroma peasant Ivan Susanin **Ива́н Суса́нин**, who purposely misguided Polish troops into the Russian forest where they perished. Once his deception was discovered, he was executed by the Poles. Glinka's opera *Ivan Susanin* (also known as *A Life for the Tsar* «**Жизнь за царя́**») has helped to fix the legend of Ivan Susanin and his patriotic sacrifice in the minds of most educated Russians.

THE ROMANOV DYNASTY   ДОМ РОМА́НОВЫХ

In 1613 with the end of the Polish intervention, an Assembly of All the Lands **Зе́мский Собо́р** elected as tsar the 16-year old Mikhail Fedorovich Romanov **Михаи́л Фёдорович Рома́нов**. His long rule (1613–45) and that of his son Aleksei Mikhailovich **Алексей Михайлович** (1645–76), called the Most Quiet **Тиша́йший**, brought a long period of relative stability to Russia and allowed the flowering of Muscovite artistic culture.

Church Schism   Церко́вный раско́л

The most significant event of the 17th century involved religious controversy. The national revival that helped to end the Time of Troubles brought with it a conservative religious revival, which was promoted by many favorites of Tsar Aleksei Mikhailovich including Archimandrite Nikon **архимандри́т Ни́кон** and the Archpriest Avvakum **протопо́п Авваку́м**. In 1652 Nikon was made Patriarch of the Russian Church. As patriarch he oversaw the correction and standardization of the texts of the church service books. Since these texts had been copied by hand throughout the medieval period, discrepancies existed between manuscripts, sometimes in small things such as spelling, sometimes in larger issues of ritual practice. To standardize church practice, Nikon could either go back to older Russian manuscripts to codify the Russian tradition, or he could use standardized printed Greek service books as a model. Nikon chose the Greek models, and in 1653, he imposed these standard Greek practices in all situations where the Russian Church had competing usages. The changes, for the most part, touched on the externals of religious observance, and they were upheld at Church councils in 1654, 1656, and by the Great Council of 1666–67 despite Nikon's fall from grace by that time.

These changes and the authoritarian manner in which they were imposed provoked a "Schism" **раско́л** in the Church, with those who rejected the changes branded as "schismatic" **раско́льник**.

This dissenting movement known as the Old Belief **ста́рая ве́ра** was led by the Archpriest Avvakum, who saw the changes as an insult to native Russian traditions and a corruption of Russia's true Orthodoxy. A fiery orator, Avvakum gave full voice to the opposition; and the text of his life story «**Житие́ протопо́па Авваку́ма**» stands as a striking testament to his struggle and the hardships of life in 17th century Muscovy. The text's colorful language and powerful narrative voice make it a milestone in the development of Old Russian literature. However, Avvakum's endless invective against the reforms and the tsars who approved of them finally wore out royal patience. In 1682 he was burned at the stake after 26 years of imprisonment and exile.

Traditions maintained by the Old Belief	Nikon's Reforms and Current Orthodox Practice
1. spell the name Jesus **Исýс**	1. spell the name Jesus **Иисýс**
2. **аллелýйя** Alleluia is repeated twice when it is spoken in the liturgy	2. **аллелýйя** Alleluia is repeated three times
3. sign of the cross is made with two fingers **двоепéрстие**	3. sign of the cross is made with three fingers **троепéрстие**
4. faithful prostrate to the ground **земнóй поклóн**	4. faithful bow to the waist **пояснóй поклóн**
5. church processions **крéстные хóды** move **пóсолонь** with the sun (that is, from east to west)	5. processions move **против сóлнца** opposite the sun (that is, from west to east)

Among those who followed Avvakum's example was the Boyar Woman Morozova **боя́рыня Морóзова**, arrested in 1671 and exiled to Borovsk for her virulent protests against the new faith. Her image is best known to Russians from Surikov's painting *Boyarinya Morozova* «**Боя́рыня Морóзова**», where **1-11** he depicts her as a strong, determined ascetic being dragged off in chains on a sledge, with her arm defiantly raised to bless the crowd with the two-fingered sign of the cross.

To some Russians and Russian historians, Avvakum and the Old Believers represented the first major social protest against the growing authoritarianism of the tsar (who, at the urging of the gentry, had imposed serfdom in 1649). Thus, Avvakum could be claimed as a prototype of a political revolutionary. For many others, the words Old Ritualist **старообря́дец** and schismatic **раскóльник** bring to mind fanatically conservative obscurantists; they prove the ignorance and backwardness of the Russian common people who failed to distinguish between the essence of religious faith and its external practices.

Because of continuing persecution from the central government, many proponents of the Old Belief moved to the frontier regions of the Muscovite state, particularly the Transvolga region and Siberia. There they continued their faith and way of life, surviving to the present day, although the modern dissenters prefer to be called Old Believers **старовéры**.

Peasant Rebellions   Крестья́нские восста́ния

Protests in the 17th century, however, were not limited to religious questions. The political instability of the first part of the century and the country's economic problems helped to fuel a number of rebellions by the peasants and lower classes. Soviet historiography tended to over-emphasize these rebellions, seeing in them the beginnings of the class struggle that would culminate in the Great October Social Revolution of 1917.

The Don Cossack chieftain Sten′ka (Stepan) Razin **атама́н Сте́нька (Степа́н) Ра́зин** became famous for leading parties of men in long boats **стру́ги** in daring raids on Persian settlements along the Caspian coast. In the spring of 1670, he and his Cossack followers turned their attention from plundering Persian cities to taking control of Muscovite holdings along the Volga River. Sailing up the Volga, they took town after town (Astrakhan, Saratov, Samara), executing government officials and members of the gentry, burning estates and proclaiming freedom to the local population. After losing to tsarist forces near Simbirsk, Razin tried to regroup his followers, but he was betrayed. On June 6, 1671 he was executed in Moscow. The memory of Razin, with his call for freedom from the landlords and the whims of tsarist officials, has found lasting embodiment in the folk tradition—where songs and stories about him abound. A very common, but highly romanticized, song is **«Из-за о́строва на стре́жень»** where the violence of Razin's rebellion is effaced by the story of Razin's treatment of a kidnapped Persian princess and the jealousy of his band of men.

Fig. 1-13.   Vasilii Surikov, *Stepan Razin* **«Степа́н Ра́зин»** (1903–10)

Песня о Стеньке Разине	Song of Sten'ka Razin
Из-за о́строва на стре́жень,	From behind an island, into the deep,
На просто́р речно́й волны́,	Into the openness of the river's waves
Выплыва́ют расписны́е,	The painted, narrowbowed boats sailed out.
Острогру́дые челны́.	
На пере́днем Сте́нька Ра́зин,	In the foremost one Stenka Razin,
Обня́вшись с свое́й княжно́й,	Embracing his princess,
Сва́дьбу но́вую справля́ет	Celebrates his new wedding,
Сам, весёлый и хмельно́й.	Merry and drunken.
Позади́ их слы́шен ро́пот:	From behind one could hear grumbling:
«Нас на ба́бу променя́л,	"He's traded us for a woman,
То́лько ночь с ней провожжа́лся,	He spent one night with her,
Сам нау́тро ба́бой стал!»	The next morning he himself was like a woman."
Этот шёпот и насме́шки	The fearsome chieftain hears
Слы́шит гро́зный атама́н	The whispers and the ridicule
И он мо́щною руко́ю	And with a powerful arm
О́бнял персия́нки стан.	He embraced the Persian woman.
А она́, поту́пя о́чи,	While she, with downcast eyes,
Ни жива́ и ни мертва́	Neither alive, nor dead,
Мо́лча слу́шает хмельны́е	Listens silently to the
Атама́новы слова́:	Chieftain's drunken words:
«Ничего́ не пожале́ю,	"I shall sacrifice everything,
Бу́йну го́лову отда́м»,	I shall lay down my rebellious head,"
Раздаётся го́лос вла́стный	Resounded the powerful voice
По окре́стным берега́м.	Against the nearby riverbanks.
«Во́лга, Во́лга, мать родна́я,	"Volga, Volga, our dear mother,
Во́лга, ру́сская река́,	Volga, the Russian river,
Не вида́ла ты пода́рка	You have yet to see a present
От донско́го казака́!»	From the Don Cossack!"
Мо́щным взма́хом поднима́ет	With a might thrust he lifted
Он краса́вицу-княжну́	His beautiful princess
И за борт её броса́ет	And threw her over the side of the ship,
В набежа́вшую волну́.	Into the oncoming wave.
«Что ж вы, бра́тцы, приуны́ли?	"Why now, brothers, have you grown sad?
Эй ты, Фи́лька, чёрт, пляши́!	Hey, you, Filka, dance, damn you!
Гря́нем пе́сню удалу́ю	Let us belt out a bold song,
На поми́н её души́!»	For the remembrance of her soul!"

1-12

THE EIGHTEENTH CENTURY

ВОСЕМНА́ДЦАТЫЙ ВЕК

Peter the Great

Пётр Пе́рвый (Вели́кий)

Fig. 1-14.   Valentin Serov, *Peter I* «Пётр I» (1907)

Beginning of his Reign

Нача́ло ца́рствования

The tensions between native traditions and foreign innovations that lurk under the surface of the religious controversy of the 17th century came to the fore in the reign of Petr Alekseevich **Пётр Алексе́евич** (1672–1725), better known as Petr I **Пётр Пе́рвый** (and, mostly parenthetically, as Peter the Great **Пётр Вели́кий**). He is the one credited with transforming the Muscovite kingdom **Моско́вское ца́рство** into the westernized Russian Empire **Росси́йская импе́рия**, adding "Emperor" **импера́тор** to the official list of his titles. Although Peter was named co-tsar with his older half-brother Ivan in 1682, the country was really ruled by his older half-sister Sofia Alekseevna **Со́фья**

Алексе́евна, who acted as regent **ре́гентша** until 1689. From 1689–94 the country was ruled in Peter's name by his mother and uncles; only in 1696, upon the death of his half-brother and co-tsar Ivan, did Peter become the sole ruler of the country. Peter's childhood was spent away from court life, and he enjoyed considerable freedom in his upbringing. In the villages of Preobrazhenskoe **Преображе́нское** and Semenovskoe **Семёновское** outside of Moscow, he taught himself about military matters, playing "soldiers" with real children from both noble and peasant families. As a youth, Peter visited Moscow's foreign quarter **неме́цкая слобода́** where he was introduced to European customs. These early connections with foreigners are often thought to have set the foundation for his later program of westernization.

In 1697–98 Peter undertook his famous "Great Embassy" **вели́кое посо́льство** to Western Europe. The purpose of this visit was to enlist the support of European powers in Moscow's struggles against the Turks, but its main benefit was to familiarize dozens of Moscow's young nobles with western military and manufacturing technology and customs and to import them into Russia. In this mission the tsar traveled "incognito" under the assumed name Petr Mikhailov **Пётр Миха́йлов**. The great embassy had to be cut short because of an uprising of the Moscow streltsy **стрельцы́** (the conservative military elite of old Moscow, who were enormously suspicious of Peter's intentions). Peter put down the rebellion mercilessly with public executions on Red Square, depicted in Surikov's famous painting *The Morning of the Strel'tsy* 🖵 **1-13** *Execution* «**У́тро стреле́цкой ка́зни**». This rebellion is often seen as the event which confirmed Peter's intentions to westernize his country.

Northern War   *Се́верная война́*

Peter's military accomplishments are well known: the lengthy Northern War **Се́верная война́** with Sweden was successfully concluded by Russia in 1721 mostly because of Peter's reforms of the Russian army and creation of a Navy **вое́нно-морско́й флот**. At the beginning of this war Sweden was the most powerful country on the Baltic Sea, and it quickly took control of the land along the Baltic coast northwest of Moscow by defeating the Russian forces at Narva **На́рва** in November 1700. The Russians countered by establishing themselves on the Gulf of Finland **Фи́нский зали́в** in 1701–02. In 1706 Sweden forced peace upon Saxony and Poland, Russia's fellow combatants in the war. Using his power over the defeated Poland, the Swedish King Charles XII **Карл XII** amassed his troops on Polish soil in 1708 and invaded Russian territory from the southwest. In June 1709 the Russians checked the invasion with their decisive victory over the Swedes at Poltava in Ukraine **Полта́вская би́тва**. This allowed the Russians eventually to take control over the territory of present-day Latvia and Estonia (known then as **Лифля́ндия** and **Эстля́ндия**), and it opened up the Baltic Sea coast for Russia's growing maritime trade with Western Europe.

Founding of St. Petersburg   *Основа́ние Петербу́рга*

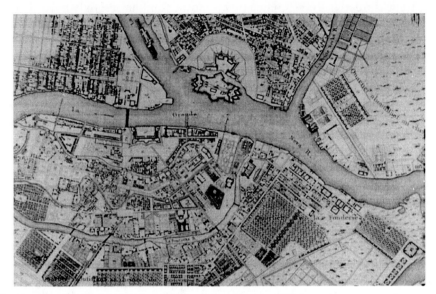

Fig. 1-15.   Bird's eye view of Petersburg from an 18th century engraving

In the course of the Northern War, Peter felt the need to establish a stronger, more permanent Russian presence in the northwest, and in 1703 he initiated the construction of the Peter-Paul Fortress **Петропа́вловская кре́пость** in the delta of the Neva River **Нева́**.

This event marks the founding of St. Petersburg **Санкт-Петербу́рг**, which has been termed Russia's "Northern Capital" **се́верная столи́ца** and its "window on Europe" (it is said Peter **«прору́би́л окно́ в Евро́пу»** "cut a window through to Europe"). In his poem "The Bronze Horseman" **Ме́дный вса́дник** (1833), a standard of the school repertoire, Pushkin formulates Peter's thoughts about the location and founding of the city.

1-14
Отсе́ль грози́ть мы бу́дем шве́ду.
Здесь бу́дет го́род заложён
На зло надме́нному сосе́ду.
Приро́дой здесь нам суждено́
В Евро́пу проруби́ть окно́,
Ного́ю твёрдой стать при мо́ре.

From here we shall threaten the Swede.
A city will be laid out here
To spite our haughty neighbor.
It was fated by nature for us to
Break out a window on Europe here,
To take a firm stand on the seacoast.

The Peter-Paul Fortress became the hub for the new, planned city to be delineated by long, broad straight avenues **проспе́кты** (**першпекти́вы** in the 18th century) and networks of canals **кана́лы**. The latter stem from geographical and engineering necessity and from the enormously positive impression that Amsterdam with its canals made on Peter. Indeed, much of Petersburg's first architecture borrowed from Dutch styles of the late 17th century. Later in the 18th century, the city's appearance was much influenced by Italian styles, and the city received the additional appellation "Venice of the North" **се́верная Вене́ция**.

From the very beginning St. Petersburg has engendered a rich mythology. Peter's first wife Evdokiia Lopukhina **Евдоки́я Лопухина́** was supposed to have cursed the city, wishing it to be desolate «**Петербу́ргу быть пу́сту**». There was great loss of life in constructing the city in such a cold and swampy environment, prone to frequent and devasting floods. The glorious image of St. Petersburg as a great planned city with a harmonious unity of architectural style competes with this darker side of the city in Pushkin's poem "The Bronze Horseman." Extensive quotes from the poem can be found in Chapter 2.

The Reforms of Peter the Great   *Петро́вские рефо́рмы*

During Peter's reign virtually all aspects of government and social life changed. While Peter is usually credited with personally implementing these changes, he did get assistance from a small inner circle (the peasant-born Menshikov **Ме́ншиков**, the noble Sheremet'ev **Шереме́тьев**, the foreigner Bruce, the Ukrainian cleric Feofán Prokopóvich **Феофа́н Прокопо́вич**—later termed "the fledglings of Peter the Great" **птенцы́ гнезда́ Петро́ва**). In place of the Boyar Council **боя́рская ду́ма**, which had advised the previous tsars, in 1711 Peter created a Senate **Сена́т** which served legislative and executive functions for the tsar. He replaced the ancient system of government offices **прика́зы** with administrative colleges **колле́гии** (that is, Military College **Вое́нная колле́гия**, The College of Foreign Affairs **Колле́гия иностра́нных дел**), which were led by councils of men. The Empire was divided into governorates **губе́рния** numbering at first 8, and then later 11. Those who populated this new bureaucracy became known as civil servants **чино́вники** (in contrast to the clerks and scribes **дья́ки/подья́чие** who ran the Muscovite **прика́зы**). These civil servants were divided into 14 levels of responsibilities, service and seniority in Peter's famous Table of Ranks **та́бель о ра́нгах**. Each of the 14 levels (1 was the highest, 14 the lowest) had a specific title with specific duties, although these varied as to whether the person served in the military, civil bureaucracy, or the courts. With only small modifications, this system of classifications remained in effect until 1917, although the social mobility that Peter wanted this classification to allow was greatly curtailed by his successors in the 18th century. Contemporary Russians may not always know the levels associated with the particular ranks, but the names of the ranks are familiar from Russian literature.

Rank **Класс**	Civil Rank **Чины́ гражда́нские**	Military Rank **Чины́ вое́нные**
1	**Ка́нцлер**	**Генерал-Фельдма́ршал**
2	**Действи́тельный сове́тник**	**Генера́л-от-кавале́рии** **Генерал-от-инфанте́рии** **Генерал-от-артилле́рии**
3	**Та́йный сове́тник**	**Генера́л-Лейтена́нт**
4	**Действи́тельный ста́тский сове́тник**	**Генера́л-Майо́р**
5	**Ста́тский сове́тник**	
6	**Колле́жский сове́тник** **Вое́нный сове́тник**	**Полко́вник**
7	**Надво́рный сове́тник**	**Подполко́вник**
8	**Колле́жский асе́ссор**	**Капита́н**
9	**Титуля́рный сове́тник**	**Штабс-капита́н**
10	**Колле́жский секрета́рь**	**Пору́чик**
11	**Корабе́льный секрета́рь**	
12	**Губе́рнский секрета́рь**	**Подпору́чик**
13	**Провинциа́льный секрета́рь**	**Пра́порщик**
14	**Колле́жский регистра́тор**	

In 1721 the administration of the Orthodox Church was similarly reformed under Peter by a document called the *Spiritual reglament* **Духо́вный регла́мент**. In place of a patriarch as head of the Russian church, he instituted the Holy Synod **Святе́йший сино́д**, a council of 10 (later 12) clerics and lay people, headed by a lay Overprocurator **Оберпрокуро́р**.

The costs of these grand projects and military campaigns were great, and financing them remained a constant problem for Peter. On the one hand, he attempted to stimulate Russian manufacturing and trade to increase tax and tariff revenues; on the other he instituted new taxes, particularly the onerous head tax **поду́шная по́дать** of 1724, which was imposed on all adult male peasants and townspeople, according to the census **реви́зия** of 1719.

In addition to these administrative changes, Peter changed many external features of Russian society. He demanded that all those serving at court and in the government should dress in a western manner, and, according to legend, he personally cut the long hems of protestors' caftans. Peter attacked the wearing of beards, a traditional Muscovite practice, and reportedly the tsar publically shaved off the beards of some who clung to their Muscovite ways. Furthermore, Peter introduced the Julian calendar, making the new year start January 1 (Old Russian practice held September 1 as the start of the new year). Peter also introduced the B.C./A.D. system of dates in place of previous way of counting years from the creation of the world (which added 5508 years to every AD date, that is, 1700 AD = 7208).

Views of Peter the Great   *Взгля́ды на жизнь и де́ятельность*
                                      Петра́ Пе́рвого

Fig. 1-16.   Etienne Falconet, *Monument to Petr I* «Па́мятник Петру́ I»
              ("Bronze Horseman" **Ме́дный вса́дник**, 1782)

That Peter the Great touched all aspects of Russian life is disputed by none; but
the evaluation of Peter's legacy and the benefits and negative ramifications of
his transformations are disputed by Russians of all stripes and philosophical
outlooks. This range of opinion is reflected in the wide variety of Peter's depic-
tions in Russian sculpture, painting, and literature. Some of the earliest negative reactions to Peter and his reign clustered around the Old Believers, who
were certain that Peter was the Antichrist **анти́христ**. Peter is sometimes a
stern and domineering father as in Ge's **Ге** painting *Peter Interrogates the Tsarevich Alexis Petrovich in Peterhof* «**Пётр I допра́шивает царе́вича Алексе́я** 🖾 **1-15**
Петро́вича в Петерго́фе». Peter's first son Alexis was no supporter of the
tsar's transformations, and he was executed for allegedly plotting against his
father. On the other hand, for most of the 18th century, Peter was eulogized by

poets and historians for having laid the foundation for Russia's continued westernization and territorial expansion. In sculpture the best known image is the majestic and determined Peter on horseback in Falconet's work the Bronze Horseman **Ме́дный вса́дник**, which Catherine the Great had erected on the banks of the Neva in St. Petersburg in 1782.

Peter is also depicted as a genius who tranformed the country and towered over all men (V. Serov's **Серо́в** painting *Peter I* **Пётр Пе́рвый**). Sometimes, as in the works of Russia's greatest poet Alexander Pushkin (1799–1837), there is some ambiguity about Peter and his legacy. In the poem "Poltava," Peter is the grand, almost divine, military leader.

1-16

Выхо́дит Петр. Его́ глаза́
Сия́ют. Лик его́ ужа́сен.
Движе́нья бы́стры. Он прекра́сен,
Он весь как бо́жия гроза́.

Peter emerges. His eyes
Shine. His visage is terrifying.
His movements are fast. He is magnificent.
His whole appearance instills the fear of God.

In the poem "The Bronze Horseman" **«Ме́дный вса́дник»**, Pushkin has Peter's statue come to life, revealing a threatening, vengeful tsar who hunts **1-17** down the poem's broken hero Evgenii since the latter has dared to grumble about Peter's city.

... Показа́лось
ему́, что гро́зного царя́,
Мгнове́нно гне́вом возгоря́
Лицо́ тихо́нько обраща́лось ...

... It seemed to him [Evgenii] that
The face of the threatening tsar,
Suddenly flaring up with fury,
Slowly turned toward him ...

Linguistically, the reign of Peter ushered in a virtual flood of western words. The vocabulary for certain industries and branches of manufacturing were borrowed wholesale—the language of sailing, ship-building and navigation, for example, was adapted from Dutch terms (although these are sometimes misidentified as German borrowings). Yet even here, we can see something of a native backlash. Perhaps because Russian peasants found the name of the new capital hard to pronounce, or, more likely, owing to the Dutch language, the name of St. Petersburg was abbreviated to "Piter" ("Pieter" in Dutch) **Пи́тер**, a form still widely used in conversation.

AFTER PETER

Anna Ioannovna

Top political power in the rest of the 18th century was dominated by empresses **императри́цы** and their favorites **фавори́ты** through palace coups **дворцо́вые переворо́ты**. Russians often think of this century as one of continual court intrigues. The first of these three distinguished empresses was Anna Ioannovna **Áнна Иоáнновна** (ruled 1730–40), daughter of Peter's half-brother Ivan. Since Anna Ioannovna spent her married life as a princess in German Courland, the highest Russian nobles thought that she could be manipulated and would easily accept secret conditions **та́йные конди́ции** that would limit her power and make her something of a constitutional monarch. To receive the throne, she accepted the conditions; but shortly thereafter, with the support of the gentry, she renounced these limitations. Under the influence of her favorite, the otherwise undistinguished Ernst-Johann Biron **Би́рон**, Anna Ioannovna's rule became cruel and strictly autocratic, marked by political repression. Germans from Courland were invited to help run her government and Russia's cultural institutions (for example, the Academy of Sciences **Акаде́мия нау́к**). This dark period is often referred to as the Bironovshchina **биро́новщина** in Russian, after the Empress's favorite.

Elizaveta Petrovna

Елизаве́та Петро́вна

A palace coup kept Anna Ioannovna's chosen successor from retaining the throne and brought to power Peter the Great's daughter Elizaveta Petrovna **Елизаве́та Петро́вна** (ruled 1741–61). While the political accomplishments of her twenty-year reign were not especially brilliant, it was under her that a westernized Russian culture finally took hold. Elizabeth's reign saw Rastrelli's rococo reconstructions of a number of major royal palaces—namely Peterhof **Петерго́ф**, the Catherine Palace **Екатери́нинский дворе́ц** at Tsarskoe Selo **Ца́рское Село́** (lit. Tsar's village), and the Winter Palace **Зи́мний дворе́ц** in St. Petersburg proper. The 1740s saw the rise of the fisherman's son Mikhail Lomonosov **Михаи́л Ломоно́сов** (1711–65), a man of such diverse intellectual talents and abilities that Pushkin labeled him "the first Russian university" **пе́рвый ру́сский университе́т**. With Lomonosov the process of the codification of a new Russian literary language took shape, and to this day his verse is considered the beginning of modern Russian poetry. He was instrumental in establishing Moscow University in 1755, an institution which today bears his name. His faith that education would lead talented Russians to make scientific discoveries of international importance is summarized in these frequently quoted lines from his *Ode of 1747* «**Ода 1747 года**»:

… мóжет сóбственных Платóнов
И бы́стрых рáзумом Невтóнов
Росси́йская земля́ рожда́ть.

… the Russian land can give birth
To its own Platos
And quick-minded Newtons.

Catherine the Great	Екатери́на Втора́я (Вели́кая)

The second most distinguished leader of the 18th century was Catherine the Second **Екатери́на Втора́я** also known as the Great **Вели́кая** (ruled 1762–96). A German princess who married into the Russian royal family, she was involved in the palace coup that ended the life and brief reign of her husband Petr III **Пётр Тре́тий** (grandson of Peter the Great). Her reign passed under the slogan of Enlightened Absolutism **просвещённый абсолюти́зм**, in which Catherine herself was the enlightened ruler. She corresponded with Voltaire and wrote plays and other artistic literature in Russian (although her native language was German, and the language of her court was French).

Fig. 1-17.   Dmitri Levitskii, *Portrait of Catherine the Great in the Temple of the Goddess of Justice* «**Портре́т Екатери́ны II, законода́тельницы в хра́ме боги́ни Правосу́дия**» (1783)

Foreign Policy   ***Внéшняя полúтика***

In foreign affairs there were two major wars with Turkey during Catherine's reign. The first, in 1768–74, brought fame to Rumiantsev **Румя́нцев** as commander of the Army and Orlov **Орло́в** as commander of the Russian fleet; the second, in 1787–92, assured General Suvorov's **Суво́ров** (1730–1800) place in history as conqueror of the Turkish fortresses at Ochakov **Оча́ков** and Ismail **Изма́йл**.[7] These victorious wars gave Russia control over Crimea and the northern coast of the Black Sea, extending from the Caucasus **Кавка́з** in the East to the River Dniester **Днестр** in the West. After the first wars, Catherine put her favorite Potemkin **Потёмкин** in charge of populating the Russian territorial gains in order to secure Russian control of them. During an inspection of the area in 1787, the new settlements impressed Catherine, Emperor Joseph II of Austria and King Stanislaw Poniatowski of Poland. From a distance, the villages looked very prosperous; in reality some of them were no more than set designs that Potemkin had erected to create the illusion of prosperity. Thus the expression "Potemkin villages" **потёмкинские дере́вни** stands for any project whose substance is only an illusion designed to impress others. To be fair, during Catherine's reign there were large-scale immigrations of German settlers which advanced Russian agricultural production. The most famous concentration of these settlers was in the lower Volga, from where the "Volga German" **пово́лжский не́мец** designation arose.

During Catherine's reign, Russia, Prussia, and Austria participated in three successive partitionings of Poland **разде́лы По́льши** (1772, 1793, 1795), which gave Russia enormous tracks of land in Lithuania, Belorussia and Ukraine, and Poland proper. With this land, Russia inherited for the first time a large Jewish population which later Tsarist authorities would restrict by instituting the Pale of Settlement **черта́ осе́длости**. This policy prohibited Jews from living outside of certain areas of the Russian Empire, except in special circumstances.

Pugachev   ***Пугачёв***

By far the most significant domestic event of Catherine's reign was the Pugachev rebellion **Пугачёвское восста́ние** (also known by the derogatory name **пугачёвщина**), which had great repercussions on internal politics. In 1773 claiming to be the Emperor Petr III (miraculously saved after the palace coup of 1762), Emel'ian Pugachev **Емелья́н Пугачёв** (1742–75) initiated a rebellion in the Urals and along the Iaik River **Яи́к**, which quickly engulfed the eastern parts of European Russia. In his proclamations which he signed as Petr III, Pugachev declared that, if returned to power, he would end serfdom and grant his supporters all the land and benefits enjoyed by the nobility. The appeal

---

[7] Suvorov is also famous for his campaigns against Napoleon's Army in Northern Italy and Switzerland in the late 1790s. See Surikov's famous painting of him crossing the Alps with his soldiers.

found rich support among the peasants, Cossacks and non-Russian peoples of the area (the Bashkirs **башки́ры**, Tatars **тата́ры**, and Kalmyks **калмы́ки** whose lot in the course of the 18th century had become quite hard. In addition to military attacks on towns such as Orenburg and Kazan', the rebellion was marked by the brutal hangings of captured army officers, government officials and nobles. Furthermore, many peasants revolted against their masters and burned their estates. By the end of 1774 Pugachev was captured and taken to Moscow, where he was executed on January 10, 1775. The rebellion is well known to Russians, especially from Pushkin's historical novel *The Captain's Daughter* **«Капита́нская до́чка»** (1836). Pushkin's insightful line about the "pointless and merciless Russian revolt" **ру́сский бунт, бессмы́сленный и беспоща́дный** is often cited by Russians with regard to this and other popular rebellions. The Pugachev rebellion was the last large-scale peasant uprising in Imperial Russia, and Catherine's government worked hard to erase all memory of it, even renaming the Iaik River, where it began, the Ural River **Ура́л**.

Domestic Policy   *Вну́тренняя поли́тика*

The Pugachev rebellion shook Catherine and her authority, and from 1775 onwards she worked to shore up her support among the Russian nobility. With the territorial expansion of the Empire, Catherine gave huge estates to her generals and favorites and extended serfdom into new areas of the Empire. In 1785 she granted the *Charter of the Nobility* **Жа́лованная гра́мота дворя́нству**, which assured the nobility of the right to petition the monarch directly, freedom from service, taxation and corporal punishment, and recognition of the nobles' full rights over their property, including serfs. The exploitation of serfs increased significantly during Catherine's reign and this led to the first exposés about the evils of serfdom, such as Alexander Nikolaevich Radishchev's (1749–1802) *Journey from St. Petersburg to Moscow* **«Путеше́ствие из Петербу́рга в Москву́»** (1790), which unfortunately fell victim to the first overt governmental book-banning in Russia. Radishchev's exposure of the horrible conditions of serfs under their overbearing masters incensed Catherine; and she had the author exiled to Siberia for 10 years. Allowed back from exile after Catherine's death in 1796, Radishchev was even asked to participate in the government's plans to reform serfdom during Alexander I's reign. The threat of new reprisals drove him to suicide. Soviet historiography celebrated Radishchev as "the first Russian revolutionary" **пе́рвый ру́сский революционе́р**.

Golden Age of the Nobility   Золото́й век дворя́нства

Life in Society   *Све́тская жизнь*

The 18th century is often known as the Golden Age of the Nobility **Золото́й век дворя́нства**, since Peter's reforms eventually led to the creation of a new class of Europeanized Russians. The ways of life for these nobles changed greatly, not only in external fashions: low-cut hoop dresses for women, frock coats and breeches for men, powdered wigs for both; but also in the very patterns of socialization. Peter was the first to establish assemblies **ассамблéи** where men and women were expected to socialize together (previously Russian noble women had been strictly segregated from male company, spending their lives in quarters known as the terem **тéрем**). In the following decades, fashions and manners became even more Europeanized, with French becoming the standard language of social occasions. The year was divided into the winter social season in the cities, and the summer retreat to the country estate (**имéние/усáдьба**). Presence in the cities (preferably Moscow or St. Petersburg) for the winter season's balls and entertainment was important even for the less affluent gentry since it provided the best venue for match-making and marriages. Visiting and receiving guests became a significant form of socializing in the second half of the 18th century, and it came to be considered "good form" for the host to be hospitable even beyond his means. Having guests necessitated elaborate, lengthy meals with exotic ingredients served with imported wines. These dinners **обéды** were followed by entertainment—often in the form of a home theater (the most famous "domestic theater" **домáшний теáтр** belonged to the Sheremet'ev counts, with performances in their Moscow palace at Ostankino **Остáнкино**) or orchestra (whose actors, singers, and musicians were trained serfs), followed by dancing, card games, billiards, walks through exquisite gardens, and so on. Extravagance in entertainment became a way of life, and expenditures for building, furnishing and maintenance of city and country homes (with all of their related outbuildings **флѝгели**) became highly significant.   📖 **1-21**

Upbringing of Children   *Воспитáние детéй*

The upbringing and education of children changed significantly in 18th century Russia. Many nobles hired foreign, usually French, governors **гувернёры** (fem. **гувернáнтка**) and tutors **учителя́** to provide primary education in the home. Such tutors provided basic instruction in reading, writing, languages, history, sciences, manners, and other activities such as fencing, dancing, and so on. As the frequent social satires of time would suggest (cf. the German tutor Wralman **Врáльман** [lit., Liar-Man] of Fonvizin's play *The Minor* **«Нéдоросль»**), these foreigners often had poor training (and sometimes no training) for their duties and little interest in their charges. After these home tutors, sons might be sent off for more formal schooling, usually military in nature, or directly into service in the army or bureaucracy. Daughters were also educated mostly at home, although there were boarding schools **пансиóны**, the most famous of which was the Institute for Girls of the Nobility **Институ́т благорóдных деви́ц** at Petersburg's Smolny Convent **Смóльный монасты́рь**.

Finances   *Фина́нсы*

Debt was a major fact of life for the gentry. Even the richest members of the nobility found themselves constantly in need of money, which they raised by: 1) performing government service for salary; 2) increasing the obligations of their peasants; 3) mortgaging their estates or selling off land, forests, or resources. The first of these options did not necessarily bring in great revenue (although there were cases of exceptional royal generosity). Nobles frequently resorted to the second possibility. Average peasant obligations in terms of both quit-rent **обро́к** and corvée **ба́рщина** grew considerably between 1760–1800; but peasant labor was not an inexhaustible resource. The third path often led to the land-owner's complete bankruptcy, since the amount of land and resources to sell was finite, and their fixed incomes created problems in repaying the interest on loans and mortgages. These considerations play important parts in many major works of Russian literature set in the first part of the 19th century. For example, in Pushkin's *Eugene Onegin* **«Евге́ний Оне́гин»** we learn about the title character's father:

🔊 1-22 | Служи́в отли́чно—благоро́дно, | Having served excellently and nobly, |
|---|---|
| Долга́ми жил его́ оте́ц, | His father lived in debt |
| Дава́л три ба́ла ежего́дно | He hosted three balls each year |
| И промота́лся наконе́ц. [1.3] | And finally went broke. |

Similarly, the young Nikolai Rostov **Никола́й Росто́в** of Tolstoy's *War and Peace* **«Война́ и мир»** has to pay off his father's debts if he wants to maintain the family's honorable name. He is saved from life as an impoverished noble only by his marriage to the wealthy heiress Princess Mar′ia **княжна́ Ма́рья Болко́нская**.

At the onset of the 19th century, many Russian nobles with small estates had to live quite frugally to avoid bankrupcy, exacting everything they could from the land and peasants they owned. These landowners **поме́щики** became the targets for frequent criticism in Russian literature (cf. Gogol's *Dead Souls* **«Мёртвые ду́ши»** and Chekhov's "Land-owners" **«Поме́щики»**), where the stereotypical landowner is shown to be hopelessly backward, narrow-minded, parsimonious, and cruel.

The westernizing changes that touched all aspects of the lives of the nobility in the 18th century affected the lives of the common folk **наро́д** very little (except for the increasing obligations of serfdom). The new culture of the elite left almost no reflection in folk culture, which continued in its traditional forms. All in all, Peter the Great's reforms, which were designed to create a single great Russian state, wound up creating virtually two separate Russian peoples. Bridging this cultural divide became a significant question for Russians in the 19th century.

The Nineteenth Century

Introduction

Девятна́дцатый век

Введе́ние

It is not unusual for the shape of history to vary widely depending on its writer; however, this is particularly true for Soviet histories of Russia's development in the 19th century. In them all national history had to be reduced and fit into a scheme leading to the inevitable Socialist Revolution of October 1917. All events in the last 117 years of Tsarist history could be classified as good or bad, depending on whether they fostered the development of Russian national consciousness, exposed the contradictions of autocracy, drew on national and popular movements, or moved the nation to a new stage on its path towards socialism. The intensely teleological nature of this historiography generally restricted the breadth of subjects covered in most history textbooks to those events which were easiest to fit into this scheme. For example, the war with Napoleon and its connection to the Decembrists were overemphasized; but there was little mention of Tsar Alexander I's early liberalism, including the freeing of serfs in the Baltic lands and Poland.

1800–25 гг.

Alexander I

Алекса́ндр Пе́рвый

Alexander I **Алекса́ндр Па́влович** (ruled 1801–25) came to power when his unpopular father Pavel I **Па́вел Пе́рвый** (ruled 1796–1801) was suffocated to death in his bed chamber by members of the royal guard. The beginning of the new tsar's reign was accompanied by a burst of enthusiasm, since it seemed likely that he would make significant reforms, putting an end to serfdom and bringing Russia in line with Western European powers. In the period 1807–12 Alexander's proposals for reforms were spearheaded by his talented assistant Mikhail Speranskii **Михаи́л Спера́нский** (1772–1839), who even proposed a constitution for Russia. Unfortunately, the "wonderful days of Alexander's beginning" **дней Алекса́ндровых прекра́сное нача́ло** (as Pushkin wrote) remained mostly an unfulfilled promise.

Patriotic War of 1812

Оте́чественная война́ 1812 г.

What claims Russians' attention most about this period are the conflicts with Napoleon, which culminated in the French invasion in June 1812. This began what is commonly known in Russia as the Patriotic War of 1812 **Оте́чественная война́ 1812 го́да**. The events of this war have fueled numerous historical novels, poems, memoirs, and movies—most notably Tolstoy's *War and Peace* **«Война́ и мир»** (both in its prose form and in the epic Soviet movie of 1966 which together serve as easily remembered sources about this war).

In face of superior French forces, the Russian armies, at first commanded by Generals Barclay-de-Tolly **Баркла́й де То́лли** and Bagration **Багратио́н**, were forced to retreat. After these initial setbacks, public opinion forced Alexander I to appoint Mikhail Illarionovich Kutuzov **Михаи́л Илларио́нович Куту́зов** (1745–1813) as supreme commander **главнокома́ндующий** of the Russian forces. Well-liked by the military, Kutuzov has been immortalized in the popular imagination as a wise old fox, who knew that patient waiting would force Napoleon to overextend himself and thus allow the Russians victory. The most famous battle of this war was fought at Borodino **Бородино́**, a village just outside of Moscow, on August 26, 1812. The casualties on both sides were extremely heavy in this one day of fighting, and Kutuzov ordered a retreat even though parts of the Russian defenses held. The battle is celebrated in Lermontov's poem "Borodino," a school standard.

Following the battle, on September 1 in a wooden hut in the village of Fili (now a district of Moscow), Kutuzov and his military council made the decision to abandon Moscow to Napoleon without another battle. Occupying Moscow for little over a month, Napoleon's army looted the deserted capital. During the occupation, many buildings burnt in the Moscow Fire **пожа́р 1812 го́да**. Although Napoleon thought that taking Moscow would force Alexander I into peace talks, the Tsar and the army remained fixed in their opposition to the French. On October 6 Napoleon decided to withdraw from Moscow and make his way back to Central Europe. Kutuzov pursued Napoleon and blocked his attempts to take a southern route through well-supplied lands. Forced to retreat along the same devastated route by which it entered the country, the Grande Armée **вели́кая а́рмия** was almost completely destroyed by December 1812, when it left Russian soil. During the occupation of Moscow and the retreat, peasant partisan groups **партиза́нские отря́ды** and small guerilla-like forces, lead by dashing figures like the Hussar Denis Davydov **гуса́р Дени́с Давы́дов**, hounded Napoleon's forces in occupied territory, capturing supplies,

Fig. 1-18.   Alexander Kivshenko, *War Council at Fili* «Вое́нный сове́т в Филя́х» (1879)

and interfering with communications. The role of such grass-roots efforts and the enormous popular support for the war have received much attention in the historical literature and have turned this war into a great *national* struggle for survival in the popular imagination.[8]

The peace treaty of the Congress of Vienna **Вéнский конгрéсс** in 1815 gave Russia a major role to play in European politics. Allying itself with European absolute monarchies, Tsarist Russia came to stand steadfastly against popular national rebellions.

Arakcheev's Policies   *Аракчéевщина*

The second half of Alexander I's reign was distinguished by a growing conservatism in his domestic policies, especially with General A.A. Arakcheev **Аракчéев** as minister of war and later prime minister. The general became infamous for his "military settlements" **воéнные поселéния** where soldiers and their families were settled on land which they were expected to farm for their subsistence. Although the plan made supporting a standing army cheaper, it had flaws: absolute military discipline extended over all aspects of family life in these settlements; and all disturbances were ruthlessly supressed. On the whole, the conservative policies of the last years of Alexander's reign became known as **аракчéевщина**.

As officialdom and the court became more conservative, many of Russia's better educated nobles (frequently veterans of the campaigns against Napoleon) looked for more progressive solutions to Russia's problems. On the model of the Free Masons **масóны**, who had been active in Russia since the 18th century, various secret societies **тáйные óбщества** formed after 1812 to discuss political issues, such as the abolition of serfdom and the creation of a constitutional monarchy or a republic in Russia.

Decembrists   *Декабрúсты*

Alexander I's accidental death in November 1825 provided an opportunity for these societies to act.[9] Since Alexander had no children, the line of succession was unclear; most assumed that the throne would go to Alexander's brother

---

[8] It is not surprising, therefore, that the destruction and reconstruction of Moscow's Cathedral of Christ the Savior **Храм Христá Спасúтеля**, a monument to the Russian victory in 1812, has been such a target of controversy. The original building (blown up in 1931 by the Soviets) was a popular monument to Russia's struggle in 1812. The popular nature of the building was emphasized by the fact that it was funded entirely by public donations **нарóдные дéньги**. With its reconstruction in 1997, this structure has emerged as a national (but not entirely popular) symbol of Russia's rebirth after Soviet rule.

[9] Legends persist that Alexander I did not die in the hunting accident in Taganrog in 1825. According to them, Alexander, supposedly feeling guilty for his part in the conspiracy against his father, arranged his "death" so that he could secretly escape his duties as tsar to live the life of a simple hermit under the name Fedor Kuz'mich.

Konstantin **Константи́н**, but he had already secretly renounced it. Few wanted Alexander's brother Nicholas **Никола́й** as the new tsar, because he was generally disliked by the military for his strict and overbearing personality. On December 14, 1825 when troops were assembled on Senate Square in St. Petersburg to swear allegiance to Nicholas as the new tsar, some divisions refused to do so.

Nicholas was already well informed about the plot; and after some attempts to end the conflict peacefully, Nicholas called in loyal troops, and the rebellion was put down by force. Of the rebels, called Decembrists **Декабри́сты**, five (Ryleev **Рыле́ев**, Pestel **Пе́стель**, Murav'ev-Apostol **Муравьёв-Апо́стол**, Bestuzhev-Riumin **Бесту́жев-Рю́мин**, Kakhovsky **Кахо́вский**) were executed; 500 other men were sentenced to hard labor **ка́торга** in Siberia, exile in distant provinces under police surveillance or active duty in the Caucasus. The Decembrist rebellion **Восста́ние декабри́стов** was easily put down because it was disorganized, had little support outside of a small group of elite military officers, and lacked a coherent plan of action.

Fig. 1-19.   K. Kol'man, *The Insurrection of December 14, 1825 on Senate Square* «**Восста́ние 14 декабря́ 1825 го́да на Сена́тской пло́щади**» (1830)

1826–60 гг.

Nicholas I   *Никола́й Пе́рвый*

The threat of revolution set the tenor for the whole conservative thirty-year reign (1825–55) of Nicholas I **Никола́й Пе́рвый**, whose ideological beliefs are captured in the three-word slogan: Orthodoxy **Правосла́вие**, Autocracy **Самодержа́вие**, Nationality **Наро́дность**. According to this official ideology, it was these three factors (Russia's historical choice of religion, the absolute authority of the tsar, and the uniqueness of the Russian national character) that made the country great, and these three special aspects of Russian life must firmly be maintained for Russia to withstand subversive foreign influences and ideologies. To keep track of potential threats, Nicholas created the hated Third Department **Тре́тье отделе́ние** or secret police, headed by Count Alexander Benckendorff **Бенкендо́рф**, whose very name stands for state repression and censorship. Nicholas established preliminary review of all books and manuscripts by a government censorship board **цензу́ра**; and the decisions of this committee touched some of the most famous works of Russian literature, including Gogol's *Dead Souls* «**Мёртвые ду́ши**». The Emperor even declared himself to be Pushkin's personal censor.

Petrashevtsy   *Петраше́вцы*

Private correspondence was regularly read by government agents, and private meetings and regular salons, when allowed, were often infiltrated by informers **доно́счики**. One famous case involved the Petersburg Petrashevtsy **Петраше́вцы** named after Mikhail Vasil'evich Butashevich-Petrashevskii **Петраше́вский** who organized meetings in his apartment. In 1849 this group, dedicated to the discussion of Christian Socialism (or Utopian Socialism **утопи́ческий социали́зм** as Soviet historians called it), was raided and all its members were arrested. Twenty-one participants, including the young writer Fedor Dostoevsky **Достое́вский**, were sentenced to death by hanging. Their lives were spared by a last-minute reprieve, designed by Nicholas for maximum dramatic effect. Dostoevsky and the others were sentenced to hard labor in Siberia, followed by military service as enlisted men.

Slavophilism and Westernism   *Славянофи́льство и за́падничество*

The politically repressive climate of the 1830s and 40s did not hinder the development of two very opposing ideologies in Russia: Slavophilism **славянофи́льство** and Westernism **за́падничество** (their respective proponents being Slavophiles **славянофи́лы** and Westernizers **за́падники**). Slavophiles (represented chiefly by Aleksei Khomiakov **Хомяко́в** and the brothers Ivan and Konstantin Aksakov **Акса́ков**) attributed Russia's problems to the westernization forcibly induced by Peter the Great. According to them this change disrupted the natural harmonious communal form of life and religious faith and practice (sobornost′ **соборность**) that had marked the lives of both peasant and noble in the times before Peter. While proponents of patriarchial traditions, the Slavophiles nonetheless thought that an end to serfdom was necessary in order to return to this balanced life. In contrast, the Westernizers were supporters of Peter the Great's reforms, although they saw a need for continued development along western models, including the abolition of serfdom and the restructuring of political power. Both of these ideological camps were populated by "men of the 40s" (that is, 1840s) **люди сороковы́х годо́в**, who were more inclined toward philosophical reflection and expression than to revolutionary propaganda, which explains why Nicholas I's government tolerated their discussions.

Thick Journals   *Тóлстые журнáлы*

These philosophical schools, together with the growth of Russian literary talent, became the basic fare of Russia's first journals, often referred to as thick journals **тóлстые журнáлы**, since each issue consisted of several hundred pages. From the 1830s onward, such journals consistently served as the main battlegrounds for political, literary, and aesthetic discussions and polemics. They fulfilled a social function: since a single copy might be widely circulated among members of a family or social circle, the journals helped develop a certain set of common, shared experiences and intellectual ideas for the developing intelligentsia **интеллиге́нция**. A few of the most famous journals were the conservative *Muscovite* **«Москвитя́нин»** (1841–56) and *Russian Messenger* **«Ру́сский ве́стник»** (1856–1906), the liberal *The Contemporary* **«Совреме́нник»** (1836–66), and *Annals of the Fatherland* **«Оте́чественные запи́ски»** (1839–84).

The Intelligentsia   *Интеллиге́нция*

In addition to these ideological camps, several intellectual figures of this time merit mention. Petr Chaadaev **Пётр Чаада́ев**, whose first *Philosophical Letter* **«Философи́ческое письмо́»** (1836) contained outspoken opinions about Russia's lack of a past, created a great stir in Russian society. He was declared a madman by Nicholas' government and was subjected to house arrest.

Alexander Herzen **Алекса́ндр Ге́рцен** (1812–70), the illegitimate son of a noble, became the most important voice against the status quo in Russian political life. Following a series of arrests and internal exiles, Herzen left his homeland in 1847 for England, where he established the Free Russian Press **Во́льная ру́сская типогра́фия** which produced numerous works to counter the heavily censored Russian press. Herzen is most closely connected with the press' newspaper *The Bell* **«Ко́локол»**, which was regularly smuggled into Russia and had a wide distribution among the Russian reading public. Herzen's London press and its publications became a vital center for anti-tsarist propaganda and revolutionary activity.

A third figure of the 1830 and 1840s is Vissarion Grigor'evich Belinskii **Виссарио́н Григо́рьевич Бели́нский** (1811–48), Russia's most famous literary critic. His radical socio-political views and readings of Pushkin, Gogol, Turgenev, and the young Dostoevsky became the standard interpretations of these authors and their works for many generations of Russians, both in the 19th century and in the Soviet period. Some of these opinions are embodied in well-known one-liners, such as this one about Pushkin's novel in verse: "*Evgenii Onegin* is the encyclopedia of Russian life" **«Евге́ний Оне́гин»—энциклопе́дия ру́сской жи́зни»**. Among Belinskii's most famous works is his "Letter to Gogol'" **«Письмо́ к Го́голю»** (1848) in which he berated the religious, mystical tones of the writer's *Selected Passages from Correspondence with Friends* **«Вы́бранные места́ из перепи́ски с друзья́ми»** which glorified the patriarchal life of the Russian nobility and peasantry. Belinskii died in 1848 from consumption (tuberculosis) **чахо́тка** (a cliché of 19th-century biographies).

Belinskii's social origins are a true sign of the changing times of the 1830s and 40s in Russia. Son of a military doctor, Belinskii was a raznochinets **разночи́нец** (that is, someone neither from the nobility nor the peasantry) who rose to his place in Russian society through his university education. Razno-chintsy and other similar social groups (for example, priests' sons **попо́вичи**) were important players in Russia's cultural life in the 19th century and contributed to the development of the country's intelligentsia.

Foreign Policy   *Вне́шняя поли́тика*

In foreign policy Nicholas I was as conservative as he was in domestic affairs. Vehemently opposed to national independence movements, he had Russian troops intervene to put down rebellions in Central Europe on several occasions, and this won him the nickname "policeman of Europe" **жанда́рм Евро́пы**. Despite these interventions, the old political order was being challenged by new directions in social, economic and political thought. The popular uprisings in several European countries in 1848 inspired Karl Marx to write the *Communist Manifesto*, which was translated into Russian as **«Манифе́ст Коммунисти́ческой па́ртии»**. Two of its famous lines are "Workers of the world, unite!" **Пролета́рии всех стран, соединя́йтесь**!, which became the motto of Lenin's newspaper *Truth* **«Пра́вда»**; and "A spectre is haunting Europe, the spectre of Communism" **При́зрак бро́дит по Евро́пе, при́зрак коммуни́зма**.

The Crimean War   *Кры́мская война́*

Towards the end of Nicholas' reign, Russia got involved in a power struggle with Turkey for dominance over the Balkans and the Black Sea. Since Russia's army was superior to Turkey's, it quickly took Moldavia **Молда́вия** and Wallachia **Вала́хия**, and Russia's fleet under the leadership of Admiral P.S.

Nakhimov **Нахи́мов** took Sinope, a Turkish port on the Black Sea. France and England, alarmed at this sudden shift in power, joined Turkey in the war, and Russia was soon overpowered. Much of the military action in the second half of the war was concentrated on Crimea **Крым** and Russia's naval base at Sevastopol **Севасто́поль** which was under siege almost 11 months before falling in August 1855. Lev Tolstoy **Лев Никола́евич Толсто́й**, who served in this campaign, described the conditions in the besieged city in his three Sevastopol sketches **Севасто́польские расска́зы**. Russia sued for peace and received poor terms, losing much influence in the Balkans and on the Black Sea. The Crimean war **Кры́мская война́** (1853–56) is remembered in Russian history as a sign of the country's military, technological, and financial weakness **бесси́лие**, decay **гни́лость**, and backwardness **отста́лость**. The only positive outcome of the war was the realization that Russia desperately needed reform.

POST-REFORM RUSSIA   ПОРЕФО́РМЕННАЯ РОССИ́Я

Abolition of Serfdom   Отме́на крепостно́го пра́ва

Fig. 1-20.   Grigorii Miasoedov, *Reading the Manifesto of February 19, 1861*
«Чте́ние манифе́ста 19 февраля́ 1861 го́да» (1873)

Alexander II, who assumed the throne in 1855, prepared great reforms **вели́кие рефо́рмы** for the country, starting with the abolition of serfdom **отме́на крепостно́го пра́ва**. After 5 years of negotiations concerning the conditions for liberation, the serfs were freed on February 19, 1861 by legislation known as the **Положе́ние 19-го февраля́ 1861 го́да,** which was announced in a royal manifesto **манифе́ст** on the same day.

With their liberation, peasants in general received about half of the land allotment **наде́л** that they had previously farmed for themselves. The tsarist government compensated the landowners for this land directly, leaving the peasants to make redemptive payments **вы́куп** to the government over a period of 49 years if they wanted actually to own the land. In the meantime, all peasant land was considered the property not of the individual peasant or his family, but of the whole village community **общи́на** (also called **мир**) which was headed by an elder **ста́роста**. The **общи́на** as a unit was responsible to the government for all of its members, which led to a system of collective responsibility (and collective cover-ups) known as **кругова́я пору́ка**. This system provided members of the community with ways to avoid responsibility for problems that arose in the community.

Collective responsibility also insured that no member of the community would "blow the whistle" on others in the community since they would all be held responsible to the outside authorities. Many point to this tradition as the root for the lack of personal responsibility that the peasants felt for meeting their obligations. Even today this expression is used to explain people's failures in meeting individual responsibilities and group cover-ups of problems and corruption. Agriculture **агра́рный вопро́с** remained a sore point right up until 1917, and made the Bolsheviks' promise of "Land for the peasants" **Земля́— крестья́нам** attractive to the peasantry.

Other Reforms   **Други́е рефо́рмы**

Following the liberation of the serfs, Alexander II, now the Tsar-Liberator **Царь-освободи́тель**, instituted a series of reforms in the military and judiciary system (including criminal trials by jury **прися́жные заседа́тели**). He also loosened his predecessor's censorship restrictions on the press, which allowed a new wave of radical thought into Russia's periodicals and gave considerable latitude to Russia's expanding universities.

The Woman Question   **Же́нский вопро́с**

Along with the discussions of the emancipation of the peasants, the liberal and left wings of Russian society from the mid-1850s onward became more concerned with the "woman question" **же́нский вопро́с**, that is, women's struggles for political and social rights. Until 1917 women had few legal rights in Russia, and they were frequently required to obtain the permission of their fathers or husbands before embarking on any undertaking, even as basic as traveling abroad. They were denied access to university-level education, until institutions such as advanced women's courses **вы́сшие же́нские ку́рсы** were created in the 1870s. Women who attended these became known as **курси́стки**. Lack of progress in the area of women's rights in the second half of the 19th century helped to radicalize Russian women which in part explains why such a large number of Russian revolutionaries were women.

Nihilists   Нигили́сты

From the second half of the 1850s many university students **студе́нты** and other young men and women were swept up in radical politics. Proclaimed "nihilists" **нигили́сты** by their opponents (since they rejected all social conventions), these new radicals, Nikolai Chernyshevsky **Никола́й Черныше́вский** (1828–89), the most famous among them, preached an atheistic gospel of utilitarianism, positivism, and realism. Written in 1862–63 in a cell of the Peter-Paul Fortress, Chernyshevsky's novel *What is to be Done?* «**Что де́лать?**» became the bible of Russian leftists, who strove to put into practice Chernyshevsky's radical vision for the transformation of society on a communal, cooperative basis where all are guided by enlightened self-interest.

Populism   Наро́дничество

By the end of the 1860s, when radical propaganda had failed to incite revolutionary change in Russia's urban centers, the radicals turned to the peasantry. In the summers of 1874–75, university students "went out to the people" **пошли́ в наро́д** to educate the peasants and spread revolutionary enlightenment among them. While this "going to the people" **хожде́ние в наро́д** was a failure (the peasants met these newcomers with great skepticism, and tsarist police cracked down on the students during the summer of 1874), the spirit of populism **наро́дничество** remained high among Russia's radicals, and they tried to build momentum for a revolt by playing on the discontent of the peasants.

The People's Will   Наро́дная во́ля

Two political groups arose following the failure of "going to the people": "Land and Freedom" **Земля́ и Во́ля** in 1876 and "The People's Will" **Наро́дная во́ля** in 1879. The latter group believed in the use of terrorism to provoke a full revolutionary uprising, and on March 1, 1881 its members assassinated Alexander II. The site of the assassination in St. Petersburg is now 1-23 marked by the ornate Church of the Savior on the Blood **Спас на Крови́**. The architectural style of this church, reminiscent of St. Basil's in Moscow, was a symbol of Alexander III's determination to oppose westernizing movements with a return to old Russian values and traditions.

Reaction Реа́кция

Shaken by the brutal murder of his father, Alexander III **Александр III** (ruled 1881–94) embarked on a reign of extreme reactionary politics, with the arch-conservative Konstantin Pobedonostsev **Победоно́сцев** leading the Russian church and carrying out the tsar's social agenda. He instituted policies of Russification **русифика́ция** of the Empire's many nationalities and fostered anti-semitic sentiment in the country, encouraging even violent attacks **погро́мы** against the Empire's Jewish population. The Russian revolutionary movement continued, but it was led primarily from abroad. In the 1880s in Geneva, Switzerland the political thinker Georgii Plekhanov **Плеха́нов** began the theoretical work of translating Marx's political and social ideas into Russian reality. The 1880s and 90s saw tremendous growth of interest in Marxism **маркси́зм** in Russia as well as the beginnings of the political career of Vladimir Il'ich Ul'ianov **Влади́мир Ильи́ч Улья́нов** (aka Lenin **Ле́нин**, 1870–1924).

Tolstoyanism Толсто́вство

At the end of the 19th century Alexander III's reactionary ideology and Marxism competed with another significant philosophical and ethical movement in Russia, Tolstoyanism **толсто́вство**. In the 1880s the writer Tolstoy **Толсто́й** experienced a deep spiritual crisis, which led him to "simplify" his life and to start personally working the land on his estate Yasnaia Poliana **Я́сная Поля́на**. With this change of life, he began to develop his social, religious, and political views (including vegetarianism **вегетариа́нство**, non-violent resistance to evil **непротивле́ние злу наси́лием**) into a new ethical religious way of life, ▣ **1-24** and he attracted followers known as Tolstoyans **толсто́вцы**. While the details of Tolstoy's political and moral development were not examined in the Soviet period, children were taught Lenin's quote that Tolstoy was a "mirror of Russian revolution" **зе́ркало ру́сской револю́ции**.

Scientific Discoveries Нау́чные откры́тия

The 19th century saw numerous technological innovations imported into Russia: the first railroad **желе́зная доро́га** was opened in 1837 between St. Petersburg and Tsarskoe Selo (a line to Moscow followed in 1851; and the Trans-Siberian tracks **транссиби́рская желе́зная доро́га** were virtually completed in 1903); coal mining grew in the Donbass, and oil deposits were found around Baku; major textile factories grew up around Moscow. Important scientific discoveries were made by Russians as well: the mathematician Lobachevskii **Лобаче́вский** (1792–1856) developed non-Euclidian geometry; the surgeon Sechenov **Се́ченов** (1829–1905) worked on the brain and reflexes; the chemist Mendeleev **Менделе́ев** (1834–1907) produced the Periodic Table of Elements; and the physiologist Pavlov **Па́влов** (1849–1936) conducted experiments on conditioned behaviors using dogs.

THE END OF THE EMPIRE	КОНЕ́Ц ИМПЕ́РИИ
Nicholas II	**Никола́й Второ́й**

Poorly educated and ill-prepared for power, Nicholas II (1868–1918) became emperor in 1894. Legend has embellished the aura of doom around the last tsar and his family, especially the ominous incident during his coronation in 1896 when thousands were crushed in a stampede at Khodynka Field **Ходы́нка** in Moscow. Despite the deaths, the new tsar continued his schedule of celebratory balls and social gatherings.

Political Parties	**Полити́ческие па́ртии**

In the late 1890s and first decades of the twentieth century Russia experienced intense industrial expansion, but there was little accompanying legislation to support and protect workers from excessive exploitation. Political revolutionaries began to join with labor organizers which gave rise to potent political parties. The SD **СД (эс-дэ)**, the Social Democrats **социа́л-демокра́ты** or officially the Russian Social-Democratic Labor Party **РСДРП Росси́йская социа́л-демократи́ческая рабо́чая па́ртия** was founded in 1898. At the Party's Second Congress in London in 1903, there was a disagreement over party organization, and the movement split into two factions: the Bolsheviks **большевики́**, led by Lenin, and the Mensheviks **меньшевики́**. Other political parties of the time were: SR **СР (эс-эр)**, the Socialist Revolutionaries **социал-революционе́ры** (who favored terrorism) and the Cadets **каде́ты** (short for Constitutional Democrats **конституцио́нные демокра́ты**), who favored a liberal constitutional monarchy or republic. On the extreme right, tsarism was supported by Monarchists **монархи́сты**, the Union of the Russian People **Сою́з ру́сского наро́да**, and vigilante squads, the Black Hundreds, **чёрные со́тни**, an individual member of which was called a "man of the Black Hundred" **черносо́тенец**. This last expression is still used today to describe people with crude (and potentially violent) nationalistic ideas.

1905 г.

Russia's embarrassing military defeats in the Russo-Japanese War **Ру́сско-Япо́нская война́** (1904–05) and the economic strains it caused both for the peasantry and industrial workers, the proletariat **пролетариа́т**, fueled considerable discontent and political unrest. On January 9, 1905, a group of workers from St. Petersburg's factories led by the priest Gapon **Гапо́н** marched to the Winter Palace to present Nicholas with a petition **пети́ция**, demanding reforms in labor laws and government policies. Troops fired on the peaceful demonstration, and the day has entered Russian history as Bloody Sunday **Крова́вое воскресе́нье**. It ignited a year of strikes, assassinations, uprisings, and rebellions in Russia's cities and countryside, referred to as the Revolution of 1905

Револю́ция 1905 го́да, summed up by Lenin as the "dress rehearsal" **гене-ра́льная репети́ция** for October 1917. Three famous incidents from this revolution were the uprising on the Battleship Potemkin **восста́ние на бронено́сце «Потёмкин»** in the Black Sea (celebrated in Eisenstein's film, see Chapter 9), **1-25** the nationwide general strike **Всеросси́йская ста́чка** in October, and the December uprising in Moscow's Presnya **Пре́сня** district with its barricades **баррика́ды** (memorialized in the names of that district's subway stations **Кра́сная Пре́сня** The Red Presnya and The Barricades **Баррика́дная**).

Nicholas made some concessions in face of this protest, the most significant being the establishment of a representative parliament **Ду́ма**, although its real power was slowly whittled away between 1905–17. Despite concessions, the revolution was put down only by brute force, organized in part by Stolypin **Столы́пин**, Nicholas' Prime Minister. Punitive expeditions **кара́тельные экспеди́ции** and executions **ка́зни** became frequent. Nooses became known as Stolypin's neckties **столы́пинские га́лстуки** and the tsar as Nicholas the Bloody **Никола́й Крова́вый**. To his credit, Stolypin also implemented major agricultural reforms **столы́пинская агра́рная рефо́рма**, which allowed individual peasants to withdraw from the peasant **общи́на** and work entirely for themselves.

Rasputin   Распу́тин

Aspects of the last tsar's family life contributed their share to his political unpopularity. In 1894 Nicholas married the German princess Alix of Hesse-Darmstadt, who was called in Russia Alexandra Fedorovna **Алекса́ндра Фёдоровна**. She was a tempermental and willful woman who remained unpopular in Russia among both the upper and lower classes. The birth of the Crown Prince Alexis **царе́вич Алексе́й** in 1904 was a long-awaited event, since Russian law prohibited the throne from being passed on to any of Nicholas' four daughters. Unfortunately, Alexis was soon discovered to suffer from hemophilia, which made it unlikely that he would ever be able to succeed his father as tsar. When medicine failed to heal Alexis, Alexandra, a believer in spiritualism and religious mysticism, looked to faith-healers. In 1906 the shadowy figure of the peasant holy man **ста́рец** Gregory Rasputin **Григо́рий Распу́тин** began to frequent the Court. In the following years, despite many reports and rumors about the holy man's scandalous behaviour, his influence over Alexandra and the royal family continued to grow.

World War I   Пе́рвая Мирова́я война́

In August 1914 Russia became embroiled in World War I **Пе́рвая Мирова́я война́**, usually characterized as the imperialist war **империалисти́ческая война́**, against Germany, Austro-Hungary, and Turkey. In a wave of patriotic feeling, Russian society initially supported the cause, and even the capital's name was changed from the Germanic sounding Petersburg **Петербу́рг** to the Slavic-based Petrograd **Петрогра́д**. Russia fought hard, but the war went badly from the middle of 1915 onwards. Rumors started to spread that blamed the tsaritsa **цари́ца** for the Russian defeats, suggesting that she was passing secret information to her royal relatives back in Germany. Rasputin continued to use his power over Alexandra to influence political decisions and ministerial appointments, and this, coupled with his scandalous behavior, further eroded the prestige of the royal family even among monarchists. In December 1916 a group of loyalists led by Prince Felix Yusupov **князь Фе́ликс Юсу́пов** murdered Rasputin, but the death of this charlatan came far too late to allow the royal family to rehabilitate itself.

The February Revolution   Февра́льская револю́ция

Because of economic problems, food shortages, low morale from military defeats, and enormous social inequalities, rioting broke out in the capital in February of 1917. When troops refused to shoot the rioters, the Romanov dynasty, which had celebrated its 300th anniversary **трёхсотле́тие до́ма Рома́новых** in 1913, collapsed. The February Revolution **Февра́льская револю́ция** forced Nicholas to abdicate the throne **отре́чься от престо́ла** for himself and his son. A Provisional Government **Вре́менное прави́тельство** (Alexander Kerensky became prime minister in July 1917) was set up to run the country until a Constituent Assembly **Учреди́тельное собра́ние** could work out a new constitution for a free and democratic Russia. The Provisional Government immediately had to compete for power with the Council of Workers' and Soldiers' Deputies **Сове́т рабо́чих и солда́тских депута́тов**, and this created an undesirable split in authority **двоевла́стие**. Two frequent slogans of the time in support of the Soviet and its outlooks were: All power to the Soviets! **Вся власть Сове́там!** and Down with the war! **Доло́й войну́**! The situation could not last indefinitely, and the Bolsheviks from their headquarters in the former Smol'nyi Institute prepared the so-called Great October Socialist Revolution **Вели́кая Октя́брьская социалисти́ческая револю́ция** or simply a coup **переворо́т** (in the opinion of their opponents). On the night of October 24–25, the battleship Aurora **кре́йсер «Авро́ра»** gave the signal for the storming of the Winter Palace **штурм Зи́мнего дворца́**, where the Provisional Government was located. The Bolsheviks quickly seized control of the government and established the Soviet state. The victory was immortalized in the slogan "Glory to October!" **Сла́ва Октябрю́**!

Fig. 1-21.   Still from Eisenstein's *October*—storming of the Winter Palace

SOVIET POWER   **СОВÉТСКАЯ ВЛАСТЬ**

First Decrees   **Пéрвые декрéты**

Lenin immediately published the decrees on peace **Декрéт о мúре** which announced Russia's conditions for an end to the war and the **Декрéт о землé**, which transferred all private land into the hands of peasant soviets. Soon after this, the new government, called the Soviet of the People's Commissars **Совéт нарóдных комиссáров** (**Совнаркóм** was its acronym, and the new regime relished acronyms), announced the abolition of all titles and privileges,[10] the separation of Church and state, the separation of the Church and schools, the nationalization of banks and industry, the abolition of private property rights and even the reform of orthography (the letters **i** and **ѣ** were replaced by **и** and **е**, and **ъ** no longer had to be written at the end of words ending in a hard consonant). Interestingly, this orthographic reform was not "revolutionary" in any political sense of the word, but was the result of the lengthy work of a reform commission. Most Russians, however, link the reform of the alphabet with the early Soviet government.

---

[10] Not only titles of the nobility (prince **князь** and count **граф**, and so on) were suppressed, but even the standard forms of address Mr./Mrs. **господúн/госпожá** were abolished, because of their class associations. The term "citizen" **гражданúн /граждáнка** was widely used at first, although it was later supplanted by the ubiquitous "comrade" **товáрищ**.

Fig. 1-22.   Vladimir Serov, *V.I. Lenin Proclaims Soviet Power* **«В.И. Ле́нин провозглаша́ет сове́тскую власть»** (1962)

In January 1918 the Soviet regime forcibly disbanded the Constituent Assembly, which gathered in Petrograd to create a constitution for Russia. In February 1918, the Julian calendar was replaced with the Gregorian used throughout the rest of the world; as a result 13 days were skipped. (All dates up to this point have been given according to the old style **по ста́рому сти́лю**, which the Russian Orthodox Church continues to use to this day.) In March the capital of the country was officially moved back to Moscow, locating political power closer to the center of traditional Russia. Also in that month the Soviets ended Russia's role in World War I with the Treaty of Brest-Litovsk **Бре́стский мир**, which resulted in enormous territorial and monetary concessions to Germany.

Civil War   Гражда́нская война́

The Sides   *Проти́вники*

The totality of the Bolsheviks' policies, together with their use of violence, created serious divisions in Russian society between pro-Bolshevik elements, the Reds **кра́сные**; anti-Bolsheviks, the Whites **бе́лые**; anarchists **анархи́сты**, the Greens **зелёные**, and other political parties. An armed civil war **Гражда́нская война́** broke out early in 1918 and was fought by the Red Army **Кра́сная а́р-**

мия and the Whites' Volunteer Army **Доброво́льческая а́рмия**. Civil war battles and campaigns are best known as the offensives and defeats of various White generals (Kornilov **Корни́лов**, Denikin **Дени́кин**, Kolchak **Колча́к**, Vrangel **Вра́нгель**). The generals were supported to some extent by troops and military aid from England, France, Japan and the U.S., which became known as the foreign military intervention **иностра́нная вое́нная интерве́нция**. [See the CD for a text of Lenin's "Address to the Red Army" and a recording of Lenin himself reading it.] Soviet military leaders who distinguished themselves at the time were Tukhachevskii **Тухаче́вский**, Budenny **Будённый**, Voroshilov **Вороши́лов** and Frunze **Фру́нзе** (and these names have been incorporated at various times into the names of many cities, military bases, schools and troop units, etc). 1-26

Chapaev   *Чапа́ев*

One legendary hero of the Civil War was cavalryman Vasilii Ivanovich Chapaev **Васи́лий Ива́нович Чапа́ев**, who became famous for his brave (almost foolhardy) exploits and was mortally wounded in battle in 1919. His cult spread through Furmanov's novel *Chapaev*, as well as the 1934 movie based on his exploits. A simple man from the people, Chapaev and his orderly Petya became the easy target for many Soviet jokes. For example: 📽 1-27

> **Пе́тька провали́лся на экза́менах в Вое́нную акаде́мию.** 🔊 1-28
> **Васи́лий Ива́нович:— Что ж ты, Пе́тька, диви́зию осрами́л?**
> **—Понима́ешь, спроси́ли, кто тако́й Нью́тон, а я сказа́л, что жеребе́ц из тре́тьего эскадро́на …**
> **—Ну и пра́вильно, что тебя́ погна́ли: Нью́тона я ещё ле́том во второ́й эскадро́н переда́л!**

Petya flunked his entrance exam for the military academy.
Vasilii Ivanovich: How could you shame our division like that, Petya?
—They asked who Newton is, and I said that he's a stallion in the third squadron.
—They were right to put you out. Last summer I transferred Newton to the second squadron![11]

Cheka   *Чека́*

Even before the armed opposition of the civil war, Soviet power created the means to ferret out secret, internal opposition. On December 7, 1917 the All-Russian Extraordinary Commission against Counterrevolution and Sabotage **Всеросси́йская чрезвыча́йная коми́ссия по борьбе́ с контрреволю́цией и**

---

[11] Dora Shturman and Sergei Tiktin, *Sovetskii Soiuz v zerkale politicheskogo anekdota* (London: Overseas Publications Interchange, Ltd, 1985), 301.

сабота́жем (ВЧК) or the Cheka **ЧК** for short, was born. Headed by the Polish-born Felix Dzerzhinskii **Фе́ликс Дзержи́нский** (known as "Iron Felix" **желе́зный Фе́ликс**, not only for his unyielding policies, but also for the statue that stood until 1991 in Lubyanka Square outside KGB headquarters), the Cheka savagely hunted down all opposition to the new regime, imprisoning, exiling, and executing masses of people. It continued its bloody work after the war, being reorganized in 1922 as the Unified State Political Administration **Объединённое госуда́рственное полити́ческое управле́ние (ОГПУ)**. In 1934 it was renamed again, becoming the People's Commissariat of Internal Affairs **Наро́дный комиссариа́т вну́тренних дел (НКВД)**. Headquartered in a massive building on Lubyanka Square **Лубя́нка** in Moscow, this institution under its different names filled the whole system of prison/labor camps, the GULag **ГУЛа́г (госуда́рственное управле́ние лагере́й)**, whose most infamous sites were Solovki **Соловки́** in the North, and Kolyma **Колыма́** and Magadan **Магада́н** in the Far East.

NEP   НЭП

The Civil War ended by the close of 1920, but it took another two years to form the USSR **СССР**, Union of Soviet Socialist Republics, **Сою́з Сове́тских Социалисти́ческих Респу́блик**. The confiscatory economic policies of the Soviet government during the Civil War, known as War Communism **Вое́нный коммуни́зм**, proved utterly disastrous, and Lenin and the Party were forced to institute the New Economic Policy (NEP) **Но́вая экономи́ческая поли́тика (НЭП)** in 1921 in order to revive the country. NEP allowed for the private ownership of small business and manufacturing and gave peasants freedom to farm their land and sell their surplus on an open market. NEP also brought foreign capital back into the country. By 1927 the country's economic production had returned to the level of 1914.

NEP created a whole new class of people—the Nepmen **нэ́пманы**—traders and small business men who made easy money, but were known for their petit-bourgeois morals **мелкобуржуа́зные/меща́нские/обыва́тельские нра́вы**.[12] Distrusted by political power, the Nepmen were not allowed to vote nor to send their children to schools or universities. The two most famous satires on this period belong to Il'f and Petrov *The Twelve Chairs* «Двена́дцать сту́льев» and *The Golden Calf* «Золото́й телёнок», with their hero Ostap Bender **Оста́п Бе́ндер**, the "Great Schemer" **Вели́кий Комбина́тор**.

Under NEP the government still maintained control over large industries and enterprises. From the beginning Soviet leaders were drawn to large-scale industrial projects; Lenin himself wanted the electrification of the country

---

[12] All three of these terms **буржу́й** (bourgeois)/**меща́нин** (originally a member of Russia's urban lower middle class **меща́нство**)/**обыва́тель** (philistine) remain insults even in post-Soviet Russian.

through hydroelectric power plants. His statement "Communism equals Soviet power plus the electrification of the whole country" **Коммунизм есть советская власть плюс электрификация всей страны** became a national slogan; and by the 1930s many hydro-electric plants were producing power for industry as well as household electric lights, known as Il'ich's light bulbs **лампочки Ильича**.

STALIN	Сталин
Struggle against Trotsky	**Борьба с Троцким**

The 1920s saw internal political struggles for leadership among the top party leaders in the Politburo **Политбюро**. By the time of Lenin's death on January 21, 1924, Joseph Stalin **Иосиф Виссарионович Сталин** (originally Dzhugashvili **Джугашвили**, 1879–1953) had worked his way up from being people's commissar for nationalities **нарком национальностей** to General Secretary **генеральный секретарь (генсек)** of the Party. Stalin's chief rival Lev Davidovich Trotsky **Лев Давидович Троцкий** (originally Bronshtein **Бронштейн**, 1879–1940) was very popular with the Petrograd garrison and served as the People's Commissar of War **нарком по военным делам** at the start of the Civil War. He organized and led the Red Army, using intimidation to fill its ranks and create discipline.

Lenin was concerned about Stalin's rise to power, and in his so-called *Testament* **«Завещание Ленина»**, he wrote that Stalin was "too crude, and that shortcoming, while bearable in the environment and discussions between us communists, becomes unbearable in the position of General Secretary" **«слишком груб, и этот недостаток, вполне терпимый в среде и в общениях** 🔊 **1-29**

между нами, коммунистами, становится нетерпимым в должности генсека». This document was never read at the 12th Party Congress, becoming widely known in Russia only after the 20th Party Congress in 1956. Despite Lenin's warnings, Stalin was able to consolidate his power; he had Trotsky expelled from the Politburo in 1927 and exiled in 1929. Until his assassination in 1940, Trotsky cast a shadow on the Party from abroad, and his "followers" the Trotskyites **троцкисты** became targets for accusations of international spying and anti-Soviet activities. After Trotsky, Stalin dealt with his lesser rivals, Bukharin **Бухарин**, Kamenev **Каменев** and others, who in turn were pushed out of positions of power, publicly discredited, and physically eliminated.

Fig. 1-23.   Joseph V. Stalin

Industrialization   Индустриализа́ция

By the late 20s, Stalin was ready to launch his master plan for transforming all aspects of the nation's life into a government-controlled socialist system. To accomplish this, the State Planning Committee **Госпла́н** worked out a five-year plan **пятиле́тка** for the economic development of the country. Stalin increased the already rosy quotas for expected economic growth and called for the production targets to be fulfilled in *four*, not five, years, giving birth to the slogan: The five-year plan in four years. **Пятиле́тку в четы́ре го́да**. (This, of course, became ironically twisted into slogans like "Five years in three days!" **Пятиле́тку в три дня**!) The main focus of the government plan was industrialization **индустриализа́ция** with rapid increases in the nation's production of coal, steel, and oil. New industrial cities, such as Magnitogorsk **Магнитого́рск**, sprang up in previously uninhabited areas. According to the slogan, the country was on a mission to "catch up to and overtake the West" **догна́ть и перегна́ть За́пад**.

Collectivization   Коллективиза́ция

Enormous structural changes, known under the general name of collectivization **коллективиза́ция**, were introduced in agriculture based in part on the Marxist belief that "industrialized" agriculture would be more efficient than individual farms. In addition, the resettling of peasants onto collective farms **колхо́зы** and state farms **совхо́зы** gave the government and party greater control over the peasantry. Finally, government control over the prices of agricultural products allowed it in the early 1930s to squeeze capital out of the population to finance grand industrial projects. To keep the peasants on collective farms, Stalin had the peasants' internal passports **паспорта́** confiscated, which effectively reintroduced serfdom, since peasants could not travel without a passport. Many peasants, however, resisted forced collectivization, and protest took many forms, especially the slaughter of farm animals. All resistance was blamed on the kulaks (literally, "fists") **кулаки́**, or rich peasants, and the state repressed them with brutal force: mass arrests, deportations, imprisonment in concentration camps, and executions. A telling slogan of the "dekulakization" **раскула́чивание** was Stalin's "liquidation of the kulaks as a class" **ликвида́ция кула́чества как кла́сса**. The pace of collectivization was slowed slightly in 1930 because famine threatened; but the policy was finally extended to all farmers by the mid-1930s creating severe famine, especially in Ukraine. From Russian literature two texts come to mind for their descriptions of the momentous change that the 1930s brought to the Russian village: Mikhail Sholokhov's **Шо́лохов** officially approved epic *Virgin Soil Upturned* «**По́днятая целина́**» (written 1932–60) and Andrei Platonov's formerly banned novel *The Foundation Pit* «**Котлова́н**».

Pavlik Morozov   Па́влик Моро́зов

One name particularly associated with collectivization is Pavlik Morozov **Па́влик Моро́зов** (1918–32). As a schoolboy, Pavlik became a member of the Young Pioneers **пионе́ры** (a national civic-awareness organization for children with many local chapters—sometimes roughly equated with the Boy/Girl Scouts) and took active part in the organization's campaigns against the kulaks in his native village Gerasimovka. Denouncing his father for helping some kulaks, Pavlik testified against him at his trial in 1930. On September 3, 1932 a band of kulaks took revenge and killed Pavlik and his younger brother. Pavlik instantly became a national martyr; and scores of parks, summer camps, and local chapters of Young Pioneers (**пионе́рские отря́ды**) were named after him.

Socialist Realism   Соцреали́зм

Stalin's program for the country included not only economic transformation, but cultural transformation as well. Following the dissolution of all artistic associations in 1932, the first Congress of Soviet Writers in 1934 proclaimed "socialist realism" **социалисти́ческий реали́зм** (or **соцреали́зм**) as the only acceptable artistic method, and it called on writers to be "the engineers of human souls" **инжене́ры челове́ческих душ**. The natural and social sciences were also subjugated to Party control: whole branches of science (sociology, genetics, psychoanalysis, and so on) were closed down, and scientists were intimidated, arrested and sometimes executed. The country's best botanist and geneticist Nikolai Vavilov **Никола́й Вави́лов** (1887–1943) died of starvation in a Saratov prison.

Personality Cult   Культ ли́чности

The signs of Stalin's personality cult **культ ли́чности** first appeared in 1929 with the celebration of his fiftieth birthday, and they continued to grow throughout the 30s and 40s. Comrade Stalin became the great leader **вели́кий вождь**,[13] the father of the peoples **оте́ц наро́дов**, and even the benefactor of children (cf. the widespread slogan "Thank you, Comrade Stalin, for our happy childhood!" **Спаси́бо това́рищу Ста́лину за на́ше счастли́вое де́тство**). His features were added to create the ubiquitous four-headed profile image: Marx-Engels-Lenin-Stalin. In 1937 the Stalinist revision of national history appeared in school textbooks, such as *Short Course on the History of the USSR* **«Кра́ткий курс исто́рии СССР»**, which placed great emphasis on the importance of the "strong leader" in Russia's past. A year later Stalin reinterpreted the history of the party in his *History of the All-Union Communist Party (of Bolsheviks): Short Course* **«Исто́рия ВКП(б): кра́ткий курс»**, where he emphasized his place in the Party's development.

---

[13] One should not forget that *вождь* in German is *Führer* and in Italian *duce*.

Fig. 1-24.   Vasilii Efanov, *An Unforgettable Meeting* **«Незабыва́емая**
              встре́ча» (1936–37)

The country developed a mania for superlatives and exaggerated historical
claims, which have been mocked in many jokes such as: Soviet watches—fastest
in the world! **Сове́тские часы́—са́мые бы́стрые в ми́ре**; Soviet paralysis is the
most progressive in the world! **Сове́тский парали́ч—са́мый прогресси́вный в**
ми́ре!; Russia is the homeland of the elephant **Росси́я ро́дина слоно́в**; Soviet
dwarves are the tallest in the world! **Сове́тский ка́рлик—са́мый высо́кий в**
ми́ре!

Stakhanov   Стаха́нов

Competitions for setting records in individual labor production became commonplace, and record-setting workers were named Stakhanovites **стаха́новцы**
after the coal miner Aleksei Stakhanov **Стаха́нов** who, in a single shift, mined
more than 14 times the expected norm. By the middle of the 1930s Stalin could
announce that "Socialism has been secured" **Социали́зм завоёван!** and prepare the country for the new socialist Constitution of 1936.

Everyday Life   Быт

Contrary to the optimistic claims of the popular 30s song "Life has gotten better, life has gotten cheerier" **Жить ста́ло лу́чше, жить ста́ло веселе́й**, the
lives of ordinary Soviet citizens grew much more difficult. Legislation on private and family matters grew more restrictive from the end of the 1920s with
the abolition of abortion and divorce and the five-year plan against religion

антирелигио́зная пятиле́тка, which promised to extirpate the very concept of God from Soviet society. The length of the work day increased; penalties for absenteeism became harsher. Since the Civil War, when private ownership of housing was abolished, the government took control over allotting living space **жилпло́щадь**, and a terrible housing shortage developed in the country's main cities. The government's response to this was to create "communal apartments" **коммуна́льные кварти́ры (коммуна́лки)** where each family was issued a separate room, but the kitchen and bathroom were shared by all. In the early Soviet period, to have a separate apartment **отде́льная кварти́ра** was a sign of extraordinary privilege. Getting a room in a communal apartment was difficult, sometimes requiring devious and extra-legal efforts (especially bribes **взя́тки**). Such efforts are frequently depicted in Soviet satire, and they form a virtual refrain throughout the works of the writer Mikhail Bulgakov **Михаи́л Булга́-ков**. While the "apartment question" **кварти́рный вопро́с** eased in the later Soviet period, communal apartments continue to exist even today in Russia.

Terror   Терро́р

The aggressive sovietization of all aspects of life had many dark sides. While some fought for the policies out of conviction and others propagandized them out of cynical opportunism, most complied with them out of fear: fear of losing a job, of losing rights to an apartment or room in a communal apartment, of being exiled to a less desirable city, of arrest and imprisonment in a concentration camp, of execution. While fear and terror were a part of Soviet power since its first days, they are most associated with the periods 1934–38, the Great Terror **Вели́кий терро́р** (to use the name first popularized in English-language scholarship). The event that launched the major campaigns against wreckers **вреди́тели**, spies **шпио́ны**, Trotskyites **троцки́сты** and other enemies of the people **враги́ наро́да** was the murder of Leningrad's party boss Sergei Kirov **Ки́ров** on December 1, 1934. This event was orchestrated by Stalin so he could remove a rival and provoke a widespread purge **чи́стка** of the Party. An excerpt from a school history textbook captures the mood of the mid 1930s:

> **Но в на́шей стране́ остава́лись ещё враги́ сове́тского наро́да, враги́ СССР. Это они́—друзья́ Тро́цкого, Зино́вьева и Ка́менева, а с ни́ми Ры́ков и Буха́рин—организова́ли в СССР ба́нду уби́йц, вреди́телей и шпио́нов. Это они́ злоде́йски уби́ли пре́данного наро́ду большевика́ Серге́я Миро́новича Ки́рова ... Троцки́сты и ры́ковцы вреди́ли, как могли́ ...Они́ мечта́ли о войне́ и вое́нном пораже́нии СССР. Сове́тская власть беспоща́дно и своевре́менно уничто́жила враго́в сове́тского наро́да. В СССР победи́л социали́зм.[14]**

🔊)) 1-30

---

[14] *Istoriia SSSR: Kratkii kurs*, ed. by Shestakov (Moscow: Uchpedgiz, 1945), 255–56.

But in our country there still remained enemies of the Soviet people, enemies of the USSR. It was they (the friends of Trotsky, Zinov'ev, and Kamenev, and Rykov and Bukharin with them) who organized a band of murderers, wreckers, and spies in the USSR. It was they who villainously murdered the Bolshevik Sergei Mironovich Kirov, who was devoted to the people. The Trotskyites and Rykovites wrecked what they could ... they dreamed about war and the military defeat of the USSR. Soviet power mercilessly and opportunely destroyed the enemies of the Soviet people. In the USSR Socialism has won.

Anyone could turn out to be a wrecker or spy—even the heads of the secret police changed with surprising speed: Yagoda **Ягода** in 1936 was replaced by Ezhov **Ежов**, who was in turn replaced by Beria **Бе́рия** in 1938. All three were infamous for their rounding up of enemies of the people and for their use of torture to extract false confessions. The Russian proverb "There's no harm in trying" **Попы́тка не пы́тка** (lit. "An attempt isn't torture.") was incorporated into the eerie punchline of a joke where Stalin says to Beria: An attempt isn't torture, isn't that true, Lavrentii Pavlovich? **Попы́тка не пы́тка, не пра́вда ли, Лавре́нтий Па́влович**? Targeted in this period were the elite of the party (show trials were orchestrated against Zinov'ev, Kamenev, Bukharin, and many others in 1936–38) and the military (Tukhachevskii **Тухаче́вский**—a hero of the Civil War, and other top miliary leaders were arrested and executed without trial in 1937). The horrors of this period, the enormous destruction of the Moscow and Leningrad intelligentsia, which left almost no family unscathed, first became known in the late 1950s during Khrushchev's Thaw **О́ттепель**. However, two of the most powerful narratives about the terror and camps, Evgeniia Ginzburg's memoir *Into the Whirlwind* **«Круто́й маршру́т»** and Varlam Shalamov's *Kolyma Tales* **«Колы́мские расска́зы»**, came out in Russia only in the late 1980s.

WORLD WAR II (1939–45)	**ВТОРА́Я МИРОВА́Я ВОЙНА́**
THE GREAT PATRIOTIC WAR (1941--45)	**ВЕЛИ́КАЯ ОТЕ́ЧЕСТВЕННАЯ ВОЙНА́**

1939 г.

Although the Soviet Union bitterly opposed Fascism in the 1930s, by the end of the decade, it found itself essentially isolated between two hostile countries, fascist Germany and imperialist Japan. In August 1939 the USSR negotiated a surprising ten-year pact of non-agression with Hilter's Germany, known as the Molotov-von Ribbentrop Pact **пакт Мо́лотова-Риббентро́па**. Reassured that the Soviet Union would not declare war, Fascist Germany invaded Poland on September 1, 1939, provoking World War II. Secret protocols in the non-aggression pact allowed the Soviet Union to occupy and annex Eastern Polish territory and to create a sphere of influence in the Baltics. In 1940 the Soviet government sponsored communist revolutions in Lithuania, Latvia, and Estonia, and the new puppet governments asked to be annexed by the Soviet Union.

Russians recall with great bitterness that it was Germany who broke the non-aggression pact and started the war by invading the Soviet Union. Once war with Germany began in 1941, all references to this pact and the division of Polish territory were banished from public discussion until the last days of the USSR, when the Soviet government finally acknowledged the pact and its secret protocols.

In addition to the new sphere of influence in Eastern Europe and the Baltics, the Soviet Union wanted to shore up the security of Leningrad and the country's north western border. When Soviet diplomacy failed to press Finland into accepting a new border some 25 miles further west of Leningrad in exchange for land in Karelia, the Finnish war **Фи́нская война́** broke out in November 1939. Although the Soviet forces incurred tremendous losses (pointing out the Soviet Army's significant weaknesses in training and shortages of supplies), the Soviet Union won the war by March 1940, forcing Finland to accept the territorial exchange.

Major Events   Гла́вные собы́тия

Germany invaded Russia on June 22, 1941, beginning the Great Patriotic War **Вели́кая Оте́чественная война́**.[15] The Soviet military and government were **1-31** unprepared for the fight, and Germany quickly cut deep into Soviet territory, killing and capturing millions of soldiers and civilians. By the middle of July 1941, Leningrad was surrounded; and, although the city was not captured, the Germans mounted a blockade **блока́да** that lasted 900 days. Those who had not been evacuated experienced horrible famine and deprivation (**го́лод и хо́лод**) and continuous enemy bombardment. Over a million residents of the city perished, most of whom were buried in mass graves at the Piskarev Cemetery **Пискарёвское кла́дбище**. By fall 1941 German forces had reached Moscow, and Soviet military and political command decided to fight off the German attack at all costs. The expression "There's nowhere else to retreat— Moscow is behind us" **Да́льше отступа́ть не́куда—позади́ Москва́** arose from the Battle of Moscow, and is heard in everyday speech: "There's an exam tomorrow. There's no where to retreat" **За́втра экза́мен. Отступа́ть не́куда**. The Red Army halted the German offensive on Moscow in December 1941; the Battle of Moscow **Моско́вская би́тва**, the first real victory for Soviet forces, showed that the Germans were not invincible. Failing to take Moscow, the Germans changed strategies and pushed toward the south (toward Kharkov, the northern Caucuses, and towards the Volga River). The turning point in the

---

[15] The beginning of Stalin's Address of 3 July 1941 and a recording of Stalin reading it can be found on the CD. Note that the words **бра́тья и сёстры!** brothers and sisters! are almost universally associated with the beginning of World War II in Russia.

war became the Battle of Stalingrad **Сталингра́дская би́тва** (commonly known as the Stalingrad Cauldron **сталингра́дский котёл**) which began on July 17, 1942. The fighting was intense: the sides fought over every block and building in the city.

The tide finally turned when the Red Army launched a counterattack against the German rear and captured Hitler's 6th Army at the beginning of February 1943. The victory at Stalingrad **Побе́да под Сталингра́дом**, celebrated in the city's (now named Volgograd **Волгогра́д**) enormous monuments on Mamai Kurgan **Мама́ев курга́н**, provided the Soviets with certainty that they would overcome the Germans. In the fall of 1944 the Red Army had pushed the Germans back beyond the 1941 border of the country. From there on, the Soviet war effort turned to liberating the countries of Eastern Europe and capturing Berlin, under the slogan of "Take Berlin!" **Даёшь Берли́н!** On April 25, 1945, Soviet troops met up with American units in the famous "Meeting on the Elbe" **Встре́ча на Э́льбе**, and Soviet troops took Berlin by May 2. The final capitulation and cease-fire came on May 8, while May was declared the official Victory Day **День Побе́ды**. Although Stalin took the title Generalissimo **Генерали́ссимус** and acted as the Supreme Commander of Armed Forces of the USSR **Верхо́вный Главнокома́ндующий Вооружёнными Си́лами СССР**, much of Russia's final military success in the war can be attributed to Marshal Georgii Zhukov **ма́ршал Гео́ргий Жу́ков** and the personal heroism of millions of Soviet citizens and soldiers. For example, Alexander Matrósov **Алекса́ндр Матро́сов**, a 19-year old soldier, threw himself onto a German machine gun to absorb its spray of bullets until his unit could take a position.

Fig. 1-25.   Street fighting in Stalingrad

Partisans   Партизáны

Two phenomena need to be mentioned about the lives of millions of Soviet citizens who ended up living in German occupied territories. The first is the Germans' horrible brutality towards Slavs, Jews and other nationalities living in these areas. Believing them to be inferior races, the Germans committed many atrocities against civilians. At Babi Yar **Бáбий яр**, a site outside of Kiev, almost 160,000 people (mostly Jews) were shot. Over four million people in occupied areas were evacuated to Germany as slave labor for German military factories. The horrors of life under the Germans helped spark a strong resistance movement of partisans **партизáны**. The movement was particularly strong in Belorussia, where whole units **отря́ды** formed to fight the Germans. Members of the resistance committed many individual acts of sabotage against the German war effort, and when they were caught, they were tortured and executed. Soviet history texts encouraged the memory of mass heroism **мáссовый герои́зм** among young Communists, and maintained cults of such martyrs. For example, Zoia Kosmodem'ianskaia **Зóя Космодемья́нская**, a 17-year old schoolgirl blew up a munitions depot; Konstantin Zaslonov **Константи́н Заслóнов** ("Uncle Kostya" **Дя́дя Кóстя**), a railroad worker in Orsha sabotaged 98 enemy trains. The memory of such individual sacrifices is woven into the composite literary character Vasilii Terkin **Васи́лий Тёркин**, the hero of A. Tvardovskii's poem by the same name.

Significance of the War   Значéние войны́

One could write much, much more about "The War" **войнá** and its heroic and tragic moments. With over 20 million people killed, thousands of square miles of the country devastated, and countless cultural monuments destroyed, it had an enormous effect on Soviet life, history and outlook. Russians have very strong personal feelings about it—virtually every family lost someone in the fighting, and people experienced enormous hardship. The depth of these feelings showed in the erection of war memorials, the visitation of cemeteries, and the establishment of the tradition of newly-weds placing flowers on the Grave of an Unknown Soldier **Моги́ла Неизвéстного Солдáта**. The war is never treated humorously; the war effort is considered sacred by the Russians. In the Brezhnev years, the devastation of the war was sometimes cynically exploited by politicians as an excuse for the country's economic problems. A safe topic, the war inspired countless books, films, TV series, memoirs, and other artistic works during the rest of the Communist era. Each of these sources adds to the truths and myths that Russians know about the period.

Post-War Years   **Послевое́нные го́ды**

Faced with the failure of his foreign policy in the wake of the German invasion of 1941, Stalin sought to boost Soviet (particularly Russian) national pride in the fight against foreigners by enlisting the support of those institutions which were most closely related to national identity. Thus, he engaged the Russian Orthodox Church, which was allowed to reopen some churches and seminaries; the search for internal wreckers quieted; rigid literary censorship was relaxed.

After the war, however, Stalin through his favorite Andrei Zhdanov **Жда́нов**, the party boss of Leningrad, launched a new wave of repressions targeting intellectual circles (particularly, Anna Akhmatova **Ахма́това** and Mikhail Zoshchenko **Зо́щенко**) which became known as Zhdanovshchina **жда́новщина**. Tensions in the international arena and the start of the Cold War **холо́дная война́** led the party in 1949 to launch its "fight against cosmopolitanism" **борьба́ про́тив космополити́зма** which clearly condemned all foreign influences (reading Western literature, listening to Western music, and so on) as harmful and made scientific and scholarly contacts with the West suspect and virtually impossible. The campaign had a strongly anti-semitic core, and Jews were branded as "stateless cosmopolitans" **космополи́ты безро́дные**.

THE KHRUSHCHEV YEARS   **ХРУЩЁВСКОЕ ДЕСЯТИЛЕ́ТИЕ**

20th Party Congress   **XX Съезд**

Only Stalin's death on March 5, 1953 started a process of healing that would take many years to complete. By 1956 Nikita Sergeevich Khrushchev **Ники́та Серге́евич Хрущёв** emerged as leader after a power struggle among Stalin's closest associates, and in his famous secret speech at the end of the 20th Party Congress **Двадца́тый съезд КПСС**, he started exposing Stalin's cult of personality **разоблаче́ние ку́льта ли́чности Ста́лина**. Attacking only the most extreme of the repressive measures used by Stalin, Khrushchev called for a "return to Leninist norms in party and government life" **возвра́т к ле́нинским но́рмам в парти́йной и госуда́рственной жи́зни**. The government security organs, by the 50s renamed KGB **КГБ** (Committee on State Security **Комите́т госуда́рственной безопа́сности**), which had formerly

Fig. 1-26.   Nikita Sergeevich Khrushchev

put people into prison, was charged to begin the rehabilitation of the repressed **реабилита́ция репресси́рованных**. Characteristically for Khrushchev's destalinization **десталиниза́ция**, not everyone was rehabilitated, and not all aspects of the totalitarian Stalinist system (usually called the **администрати́вно-кома́ндная систе́ма** in Russian) were deemed bad—for example, collectivization of agriculture remained unquestioned.

Agriculture	Земледе́лие

Personally, Khrushchev was more humane than Stalin. Coming from rural Ukraine, he took a real interest in agricultural questions and the plight of the kolkhoz workers **колхо́зники**. Certain concessions were made to them—they were allowed to retain a small plot of land **уча́сток** for their own use as well as a limited number of farm animals. With the inefficiency of collectivized agriculture, it was often the produce from these individual plots sold in the farmers' markets **колхо́зный ры́нок** that kept urban Russians supplied with food. Those working on the kolkhoz received internal passports, which allowed them to travel and possibly move to urban areas for a better life.

Under Khrushchev Soviet agriculture expanded into the "virgin soil" **целина́** regions of the country. In the 1950s young people gathered by the trainload to go off to these large tracts of semi-arid land mostly in Kazakhstan and Western and Southern Siberia and to start a new life. In the first years, the virgin soil was very productive, but after that production levels fell sharply.

Khrushchev became the first Soviet leader ever to visit the United States, and he was completely taken with corn **кукуру́за** during his visit to an Iowa farm. He propagandized corn for Soviet agriculture, and soon corn was being planted even as far north as the Arctic. This mania for corn even inspired parodies, such as the following, to the tune of the song "Little Light" **«Огонёк»**:

Я броди́л ме́жду скал,	I wandered among the crags,
Я Хрущёва иска́л,	I was looking for Khrushchev,
А Хрущёв ме́жду скал	But Khrushchev was planting
Кукуру́зу сажа́л.	Corn among the crags.

Khrushchev often peppered his speech with blunt expressions—responding to Western criticism of Soviet agricultural production he threatened, **«Мы вам ещё пока́жем ку́зькину мать»** "We'll show you a thing or two," and he famously threatened the West with the phrase **«Мы вас похоро́ним»** "We'll be performing funeral rites for you!"

Censorship	Цензу́ра

Socially, the period was looked upon as a hopeful time, as a "Thaw" **О́ттепель** (often called the "Khrushchev thaw" **хрущёвская о́ттепель**). Liberalization did occur in various aspects of public policy and discourse, the arts and literature in this period, although there are equally famous cases of censorship—the persecution of Boris Pasternak **гоне́ние на Пастерна́ка** in 1957 for the foreign publication of his novel *Doctor Zhivago* «**До́ктор Жива́го**». During a visit to an art exhibition at Moscow's Manege **Мане́ж** in 1962, Khrushchev personally attacked the formalism **формали́зм** of certain artists "**у кото́рых мозги́ набекре́нь**" (roughly, "whose brains were knocked sideways"). Khrushchev later regretted the harsh criticism he aimed at one of the Manege artists, the sculptor Ernest Neizvestnyi **Эрнст Неизве́стный**, and in his will Khrushchev asked to commission the sculptor to make a momument for his tomb. In contrast, Khrushchev was deeply impressed by Solzhenitsyn's *A Day in the Life of Ivan Denisovich* «**Оди́н день Ива́на Дени́совича**», which described conditions in a post-War prison camp, and allowed its publication in 1962.

Scientific Discoveries   Нау́чные откры́тия

On the whole, Russia's first postwar "generation of victors" **поколе́ние победи́телей** had reason to hope that the future would be better. Under Khrushchev the Soviets made important discoveries and reached major milestones in space: in 1957 they launched the first artificial satellite **иску́сственный спу́тник**; and four years later cosmonaut Yuri Gagarin **космона́вт Ю́рий Гага́рин** became the first human being to go into space. The Soviets also made important discoveries in the use of atomic energy for peaceful purposes **ми́рный а́том**, opening the first atomic power plant in 1954, and developing the nuclear-powered ice-breaker "Lenin" **а́томный ледоко́л «Ле́нин»** in 1957. Many of the scientific discoveries which led to these "firsts" were produced at secret scientific-research institutions, known as "post office boxes" **почто́вые я́щики**, as their locations were designated only by numbers.

Everyday Life   Быт

Beginning with Khrushchev, the Soviets made concerted attempts to deal with the difficult living conditions in Russia's cities, especially housing. The external grandeur and ornamentation of the Stalinist "Empire" Style apartment buildings[16] were rejected in favor of plain five-story walk-ups, known as "Khrushchev's slums" **хрущёбы** (a play on the word **трущо́бы** slums). While they provided many people with their first separate apartment, these buildings are often criticized in comparison with Stalinist buildings for their shoddy workmanship and small size. Nevertheless, there was visible improvement in people's lives, and this continued to raise their expectations for the future. The slogan of the time was «**Ны́нешнее поколе́ние сове́тских люде́й бу́дет жить при коммуни́зме**» "The current generation of Soviet people will live under Communism."

---

[16] This style is sometimes called by the pun **ста́линский ампи́р (во вре́мя чумы́)** Stalin's Empire (at the time of the plague), which plays on the title of Pushkin's drama «**Пир во вре́мя чумы́**» *A Feast at the Time of the Plague.*

Foreign Policy   Вне́шняя поли́тика

In foreign policy after World War II, tensions with the West developed into the Cold War **холо́дная война́**, and Churchill's famous "Iron Curtain" **желе́зный за́навес** descended upon Europe, creating a Soviet sphere of influence throughout central Europe. Thus, Poland, Czechoslovakia, Hungary, Rumania, Bulgaria, and East Germany became "brother countries" **бра́тские стра́ны**, linked to the Soviet Union economically by the 1949 Council of Mutual Economic Assistance (COMECON) **Сове́т экономи́ческой взаимопо́мощи (СЭВ)** and politically by the 1955 Warsaw Pact **Варша́вский догово́р**. While extending and consolidating Soviet influence throughout the world, Khrushchev spoke theoretically of peaceful coexistence **ми́рное сосуществова́ние**, according to which Communist ideological, political, and economic systems would compete peacefully with the West until the inevitable fall of Capitalism. While competition was supposed to happen without war, several incidents (the building of the Berlin Wall **берли́нская стена́** and the Cuban Missile Crisis **Кари́бский кри́зис**) almost provoked one.

BREZHNEV   БРЕ́ЖНЕВ

Khrushchev's Forced Departure   Наси́льственная отста́вка Хрущёва

Fig. 1-27.   Leonid Il'ich Brezhnev

In 1964 dissatisfaction with Khrushchev's domestic and foreign policy (the bad harvest of 1963 and the bloody suppression of protest in Novocherkassk **Ново-черка́сск** over price increases) led a small group of party leaders to force him to "retire for health reasons" **уйти́ на пе́нсию по состоя́нию здоро́вья**.

Leonid Il'ich Brezhnev **Леони́д Ильи́ч Бре́жнев** assumed Khrushchev's role as First Secretary of the Communist Party **Пе́рвый секрета́рь КПСС** (and later, General Secretary **Генера́льный секрета́рь КПСС**), while Andrei Kosygin **Андре́й Косы́гин** became the Head of the Council of Ministers **Председа́тель Сове́та Мини́стров**. The years of Brezhnev's reign, officially passing as the period of Developed Socialism **развито́й социали́зм**, later became characterized as the Epoch of Stagnation **эпо́ха засто́я/засто́йное вре́мя**. While many of those who came of age in the 1960s with the legacy of 20th Party Congress still fresh (the so-called people of the 60s **шестидеся́тники** or children of the 20th Congress **де́ти XX съе́зда**) hoped for continued liberalization, Brezhnev and the country's ruling class or "nomenclature" **номенклату́ра** moved in a conservative direction in domestic policies and returned to more confrontational stances in foreign policy. In 1965 under Brezhnev the writers Sinyavskii **Синя́вский** (pseudonym Abram Tertz **Абра́м Терц**) and Daniel′ **Дание́ль** received severe sentences for criticizing the Soviet system in works published abroad. In August 1968 the Soviet Union led the armed suppression of the "Prague Spring" **Пра́жская весна́** (the movement of Czech reformers who had promised to create "socialism with a human face" **социали́зм с челове́ческим лицо́м**). By 1970 A. Tvardovskii, editor of the liberal journal *The New World* **«Но́вый мир»**, was removed from his post. Taken together these events signaled a clear end to the political moderation of Khrushchev's days.

Soviet Society   Сове́тское о́бщество

Socially, beginning with the 60s the Soviet Union experienced the separation of society into two realms: the official, where people paid careful attention to the Party and its ideology; and the domestic, where, at home in the kitchen, like-minded people **свой круг** gathered to talk and discuss topics in literature, art

Fig. 1-28.   Party Congress at the Kremlin's Palace of Congresses

and politics that might not be officially sanctioned. In comparison with Stalinist times, the regime and its security organs tended to be more selective in ferreting out private opinions, although any public protest against officialdom could get a person branded as a "dissident" **диссиде́нт**. Even private discussions could bring disaster if an informer **стука́ч** were present. The regime varied the punishments it inflicted on dissenters: from the relatively mild (expulsion from work or school) to the more serious (imprisonment, confinement in a mental hospital, or banishment from the country).

Censorship   Цензу́ра

Censorship during the Brezhnev years took many guises. Books could be banned outright, or they could be published in small editions (**малотира́жные изда́ния**) so that few people would have access to their ideas. Films could be shelved (**положи́ть фи́льм на по́лку**), or they could be shown rarely in small, special theatres. People sometimes would write even if they had no chance for publication, and this practice became known as "writing for the desk" **писа́ть в стол**. Nevertheless, people who wanted information could get it through various unofficial sources: there were samizdat **самизда́т** (secret printings or typed copies of manuscripts of forbidden works done in Russia by the author), tamizdat **тамизда́т** (forbidden books printed in Russian abroad and smuggled into Russia), and foreign news broadcasts, especially the Voice of America **Го́лос Аме́рики**, and the BBC **Би-би-си**, which people could catch on shortwave radios. The tape-recorder revolution **магнитофо́нная револю́ция** allowed people to listen to the unofficial concerts of many singers like Bulat Okudzhava **Була́т Окуджа́ва**, Vladimir Vysotsky **Влади́мир Высо́цкий** and Alexander Galich **Алекса́ндр Га́лич**. But perhaps the most widespread form of "dissident" expression in these years were jokes **анекдо́ты**, which spread rapidly in all layers of society and mocked all aspects of Soviet society including Brezhnev himself.

Sakharov and Solzhenitsyn   Са́харов и Солжени́цын

The list of cultural figures officially proclaimed "dissidents" in this period would be a long one, and a list of people considered "ideologically dubious" **сомни́тельные в идеологи́ческом отноше́нии** would be far longer. Two names deserve mention: the physicist and academician Andrei Dmitrievich Sakharov **Андре́й Дми́триевич Са́харов** (1921–89) and the writer Alexander Isaevich Solzhenitsyn **Алекса́ндр Иса́евич Солжени́цын** (b. 1918). At the height of his work in physics, Sakharov openly started to criticize Soviet policies on nuclear weapons. From there he turned his attention to human rights violations **наруше́ния прав челове́ка** in the USSR for which in 1975 he received the Nobel Peace Prize. For protesting the Soviet invasion of Afganistan in 1979, he was exiled to Gorky **Го́рький** (now Nizhny Novgorod **Ни́жний**

Но́вгород), a "closed" city **закры́тый го́род** where foreigners were not allowed to travel.

Solzhenitsyn's first work *A Day in the Life of Ivan Denisovich* drew from his own experiences of being confined to a Soviet labor camp after he had written a letter to a friend criticizing Stalin. His following works (*First Circle* «**В кру́ге пе́рвом**», *The GULag Archipelago* «**Архипела́г ГУЛаг**») went on to call into question not only the excesses of the Soviet system, but its core values and ideas. In 1974 he was exiled from the country, returning only in 1994.

Corruption   Корру́пция

Officialdom in both Government and Party structures (**бюрокра́тия** and **аппара́т** respectively) flourished under Brezhnev, while real power grew more and more concentrated in the hands of a narrow group of the elite whose main goal was to preserve its privileged position. Signs of special status were: **госда́чи** goverment-owned country houses; **автомаши́ны** cars; **спецпайки́** special grocery bundles; and trips abroad **заграни́чные пое́здки**. Bribes (a perennial problem in Russia) were simply expected as part of doing business with officialdom. Pompous, self-congratulatory public events nurtured the egos of Brezhnev and his entourage. Brezhnev arranged for himself to win the Lenin Prize **ле́нинская пре́мия** in Literature for his ghost-written autobiographical trilogy.

At most places of work absenteeism was high, and people sometimes took advantage of their positions. This ranged from the relatively harmless activity of shopping during work hours to major graft and corruption. As economic growth in the country slowed in the 1970s, shortages **дефици́т** became even more common; lines **о́череди** appeared for many goods; people used connections **свя́зи/блат** to obtain goods and services. Unsurprisingly, people stopped using the word "to buy" **купи́ть**, replacing it with the word "to obtain" **доста́ть**. Appropriating official supplies and property for personal use helped feed the "shadow economy" **теневáя эконо́мика** or the black market **чёрный ры́нок**, since these goods could be resold or traded for other hard to get goods. The following two-liner is very telling:

> **Товáрищ! Неси́ с рабо́ты кáждый гвоздь!**
> **Ты тут хозя́ин, а не гость!**

Comrade! Steal every nail from your place of work;
You're the boss here, not a guest!

Officialdom tried to place the blame for these "temporary" economic difficulties on speculators **спекуля́нты** and parasites **тунея́дцы**, and exhorted the nation to resist **вещи́зм** (lit. "thing-ism") and **ве́щный фетиши́зм** (lit. "property fetishism"). Talk about "temporary" economic difficulties sparked the following joke: «**Еди́нственное, что в Сове́тском Сою́зе постоя́нно — э́то**

вре́менные тру́дности». "The only thing that is constant in the Soviet Union are temporary difficulties."

Foreign Policy	**Вне́шняя поли́тика**

The early 1970s brought a relaxation in Soviet-American relations that became known by the French word *détente* in the West and **разря́дка** in Russia. Cooperation extended even to space where an American Apollo ship docked with a Soviet Soiuz **Сою́з** ship. In the 1970s Jews were allowed to leave the Soviet Union for their "historical homeland" **истори́ческая ро́дина**. This began the so-called "third wave" **тре́тья волна́** of massive emigration from the Soviet Union (the first wave **пе́рвая волна́** refers to those who left after the revolution of 1917 and the second **втора́я волна́** to those who, displaced during World War II, chose not to return to the USSR after the war). Once they initiated the emigration process, Jews usually faced a number of serious consequences (for example: loss of employment, restriction of educational opportunities), and, if they were ultimately denied permission to leave, they were doomed to live in the USSR as traitors to the country. By the late 70s tension again grew in foreign affairs due to the Soviet military intervention in Afganistan, beginning in December 1979, and Soviet influence on Jaruzielski's imposition of martial law in Poland in December 1980.

THE BREAKUP OF THE SOVIET UNION	**РАСПА́Д СОВЕ́ТСКОГО СОЮ́ЗА**
Gorbachev	**Горбачёв**

After Brezhnev's death in 1982, the Soviet Union was ruled by two short-lived figures, Yuri Andropov **Ю́рий Андро́пов** and Konstantin Chernenko **Константи́н Черне́нко.** In March 1985 Mikhail Gorbachev **Михаи́л Серге́евич Горбачёв** was elected General Secretary of the Central Committee of the Communist Party **генера́льный секрета́рь Центра́льного комите́та КПСС.** Gorbachev became best known for the policies of

Fig. 1-29. Mikhail Sergeevich Gorbachev

"perestroika" **перестро́йка**, referring to a fundamental socialist restructuring of the economy, and "glasnost" **гла́сность**, which referred to an opening of discussion on social and political issues. While perestroika failed to provide the change needed for maintaining the Soviet system, glasnost succeeded beyond

Gorbachev's wildest dreams. From 1987 each successive issue of newspapers and magazines (especially *Moscow News* «**Моско́вские но́вости**» and *Ogonek* «**Огонёк**») chipped away at formerly forbidden topics **запре́тные те́мы**. The problems of everyday life, historical injustices, mass repressions, and hitherto forbidden novels and essays became everyday reading. Gorbachev had a difficult time keeping firm central control over the reins of power as glasnost allowed people to discuss political problems, such as the Armenian-Azerbaijan conflict in Nagorny Karabakh **Наго́рный Караба́х** and economic problems, but it did nothing to find solutions to these problems. Furthermore, glasnost prevented Gorbachev from using the old repressive administrative measures to force solutions on the populace. Gorbachev tried various political maneuvers to solidify his authority, having himself elected to government posts (not just party positions). He became Chair of the Supreme Soviet of the USSR **Председа́тель Верхо́вного Сове́та СССР** and then later President of the USSR **Президе́нт СССР**.

Sovereignty of the RSFSR   **Суверените́т РСФСР**

Following the change of governments in the former satellite states of Eastern Europe in the fall of 1989, Soviet republics began to claim more and more of their sovereignty **суверените́т** beginning with Lithuania, which declared its independence in March 1990. On June 12, 1990 the Russian Federation (RSFSR) **Росси́йская Сове́тская Федерати́вная Социали́стическая Респу́блика (РСФСР)** declared its sovereignty, and that date is now celebrated as Russia's official "Independence Day" **День Незави́симости**. In 1991 on that date the citizens of the Russian Federation (now called **россия́нин**/pl. **россия́не**; in contrast to the ethnic designation **ру́сский/ру́сские**) elected Boris Nikolaevich Yeltsin **Бори́с Никола́евич Ельцин** as president.

Fig. 1-30.   Boris Nikolaevich Yeltsin with the Kremlin's Savior Tower in the background

August Coup   **Августовский путч**

Fig. 1-31.   Defenders of the White House, August 1991

The proclaimed independence of the Russian Federation gained true significance only after the attempted coup in August 1991 **а́вгустовский путч**. On August 19, while Gorbachev was on vacation in Crimea, seven highly-placed conservative government ministers announced an "extraordinary situation" **чрезвыча́йное положе́ние** during which they tried to seize control of the country and push Gorbachev out of power. The coup provoked storms of protest, including that of the popular Russian President Yeltsin. Fearing that the coup plotters **загово́рщики** would attempt to crush him and the opposition, thousands of Muscovites headed to defend the "White House" **защища́ть Бе́лый дом** where the government of the Russian Federation was housed. The coup plotters found little support in the country and army for their action, and within four days they were arrested.

INDEPENDENT RUSSIA   **НЕЗАВИ́СИМАЯ РОССИ́Я**

The failed coup was the end for the USSR, the control of the Communist Party, and the political authority of Gorbachev. With the signing of the Belovezhskoe Accord **Белове́жское соглаше́ние** in December 1991, the Soviet Union was officially dissolved and replaced by a loose confederation of states called the Commonwealth of Independent States **Содру́жество Незави́симых Госуда́рств (СНГ)**. The RSFSR became a totally free and independent state, renamed the Russian Federation **Росси́йская Федера́ция**, or just Russia **Росси́я**.

    In the fall of 1991 there was a massive campaign to wipe away Communist institutions in Russian life. While it was easy to remove monuments of Soviet heros and change the names of streets, cities and public institutions, the legacy of the Soviet mindset (epitomized in the word **совóк/совкóвый**—pejorative labels denoting Soviet stupidity and closed-mindedness) has been harder to erase. Nevertheless, since 1991 Russia **Россúя** continues in its attempts to establish itself as a democratic, law-based state **демократúческое правовóе государство**.

APPENDIX: MILITARY TERMS   ВОÉННЫЕ ТÉРМИНЫ

Since history has traditionally focused on ruling political powers and their struggles with foreign enemies and internal conflicts, the following commonly used terms may be helpful in reading history texts and fictional accounts of battles. The most general word for "war" is **войнá** and "to conduct a war"— **воевáть**. A "battle" is **сражéние** and its related verb is **сражáться**. "Fighting" or "action" is **бой** (**убúт в бою** = killed in action). Other words for "battle" all carry stylistic nuances. **Бúтва** is a "grand battle," reserved for the names of certain key historical confrontations, such as Peter the Great's Poltava Battle in 1709 **Полтáвская бúтва** and the Battle at Borodino against Napoleon in 1812 **Бородúнская бúтва**. **Побóище** is a distinctly medieval term suggesting the complete rout of the enemy and is used when describing Alexander Nevsky's Battle on the Ice in 1242 **Ледóвое побóище** and Dmitri Donskoi's Battle with Mamai in 1380 **Мамáево побóище**. **Борьбá** is used for "battle" or "struggle" in a non-military sense. In a war there are the front **фронт** and the rear **тыл**, while the fighting forces **войскá** (usually *pl.*) can go on an offensive **наступлéние**, or retreat **отступлéние**, or maintain the defense of an area **оборóна**. A stalemate might lead to a blockade **блокáда** or a siege **осáда**, leaving a city under siege **в осáдном положéнии**. Troops might live in barracks **казáрма**, dug-outs **земля́нка**, bunkers **бýнкер** or in trenches **окóпы**. Wars start with an enemy **враг** or an opponent **протúвник** and end with victors **победú-тели** and the conquered **побеждённые**. Victory is **побéда**, and the loss of a battle or war can be a defeat **пораже́ние** or a rout **разгрóм**. Invading and occupying armies are referred to as **захвáтчики** (*literally* snatchers), a term liberally applied in Soviet histories.

Weapons (**орýжие**, always sing.) can range from the medieval: sword **меч**, spear **копьё**, bow **лук**, arrow **стрелá**; to the more modern: cannon **пýшка**, saber **сáбля**, gun **ружьё**, bayonet **штык**, pistol **пистолéт**, sub-machine-gun **автомáт**, machine-gun **пулемёт**, bomb **бóмба**, shell or grenade **гранáта** (note the feminine gender; the masculine noun **гранáт** is a pomegranate or the semi-precious stone garnet), mine **мúна**, tank **танк**. Bullet is **пýля**, or more archaically and poetically **свинéц** (*lit.* lead).

The Soviet period highlighted revolutionary struggle **революциóнная борьбá** describing rebellions **бýнты**, uprisings **восстáния**, coups **перевóроты/пýтчи**, and revolutions **революцúи**. The participants in those are respectively: **бунтовщúк, повстáнец, путчúст, революционéр**. Russian history has also been shaped by conspiracies **зáговоры** and conspirators **заговóрщики**.

Part 2. Contexts in Language

Язык — материал литературы.

Ю. Лотман

Language is the raw material of literature.

Iu. Lotman

*When Russians get together and don't drink
wine or play cards, they talk about literature or
death.*

M. Artsybashev, *Jealousy*

Fig. 1.   "Moscow! How much converges in that name for every Russian!"
(from Pushkin's *Eugene Onegin*)

Russians like to say that they are the most reading country in the world (**са́мая читáющая странá в ми́ре**). One of the reasons why reading is so popular in Russia is suggested by the similarity between such expressions as **пить запóем** "to have a drinking fit" and **читáть запóем** "to read avidly." Like alcohol, reading has provided for generations of Russians a readily available magic door through which one slips away from drab and depressing reality. Perhaps, the major reason for all this reading is that being well-read and able to talk about it was accepted and expected **при́нято** in educated society. It was the normal thing to do. If you could not talk about Bulgakov or Solzhenitsyn then you could not mix comfortably with those who did. The power of words and writing was augmented by Russia's pre- and post-Revolutionary governments who took the trouble to watch and then punish writers whose only offense was to ignore ideology in their writing. (The Communist government even forced libraries to cleanse encyclopedias by cutting out offensive articles, with scissors.) At first, what was written mattered *primarily* to anyone who could read (that is, the educated upper classes), and then, when everyone could read (as literacy expanded under the Soviets), the importance of these wronged writers only grew. After all, forbidden fruit is sweet **запре́тный плод сла́док**. To fuel the fires of silent protest, an army of intellectual desperadoes typed multiple copies of banned books, and sold them for sustenance in a system called Samizdat **самизда́т** or self-publishing. Possessors of banned books rented or lent them out for unimagineably short periods and everyone involved ran the risk of confiscation and arrest. Writers of forbidden literature were sometimes temporarily exiled, permanently banished, or killed. The importance of the printed word was thus permanently fixed in the Russian mind, and literature turned into a clandestine forum for free thought, and in so doing, gave Russians a sense of their own human worth.

Fig. 2.   The cover of the magazine *New Time*, with a variation on the same quote

Educated Russians carry a virtual library around with them, not necessarily because of an innate interest in literature, but because their teachers (and sometimes parents) made sure it would be carried around: practically everyone in the country has been required to memorize essentially the same bits of poetry and prose. (Scratch a Russian, any Russian, and you can hear about a green oak tree at the seaside with a golden chain around it.) Such memorization led to a *shared* interest in and understanding of literature, which then became a way for people to communicate with one another. This led in turn to a sense of community felt at poetry readings and other literary events. This fodder for allusions is therefore readily available to all, and is found everywhere in Russian life: in speech, in advertising, and in journalism.

Генеральная лицензия ЦБ РФ №41

«Москва! Как много в этом звуке для сердца русского слилось, как много в нем отозвалось...» Упоминаемая в старинных сказаниях и песнях, хранящая в своем сердце историю России, испытавшая и тяготы поражений, и светлые минуты побед – Москва отмечает 850 лет своей удивительной судьбы. Город, возведенный в 12 веке Юрием Долгоруким, стал оплотом многих битв и сражений, его образ берег в сердце каждый, кто хоть раз оказывался здесь, на семи холмах. На протяжении восьми с половиной сотен лет он привлекал внимание поэтов, композиторов и художников. В его честь слагали былины, сочиняли поэмы и симфонии... Москва жила, росла, менялась. И с каждым прожитым годом все дороже становились для нас потертые шероховатые камни старых зданий, овеянные памятью прошлого, вековые дубы и тополя – молчаливые свидетели минувших дней. Время преобразило облик Москвы, но не сумело разрушить связь поколений. Это наш город, в котором жили наши предки, живем мы и будут жить наши дети... С праздником, Москва!...

Банк
МЕНАТЕП
ОФИЦИАЛЬНЫЙ БАНК ПРАЗДНОВАНИЯ
850-летия основания Москвы

Figure. 3. The same quotation is cleverly used in this ad for Bank MENATEP

In contemporary Russia, despite the fact that people's free time is severely limited by concerns of economic survival, and although the younger generation is more than ever attracted to pop culture and TV, educated people are still expected to be well-read in the Russian classics, even when their professions lie altogether outside the humanities. "I used to be able to recite all of Eugene Onegin by heart" is a not infrequent boast among people whose specialization is quite technical. Literary quotations fly back and forth in informal conversations among close friends (much in the way quotations from TV commercials are in the United States), and they also adorn lectures, political speeches and interviews.

Chapters 2 and 3 contain those quotations from literature that the educated Russian carries in his head, and that a student of Russian will encounter not only in everyday conversations with Russians, but when he picks up a newspaper or turns on the television. An analysis of quotations in the press showed that one issue of the Moscow newspaper "Kommersant" (1991) contained no less than eighteen headlines based on literary quotations, mostly from poetry. The most quoted poet was Pushkin, followed by Lermontov, Griboedov and Mayakovsky; the most cited prose writers were Bulgakov and Gogol. The author and editors have tried to provide you a resource for identifying those authors and quotes you'll most likely need to look up after you've heard or read them. What we do here is try to determine what Russian literature is, for Russians, so that non-Russians can have an intimation of its range and character.

The two chapters offer a selection of the most frequent and familiar literary quotations arranged chronologically by author. All works are numbered: an author is assigned a number. Each of his works is assigned a number, and each quotation from the work has its own number. For instance: Alexander Pushkin is author #7. His work *Eugene Onegin* is the 27th to be quoted in the section on Pushkin. Thus *Onegin* can be found in the poetry chapter under 7.27. Each quote from *Onegin* is further sub-listed. The famous line "My uncle is a man of the strictest morals" happens to be the fifth quote listed from *Onegin*, and it is numbered 7.27.5. The parts of quotations that are universally remembered verbatim are given in italics. Each quotation is followed by illustrations of its use in speech (informal conversations are full of irreverent humorous distortions of well-known lines, and the mutual pleasure of recognition shines through each of these exchanges), media (practically any issue of a newspaper or magazine will contain either a direct quotation from or a reference to a literary work–often with humorous effect) or literature (many quotations are well-known because they are quoted in other works of literature).

Quoting Russian Poetry   **2**   **Ру́сская поэ́зия в цита́тах**

Valentina Zaitseva

1. Mikhail Vasilievich Lomonosov (1711–65)

Михаи́л Васи́льевич Ломоно́сов

(Also see Chapter 1, 33; Chapter 10, 32.)

A scientist, scholar and poet, Lomonosov is Russia's great Renaissance man. A fisherman's son with a legendary thirst for knowledge, Lomonosov had to conceal his low social origin in order to be permitted to enroll in the Slavo-Greco-Latin Academy in Moscow. A few decades later he was a renowned scholar and a

Fig. 2-1.

founder of Moscow University. His poetry (mostly in the genre of the ode) was important for the development of Russian verse, but to the modern ear it sounds heavy or clumsy. A few lines survive, however, and immediately float into one's memory at the mention of Lomonosov's name.

1.1. Most frequently cited are the following lines from his poem «**Ода 1747 года**» "Ode of 1747":

> Что мо́жет со́бственных Плато́нов
> И бы́стрых ра́зумом Невто́нов
> Росси́йская земля́ рожда́ть.

 2-1

The Russian land can give birth to its own Platos and quick-minded Newtons.

Use: This quotation embellishes many a patriotic speech.

> *Нау́ки ю́ношей пита́ют,*
> Отра́ду ста́рым подаю́т, …

Scholarship nurtures the young, it gives joy to the old.

Illustration: Headline **«Наде́жды ю́ношей пита́ют»** "Hopes nurture the young" in ***Ито́ги***, November 1996. The article reported on a sociological poll aiming to find out whether young people believe that their standard of life may improve in the future.

2. Ippolit Fedorovich Bogdanovich (1743–1803)

Ипполи́т Фёдорович Богдано́вич

His major work is **«Ду́шенька»** "Dushenka" (1783), a long poem about Psyche and Cupid. Psyche is **душа́** (soul); its diminutive **ду́шенька** is used as a term of endearment (= "dear, sweet-heart").

Fig. 2-2.

2.1. The following line is especially famous, partly because it was used by Pushkin as the epigraph to his story **«Ба́рышня-крестья́нка»** "The Peasant Miss."

🔊 2-2   **Во всех ты, Ду́шенька, наря́дах хороша́.**

You, Dushenka (sweetheart), look pretty in all dresses.

Use: Often quoted to compliment a female friend's outfit.

3. Gavrila Romanovich Derzhavin (1743–1816)

Гаври́ла Рома́нович Держа́вин

Derzhavin is considered one of the greatest poets of the 18th century. A son of poor landowners, he became one of the highest officials during the reign of Catherine II. In his diaries he described the dangers and humiliation of the life of a poet close to the rulers, and of a statesman trying to be honest in a world of corruption. Derzhavin was present at Pushkin's graduation and was impressed with the talent of the young poet. [See the reference to the event in Pushkin's *Eugene Onegin*, 7.27.20.]

Fig. 2-3.

3.1. From the ode **«На смерть кня́зя Мещёрского»** "On Prince Meshchersky's Death" (1779):

> **Глаго́л времён; ... мета́лла звон!**
> **Твой стра́шный глас меня́ смуща́ет.**

2-3

The voice of the ages! [Lit.: A word of the times!] The ring of metal! Your horrific voice troubles me.

3.2. From the ode **«Бог»** "God" (1784):

> **Я царь—я раб, я червь—я бог.**

2-4

I am a king, and I am a slave, I am a worm, and I am a god.

4. NIKOLAI MIKHAILOVICH KARAMZIN[1]
(1766—1826)

НИКОЛА́Й МИХА́ЙЛОВИЧ КАРАМЗИ́Н

«Посла́ние к Алекса́ндру Алексе́евичу Плеще́еву» "Letter to Alexander Alekseevich Pleshcheev" (1796):

> *Смея́ться, пра́во, не грешно́*
> *Над всём, что ка́жется смешно́.*

2-5

It is really not a sin to laugh at anything that seems funny.

Fig. 2-4.

5. IVAN ANDREEVICH KRYLOV
(1769–1844)

ИВА́Н АНДРЕ́ЕВИЧ КРЫЛО́В

(Also see Chapter 4.)

While his work as journalist, playwright and translator has been completely forgotten, Krylov's popularity as a writer of fables remains enormous: he has been **де́душка Крыло́в** "Granddaddy Krylov" to many generations of

Fig. 2-5.

---

[1] See Chapter 3 for biographical details.

Russians from the beginning of the 19th century to this day. In fact, his name became so firmly linked with the whole genre of fable, that one of Dostoevsky's characters in *The Possessed*, Captain Lebyadkin, simply attaches it to the word "fable," announcing: "**Я написа́л ба́сню Крыло́ва,**" that is, "I wrote a Krylov-fable." Traditionally, the main personages of fables are animals acting out human weaknesses and vices. After Krylov, no Russian can think of the animal kingdom without making immediate associations with his little masterpieces, many of which have obtained the status of proverbs.

5.1. «**Воро́на и Лиси́ца**» "The Crow and the Fox." Almost the whole fable is usually remembered:

2-6 [...]

Воро́не где-то Бог посла́л кусо́чек сы́ру.
На ель воро́на взгромоздя́сь,
Позáвтракать было совсе́м уж собрала́сь,
Да позаду́малась, а сыр во рту держа́ла.
На ту беду́ лиса́ близёхонько бежа́ла:
Вдруг сы́рный дух лису́ останови́л:
Лиси́ца ви́дит сыр—лиси́цу сыр плени́л.
Плуто́вка к де́реву на цы́почках подхо́дит,
Верти́т хвосто́м, с воро́ны глаз не сво́дит,
И говори́т так сла́дко, чуть дыша́:
«Голу́бушка, как хороша́!
Ну, что за ше́йка, что за гла́зки!
Расска́зывать, так, пра́во, ска́зки!
Каки́е пёрышки! Како́й носо́к!
И, ве́рно, а́нгельский быть до́лжен голосо́к!
Спой, све́тик, не стыди́сь! **Что, е́жели, сестри́ца,**
При красоте́ тако́й и петь ты мастери́ца,
Ведь ты б у нас была́ царь-пти́ца!»
Вещу́ньина с похва́л вскружи́лась голова́,
От ра́дости в зобу́ дыха́нье спёрло,
И на приве́тливы лиси́цыны слова́
Воро́на ка́ркнула во всё воро́нье го́рло:
Сыр вы́пал—с ним была́ плуто́вка такова́.

Fig. 2-6.   The Crow and the Fox

Once a crow happened upon a piece of cheese. The crow perched at the top of a spruce tree and was about to begin its breakfast, but started to think, a piece of cheese in its mouth. Unfortunately, a fox was running by. Arrested by the smell of cheese, it looked up. The fox saw the cheese, the cheese attracted the fox. The scoundrel tiptoed to the tree, waved its tail, unable to tear its eyes away from the crow, and said sweetly, barely breathing: "O how beautiful you are, my dear!

What a neck, what eyes! They are of fabulous beauty. What feathers! What a beak! I bet you have an angelic voice, too. Sing for me, dearest! Don't be ashamed! What if in addition to such beauty you are also a master of singing—why, then you would become our Queen-Bird!" The crow's head began to spin from all the praise; choking with joy [lit.: its breath caught in its crop from joy], the crow opened its mouth wide and cawed loudly. The cheese fell, and the fox vanished with it.

Use: The fable is a source of many jokes:

(a) Taking food out of the refrigerator, one might say: **Вороне где-то Бог послал кусочек сыру** "Once a crow happened upon a piece of cheese."

(b) When persuading a friend to perform, one might say: **Спой, светик, не стыдись!** "Sing for me, dearest! Don't be ashamed!"

(c) In describing one's enthusiastic reaction to something, one might say with self-irony: **У меня от радости в зобу дыханье сперло** "I was breathless with joy."

(d) Here is an anecdote of pre-perestroika times, when there was a severe shortage of food:

Вовочка учит наизусть: "вороне где-то бог послал кусочек сыру" ... —Папа, а разве есть бог? —А разве есть сыр? Это же басня, сынок. Little Vovochka is memorizing: "Once God helped a crow to scavenge a piece of cheese ..." "But daddy, there is no God, is there?" "Hey, there is no cheese either, is there? This is a fable, son."

Fig. 2-7.   Monument to Krylov in St. Petersburg

5.2. «Лебедь, Рак и Щу́ка» "The Swan, the Crayfish and the Pike."

🔊 2-7 *Одна́жды Ле́бедь, Рак да Щу́ка*
Везти́ с покла́жей воз взяли́сь
И вме́сте тро́е все в него́ впрягли́сь;
Покла́жа бы для них каза́лась и легка́:
Да Ле́бедь рвётся в облака́,
Рак пя́тится наза́д, а Щу́ка тя́нет в во́ду.
Кто винова́т из них, кто прав—суди́ть не нам;
Да то́лько воз и ны́не там.

Once, a swan, a crayfish and a pike agreed to draw a cart loaded with
freight, so they harnessed themselves to the cart as a team. Although
the burden seemed light, they had no success: the swan flies to the sky,
the crayfish moves backwards, and the pike pulls towards the water.
We cannot judge which of them is right, but the cart is still there.

Illustration:

(a) You can imagine the number of jokes playing on the last name of
     General Lebed' [ле́бедь, " swan"] since he became prominent on the
     political scene.

(b) Headline in *Пра́вда* (1994): «Ле́бедь, рак и щу́ка. А́нгло-америка́н-
     ская ссо́ра из-за Бо́снии обостря́ется». "A swan, a crayfish and a
     pike: the American-British argument over Bosnia is getting sharper."

(c) From a conversation between TV talk-show anchor Boris Notkin and
     his guest, Alexander Shokhin (March 1994):

Б.Н.: «Вы / се́рдце/ Вы мозг // Вы еди́нственный челове́к, кото́рый
мо́жет прекрати́ть ха́ос // когда́ все тя́нут одея́ло на себя́/как
ле́бедь / рак и щу́ка».

"You are the heart, you are the brain, you are the only person who can
stop the chaos at a time when everyone pulls the blanket in their own
direction, like the swan, the crayfish, and the pike."

(d) «А воз и ны́не там» "And the cart is still there" can be said about any
     business long undone.

🔊 2-8 **5.3.** "Услу́жливый дура́к опа́снее врага́" "An obliging fool is more dangerous
than an enemy." A popular line from the fable «Пусты́нник и Медве́дь» "The
Hermit and the Bear."

Illustration: Headline in *Но́вое вре́мя*, August 1995: «Опа́снее врага́. Па́ртия
дурако́в угрожа́ет перегово́рам в Чечне́, счита́ет Арка́дий Во́льский».
"More dangerous than an enemy: The party of fools is a menace to peace talks
in Chechnya, according to Arkady Volsky."

Fig. 2-8. The Cuckoo and the Rooster

5.4. From the fable «**Куку́шка и Пету́х**» "The Cuckoo and the Rooster":

За что же, не бойсь греха́, 🔊 **2-9**
Куку́шка хва́лит Петуха́?
За то, что хва́лит он Куку́шку.

Why does the cuckoo praise the rooster so shamelessly (lit.: without being afraid of falling into sin [lying])? Because the rooster praises the cuckoo.

5.5. «**Три́шкин кафта́н**» "Trishka's Coat." This is a fable about Trishka, who cut the lower parts of his sleeves to make patches for the holes in the elbows; when the sleeves turned out to be too short, he used the lapels of his coat to make the sleeves longer. "Trishka's Coat" is used as an expression to mean short-sighted efforts.

Illustration: Headline in **Аргуме́нты и фа́кты**. Aug. 1996: «**Три́шкин** 🔊 **2-10** **кафта́н краево́го бюдже́та**» "Trishka's coat of the regional budget."

5.6. «**Слона́-то я и не приме́тил**» from the fable "**Любопы́тный**" "The 🔊 **2-11** Curiosity Lover." A man is recounting his impressions of all the wonderful little insects and other small things he saw in a new museum. When asked what he thought of an elephant, the man answered: «**Слона́-то я и не приме́тил**» "As for the elephant, I never noticed him."

Use: to point out that someone missed the most obvious point.

5.7. «**Хоть ви́дит о́ко, да зуб неймёт**» "Although the eye sees it, the tooth 🔊 **2-12** can't get it." From the fable «**Лиси́ца и виногра́д**» "The Fox and the Grapes."

5.8. «**Кварте́т**» "The Quartet." A fable in which a monkey, an ass, a goat and a bear decide to play a quartet in order "to charm the world with their art" «**пленя́ть свои́м иску́сством свет**». After struggling with the music they decided to switch places, which didn't help.

5.8.1. A nightingale explained to them that more than a change of seating arrangement is needed:

А вы, друзья́, как ни сади́тесь 🔊 **2-13**
Всё в музыка́нты не годи́тесь.

And you, my friends, are not musicians no matter how you sit.

5.9. «Марты́шка и очки́» "The Monkey and the Spectacles." A monkey heard that spectacles help one see better. It got several pairs, but did not know how to use them: smelling and licking spectacles did not improve the monkey's vision. Then it got very angry and smashed all of them to pieces.

5.9.1. This line is often used as a joke whenever one complains of bad vision:

🔊 2-14   **Марты́шка к ста́рости слаба́ глаза́ми ста́ла; ….**

The Monkey in old age found that her sight grew weak.

🔊 2-15

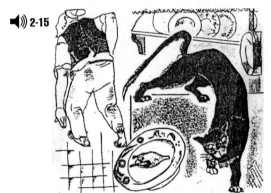

Fig. 2-9.   The Cat and the Cook

5.10. «А Ва́ська слу́шает да ест» "And Vas'ka listens, but keeps eating." (the fable **«Кот и По́вар»** "The Cat and the Cook"). **Ва́ська**, a pejorative form of **Васи́лий**, is a traditional name for a cat. The cook gives the cat a sermon about how bad it is to steal food. While the cook goes on and on, excited by his own eloquence, the cat keeps eating the stolen food. The line is used to point out that words are not enough to change someone's behavior.

6. YEVGENY ABRAMOVICH BARATYNSKY (1800–44)

ЕВГЕ́НИЙ АБРА́МОВИЧ БАРАТЫ́НСКИЙ

Baratynsky is famous for his philosophical poetry. He belonged to Pushkin's circle and was his close friend. A few lines from his poetry are frequently quoted:

6.1. From the poem **«Разуве́ние»** "Dissuasion" (1821). The poem is all the more familiar to Russians thanks to a popular song based on it.

Fig. 2-10.

🔊 2-16   *Не искуша́й меня́ без ну́жды*
            Возвра́том не́жности твое́й: ….

Don't tempt me needlessly by showing me your tenderness again [literally, by returning your tenderness].

...Уж я не ве́рю увере́ньям,
Уж я не ве́рую в любо́вь ....

I no longer believe the assurances, I no longer believe in love.

6.2. «Мой дар убо́г ...» "My gift is meager ..." (1828)

Мой дар убо́г, и го́лос мой не гро́мок,
Но я живу́, и на земле́ мое́
Кому́-нибудь любе́зно бытие́:
Его́ найдёт далёкий мой пото́мок
В мои́х стиха́х; как знать? душа́ моя́
Ока́жется с душо́й его́ в сноше́ньи,
И как нашёл я дру́га в поколе́ньи,
Чита́теля найду́ в пото́мстве я.

🔊 2-17

My gift is meager and my voice is not loud, but I live, and there is someone on this earth to whom my existence is pleasing; my remote descendant will find it in my poems; who knows, perhaps my soul will communicate with his. And as I found a friend in my generation, I will find a reader in posterity.

6.3. From the poem «Му́за» "My Muse" (1829):

Не ослеплён я му́зою мое́ю:
Краса́вицей её не назову́т,
[...]
Но поражён быва́ет ме́льком свет
Её лица́ необщим выраже́ньем,
Её рече́й споко́йной простото́й;

🔊 2-18

I am not dazzled by my muse: no one would call her a beauty [...] But the world at times is struck by the uncommon expression on her face, by the calm simplicity of her words.

Illustration: Two pages in **Кура́нты** Aug./Sept. 1997 present the work of domestic fashion-designers; the caption uses Baratynsky's line to sum up their efforts: "As is well known, Russians wish to have an uncommon expression on their faces. For that reason Russian designers and clothesmakers have persistently worked (and some still continue to work) on the creation of exactly this kind of face."

7. ALEXANDER SERGEEVICH PUSHKIN (1799–1837)

АЛЕКСА́НДР СЕРГЕ́ЕВИЧ ПУ́ШКИН

Fig. 2-11. O. Kiprensky's famous portrait of Pushkin

2-18   • Пу́шкин—на́ше всё.
             (Аполло́н Григо́рьев)

Pushkin is our everything.
(Apollon Grigoriev)

• Пу́шкин есть явле́ние чрезвыча́йное и, мо́жет быть, еди́нственное явле́ние ру́сского ду́ха: это ру́сский челове́к в его́ разви́тии, в како́м он, мо́жет быть, я́вится че́рез две́сти лет.
(Го́голь)

Pushkin is an extraordinary phenomenon, and perhaps a unique manifestation of the Russian spirit: this is the Russian as he will perhaps appear [become] after two hundred years of development.
(Gogol)

• An entry in Tsar Nicholas I's diary after talking to Pushkin: **Сего́дня я разгова́ривал с умне́йшим му́жем Росси́и.** "Today I spoke with the most intelligent man in Russia."

Pushkin is a Russian national idol. No other poet or writer has attracted as much public attention to his work, personal life, character, drafts (including the doodles on their margins), and personal letters to his wife, friends and enemies, as Pushkin. No other writer is as revered or as widely quoted as Pushkin. Russian scholars consider him the founder of contemporary Russian literature and the creator of a literary language.

Russia celebrates the anniversaries (dates are given in New Style) of his birth (June 6) and death (February 10)—not only officially but often in private. One of the most fruitful and inspired periods of Pushkin's life, the fall of 1830 that he spent in his little village of Boldino, became a synonym for a season of productive work of the highest quality: **Бо́лдинская о́сень.** [See also Chapter 10]

Figs. 2-12, 2-13.   Pushkin's estate at Boldino

Pushkin's short life, his astounding work, his development as a writer and thinker have been studied and described by generations of scholars, literary critics and writers. His mother, **Надéжда Óсиповна Ганнибáл** (Nadezhda Osipovna Hannibal), was a granddaughter of the Abyssinian prince Ibragim Hannibal, a captive given to Peter the Great by the Turkish sultan; Ibragim became a favorite of the tsar and attained the rank of general. Pushkin's pride in these biographical ties with Peter the Great shows in his unfinished novel, *The Moor of Peter the Great,* «**Арáп Петрá Велúкого**». His father, **Сергéй Львóвич**, Sergey L'vovich, was an impoverished descendant of one of the oldest aristocratic families; the Pushkins are mentioned in *The Chronicles,* «**Пóвесть временнýх лет**» and appear in Pushkin's *Boris Godunov.* As a child,

Fig. 2-14.   The house of Pushkin's
              Nanny in Mikhailovskoe

Pushkin did not receive much attention from his parents; instead, he was adored by his old nanny Arina Rodionovna, a peasant woman, a serf, who told him countless folk stories and fairy-tales; his affection for her is reflected in his poems "**К нянe**" [see 5.11] and «**Бýря мглóю нéбо крóет**» [see 5.6]. As soon as one hears the words **няня Арúна Родиóновна** Nanny Arina Rodionovna, they inevitably trigger the line from Pushkin's letter to his brother cited in

every textbook: «**Что за прéлесть эти скáзки! Кáждая есть поэма!**» "What a delight these fairy-tales are! Each is a poem!"

Pushkin began to write very early; his first poems, published at the age of 15, were instantly recognized as outstanding. During his Lyceum period, while still very young, he became a cherished and admired friend of liberal-minded intellectual army officers, many of whom were later implicated in a failed revolt against Tsar Nicholas I (December 14, 1825).

Pushkin's liberalism, independence, his scandalous duels, and his rising literary fame (including the popularity of his privately-circulated blasphemous poems and epigrams) infuriated Tsar Alexander I, who sent the poet into exile—twice (first to the south of Russia, the Caucasus, and the second time to the poet's own village, Mikhailovskoe).

Pushkin's marriage to one of the most beautiful women of his time, Natal'ia Nikolaevna Goncharova **Ната́лья Никола́евна Гончаро́ва**, the untoward attention paid her by Tsar Nicholas I, Pushkin's tragic death from a lethal wound received in a duel with

Fig. 2-15. Pushkin's wife, N. Goncharova

Georges D'Anthés, the Frenchman who widely advertised his passion for Pushkin's wife—all this is part of the Russian Everyman's knowledge of Pushkin, and a subject of fascinating studies and speculations on the part of scholars.

◀))) 2-20

Fig. 2-16. V. Serov, *Pushkin in the Park*

The wide use of the name "Pushkin" as a humorous reproach to someone refusing to take personal responsibility is mirrored in a very popular satirical puppet show called *Puppets* «Ку́клы», in which the puppets represent Yeltsin and other prominent political figures:

—**А на культу́ру кто бу́дет дава́ть, Пу́шкин?**

"And who is going to give money to support culture, Pushkin?"

(This is a play on a line from *The Happy Guys* **Весёлые ребя́та** (1934), a film by Aleksandrov: see Chapter 9.)

Fig. 2- 17.   Magazine cover depicting Pushkin as an avant-gardist

Here are jokes testifying to Pushkin's popularity:

(a)   **Два францу́зских тури́ста—у па́мятника Пу́шкину:**   🔊🌒 **2-21**

**—Ну скажи́те, кака́я несправедли́вость,—попа́л Данте́с, а па́-
мятник поста́вили Пу́шкину!**

Two French tourists are standing near the Pushkin monument, and one
says "How unfair; it was D'Anthés who hit the target, but they erected
a monument to Pushkin!"

(b) **В связи́ с юбиле́ем А.С. Пу́шкина Ста́лин объяви́л ко́нкурс на
прое́кт па́мятника вели́кому поэ́ту. Тре́тью пре́мию получи́л
прое́кт, изобража́ющий Пу́шкина, кото́рый чита́ет том сочине́ний
Ста́лина.**

Втору́ю пре́мию — Ста́лин, чита́ющий том Пу́шкина.

**Пе́рвую пре́мию получи́л прое́кт, изобража́ющий Ста́лина,
чита́ющего Ста́лина.**

In connection with the anniversary of A.S. Pushkin, Stalin announced a
competition for the best design of a monument to the great poet. The
third prize was won by a monument depicting Pushkin reading a volume of Stalin's work; the second by one with Stalin reading Pushkin;
the first prize went to one with Stalin reading Stalin.

One of the poems that best illustrates just how far Pushkin and his work
have infiltrated the Russian mind and speech is **«К Чаада́еву»** "To Chaadaev"
(1818). Petr Iakovlevich Chaadaev was Pushkin's free-thinking, Western-
oriented philosopher friend. His unorthodox views led to his being declared
insane.

 2-22

Fig. 2-18.   P.Ia. Chaadaev

Любви́, наде́жды, ти́хой сла́вы
Недо́лго не́жил нас обма́н,
Исче́зли ю́ные заба́вы,
Как сон, как у́тренний тума́н;
Но в нас гори́т ещё жела́нье,
Под гнётом вла́сти роково́й
Нетерпели́вою душо́й
Отчи́зны вне́млем призыва́нье.
Мы ждём с томле́ньем упова́нья
Мину́ты во́льности свято́й,
Как ждёт любо́вник молодо́й
Мину́ты ве́рного свида́нья.
Пока́ свобо́дою гори́м,
Пока́ сердца́ для че́сти жи́вы,
Мой друг, отчи́зне посвяти́м
Души́ прекра́сные поры́вы!
Това́рищ, верь: взойдёт она́,
Звезда́ плени́тельного сча́стья,
Росси́я вспря́нет ото сна,
И на обло́мках самовла́стья
Напи́шут на́ши имена́!

We did not revel in the illusions of love, of hope, and of peaceful fame
for long; the amusements of youth soon vanished like a dream, like
morning mist. But our hearts still burn with yearning; under the yoke
of oppression we await the call of the fatherland. In an anguish of anti-

cipation, we long, like a young lover would long for an agreed-upon rendezvous, for the moment when sacred freedom will come. While freedom still inflames us, while our hearts are still devoted, let us, my friend, dedicate to our fatherland our soul's noble impulses! Believe, my friend: the star of enchanting happiness will rise, Russia will rouse herself from her long sleep, and on the ruins of tyranny the nation will write our names.

The sincerity and ardor of this poem can bring tears to the eyes of any Russian; just to say the words **«звезда́ плени́тельного сча́стья»** "the star of enchanting happiness" or **«души́ прекра́сные поры́вы»** "the soul's noble impulses" is to step into a magic world of happiness and hope. This, however, does not prevent a Russian from enjoying the sacrilegious use of the same lines to mock the hypocrisy of the authorities, as in an old pre-perestroika joke:

—Почему́ у вас в КГБ на стене́ виси́т портре́т Пу́шкина, а не Дзержи́нского? ◀)) 2-23

   —Потому́ что Пу́шкин пе́рвый сказа́л: «Души́ прекра́сные поры́вы!»

"Why do you have Pushkin's portrait on the wall in the KGB office? Why not Dzerzhinsky's [founder of the KGB]?"

   "Because he was the first to say 'Strangle the noble impulses!' [= 'The soul's noble impulses']."

This quotation has to be pronounced with the intonation of an imperative. The punchline is based on the coincidence between the Genitive of **душа́** ('soul') and the imperative of the verb **души́ть** ('strangle, repress'), which is of course lost in translation. Another joke of the perestroika period shows people's bewilderment and mistrust of the entire concept of *glasnost*:

Това́рищ, верь: пройдёт она́, ◀)) 2-23
Эпо́ха горбачёвской гла́сности,
И Комите́т Госбезопа́сности
Запо́мнит на́ши имена́.

Comrade, trust me: the era of Gorbachev's *glasnost* will pass,
and the KGB will remember our names.

Another joke makes use of lines from the poem to convey people's disillusion with perestroika:

О перестро́йке: «Любви́, наде́жды, ти́хой сла́вы ◀)) 2-23
Недо́лго не́жил нас обма́н».

About perestroika: We did not revel in the illusions of love, of hope, and peaceful fame for long.

The same poem is quoted on a perestroika-era poster voicing ecological concerns. The poster promises that after purifying filters are installed "a grateful posterity will write our names":

> «Очистны́е сооруже́ния—досро́чно!
> И благода́рные пото́мки напи́шут на́ши имена́».
> (V. Cherenov, S. Uvarov and V. Kozlov. *Environmental Pollution*)

7.1. From «У́зник» "A Prisoner" (1822):

🔊 2-24   Сижу́ за решёткой в темни́це сыро́й,
            Вскормлённый в нево́ле орёл молодо́й.

A young eagle brought up in captivity, I am behind bars in a damp dungeon.

Use: Since there are two expressions with the same verb **сиде́ть** "sit": **сиде́ть в тюрьме́** "to be in prison," and **сиде́ть до́ма** "to stay home," the above lines are often used as a joke implying that one has to stay home (that is, doing some tedious work).

7.2. From «Разгово́р книгопродавца́ с поэ́том» "Conversation between a Publisher and a Poet" (1824):

🔊 2-25   Не продаётся вдохнове́нье,
            Но мо́жно ру́копись прода́ть.

The inspiration is not for sale, but the manuscript is.

Illustration: Headline in a weekly newspaper *Собесе́дник* (*Interlocutor*) No. 24, 1993: «Дми́трий Бы́ков: Разгово́р поэ́та с книгопродавца́ми» "Dmitri Bykov: a conversation between a poet and booksellers."

🔊 2-26   7.3. «Что пройдёт, то бу́дет ми́ло» "Whatever passes will be remembered as sweet." A universally remembered line from the short poem «Е́сли жи́знь тебя́ обма́нет, не печа́лься, не серди́сь» "If life deceives you, don't be sad, don't be angry" (1825).

7.4. From «Вакхи́ческая пе́сня» "Bacchic Song" (1825):

🔊 2-27   *Что смо́лкнул весе́лия глас?*

Why did the sound [lit: voice] of merriment quiet down?

7.5. From «Зи́мний ве́чер» "Winter Evening" (1825):

7.5.1.

🔊 2-28   Бу́ря мгло́ю не́бо кро́ет,
            Ви́хри сне́жные крутя́.
            То, как зверь, она́ заво́ет,
            То запла́чет, как дитя́.

A blizzard covers the sky with gloom, now howling like a wild beast, now crying like a baby.

Illustration:

(a) A passage from Bulgakov's *Master and Margarita*, in which the mediocre poet Riukhin looks at Pushkin's monument with envy and produces the following monologue:

> … [В]от приме́р настоя́щей уда́чливости. […] —како́й бы шаг он ◀))) 2-28
> ни сде́лал в жи́зни, что бы ни случи́лось с ним, всё шло ему́ на
> по́льзу, всё обраща́лось к его́ сла́ве! Но что он сде́лал? Я не
> постига́ю … Что-нибу́дь осо́бенное есть в э́тих слова́х: «бу́ря
> мгло́ю …»? Не понима́ю!.. Повезло́, повезло́! —вдруг ядови́то за-
> ключи́л Рю́хин […] —стреля́л, стреля́л в него́ э́тот белогварде́ец
> и раздроби́л бедро́ и обеспе́чил бессме́ртие …

Here is an example of real luck […], whatever step he took in his life, whatever happened to him—everything benefited him, everything tended to his glory! But what did he do? Inconceivable! Is there anything special in these words: 'The storm covers the sky with gloom?' I don't get it! … Luck, pure luck!" Riukhin concluded with sudden venom. "That White Guard shot and shot at him, and smashed his hip and guaranteed his immortality …"

(b) The second line of the poem, **«То как зверь она́ заво́ет, то запла́чет, как дитя́»** "now howling like a wild beast, now crying like a small baby," is often used without change to refer to poor singing (or any other loud out-of-place noise, for example, a car which refuses to start).

7.5.2.

◀))) 2-29

Вы́пьем, до́брая подру́жка
Бе́дной ю́ности мое́й,
Вы́пьем с го́ря; где же кру́жка?
Се́рдцу бу́дет веселе́й.

Let's drink, O dear friend of my poor youth, let's drink to forget our grief. Where is the cup? It will cheer our hearts.

Illustration:

(a) The line: **«Вы́пьем с го́ря. Где же кру́жка»?** is, naturally, often ◀))) 2-29 quoted in a country like Russia where alcoholism is a serious problem and alcohol consumption is surrounded with elaborate rituals. You can cheer up any Russian by quoting this line whenever a drink is offered (even if the beverage is not alcoholic).

(b) A coy advertisement in *Огонёк* March 1997 slightly changes the immortal line: «**Вы́пьем ЧАЮ, где же кру́жка, се́рдцу бу́дет веселе́й ... (мог бы сказа́ть поэ́т). Путь к се́рдцу россия́нина лежи́т ... че́рез ча́шку ча́я**» "'Let us have some TEA, where is the cup, it'll cheer up our hearts ...' (the poet might have said). The way to a Russian's heart is through a cup of tea."

7.6. The poem «**19 октября́**» "October 19th" (1825) is dedicated to the reunion of Pushkin's school-mates, the first graduates of the Lyceum **лице́й**, a very special higher-education school for children of the Russian nobility, where Pushkin studied with other gifted young aristocrats. It was hoped that the tsar would invite graduates of the Lyceum to form an enlightened council. The establishment of the Lyceum next to the tsar's summer residence in Tsar's Village (**Ца́рское Село́**) near Petersburg was taken by Russian society almost as a promise to transform the autocratic government into a constitutional monarchy. This never happened. Many of Pushkin's Lyceum friends joined the secret society and participated in the December uprising on Senate Square **Сена́тская пло́щадь**. Some of the Lyceists became prominent poets (Delvig, Kiukhel'beker), others government officials—but all cherished their Lyceum memories and great affection for each other throughout their lives.

7.6.1.

🔊 2-30   **Друзья́ мои́, прекра́сен наш сою́з!**
         Он как душа́ нераздели́м и ве́чен—

My friends, how beautiful is our union! Like one's soul, it is indivisible and eternal.

Illustration:

(a) The line **Друзья́ мои, прекра́сен наш сою́з!** is often repeated as a toast when drinking to the health of friends.

(b) One of the episodes of the TV show «**Ку́клы**» (October 1996) was entirely based on Pushkin's poem «**19 октября́**»; at some point Зю́га, the puppet representing Zyuganov, the communist rival of Yeltsin, exclaims: «**Друзья́ мои́! Прекра́сен наш Сою́з!**» "My friends! Our Union [the Soviet Union] is beautiful." The puppet representing Yeltsin is called **Бори́ска**, a diminutive/pejorative form of the name Boris that is an easily recognizable reference to Pushkin's drama «**Бори́с Годуно́в**», in which the dissatisfied boyars refer disrespectfully to Tsar Boris as Boriska behind his back. Boriska laments the lack of loyal friends like Pushkin's and imagines how all of his comrades-in-arms would behave if he were Pushkin and they Decembrists: not a single one of them would go to Senate Square, there would be no uprising, and the whole of Russian history would have been different.

Fig. 2-19.   The Yeltsin puppet from the television show *Puppets*

7.6.2.

Куда́ бы нас ни бро́сила судьби́на,   🔊)) 2-31
И сча́стие куда́ б ни повело́,
Всё те же мы: нам це́лый мир — чужби́на;
Оте́чество нам — Ца́рское Село́.

Wherever chance and fortune cast us and destiny bids us go, we stay
the same: to us the whole world is alien, our Fatherland is Tsarskoe
Selo.

7.6.3.

Служе́нье муз не те́рпит суеты́;   🔊)) 2-32
Прекра́сное должно́ быть велича́во.

Serving the Muses is irreconcilable with fussiness; beauty must have
majesty.

7.7. The poem «К ***» "To ***" (1825) is dedicated to **А́нна Петро́вна Керн**
Anna Petrovna Kern:

7.7.1.

Я по́мню чу́дное мгнове́нье: 🔊)) 2-33
Передо мной яви́лась ты,
Как мимолётное виде́нье,
Как ге́ний чи́стой красоты́.

I remember a wonderful moment: you appeared before me, like a fleeting
vision, like the embodiment of pure beauty.

Fig. 2-20.   A.P. Kern

Use:

(a) Whenever someone begins a sentence with «**Я по́мню ...**» "I remember ..." the person risks being interrupted with the continuation of Pushkin's line: «**чу́дное мгнове́нье**» "a wondrous moment."

(b) If someone drops by a friend's house for a very short time, someone is bound to comment «**Ну, ты как мимолётное виде́нье!**» "Well, you are like a fleeting vision."

7.7.2.

◀)) 2-34
В глуши́, во мра́ке заточе́нья
Тяну́лись ти́хо дни мои́
Без божества́, без вдохнове́нья,
Без слёз, без жи́зни, без любви́.

In my remote corner, in the gloom of isolation, my days dragged, without divinity or inspiration, without tears, life, or love.

Use: «**без божества́, без вдохнове́нья**» can be said about any piece of writing, movie and so on, to indicate that it is dull and uninspiring.

7.8. From «**Проро́к**» "The Prophet" (1826)

7.8.1.

◀)) 2-35
Духо́вной жа́ждою томи́м,
В пусты́не мра́чной я влачи́лся,
И шестикры́лый серафи́м
На перепу́тьи мне яви́лся.

Tormented by a spiritual thirst, I dragged myself through a gloomy desert, and a six-winged seraph appeared before me.

7.8.2.

◀)) 2-36
И Бо́га глас ко мне воззва́л:
«**Восста́нь, проро́к, и виждь, и вне́мли,**
Испо́лнись во́лею мое́й,
И, обходя́ моря́ и зе́мли,
Глаго́лом жги сердца́ люде́й».

And then the voice of God called upon me: "Arise, my prophet! See and hear, fulfill my will! Cross the lands and seas, inflame people's hearts with your words

Illustration: An article under the headline **«Глаго́лом жечь сердца́ люде́й …»** "To inflame people's hearts with a word" in ***Огонёк***, February 1997 criticizes the poor quality of advertisements. The solemn headline is hilariously funny in view of the fact that the advertisements that were supposed to "inflame people's hearts" were displayed on match-boxes.

7.9. Lines from the poem **«Ня́не»** "To My Nanny" (1827):

Подру́га дней мои́х суро́вых,
Голу́бка дря́хлая моя́!

🔊)) 2-37

A loyal friend of my bleak days, my decrepit old dear!

Fig. 2-21.   *Winter Evening*, a depiction of Pushkin and his Nanny

Use: These two lines are often addressed with humorous affection to a female friend (**Приве́т, подру́га дней мои́х суро́вых!**) "Hi, loyal friend of my bleak days!" or in introducing her to someone: **«А э́то Та́ня, подру́га дней мои́х суро́вых, голу́бка дря́хлая моя́!»** "And this is Tanya, a loyal friend of my bleak days, my decrepit old dear!"

7.10. The poem **«Во глубине́ сиби́рских руд»** "In the depth of Siberian mines" (1827) had to be memorized in Soviet schools. Pushkin addressed it to his friends the Decembrists, sentenced to hard labor in Siberia for rising against the tsar in December 1825.

7.10.1. **«Не пропадёт ваш ско́рбный труд»** "Your sorrowful labor will not go for nothing." This particular line from the poem became especially popular and is used whenever one is jokingly thanking somebody for something. The full quotation is:

🔊 2-38 Во глубине́ сиби́рских руд
Храни́те го́рдое терпе́нье,
Не пропадёт ваш ско́рбный труд
И дум высо́кое стремле́нье.

In the depth of Siberian mines keep your proud patience. Your sorrowful labor and the lofty aspiration of your thoughts will not go for nothing.

Illustration: Vladimir Fedorovich Odoevsky **Одо́евский**, a poet and one of the Decembrists, wrote an answer to Pushkin's poem entitled **«А.С. Пу́шкину»** or **«Отве́т на посла́ние А.С. Пу́шкина»** "To Pushkin (An Answer to the Missive of A.S. Pushkin)" (1827):

🔊 2-38 **Наш ско́рбный труд не пропадёт:**
Из и́скры возгори́тся пла́мя.

Our sorrowful labor will not go for nothing, the spark will kindle a flame.

The line **«Из и́скры возгори́тся пла́мя»** "the spark will kindle a flame" was made popular by Lenin, who took it as a motto for his first political newspaper, **И́скра** *The Spark.*

🔊 2-39 7.10.2.
Темни́цы ру́хнут — и свобо́да
Вас при́мет ра́достно у вхо́да, ...

The prisons will collapse and Freedom will greet you joyfully at the door.

Illustration: Headline in ***Общая газета***, Aug. 1997, to an article about the disastrous state of the prisons: **«Темни́цы ру́хнут и ...»** "The prisons will collapse and ..."

7.11. The whole text of the poem **«Ты и Вы»** "Thou [singular] and You [plural]" (1828) used to be memorized:

🔊 2-40 Пусто́е *вы* серде́чным *ты*
Она, обмо́лвясь, замени́ла
И все счастли́вые мечты́
В душе́ влюблённой пробуди́ла.
Пред ней заду́мчиво стою́,
Свести́ оче́й с неё нет си́лы;
И говорю́ ей: как *вы* ми́лы!
И мы́слю: как *тебя́* люблю́!

The empty *you are* by the heartfelt *thou art* she substituted through a slip of the tongue, and has awakened in my enamored heart all sorts of happy dreams. I stand before her, day-dreaming, unable to tear my eyes away from her, and tell her: "how sweet *you* are!" while thinking: "how much I love *thee* !"

7.12. **«Зимнее утро»** "Winter Morning" (1829) was supposed to be memorized in schools; many remember more than the few lines below, which come to everyone's mind on a crisp-cold winter morning full of sunshine:

7.12.1.

Мороз и солнце; день чудесный!   🔊 2-41
Ещё ты дремлешь, друг прелестный —
Пора, красавица, проснись:
Открой сомкнуты негой взоры,
Навстречу северной Авроры,
Звездою севера явись!

The frost and the sun. The day is wonderful. Are you still sleeping, my charming friend? It's time, my beauty, wake up! Open your eyes shut in sweet sleep, rise like the North Star to meet the Northern Aurora [that is, dawn].

7.12.2.

Под голубыми небесами   🔊 2-42
Великолепными коврами,
Блестя на солнце, снег лежит;

Under the bright blue sky, the snow lies, sparkling under the sun like a splendid carpet.

7.13. **«Я вас любил ...»** "I loved you ..." (1829) is a poem every Russian knows by heart from beginning to end:

Я вас любил: Любовь ещё, быть может,   🔊 2-43
В душе моей угасла не совсем;
Но пусть она вас больше не тревожит;
Я не хочу печалить вас ничем.
Я вас любил безмолвно, безнадёжно,
То робостью, то ревностью томим;
Я вас любил так искренно, так нежно,
Как дай вам Бог любимой быть другим.

I loved you once. This love might not yet be extinguished in my heart, but don't let it distress you any more. I do not want to sadden you with anything. I loved you silently, without a hope, tormented at times with shyness, at times jealously. I loved you once so sincerely, so gently as I pray God grant you to be loved by another.

Illustration:

(a)   The title of an article in ***Итоги***, December 1996, about troubles with the shares of a company plays on the phonetic similarity of the pronoun VAS "you" and the company's name, AutoVAZ: **«Я ВАЗ любил ...»** "I loved VAZ once ..."

(b)   A sketch on the television show, **«Куклы»** *Puppets*, 1996, shows the puppet Lenin giving an examination in Russian literature to **Бориска**, a puppet representing Yeltsin. Boriska begins:

🔊)) 2-44   —Пу́шкин. Ли́рика. Ли́рика у Пу́шкина быва́ет гражда́нская и любо́вная. Гражда́нская, значит, обращена́ к гра́жданам, а любо́вная—к гражда́нкам. Наприме́р: «Я вас люби́л ...»
Ле́нин: —Меня́?
Бори́ска: —Ну, вас когда́-то все люби́ли ... Причём —любо́вь ещё быть мо́жет!
Ле́нин: —Да́льше!
Бори́ска: Но-о ... Пусть она вас бо́льше не трево́жит!

"So. Pushkin. Lyrical poems. Pushkin's lyrical poems are either civic or love poems. Civic poems, e-e-er, are addressed to male citizens, and the love poems to female citizens. For example: 'I loved you once.'"
Lenin: "Me?"
Boriska: "There was a time when everyone loved you. And by the way, may still love you."
Lenin: "Go on."
Boriska: " 'But e-e-er don't let it distress you any more.
In this sketch Yeltsin is depicted as a complete ignoramus who confuses the two senses of the word **гражда́нский** ('civic' vs. 'citizen's').

7.14. The poem **«Мадо́нна»** "Madonna" (1830) is dedicated to Pushkin's wife, Natal'ia Goncharova **Ната́лья Никола́евна Гончаро́ва**:

🔊)) 2-45   Испо́лнились мои́ жела́ния. Творе́ц
Тебя́ мне ниспосла́л, тебя́, моя́ Мадо́нна,
Чисте́йшей пре́лести чисте́йший образе́ц.

My wishes are fulfilled. The Creator sent you to me, my Madonna, the purest specimen of the purest charm.

7.15. From **«Эле́гия»** "Elegy" (1830):

🔊)) 2-46   Но не хочу́, о дру́ги, умира́ть;
Я жить хочу́, чтоб мы́слить и страда́ть ....

I do not want, O dear friends, to die; I want to be alive to think and suffer [lit.: in order to think/ reason/ contemplate and suffer].

[Note that this is not a masochistic craving for suffering, often erroneously regarded as stereotypically Russian. What is meant here is: thinking and understanding is life's greatest gift, even if it brings pain and suffering. Thus, to a Russian, these lines imply courage, love of life and the sadness of wisdom.]

7.16. From the poem «**Герой**» "A Hero" (1830):

Тьмы ни́зких и́стин мне доро́же 🔊 2-47
Нас возвыша́ющий обма́н ...

A lie that uplifts us is much dearer to me than thousands of base truths.

Illustration: Headline in *Но́вое время* Dec. 1996: «**Нас возвыша́ющий цини́зм. Жа́жда нра́вственной поли́тики как детона́тор социа́льного взры́ва**». "'Cynicism that uplifts us:' the longing for moral politics as detonator of a social explosion."

7.17. From «**Поэ́ту**» "To a Poet" (1830):

[…] Ты сам свой вы́сший суд; 🔊 2-48
Всех стро́же оцени́ть уме́ешь ты свой труд.
Ты им дово́лен ли, взыска́тельный худо́жник?
Дово́лен? Так пуска́й толпа́ его брани́т, ….

You are your own highest judge. You are able to evaluate your own work more strictly than anyone else. Are you satisfied with it, demanding artist? Are you? Then let the mob curse it ….

7.18. From «**Óсень**» "Autumn" (1833):

7. 18.1.

Октя́брь уж наступи́л—уж ро́ща отряха́ет 🔊 2-49
Последние листы́ с наги́х свои́х ветве́й;

October is here already: the grove shakes off the last leaves from its naked limbs.

Use: The extent to which Pushkin's poetry shaped the Russian mentality is amazing: perception of the seasons, for example, is unthinkable without associations with Pushkin's lines. Thus either the word "October" or the sight of bare autumnal trees would immediately trigger the above lines.

7.18.2.

Ох, ле́то кра́сное! люби́л бы я тебя́, 🔊 2-50
Когда́ б не зной да пыль, да комары́, да му́хи.

O beautiful summer! How much I would love you if not for heat and dust and mosquitoes and flies.

7. 18.3.

◀))) 2-51

Уны́лая пора́! очей очарова́нье!
Прия́тна мне твоя́ проща́льная краса́— ....

Oh, doleful season, enchantment for the eyes!
You bring me sweetness in your parting beauty [lit.: your farewell
beauty is pleasing to me].

Illustration:

(a) «**Оче́й очарова́нье**» "enchantment for the eyes" can be said about
anything visually pleasing.

(b) In the newspaper **Сего́дня**, September 1993, the headline «**Авто-
сало́нная пора́—оче́й очарова́нье**» "Car-show season—enchantment for the eyes" lends a tone of irony and admiration to an article
about the fall exhibition of new models of cars.

7. 18.4.

◀))) 2-52

И мы́сли в голове́ волну́ются в отва́ге,
И ри́фмы лёгкие навстре́чу им бегу́т,
И па́льцы про́сятся к перу́, перо́ к бума́ге,
Мину́та—и стихи́ свобо́дно потеку́т.

And the thoughts in my head are crowded in courageous excitement,
and the light rhymes are running to meet them, my fingers beg for a
pen, the pen for paper; one more minute—and the verses will flow
freely.

Illustration: An advertisement in **База́р** *Bazaar*, September 1997, (see Fig.
2-22) cleverly combines these lines with a quotation from Chekhov [see
Chapter 3, 13.1] to promote pens and various desk paraphernalia from Western
companies:

◀))) 2-52

**И ру́ки тя́нутся к перу́, перо́—к бума́ге ... На ва́шем рабо́чем
столе́ всё должно́ быть прекра́сно .... Мо́жет быть, что тако́е
окруже́ние благотво́рно поде́йствует и на мы́сли, кото́рые
потре́буется неме́дленно записа́ть. Оста́нется лишь протяну́ть
ру́ку к перу́ Mont-Blanc, Waterman или Shaeffer.**

"And hands are stretching to reach for a pen, the pen for paper...
Everything on your desk should be beautiful .... It may happen that
such a noble environment would beneficially influence your thoughts,
and you would need to jot them down. It only remains to stretch out
your hand for a Mont-Blanc, Waterman or Shaeffer pen."

Fig. 2-22.

7.19. **«Порá, мой друг, порá!»** "Tis time, my friend, tis time!" (1834):

🔊)) **2-53**

Порá, мой друг, порá! покóя сéрдце прóсит —
Летя́т за дня́ми дни, и кáждый час унóсит
Частúчку бытия́, а мы с тобóй вдвоём
Предполагáем жить, и глядь, как раз умрём.
На свéте счáстья нет, но есть покóй и вóля.
Давнó завúдная мечтáется мне дóля —
Давнó, устáлый раб, замы́слил я побéг
В обúтель дáльнюю трудóв и чúстых нег.

Tis time, my friend, tis time! My heart is begging for rest — and with
each hour a small part of existence is carried off. Both of us, you and I,
resolved to live. And in a blink of an eye, we die. There is no happiness
on earth, but there is peace and freedom. How long I've dreamt of an
enviable lot — how long I, a weary slave, have planned an escape to the
remote refuge of toil and pure delight.

Illustration:

(a) The first line is one of the most frequently repeated quotations and is
     used without change when one is about to leave a party or other social
     gathering.

(b) The magazine cover below (***Огонёк***, April 1996) shows at the bottom
     a new Volvo bus, accompanied by the words **«На све́те сча́стья нет, /
     но есть поко́й и Во́льво»** "There is no happiness on earth, but there
     is peace and Volvo."

Fig. 2-23.

7.20. From «**... Вновь я посети́л ...**» "... I visited anew ..." (1835):

7.20.1.

**... Вновь я посети́л
Тот уголо́к земли́, где я провёл
Изгна́нником два го́да незаме́тных.**

🔊 2-54

... I visited anew that spot on earth where I spent two unnoticed years as an outcast.

7.20.2.

**[...] *Здра́вствуй, пле́мя,
Младо́е, незнако́мое!***

🔊 2-55

I greet you, young and unfamiliar generation!

Illustration: A headline in **Огонёк**, June 1997, introduces into this quotation a reproach to the young generation: «**Эх вы, пле́мя младо́е. Путеше́ствие на ро́дину Пу́шкина**». "Oh, you, the young generation. A trip to Pushkin's birthplace." (To say: **Эх вы!/эх ты!** "Oh, you" is to express disappointment/ exasperation with someone.)

7.21. A well-remembered line from the poem «**Стихи́, сочинённые но́чью во вре́мя бессо́нницы**» "Verses Composed at Night during Insomnia" (1830) is:

Жи́зни мы́шья беготня́.

🔊 2-56

Life's rustle, like the sound of mice running around.

7.22. From «**Я па́мятник себе́ воздви́г нерукотво́рный ...**» "I have erected a monument to myself ..." (1836):

7.22.1.

**Я па́мятник себе́ воздви́г нерукотво́рный.
К нему́ не зарастёт наро́дная тропа́.
Вознёсся вы́ше он главо́ю непоко́рной
Александри́йского столпа́.**

🔊 2-57

I have erected a monument to myself not built by hands. There will always be a well-trodden path leading to it. It raises its defiant head higher than Alexander's Column.

Illustration:

(a) Once in Russia the writer saw the following philosophically stated graffiti on the door of a public restroom: «**Сюда́ не зарастёт наро́дная тропа́**» "There will always be a well-trodden path leading here."

(b) A sketch on the TV show «**Ку́клы**» depicts the office of the president of the Central Bank and a long line of petitioners asking for money. The secretary comments in a melancholy tone: «**К нему́ не зарастёт наро́дная тропа́**».

7.22.2.

🔊 2-58   *Слух обо мне́ пройдёт по всей Руси́ вели́кой,*
И назовёт меня всяк су́щий в ней язы́к,
И го́рдый внук славя́н, и финн, и ны́не ди́кой
Тунгу́с, и друг степе́й калмы́к.

They will hear of me all over Great Russia/Rus′, and every people living in it shall know my name: the proud descendant of the Slavs, the Finn, the still uncivilized Tungus, and the Kalmyk, friend of the steppes.

7.22.3.

🔊 2-59   **И до́лго бу́ду тем любе́зен я наро́ду,**
Что чу́вства до́брые я ли́рой пробужда́л,
Что в мой жесто́кий век воссла́вил я свобо́ду
И ми́лость к па́дшим призыва́л.

And for a long time I will be loved by people because I evoked kind feelings with my lyre, because I, in my cruel century, glorified freedom and asked for mercy for the fallen ones.

7.22.4.

🔊 2-60   **Веле́нью Бо́жию, о Му́за, будь послу́шна, [...]**
Хвалу́ и клевету́ прие́мли равноду́шно,
И не оспо́ривай глупца́.

O my Muse, obey God's will .... Take either praise or slander with equal indifference and never dispute a fool's opinion.

Illustration: This is a good example of how a line from a poem written almost two centuries ago can be adapted to present-day needs. When General Alexander Lebed, known as "a man of action," quoted Pushkin during an interview, the journalist was so impressed that this became the headline of his article: «Алекса́ндр Ле́бедь: хвалу́ и клевету́ прие́мли равноду́шно ...» "Alexander Lebed: Take either praise or slander with equal indifference." By citing this particular line, General Lebed added to his public image an unexpected side, that of a cultured person, and at the same time implied that all the accusations against him were merely "slander"—and he did all this without taking any legal responsibility for the act (after all, a quotation is a quotation).

7.23. «Русла́н и Людми́ла» *Ruslan and Liudmila*, a mock-epic fairy-tale (1817–20) [See also Chapter 4 and Chapter 7.]

7.23.1. Проло́г Prologue. Almost the entire prologue to the poem is universally remembered:

У лукомо́рья дуб зелёный;
Злата́я цепь на ду́бе том:
И днём и но́чью кот учёный
Всё хо́дит по́ цепи круго́м;
Идёт напра́во—песнь заво́дит,
Нале́во—ска́зку говори́т.

Там чудеса́: там ле́ший бро́дит,
Руса́лка на ветвя́х сиди́т;
Там на неве́домых доро́жках
Следы́ неви́данных звере́й;
Избу́шка там на ку́рьих но́жках
Стои́т без о́кон, без двере́й;
[...]
В темни́це там царе́вна ту́жит,
А бу́рый волк ей ве́рно слу́жит;
Там сту́па с Ба́бою Яго́й
Идёт, бредёт сама́ собо́й;
Там царь Каще́й над зла́том ча́хнет;
Там ру́сский дух ... там Ру́сью па́хнет!

By the curving shore of the sea there grows a green oak, and on that oak there is a golden chain. Day and night, a learned [trained] cat paces that chain. When walking to the right, he begins a song, when walking to the left, he tells a fairy-tale. There are miracles there, a forest-goblin roams there, a mermaid sits on the branches [of that tree]. On the unknown paths there are foot-prints of unfamiliar beasts; there stands a hut on chicken legs, without windows or doors. There is a princess despairing in the dungeon, with a brown wolf loyally serving her; there is a mortar carrying Baba Yaga, moving all by itself. There Tsar Scrag withers away over his gold; there is a Russian spirit there ... it smells of Rus' there!

Illustration:

(a) See comments on fairy-tale characters in Chapter 3, Section 1.

(b) In the science-fiction novel by the brothers Strugatsky, *Monday Begins on Saturday*, there is an entire research institute working on scientific explanation of fairy-tale phenomena. Baba Yaga is a museum keeper, and the learned cat still tells an enormous number of fairy-tales, only he can't finish a single one: the poor animal suffers from senility.

7.23.2. Pushkin's translation of lines from the Scottish poet James MacPherson, used in *Ruslan and Liudmila*:

🔊 2-62   **Дела́ давно́ мину́вших дней,**
           Преда́нья старины́ глубо́кой.

A tale of the times of old! …
The deeds of days of other years! …

7.23.3.

🔊 2-63   **О по́ле, по́ле, кто тебя́**
           Усе́ял мёртвыми костя́ми?

O, field, field, who has covered you with dead bones?

Fig. 2-24.   V. Vasnetsov, *After Igor's Battle with the Polovetsians*

7.24. In the long romantic poem **«Цыга́ны»** "Gypsies" (1824) the hero, Aleko, abandons urban civilization and embraces the simple natural life of the Gypsies.

7.24.1.

🔊 2-64   *Цыга́ны шу́мною толпо́й*
           По Бессара́бии кочу́ют.

A noisy crowd of gypsies roams through Bessarabia.

Use: These lines are often quoted upon seeing a noisy group of people, or even by someone in that noisy group.

7.24.2.

🔊 2-65   *Пти́чка бо́жия не зна́ет*
           Ни забо́ты, ни труда́; ….

God's little bird knows neither care nor toil.

Use: A rather negative reference to someone living irresponsibly.

7.24.3.

**И всю́ду стра́сти роковы́е
И от суде́б защи́ты нет.**

🔊)) 2-66

And fatal passions reign everywhere, and there is no protection from the Fates.

7.25. «Полта́ва» "Poltava" (1828–29) is a long poem about Peter the Great's war with Sweden.

7.25.1.

*В одну теле́гу впрячь не мо́жно
Коня́ и тре́петную лань.*

🔊)) 2-67

It is impossible to harness to one cart a horse and a trembling fallow deer.

Use: These lines are often used to refer to any two people who would not make a good team (whether marital or working).

7.25.2.

Тиха́ укра́инская ночь.
**Прозра́чно небо. Звёзды бле́щут.
Свое́й дремо́ты превозмо́чь
Не хо́чет во́здух ....**

🔊)) 2-68

Quiet is the Ukrainian night. The sky is translucent. The stars shine. The air doesn't want to overcome its drowsiness.

Illustration: An article about the shortage of electricity in Ukraine had the following headline in the newspaper *Изве́стия* (1993): «Темна́ укра́инская ночь» "Dark is the Ukrainian night."

7.25.3. [Also see Chapter 1.]

[...] Из шатра́,
Толпо́й люби́мцев окружённый,
Выхо́дит Пётр. *Его глаза́*
Сия́ют. Лик его ужа́сен.
Движе́нья бы́стры. Он прекра́сен.
Он весь, как бо́жия гроза́.

🔊)) 2-69

Peter comes out of the tent, surrounded by a crowd of favorites. His eyes are shining. His face is terrifying. His movements are fast. He is magnificent. He is like a storm of God.

7.25.4.

◀)) 2-70   *Швед, ру́сский — ко́лет, ру́бит, ре́жет.*

A Swede, a Russian stab, chop, cut.

7.26. **«Ме́дный вса́дник»** "The Bronze Horseman" (1833) is a long poem about the flood in St. Petersburg, during which the bronze statue of Peter the Great chases a poor man named **Евге́ний** Eugene through the empty streets.

7.26.1. He = Peter:

◀)) 2-71   *На берегу́ пусты́нных волн*
            Стоя́л он, дум вели́ких полн,
            И вдаль гляде́л ....

On the bank of desolate waves, *he* stood, full of great thoughts, and gazed into the distance.

◀)) 2-72   7.26.2.

            И ду́мал он:
            Отсе́ль грози́ть мы бу́дем шве́ду.
            Здесь бу́дет го́род заложён
            На зло надме́нному сосе́ду.
            Приро́дой здесь нам суждено́
            В Евро́пу проруби́ть окно́, ...

And he thought: "We are going to threaten the Swedes from this very place. Here a city will be founded to spite the arrogant neighbor. Nature itself decrees that we carve out a window to Europe here.

Illustration:

◀)) 2-72   (a) An article in the newspaper ***Черномо́рская здра́вница*** (1997) about Philip Morris as a sponsor of a provincial art festival has the headline: **«В Росси́ю проруби́ть окно ...»** "To carve out a window to Russia ..."

            (b) Headline in ***Огонёк***, December 1996: **«Обернётся ли 'окно в Евро́пу' ли́нией Маннерге́йма?»** "Will a 'window to Europe' turn into a 'Mannerheim line'?" — An article on a conflict with the Finns concerning the highways on the border.

            (c) From an article in ***Ито́ги***, December 1996, "Russia lost its fleet": **«Корабли́ у нас со времён Петра́ Пе́рвого стро́или непло́хо, о́кон морски́х то́же напроруба́ли доста́точно»** "From the time of Peter the Great, we haven't been bad at building ships; many naval windows were carved out, too."

Все флаги в гости...

Мир российской моды в волнении:
пройдет совсем немного времени,
и впервые в нашей стране, в Москве,
будет проходить международный конкурс
профессиональных манекенщиц
«Топ-модель мира-95».
Лучшие манекенщицы из пятидесяти
стран мира продемонстрируют коллекции
известных кутюрье Анны Молинари

и Реджины Шрекер из Италии,
а также наших соотечественников

Fig. 2-25.

7.26.3.

Сюда́ по но́вым им волна́м
Все фла́ги в го́сти бу́дут к нам.

🔊 2-73

The flags of all nations will navigate these new waters, to visit us here [ships of all nations will come visit us here].

Illustration: **Крестья́нка** (1995) has the headline to an article about an international competition of professional models in Moscow: **«Все фла́ги в го́сти ... Топ-моде́ль ми́ра-95».** "'The flags of all nations will visit ...' World Top Model-95." [see left]

7.26.4.

Люблю́ тебя́, Петра́ творе́нье,
Люблю́ твой стро́гий,
       стро́йный вид, ...

🔊 2-74

I love you so, Peter's creation, I love your stern, elegant appearance.

7.26.5. A description of "white nights" in Petersburg; **Адмиралте́йство** is The Admiralty, a beautiful building with a golden spire:

И я́сны спя́щие грома́ды
Пусты́нных у́лиц, *и светла́*
Адмиралте́йская игла́ ....

🔊 2-75

And sleeping massive forms in the deserted streets are clearly seen, and the spire of the Admiralty shines bright.

7.26.6.

Одна́ заря́ смени́ть другу́ю
Спеши́т, дав но́чи полчаса́.

🔊 2-76

Sunrise hastens to replace sunset, having allowed the night only half an hour.

[Since in Russian **заря́** 'dawn' may mean either sunrise or sunset—**у́тренняя заря́** or **вече́рняя заря́**—Pushkin uses the same word for both.]

7.26.7.

🔊 2-77   *Красу́йся, град Петро́в, и стой*
          Неколеби́мо, как Росси́я, ….

Stand in beauty, O Peter's city, stand unwavering, like Russia.

7.26.8. Words addressed to the statue of Peter the Great, The Bronze Horseman:

🔊 2-78   *Куда́ ты ска́чешь, го́рдый конь,*
          И где опу́стишь ты копы́та?

Where are you galloping to, O proud steed, and where will you rest your hooves?

7.27. **«Евге́ний Оне́гин»** *Eugene Onegin,* a novel in verse (1823–30).

7.27.1. The line from Pushkin's letter to a friend: **«Пишу́ рома́н, не в про́зе, а в**
🔊 2-79   **стиха́х: дья́вольская ра́зница!»** "I am writing a novel, not in prose but in verse: it makes a hell of a difference!" has became a part of common knowledge, and people use the phrase with gusto and on any imaginable occasion.

🔊 2-80   7.27.2. **«Энциклопе́дия ру́сской жи́зни»** (**В.Г.**  **Бели́нский**) "Encyclopedia of Russian life" is a famous definition of *Eugene Onegin* given by V.G. Belinsky, one of the best-known critics of the 1830s and 1840s.

7.27.3. The epigraphs to some chapters of *Onegin* taken by Pushkin from different authors are also frequently cited:

🔊 2-81   **И жить торо́пится и чу́вствовать спеши́т.**
          (Вя́земский, «Пе́рвый снег», эпи́граф
          к 1-й главе́)

He hastens to live, he rushes to feel.
(Viazemsky, "The First Snow," epigraph
to the first chapter)

Fig. 2-26. V.G. Belinsky

7.27.4. Epigraph to chapter 8:

🔊 2-82   **Проща́й, и е́сли навсегда́, то навсегда́ проща́й.**
          (Ба́йрон)

Fare thee well, and if forever,
Still forever fare thee well.
    (Byron)

7.27.5. The first lines of chapter 1 are ingrained in many a Russian's memory:

Мой дя́дя са́мых че́стных пра́вил,   🔊 **2-83**
Когда́ не в шу́тку занемо́г,
Он уважа́ть себя́ заста́вил,
И лу́чше вы́думать не мог;

My uncle was a man of the strictest morals; when he got seriously sick, he suddenly made everyone appreciate him, and could not have invented a better trick.

Illustration: The extent to which the first line is familiar is well demonstrated by the following sales gimmick printed in ***Огонёк***, February 1996:

«Кста́ти, в связи́ с годовщи́ной сме́рти Пу́шкина наш вопро́с: 🔊 **2-83**
каку́ю профе́ссию име́л са́мый упомина́емый в Росси́и дя́дя?
Пе́рвого, кто отве́тит пра́вильно ..., по предъявле́нии квита́нции о
подпи́ске ожида́ет приз».

"By the way, in connection with the anniversary of Pushkin's death we have a question for you: What was the profession of the uncle most frequently mentioned in Russia? A prize awaits the first person who answers this question after showing proof of subscription to our magazine."

7.27.6. From chapter 1, stanza 5:

Мы все учи́лись понемно́гу,   🔊 **2-84**
Чему́-нибу́дь и как-нибу́дь:
Так воспита́ньем, сла́ва Бо́гу,
У нас немудрено́ блесну́ть.

We all studied precious little: something here, something there; so it is not difficult, thank God, to make an impression [lit: to shine] with one's education.

7.27.7. From chapter 1, stanza 25:

Быть мо́жно де́льным челове́ком   🔊 **2-85**
И ду́мать о красе́ ногте́й: ....

One can be a sensible person and still care about the beauty of one's nails.

Illustration:

(a) These lines were displayed in the window of a store selling products for taking care of one's nails.
(b) The magazine ***Крестья́нка***, 1996, offers various tips for taking care of one's nails without professional help under the headline: **«Немно́го о красе́ ногте́й»**. "A little bit on the beauty of one's nails."

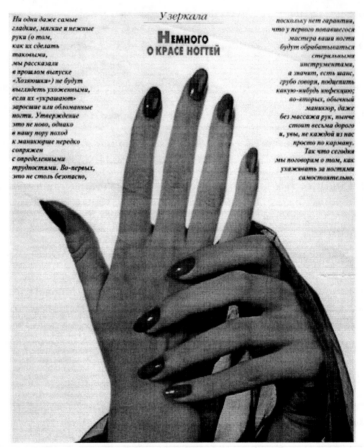

Fig. 2-27.

7.27.8. From chapter 2, stanza 1:

🔊 2-86   *Дере́вня, где скуча́л Евге́ний,*
          Была́ преле́стный уголо́к; ….

The village in which Eugene languished was a charming little place [lit.: corner].

7.27.9. From chapter 2, stanza 13:

🔊 2-87   **Они́ сошли́сь. Волна́ и ка́мень,**
          Стихи́ и про́за, лёд и пла́мень
          Не столь разли́чны меж собо́й.

They made friends. A rock and a wave, prose and poetry, ice and flame were not as unlike as these two men were.

7.27.10. From chapter 2, stanza 25:

И та́к она́ звала́сь Татья́ной.
Ни красото́й сестры́ свое́й,
Ни све́жестью её румя́ной
Не привлекла́ б она́ оче́й. [...]
Она́ в семье́ свое́й родно́й
Каза́лась де́вочкой чужо́й.

🔊) 2-88

And her name was Tatiana. She would not attract your eyes either with beauty like her sister's or with her sister's rosy freshness.[...] In her own family she seemed someone else's child.

7.27.11. From chapter 3, stanza 28:

Как уст румя́ных без улы́бки,
Без граммати́ческой оши́бки
Я ру́сской ре́чи не люблю́.

🔊) 2-89

Like rosy lips without a smile, I don't like Russian speech without a grammatical mistake.

7.27.12. From chapter 3, stanza 31 (**Письмо́ Татья́ны к Оне́гину** Tatiana's letter to Onegin):

Я к вам пишу́ — чего́ же бо́ле?
Что я могу́ ещё сказа́ть?
Тепе́рь я зна́ю, в ва́шей во́ле
Меня́ презре́ньем наказа́ть.

🔊) 2-90

I write to you—what more can be said? What else can I add to that? Now, I know, it is in your power to punish me with your contempt.

Illustration:

(a) Headline: **«Я к вам пишу́ — чего́ вам сде́лать?»** Subheading: **«Что пи́шут и рекоменду́ют президе́нту Горбачёву»**, *Изве́стия*, 1991. "I write to you—what's there for you to do?" with the subheading "What people write and recommend to President Gorbachev." Notice the use of colloquial **чего́** instead of standard **что**, which produces a humorous clash in styles.

🔊) 2-90

(b) **«Я к вам пишу́ ...»** "I write to you ..." This is the title under which letters to the editor are published in the journal *Огонёк*.

7.27.13. Continuation of Tatiana's letter:

Вообрази́: я здесь одна́
Никто́ меня́ не понима́ет,
Рассу́док мой изнемога́ет
И мо́лча ги́бнуть я должна́.

🔊) 2-91

Imagine: I am here alone, no one understands me; my reason fails me, and I must perish silently.

7.27.14. From chapter 4, stanza 7:

🔊 2-92

Чем ме́ньше же́нщину мы лю́бим,
Тем ле́гче нра́вимся мы ей,
И тем её верне́е гу́бим
Средь обольсти́тельных сете́й.

The less we love a woman, the more [lit.: easier] she likes us, and the surer we destroy her in the nets of seduction.

7.27.15. From chapter 4, stanza 16 (Onegin meets Tatiana in the garden and tells her what he thinks of her letter):

🔊 2-93

Я вас люблю́ любо́вью бра́та
И, мо́жет быть, ещё нежне́й.
                    ******
Учи́тесь вла́ствовать собо́ю,
Не вся́кий вас, как я, поймёт:
К беде́ нео́пытность ведёт.

I love you with the love of a brother, and, perhaps, even more tenderly … Learn to control yourself, not everyone will understand you as I do: your inexperience may lead you into trouble.

7.27.16. From chapter 5, stanza 2:

🔊 2-94

Зима́! Крестья́нин, торжеству́я,
На дро́внях обновля́ет путь.
Его́ лоша́дка, снег почу́я,
Плетётся ры́сью как-нибу́дь.

Here's winter! The triumphant peasant tries out the road on his sled. His horse, sensing snow, trots along lazily.

Illustration: Headline in *Аргуме́нты и фа́кты*, 1996: **«Весна́! … Моше́нник торжеству́ет …»** "Here's spring! A scoundrel triumphs …"

7.27.17. From chapter 6, stanza 21 (Lensky's verses, composed on the eve of his duel with Onegin):

🔊 2-95

Куда́, куда́ вы удали́лись,
Весны́ мое́й златы́е дни?
Что день гряду́щий мне гото́вит?

Where, where have you gone, O golden days of my spring? What does the coming day have in store for me? [lit: what is the coming day preparing for me?]

Illustration:

(a) A political forecast in ***Огонёк***, March 1996, has the headline: **«Что год грядущий нам готовит?»** "What does the coming year have in store for us?"

(b) The same heading in ***Новое время***, Feb.1997, forecasts the financial future.

(c) The line **«Что день грядущий мне готовит?»** is used to head a commercial article about the salon of a clairvoyant in ***Московский комсомолец***, 1997.

Fig. 2-28.

7.27.18. From chapter 6, stanza 43:

Лета́ к суро́вой про́зе кло́нят,
Лета́ шалу́нью ри́фму го́нят.

🔊 2-96

The years incline one to sober prose;
The years drive away mischievous rhymes.

Illustration: Headline in ***Куранты***, 1996: **«Года́ к суро́вой про́зе кло́нят»** "The years incline one to sober prose."

7.27.19. From chapter 6, stanza 44:

Мечты́, мечты́! Где ва́ша сла́дость?
Где, ве́чная к ней ри́фма, мла́дость?

🔊 2-97

Dreams, dreams, where is your sweetness? Where is your rhyme, youth's fleetness? [Lit.: Dreams, dreams! Where is your sweetness? Where's your eternal rhyme, youth?]

7.27.20. From chapter 8, stanza 2:

◀))) 2-98   **Стари́к Держа́вин нас заме́тил**
             И, в гроб сходя́, благослови́л.

Old Derzhavin noticed me [Lit.: us] and descending to his grave gave his blessing.

7.27.21. From chapter 8, stanza 10:

◀))) 2-99   *Блаже́н, кто сма́лоду был ма́лод,*
             Блаже́н, кто во́время созре́л, ...

Blessed is the one who felt young while young, blessed is the one who matured in time.

7.27.22. From chapter 8, stanza 20 (Onegin's exclamation upon finding Tatiana a fashionable lady of Petersburg's high society):

◀))) 2-100   *Уже́ль та са́мая Татья́на ...*

Could it be the same Tatiana?

Illustration:

   (a)   Headline in *Но́вое вре́мя*, May 1997: «**Уже́ль та са́мая Татья́на. О тру́дной де́вочке, нево́льном престу́пнике и у́мных милицио-не́рах**». "Could it be the same Tatiana? A story about a difficult teenage girl, an involuntary criminal and clever policemen."

   (b)   Headline in *Комсомо́льская пра́вда,* 1997: « **Уже́ль та са́мая Татья́на? Одну́ из гла́вных роле́й в голливу́дской экраниза́ции Евге́ния Оне́гина сыгра́ет дочь ли́дера "Аэросми́та"**. "'Could it be the same Tatiana?' One of the major roles in the Hollywood screen version of *Eugene Onegin* will be played by the daughter of Aerosmith's lead singer."

7.27.23. From chapter 8, stanza 29:

◀))) 2-101   *Любви́ все во́зрасты поко́рны,*
             Но ю́ным, де́вственным сердца́м
             Её поры́вы благотво́рны, ...

Love conquers all ages; but only to young, innocent hearts are love's impulses beneficial.

Illustration: Heading in *Изве́стия*, 1992: «**Взя́тке все во́зрасты поко́рны**» "A bribe conquers all ages."

7.27.24. From chapter 8, stanza 17:

Скажи́ мне, князь, не зна́ешь ты,
Кто там в мали́новом бере́те
С посло́м испа́нским говори́т?

🔊 2-102

Tell me, Prince, do you know who the lady in the raspberry-colored beret talking with the Spanish Ambassador is?

7.27.25. From chapter 8, stanza 32 (**Письмо́ Оне́гина к Татья́не**, Onegin's letter to Tatiana):

Предви́жу всё: вас оскорби́т
Печа́льной та́йны объясне́нье.

🔊 2-103

I foresee all: my sad secret will insult you.

7.27.26. From chapter 8, stanza 32:

Бо́же мой!
Как я оши́бся, как нака́зан ...
Я зна́ю: век уж мой изме́рен;
Но чтоб продли́лась жизнь моя́
Я у́тром до́лжен быть уве́рен,
Что с ва́ми днём уви́жусь я.

🔊 2-104

My God, what a mistake I've made, how severely I've been punished ... I know my lifespan is predestined [measured], but for my life to continue I have to be certain in the morning of seeing you by afternoon.

7.27.27. From chapter 8, stanza 43 (**отве́т Татья́ны**):

«Оне́гин, я тогда́ моло́же,
Я лу́чше, ка́жется, была́.
И я люби́ла вас; и что же?
Что в се́рдце Ва́шем я нашла́?
Како́й ответ? Одну́ суро́вость.»

🔊 2-105

Onegin, I was younger then and, perhaps, better; and I loved you; and so what did I find in your heart? What kind of answer? There was only coldness.

7.27.28. From chapter 8, stanza 47. (**ответ Татьяны**, Tatiana's answer):

«А сча́стье бы́ло так возмо́жно,
Так бли́зко! ...»

🔊 2-106

And happiness was so real, so near!

Illustration: From Chekhov's story **«Ковёр»** "The Rug": **«А ведь сча́стье бы́ло так бли́зко, так возмо́жно! —поду́мал секрета́рь, загляну́в в откры́вшуюся дверь»** "And wasn't the happiness so near, so real," thought the secretary, after stealing a glance through the open door.

7.27.29. From chapter 8, stanza 47 (**отве́т Татья́ны**, Tatiana's answer):

2-107

> *«Я вас люблю́ (к чему́ лука́вить?)*
> *Но я друго́му отдана́;*
> *Я бу́ду век ему́ верна́».*

I love you–why pretend? But I am given to another, I will be faithful to him all my life.

7.27.30. From chapter 8, stanza 51:

2-108

> **Но те, кото́рым в дру́жной встре́че**
> **Я стро́фы пе́рвые чита́л …**
> *Ины́х уж нет, а те дале́че,*
> *Как Са́ди не́когда сказа́л.*

But those in whose friendly circle I read the first stanzas … Some of them are no more, others are far away, as Saady said a long time ago.

Pushkin is referring to his Decembrist friends, in particular his friend Del'vig, who died in 1831. In Soviet times the phrase "some of them are no more, others are far away" was a cryptic way of referring to people arrested for political reasons.

8. MIKHAIL IURIEVICH LERMONTOV (1814–41)

МИХАИ́Л Ю́РЬЕВИЧ ЛЕ́РМОНТОВ

Lermontov's mother, a rich aristocrat, died when he was three; he was brought up by his doting grandmother who could not stand Lermontov's father, a poor army officer; she insisted that father and son never see each other. He began to write at fourteen, and some of his best and most anthologized poems were written when he was fifteen. His heroes were Byron and Napoleon. He worshipped Pushkin.

Fig. 2-29.

The poem which brought Lermontov overnight fame also cost him his freedom; it was "The Death of a Poet," written immediately after Pushkin's death in 1837. In it, Lermontov, a twenty-three-year-old Hussar officer, directly accused the tsar and his court of orchestrating Pushkin's destruction. Copies of the poem circulated in Petersburg in handwritten form reached the tsar; Lermontov was at once sent to the Caucasus where at the time Russia was waging war against the Chechens. The remaining four years of his life Lermontov filled with battles, duels, love affairs and several volumes of poems, dramas and prose, which changed the direction of Russian literaure and placed his name right next to Pushkin's. In 1841, Lermontov was killed in a duel in Piatigorsk by his former classmate Martynov.

8.1. From «Смерть Поэ́та» "The Death of a Poet" (1837)

8.1.1.

Поги́б Поэ́т! —нево́льник че́сти—
Пал, оклеве́танный молво́й,
С свинцо́м в груди́ и жа́ждой ме́сти,
Пони́кнув го́рдой голово́й!..
Не вы́несла душа́ Поэ́та
Позо́ра ме́лочных оби́д,
Восста́л он про́тив мне́ний све́та
Оди́н, как пре́жде … и уби́т! …

🔊 2-109

The Poet perished!—the slave of honor—he fell, vilified by rumors, with a bullet in his chest and a thirst for revenge, his proud head drooping. The Poet's soul could not endure the shame of petty insults, he rose against the opinions of high society, alone, as before—and is killed!

8.1.2.

Его́ уби́йца хладнокро́вно
Навёл уда́р … спасе́нья нет:
Пусто́е се́рдце бьётся ро́вно,
В руке́ не дро́гнул пистоле́т.
И что за ди́во? … издалёка,
Подо́бный со́тням беглецо́в,
На ло́влю сча́стья и чино́в
Забро́шен к нам по во́ле ро́ка;
Смея́сь, он де́рзко презира́л
Земли́ чужо́й язы́к и нра́вы;
Не мог щади́ть он на́шей сла́вы;
Не мог поня́ть в сей миг крова́вый,
На что он ру́ку поднима́л! …

🔊 2-110

His murderer cold-bloodedly aimed his shot—there is no help ... the [murderer's] empty heart beats evenly, the pistol in his hand did not waver. And what kind of wonder [is his murderer]? From afar, like so many refugees, he is thrown into our country by the will of the fate, to fish for his fortune and the higher ranks; laughing, he insolently despised the alien language and traditions; he could not have mercy on our glory, he could not understand at this bloody moment against what he raised his hand!

8.1.3.

◀))) 2-111

А вы, надме́нные пото́мки
Изве́стной по́длостью просла́вленных отцо́в,
[...]
Вы, жа́дною толпо́й стоя́щие у тро́на,
Свобо́ды, Ге́ния и Сла́вы палачи́!
Таи́тесь вы под се́нию зако́на,
Пред ва́ми суд и пра́вда—всё молчи́! ...
Но есть и бо́жий суд, напе́рсники развра́та!
Есть гро́зный суд: он ждёт;
Он не досту́пен зво́ну зла́та,
И мы́сли и дела́ он зна́ет наперёд.
Тогда́ напра́сно вы прибе́гнете к злосло́вью:
Оно́ вам не помо́жет вновь,
И вы не смо́ете всей ва́шей чёрной кро́вью
Поэ́та пра́ведную кровь!

And you, arrogant descendants of fathers notorious for their baseness, ... you, standing near the throne in a greedy crowd, executioners of Freedom, Glory, and Genius! You are hiding under the cover of law; truth and justice—everything should be silenced before you! But there is God's judgment, O confidantes of corruption! There is a terrible judgment: it waits, it is not accessible to the jingling of gold, it knows one's thoughts and deeds ahead of time. Then in vain will you resort to slander; it will not help you again, and you won't be able to wash off the sacred blood of the Poet with all your black blood!

Illustration:

◀))) 2-112

(a) In Russian, the word **суд** can mean either 'judgment' or 'trial.' Both meanings are combined in the title of a review of a new book by a famous dissident, Vladimir Bukovsky Буко́вский, *Моско́вский про-це́сс, Moscow Trial*: «Но есть, есть бо́жий суд, напе́рсники развра́та!» "But there is, there is God's judgment, O confidantes of corruption!

(b) Lermontov's name became strongly associated with Pushkin's. In the minds of Russians "Pushkin and Lermontov" is as immediate an association as "bread and butter." There are numerous anecdotes beginning with «Одна́жды Пу́шкин и Ле́рмонтов ...» "Once, Pushkin and Lermontov ...." An author of funny rhymes and hilarious math problems, G. Oster, uses this association to create entertaining math problems for children:

Пу́шкин роди́лся в 1799 году́, а Ле́рмонтов—на 15 лет по́зже. Ско́лько лет бы́ло бы Пу́шкину и Ле́рмонтову в 1850 году, если бы Марты́нов и Данте́с прома́зали?

Pushkin was born in 1799, and Lermontov, fifteen years later. How old would be Pushkin and Lermontov in 1850 if both Martynov and D'Anthés turned out to be bad shots?

Fig. 2-30.   Illustration to accompany the problem above

8.2. From «Ни́щий» "Beggar" (1830):

Куска́ лишь хле́ба он проси́л
И взор явля́л живу́ю му́ку,
И кто-то ка́мень положи́л
В его́ протя́нутую ру́ку.

🔊)) 2-113

He asked only for a piece of bread, and his gaze showed great pain, but somebody placed a rock in his outstretched hand.

8.3. From «Жела́нье» "A Wish" (1832):

Отвори́те мне темни́цу,
Да́йте мне сия́нье дня,
Черногла́зую деви́цу,
Черногри́вого коня́.

🔊)) 2-114

Open up my prison, give me the shining of day, [give me] a dark-eyed girl, [and] a black-maned steed.

8.4. Russians can often recite the entire poem «Па́рус» "The Sail" (1832) from memory.

Беле́ет па́рус одино́кой
В тума́не мо́ря голубо́м! ...
Что и́щет он в стране́ далёкой?
Что ки́нул он в краю́ родно́м? ...

🔊)) 2-115

Игра́ют во́лны—ве́тер сви́щет,
И ма́чта гнётся и скрыпи́т ...
Увы! он сча́стия не и́щет
И не от сча́стия бежи́т!

Под ним струя́ светле́й лазу́ри,
Над ним луч со́лнца золото́й ...
А он, мяте́жный, про́сит бу́ри,
Как бу́дто в бу́рях есть поко́й!

There is a lonely white sail in the blue mist of the sea. What is it seeking in a far-away country? What did it abandon in its own land? The
waves are playing, the wind whistles, the mast bends and creaks. Alas!
It is not looking for happiness and it is not from happiness that it runs
away. Under it is a stream lighter than azure, above it is a ray of the
sun, but it, rebellious, is asking for a storm—as if there were peace in
storms.

Illustration: An article about problems experienced by the Russian Far East
Fleet, published in ***Ито́ги***, Dec. 1996, uses Lermontov's line as a subheading:
«Увы́, он сча́стия не и́щет» "Alas! It does not look for happiness ..."

8.5. **«Бородино́»** "Borodino" (1837) is a long poem about the famous battle
near the village Borodino, where the Russian army fought Napoleon's army
fiercely before surrendering Moscow. Many know the whole poem by heart;
passages from it were memorized in schools.

8.5.1.

🔊 2-116
—Скажи́-ка, дя́дя, ведь не да́ром
Москва́, спалённая пожа́ром,
Францу́зу отдана́?
Ведь бы́ли ж схва́тки боевы́е,
Да, говоря́т, ещё каки́е!
Неда́ром по́мнит вся Росси́я
Про день Бородина́!

Say, old man [lit: "uncle"], was it for a reason that Moscow, burnt by
the fire, was surrendered to the French? There were battles, weren't
there? Yes, and great ones! It is not for nothing that all Russia remembers the day of Borodino!

Illustration: Headline in ***Изве́стия***, 1993: **«Скажи́-ка, дя́дя, ведь неда́ром?»**
The article describes the kidnapping of a rich businessman's nephew and the
$300,000 requested as a ransom. Lermontov's **«не да́ром»** ('not in vain, for a
reason, not for nothing') next to the astronomic sum of the ransom reads as
"not for free" and acquires a gleeful and sinister tone.

8.5.2.

Тогда́ счита́ть мы ста́ли ра́ны,
Това́рищей счита́ть.

🔊)) 2-117

Then we began to count our wounds, to count our comrades …

Illustration: Headline in ***Изве́стия***, 1992: «**… Тогда́ счита́ть мы ста́ли де́ньги**». "… Then we began to count our money," with the subheading: «**Зарпла́та и це́ны**» "Salaries and prices."

8.6. From «**Бегле́ц**» "The Deserter" (1838):

Га́ру́н бежа́л быстре́е ла́ни,
Быстре́й, чем за́яц от орла́;

🔊)) 2-118

Garun fled faster than a gazelle, faster than a rabbit from an eagle.

Illustration: Headline in ***Труд***, Aug. 1997: «**Бежа́л солда́т быстре́е ла́ни**» "A soldier fled faster than a gazelle," an article about a deserter from the army.

8.7. From «**Ду́ма**» "Meditation" (1838):

8.7.1.

Печа́льно я гляжу́ на на́ше поколе́нье!
Его́ гряду́щее—иль пу́сто, иль темно́ ….

🔊)) 2-119

I look sadly at our generation: its future is either empty or dark.

8.7.2.

Бога́ты мы, едва́ из колыбе́ли,
Оши́бками отцо́в и по́здним их умо́м
И жизнь уж нас томи́т,
Как ро́вный путь без це́ли,
Как пир на пра́зднике чужо́м.
К добру́ и злу посты́дно равноду́шны,
В нача́ле по́прища мы вя́нем без борьбы́; […]

🔊)) 2-120

И ненави́дим мы, и лю́бим мы случа́йно,
Ниче́м не же́ртвуя ни зло́бе, ни любви́,
И ца́рствует в душе́ како́й-то хо́лод та́йный,
Когда́ ого́нь кипи́т в крови́.

We are rich, from the cradle, with our fathers' mistakes and their tardy wisdom, and already life bores us, like an even road without direction, like a feast at a stranger's celebration. Shamelessly indifferent to good and evil, we perish at the beginning of life's road without a struggle.

We hate and love by accident, sacrificing nothing either for malice or for love; and there reigns a secret coldness in our breasts while fire boils in our blood.

8.7.3.

🔊 2-121   **И прах наш, с стро́гостью судьи́ и граждани́на,**
             Пото́мок оскорби́т презри́тельным стихо́м,
             Насме́шкой го́рькою обма́нутого сы́на
             Над промота́вшимся отцо́м.

And our descendant, with the strictness of judge and citizen, will insult
our dust by his contemptuous verse, in a deceived son's bitter mockery
of his father who squandered all he had.

8.8. From «Де́мон» "The Demon" (1829–38):

8.8.1.

🔊 2-122   *Печа́льный де́мон, дух изгна́нья,*
             Лета́л над гре́шною землёй,
             И лу́чших дней воспомина́нья
             Пред ним тесни́лися толпо́й; ….

A sad Demon, the spirit of exile, flew over the sinful earth, and memories of the best days crowded upon him.

Fig. 2-31.   M. Vrubel', *The Demon and Tamara*

8.8.2.

И на челе́ его высо́ком
Не отрази́лось ничего́.

🔊 2-123

His high forehead expessed nothing.

8.8.3.

На возду́шном океа́не,
Без руля́ и без ветри́л,
Ти́хо пла́вают в тума́не
Хо́ры стро́йные свети́л; ….

🔊 2-124

On the airy ocean, without rudder and without a sail, choirs of luminaries quietly float in the mist.

8.9. From **«Есть ре́чи—значе́нье …»** "There are words …" (1839):

Есть ре́чи—значе́нье
Темно́ или ничто́жно,
Но им без волне́нья
Внима́ть невозмо́жно.

🔊 2-125

There are words [lit.: speeches] whose meaning is either dark or insignificant, but one cannot take them in without excitement.

8.10. The entire poem **«И ску́чно, и гру́стно …»** "I am bored and sad …" (1840) is well-remembered:

И ску́чно и гру́стно, и не́кому ру́ку пода́ть
В мину́ту душе́вной невзго́ды …
Жела́нья!..что по́льзы напра́сно и ве́чно жела́ть? …
А го́ды прохо́дят—всё лу́чшие го́ды!
Люби́ть …но кого́ же? … на вре́мя—не сто́ит труда́,
А ве́чно люби́ть невозмо́жно.
В себя́ ли загля́нешь?—там про́шлого нет и следа́:
И ра́дость, и му́ки, и всё там ничто́жно …

🔊 2-126

Что стра́сти?—ведь ра́но иль по́здно их сла́дкий неду́г
Исче́знет при сло́ве рассу́дка;
И жизнь, как посмо́тришь с холо́дным внима́ньем вокру́г,—
Така́я пуста́я и глу́пая шу́тка …

I am bored and sad, and there is no one to proffer a hand in a moment of distress. Desire! What is the use of forever desiring in vain! And the years fly by—the best years. One can love … but who is there to love? It's not worth it to love for only a while, but to love forever is impossible. And if I look inside myself? There is not a trace of the past: joy and pain and all that is there is so insignificant … What of passions?

Their sweet ailment sooner or later will vanish at the first word of reason, and life, if you look with cold attention around you, is such an empty and stupid joke.

🔊 **2-127** *Illustration:* «**Ложь и обма́н открыва́ются в первозда́нной приро́де, сто́ит то́лько взгляну́ть вокру́г с холо́дным внима́ньем**». "Lies and deceit are found in pristine nature if one but looks around with cold attention." From an article in ***Огонёк***, June 1996, entitled «**Эволю́ция лжи. Обма́н как страте́гия успе́ха**». "Evolution of lies. Deceit as a strategy for success."

НАУКА И ТЕХНИКА
Очевидное-невероятное

ЭВОЛЮЦИЯ ЛЖИ
Обман как стратегия успеха

Кро́шечные самцы светлячков в поисках пары порхают над травкой, посылая свои световые сигналы: вспышка длится 0,3 секунды, 455 мерцаний на километр полета. Самочки отвечают «подмигиванием» специфической яркости и частоты (каждый из почти 2000 видов имеет свой световой код), и кавалер обретает невесту. Но при этом — коварство и любовь! — некоторые становятся жертвой ужасного обмана: самки хищного вида Photuris, крупные и прожорливые, ловко имитируют зов любви, так что иной легковерный жених вместо брачного ложа попадает в объятия смерти.

Рядом, в бархатной темноте, самцы вида Macdermotti старательно подражают сигналам хищницы Photuris, стремясь отпугнуть конкурентов собственного роду-племени и получить преимущество в поисках пары, поскольку женские особи Macdermotti встречаются крайне редко. А самцы

выживания в суровой борьбе за существование между отдельными видами.

Так продолжалось до 1988 года, пока двое шотландских ученых — Ричард Берн (Byrne) и Эндрю Уайтен (Whiten) не опубликовали совместный труд под названием «Макиавеллистический разум», где описаны факты обмана обезьянами собственных соплеменников. Обезьяны, как выяснилось, прекрасно умеют манипулировать поведением своих собратьев. При виде чего-нибудь вкус-

Ложь и обман открываются в первозданной природе, стоит только взглянуть вокруг с холодным вниманьем.

Fig. 2-32.

8.11. From **«А.О. Смирно́вой»** "То А.О. Smirnova" (1840):

Что ж де́лать?.. Ре́чью неиску́сной
Заня́ть ваш ум мне не дано́ …
Всё это бы́ло бы смешно́,
Когда́ бы не́ было так гру́стно …

What shall I do? It is not given to me to entertain your mind with my artless speech. All this would have been funny if it weren't so sad.

8.12. The entire poem **«Го́рные верши́ны (Из Гёте)»** "Mountain Summits (from Goethe)" (1840) is usually remembered:

Fig. 2-33. Artist unknown. *Portrait of A.O. Smirnova*

Го́рные верши́ны
Спят во тьме ночно́й;
Ти́хие доли́ны
По́лны све́жей мглой;
Не пыли́т доро́га,
Не дрожа́т листы́ …
Подожди́ немно́го,
Отдохнёшь и ты.

Mountain summits slumber in the night darkness. Quiet valleys are filled with moist gloom. The dust on the road is still, the leaves do not tremble; wait a while — and you, too, will rest.

8.13. Though the epigraph to the poem **«Мцы́ри»** "Mtsyri" (1840) is taken from the Bible, it became strongly associated with the poem:

Вкуша́я, вкуси́х ма́ло мёда, и се аз умира́ю.
(1-я Кни́га Царств)

Eating, I have eaten little of honey and now I am dying.
(1 Kings)

8.13.1.
Я знал одно́й лишь ду́мы власть,
Одну́ — но пла́менную стра́сть …

I knew the power of one thought only, I had a single but flaming passion.

8.14. From **«Ро́дина»** "Motherland" (1841):

Люблю́ отчи́зну я, но стра́нною любо́вью!

I love my native land, but my love is strange.

8.15. «**Проща́й, немы́тая Росси́я ...**» "Farewell, unwashed Russia ..." (1841):

🔊 2-133   *Проща́й, немы́тая Росси́я,*
Страна́ рабо́в, страна́ госпо́д,
И вы, мунди́ры голубы́е,
И ты, им пре́данный наро́д.

Farewell, unwashed Russia, the country of slaves and masters, and you, blue uniforms [a reference to police uniforms], and you, the masses loyal to them.

Illustration: An article about the forced emigration of V. Orekhov with his wife to the USA in ***Но́вое вре́мя***, April 1997, is headed: «**Проща́й, немы́тая конто́ра**» "Farewell, unwashed office."

8.16. From «**Тама́ра**» "Tamara" (1841):

🔊 2-134   **В той ба́шне высо́кой и те́сной**
Цари́ца Тама́ра жила́:
Прекра́сна, как а́нгел небе́сный,
Как де́мон, кова́рна и зла.

In that tall and narrow tower lived the tsarina Tamara, beautiful as a heavenly angel, perfidious and wicked as a demon.

8.17. From «**Догово́р**» "Agreement" (1841):

🔊 2-135   *Была́ без ра́достей любо́вь,*
Разлу́ка бу́дет без печа́ли.

The love was without joy, the parting will be without sorrow.

8.18. The first line of the poem «**Выхожу́ оди́н я на доро́гу**» "I go out alone on the road ..." (1841) is frequently heard, and many know the entire poem by heart. It is also a well-known song.

🔊 2-136   *Выхожу́ оди́н я на доро́гу;*
Сквозь тума́н кремни́стый путь блести́т;
Ночь тиха́. Пусты́ня вне́млет Бо́гу,
И звезда́ с звездо́ю говори́т.

В небеса́х торже́ственно и чу́дно!
Спит земля́ в сия́нье голубо́м ...
Что же мне так бо́льно и так тру́дно?
Жду ль чего́? Жале́ю ли о чём?

Уж не жду́ от жи́зни ничего́ я,
И не жаль мне про́шлого ничу́ть;
Я ищу́ свобо́ды и поко́я!
Я б хоте́л забы́ться и засну́ть!

Но не тем холо́дным сном моги́лы …
Я б жела́л наве́ки так засну́ть,
Чтоб в груди́ дрема́ли жи́зни си́лы,
Чтоб, дыша́, вздыма́лась ти́хо грудь;

Чтоб всю ночь, весь день мой слух леле́я,
Про любо́вь мне сла́дкий го́лос пел,
Надо мной чтоб, ве́чно зелене́я,
Тёмный дуб склоня́лся и шуме́л.

I go out alone on the road. The rocky way shines before me. The night is quiet. The deserted world listens to God, and a star speaks to a star. The skies are solemn and wonderful! The earth sleeps in blue light … Why is it that I feel such pain and am so troubled? Am I expecting something to happen? Or maybe there is something I regret?

No, I don't expect anything from life, and I don't regret the past in the least; I am seeking freedom and peace! I would like to lose myself in oblivion and to fall asleep! But I do not wish to sleep the sleep of the grave … I would like to slumber forever in such a way that life's forces would still be dozing in my breast, so that my chest would quietly rise, breathing; so that all night, all day, delighting my ear, there would be a sweet voice singing to me about love; and a dark oak, eternally green, would bend and rustle its boughs over me.

Illustration: In his tragic poem, «**Конце́рт на вокза́ле**» "Railway Station Concert" Osip Mandelshtam uses Lermontov's line «**И звезда́ с звездо́ю говори́т**» to create a powerful image of despair:

Нельзя́ дыша́ть, и твердь киши́т червя́ми,
И ни одна́ звезда́ не говори́т.

🔊)) 2-137

It is impossible to breathe, and the firmament swarms with worms, and not a single star speaks.

9. FEDOR IVANOVICH TIUTCHEV (1803–73)

Фёдор Ива́нович Тю́тчев

Fig. 2-34.

Tiutchev is one of the most original Russian poets, whose poetry combines profound philosophical thought with passionate feeling. He was born into a very cultivated old aristocratic family. As a member of the aristocracy, Tiutchev spoke very little Russian. When he was 18, he was appointed ambassador to

Bavaria and spent about twenty years abroad. In 1836 Tiutchev sent a few of his poems to Russia, but never took his poetic career seriously and thought of himself first and foremost as a political thinker. Like Dostoevsky, Tiutchev believed in a special messianic role for Russia in the world. Pushkin published Tiutchev's poems in his journal ***Современник*** *The Contemporary* under the title «**Стихотворе́ния, при́сланные из Герма́нии**» "Poems Sent from Germany." This was the last issue before Pushkin's death. Tiutchev's poetry remained largely unknown to his contemporaries, though he was famous for his brilliant wit; many of his aphorisms were repeated in the salons of Petersburg. Only in 1854 did he publish a volume of his poems, about which Fet wrote:

◀))) 2-138   **Вот э́та кни́жка небольша́я,**
                 Томо́в премно́гих тяжеле́й.

Here is this modest [lit: "not large"] book, which is heavier than a great number of other volumes.

9.1. The poem «**Весе́нняя гроза́**» "Spring Thunderstorm" (1828) was memorized in schools. Everyone remembers at least the first stanza:

◀))) 2-139   **Люблю́ грозу́ в нача́ле ма́я,**
                 Когда́ весе́нний пе́рвый гро́м,
                 Как бы резвя́ся и игра́я,
                 Грохо́чет в не́бе голубо́м.

I love a thunderstorm in the beginning of May, when the first spring thunder, as if romping and playing, rumbles in the blue sky.

9.2. «**Весе́нние во́ды**» "Spring Waters" (1830) was set to music by Rakhmaninov:

◀))) 2-140   **Ещё в поля́х беле́ет снег,**
                 А во́ды уж весно́й шумя́т— ….

There is still snow whitening the fields, but spring is already heard in the waters.

9.3. From «**Певу́честь есть в морски́х волна́х**» "There is melodiousness in the sea-waves …":

◀))) 2-141   **[…]**
                 Так отчего́ же в о́бщем хо́ре
                 Душа́ не то́ поёт, что мо́ре,
                 И ро́пщет мы́слящий тростни́к?

So why then in the common chorus does the soul not sing what the sea [sings], and the thinking reed grumbles?

Comment: "The thinking reed" is a definition of a human being given by the French mathematician and philosopher Blaise Pascal.

9.4. From «**Цицеро́н**» "Cicero" (1830):

Счастли́в, кто посети́л сей мир 🔊 2-142
В его́ мину́ты рокови́е—
Его́ призва́ли всеблаги́е,
Как собесе́дника на пир; ….

Happy is he who visited this world in its fateful moments: he, as their peer in conversation, was summoned to their feast by the omnigracious gods.

9.5. From «Silentium» "Silence" (1830):

9.5.1.

Молчи́, скрыва́йся и тай 🔊 2-143
И чу́вства и мечты́ свои́!

Be silent, don't show yourself, hide your feelings and your dreams!

9.5.2.

Мы́сль изрече́нная есть ложь. 🔊 2-144

A thought expressed [in words] is a lie.

9.6. «**Умо́м Росси́ю не поня́ть …**» "One cannot comprehend Russia rationally …" (1866):

Умо́м Росси́ю не поня́ть, 🔊 2-145
Арши́ном о́бщим не изме́рить:
У ней осо́бенная стать—
В Росси́ю мо́жно то́лько ве́рить.

One cannot comprehend Russia rationally, one cannot measure her with a common yardstick. She has a special stature—one can only believe in Russia.

Illustration:

(a) Headline in *Изве́стия*, 1993: «**Умо́м росси́йский ры́нок не поня́ть**» 🔊 2-146 "One cannot comprehend rationally the Russian market."

(b) Headline in *Незави́симая газе́та,* 1993: «**В Росси́ю мо́жно то́лько ве́рить?**» "Can one only believe in Russia?"

(c) In his obscene epigram, Igor′ Guberman **И́горь Губерма́н** suggests a more rational approach to interpretation of Russia:

Давно́ пора́, ядрёна мать,
Умо́м Росси́ю понима́ть!

"It's about freakin' time to comprehend Russia rationally!"

(d)   A joke in ***Новое время***, February 1996:

—Почему́ у нас сто́лько дурако́в?
—Умо́м Росси́ю не поня́ть!

"Why do we have so many fools?"—"Because one can't comprehend
Russia rationally!"

В Россию можно только верить

Fig. 2-35.   Queen Elizabeth II of Great Britain and Boris Yeltsin

9.7. The poem «**К.Б.**» "K.B." (1870) is dedicated to Baroness Amalia Kriudner.
This poem is also well-known as a song.

🔊 2-147   Я встре́тил вас—и всё было́е
В отжи́вшем се́рдце ожило́,
Я вспо́мнил вре́мя золото́е—
И се́рдцу ста́ло так тепло́ ...

I met you—and all the past came alive in my tired heart; I recalled that
golden time—and my heart warmed.

9.8. «Нам не дано́ предугада́ть …» "We are not destined to foretell …" (1869):

Нам не дано́ предугада́ть,   🔊 2-148
Как сло́во на́ше отзовётся, —
И нам сочу́вствие даётся,
Как нам даётся благода́ть …

We are not destined to foretell how our words will be received [lit. how our word will echo (back to us)], and other people's understanding is given to us like a blessing [lit.: and compassion is given to us like a blessing].

Illustration: Headline in ***Аргуме́нты и фа́кты***, 1996: «**Что обеща́ет разво́д с Чечнёй**» "What our divorcing Chechnya portends," with the subtitle: «**Как сло́во наше отзовётся**».

9.9. From «**В ду́шном во́здуха молча́нье …**» "In the Sultry Silence of the Air" (1836):

В ду́шном во́здуха молча́нье   🔊 2-149
Как предчу́вствие грозы́
Жа́рче роз благоуха́нье,
Зво́нче го́лос стрекозы́ …

In the sultry silence of the air a thunderstorm gathers. The fragrance of roses grows hotter, the voice of a dragonfly is more shrill.

Illustration: Here is an example of a reference to these lines wandering from poet to poet:

(a)   Mandelshtam (1932):

Да́йте Тю́тчеву стрекозу́, —   🔊 2-150
Догада́йтесь, почему́!

Give Tiutchev a dragonfly. Guess why!

(b)   Timur Kibirov (1993):

Дай же При́гову стреко́зу,   🔊 2-150
не жиди́сь и не жале́й!
Ми́ше дай стреко́зу то́же.
Мне — четы́рнадцать рубле́й!

Give Prigov a dragonfly, don't be stingy, don't be tight! To Misha, too, give a dragonfly. Me? Give me 14 rubles.

10. AFANASII AFANASIEVICH FET (1820–92)

АФАНА́СИЙ АФАНА́СЬЕВИЧ ФЕТ (ШЕНШИ́Н)

Fet's last name came from his German mother, who left her husband for the Russian nobleman Afanasii Shenshin. The Russian church would not acknowledge the legitimacy of Fet's birth and his right to inherit the aristocratic title of his father. Only a special decree by tsar Alexander II restored him to his hereditary rights and allowed him to use the last name Shenshin. But by that time he had already become known as one of the finest Russian poets, Afanasii Fet. Fet's poetry is associated with the movement "art for art's sake," which emphatically opposed the use of civic motifs in poetry.

Fig. 2-36.

10.1. «**Я пришёл к тебе́ с приве́том ...**» "I came to you with a greeting ..." (1843):

🔊 2-151
Я пришёл к тебе́ с приве́том,
Рассказа́ть, что со́лнце вста́ло,
Что оно́ горя́чим све́том
По листа́м затрепета́ло;

Рассказа́ть, что лес просну́лся,
Весь просну́лся, ве́ткой ка́ждой,
Ка́ждой пти́цей встрепену́лся
И весе́нней по́лон жа́ждой;

Рассказа́ть, что отовсю́ду
На меня́ весе́льем ве́ет.
Что не зна́ю сам, что бу́ду
Петь—но то́лько пе́сня зре́ет.

I came to you with a greeting, to tell you that the sun is risen, that it quivers with its hot light on the leaves; To tell you that the forest is awake, all of it awake, every bough; it arose with every bird and is breathing with spring thirst; I tell you that joy wafts around me from everywhere, and that I don't even know what I am going to sing—only that a song is welling up within me.

Illustration: The following passage from Il'f and Petrov's *Twelve Chairs* [see Chapter 3, 16.1.2] uses some lines from the poem.

🔊 2-152
Оста́п раскры́л глаза́ .... —С до́брым у́тром, Ки́са, —сказа́л он, дава́сь зево́той. —Я пришёл к тебе́ с приве́том, рассказа́ть, что со́лнце вста́ло, что оно́ горя́чим све́том по чему́-то там затрепета́ло ...

Ostap opened his eyes …. "Good morning, Kisa," he said, choking with a yawn. "I came to you with a greeting, to tell you that the sun is risen, that it quivered with its hot light on something or other."

10.2. «Шёпот, ро́бкое дыха́нье … » "A whisper, the faintest breath …" (1850):

Шёпот, ро́бкое дыха́нье,   🔊 2-153
Тре́ли соловья́,
Серебро́ и колыха́нье
Со́нного ручья́,

Свет ночно́й, ночны́е те́ни,
Те́ни без конца́,
Ряд волше́бных измене́ний
Ми́лого лица́,

В ды́мных ту́чках пу́рпур ро́зы,
О́тблеск янтаря́,
И лобза́ния, и слёзы,
И заря́, заря́!..

A whisper, the faintest breath, warbling of a nightingale; the silver rippling of a sleepy creek; the light of night, nocturnal shadows, endless shadows; a series of magic changes in the sweet face; in the smoky clouds a crimson rose, the gleam of amber; and kisses and tears and the dawn, the dawn!

Illustration: Lidia Chukovskaya in her memoirs about Anna Akhmatova describes an episode when Akhmatova was supposed to meet with an editor to state her objections to his corrections: "I asked how the meeting with the editor ended, how he received her reproaches." Akhmatova answered with Fet's words: «И лобза́ния, и слёзы, и заря́, заря́!»

11. Nikolai Alekseevich Nekrasov (1821–78)

Никола́й Алексе́евич Некра́сов

Nekrasov was a god of the Russian radical intelligentsia in the 1850s and 1860s. He was the son of a rich nobleman and spent his childhood at an enormous estate near the Volga. His melodious poems, with masterful use of folklore and colloquial language, described the misery of the peasants and passionately condemned social injustice. As an editor and the owner of leading literary journals which

Fig. 2-37.

published works of Turgenev, Tolstoy and Dostoevsky, Nekrasov was one of the most influential figures in literary circles. Nowadays Russians usually know and love Nekrasov's poetry, and they sometimes mistake them for folksongs. No description of Nekrasov's poetry ever fails to mention that his Muse is «Му́за ме́сти и печа́ли» "A muse of revenge and sorrow."

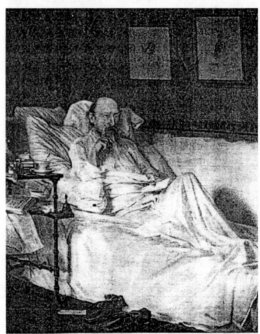

Fig. 2-38.   N. Kramskoi, *N.A. Nekrasov Ill*

11.1. From «Поэ́т и граждани́н» "Poet and Citizen" (1856):

🔊 2-154   **Поэ́том мо́жешь ты не быть,**
Но граждани́ном быть обя́зан.

You may not be a poet, but a citizen you must be.

Illustration: An article about problems with Lithuanian citizenship for Russians
🔊 2-154   had the headline: «Но граждани́ном быть не мо́жешь!» "But you can't be a citizen!" —*Новое Время*, June 1997.

11.2. From «Се́ятелям» "To the Sowers" (1876):

🔊 2-155   *Се́йте разу́мное, до́брое, ве́чное,*
Се́йте! Спаси́бо вам ска́жет серде́чное
Ру́сский наро́д ...

Sow [disseminate] the meaningful, the kind, the eternal; sow! The Russian people will give you their heartfelt thanks.

Illustration:

(a) Headline in *Известия*, 1995: «Разу́мное, до́брое, ве́чное, но на 🔊 2-155 забо́ре» "The meaningful, the kind, the eternal, but on the fence." The article describes a person who felt a need to support his fellow-citizens and who secretly, at night, would go out in the streets to write on fences some reassuring messages like "People, all will be well."

(b) Ostap Bender, a character from Il'f and Petrov's *Golden Calf* [see Chapter 3, 16] mocks his companion: «... почему́ вы не чита́ете газе́т? Их ну́жно чита́ть. Они́ дово́льно ча́сто се́ют разу́мное, до́брое, ве́чное» "Why don't you read newspapers? One should read them. They fairly often sow the meaningful, the kind, the eternal."

11.3. From «Размышле́ния у пара́дного подъе́зда» "Contemplations at the Front Door" (1858):

11.3.1.

... Родна́я земля́! 🔊 2-156
Назови́ мне таку́ю оби́тель,
Я тако́го угла́ не вида́л,
Где бы се́ятель твой и храни́тель,
Где бы ру́сский мужи́к не стона́л?

My native land! Name for me such an abode, I have never seen such a place, where your sower and keeper, where the Russian peasant would not moan.

Illustration: An essay about male-female relationships in *Крестья́нка,* 1997, 🔊 2-156 describes a woman complaining to her friend of her husband's cheating on her. In response, she receives the following "consolation": **«Ах, измени́л, да укажи́ мне таку́ю оби́тель, где бы муж или жена́ не измени́ли ни ра́зу»** "Oh, he cheated, big deal. Just point out to me such an abode, where a husband and wife never cheated on each other."

11.3.2.

Выдь на Во́лгу: чей стон раздаётся 🔊 2-157
Над вели́кою ру́сской реко́й?
Этот стон у нас пе́сней зовётся—
То бурла́ки иду́т бечево́й!..

Come out to the shore of the Volga: whose moan is resounding over the great Russian river? This moan we call a song—it is barge-haulers going along, pulling the rope!

Illustration: Heading in *Огонёк*, September 1996: «Ски́дка по-ру́сски. Э́тот 🔊 2-157 стон у нас пе́сней зовётся» "A sale, Russian-style. This moan we call a song."

11.4. From «Ры́царь на час» "A Knight for an Hour" (1862):

🔊 2-158
От лику́ющих, пра́здно болта́ющих,
Обагря́ющих ру́ки в крови́
Уведи́ меня́ в стан погиба́ющих
За вели́кое де́ло любви́!

Take me away from the rejoicing ones, from the idly chatting, from those steeping their hands in blood; lead me to the camp of those perishing for the great cause of love!

11.5. From **«Па́мяти Добролю́бова»** "To Dobroliubov's Memory" (1864):

11.5.1.

🔊 2-159
Суро́в ты был, ты в молоды́е го́ды
Уме́л рассу́дку стра́сти подчиня́ть.

You were austere; in your younger years you knew how to subordinate your passions to reason.

11.5.2.

🔊 2-160
Како́й свети́льник ра́зума уга́с!
Како́е се́рдце би́ться переста́ло!

What ray of reason has been extinguished! What a heart has stopped beating!

11.6. From **«Забы́тая дере́вня»** "A Forgotten Village" (1855):

🔊 2-161
У бурми́стра Вла́са ба́бушка Нени́ла
Почини́ть избёнку ле́су попроси́ла.
Отвеча́л: нет ле́су, и не жди—не бу́дет!
«Вот прие́дет ба́рин—ба́рин нас рассу́дит,
Ба́рин сам уви́дит, что плоха́ избу́шка,
И вели́т дать ле́су», —ду́мает стару́шка.

Grandma Nenila asked the steward Vlas for wood to fix her hut. He answered: "There's no wood, and don't expect any!" "Now, as soon as the landowner comes, he will settle our dispute; the landowner will see for himself that the hut is about to collapse—and he will order him to give me some wood," the old lady thinks. [In reality this would not happen. The allusions to the **ба́рин** reveal the old woman's futile hopes.]

Illustration:

(a) Headline in ***Огонёк***, November 1996: **«Два ми́ра—два кефи́ра»** "Two worlds—two kefirs," with the subtitle: **«Ба́рин нас рассу́дит».** The article discusses problems in a milk-processing factory.

(b) A huge photo on the front page of ***Аргуме́нты и фа́кты***, 1997, depicts a long line circling Red Square, which has a telephone in place of the Mausoleum. Across the photo is written:

Вот услы́шит Е́льцин,
Ельцин нас рассу́дит …

As soon as Yeltsin hears us, he will settle our dispute.

11.7. **«В по́лном разга́ре страда́ дереве́нская»** "The hard work of harvest time is in full swing" (1862) is a poem about a peasant woman working hard in the field where she had to take her infant baby. The poem became a popular song.

11.7.1.

В по́лном разга́ре страда́ дереве́нская …   🔊 2-162
До́ля ты! ру́сская до́люшка же́нская!
Вряд ли трудне́е сыска́ть.

The hard work of harvest time is at its full height. O you, fate, the heavy fate of a Russian woman! It's impossible to find a harder one.

11.7.2.

Вку́сны ли, ми́лая, слёзы солёные   🔊 2-163
С ки́слым кваско́м попола́м? …

Do you like, my dear, the taste of your salty tears mixed with sour kvas? [kvas is a drink made of fermented bread]

11.8. **«Крестья́нские де́ти»** "Peasant Children" (1861) is a narrative poem in which the first-person protagonist relates his various encounters with peasant children; the excerpt below is usually remembered verbatim and often quoted:

Одна́жды, в студёную зи́мнюю по́ру,   🔊 2-164
Я и́з лесу вы́шел; был си́льный моро́з.
Гляжу́, поднима́ется ме́дленно в го́ру
Лоша́дка, везу́щая хво́росту воз.
И, ше́ствуя ва́жно, в споко́йствии чи́нном,
Лоша́дку ведёт под уздцы́ мужичо́к
В больши́х сапога́х, в полушу́бке овчи́нном,
В больши́х рукави́цах … а сам с ногото́к!
—Здоро́во, парни́ще! —«Ступа́й себе́ ми́мо!»
—Уж бо́льно ты гро́зен, как я погляжу́!
Отку́да дрови́шки? —«Из ле́су, вести́мо;
Оте́ц, слы́шишь, ру́бит, а я отвожу́».
(В лесу́ раздава́лся топо́р дровосе́ка).
—А что, у отца́-то больша́я семья́?
«Семья́-то больша́я, да два челове́ка
Всего́ мужико́в-то: оте́ц мой да я …»
—Так вот оно что! А как звать тебя́? —«Вла́сом».
—А кой тебе́ го́дик? —«Шесто́й минова́л …
Ну, мёртвая!» —кри́кнул малю́точка ба́сом,
Рвану́л под уздцы́ и быстре́й зашага́л.

Once in the cold winter, I came out of the forest; it was freezing. Suddenly I saw a horse, slowly struggling up the hill, pulling a cart loaded with brushwood. And stalking along, ceremoniously calm, was a little peasant leading the horse by the bridle. He was wearing huge boots, a sheepskin coat, huge mittens—himself being the size of a fingernail. "Hey there, my lad!" "Go on by! "Aren't you fearsome, I see! Where's this firewood from?" "From the forest, obviously. My father— hear the sound?—chops the wood and I take it home." (There was a sound of chopping coming from the forest.) "So, your father—does he have a large family?" "The family—it's large all right, but there are only two men in it: my father and I." "So, that's how it is! And what's your name?" "Vlas." "And how old are you?" "Coming on seven … Hey, you, dead meat!" shouted the little guy in a low bass, pulled the bridle and hastened his pace.

Illustration:

🔊 **2-165** (a) An article about the illegal circulation of weapons in ***Российская газета***, 1997, had the headline: **«Откýда ружьúшко? Со склáда, вестúмо»** "Where's the rifle from? From the warehouse, obviously."

(b) A weekly newspaper, ***Собесéдник***, 1997, published an article with the following headline: **«Откýда парнúшки? Из 'Юниóра', вестúмо. Расскáз о том, как в УПК (учéбно-производствéнный комбинáт) дéлают дéньги и ýчат людéй».** "Where are these lads from? From 'Yunior,' obviously. A story about making money and teaching people at vocational school."

11.9. **«Морóз Крáсный Нос»** "Red-Nosed Frost" (1863) is a narrative poem about a peasant woman who has just buried her husband and now has to do all the hard work alone. She goes to the forest to chop wood and Father Frost (a fairytale figure) mercifully casts over her a dream-spell, under which she freezes to death.

🔊 **2-166** **11.9.1.**
> *Есть жéнщины в рýсских селéньях*
> *С спокóйною вáжностью лиц,*
> *С красúвою сúлой в движéньях,*
> *С похóдкой, со взглядом царúц,—….*

There are women in Russian villages with calm self-possession in their faces, with a graceful strength in their movements, with the gait and gaze of a queen.

🔊 **2-166** *Illustration: Огонёк*, June 1996, published an article about Norwegian men seeking Russian wives under the heading: **«Есть Нúны в норвéжских селéньях»** "There are Ninas in Norwegian villages."

11.9.2.

Их ра́зве слепо́й не заме́тит,
А зря́чий о них говори́т:
«Пройдёт—сло́вно со́лнце осве́тит!
Посмо́трит—рублём подари́т»!

🔊 **2-167**

Only a blind man wouldn't notice them; and those who have eyes would say about them: "She walks by—and it's like the sun shines upon you! She looks at you—and it's like she gave you a gift of a ruble!"

11.9.3.

Иду́т они той же доро́гой,
Како́й весь наро́д наш идёт.
Но грязь обстано́вки убо́гой
К ним сло́вно не ли́пнет. Цветёт

🔊 **2-168**

Краса́вица, ми́ру на ди́во,
Румя́на, стройна́, высока́,
Во вся́кой оде́жде краси́ва,
Ко вся́кой рабо́те ловка́.

They follow the same path as all our folk, but it's as if the dirt of the squalid surroundings does not stick to them. A beauty, she blooms, making the world gasp; she is rosy-cheeked, tall and slender, beautiful in any dress, deft at any work.

11.9.4.

В игре́ её ко́нный не сло́вит,
В беде́—не сробе́ет,—спасёт:
Коня́ на скаку́ остано́вит,
В горя́щую и́збу войдёт!

🔊 **2-169**

In a game one would not be able to catch her even on horseback; in trouble she would never falter, she'll save you; she would stop a galloping steed, she would walk into a burning hut.

Illustration: A contemporary poet, Naum Korzhavin **Нау́м Коржа́вин**, uses Nekrasov's lines to show that Russian life still does not give Russian women a break; they still have to be heroic, because:

А ко́ни всё ска́чут и ска́чут,
А и́збы горя́т и горя́т …

🔊 **2-169**

And the steeds still keep galloping, and the huts still keep burning….

11.10. **«Кому́ на Руси́ жить хорошо́»** "Who lives well in Russia" [lit: "For whom life is good in Rus'"] (1863–77) is a narrative poem with folklore elements describing seven peasants who set off on a long journey to find a happy person in Russia. The title itself is quoted often.

Illustration:

   (a) Headline in ***Аргуме́нты и ф а́кты***, 1997: «**Кому́ в СНГ жить хорошо́**» "Who lives well in the Commonwealth of Independent States."

   (b) A well-known photo of Boris Yeltsin comforting an old-age pensioner carries the caption «**Пока́ на Руси́ жить нелегко́**». "It is not easy to live in Russia these days."

Пока на Руси жить нелегко

Fig. 2-39.

11.10.1.

🔊 2-170   **На столбово́й доро́женьке**
         Сошли́сь семь мужико́в:
         [...]
         Сошли́ся—и заспо́рили:
         Кому́ живётся ве́село,
         Вольго́тно на Руси́?

Seven peasants got together on a high road. [...] They came together and began to argue: who in Rus' lives free, who enjoys life?

11.10.2.

2-171

Рома́н сказа́л: поме́щику,
Демья́н сказа́л: чино́внику,
Лука́ сказа́л: попу́.
Купчи́не толстопу́зому! —
Сказа́ли бра́тья Гу́бины,
Ива́н и Митродо́р.
Стари́к Пахо́м поту́жился
И мо́лвил, в зе́млю гля́дючи:
Вельмо́жному боя́рину,
Мини́стру госуда́реву.
А Пров сказа́л: царю́ …

Roman said: " a landlord," Demian said: "an official," Luka said, "a priest"; "a pot-bellied merchant!" said Ivan and Mitrodor, the brothers Gubin. Old Pakhom first pondered and then said, looking down: "a noble magnate, the tsar's minister." Prov said: "the tsar."

Illustration: Литературная газета, 1989, parodies the excessive use of foreign words in contemporary media, following Nekrasov's rhymes and verse patterns:

2-172

Колло́квиум шторми́ло.
Схвати́лись дискусса́нты,
Оди́н сказа́л:
—Марке́тинг!
Друго́й отре́зал:
—Бри́финг!
А тре́тий ря́вкнул:
—Кли́ринг!
И гро́хнул кулако́м.
Так в на́шем регио́не
Дости́гнут был консе́нсус
Посре́дством плюрали́зма,
Хотя́ и эксклюзи́вно,
Но что весьма́ прести́жно—
Без спо́нсоров прито́м!

The *colloquium* stormed. The *discussants* began to fight. One said: *Marketing*! Another cut him off: *Briefing*! The third roared: *Clearing*! and banged the table with his fist. Thus in our *region* there was *consensus* reached, by means of *pluralism*, although *exclusively*, but what was especially *prestigious*—without the *sponsors* at that!

11.10.3.

◀)) 2-173 **Ку́шай, тю́рю, Я́ша,—молочка́-то нет.**
—Где ж коро́вка на́ша? —Увели́, мой свет!

"Eat tiuria, Yasha, there is no milk any more." "And where is our
cow?" "They took it away, my dear!" [Tiuria is the cheapest peasant
soup, made of bread, water, and onion; Yasha is a diminutive of
Yakov.]

◀)) 2-173 *Illustration:* An article in ***Аргументы и факты,*** 1997, about the expensive
tastes of Russian politicians (contrary to their declaration about their love for
simple Russian food) has a headline with the sarcastic suggestion: **«Ку́шай,
Ге́на, тю́рю»** "Eat tiuria, Gena." [Gena is a diminutive of the name Gennadii,
a reference to Gennadii Ziuganov.]

12. ALEXANDER ALEKSANDROVICH BLOK (1880–1921)

АЛЕКСА́НДР АЛЕКСА́НДРОВИЧ БЛОК

◀)) 2-174   **Траги́ческий те́нор эпо́хи**
                                    (Анна Ахма́това)

                            Tragic Tenor of an Epoch
                                (Anna Akhmatova)

Blok was born into a highly cultivated family
and led a sheltered and happy childhood
even though his parents were divorced when
he was about one year old. His maternal
grandfather was the Rector [akin to university president] of St. Petersburg university,

Fig. 2-40. K. Somov, Portrait of
Alexander Blok

and his father was a professor of law. A major figure of Russian Symbolism,
Blok is considered one of the best Russian poets of the 20th century. His first
collection of several hundred love poems **«Стихи́ о Прекра́сной Да́ме»**
"Verses about a Beautiful Lady," was inspired by his future wife Liubov
Dmitrievna Mendeleeva (daughter of the creator of the Periodic Table of the
Elements Dmitri Mendeleev **Менделе́ев**), and are full of mystic reverence. The
Beautiful Lady of the poems emerges as Eternal Femininity and Wisdom
(categories from the philosophy of the Russian philosopher Vladimir Soloviev).
Blok's long poems about Russia's past and present, of Russia's place in the

world made him a true national poet: they are filled with such love, pain, vigorous beauty and sense of history that it has become almost impossible for Russians to talk about what they feel about their motherland without allusions to Blok's poetry.

12.1. From **«Дéвушка пéла в церкóвном хóре»** "A young girl sang in the church choir" (1905):

> **Дéвушка пéла в церкóвном хóре**   🔊)) 2-175
> **О всех устáлых в чужóм краю́,**
> **О всех корабля́х, ушéдших в мóре,**
> **О всех, забы́вших рáдость свою́.**

A young girl sang in the church choir about all the weary people in alien lands, about all the ships gone to sea, about all those who have forgotten their joy.

Illustration: A headline in **Огонёк**, May 1997: **«Дéвушка пéла в церкóвном хóре»** precedes an article about a violin-player, Tatiana Grindenko.

12.2. From **«Незнакóмка»** "The Stranger" (1906):

12.2.1.   🔊)) 2-176
> **По вечерáм над рестораáнами**
> **Горя́чий вóздух дик и глух, ...**

In the evenings, over the restaurants the hot air is wild and muffled.

Illustration: The newspaper **Коммерсантъ**, 1991, published a note about the work of The House of Journalists under the heading: **«По вечерáм над рестораáнами»**.

12.2.2.   🔊)) 2-177
> **И пья́ницы с глазáми крóликов**
> **"In vino veritas!" кричáт.**

And drunkards with rabbit red eyes shout: "In vino veritas!" [Latin for: Truth is in wine]

12.2.3.   🔊)) 2-178
> **И кáждый вéчер, в час назнáченный**
> **(Иль это только снится мне?)**
> **Деви́чий стан, шелкáми схвáченный,**
> **В тумáнном дви́жется окнé.**

And every evening, at the appointed hour (or is it only my dream?) a young girl's figure sheathed in silks moves behind the fogged window.

12.2.4.

◀))) 2-179   **И ме́дленно, пройдя́ меж пья́ными,**
                    Всегда́ без спу́тников, одна́,
                    Дыша́ духа́ми и тума́нами,
                    Она́ сади́тся у окна́.

And slowly passing the drunks, always without companions, breathing
perfumes and mists, she sits down near the window.

Illustration: According to the memoirs of Mayakovsky's friend, Lily Brik, he
◀))) 2-179 quoted these lines, jokingly distorting them into: «**И ме́дленно, пройдя́ меж**
пья́ными, среди беспу́тников одна́ ...» "And slowly passing the drunks, alone
among the rakes ..."

12.2.5.

◀))) 2-180   **И ве́ют дре́вними пове́рьями**
                    Её упру́гие шелка́,
                    И шля́па с тра́урными пе́рьями,
                    И в ко́льцах у́зкая рука́.

And her tight silks breathe with ancient legends, her hat with mourning
feathers and her narrow hand with rings.

Illustration: The women's magazine **Крестьянка,** 1996, uses Blok's lines as the
title of an article about the use of fabric in female fashion and clothes design:

Fig. 2-41.

12.2.6.

Я зна́ю: и́стина в вине́.   🔊)) **2-181**

I know: the truth is in wine.

12.3. From **«В рестора́не»** *In the Restaurant* (1910):

12.3.1.

Я сиде́л у окна́ в перепо́лненном за́ле.   🔊)) **2-182**
Где-то пе́ли смычки́ о любви́.
Я посла́л тебе́ чёрную ро́зу в бока́ле
Золото́го, как не́бо, ай.

I sat in a crowded room near the window. Somewhere the fiddles sang
of love. I sent you a black rose in a wineglass full of golden-as-the-sky
Ay [champagne].

12.3.2.

Ты рвану́лась движе́ньем испу́ганной пти́цы,   🔊)) **2-183**
Ты прошла́, сло́вно сон мой легка́ ...

You sprang with the motion of a frightened bird, you passed by, light,
like my dream ...

Illustration: A St. Petersburg friend of mine was telling me about an American
who was in love with a Russian girl, but didn't want his Russian friends to meet
her. This is how my friend reported seeing them together in line at the super-
market: **«Я подошёл к ним. Тут он рвану́лся движе́ньем испу́ганной пти́цы,** 🔊)) **2-183**
и загороди́л её». "I approached them—and then he 'sprang with the motion of
a frightened bird' to get in front of her."

12.4. From the cycle **«Пля́ски сме́рти»** *Danse Macabre*, **«Ночь, у́лица,**
фона́рь, апте́ка ...» "Night, the street, a streetlamp, the drugstore ..." (1912).
Many Russians can recite the entire poem from memory:

Ночь, у́лица, фона́рь, апте́ка,   🔊)) **2-184**
Бессмы́сленный и ту́склый свет.
Живи́ ещё хоть че́тверть ве́ка—
Всё бу́дет так. Исхо́да нет.

Night, the street, a streetlamp, the drugstore, a meaningless and dismal
light. Even if you live a quarter century more—all will be the same.
There is no escape.

Illustration: An **Изве́стия**, 1993, headline to an article describing the situation 🔊)) **2-184**
in Moscow after the coup, uses Blok's line: **«Ночь. У́лица. ОМО́Н»** "Night.
Street. OMON [Special Forces]."

12.5. From «**На по́ле Кулико́вом**» "On the Kulikovo Field" (1908):

12.5.1.

◀)) 2-185
О, Русь моя́! Жена́ моя́! До бо́ли
Нам я́сен до́лгий путь!
Наш путь—стрело́й тата́рской дре́вней во́ли
Пронзи́л нам грудь.

O, my Rus′! My wife! How painfully clearly we see our long path! Our path pierced our hearts with an arrow of the ancient Tartar will.

12.5.2.

◀)) 2-186
И ве́чный бой! Поко́й нам то́лько сни́тся
Сквозь кровь и пыль …
Лети́т, лети́т степна́я кобыли́ца
И мнёт ковы́ль …

And ceaseless battle! Peace is for us but a dream vision we discern through blood and dust … Here flies a wild mare of the steppes, stamping the feather grass.

12.6. From the cycle «**Росси́я**» *Russia* (1908):

12.6.1.

◀)) 2-187
Росси́я, ни́щая Росси́я,
Мне и́збы се́рые твои́,
Твои́ мне пе́сни ветровы́е—
Как слёзы пе́рвые любви́!

Russia, poverty-ridden Russia! Your gray huts, your windy songs for me are like the first tears of love!

12.6.2. «**Рождённые в года́ глухи́е**» (**З.Н. Гиппиус**) "Those Born in God-forsaken Years" (to Z.N. Gippius) (1914):

◀)) 2-188
Рождённые в года́ глухи́е
Пути́ не по́мнят своего́.
Мы—де́ти стра́шных лет Росси́и—
Забы́ть не в си́лах ничего́.

Those born in godforsaken years, they do not remember their path. We, the children of Russia's terrible years—we are unable to forget anything.

12.7. «**Двена́дцать**» *The Twelve* (1918) is a narrative poem blessing the Revolution despite its cruelty. In the poem, twelve armed revolutionary workers (like twelve apostles) march through desolate Petrograd (or is it the whole of Russia?) and through a blizzard; they are free of the old moral rules; one of them kills his lover, who had betrayed him. Shockingly, the poem ends with the figure of Jesus Christ with a red flag, barely seen through the blizzard, marching ahead of the twelve.

12.7.1.

Чёрный ве́чер.
Бе́лый снег,
Ве́тер, ветер!
На нога́х не стои́т челове́к.
Ве́тер, ве́тер—
На всём Бо́жьем све́те!

🔊 2-189

Black evening, white snow. Wind, wind! One can't stand on one's feet. There is wind, wind—over all God's world!

12.7.2.

Свобо́да, свобо́да,
Эх, эх, без креста́!

🔊 2-190

Freedom, freedom, oh, without the cross!

12.7.3.

Революцьо́нный держи́те шаг!
Неугомо́нный не дре́млет враг!

🔊 2-191

Keep your revolutionary step, the indefatigable enemy does not dawdle!

12.7.4.

Мы на го́ре всем буржу́ям
Мирово́й пожа́р разду́ем, ...

🔊 2-192

To the woe of all bourgeois, we will fan the flames of world fire.

12.7.5.

Стои́т буржу́й, как пёс голо́дный,
Стои́т безмо́лвный, как вопро́с.
И ста́рый мир, как пёс безро́дный,
Стои́т за ним, поджа́вши хвост.

🔊 2-193

A bourgeois stands, like a hungry dog, stands silent as a question mark. And the old world stands behind him, like an orphaned dog with his tail between his legs.

12.7.6.

... Так иду́т держа́вным ша́гом—
Позади́—голо́дный пёс,
Впереди́—с крова́вым фла́гом,
И за вью́гой невиди́м,
И от пу́ли невреди́м,

🔊 2-194

Не́жной по́ступью надвью́жной,
Сне́жной ро́ссыпью жемчу́жной,
В бе́лом ве́нчике из роз—
Впереди́—Ису́с Христо́с.

Thus they walk in solemn step, behind them—the hungry dog, ahead of
them—someone with a bloody flag, invisible through the blizzard, in-
vulnerable to bullets, with gentle steps above the storm, through snowy
heaps of pearls, in a wreath of white roses, ahead of them—is Jesus
Christ.

12.8. **«Ски́фы»** "Scythians" (1918) is a long poem about the role of Russia in
the world as a shield between the West and the East (a favorite idea of the
Slavophiles). Russia combines features of both worlds, and woe to the West, if
it turns against Russia, forcing it to side with the East. The West should consider peace before it's too late. "Scythians" was the name given to ancient
tribes by the ancient Greeks.

12.8.1.

🔊)) 2-195   Милльо́ны—вас. Нас—тьмы́, и тьмы́, и тьмы́.
Попро́буйте, срази́тесь с на́ми!
Да, ски́фы—мы! Да, азиа́ты—мы,
С раско́сыми и жа́дными оча́ми!

There are millions of you. There are billions and billions of us! Try,
fight us! Yes, we are Scythians! Yes, we are Asians, with our slanted
and greedy eyes!

13. SERGEI ALEKSANDROVICH ESENIN (1895–1925)

СЕРГЕ́Й АЛЕКСА́НДРОВИЧ ЕСЕ́НИН

The son of peasants, Esenin made his peasant heritage
the main theme of his poetry. In 1915 he came to St.
Petersburg and soon became one of the leaders of Im-
aginism. There are many legends about his bohemian
life, alcoholism, scandalous love affairs and marriages,
the first of which was to the American dancer Isadora
Duncan. Despite his folksiness, Esenin was treated by
the Soviet authorities as ideologically "confused."
Weary and lonely, he took his own life by hanging

Fig. 2-42.

himself after opening his veins. In recent years there have appeared speculations about his death having been orchestrated by the NKVD [secret police].

13.1. From **«Письмо́ ма́тери»** "Letter to My Mother" (1924):

Ты жива́ ещё, моя́ стару́шка? 🔊)) 2-196
Жив и я. Приве́т тебе́, приве́т!
Пусть струи́тся над твое́й избу́шкой
Тот вече́рний несказа́нный свет.

Are you still alive, my old dear ? I too am still around. Greetings, greetings to you! May that evening light, unspeakably beautiful, still stream over your hut.

(This poem, and 13.3 are also well-known as songs.)

13.2. From **«Мы тепе́рь ухо́дим понемно́гу …»** "We leave slowly" … (1924):

Сча́стлив тем, что целова́л я же́нщин, 🔊)) 2-197
Мял цветы, валя́лся на траве́
И зверьё, как *бра́тьев на́ших ме́ньших*,
Никогда́ не бил по голове́.

I am happy that I kissed women, ruffled flowers, lay about on the grass, and that I never hit our little brothers of the animal kingdom on their heads.

Illustration: Headline in *Аргуме́нты и фа́кты*, 1997: **«Как не зарази́ться от бра́тьев на́ших ме́ньших»** "How not to catch infection from our little brothers of the animal kingdom."

13.3. **«Отговори́ла ро́ща золота́я …»** "The golden grove has ceased talking …" (1924):

Отговори́ла ро́ща золота́я 🔊)) 2-198
Берёзовым, весёлым языко́м,
И журавли́, печа́льно пролета́я,
Уж не жале́ют бо́льше ни о ком.

The golden grove has ceased talking in its birch-tree merry tongue, and the cranes, sadly flying past, do not grieve for anyone any longer.

13.4. **«Письмо́ к же́нщине»** "Letter to a Woman" (addressed to Isadora Duncan, 1924):

⏮ 2-199

13.4.1.

Вы по́мните,
Вы всё, коне́чно, по́мните.
Как я стоя́л,
Прибли́зившись к стене́;
Взволно́ванно ходи́ли вы по
    ко́мнате
И что-то ре́зкое
В лицо́ броса́ли мне.

You remember, of course you remember everything. How I stood, having approached the wall … you in agitation paced the room and threw some sharp words in my face.

13.4.2.

⏮ 2-200

Лицо́м к лицу́
Лица́ не увида́ть.
Большо́е ви́дится на
    расстоя́ньи.

Face-to-face, it is impossible to see a face. Something big is easier to see at a distance.

Fig. 2-43.   Esenin with Isadora Duncan, 1922

13.5. From «**Не жале́ю, не зову́, не пла́чу …**» "I do not regret, do not call out, do not cry …" (1921):

⏮ 2-201   Не жале́ю, не зову́, не пла́чу,
Всё пройдёт, как с бе́лых я́блонь дым.
Увяда́нья зо́лотом охва́ченный,
Я не бу́ду бо́льше молоды́м.

I do not regret, do not call out, do not cry; all will pass like clouds from white blooming apple-trees. Seized with the gold of fading, I will never be young again.

Illustration: Headline in ***Но́вое вре́мя***, Feb. 1997: «**Не жале́ет. Не зовёт, не пла́чет**» "She does not regret, call out, cry." An article about the journalist Elena Suponina who received a prize for her work and who explained that the principles of Islam she adopted can be best expressed in this Russian formula: «**Не жале́ю, не зову́, не пла́чу … »**

13.6. The poem «Клён ты мой опа́вший» "O you, my maple tree with fallen leaves" (1925) provided the lyrics for a popular song.

Клён ты мой опа́вший, клён заледене́лый,
Что стои́шь нагну́вшись под мете́лью бе́лой?
🔊 2-202

O you, my maple tree whose leaves have fallen, frozen maple, why do you bend under the white blizzard?

Illustration: An article in ***Труд***, 1997, about revaluation of the ruble has the headline: «Но́ль ты мой опа́вший» "O, you, my fallen zero."

13.7. From «До свида́нья, друг мой, до свида́нья …» "Goodbye, my friend, goodbye …" (1925). This is the poem Esenin wrote before his suicide. He wrote it in his own blood.

До свида́нья, друг мой, без руки́ и сло́ва,
Не грусти́ и не печа́ль брове́й, —
В э́той жи́зни умира́ть не но́во,
Но и жить, коне́чно, не нове́й.
🔊 2-203

Goodbye, my friend, without a handshake or a word; don't be sad, don't knit your brows with sorrow—In this life, dying is not new, but then of course to live is not any newer.

Illustration:

(a) The disillusionment and pessimism of the poem, and especially its aphoristic force, were out of place in the young Soviet state. The poet Vladimir Mayakovsky felt compelled to counterbalance that with something equally vigorous and aphoristic. Hence his poem «Серге́ю Есе́нину» "To Sergei Esenin," which ends in the following way:

Для весе́лия
          планéта на́ша
                   ма́ло обору́дована.
На́до
      вы́рвать ра́дость
               у гряду́щих дней.
В э́той жи́зни
          помере́ть
               не тру́дно.
Сде́лать жизнь
          значи́тельно трудне́й.
🔊 2-204

For merriment, our planet is poorly equipped. You have to snatch joy from the future years. In this life, it is not difficult to die. To make life is considerably more difficult.

(b) One of the characters in Aksyonov's satirical long story «**Зато-варенная бочкотáра**» *The Over-Stocked Barrel*, the romantic truck driver Vladimir Teleskopov, writes his sweetheart a note which he ends with these words: «**До свидáнья, Сúма, не грустú и не печáль бровéй, а éсли чегó узнáю, не обижáйся**».

"Goodbye, Sima, do not be sad, do not knit your brows with sorrow and if I hear something don't be offended."

14. VLADIMIR VLADIMIROVICH MAYAKOVSKY (1893–1930)

ВЛАДИ́МИР ВЛАДИ́МИРОВИЧ МАЯКО́ВСКИЙ

🔊 2-205
- **Лу́чший, талáнтливейший поэ́т нáшей совéтской эпóхи**

  (Стáлин)

  The best, the most talented poet of our Soviet epoch.

  (Stalin)

Fig. 2-44.

- **Маякóвского стáли вводи́ть принуди́тельно, как картóфель при Екатери́не. Э́то бы́ло егó вторóй смéртью. В ней он не винóвен.**

  (Пастернáк)

  They began to introduce Mayakovsky by force, like potatoes under Catherine the Great. That was his second death. He is not to be blamed for it.

  (Pasternak)

One of the greatest poets of the 20th century, a leader of Russian Futurism and the avant-garde, a rebel denouncing bourgeois values, Mayakovsky embraced the Revolution and proclaimed his poetry at the service of the "masses." In the minds of readers, there are two Mayakovskys. One is a great poet of overwhelming vigor and lyrical force, a king of shocking metaphors combining the highest and lowest levels of language, the one who began as the author of the narrative poems «**Флéйта-позвонóчник**», "The Backbone Flute," «**О́блако в штанáх**», "A Cloud in Pants," «**Человéк**» "Man," and the experimental drama «**Влади́мир Маякóвский, трагéдия**» *Vladimir Mayakovsky, a Tragedy*. The other Mayakovsky dedicated his talents to producing numerous rhymed political slogans that glorified the regime, criticized petty bureaucrats and anti-hygienic habits; this is the author of the long poem «Влади́мир Ильи́ч Ле́нин» "Vladimir Il'ich Lenin" written after Lenin's death and «Хорошо́!» "It Is Good!" written on the tenth anniversary of Soviet power. In 1930 Mayakovsky committed suicide. After his death he was canonized by the Soviet regime and proclaimed by Stalin the best Soviet poet. His poetry (especially of the second period) and the official version of his biography were studied in detail, and as a result many lines entered the stock of frequent quotations.

14.1. From «А вы могли́ бы?» "And Could You?" (1913):

А вы   ◀)) 2-206
нокти́юрн сыгра́ть
могли́ бы
на фле́йте водосто́чных труб?

And could you play a nocturne using drainpipes as a flute?

14.2. From «Послу́шайте!» "Listen!" (1913):

Послу́шайте!   ◀)) 2-207
Ведь е́сли звёзды зажига́ют,
зна́чит—э́то кому́-нибудь ну́жно? ...
Зна́чит—кто-то называ́ет
э́ти плево́чки
жемчу́жиной?

Listen! Listen, if they lit the stars, then it means that someone needs it, right? Then it means that someone calls this spit pearls?

Illustration:

(a) Headline in *Огонёк*, April 1996: «Е́сли а́томные ста́нции не ◀)) 2-207 взрыва́ют, зна́чит э́то никому́ не ну́жно?» "If they don't blow up the nuclear stations, then it means that no one needs it?"

(b) An article in *Собесе́дник* Nov. 1997, about the mosaic portraits of pop-stars on the streets had a playful headline: «Если звёзд закла́дывают, зна́чит, э́то кому́-нибудь ну́жно?» "If they put the stars into the foundation, then it means that someone needs it?" This is a play on two meanings of the verb закла́дывать: "to lay a foundation" and the slang meaning "to inform on someone."

14.3. From «Óблако в штанáх» "A Cloud in Pants" (1914–15):

14.3.1.

🔊 2-208

**Мир огрóмив мóщью гóлоса,
идý—красúвый,
двадцатидвухлéтний.**

Having deafened the world with the power of my voice, here I come: a handsome twenty-two year old.

14.3.2.

🔊 2-209

**Хотúте—
бýду от мя́са бéшеный,
—и, как нéбо, меня́я тонá,—
хотúте—
бýду безукорúзненно нéжный,
не мужчúна, а—óблако в штанáх!**

Fig. 2-45. Mayakovsky (but at 16, not 22)

If you want, I will be crazy like a meat-eater, and—changing colors, like the sky—if you wish, I will be impeccably tender, not a man, but a cloud in pants!"

14.3.3.

🔊 2-210

**Аллó!
Кто говорúт?
Мáма?**

**Мáма!
Ваш сын прекрáсно бóлен! …
У негó пожáр сéрдца.
Скажúте сёстрам, Лю́де и Óле,—
емý уже нéкуда дéться.
Кáждое слóво,
дáже шýтка,
котóрые изрыгáет обгорáющим ртом он,
выбрáсывается, как гóлая проститýтка
из горя́щего публúчного дóма.**

Hello! Who is speaking? Mama? Mama! Your son is beautifully sick. His heart is on fire. Tell his sisters, Liuda and Olia, that there is no escape for him. Every word, even a joke, that he disgorges from his scorched mouth throws itself out like a naked prostitute from a burning whorehouse.

14.3.4.

Эй, вы! 🔊 **2-211**
Не́бо!
Сними́те шля́пу!
Я иду́!

Глу́хо.

Вселе́нная спит,
положи́в на ла́пу
с клеща́ми звёзд огро́мное у́хо.

Hey you, heaven! Take off your hat! I am coming! Silence. The Universe sleeps, putting its huge ear with ticks made of stars on his paw.

Illustration: An article in **Огонёк**, March 1997, on the definition and meaning of pornography is entitled «**О́блако в штана́х**».

14.4. From «**Фле́йта-позвоно́чник**» "The Backbone Flute" (1915):

Всё ча́ще ду́маю — 🔊 **2-212**
не поста́вить ли лу́чше
то́чку пу́ли в своём конце́.

I am thinking more and more often whether it wouldn't be better to put a bullet's period at the end [of my life].

14.5. From the poem «**А всё-таки**» "Anyway" (1914):

У́лица провали́лась, как нос сифили́тика … 🔊 **2-213**

The street caved in, like the nose of a syphilitic.

Illustration: A headline preceding a group of articles about venereal diseases in **Огонёк**, April 1997: «**Друзья́ и враги́ Вене́ры. Улица провали́лась, как нос сифили́тика …**» "The friends and enemies of Venus. 'The street caved in, like the nose of a syphilitic.' "

14.6. «**Ешь анана́сы …**» "Eat pineapples …" (1917):

Ешь анана́сы, ря́бчиков жуй, 🔊 **2-214**
день твой после́дний прихо́дит, буржу́й!

Eat pineapples, munch on grouse, your last day is coming, bourgeois!

Illustration: Headline in **Аргуме́нты и фа́кты**, 1997: «**Ешь анана́сы, ря́бчиков жуй**» "Eat pineapples, munch on grouse." The article is about homeless people quarreling over food leftovers in garbage cans. One of them stated that the quality of leftovers now is higher than under socialism.

Fig. 2-46.   Mayakovsky and Lily Brik, 1922

14.7. From «Хорóшее отношéние к лошадя́м» "A Good Attitude Towards Horses" (1918):

2-215   **Дéточка,**
все мы немнóжко лóшади,
кáждый из нас по-своéму лóшадь.

Little one, we are all somewhat horses, each of us is a horse in our own way.

14.8. From «Лéвый марш» "Left March" (1918):

14.8.1.

2-216   **Довóльно жить закóном,**
дáнным Адáмом и Éвой.
Кля́чу истóрии загóним!
Лéвой!
Лéвой!
Лéвой!

Enough of living by the law given to us by Adam and Eve. Let's ride the jade of history to death. Left, left, left!

14.8.2.

2-217   **Кто там шагáет прáвой?**
Лéвой!
Лéвой!
Лéвой!

Hey, who's there stepping with the right foot? Left, left, left!

Illustration: Headline in *Нóвое врéмя*, Feb. 1997: «Лéвый демáрш. Кто там
2-217   шагáет?.. Геннáдию Андрéевичу [Зюгáнову] мешáют рабóтать» "Left de-march. Hey, who's there stepping? … They 'wouldn't let Gennady Andreevich [Ziuganov] work.'"

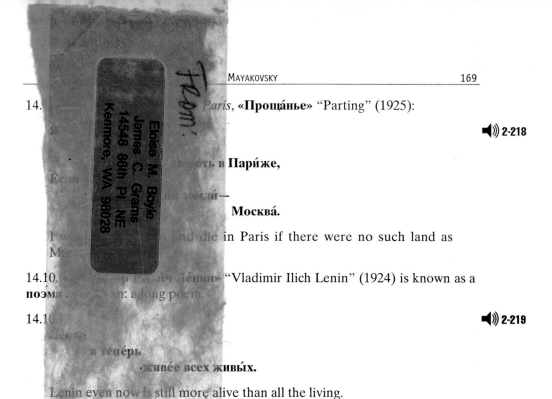

14. _____ *Paris*, «Проща́нье» "Parting" (1925):

◀)) 2-218

_____ ть в Пари́же,

_____

Москва́.

I w_____ nd die in Paris if there were no such land as
M_____

14.10. «_____ Ле́нин» "Vladimir Ilich Lenin" (1924) is known as a
поэ́ма _____ n: a long poem.

14.1_____

◀)) 2-219

_____

и тепе́рь

·живе́е всех живы́х.

Lenin even now is still more alive than all the living.

Illustration:

(a) An article in *Изве́стия*, 1992, about the reburial of Lenin places a ◀)) 2-219
question mark at the end of the quotation in the headline: «Ле́нин и
тепе́рь живе́е всех живы́х?» "Is Lenin even now still more alive than
all the living?"

(b) Headline in *Комсомо́льская пра́вда*, 1997: «Пре́сли и тепе́рь жи-
ве́й ины́х живы́х. Роковая да́та для люби́телей ро́ка: в э́тот день
20 лет наза́д сконча́лся их и́дол Э́лвис Пре́сли» "Presley even now
is still more alive than some living. A fatal date for rock-lovers: this
day 20 years ago their idol, Elvis Presley, passed away."

14.10.2. ◀)) 2-220

Что он сде́лал,

кто он

и отку́да

э́тот

са́мый челове́чный челове́к?

What did he do, who is he and from where—this most humane human?

Illustration: The following joke makes fun of the "most humane human": An
old Bolshevik is invited to a school to tell the young pioneers about his encounter with the great leader of the proletariat, V.I. Lenin. The old Bolshevik
begins:

🔊 2-220 «В 1917-м году́ я встре́тил Влади́мира Ильича́ в обще́ственном туале́те. Он стоя́л ря́дом со все́ми и де́лал то же, что и все. Но как про́сто, как челове́чно он э́то де́лал!»

"In the year 1917 I met V.I. Lenin in a public restroom. He stood next to everyone and did what everyone did. But how simply, how humanely he did it!"

14.10.3.

🔊 2-221 Па́ртия и Ле́нин —
　　　　　　　близнецы́-бра́тья,
кто бо́лее
　　　　ма́тери-исто́рии це́нен?
Мы говори́м — Ле́нин,
　　　　　　　подразумева́ем —
　　　　　　　　　　　　па́ртия,
мы говори́м
　　　　па́ртия,
　　　　　　　подразумева́ем —
　　　　　　　　　　　Ле́нин.

The party and Lenin are twin brothers. Which of them is more precious for Mother History? When we say "Lenin," we mean "the party," when we say "the party," we mean "Lenin."

Illustration:

(a)　An old joke uses Mayakovsky's lines to attack doublespeak:

🔊 2-222 **Мы говори́м Ле́нин — подразумева́ем «партия». Мы говорим «партия» — подразумева́ем «Ле́нин». И так се́мьдесят лет: говори́м одно́, а подразумева́ем друго́е.**

When we say "Lenin," we mean "the party," when we say "the party," we mean "Lenin." And we go on like that for seventy years: we say one thing, and mean another.

(b)　An article in ***Комсомо́льская пра́вда***, 1997, about a Japanese company producing Barbie dolls in the likeness of Marilyn Monroe has the headline: **«Ба́рби и Ме́рилин — близнецы-сёстры?»** "Barbie and Marilyn — are they twin sisters?"

(c)　Headline in ***Огонёк***, March 1996: **«Говори́м 'Верво́льф' — подразумева́ем, Па́мять»** "When we say 'Werewolf' we imply 'Memory'" [the name of the fascist organization in Russia].

14.11. The title of the poem **«Това́рищу Не́тте, парохо́ду и челове́ку»** "To 🔊 **2-223** Comrade Nette, a Steamship and a Person" (1926) is widely quoted.

Illustration:

(a) Headline in ***Огонёк***, March 1997: **«Ри́чарду Ни́ксону, президе́нту и челове́ку»** "To Richard Nixon, a president and a person."

(b) Headline in the newspaper ***На гра́ни невозмо́жного***, 1997: **«Ха́ббл—телеско́п и челове́к».** "Hubble, a telescope and a person."

14.12. From **«Разгово́р с фининспе́ктором о поэ́зии»** "A Talk with the Taxman about Poetry" (1926):

> —Поэ́зия   🔊 **2-224**
> 　　　　—вся!—
> 　　　　　　　　езда́ в незна́емое.
> **Поэ́зия–**
> 　　　　та же добы́ча ра́дия.
> **В грамм добы́ча,**
> 　　　　　　в год труды́.**

Poetry—all of it!—is a ride into the unknown. Poetry is the same as extraction of radium. One gram of output, a year of labor.

14.13. After Mayakovsky visited the United States he wrote a poem cycle entitled **«Стихи́ об Аме́рике»** *Verses About America.* **«Бродве́й»** "Broadway" (1925) is one of the poems in the cycle.

14.13.1.

> **Нале́во посмо́тришь—**   🔊 **2-225**
> 　　　　　　ма́мочка мать!**
> **Напра́во—**
> 　　　　мать моя́ ма́мочка!**

You look to the left—mother dear! You look to the right—my dear mother! [intended obscene association].

14.13.2.   🔊 **2-226**

> **Я в восто́рге**
> 　　　　　от Нью-Йо́рка го́рода.**
> **Но**
> 　　　**кепчо́нку**
> 　　　　　　не сдёрну с виска́.**
> **У сове́тских**
> 　　　　со́бственная го́рдость:**
> **на буржу́ев**
> 　　　　смо́трим свысока́.**

I am in rapture over the city of New York. But I will not pull my cap off my head. The Soviet people have their own pride: we look down on the bourgeoisie.

Illustration:

(a) A headline to the article in ***Огонёк***, March 1996, about a special breed of sheep producing cheese ferment: **«У расе́йской овцы́ со́бственная го́рдость»** "Russian sheep have their own pride." The spelling of **росси́йской** reflects dialectal pronunciation.

(b) An article in ***Огонёк***, June 1996, about an unusually tall man from Tunis who came to Russia to find himself a wife has a headline playing on Mayakovsky's line: **«Родуа́н не смо́трит на же́нщин свысока́»** "Rodwan does not look down on women."

14.14. «Хорошо́! Октя́брьская поэ́ма» "It Is Good! The October Poem" (1927):

14.14.1.

🔊 2-227   **«Кото́рые тут вре́менные?**

                        Слазь!

Ко́нчилось ва́ше вре́мя ....»

"Who's temporary here? Get down. Your time is up." [In the poem, a sailor shouts these words to the Provisional Government during the storming of the Winter palace.]

14.14.2.

🔊 2-228   **Я**

         земно́й шар

чуть не весь

                обошёл,—

и жизнь

            хороша́,

и жить

            хорошо́.

I walked around almost the entire globe, and life is good, and it is good to live.

14.14.3.

🔊 2-229   **Моя́**

            мили́ция

меня́

            бережёт.

My police force guards me.

Fig. 2-47.   Mayakovsky in 1925

Illustration: Headline in the newspaper *Завтра*, 1997: «**Моя́ юсти́ция меня́ бережёт**» "My justice system guards me."

14.14.4.

Жизнь прекра́сна

      и

          удиви́тельна.

🔊)) 2-230

Life is beautiful and amazing.

14.14.5.

Лет до ста́

     расти́

нам

     без ста́рости.

🔊)) 2-231

We shall grow till we are about a hundred years old without getting old.

Illustration:

(a) «**Лет до трехсо́т расти́ нам без ста́рости. Америка́нские учёные откры́ли ген долголе́тия**». "American scientists discover the gene for longevity. We shall grow till we are three hundred years old without getting old." 🔊)) 2-231

(b) Headline in *Кура́нты*, Aug./Sept. 1997: «**Лет до ста расти́ … е́сли в тре́звости**». "We shall grow till we are about a hundred years old … if we are sober."

14.15. From «**Стихи́ о сове́тском па́спорте**» "A Poem About the Soviet Passport" (1929):

14.15.1.

Я во́лком бы

     вы́грыз

          бюрократи́зм.

К манда́там

     почте́ния не́ту.

К любы́м

     чертя́м с матеря́ми

          кати́сь

люба́я бума́жка.

     Но эту́ …

🔊)) 2-232

I would gnaw out, like a wolf, the bureaucratism; I have no respect for mandates. Let any document go to any devil and his mother. But this one …

🔊 2-233

14.15.2.

Я
> **достаю́**
>> **из широ́ких штани́н**
>
> **дубликáтом**
>> **бесцéнного грýза.**
>
> **Читáйте,**
>> **завúдуйте,**
>>> **я—**
>>>> **граждани́н**
>
> **Совéтского Сою́за.**

I take [my passport] out of my wide pants as a piece of priceless cargo. Read, envy me, I am a citizen of the Soviet Union!

Illustration: Headline in *Аргумéнты и фáкты*, 1997: «**Как получи́ть заграни́чный пáспорт?**» with the subheading: «**Что я достаю́ из широ́ких штани́н?**» "How to get a foreign passport: What is it that I take out of my wide pants?"

🔊 2-233

Fig. 2-48. A. Rodchenko's photo of Mayakovsky

14.16. From «**Во весь гóлос**» "At the Top of My Voice" (unfinished, 1929–30):

14.16.1.

🔊 2-234

Профéссор,
> **сними́те очки́-велосипéд! ...**
>
> *Я сам расскажý*
>> *о врéмени*
>>> *и о себé.*

Professor, take off your bicycle-like glasses! I will tell you myself about time and about myself.

Illustration: Headline in *Нóвое врéмя*, November 1996: «**Пáпа Ри́мский о врéмени и о себé**» "The Pope of Rome about the time and himself."

14.16.2.

    Но я   🔊 **2-235**

        себя́

             смиря́л,

                  станов́ясь

    на го́рло

        со́бственной пе́сне.

But I constrained myself, stepping on the throat of my own song.

14.16.3.

Слу́шайте,   🔊 **2-236**

        това́рищи пото́мки,

агита́тора,

        горла́на-главар́я.

Заглуша́

        поэ́зии пото́ки,

я шагну́

        через лири́ческие то́мики,

как живо́й

        с живы́ми говоря́.

Listen to me, comrade descendants, to the agitator, bawler, ring-leader. Drowning the currents of poetry, I will step out of my lyrical volumes, still alive, speaking to the living.

Illustration: Headline in ***Огонёк***, June 1996: «**Агита́торы, горла́ны и главари́ мину́вшей неде́ли**» "Agitators, bawlers, ring-leaders of the past week."

14.17. From the unfinished poem addressed to Tatiana Yakovleva, written before his suicide (1930):

Как говоря́т, инциде́нт испе́рчен.   🔊 **2-237**
Любо́вная ло́дка разби́лась о быт.
С тобо́й мы в расчёте. И не́ к чему пе́речень
взаи́мных бо́лей, бед и оби́д.

As they say, the incident is over [Mayakovsky distorts the cliché **инциде́нт исче́рпан** lit.: 'the incident is exhausted' resulting in a pun: **инциде́нт испе́рчен** 'the incident is peppered all over']; the boat of love has crashed on the shores of life. We don't owe each other anything, and there is no use in a list of mutual pains, griefs and injuries.

15. ANNA ANDREEVNA AKHMATOVA (1889–1966)

ÁNNA ANDRÉEVNA AKHMÁTOVA

Fig. 2-49. Petrov-Vodkin, *Portrait of Anna Akhmatova*, 1922

🔊 2-238

- **Мýза плáча**
  (Цветáева)

  The Muse of lamentation

  (Tsvetaeva)

- **Есть жéнщины, сырóй землé роднýе.**
  И кáждый шаг их— гýлкое рыдáнье.
  (Мандельштáм)

  There are women with an affinity for mother earth. And each of their steps is a resounding sob.

  (Mandelshtam)

- **… взбесúвшаяся бáрынька, мéчущаяся между будуáром и молéльней**

  … a crazed lady running back and forth between her boudoir and the chapel.

  (Leningrad Communist Party boss Zhdanov)

Anna Akhmatova is one of the greatest poets of the 20th century. She gave Russians a new language for expressing all shades of love, personal grief and national tragedy. The magical simplicity of her poems is as hard to translate into another language as that of Pushkin. Born as Anna Gorenko near Odessa on the Black Sea, Akhmatova took for a pen-name her Tartar great-grand-mother's surname, under which she published her first collection of poems, **«Вéчер»** *Evening* in 1910. She joined the literary movement called Acmeism, founded by Nikolai Gumilev and Osip Mandelshtam, which the Communists found ideologically "alien." In 1925, publication of her work was forbidden by the Central Committee of the Communist Party. After Stalin's death, only a few scanty collections of poems appeared in the press, but her major work, *Requiem*, secretly circulated in Samizdat, was published in Russia only in 1987.

Most of her biography seems a monotonous repetition of arrests, executions and persecutions of loved ones: her ex-husband, the well-known poet Nikolai Stepanovich Gumilev, suspected of conspiracy against the Bolsheviks, was arrested and executed in 1921; during Stalin's reign, her only son, Lev Gumilev, was arrested several times and for many years imprisoned in labor camps; he was freed only after Stalin's death. Her second husband, Nikolai Punin, arrested in 1938, perished in a concentration camp.

Fig. 2-50.   Akhmatova with her husband, N. Gumilev, and son Lev

Unlike many poets and writers of her generation who displeased the authorities and were killed or imprisoned, Akhmatova was lucky enough to live to an old age and to die in her own bed. While she could not publish her own poetry, Akhmatova was allowed to support herself with translation work, which she did *en masse* and which cost her much of her health. She felt that for a poet to translate poetry while working on one's own was "the same as eating one's own brain."

In the last five years of her life she received world recognition: she was nominated for the Nobel prize (which eventually went to Robert Frost), received the Taormina prize in Italy and was awarded an honorary degree by Oxford University.

15.1. From the cycle **«Ве́чер»** *Evening*: **«Сжа́ла ру́ки под тёмной вуа́лью …»** "I wrung my hands under the dark veil …" (1912):

> **Задыха́ясь, я кри́кнула: «Шу́тка**   ◀)) 2-239
> **Всё, что бы́ло. Уйдёшь, я умру́».**
> **Улыбну́лся споко́йно и жу́тко**
> **И сказа́л мне: «Не стой на ветру́».**

Out of breath, I shouted: "It was a joke, all that has happened. If you leave, I'll die." He smiled calmly and terrifyingly and said: "Go inside. It's windy here."

15.2. **«Пе́сня после́дней встре́чи»** "Song of the Last Tryst" (1912):

> **Так беспо́мощно грудь холоде́ла,**   ◀)) 2-240
> **Но шаги́ мои́ бы́ли легки́.**
> **Я на пра́вую ру́ку наде́ла**
> **Перча́тку с ле́вой руки́.**
>
> **Показа́лось, что мно́го ступе́ней,**
> **А я зна́ла—их то́лько три!**

My chest helplessly turned cold, but I kept my walk light. I put the left-hand glove on my right hand. The staircase seemed so long, but I knew—there were only three steps!

15.3. From the cycle «**Смяте́ние**» *Confusion* (1913):

◀))) 2-241

Не лю́бишь, не хо́чешь смотре́ть?
О, как ты краси́в, прокля́тый!
И я не могу́ взлете́ть,
А с де́тства была́ крыла́той.
Мне о́чи за́стит тума́н,
Слива́ются ве́щи и ли́ца,
И то́лько кра́сный тюльпа́н,
Тюльпа́н у тебя́ в петли́це.

You don't love me, you don't want to look? Oh how beautiful you are, damned one! And I cannot soar off, although winged since my childhood. A fog clouds my eyes; faces and things blur; and only a red tulip, a red tulip in your lapel.

Fig. 2-51.   N. Altman, *Portrait of Anna Akhmatova* (1914)

15.4. From **«Ве́чером»** "In the Evening" (1913):

Звене́ла му́зыка в саду́   🔊 2-242
Таки́м невырази́мым го́рем.
Свежо́ и о́стро па́хли мо́рем
На блю́де у́стрицы во льду.

The music in the park rang with such inexpressible grief. The oysters
on ice smelled, fresh and pungent, of the sea.

15.5. **«Настоя́щую не́жность не спу́таешь…»** "Real tenderness can't be confused …" (1913):

Настоя́щую не́жность не спу́таешь   🔊 2-243
Ни с чем, и она́ тиха́.
Ты напра́сно бе́режно ку́таешь
Мне пле́чи и грудь в меха́.

Real tenderness can't be confused with anything. And it's quiet. In vain
you solicitously wrap my shoulders in furs.

15.6. The poem **«Я пришла́ к поэ́ту в го́сти»** "I visited the poet" (1914) is addressed to Blok.

15.6.1.

Я пришла́ к поэ́ту в го́сти.   🔊 2-244
Ро́вно по́лдень. Воскресе́нье.
Ти́хо в ко́мнате просто́рной,
А за о́кнами моро́з.

I came to visit the poet. Exactly noon. Sunday. It is quiet in the spa-
cious room, and there is frost beyond the windows.

Illustration: An article in **Огонёк**, Feb. 1997, describing the author's
visit to the poet Voznesensky begins with the following words: **«Я
пришла́ к Вознесе́нскому в го́сти по иро́нии судьбы́ ро́вно в   🔊 2-244
по́лдень, в воскресе́нье. И за окнами моро́з».** "I came to visit
Voznesensky, by an irony of fate, exactly at noon, Sunday. And there
was frost beyond the windows."

15.6.2.

У него́ глаза́ таки́е,   🔊 2-245
Что запо́мнить ка́ждый до́лжен,
Мне же лу́чше, осторо́жной,
В них и во́все не гляде́ть.

He has such eyes that everyone should remember them. It is better for
me, the cautious one, not to look into them at all.

15.7. «Му́за» "Muse" (1924):

◀))) 2-246
Когда́ я но́чью жду её прихо́да,
Жизнь, ка́жется, виси́т на волоске́.
Что по́чести, что ю́ность, что свобо́да
Пред ми́лой го́стьей с ду́дочкой в руке́.
И вот вошла́. Отки́нув покрыва́ло,
Внима́тельно взгляну́ла на меня́.
Ей говорю́: «Ты ль Да́нту диктова́ла
Страни́цы А́да?» Отвеча́ет: «Я».

When at night I am waiting for her to come, my life, it seems, is hanging by a thread. What are honors, what's youth, what's freedom in the face of the sweet guest with a flute in her hand. And here she enters. Throwing her veil off her face, she looks at me intently. I say to her: "Were you the one who dictated to Dante the pages of his *Inferno*?" And she answers: "It was I."

15.8. From «Ре́квием» *Requiem* (1935–40):

15.8.1.

◀))) 2-247
Нет, и не под чу́ждым небосво́дом,
И не под защи́той чу́ждых крыл —
Я была́ тогда́ с мои́м наро́дом,
Там, где мой наро́д, к несча́стью, был.

No, neither under an alien sky nor under the protection of alien wings—then I was there with my people, where my people unfortunately were.

15.8.2.

◀))) 2-248
Звёзды сме́рти стоя́ли над на́ми
И безви́нная ко́рчилась Русь
Под крова́выми сапога́ми
И под ши́нами чёрных мару́сь.

Stars of death stood over us and innocent Russia writhed under bloodstained boots and the tires of the Black Marias [чёрная мару́ся, Black Maria is a euphemism for vans transporting arrested people].

15.8.3.

◀))) 2-249
Эта же́нщина больна́,
Эта же́нщина одна́.
Муж в моги́ле, сын в тюрьме́,
Помоли́тесь обо мне́.

This woman is sick, this woman is alone. My husband is in his grave, my son is in prison, pray for me.

15.9. The poem «Па́мяти поэ́та» "To the Memory of the Poet" (1960) is dedicated to Boris Pasternak.

🔊))) 2-250

Умо́лк вчера́ неповтори́мый го́лос,
И нас поки́нул собесе́дник рощ.
Он преврати́лся в жизнь даю́щий ко́лос
Или в тонча́йший, им воспе́тый дождь.

An inimitable voice was silenced yesterday, and the interlocutor of groves left us. He turned into a life-giving wheat-ear, or into the thinnest rain he glorified in his poems.

15.10. «Поэ́ма без геро́я» *A Poem Without a Hero* is a long poem on which Akhmatova worked almost until her dying day. To a great degree autobiographical, it is also a tribute to the epoch she lived in.

🔊))) 2-251

… а так как мне бума́ги не хвати́ло
Я на твоём пишу́ черновике́.
И вот чужо́е сло́во проступа́ет …

… and since I've run out of paper, I write on your drafts. And suddenly somone else's words start showing through.

Illustration: In **Но́вое вре́мя**, Feb. 1997. V. Novodvorskaia uses the title of 🔊))) 2-251
Akhmatova's poem in her discussion of Greek tragedies in contrast with Russian history and literature; in the end, she arrives at a bitter conclusion: «Ру́сские траге́дии — поэ́мы без геро́ев». "Russian tragedies are poems without heroes."

Fig. 2-52. Akhmatova in the 1960s

15.11. «После́дняя ро́за» "The Last Rose" (1962):

🔊))) 2-252

Го́споди! Ты ви́дишь, я уста́ла
Воскреса́ть, и умира́ть, и жи́ть.
Всё возьми́, но э́той ро́зы а́лой
Дай мне све́жесть сно́ва ощути́ть.

Lord! You see that I am too tired to resurrect, and to die and to live again. Take away everything, but let me feel again the redness of this rose.

16. OSIP EMILIEVICH MANDEL′SHTAM (1891–1938)

О́СИП ЭМИ́ЛЬЕВИЧ МАНДЕЛЬШТА́М

2-253

• А в ко́мнате опа́льного по э́та
  Дежу́рят страх и Му́за в свой черёд.
                                    (Ахматова)

And in the room of an ostracized poet,
the Muse and fear keep watch in shifts.
                                    (Akhmatova)

Fig. 2-53. O. Mandel′shtam

• И нам Петра́рку у костра́ чита́ет
  Фарто́вый па́рень О́ська Мандельшта́м

And a cool guy, Os′ka Mandel′shtam, reads Petrarch to us beside a
bonfire. [Anonymous addition to Yuz Aleshkovsky's popular (and illegal) inmate song.]

Mandel′shtam was born in Warsaw and grew up in Petersburg, where he studied in one of the most cultural schools of the time, Tenishev Commercial
School. As an Acmeist he was to the Bolsheviks "ideologically alien," and, like
Akhmatova, was prohibited from publishing his works by the same official
Party document of 1925. Poetry written by Mandel′shtam after 1925 survived
due to the heroic efforts of his wife, Nadezhda Yakovlevna, who managed to
hide the manuscripts through all the KGB searches and the nomadic life forced
on her; not trusting hiding places, she memorized all his poetry and prose. In
1934 Mandel′shtam was arrested for a poem presenting Stalin as an executioner
enjoying his executions. Given the offense, his punishment was mild: exile to
Cherdyn′ (Че́рдынь, a small, old town 100 km north of Solikamsk in the Perm
district. The main industry is forestry, and it is synonymous with prison labor),
and later to Voronezh, for three years altogether. His wife was allowed to follow him. In 1938 Mandel′shtam was arrested again, and this time was sent to a
concentration camp. According to some survivors, he was buried in a mass
grave.

   Mandel′shtam's poetry turns world culture into an intimate personal diary
in which Ovid, Dante, Bach, Shakespeare, Darwin, Lamarck, Goethe are emotions, events, contemporaries. In Mandel′shtam's world, an individual lives in
intense awareness of inspired affinity with the universe, and the line between
today and history almost does not exist; what exists is human dignity, honor and

other "unwavering values " towering over "the tedious mistakes of the centuries."

One of Mandel'shtam's sayings (known through his wife's memoirs) is quoted whenever the topic of Russian poetry in the Soviet epoch emerges:

Поэзию уважа́ют то́лько у нас—за неё убива́ют.

Only in our country do they really respect poetry: they kill for it.

16.1. **«О́браз твой, мучи́тельный и зы́бкий ...»** "Thine image, torturous and vacillating ..." (1912):

> **О́браз твой, мучи́тельный и зы́бкий**   🔊)) **2-254**
> **Я не мог в тума́не осяза́ть.**
> **«Го́споди!»—сказа́л я по оши́бке,**
> **Сам того́ не ду́мая сказа́ть.**
> **Бо́жье и́мя, как больша́я пти́ца,**
> **Вы́летело из мое́й груди́.**
> **Впереди́ густо́й тума́н клуби́тся**
> **И пуста́я кле́тка позади́.**

Your image, tormenting and vacillating, I could not touch in the fog. "O, Lord!" I said inadvertently, not intending to say what I said. God's name, like a huge bird, flew out of my breast. In front a dense fog swirls, behind is an empty cage.

16.2. From **«Есть це́нностей незы́блемая ска́ла ...»** "There is an unshakeable scale of values ..." (1914):

> **Есть це́нностей незы́блемая ска́ла**   🔊)) **2-255**
> **Над ску́чными оши́бками веко́в.**

There is an unshakeable scale of values above the tedious mistakes of the centuries.

16.3. From **«Tristia»** (1918):

> **Всё бы́ло встарь, всё повтори́тся сно́ва**   🔊)) **2-256**
> **И сла́док нам лишь узнава́нья миг.**

Everything has already been in the past, everything will repeat itself anew, and the only sweet thing for us is the glimpse of recognition.

16.4. **«Бессо́нница. Гоме́р. Туги́е паруса́ ...»** "Insomnia. Homer. Taut sails ..." (1915):

16.4.1.

> **Бессо́нница. Гоме́р. Туги́е паруса́.**   🔊)) **2-257**
> **Я спи́сок корабле́й прочёл до середи́ны.**
> **Сей дли́нный вы́водок, сей по́езд журавли́ный,**
> **Что над Элла́дою когда́-то подня́лся.**

Insomnia. Homer. Taut sails. I read the list of ships up to the middle, this long brood, this train of cranes that rose one day over Hellas.

16.4.2.

🔊 2-258

Куда́ плывёте вы? Когда́ бы не Еле́на,
Что Тро́я вам, ахе́йские мужи́?

И мо́ре, и Гоме́р, всё дви́жется любо́вью.
Кого́ же слу́шать мне? И вот Гоме́р молчи́т,
И мо́ре Чёрное, вити́йствуя, шуми́т
И с тя́жким гро́хотом подхо́дит к изголо́вью.

Where are you sailing? If it were not for Helen, what would Troy be to you, Achaean men? Both the sea and Homer are set in motion by love. Whom shall I listen to? And here Homer falls into silence, and the Black Sea, soliloquizing, reaches my pillow heavily rumbling.

16.5. «Ла́сточка» "The Swallow" (1920):

🔊 2-259

Я сло́во позабы́л, что я хоте́л сказа́ть,
Слепа́я ла́сточка в черто́г тене́й вернётся,
На кры́льях сре́занных, с прозра́чными игра́ть.
В беспа́мятстве ночна́я песнь поётся.

Не слы́шно птиц. Бессме́ртник не цветёт.
Прозра́чны гри́вы табуна́ ночно́го.
В сухо́й реке́ пусто́й челно́к плывёт.
Среди́ кузне́чиков беспа́мятствует сло́во. […]

I forgot something that I wanted to say. A blind swallow will return on its severed wings to the palace of shadows, to play with the transparent ones. In oblivion a nocturnal song is sung. No birds are heard. Immortelle doesn't bloom. The manes of a nighttime herd of horses are transparent. In the dry river floats an empty boat. The word lost consciousness among the grasshoppers.

16.6. «Я верну́лся в мой го́род …» "I returned to my city …" (1930)

16.6.1.

🔊 2-260

Я верну́лся в мой го́род, знако́мый до слёз,
До опу́хших прожи́лок, до де́тских желёз.
Ты верну́лся сюда́, так глота́й же скоре́й
Ры́бий жир ленингра́дских речны́х фонаре́й.

I returned to my city, familiar to the point of tears, swollen veins, a child's glands. You returned here, so hurry—swallow the codliver oil of the Leningrad river lanterns.

16.6.2.

Петербу́рг, я ещё не хочу́ умира́ть.
У тебя́ телефо́нов мои́х номера́,
Петербу́рг, у меня́ ещё есть адреса́,
По кото́рым найду́ мертвецо́в голоса́.

(( )) 2-261

Petersburg, I don't want to die yet. You still have my telephone numbers. Petersburg, I still have addresses by which I will find the voices of the dead.

17. BORIS LEONIDOVICH PASTERNAK (1890–1960)

БОРИ́С ЛЕОНИ́ДОВИЧ ПАСТЕРНА́К

No other Russian poet has such reverence for the miracle of life as Pasternak. Like St. Francis of Assisi, famous for a sermon to birds in which he addressed them as "my sisters the birds," Pasternak talks to rain, trees and clouds and calls life "My Sister Life." His complex associations and metaphors, especially in his early poetry, are not always easy to comprehend, but even then their sweeping passion is always effective.

Fig. 2-54.

While Pasternak was always "ideologically suspicious" to the Soviet authorities, he was officially recognized as a great master even though often criticized for lack of ideological enthusiasm. His poetry has only recently been studied in schools and many Soviet people heard his name for the first time in 1958, when a huge political scandal broke out around his novel *Doctor Zhivago,* which was awarded the Nobel Prize. Pasternak's dacha in Peredelkino (the writers' village near Moscow) is now a revered memorial museum.

Pasternak also wrote works in prose, among which the most important are: «**Де́тство Лю́верс**» *Zhenya Luvers' Childhood*, the autobiographical «**Охра́нная гра́мота**» *Safe Conduct* and the novel «**До́ктор Жива́го**» *Doctor Zhivago.*

17.1. «**Февра́ль. Доста́ть черни́л и пла́кать!**» "February. Get the ink and cry!" (1912):

Февра́ль. Доста́ть черни́л и пла́кать!
Писа́ть о феврале́ навзры́д,
Пока́ грохо́чущая сля́коть
Весно́ю чёрною гори́т.

(( )) 2-262

February. Get the ink and cry! Write about February sobbing violently, while the thundering slush is burning with the black spring.

Illustration: Headline in *Нóвое врéмя*, Feb. 1997: «Арткалендáрь февраля́ … Достáть черни́л и плáкать. Сегóдняшняя афи́ша посвящена́ в основнóм литератýре». "Art-calendar for February … Get the ink and cry. Today's poster is dedicated mainly to literature."

17.2. «Пиры́» "Feasts" (1913):

🔊)) 2-263

Пью гóречь туберóз, небéс осéнних гóречь
И в них твои́х измéн горя́щую струю́.
Пью гóречь вечерóв, ночéй и лю́дных сбóрищ,
Рыдáющей строфы́ сырýю гóречь пью.

I drink the raw bitterness of tuberoses, the raw bitterness of the autumnal sky and in it the burning stream of your betrayals. I drink the bitterness of evenings, of the nights and crowded gatherings, I drink the damp bitterness of the sobbing stanza.

17.3. «Мéльницы» "Windmills" (1915):

🔊)) 2-264

[…]
Тогдá просыпáются мéльничные тéни,
Их мы́сли ворóчаются, как жерновá.
И они́ огрóмны, как мы́сли гéниев,
И несоразмéрны, как их правá.

Then the windmills' shadows awaken, their thoughts turn like millstones; and they are immense like thoughts of geniuses and disproportional like their rights.

17.4. «Мáрбург» "Marburg" (1916):

17.4.1.

🔊)) 2-265

Я вздрáгивал. Я загорáлся и гас,
Я тря́сся. Я сдéлал сейчáс предложéнье,—
Но пóздно, я сдрéйфил, и вот мне—откáз.
Как жаль её слёз! Я свято́го блажéнней!

I shuddered. A fire would burn me and die out. I shook all over. I've just made a proposal. Too late, I chickened out, and was rejected. How sorry I am for her tears! I am more blessed than a saint.

17.4.2.

🔊)) 2-266

В тот день всю тебя́, от гребёнок до ног,
Как трáгик в прови́нции дрáму Шекспи́рову,
Носи́л я с собóю и знал назубóк,
Шатáлся по гóроду и репети́ровал.

That day I carried with me all of you, from combs to feet, like a provincial tragic actor carries around a Shakespeare drama; I knew you by heart, I roamed the town and rehearsed you.

17.5. «**Про э́ти стихи́**» "About These Verses" (1917):

17.5.1.

🔊 **2-267**

> **На тротуа́рах истолку́**
> **С стекло́м и со́лнцем попола́м.**
> **Зимо́й откро́ю потолку́**
> **И дам чита́ть сыры́м угла́м.**
>
> **Задеклами́рует черда́к**
> **С покло́ном ра́мам и зиме́.**

I will pound them on the pavement into tiniest pieces, half-and-half with glass and the sun; when winter comes, I will open them up for the ceiling and let the damp corners read them. The attic will burst into declamation, with a bow to the window-frames and the winter.

17.5.2.

🔊 **2-268**

> **[...]**
> **В кашне́, ладо́нью заслоня́сь,**
> **Сквозь фо́ртку кри́кну детворе́:**
> **—Како́е, ми́лые, у нас**
> **Тысячеле́тье на дворе́?**
>
> **Кто тро́пку к две́ри протори́л,**
> **К дыре́, засы́панной крупо́й,**
> **Пока́ я с Ба́йроном кури́л,**
> **Пока́ я пил с Эдга́ром По?**

Wrapped in a scarf, shielding my face with my palm, I will shout to the children through the window vent: "What millennium is it, my dears, that we have out there? Who beat a path to my door, to a hole covered with sleet, while I was smoking with Byron, while I was drinking with Edgar [Allan] Poe?"

Illustration: Headline in **Кура́нты**, Aug. 1996: «**Како́е, ми́лые, у нас тысяче-ле́тье во дворе́?**»

17.6. «**Сестра́ моя́—жизнь ...**» "Life is my sister ..." (1917):

17.6.1.

🔊 **2-269**

> **Сестра́ моя́—жизнь и сего́дня в разли́ве,**
> **Расши́блась весе́нним дождём обо всех,**
> **Но лю́ди в брело́ках высо́ко брюзгли́вы**
> **И ве́жливо жа́лят, как зме́и в овсе́.**

Life is my sister, and today in its flood it broke, like a spring rain, against everyone. But people wearing trinkets are condescendingly grumpy; they politely sting you, like snakes in the oats.

17.6.2.

🔊 2-270   **У ста́рших на э́то свой есть резо́ны.**
Беспо́рно, беспо́рно смешо́н твой резо́н,
Что в гро́зу лило́вы глаза́ и газо́ны
И па́хнет сыро́й резедо́й горизо́нт.

Grownups have their reasons for that. And doubtless, doubtless, your reason is ludicrous: that during a thunderstorm eyes and lawns are of lilac color, and the horizon smells of damp mignonettes [famous for their strong and pleasant scent—see Gerhart, *The Russian's World*, 2nd ed.].

17.7. **«Сложа́ вёсла»** "Crossing the Oars" (1917):

🔊 2-271   **Ло́дка коло́тится в со́нной груди́,**
И́вы нави́сли, целу́ют в ключи́цы,
В ло́кти, в уклю́чины,—о, погоди́,
Это ведь мо́жет со вся́ким случи́ться!

A boat thumps in my sleepy chest. The willows bend over, kissing me on the collarbones, on the elbows, on oar locks—oh, wait! This, you know, can happen to anyone.

17.8. **«Звёзды ле́том»** "Stars in the Summertime (1917):

17.8.1.

🔊 2-272   **[...]**
Тишина́, ты—лу́чшее
Из всего́, что слы́шал.

Silence, you are the best of everything that I've heard.

17.8.2.

🔊 2-273   **[...]**
Ве́тер ро́зу про́бует
Приподня́ть по про́сьбе
Губ, воло́с и о́буви,
Подоло́в и про́звищ.

The wind tries to lift a rose, obeying the request of lips, hair and shoes, hems and nicknames.

17.9. **«Как усыпи́тельна жизнь!»** "How somnolent is life!" (1917):

17.9.1.

🔊 2-274   **Как усыпи́тельна жизнь!**
Как открове́нья бессо́нны!

How somnolent is life! How sleepless are revelations!

17.9.2.

Я с ни́ми не знако́м. 🔊 2-275
Я по́слан бо́гом му́чить
Себя́, родны́х и тех,
Кото́рых му́чить грех.

I am not acquainted with them. I am sent by God to torture myself, my
relatives and those whom it is a sin to torture.

17.9.3.

Чтоб разрыда́ться, мне 🔊 2-276
Не так уж мно́го на́до,—
Дово́льно мух в окне́.

I don't need all that much to burst into sobs—it is enough for me to see
flies on the window-glass.

17.10. «Пла́чущий сад» "Crying Garden" (1917):

Ужа́сный!—Ка́пнет и вслу́шается: 🔊 2-277
Всё он ли оди́н на све́те
Мнёт ве́тку в окне́, как кру́жевце,
Или есть свиде́тель.

The horrible one! It'll drop a drop and listen hard to see if it is still
alone in the world, crumpling a branch in the window like a piece of
lace, or if there is a witness.

17.11. «Ро́слый стрело́к, осторо́жный охо́тник ...» "Tall shooter, careful
hunter ..." (1928):

Ро́слый стрело́к, осторо́жный охо́тник, 🔊 2-278
При́зрак с ружьём на разли́ве души́!
Не добира́й меня со́тым до со́тни,
Чу́вству на корм по частя́м не кроши́.

Дай мне подня́ться над сме́ртью позо́рной.
С но́чи оде́нь меня в та́льник и лёд.
У́тром спугни́ с мочажи́ны озёрной.
Це́лься, всё ко́нчено! Бей меня в лёт.

За высоту́ ж э́той зво́нкой разлу́ки,
О пренебре́гнутые мои́,
Благодарю́ и целу́ю вас, ру́ки
Ро́дины, ро́бости, дру́жбы, семьи́.

Tall shooter, careful hunter, apparition with a rifle at the flood of my
soul! Do not make me the hundredth to round your hundred; do not
crush me to pieces to feed, piece by piece, to your feelings. Let me rise

above shameful death. At night, dress me in willow thicket and ice. In the morning, scare me off from the lake marshes, aim, and that will be all! Shoot me in flight. And for the height of this resounding parting, O my neglected, I thank you and kiss you, the hands of the Motherland, of shyness, of friendship, of family.

17.12. «Зимняя ночь» "Winter Night" (1946):

◀)) 2-279

Мело́, мело́ по всей земле́
Во все преде́лы.
Свеча́ горе́ла на столе́,
Свеча́ горе́ла.

Как ле́том ро́ем мошкара́
Лети́т на пла́мя,
Слета́лись хло́пья со двора́
К око́нной ра́ме.

Мете́ль лепи́ла на стекле́
Кружки́ и стре́лы.
Свеча́ горе́ла на столе́,
Свеча́ горе́ла.

На озарённый потоло́к
Ложи́лись те́ни,
Скреще́нья рук, скреще́нья ног,
Судьбы́ скреще́нья.

И па́дали два башмачка́
Со сту́ком на́ пол.
И воск слеза́ми с ночника́
На пла́тье ка́пал.

И всё теря́лось в сне́жной мгле,
Седо́й и бе́лой.
Свеча́ горе́ла на столе́,
Свеча́ горе́ла.

На све́чку ду́ло из угла́,
И жар собла́зна
Вздыма́л, как а́нгел, два крыла́
Крестообра́зно.

Мело́ весь ме́сяц в феврале́
И то и де́ло
Свеча́ горе́ла на столе́,
Свеча́ горе́ла.

The blizzard swept and swept all over the earth, into all lands. The candle was burning on the table, the candle was burning. As a swarm of midges in the summer flies into the flame, the snowflakes came flying from the yard to the window-frame. The blizzard shaped circles and arrows on the glass. The candle was burning on the table, the candle was burning. Onto the lit ceiling the shadows fell, the crossings of arms, the crossings of legs, the crossings of destinies. And two shoes fell on the floor with a knock. And the wax from the nightlight dripped its tears on the dress. And everything lost itself in a snow haze, grey and white. The candle was burning on the table, the candle was burning. A draft blew on the candle from the corner, and the flame of temptation raised like an angel two wings, cross-like. The blizzard swept all month long in February. And now and then the candle was burning on the table, the candle was burning.

Illustration: Moscow poet Vera Pavlova describes lovers trying to imitate the experience of Pasternak's heroes:

🔊)) 2-280

Свеча́ горе́ла на столе́,
а мы стара́лись так уле́чься,
чтоб на како́й-то потоло́к
ложи́лись те́ни. Бесполе́зно!
Ра́зве что сто́я над столо́м,
о стол рука́ми опира́ясь
и нависа́я над свечо́й,—
так—да. Но то́лько рук скреще́нья.

The candle was burning on the table, and we kept trying to lie in such a way that onto some kind of ceiling would fall our shadows. That was useless! Only by standing over the table, pushing against the table with our hands and hovering over the candle—in that position: yes. But only the crossings of the hands.

17.13. «**Ночь**» "Night" (1956):

🔊)) 2-281

Не спи, не спи, худо́жник,
Не предава́йся сну,—
Ты—ве́чности зало́жник
У вре́мени в плену́!

Don't sleep, don't sleep, artist, do not indulge in sleep–you are a hostage of eternity in the captivity of time.

17.14. «Во всём мне хочется дойти …» "In everything I wish to reach …" (1956):

◀»)) 2-282

Во всём мне хо́чется дойти́
До са́мой су́ти.
В рабо́те, в по́исках пути́,
В серде́чной сму́те.

In everything I wish to reach the very essence—in my work, in search of my path, in confusion of the heart.

17.15. «Люби́ть ины́х тяжёлый крест …» "To love some people is a heavy cross …":

◀»)) 2-283

Люби́ть ины́х тяжёлый крест,
А ты прекра́сна без изви́лин.

To love some people is a heavy cross, but you are beautiful without convolutions.

17.16. «В больни́це» "In the Hospital" (1956).

17.16.1.

◀»)) 2-284

О Го́споди, как соверше́нны
Дела́ Твои́,—ду́мал больно́й,—
Посте́ли, и лю́ди, и сте́ны,
Ночь сме́рти и го́род ночно́й.

Fig. 2-55. Pasternak's grave in Peredelkino

"O Lord, how perfect are all Your deeds," thought the patient, "the beds, the people, the walls, the night of death and the city at night."

17.16.2.

◀»)) 2-285

Я при́нял снотво́рного до́зу
И пла́чу, плато́к теребя́.
О Бо́же, волне́ния слёзы
Меша́ют мне ви́деть Тебя́.

I took a dose of sleeping pills and am crying, fidgeting with the hand-kerchief. O Lord, tears of agitation prevent me from seeing You.

17.16.3.

Конча́ясь в больни́чной посте́ли,
Я чу́вствую рук твои́х жар.
Ты де́ржишь меня́, как изде́лье,
И пря́чешь, как пе́рстень, в футля́р.

🔊 2-286

Expiring in the hospital bed, I feel the heat of Your hands. You are holding me like something handmade, and are hiding me, like a precious ring, in a case.

17.17. «Га́млет» "Hamlet" (1954):

Гул зати́х. Я вы́шел на подмо́стки.
Прислоня́сь к дверно́му косяку́,
Я ловлю́ в далёком отголо́ске,
Что случи́тся на моём веку́.

🔊 2-287

На меня́ наста́влен су́мрак но́чи
Ты́сячью бино́клей на оси́.
Если то́лько мо́жно, А́вва О́тче,
Ча́шу э́ту ми́мо пронеси́.

Я люблю́ твой за́мысел упря́мый
И игра́ть согла́сен э́ту роль.
Но сейча́с идёт друга́я дра́ма,
И на э́тот раз меня́ уво́ль.

Но проду́ман распоря́док де́йствий,
И неотврати́м коне́ц пути́.
Я оди́н, всё то́нет в фарисе́йстве.
Жизнь прожи́ть — не по́ле перейти́.

The hum quieted down. I came out on the boards of the stage. Leaning against the doorpost, I am trying to catch in a distant echo what will happen in my life. The darkness of the night aims at me with a thousand binoculars on their axis. Grant, Abba Father, that this cup pass me by. I love Your stubborn design, I agree to play this role, but another drama is taking place now, and this time spare me. But the order of acts is thought through and the end of my path is inevitable. I am alone, everything is drowning in Pharisaism. To live life is not as simple as to cross a field.

18. Marina Ivanovna Tsvetaeva (1892–1941)

Марина Ивановна Цветаева

2-288

- Мне так же трудно до сих пор
  Вообразить тебя умершей,
  Как скопидомкой мильонершей
  Средь голодающих сестёр.
  (Пастернак)

  I still have trouble imagining you dead; to me it is the same as imagining you a miser-millionaire among your starving sisters.
  (Pasternak)

Fig. 2-56.

Marina Tsvetaeva's early love lyrics are full of untamed romantic passion and bewitching melodious rhythms; the passions of the mature Tsvetaeva are strengthened by epic and folklore dimensions. Her life was difficult and tragic. Nadezhda Mandelshtam wrote about her: "I don't know a fate more horrible than that of Marina Tsvetaeva."

Tsvetaeva was born in Moscow. Her father, a professor at Moscow University and a director of the Rumiantsevskii Museum, devoted his life to the creation of a Museum of Fine Arts (now the Pushkin Museum). Tsvetaeva's mother, a culturally refined person and a talented pianist, lived for her children. Tsvetaeva described her happy childhood in the autobiographical stories **«Мать и музыка»** "My Mother and Music" and **«Дом у Старого Пимена»** "The House at Old Pimen [Street]." Tsvetaeva began writing poetry at six, not only in Russian but also French and German; her first book of poetry, **«Вечерний альбом»** *Evening Album*, was published in 1910 and was immediately noticed and appreciated. In 1941, fleeing World War II and the Nazis' bombing of Moscow, Tsvetaeva and her son evacuated to Elabuga. There, finding herself in complete isolation, without money or job, a desperate Tsvetaeva committed suicide by hanging herself, having written letters to friends entrusting her orphan son to their care.

18.1. **«Моим стихам, написанным так рано»** "My poems, written so early …" (1913)

2-289

Моим стихам, написанным так рано,
Что и не знала я, что я—поэт,
Сорвавшимся, как брызги из фонтана,
Как искры из ракет,

Ворвавшимся, как маленькие черти,
В святилище, где сон и фимиам,
Моим стихам о юности и смерти,
—Нечитанным стихам!—

Разбро́санным в пыли́ по магази́нам,
(Где их никто́ не брал и не берёт!)
Мои́м стиха́м, как драгоце́нным ви́нам,
Наста́нет свой черёд.

My poems, written so early that I didn't even know that I was a poet,
for my poems flying off, like splashes fly from a fountain, like sparks
from fireworks; for my poems, bursting, like little devils, into a sanctu-
ary full of incense and sleep; my poems about youth and death—my
unread poems!—lying around in the dust in the stores (where no one
bought them and still no one buys them!), my poems, like precious
wines, will have their day.

18.2. **«Мне нра́вится, что вы больны́ не мной ...»** "I like it that you are
lovesick not over me ..." (1915):

Мне нра́вится, что вы больны́ не мной,   🔊 **2-290**
Мне нра́вится, что я больна́ не ва́ми,
Что никогда́ тяжёлый шар земно́й
Не уплывёт под на́шими нога́ми.

I like it that you are [love-] sick not over me, I like it that I am [love-]
sick not over you, that the heavy globe will never float away from under our feet.

18.3. From the cycle **«Бессо́нница»** *Insomnia.* **«Вот опя́ть окно́ ... »** "Here
again is a window ..." (1916):

Вот опя́ть окно́,   🔊 **2-291**
Где опя́ть не спят.
Мо́жет—пьют вино́,
Мо́жет—так сидя́т.
Или про́сто—рук
Не разни́мут дво́е.
В ка́ждом до́ме, друг,
Есть окно́ тако́е.

Крик разлу́к и встреч,
Ты, окно́ в ночи́!
Мо́жет—со́тни свеч,
Мо́жет—три свечи́ ...
Нет и нет уму́
Моему́—поко́я.
И в моём дому́
Завело́сь тако́е.
Помоли́сь, дружо́к, за бессо́нный дом,
За окно́ с огнём!

Here again is a window, where they again don't sleep. Maybe they are drinking wine, maybe just sitting. Or they're simply a couple who can't take their hands apart. Every house, my friend, has a window like that. There the darkness is lit not by lamps or candles–but by sleepless eyes. You, the window in the night, you are a cry of partings and meetings! Maybe there are a hundred candles [meaning a celebration], maybe three candles [meaning death]. I can't get it off my mind. My house, too, has a window like that. Pray, my dear friend, for a sleepless house, for a window with a light.

18.4. The poem **«Никто́ ничего́ не о́тнял ...»** "Nobody took away any thing ..." (1916) is addressed to Osip Mandelshtam.

◀)) 2-282 **Никто́ ничего́ не о́тнял—**
     Мне сла́достно, что мы врозь!
     Целу́ю вас через со́тни
     Разъединя́ющих вёрст.

     Я зна́ю, наш дар—нера́вен.
     Мой го́лос впервы́е—тих.
     Что вам, молодо́й Держа́вин,
     Мой невоспи́танный стих!

Nobody took away anything—It is sweet to me, that we are apart! I kiss you through hundreds of separating miles. I know our talents are not equal. My voice for the first time is quiet. What is my bad-mannered verse to you, a young Derzhavin!

18.5. **«Ты запроки́дываешь го́лову ...»** "You throw back your head ..." (1916):

◀)) 2-283 **Ты запроки́дываешь го́лову—**
     Зате́м что ты горде́ц и враль.
     Како́го спу́тника весёлого
     Привёл мне ны́нешний февра́ль!

You throw back your head, because you're arrogant and a story-teller. What a jolly companion this February has brought me!

18.6. From the cycle **«Стихи́ о Москве́»** *Verses About Moscow* (1916).

18.6.1. The first poem in the cycle is addressed to Tsvetaeva's daughter Alia :

◀)) 2-284 **Облака́—вокру́г,**
     Купола́—вокру́г.
     Надо всей Москво́й—
     Ско́лько хва́тит рук!—
     Возношу́ тебя́, бре́мя лу́чшее,
     Деревцо́ моё
     Невесо́мое!

Clouds are all around, cupolas are all around; I am raising you up, over the whole of Moscow—as high as my arms will stretch—you, my best burden, my weightless little tree!

18.6.2.

8.   ◀)) 2-295

Москва́! Како́й огро́мный
Странноприи́мный дом!
Всяк на Руси́—бездо́мный.
Мы все к тебе́ придём.

Moscow! What a huge homeless shelter! Everyone in Russia is homeless. We all will come to you.

18.6.3.

9.   ◀)) 2-296

Кра́сною ки́стью
Ряби́на зажгла́сь.
Па́дали ли́стья.
Я роди́ла́сь.

Спо́рили со́тни
Колоколо́в.
День был суббо́тний:
Иоа́нн Богосло́в.

Мне и доны́не
Хо́чется грызть
Жа́ркой ряби́ны
Го́рькую кисть.

A rowan-tree[2] was set afire by clusters of berries. Its leaves fell. There *I* was born. Hundreds of church-bells argued. The day was a Saturday: St. John the Divine. To this day I still feel like nibbling a bitter cluster of hot rowan berries.

18.7. From the cycle «**Стихи́ к Бло́ку**» *Verses Addressed to Blok* (1916):

18.7.1.   ◀)) 2-297

Ду́мали—челове́к!
И умере́ть заста́вили.
Умер тепе́рь. Наве́к.
Пла́чьте о мёртвом а́нгеле!

You thought he was a man. And you made him die. Now he has died. Forever. Cry for the dead angel!

---

[2] Mountain ash in American English.

18.7.2.

🔊 2-288
**О, погляди́те — как
Ве́ки ввали́лись тёмные!
О, погляди́те — как
Кры́лья его полома́ны!**

Oh, look how his eyelids are sunken! Oh, look how his wings are broken!

18.8. From the cycle «**Ахма́товой**» *To Akhmatova* (1916):

18.8.1.

🔊 2-289
**1.
О му́за пла́ча, прекра́снейшая из муз!
О ты, шально́е исча́дие но́чи бе́лой!
Ты чёрную насыла́ешь мете́ль на Русь,
И во́пли твои́ вонза́ются в нас, как стре́лы.**

O Muse of lament, the most beautiful of Muses! O you, mad fiend of the white night! You send over Russia a black blizzard. And your wails pierce us like arrows.

18.8.2.

🔊 2-300
**4.
Ты со́лнце в вы́си мне за́стишь,
Все звёзды в твое́й горсти́!
Ах, е́сли бы — две́ри на́стежь —
Как ве́тер к тебе́ войти́!**

You obstruct the sun in the sky for me, all the stars are in the hollow of your hand! Oh, if only–doors ajar!–I could come to you like a wind.

18.9. «**Не самозва́нка — я пришла́ домо́й**» "Not an imposter — I came home …" (1918):

🔊 2-301
**1.
Не самозва́нка — я пришла́ домо́й,
И не служа́нка — мне не на́до хле́ба.
Я — стра́сть твоя́, воскре́сный о́тдых твой,
Твой день седьмо́й, твоё седьмо́е не́бо.**

Not an imposter — I came home, not a maid — I don't need bread. I am your passion, your Sunday rest, your seventh day, your seventh heaven.

18.10. «**Кто со́здан из ка́мня, кто со́здан из гли́ны**» "Some are created of stone, some are created of clay …" (1920):

Кто со́здан из ка́мня, кто со́здан из гли́ны, —
А я серебрю́сь и сверка́ю!
Мне де́ло — изме́на, мне и́мя — Мари́на,
Я — бре́нная пе́на морска́я.

🔊 2-302

Some are created of stone, some are created of clay, but I shine with silver and sparkle! What I do is change, my name is Marina, I am a fleeting sea-foam.

18.11. From the cycle «Пе́сенки» *Songs* (1920) «Вчера́ ещё в глаза́ гляде́л ...» "Only yesterday he looked into my eyes ...":

Вчера́ ещё в глаза́ гляде́л,
А ны́нче — всё ко́сится в сто́рону!
Вчера́ ещё до птиц сиде́л, —
Все жа́воронки ны́нче — во́роны!

🔊 2-303

Я глу́пая, а ты умён,
Живо́й, а я остолбене́лая.
О во́пль же́нщин всех времён:
«Мой ми́лый, что тебе́ я сде́лала?»

Only yesterday he looked into my eyes, and today he keeps looking away! Only yesterday he sat up till birdsong, today all the larks are crows! I am stupid, you are smart; you are alive, I'm turned to a pillar. O wail of women of all times: "My darling, what have I done to you?!"

18.12. «Есть не́кий час — как сбро́шенная кла́жа ...» "There is a certain hour ..." (1921):

Есть не́кий час — как сбро́шенная кла́жа:
Когда́ в себе́ горды́ню укроти́м.
Час учени́чества — он в жи́зни ка́ждой
Торже́ственно-неотврати́м.

🔊 2-304

There is a certain hour like a discarded load, when we tame our pride. The hour of becoming a pupil: in every life it's solemnly inevitable.

18.13. «Ты, меня́ люби́вший фа́льшью ...» "You, who loved me with false ness ..." (1923):

Ты, меня́ люби́вший фа́льшью
И́стины — и пра́вдой лжи,
Ты, меня́ люби́вший — да́льше
Не́куда! — За рубежи́!
Ты, меня́ люби́вший до́льше
Вре́мени. — Десни́цы взмах! —
Ты меня́ не лю́бишь бо́льше:
И́стина в пяти́ слова́х.

🔊 2-305

You, who loved me with the falseness of truth—and with the truth of falseness; you, who loved me beyond—beyond the impossible!—beyond all the limits! You, who loved me longer than time itself. A wave of your right arm; you don't love me anymore: the truth is in these five words.

18.14. From **«Рас-стоя́ние: вёрсты, ми́ли ...»** "Dis-stance: versts, miles ..." (To Boris Pasternak) (1925):

🔊 2-306

Рас-стоя́ние: вёрсты, ми́ли ...
Нас рас-ста́вили, рас-сади́ли,
Чтобы ти́хо себя́ вели́
По двум ра́зным конца́м земли́.

Dis-stance: versts, miles ... They placed us apart, they sat us apart, so that we would behave sedately at opposite ends of the earth.

18.15. From the cycle **«Поэ́ты»** *Poets* (1923):

🔊 2-307

1.
Поэ́т—издалека́ заво́дит речь.
Поэ́та—далеко́ заво́дит речь.

A poet takes his speech from afar. A poet's speech takes him far.

19. KONSTANTIN SIMONOV (1915–79)   КОНСТАНТИ́Н СИ́МОНОВ

Konstantin Simonov was popular both as a poet and a fiction writer. His most well-known novel is **«Дни и но́чи»** *Days and Nights*, about the seige of Stalingrad. He was adept at presenting the official view of the world in his writings, and for his labors on behalf of the state he received six Stalin Prizes and one Lenin Prize. He was the conservative editor of the literary journal **Но́вый мир** *New World* from 1946–50 and 1954–58. He is best known for two things: his attacks on writers such as Il'ia Ehrenburg and Anna Akhmatova, and his 1941 poem, **«Жди меня́ и я верну́сь»** *Wait for me and I'll come back.* The poem was wildly popular during World War II, though today most Russians can quote only the first two lines. They use them, jokingly and not, when asking someone else to wait for them:

🔊 2-308

Жди меня́ и я верну́сь.
То́лько о́чень жди,
Жди, когда́ наво́дят грусть
Жёлтые дожди́,

Жди, когда́ снега́ мету́т,
Жди, когда́ жара́,
Жди, когда́ други́х не ждут,
Позабы́в вчера́.

Жди, когда́ из да́льних мест
Пи́сем не придёт,
Жди, когда́ уж надое́ст
Всем, кто вме́сте ждёт.

Wait for me and I'll come back; but wait very hard. Wait when the yellow rains bring you sorrow,wait when the snow flies, wait in a heat wave, wait when others do not wait, having forgotten yesterday. Wait when no letters come from that far-off place, wait even when everyone else is sick of waiting.

20. IOSIF BRODSKY (1940–96)

Ио́сиф Бро́дский

Brodsky was the center of a group of talented young non-conformist Leningrad poets (Bobyshev, Naiman, Rein). They were great admirers of Anna Akhmatova and her personal friends. In 1964 Brodsky was arrested and tried for "parasitism," the official pretext for getting someone too independent into line. He was sentenced to five years hard labor, a sentence later commuted to exile in a village in the Arkhangelsk region under pressure from the literary elite. In

Fig. 2-57.

1972 Brodsky was expelled from the Soviet Union and settled in the United States, where he taught Russian literature in various universities and continued to write poetry. In 1987 he was awarded the Nobel Prize. He died in New York and was buried in his beloved Venice.

From «Ста́нсы» "Stanzas" (1962):

🔊 2-309

Ни страны́, ни пого́ста
не хочу́ выбира́ть.
На Васи́льевский о́стров
я приду́ умира́ть ...

I don't want to choose either country or cemetery. I will come to die on Vasilievsky Island.

Illustration:

(a) After Brodsky's death the Russian government approached his widow with the request that his body be transported to Russia and buried in Petersburg, on Vasilievsky Island, treating the lines above as Brodsky's will. The widow denied their request.

(b) These lines are quoted in the article **«Бро́дский в земле́ Вене́ции»** "Brodsky is in the Earth of Venice," describing his funeral (***Аргуме́нты и фа́кты***, 1997).

(c) From Dovlatov's (1941–90) "Solo on an Underwood":

◀))) 2-310

У Ио́сифа Бро́дского есть таки́е стро́чки: «Ни страны́, ни пого́ста не хочу́ выбира́ть, // На Васи́льевский о́стров я приду́ умира́ть …» Так вот, Бакаю́тов спроси́л у Гру́бина:

Ты не зна́ешь, где живёт Бро́дский?
—Не зна́ю. Умира́ть хо́дит на Васи́льевский …

Iosef Brodsky has the following lines: "I don't want to choose either country or cemetery. I will come to die on Vasilievsky Island." So, Bakaiutov asks Grubin: "Do you know by any chance where Brodsky lives?" "Have no idea. I only know that he regularly comes to die on Vasilievsky Island."

CONCLUSION

No one can write down all the knowledge that a native speaker of a language has about a subject, and the author and editors have included herein that which is *most* common of the common knowledge. You may well hear Russians quote from Pushkin's **«На хо́лмах Гру́зии»** "On the Georgian Hills," or his **«Бе́сы»** "The Devils," and **«Не пой, краса́вица, при мне»** "Don't Sing in front of Me, My Beauty." Some Russians will know the poetry of Gumilev, Bagritskii, and Zabolotskii. Many may quote Evtushenko or Voznesenskii. (These authors are listed here only as examples.)

<table>
<tr><td>

Quoting Russian Prose

</td><td>

3

</td><td>

Ру́сская про́за в цита́тах

</td></tr>
</table>

Valentina Zaitseva

1. FOLKLORE*

ФОЛЬКЛО́Р

Russian folklore is one of the major sources of common knowledge. Its language evolved from ancient oral tradition and embodies all that is distinctly Russian, both culturally and structurally, which explains why it is often so difficult to translate. Here are some of the formulaic expressions from fairy-tales regularly used in poetry, literary prose and a variety of other oral and written genres—from a chat with a friend to a newspaper article.

1.0. Names of Characters in Fairy-tales Often Used to Describe Someone

1.01. **Ива́н-дура́к (Ива́нушка-дурачо́к)** John the Fool/Simple Simon. A stupid ◀))) **3-1** good-for-nothing in the eyes of others, in some interpretations **Иван-дура́к** gets the princess and a kingdom because he acts out of the goodness of his heart. He is usually the youngest brother, not too bright, and mistreated by his older brothers. He gets his rewards with the assistance of some magic helpers. Variant: **Еме́ля-дурачо́к** Emelia the Simpleton.

1.02. **Ба́ба-Яга́, костяна́я нога́** Baba-Yaga Boney Leg. A witch with a mixture ◀))) **3-2** of comical and sinister features; she flies around in her iron mortar and lives in the **избу́шка на ку́рьих но́жках**—a shabby hut placed on gigantic chicken legs.

Use: humorous reference to someone's appearance: "In this scarf I look like Baba Yaga." Mentioning Baba Yaga's name to children is supposed to scare them into obedience. Hence the joke:

> —Е́сли ты не бу́дешь есть ма́нную ка́шу, то я позову́ Ба́бу-Ягу́. ◀))) **3-2**
> —Мам, неуже́ли ты ду́маешь, что она́ бу́дет её есть?

"If you won't eat your cream of wheat (cereal), I'll call Baba-Yaga."
"Mama, do you really think she'd eat it?"
(Russian children do not like to eat their **ма́нная ка́ша**.)

---

* See also Chapter 4, 2–12.

Fig. 3-1.   **Ба́ба Яга́ и Ива́н-царе́вич** Baba Yaga and Ivan-tsarevich

🔊 **3-3** 1.03. **Змей Горы́ныч** Serpent Gorynych; Gorynych is his patronymic. He looks like a dragon and may have several heads disgorging smoke and fire.

Use: Any smoker can be called **Змей Горы́ныч**.

Fig. 3-2.   **Змей Горы́ныч и Ива́н-царе́вич** Serpent Gorynych and Ivan-tsarevich

🔊 **3-4** 1.04. **Коще́й/Каще́й Бессме́ртный** Scrag the Immortal [**кощей** from **кость** bone]; male equivalent of Baba-Yaga; steals princesses and other beauties.

🔊 **3-4** *Use:* reference to a thin, scrawny person. In Russian folk tradition, to be thin is to look ugly, so if you eat with a Russian family, you may hear a hostess insisting that you take more food and waving aside any dieting considerations: "Eat! you are thin enough, you already look like Scrag the Immortal" **«Ешь, ешь! Куда́ тебе́ худе́ть, и так то́щий как Коще́й!»**

Fig. 3-3. **Васили́са Прекра́сная и Коще́й Бессме́ртный** Vasilisa the Beautiful and Scrag the Immortal

1.05. Other female protagonists in fairy-tales: **Васили́са Прекра́сная** Vasilisa the Beautiful; **Еле́на Прему́драя** Helena the Wise; and **Царе́вна-Лягу́шка** Frog-Princess (tsarevna is the daughter of a tsar), a princess turned into a frog through black magic, who turns back into a princess when her suitor finds her after a journey into the nether world.

The following joke makes use of these names:

Встре́тились два дру́га. Оди́н спра́шивает:
—Как рабо́тается?
—Как в лесу́! Что ни нача́льник — дуб, что ни подчинённый — пень, что ни бума́га — ли́па.
—А как живёшь?
—Как в ска́зке! До́ма тёща — Ба́ба-Яга́, жена́ — ве́дьма, сосе́дка — Царе́вна-Лягу́шка, а её муж — Ива́нушка-дурачо́к.

Two friends meet. One says: "How are things at work?" "Exactly like in the woods! Every boss is an oak (slang: blockhead), every subordinate is a stump (slang: dummy), all the paperwork is a linden tree (slang: phony)." "And how's life at home?" — "Oh, I live in a fairy-tale (= fabulously): my mother-in-law is a Baba-Yaga, my wife's a witch, a neighbor is a Frog-Princess, and her husband is a Simple Simon."

Fig. 3-4.   V. Vasnetsov, *Three Bogatyrs* «Три богатыря́»

🔊 **3-6** 1.06. A handsome brave young man is always referred to as **до́брый мо́лодец**; a mighty fighter is a **богаты́рь**, equivalent to a knight.

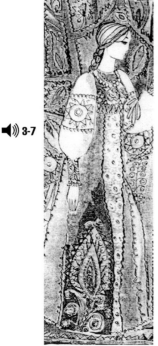

🔊 **3-7** A beautiful maiden is **кра́сна де́вица** (note that **красна** here means "beautiful" rather than "red").

Use: **кра́сна де́вица** usually stands for someone easily embarrassed. «**Сын у него́ высо́кий, плечи́стый, настоя́щий богаты́рь, но засте́нчив, как кра́сная де́вица**». "His son is a tall guy with broad shoulders, but he is bashful as a beautiful maiden."

Fig. 3-5.   Beautiful Maiden

1.1. Fixed Descriptions of Nature

1.1.1. **Мать сыра́ земля́** "mother earth," a very important figure in Russian ◀)) 3-8 culture, the goddess of a pagan matriarchal religion. She greatly contributes to the cult of the mother, alive to this day. Use of the word **мать** can be an act of blasphemy.

1.1.2. **Моло́чные ре́ки, кисе́льные берега́** (kisel is a kind of starchy jelly, tra- ◀)) 3-9 ditional Russian dessert) literally "milk rivers, kisel shores," is a symbol of fabulous prosperity, an equivalent of the English "land flowing with milk and honey." There is a second meaning to this phrase, since **кисе́льный** also means "weak" or "flabby."

Illustration: An article about the troubles with Russian fleet in *Ито́ги*, Dec. 1996, has the ironic headline: «**Моло́чные ре́ки, кисе́льные корабли́**».

1.2. Other fixed attributes: a field is always "clean," that is, a vast space with no obstruction of the view: **чи́сто по́ле**; the wide world is "white world": **бе́лый** ◀)) 3-10 **свет**; the moon, or rather the crescent moon, is always "clear": **я́сный ме́сяц**, while the sun, usually in the affectionate diminutive form, is "red": **кра́сно(е) со́лнышко**.

1.3. Magic Objects

A magic wand: **волше́бная па́лочка**; a tablecloth that sets itself with delicious ◀)) 3-11 food upon demand: **ска́терть-самобра́нка**; a flying carpet: **ковёр-самолёт**; seven-league boots, literally, "fast-walking" boots: **сапоги́-скорохо́ды**; the hut on chicken legs: **избу́шка на ку́рьих но́жках** (see 1.02).

1.4. Fixed Expressions and Phrases:

1.4.1. **В не́котором ца́рстве, в не́котором госуда́рстве жил-был царь.** "In a ◀)) 3-12 certain kingdom, in some country there was/lived a tsar." English equivalent: "Once upon a time there lived a king."

1.4.2. **Жи́ли-бы́ли стари́к со стару́хой.** "Once upon a time there lived an old ◀)) 3-13 man and an old woman."

Use: Beginning someone's life story with **жил-был … or жил да был …** gives it a folklore/epic ring. This may sound funny if you are telling a story about a mutual friend.

1.4.3. **Ско́ро ска́зка ска́зывается, да не ско́ро де́ло де́лается.** "To do the ◀)) 3-14 deed takes more time than to tell (about) it." Literally: "the fairytale goes fast but the deed does not."

Use: Often applied to narratives of bureaucratic, or other delays:

> **Мы вы́звали водопрово́дчика. Ско́ро ска́зка ска́зывается, да не ско́ро де́ло де́лается. Он яви́лся через две неде́ли.** "I called the plumber. It is sooner said than done: it took him two weeks to get here."

3-15 1.4.4. **Что, Ива́нушка, не ве́сел, что голо́вушку пове́сил?** "Why are you so sad, Ivanushka (diminutive of Ivan), why do you hang your head?" In fairytales these words are usually said by someone with magic power who intends to help the hero in his trouble.

Use: Appropriate in any situation where you can say to your friend in English: "Hey, what's up? Why are you looking so sad?" The Russian line conveys affectionate concern colored with friendly humor.

3-16 1.4.5. **По щу́чьему веле́нию, по моему́ хоте́нию** "By the pike's order, by my wish." In the fairy-tale a hero, **Еме́ля-дурачо́к** Emelia the Simpleton, catches a pike endowed with magic powers and the ability to speak. In return for setting the pike free Emelia is granted a wish any time he uses these magic words.

Use: this phrase, especially its first part, became equivalent to "as if by magic" or "presto!" **«И в эту секу́нду, как по щу́чьему веле́нию, вошла́ Ма́ша»** And at this moment, as if by magic, Masha entered."

Illustration: An advertisement in *Изве́стия*, Sept. 1997, uses the image of Emelia the Simpleton to promote electronic office supplies of the Sharp company. A laptop computer displays an image of the pike, Emelia enjoys his leisure while things get done by magic, and the caption under the picture says: **«Волше́бная те́хника для ва́шего о́фиса»** "Magic technology for your office."

Fig. 3-6.

1.4.6. Пойди́ туда́, не зна́ю куда́, принеси́ то, не зна́ю что. "Go there, I know ◀)) **3-17** not where; bring me something, I know not what." This is an impossible as-signment, given by an evil tsar to a hunter to get him away from home so that the tsar can steal the hunter's beautiful wife.

Use: a reaction to a thoughtless and impossible order, as in a heart-breaking document (1996) describing the plight of Russian refugees from Chechnya try-ing to settle in Russia:

> **«Как вы́жить в Росси́и. Сове́ты переселе́нцев переселе́нцам»** ◀)) **3-17**
> **... Ду́майте за чино́вников—они́ давно́ не ве́дают, что творя́т. А све́рху им спуска́ют всё но́вые директи́вы: «Пойди́ туда́, не зна́ю куда́. Найди́ то, не зна́ю что и где. Но что́бы за́втра всё бы́ло». Помога́йте им (то́ есть себе́), ду́майте за них, убежда́йте, осущест-вля́йте. Увы́, спасе́ние утопа́ющих—де́ло рук сами́х утопа́ющих.**

How to Survive in Russia. Tips to Refugees from Refugees:
Think for the officials, for they don't know what they are doing, and it has been like that for a long time. And they themselves keep re-ceiving new instructions from the top authorities, instructions like "go there, I don't know where; bring me something, I know not what. But it all has to be here by tomorrow." So, help them (that is, yourselves), think for them, convince them, make it happen. Alas, he who is drown-ing is responsible for his own rescue." [The last line is a quotation from Il'f and Petrov, see 15.1.6.]

1.4.7. Пошёл, куда́ глаза́ глядя́т. "And he went where his eyes led him." In ◀)) **3-18** fairytales, said of someone turned out from home. Use: either in reference to a turned-down petitioner, or as a description of an aimless walk for pleasure: **«Перед мои́м но́сом закры́ли дверь, и пошёл я куда́ глаза́ глядя́т. / Мы шли по́ лесу куда́ глаза́ глядя́т».** "They closed the door in my face and I had to go where my eyes led me." "We strolled in the woods, walked anywhere our eyes led us."

1.4.8. ... ни в ска́зке сказа́ть, ни перо́м описа́ть. "Neither a fairy-tale can de- ◀)) **3-19** scribe it nor a pen." This is said of something extraordinary either in a good or a bad sense:

> **Она́ така́я краса́вица, что ни в ска́зке сказа́ть, ни перо́м опи-са́ть./Что они́ творя́т—уму́ непостижи́мо: ни в ска́зке сказа́ть, ни перо́м описа́ть.**

"She is a beauty beyond any description." "The things they are doing are mind-boggling, just indescribable."

🔊 3-20 1.4.9. **Ста́ли они́ жить-пожива́ть и добра́ нажива́ть.** "And they lived happily ever after." Literally: "And they began to live to their pleasure and to increase their fortune."

🔊 3-21 1.4.10. **И я там был, мёд-пи́во пил, по уса́м текло́, а в рот не попа́ло..** "I, too, was there, drank honey and beer, all of it ran down my mustache and did not get into my mouth." A traditional conclusion of a fairy-tale.

2. *THE TALE OF BYGONE YEARS*   «ПО́ВЕСТЬ ВРЕМЕННЫ́Х ЛЕТ»

This is an old Russian chronicle (compiled around 13th century).

🔊 3-22 2.1. **Иду́ на вы** "Beware, I am coming to get you" (Literally: "I am coming at you"). According to the chronicles, Prince Svyatoslav (12th century) always warned his enemies before attacking them (**вы** here is in the old accusative case, which did not have the animate form).

Illustration: A song from the popular film *Assa:*

🔊 3-22   **В по́ле зре́ния появля́ется но́вый объе́кт.**
          В на́шем по́ле зре́ния появля́ется но́вый объе́кт.
          Иду́ на ты, иду́ на ты, иду́ на ты …

          "There is a new object coming into view,
          A new object appears in our field of vision,
          Beware, I am coming to get you, coming to get you, coming to get
          you …"

3. ALEXANDER RADISHCHEV (1749–1802)   АЛЕКСА́НДР РАДИ́ЩЕВ

3.1. *Journey from*   «Путеше́ствие из
   ***St. Petersburg to Moscow* (1790)**   Петербу́рга в Москву́»

🔊 3-23 Radishchev is known to generations of Russian readers for his 1790 work *Journey from St. Petersburg to Moscow*. In it, he damns aristocratic landowners who beat, rape, and often kill their serfs; in fact, he condemns the institution of serfdom (and, implicitly, the government for allowing it to exist) as inhuman. Radishchev rails against tsarist censorship, and presents a chillingly bleak picture of Russian life in the 18th century. The fact that the Soviet authorities hailed the book as an exposé of tsarist-era abuses should in no way discount its importance: *Journey from St. Petersburg to Moscow* was a courageous, revolutionary work for its time—in Russia. Not surprisingly, the book incurred the wrath of Catherine II who, despite her claims of "enlightenment," had Radishchev exiled to Siberia for ten years (originally he was condemned to death). Radishchev committed suicide in 1802.

4. NIKOLAI MIKHAILOVICH KARAMZIN (1766—1826)

НИКОЛА́Й МИХА́ЙЛОВИЧ КАРАМЗИ́Н

Karamzin is an important figure in Russian culture: he was a writer, a historian and a journalist. As a writer, he was the founder of Russian Sentimentalism, a literary movement which placed the highest value on the emotional life of individuals, independently of their social status (recall that this was the time of serfdom in Russia), and on compassion toward fellow human beings. As a journalist, he was instrumental in disseminating the ideas of the French Enlightenment. Karamzin's fundamental 12-volume *History of the Russian State* **«Исто́рия госуда́рства Росси́йского»** was the first work of its kind in Russia. He is also credited with a great contribution to the development of Russian literary language.[1] Among his works, most remembered today are *Letters of a Russian Traveler* **«Пи́сьма ру́сского путеше́ственника»** (1791) and especially *Poor Liza* **«Бе́дная Ли́за»** (1792).

4.1. *Poor Liza*   **«Бе́дная Ли́за»**

The title of Karamzin's story is often used ironically to stand for "pure innocent abused maiden," or as a reference to someone trying to exploit other people's compassion. In the story, Liza is a beautiful and sensitive peasant girl who falls in love with a nobleman and commits suicide after he abandons her.

Illustration: **«Бе́дная Ли́за»**, headline in the newspaper *Труд,* 1997, to the following short note:

> **237 лет наза́д росси́йская императри́ца Елизаве́та издала́ ука́з, в кото́ром потре́бовала искорени́ть «зло́ и привы́чку смотре́ть на слу́жбу госуда́реву как на кормле́ние».**   ◀ঝ)) 3-24

> 237 years ago the Russian empress Elizabeth issued a decree in which she required the eradication of the " bad and evil custom of viewing one's job in the tsar's service as a legitimate source of bribes."

The headline implies that in modern Russia corruption is boundless and universal. The tsaritsa failed with her decree: Poor Liza! Little did she know how en-

---

[1] The efforts of Karamzin will be more appreciated if we recall that at the time it was customary for Russian educated gentry to communicate in French. While spoken Russian was well-developed, it was used mainly for mundane purposes. Written Russian yet had to break from lofty Church Slavonic and was flooded with expressions from Latin, German, French and other languages (see Chapter 1). Russian lacked words and structures necessary to discuss abstract notions in such areas as art, philosophy, science, administration, and other aspects of social life. In the words of Karamzin's contemporary, describing the gap between everyday Russian and lofty Church Slavonic: "We theorize in German, we joke in French and we use Russian only to pray to God and scold our servants" (Kaisarov).

trenched the evil custom was. This is also a pun, since Liza is a diminutive of the tsaritsa's name.

🔊 **3-25** 4.1.1. **И крестьянки любить умеют!** "Peasant women, too, know how to love!" A line from Karamzin's *Poor Liza* often used as a humorous riposte to someone's patronising praise, or to say something to the effect of "See, I can do it too!"

5. ALEXANDER SERGEEVICH PUSHKIN (1799–1837)[2]

АЛЕКСА́НДР СЕРГЕ́ЕВИЧ ПУ́ШКИН

5.1. *The Captain's Daughter* (1833–36)

«Капита́нская до́чка»

As was also the case with *Eugene Onegin*, some of the epigraphs preceding chapters of *The Captain's Daughter* became associated with Pushkin's work.

🔊 **3-26** 5.1.1. **Береги́ честь смо́лоду.** "Guard your honor from the time you are young." This is the epigraph to the first chapter. Although this is a proverb, it is perceived as a part of *The Captain's Daughter*.

Illustration: This particular proverb becomes the topic of endless school compositions and oral class-presentations when school programs cover *The Captain's Daughter*. No wonder it has become an active model generating new maxims like the one in a headline in **«Ва́ше пра́во»**, the supplement to the magazine *Социа́льная защи́та*: **«Береги́те не́рвы смо́лоду»** "Guard your nerves from the time you are young."

🔊 **3-27** 5.1.2. **Я приближа́лся к ме́сту моего́ назначе́ния** "I was approaching the place of my appointment."

Illustration: This sentence became especially famous through other works of literature quoting it. For example, the Strugatsky brothers begin their well-known satirical novel *Monday Begins on Saturday* exactly this way: **Я приближа́лся к ме́сту моего́ назначе́ния.**

🔊 **3-28** 5.1.3. **Не приведи́ Бог ви́деть ру́сский бунт, бессмы́сленный и беспоща́дный!** "God save us from seeing a Russian riot, meaningless and merciless!" This line is often quoted when a political situation in the country is fraught with civil unrest.

5.2. *The Queen of Spades* (1833)

«Пи́ковая да́ма»

🔊 **3-29** 5.2.1. **Тро́йка, семёрка, туз.** "Three, seven, ace" (names of cards). In Pushkin's *The Queen of Spades,* betting on these three cards was supposed to bring certain luck to Hermann, the main character in the story. Unfortunately, whether by mistake or through the interference of supernatural forces, he pulled a Queen of Spades instead of an ace.

---

[2] See Chapter 2 for biographical information.

Fig. 3-7.   **Пи́ковая да́ма** The Queen of Spades

Illustration:

(a)   «**Тро́йка, пятёрка … кто туз? Вы́боры в Чечне́: раскла́д** 🔊 3-29
       игроко́в» (**Но́вое вре́мя,** January 1997). "Three, five … and who is
       going to be the ace? Elections in Chechnia: the arrangement of the
       players."

(b)   «**Тро́йка, семёрка, туз. Что на́ша жизнь? —игра́**». "Three, seven,
       ace. What's our life? It's a game." Subtitle in an article about politi-
       cal games involving Russia, China and the USA (**Но́вое вре́мя,**
       May 1997).

5.3. *A Trip to Arzrum* (1836)   «**Путеше́ствие в Арзру́м**»

Мы лени́вы и не любопы́тны…. We are lazy and not curious.   🔊 3-30

6. MIKHAIL YURIEVICH LERMONTOV (1814–41)[3]

МИХАЙЛ Ю́РЬЕВИЧ ЛЕ́РМОНТОВ

Lermontov's prose is considered as important as his poetry.

Fig. 3-8.

6.1. *A Hero of Our Time* (1840)   «Геро́й на́шего вре́мени»

This is the title of the most famous novel by Lermontov. The protagonist, Pechorin **Печо́рин**, who is rather an anti-hero, in many ways echoes Pushkin's Eugene Onegin. The name Pechorin is often used to refer to a man whom women find irresistible.

🔊 3-31 *Illustration:* Headline in ***О́бщая газе́та***, 1997: «Геро́и вчера́шнего вре́мени: почему́ же́ртвами перестро́йки называ́ют себя́ не ста́рые парти́йные нача́льники, а те, кто в конце́ 80-х ещё ходи́л в шко́лу?» "Heroes of a by-gone time: How is it that the people who at the end of the eighties were still going to high school—they rather than the old party bosses—call themselves 'victims of perestroika'?"

7. NIKOLAI VASILIEVICH GOGOL (1809–52)

НИКОЛА́Й ВАСИ́ЛЬЕВИЧ ГО́ГОЛЬ

One of the three giants of 19th century Russian prose (the other two are Tolstoy and Dostoev-sky), Gogol is the most enigmatic and hard-to-place writer, claimed as forefather by Realism, Symbolism and Post-Modernism. His strange and beautiful prose is resistant to translation; it is a masterful mixture of the comical, phantasma-goric, satirical, romantic, sinister, and poetic.

Fig. 3-9.

---

[3] See Chapter 2 for biographical information.

Gogol was born in Ukraine, but for many years lived in his beloved Italy, making occasional trips to Russia. His first collection of stories, *Evenings on a Farm near Dikanka* «**Вечера́ на ху́торе близ Дика́ньки**» (1831–32), made all of Russia fall in love with Ukraine. The stories were so hilarious that the printers, who were doubling up with laughter, had trouble type-setting the book. But his most famous work is *Dead Souls* «**Мёртвые ду́ши**» (1835–52), a searing look at Russia, "warts and all." After Gogol read the first draft of *Dead Souls* to Pushkin, Pushkin exclaimed: «**Бо́же, как грустна́ на́ша Росси́я!**» "God, what a sad place our Russia is!"

7.1. *Evenings on a Farm near Dikan'ka* (1831–32)   «Вечера́ на ху́торе близ Дика́ньки»

All the stories in the collection are based on Ukrainian folklore, mythology and history. They take place in the settlements of Dnieper Cossacks, **запоро́жские каза́ки**. All the quotations under (6.1.–6.1.3) are from various stories in this collection.

7.1.2. In "The Night before Christmas" «**Ночь пе́ред Рождество́м**», the devil steals the moon from the sky and the blacksmith Vakula restores it.

Fig. 3-10.   Instructions for cross-stitching *The Night before Christmas*

Illustration: You can judge for yourself how popular the story is, if a magazine for women, ***Крестьянка***, January 1997, offers its readers a pattern for embroidery under the title **«Ночь пе́ред Рождество́м»**, upgrading a rather mediocre drawing by linking it to the lighthearted poetic atmosphere of Gogol's story.

🔊 **3-32** **7.1.3. Зна́ете ли вы украи́нскую ночь? О, вы не зна́ете украи́нской но́чи!** "Do you have any idea of what a Ukrainian night is? Oh, you don't know what it is! " A very popular quotation from "A Night in May, or The Drowned Maiden" **«Ма́йская ночь, или Уто́пленница»**.

7.2. "A Terrible Vengeance" **«Стра́шная месть»**. Horror movies pale next to this story. The dead gnaw each other, a father has diabolic power over the soul of his daughter, and this is all mixed with enchanting descriptions of landscapes. The title itself became proverbial, and the passage below with a description of the Dnieper had to be memorized in high schools. You can count on the presence of at least the first and last sentences in everyone's mind as soon as you say "Dnieper."

🔊 **3-33** **7.2.1. Чу́ден Днепр при ти́хой пого́де, когда́ во́льно и пла́вно мчит сквозь леса́ и го́ры по́лные во́ды свои́. Ни зашелохнёт; ни прогреми́т. Гляди́шь и не зна́ешь, идёт или не идёт его́ велича́вая ширина́, и чу́дится, бу́дто весь вы́лит он из стекла́, и бу́дто голуба́я зерка́льная доро́га, без ме́ры в ширину́, без конца́ в длину́, ре́ет и вьётся по зелёному ми́ру. Лю́бо тогда́ и жа́ркому со́лнцу огляде́ться с вышины́ и погрузи́ть лучи́ в хо́лод стекля́нных вод, и прибере́жным леса́м я́рко отсвети́ться в во́дах. Зеленоку́дрые! они́ толпя́тся вме́сте с полевы́ми цвета́ми к вода́м, и наклони́вшись, гляди́т в них и не нагляди́тся, и не налюбу́ются све́тлым свои́м зра́ком, и усмеха́ются к нему́, и приве́тствуют его́, кива́я ветвя́ми. В середи́ну же Днепра́ они́ не сме́ют гля́нуть: никто́, кро́ме со́лнца и голубо́го не́ба, не гляди́т в него́. Ре́дкая пти́ца долети́т до середи́ны Днепра́.**

"How fabulous is the Dnieper on a quiet day, when it streams its full waters gently and powerfully through woods and mountains. Nothing stirs there, nothing rustles. You look at it and you don't know whether its magnificent breadth moves or not, and you have the impression that its entire surface is made of glass, and like a measureless never-ending road made of blue mirror it soars and winds through a green world. At such times, how happy is the hot sun to gaze at it from above and to sink its rays in the coolness of the glassy waters, how happy are the river-side woods to cast their radiant reflections in them. Oh, green-curled trees! Together with field flowers, they flock to the waters and bend over to gaze into them, endlessly admiring the reflection of their shiny eyes and smiling at it, and greet it with waving boughs. But they dare not steal a glance at the middle of the Dnieper: no one except the sun and the blue sky ever looks into it. It is a rare bird that can reach the middle of the Dnieper."

Illustration: The last line of Gogol's quotation acquires an eerie and tragic sense in a poem by Lev Losev, "From a wireless interception. Nocturne" **«Из радиоперехва́тов. Ноктю́рн»**, describing the Chernobyl catastrophe and its horrible aftermath for people and animals:

> … тре́тий день обостри́тся
> поно́с, выпаде́нье пера́.
> Повторя́ю: ре́дкая пти́ца
> долети́т до середи́ны Днепра́.

🔊 3-34

… [the] third day will bring acute diarrhea, and feathers will fall. I repeat: It is a rare bird that can reach the middle of the Dnieper.

7.3. *Mirgorod* (1835) «Ми́ргород»

Literally "Peaceful Town," this is Gogol's second collection of stories in a Ukrainian setting. His Mirgorod is a provincial town in the middle of nowhere, with a huge muddy puddle in front of the city hall. Nothing ever happens in Mirgorod. These are the implications behind a reference to any town or city as "Mirgorod."

7.4. "Viy" «Вий» (1835). The story is even eerier than «Стра́шная месть» (7.1.3). It is full of Halloween-type horrors, but, like Poe's somber "Fall of the House of Usher," it lacks the relief of Halloween's humor.

7.4.1. Подыми́те мне ве́ки! "Lift my eyelids!" These are the words of **Вий** Viy, the ghastly king of all the evil spirits. To appreciate this line, imagine the dreadful experience of **Хома́ Брут** Khoma Brut, a young theology student, muttering prayers in a lit church within a protecting holy circle. He does not dare to raise his eyes, because a coffin with the dead body of a beautiful girl, transformed into a ghoulish witch, swooshes around the church trying to get him. Invisible to her and other uncanny creatures, Khoma survives for two nights. But on the third, they bring Viy and the horrible end follows. This is how Viy is described:

🔊 3-35

> Весь был он в чёрной земле́. Как жи́листые, кре́пкие ко́рни, выдава́лись его засы́панные землёю но́ги и ру́ки. Тяжело́ ступа́л он, помину́тно оступа́ясь. Дли́нные ве́ки опу́щены бы́ли до са́мой земли́. С у́жасом заме́тил Хома́, что лицо́ бы́ло на нём желе́зное. Его привели́ по́д руки и пря́мо поста́вили к тому́ ме́сту, где стоя́л Хома́.
> —Подыми́те мне ве́ки: не ви́жу! —сказа́л подзе́мным го́лосом Вий—и всё со́нмище ки́нулось подыма́ть ему́ ве́ки. […] —Вот он! —закрича́л Вий и уста́вил на него́ желе́зный па́лец.

He was covered with black earth. His arms and legs bulged from under the mud like mighty twisted roots. He walked heavily, stumbling with each step. His eyelids were so long that they reached the ground.

Khoma noticed with horror that he had a face made of iron. "Lift my eyelids for me: I cannot see! " said Viy in his subterranean voice, and the host of creatures rushed to lift his eyelids. "There he is!" screamed Viy and pointed his iron finger at him.

Illustration:

(a) In his "The Fourth Prose" «**Четвёртая про́за**» Osip Mandelshtam exclaims: «**Подними́те мне ве́ки! да́йте мне ЦК**». "Lift my eyelids for me! Give me the Central Committee of the Communist Party." Written at the peak of Stalin's purges, these ironic words of a poet driven to bitterness and despair acquire a blood-curdling ring. Mandelshtam's text was for a long time illegal and circulated in samizdat.

3-36

(b) An article in the magazine ***Огонёк***, April 1997, mocks believers in psychics: «**Подними́те мне ве́ки! —проси́л Вий. Да́же он не мог ви́деть с закры́тыми глаза́ми**». "'Lift my eyelids,' asked Viy. Even he could not see with his eyes closed."

7.5. *Taras Bulba* «**Тара́с Бу́льба**» (1835), a short historic novel taking place in 17th-century Ukraine, which romanticizes the Cossacks and their heroic battles against the Poles.

3-37   7.5.1. **А повороти́сь-ка, сын! Э́кой ты смешно́й како́й!** "Turn around, son! Don't you look funny!" With these words old Taras greeted his sons, dressed in student robes, upon their arrival home for their first summer vacation. This quotation has become a standard joke addressed to a friend (whether male or female) parading in new clothes.

3-38   7.5.2. **Я тебя́ породи́л, я тебя́ и убью́!** "'Tis I who begot you and 'tis I who shall kill you." Taras Bulba says these words to his son Andriy before killing him for treason.

Illustration:

(a) Everyone enjoys repeating a notorious mistake from a school composition on *Taras Bulba*, in which a student apparently got carried away with the parallelism of the comparative construction in Bulba's words: «**Чем тебя́ породи́л, тем тебя́ и убью́!**» "What I begot you with, that I shall kill you with."

3-39

(b) A note on crime in the newspaper *Аргуме́нты и фа́кты,* 1996, entitled «**Я тебя́ породи́л ...**» uses Gogol's line to lighten up the description of a gruesome murder: «**Оте́ц из своего́ ружья́ вы́стрелил 24-ле́тнему сы́ну пря́мо в грудь. Стреля́вшего посади́ли в изоля́тор вре́менного содержа́ния, так что вре́мени для размышле́ния о правоме́рности го́голевского—я тебя́ породи́л, я тебя́ и убью́—у него́ в доста́тке, то́лько вот сы́на уже́ не верну́ть**». A father fired his rifle through the chest of his 24-year-old son. The father is under arrest and kept in solitary confinement, so now he can have plenty of time to contemplate the inescapable truth of the Gogolian "Tis I who begot you and tis I who shall kill you." What he cannot do, though, is return his son from the dead.

(c)   Headline in **Но́вое вре́мя**, April 1997: **«Торго́вля полити́ческими беглеца́ми. Мы их породи́ли, мы их и продади́м».** "The trading of political refugees. 'Tis we who begot them, 'tis we who shall sell them."

Fig. 3-11.

7.5.3. **Есть ещё по́рох в пороховни́цах!** "There is still gunpowder in our pow- 🔊 **3-40** der-flasks!" This is the cossacks' answer to Taras Bulba, assuring him that they still have strength to continue the fight.

7.6. **Ску́чно на э́том све́те, господа́!** "This world is dreary, gentlemen!" These 🔊 **3-41** are the last words in the funniest story Gogol ever wrote, **«По́весть о том, как Ива́н Ива́нович поссо́рился с Ива́ном Ники́форовичем»** "The Story of How Ivan Ivanovich Quarreled with Ivan Nikiforovich." Two friends, inhabitants of Mirgorod, Ivan Ivanovich and Ivan Nikiforovich, become bitter enemies over a trifle: one called the other a goose.

🔊 **3-42** **7.7. Мартобря́ 86 числа́, между днём и но́чью.** "Marchember 86, between day and night," a line from Gogol's short novel *The Diary of a Madman* **«Запи́ски сумасше́дшего»** (1835), showing the Madman's confusion of the names of the months.

Use: The quotation is used to show that one does not remember the exact date, for example:

🔊 **3-43**

    (a) **—Како́е сего́дня число́? —Пятна́дцатое мартобря́.** "What date is it today?" "The 15th of Marchember";

    (b) The first line of Brodsky's poem **«Ниотку́да с любо́вью, на́дцатого мартобря́ ...»** "From nowhere with love, Umpteenth of Marchember ..."

7.8. *Dead Souls. A Poem* (1835–52)   «Мёртвые ду́ши» (Поэ́ма)

The title has nothing to do with supernatural forces. Although the word **душа́** means "soul," its other meaning is "a person." Thus the number of serfs one owned was referred to as **коли́чество душ**. In the novel, the main character, Pavel Ivanovich Chichikov, a great swindler with a respectable appearance, travels around buying serfs who have actually died but on paper still count as alive until the next official census. Since their owners have to pay a tax for the dead, they sell them to Chichikov gladly and at a symbolic price. In return, Chichikov gets the documents proving that he owns a great number of serfs. This should upgrade his social status and give him the right to take out mortgages and the prospect of marrying a rich heiress. Thus the plot strings out Chichikov's encounters with all sorts of characters, shown in the light of Gogol's unsurpassed gift for the comical and satirical. The novel, however, is not just a satire. Gogol called it a poem intending to capture Russia in its entirety, at its worst and best. The best part was to come in the second volume, with which Gogol was dissatisfied and which he burnt in a moment of frustration. Glimpses of what is best about Gogol's Russia are found in lyrical digressions interwoven in the text of the first volume.

Illustration:

🔊 **3-44**

    (a) An article about high prices for funeral services is entitled "What is the price of *Dead Souls*? **«Почём 'Мёртвые ду́ши'?»** in the magazine *Семья́*, 1997.

    (b) During the 1996 presidential campaign the magazine *Огонёк*, 1996, discussed rumors about candidates trading votes: **«Да и вообще́, большинство́ претенде́нтов ны́нче в стремле́нии повы́годнее загна́ть свой эфеме́рный това́р весьма́ сма́хивают на Чи́чикова. [...] Избира́телям же остаётся лишь гру́стно, по-го́голевски, улыба́ться».** "In fact, most candidates nowadays greatly resemble Chichikov in their aspiration to get a bargain on their ephemeral merchandise.[…] In response to that, the voters can do nothing but wear a sad Gogolian smile." [See 6.8.2.]

(c) The crime section in *Огонёк*, March 1996, describes a brutal murder under the title **«Мёртвые у́ши»** "Dead Ears."

7.8.1. A famous line from one of Gogol's "lyrical digressions":

… и то, что пробуди́ло бы в пре́жние го́ды движе́нье в лице́, смех и немо́лчные ре́чи, то скользи́т тепе́рь ми́мо, и безуча́стное молча́ние храня́т мои уста́. *О, моя́ ю́ность! о, моя́ све́жесть!* 📢 3-45

… what in earlier years would produce a change in my face, would make me laugh and talk incessantly—all this passes by without touching me and an impassive silence seals my lips. Oh, my youth! Oh, my naiveté!

7.8.2. **Смех сквозь слёзы.** "Laughter through tears." A frequently cited abbre- 📢 3-46 viated version of another "lyrical digression" from *Dead Souls*:

И до́лго ещё определено́ мне чу́дной вла́стью идти́ о́б руку с мои́ми стра́нными геро́ями, озира́ть всю грома́дно-несу́щуюся жизнь, озира́ть её сквозь ви́дный ми́ру смех и незри́мые, неве́домые ему слёзы!

By design of some miraculous forces I am to follow my strange characters hand-in-hand for a long time yet, I am to watch the entire vast life whirling by; to watch it through laughter apparent to the world and through tears unseen and unknown to it!

Illustration: The magazine ***Но́вое вре́мя*** has a regular column called **«Смех сквозь слёзы»**.

7.8.3. The names of the characters have acquired proverbial status: to say "He is a real Nozdrev/Sobakevich/Manilov" is to state your opinion of a particular person and in addition, to have a free ride on Gogol's humor, for it surely would make your addressee smile if not roar with laughter.

Петру́шка. Petrushka (diminutive of **Пётр**). Petrushka, Chichikov's valet, 📢 3-47 enjoys the process of reading as such and devours any printed matter that comes his way with equal passion, be it a love story, an ABC book, a prayer book or chemistry textbook. To imply that someone had read a story without paying much attention to its content one would say: **«Он чита́ет, как го́голевский Петру́шка».**

Плю́шкин. Pliushkin is described by Gogol as **«проре́ха на челове́честве»** "a 📢 3-48 hole in the fabric of humanity." Enormously rich and miserly to the point of de- mentia, Pliushkin wears clothes suitable for a beggar; he would rather die than part with as much as a scrap of paper. He prudently brings home and piles up all sorts of useless junk: rusty nails, rags, fragments of broken glass, and so on. Thus a person referred to as **настоя́щий Плю́шкин** is not only stingy, but a pack-rat.

Мани́лов. Sugary-pleasant, empty-headed Manilov is given to daydreaming about various complicated and impractical projects (like building a tunnel from the porch of his house to the nearby pond, or else erecting a bridge across that pond; and wouldn't it be nice if on the bridge there were a row of merchants selling their goods to Manilov's peasants …).

Illustration:

(a) The scene in which Manilov and Chichikov for several minutes stand at the door trying to persuade each other to enter the room first is often humorously acted out by a host and a guest:

3-49

—Нет, то́лько по́сле вас. Сде́лайте ми́лость, не беспоко́йтесь так для меня́, я пройду́ по́сле, —говори́л Чи́чиков.

—Нет, Па́вел Ива́нович, нет, вы гость, —говори́л Мани́лов, пока́зывая ему́ руко́ю на дверь.

—Не затрудня́йтесь, пожа́луйста, не затрудня́йтесь. Пожа́-луйста, проходи́те, —говори́л Чи́чиков.

—Нет уж извини́те, не допущу́ пройти́ позади́ тако́му при-я́тному, образо́ванному го́стю. ….

"No, after you. Do me a favor, don't trouble yourself so for my sake, I will enter after you," said Chichikov. "No, Pavel Ivanovich, you are a guest," said Manilov, pointing at the door. "Don't trouble yourself, please, don't trouble yourself, go in first," said Chichikov. "Oh, no, you would have to pardon me, I would not dream of letting such a pleasant and highly educated guest enter after me."

The exact words of Gogol's dialogue are not essential, in fact only "**Нет, то́лько по́сле вас**" would go unchanged—the rest either dropped or embellished according to one's taste. Some go as far as ending the scene by squeezing through the doorway together, reenacting Manilov's and Chichikov's brilliant solution.

(b)   An article in *Аргуме́нты и фа́кты*, 1996, expresses misgivings about the Mayor's fiscal intentions:

«… наде́емся, он не ста́нет распыля́ть городско́й бюдже́т на мани́ловские проже́кты». We hope that he will not squander the municipal budget on Manilov-like projects.

(c)   A headline in *Но́вое вре́мя*, July 1996:

«**О́стров сокро́вищ. Чтобы Сахали́н стал им, нужны́ робинзо́ны, а не мани́ловы**». "Treasure Island [reference to Robert Louis

Stevenson]. For Sakhalin to become a real treasure island, we need Robinsons [reference to Robinson Crusoe] rather than Manilovs."

Собакéвич. Sobakevich «**похóж на срéдней величины́ медвéдя**» "looks like a 🔊 **3-50** medium size bear"; all his possessions are heavy, sturdy and practical. He would never say a good word about anyone in his town; the most flattering thing he ever said was:

> «**Одúн там тóлько есть поря́дочный человéк—прокурóр, да и тот, éсли сказáть прáвду, свинья́**». "There is only one decent person here—the Public Prosecutor, but even he, to tell you the truth, is a swine."

Another famous saying of Sobakevich, used when the speaker wishes to indicate that s/he does not fall for some cleverly camouflaged deceit:

> «**… я гáдостей не стáну есть. Мне лягу́шку хоть сáхаром облепú, не возьму́ её в рот**». "I would never eat the yucky stuff. For all I care, they can cover a frog with sugar: I would not put it in my mouth."

Ноздрёв. Nozdrev is an impertinent carouser, a gambler, and a rogue. He im- 🔊 **3-51** poses his boorish friendship upon everyone only to end up in a fight, often physical, after which his side-whiskers look thinner on one side.

7.8.4. Дáма прия́тная во всех отношéниях и прóсто прия́тная дáма "A lady 🔊 **3-52** pleasant in all respects and a simply pleasant lady."

Illustration: Boris Notkin, popular anchor of a TV show, was referred to as «**прия́тный во всех отношéниях**» "pleasant in all respects" in the newspaper *Труд,* 1997.

7.8.5. … глáзки и лáпки "bird's eyes, bird's feet" is a fragment of a conversa- 🔊 **3-53** tion of two pleasant ladies about a fabric pattern. Their discussion is often cited as a classical example of an empty conversation:

> … **вообразúте себé: полóсочки у́зенькие …. какúе тóлько мóжет предстáвить воображéние человéческое, фон голубóй и через полóску всё глáзки и лáпки, глáзки и лáпки, глáзки и лáпки …**

> Just imagine: there are stripes as narrow as human fancy can envision, a sky-blue background and across the stripes there are bird's eyes and bird's feet, bird's eyes and bird's feet, bird's eyes and bird's feet.

"**Глазки и лапки**" repeated three times creates an impression of incessant **ла-ла-ла**: blah-blah-blah …

7.8.6. This lengthy passage is one of the most famous "lyrical digressions" in *Dead Souls;* it also had to be memorized in high school. The most often cited lines are given in italics:

🔊 3-54

И какой же русский не любит быстрой езды? Его́ ли душе́, стремя́щейся закружи́ться, загуля́ться, сказа́ть иногда́ чорт побери́ всё! его́ ли душе́ не люби́ть её? Её ли не люби́ть, когда́ в ней слы́шится что́-то восто́рженно-чу́дное? Кажи́сь, неве́домая си́ла подхвати́ла тебя́ на крыло́ к себе́, и сам лети́шь, и всё лети́т: летя́т вёрсты, летя́т навстре́чу купцы́ на облучка́х свои́х киби́ток, лети́т с обе́их сторо́н лес с тёмными стро́ями е́лей и со́сен, с топо́рным сту́ком и воро́ньим кри́ком, лети́т вся доро́га ниве́сть куда́ в пропада́ющую даль, и что́-то стра́шное заключено́ в сем бы́стром мелька́ньи, где не успева́ет озна́читься пропада́ющий предме́т, то́лько не́бо над голово́ю, да лёгкие ту́чи, да продира́ющийся ме́сяц одни́ ка́жутся недви́жны. *Эх тро́йка! пти́ца тро́йка, кто тебя́ вы́думал?* знать, у бо́йкого наро́да ты могла́ то́лько роди́ться, в той земле́, что не лю́бит шути́ть, а ро́внемгла́днем разметну́лась на полсве́та, да и ступа́й счита́ть вёрсты, пока́ не заряби́т тебе́ в о́чи. И не хи́трый, кажи́сь, доро́жный снаря́д, не желе́зным схва́чен винто́м, а на́скоро живьём с одни́м топоро́м да долото́м снаряди́л и собра́л тебя́ яросла́вский расторо́пный мужи́к. Не в неме́цких ботфо́ртах ямщи́к: борода́ да рукави́цы и сиди́т чорт зна́ет на чём; а привста́л да замахну́лся, да затяну́л пе́сню—ко́ни ви́хрем, спи́цы в колёсах смеша́лись в оди́н гла́дкий круг, то́лько дро́гнула доро́га, да вскри́кнул в испу́ге останови́вшийся пешехо́д! и вон она́ понесла́сь, понесла́сь, понесла́сь!.. И вон уже́ ви́дно вдали́, как что́-то пыли́т и сверли́т во́здух.

Не так ли и ты, Русь, что бо́йкая необгони́мая тро́йка несёшься? Ды́мом дыми́тся под тобо́ю доро́га, гремя́т мосты́, всё отстаёт и остаётся позади́. Останови́лся поражённый бо́жьим чу́дом созерца́тель: не мо́лния ли э́то, сбро́шенная с не́ба? что зна́чит э́то наводя́щее у́жас движе́ние? и что за неве́домая си́ла заключена́ в сих неве́домых све́том коня́х? *Эх, ко́ни, ко́ни, что за ко́ни!* Ви́хри ли сидя́т в ва́ших гри́вах? Чу́ткое ли у́хо гори́т во вся́кой ва́шей жи́лке? Заслы́шали с вышины́ знако́мую пе́сню, дру́жно и ра́зом напрягли́ ме́дные гру́ди и, почти́ не тро́нув копы́тами земли́, преврати́лись в одни́ вы́тянутые ли́нии, летя́щие по во́здуху, и мчи́тся вся вдохнове́нная бо́гом!.. *Русь, куда́ ж несёшься ты, дай отве́т? Не даёт отве́та.* Чу́дным зво́ном залива́ется колоко́льчик; греми́т и стано́вится ве́тром разо́рванный в куски́ во́здух; *лети́т ми́мо всё, что ни есть на земли́, и кося́сь посторо́ниваются и даю́т ей доро́гу други́е наро́ды и госуда́рства.*

"And what Russian does not love riding fast? Is it not in his soul to long for a whirlwind, to let himself loose, to say sometimes, "to hell with it all!" Can one help but love it, when there is something exaltingly wonderful in it? As if some unknown power has lifted you up close on its wing and you take off, and everything takes flight: the miles fly by, the merchants rush toward you sitting high on their coachman's seats, the forest flies on either side, the tall dark rows of spruce and pine, with the sound of an axe, and the cry of the crow, the whole road is flying to nowhere, to an unknown disappearing length; and something frightening is hidden in the flickering quickness, in which objects do not have the time to form before they trail off in the distance, only the sky overhead, the feathery clouds and the peering crescent moon seem still.

Oh troika! bird-like troika! who invented you? Only out of a feisty people could you have been born, only in a humorless land that spreads out and glides smoothly across half the world: go ahead and count the miles until your vision blurs. And not too complex this riding equipage, not fashioned with an iron screw, but haphazardly with an axe and a chisel by a handy peasant. The coachman is not wearing foreign riding boots, but a Russian beard and mittens, God knows what he sits on, but when he rises and waves his whip, and then strikes up a song, the horses dash like the wind, the spokes come together into one smooth disk, and the road barely begins trembling and already a startled passerby cries out and stops short. And on and on it goes charging and racing, and way up ahead now something can be seen raising the dust and drilling through the air.

And are you not, Rus', like the boisterous unbeatable troika racing forward?

The road clouds in smoke underneath you, bridges groan, everything falls away and is left behind. The beholder, astounded, looking on this godly wonder, thinks: can it be a thunderbolt, thrown from the heavens? What is the meaning of this movement, bringing on such terror? What great unknown force is hidden in these unearthly horses? And oh, what horses! such horses! Is there a whirlwind in your manes? Does a keen sense run burning through your very veins? As the familiar song is heard from up above, they start off together, strain their bronze chests as one, and almost not touching hooves to the ground, stretch into a long line that flies through the air and the troika races onward, filled with divine inspiration.

Oh, Rus'! Where are you rushing to? Answer me! There is no answer. The harness bells chime sweetly, the air roars and thunders, becoming a wind-storm; everything flies past, all that is in this world, and stepping to the side, looking askance, all other nations and countries make way.

Illustration: The popularity of the first line from this passage is enormous, as can be seen from the following headlines:

◀))) 3-55 (a) «Конгре́сс сооте́чественников: како́й же ру́сский не лю́бит кла́ссовой борьбы́?» "A Congress of our compatriots: what Russian does not love class-struggle?" —*Коммерсáнтъ*, 1991;

(b) «Како́й же люби́тель бы́строй езды́ бы́стро отдаёт долги́?» "What lover of driving fast repays his debts quickly?" —*Огонёк*, June 1996;

(c) «Како́й ру́сский не лю́бит бы́строй езды́ без биле́та? Го́голь (по слу́хам)». "'What Russian does not love fast driving without a ticket? Gogol (according to the rumors)." —An epigraph to a humorous story in *Крестья́нка*, 1995;

(d) «Како́й мужчи́на не мечта́ет огра́бить банк!» "What man does not dream of robbing the bank!" —*Огонёк*, January 1997;

(e) «Эх, прокачу́! Како́й же ру́сский не лю́бит бы́строй езды́», —An article about the slow speed of Russian trains in *Огонёк*, February 1997;

(f) «Како́й же настоя́щий ру́сский национа́л-патрио́т ещё не 'засвети́лся' на ТВ?» "What real Russian nationalistic patriot has not flashed his face on TV yet?" —*Огонёк*, March 1996;

(g) The image of a troika **тро́йка** flying in the air as a symbol of Russia has been reproduced endlessly and in all sorts of media (pictures on chocolate bars, Khokhloma boxes, posters and movies). There are novels, plays and stories using the imagery of this passage. Thus, a character in a Shukshin story, a peasant man with no education to speak of, is struck by the thought that if the troika is a proud symbol of Russia, what's there to be so proud of: doesn't that troika carry in it the swindler Chichikov? In Bulgakov's «Похожде́ния Чи́чикова» *The Adventures of Chichikov*, Chichikov appears with his troika in the Soviet Russia of the twenties and comfortably continues his machinations.

7.9. "The Overcoat" (1835)   «Шине́ль»

The story of a demented petty official. One of the writers of the post-Gogolian period (the quote is anonymous, though commonly attributed to Dostoevsky) acknowledged the debt of Russian literature to this story: «Все мы вы́шли из Го́голевской шине́ли». "All of us came out of Gogol's overcoat."

◀))) 3-56 *Illustration:* A joke in *Литерату́рная газе́та*, 1996: «Все мы вы́шли из шине́ли, то́лько одни́ из го́голевской, други́е из ста́линской». "All of us came out of an overcoat, only some of us came out of Gogol's overcoat, others, out of Stalin's."

8. ALEXANDER IVANOVICH HERZEN (1812–70)

АЛЕКСА́НДР ИВА́НОВИЧ ГЕ́РЦЕН

Herzen was a writer, thinker and journalist with immense political influence. He emigrated from Russia to London and founded there two revolutionary periodicals: *Polar Star* **Поля́рная звезда́** (which had on its cover the profiles of the five Decembrists executed by Nikolas I) and the newspaper *The Bell* **Ко́локол**. Both were widely—and illegally—circulated in Russia. This is the "Bell" which, according to Lenin, "woke up Russia."

Fig. 3-12.

8.1. *The Past and Thoughts* (1868)

«Было́е и ду́мы»

Brilliantly written, Herzen's memoirs capture the essence of intellectual, political and personal life in Russia of the 1850s and 1860s. The episodes most remembered by the general public describe Herzen's ideal friendship with his

Fig. 3-13. Herzen and Ogarev

lifelong friend, the poet Ogarev: their friendship did not end even after Ogarev's wife left him for Herzen.

Illustration: **Крестья́нка** has a regular section dedicated to sweethearts of famous writers and poets entitled «Было́е и да́мы» "The Past and Ladies." The March issue of 1996 describes the life of Anna Petrovna Kern, to whom Pushkin dedicated his famous poem «Я по́мню чу́дное мгнове́нье» "I remember a wonderful moment" [see Chapter 2, 7.7.1]. The issue of March 1997 has a story entitled «Бе́дная Ка́тя, принце́сса сиа́мская» "Poor Katia, the Siamese princess" [reference to poor Lisa, see 3.1].

🔊 3-57

Fig. 3-14.   Story from the magazine *Крестьянка*

8.2. *Who Is to Blame?* **(1847)**   «Кто винова́т?»

While the plot and the story are nearly forgotten, the title is widely quoted:

🔊 **3-58** *Illustration:* «**Кто винова́т и что де́лать?**» "Who is to blame and what's to be done?" Headline in *Огонёк,* 1997 [see also Chernyshevsky, 12.1].

9. IVAN GONCHAROV (1812–91)   ИВА́Н ГОНЧАРО́В

9.1. *Oblomov* **(1859)**   «Обло́мов»

Goncharov's chief contribution to Russian literature is the remarkable novel *Oblomov*. The work tells the story of Il'ia Oblomov, a pampered, intelligent child who grows up on the estate of Oblomovka **Обло́мовка**. His entire existence is conditioned by indolence, and the themes of sleep and dreaming pervade the work. Oblomov spends most of his day in bed. It seems that everyone in Oblomovka is sleepy and naps are interrupted only by meals.

　　　Mention Oblomov to Russian readers and most will recognize Oblomov as a type: languid, dreaming of comfort and good food; and Oblomovka as a 🔊 **3-59** dream-like place. The term **«обло́мовщина»** "Oblomovism" refers to chronic inertia.

10. IVAN SERGEEVICH TURGENEV (1818–83)

ИВА́Н СЕРГЕ́ЕВИЧ ТУРГЕ́НЕВ

Fig. 3-15.

A moderate liberal, a passionate Westerner and a perfect gentleman, Turgenev was the acclaimed top writer of the fifties and sixties, gradually eclipsed by Dostoevsky and Tolstoy. Turgenev was a personal friend of Flaubert, Zola and Henry James, and he advocated Russian culture in the West. His novels focused on the social problems of his time. His female characters have shaped the national concept of the Russian woman: she is either a mysterious, dangerous seductress, or pure, beautiful, young and very strong, always inspired to action and self-sacrifice by an eloquent, idealistic man who in the end cannot rise to his own ideals.

10.1. *Notes of a Hunter* (1852)   «Запи́ски охо́тника»

A masterpiece presenting serfs as human beings worthy of respect and admiration, which had the same explosive effect in Russia as Stowe's *Uncle Tom's Cabin* did in the United States. 🔊 3-60

10.2. "Mumu" (1852)   «Муму́»

The touching story of a deaf and dumb serf, Gerasim, whose only joy in life was his little dog Mumu. His cruel landlady, disturbed by Mumu's barking at night, ordered the dog killed. After unsuccessful attempts to hide Mumu, Gerasim ends up drowning his pet with his own hands.

Illustration:

(a) From the jokes about Vovochka, notorious bad boy (equivalent of Bart Simpson):

Во́зле па́мятника Алекса́ндру Серге́евичу Пу́шкину стоя́т два пио- 🔊 3-61
не́ра. Подхо́дит к ним Во́вочка и спра́шивает: —Кому́ па́мятник?
    Пионе́ры отвеча́ют: —Пу́шкину.
    —Э́то кото́рый "Муму́" написа́л?
    —Ты что, дура́к? «Муму́» Турге́нев написа́л, а это—Пу́шкин.
    Во́вочка заду́мался. Пото́м говори́т: —Что́-то я вас не пойму́.
«Муму́» Турге́нев написа́л, а па́мятник Пу́шкину поста́вили?

Two young pioneers are standing near Pushkin's monument. Vovochka approaches them with a question: "Whose monument is this?" The pioneers answer: "This is Pushkin's monument." "Pushkin? The one who wrote 'Mumu'?" "Are you crazy? 'Mumu' was written by Turgenev. This is Pushkin." Vovochka falls to thinking and then says: "I don't get it. *Turgenev* wrote 'Mumu' and they erect a monument to *Pushkin*?"

(b) Another joke treats this story as a bare minimum of literary knowledge:

3-62

Муж и жена́ вы́шли на прогу́лку. Муж мра́чно молчи́т. Жена́ пыта́ется завяза́ть разгово́р:
–Кака́я же́нщина была́ А́нна Каре́нина! Каки́е чу́вства!
Муж молчи́т.
–Да ты что, А́нну Каре́нину не чита́л?
–Не чита́л.
–А что ж ты чита́л?
–«Муму́»! А е́сли бу́дешь пристава́ть—утоплю́!

A husband and a wife are taking a walk. The husband is gloomily silent. The wife is trying to strike up a conversation: "What a woman Anna Karenina was! What emotions!" The husband does not respond. "You mean you haven't read Anna Karenina?" "I have not." "What on Earth have you read then?" "I've read 'Mumu.' And if you keep bothering me, I'll drown you!"

(c) A popular cartoon in *Но́вое вре́мя*, Jan. 1997, and later in *Крестья́нка*:

3-63

Здесь жила́ Муму́, траги́чес-ки поги́бшая в конце́ Х1Х ве́ка. Па́мятник старины́. Охраня́ется госуда́рством.

"Here lived Mumu, who tragically perished in the end of the 19th century. A historical monument, protected by law."

Fig. 3-16.

3-64 **10.3. *Fathers and Sons* (1862)**   **«Отцы́ и де́ти»**
[literally: Fathers and Children]

The title of this novel became synonymous with the conflict between generations. The "sons" are represented by a positivist and nihilist, Bazarov, who does not believe in God, despises art and social conventions, and is devoted to science.

10.4. *The Nest of the Gentry* (1859)   «Дворя́нское гнездо́» ◀))) 3-65

The title of Turgenev's short novel stands for the bygone poetic, almost pastoral life of the Russian gentry.

10.5. *The Diary of A Superfluous Man*   «Дневни́к ли́шнего челове́ка»

The term «ли́шние лю́ди» "superfluous people" was first used by Turgenev in ◀))) 3-66 this story, and later became a standard reference to a series of literary characters (like Pushkin's Onegin, Lermontov's Pechorin) or people in real life. They are ironic "outsiders" in any society and don't know what to do with themselves despite their usually considerable talents, education and sophisticated views of life.

10.6. *Poems in Prose*   «Стихотворе́ния в про́зе»

In the last years of his life, Turgenev wrote a series of these poems in prose. The one cited below had to be memorized in schools:

> Во дни сомне́ний, во дни тя́гостных разду́мий о су́дьбах мое́й ◀))) 3-67
> ро́дины — ты оди́н мне опо́ра и подде́ржка, о вели́кий, могу́чий,
> правди́вый и свобо́дный ру́сский язы́к. Не будь тебя́, как не впасть
> в отча́яние при ви́де того́, что соверша́ется до́ма? Но нельзя́
> ве́рить, чтобы тако́й язы́к не́ был дан вели́кому наро́ду!

In the days of doubt, in the days of painful reflections on the destiny of my motherland, you alone are my support and my buttress, oh great, powerful, truthful, and free Russian language. If not for you, how is one not to fall into despair at the sight of what is going on at home? But it is impossible to believe that such a language was not given to a great people.

Illustration:

(a) This lyrical piece is so well-known that the words вели́кий, могу́- ◀))) 3-68
чий are often used as synonyms for the Russian language (e.g: «Ну
как э́то сказа́ть на на́шем могу́чем и вели́ком?» "How does one
express it in our great and powerful [language]?"

(b) An article in the newspaper *За́втра*, 1997, entitled «Как не впасть
в отча́янье …» "How not to fall into despair" discusses a new law
in Kazakhstan requiring that a full 50% of any broadcast in any
audio-visual medium has to be in the Kazakh language.

11. FEDOR MIKHAILOVICH DOSTOEVSKY (1821–81)

ФЁДОР МИХА́ЙЛОВИЧ ДОСТОÉВСКИЙ

Certain facts of Dostoevsky's biography are known by all educated Russians: he suffered from epilepsy (and so did some of his characters: Myshkin in *The Idiot*, Smerdiakov in *The Brothers Karamazov*); his first novel *Poor Folks* «Бе́дные лю́ди» (1846) brought him overnight fame but not fortune, thus he was chronically short of money and debt-ridden, and his publishers paid precious little for his masterpieces; he participated in a secret society whose activity consisted mainly in heated discussions about Utopian socialism; was arrested together with his idealistic friends and condemned to death; endured the horror of standing in the city square facing the firing squad; at the last moment there arrived a messenger with the melodramatic announcement of the tsar's clemency: instead of death, prison and exile in Siberia. Out of this experience came his *Notes from the House of the Dead* «Запи́ски из мёртвого до́ма». He had a tormented affair with Apolinaria Suslova, *la femme fatale* of his life. He followed Suslova to Germany and France and tried to cure his financial problems at casinos where he became addicted to gambling. At age 44 Dostoevsky married Anna Grigorievna Snitkina, his 20-year-old stenographer to whom he dictated his novel *The Gambler* «Игро́к». She helped her husband finish the work, and he thus was able to meet the publisher's deadline (if he had been late, his publisher would get the manuscript free!). His public speech about Pushkin turned into an ecstatic celebration of Dostoevsky.

Fig. 3-17.

No one before Dostoevsky investigated moral and philosophical truths in a work of literary fiction with such fervor and suspense. Each of his novels is a philosophical treatise intertwined with murder, scandals, hysterical confessions and fits of self-sacrifice.

11.1. *The Insulted and Injured* (1861)   «Уни́женные и оскорблённые»

◀))) 3-69 The title of one of Dostoevsky's earlier novels is often quoted when social injustice is the topic. Thus, an article in ***Но́вое вре́мя***, March 1997, about the troubles of Russian citizens living in Lithuania has the headline «Уни́женные и оскорблённые».

11.2. *Crime and Punishment* (1866)   «Преступле́ние и наказа́ние»

Rodion Raskol′nikov, a poor and ambitious young man, commits a sordid premeditated murder, killing an insignificant and mean old lady with an axe. He does it not so much for her money as to prove to himself that he belongs to the same exceptional group of people as Napoleon, who dare break the rules of human conduct to attain their great goals, which are possibly beneficial for humanity.

Illustration:

(a) An article with the headline **«Преступле́ния и наказа́ния»** in ***Аргуме́нты и фа́кты***, 1997, discusses corruption at all levels of society and the problems with implementing a law to punish the offenders.

(b) A letter to the magazine ***Крестья́нка***, April 1997, written in response to the magazine's previous editorial, defends the values of modern young people: ◀))) **3-70**

> **Вас трево́жит «жёсткая ориента́ция» молодёжи на «неме́дленное обогаще́ние». И гло́жет ностальги́я по «суса́льному» про́шлому, где всё бы́ло присто́йно, идилли́чески разме́ренно. Почита́ешь: вы, ста́ршее поколе́ние, пря́мо в раю́ жи́ли. А мы,—молодёжь,—сплошь «Раско́льниковы с топора́ми».**

You are worried by a "hard determination" of the younger generation "to get rich immediately." You are gnawed by nostalgia for the sugary past, for the time when life was orderly and idyllically measured. One only has to read what you wrote to get the impression that you, the older generation, lived right in paradise. And of course we, the younger generation, are nothing but Raskol′nikovs with axes.

11.3. *The Brothers Karamazov* (1880)   «Бра́тья Карама́зовы»

The plot of the last and most profound of Dostoevsky's novels is structured around patricide. The brothers are Ivan, the intellectual rebel; impulsive Dmitri; an illegitimate son and servant in the house, Smerdiakov; and the youngest, Alyosha, preparing to become a monk.

11.3.1. **Широ́к челове́к! Я бы су́зил ...** Literally: "A human being is too ◀))) **3-71** broad. I would narrow him down ..." Meaning: there is room for too many opposite values in the human soul (spoken by Dmitri).

11.3.2. **Всё позво́лено** "everything is permitted." This is a part of Ivan's argu- ◀))) **3-72** ment that if God does not exist there are no moral restraints, everything is permitted.

◀》 **3-72** *Illustration:* ***Новое время,*** February 1997: «Оста́вшись по́сле кра́ха комму-
ни́зма еди́нственной глоба́льной идеоло́гией, капитали́зм ведёт себя́ как
победи́тель, кото́рому дозво́лено всё». "Having remained the only global
ideology after the downfall of Communism, Capitalism behaves like a victor for
whom everything is permitted."

◀》 **3-73** 11.3.3. **С у́мным челове́ком и поговори́ть прия́тно.** "It is always a pleasure to
talk to an intelligent man." This quotation is often used when the speaker
wishes to say, "I believe we understand each other perfectly."

◀》 **3-74** 11.3.4. **Слези́нка ребёнка** "a child's tiny tear." The weightiest argument in
Ivan's rebellion against God: if God allows abuse of innocent children who
have had no time to sin yet, then the idea of happiness and harmony in the
afterlife does not make sense: how could anyone be happy if happiness were
bought at such a price as one tiny tear from an abused child?

Illustration:
(a) A popular satirical TV show, **«Ку́клы»** *Puppets*, ridiculed the
ignorance of the political leaders in the sketch **«Экза́мен»**. All the
puppets are to have an oral exam in Russian literature and discuss the
topics they have just received. **Зю́га**, the puppet representing
Ziuganov, reads his aloud:

◀》 **3-74** **И у меня́ хоро́шая те́ма—сча́стье всего́ челове́чества. Это я сдам
(смо́трит в биле́т, озада́ченно): тут ещё про слези́нку ребёнка …
Достое́вщина кака́я-то!**

I, too, got a nice topic: the happiness of all humanity. This I know how
to answer (looks at card with exam topics, puzzled): There is something
here about a tiny tear of a child … Some kind of Dostoevskianism!

◀》 **3-75** 11.3.5. The main character in Ivan's story about the Catholic church in the middle ages is **Вели́кий Инквизи́тор** "The Grand Inquisitor." His power is so
great that when Christ suddenly appears in the streets, the Grand Inquisitor
orders Him arrested, and although everyone instantly recognizes Christ, people
do not dare disobey the Grand Inquisitor and do as they are told.

11.4. *The Idiot* **(1868)**   «Идио́т»

◀》 **3-76** **Красота́ спасёт мир** "Beauty will save the world."

12. NIKOLAI GAVRILOVICH CHERNYSHEVSKY (1828–89)

НИКОЛА́Й ГАВРИ́ЛОВИЧ ЧЕРНЫШЕ́ВСКИЙ

A revolutionary, a radical literary critic, an economist and a writer of dubious literary merit but immense influence on several generations of young people, Lenin among them, inflamed by his ideas of social justice and ways to achieve it. Chernyshevsky died after many years of prison and hard labor in Siberia. He became an

Fig. 3-18.

official icon in Soviet times, was ridiculed by Nabokov in his novel «Дар» *The Gift*, and still is respected not so much as a thinker and writer but as a man of civic courage.

12.1. *What Is to Be Done?* (1863)   «Что де́лать?» 🔊)) 3-77

Lenin borrowed Chernyshevsky's title for his revolutionary pamphlet (also studied in Soviet schools) in which he claimed that Russian literature produced two most important questions: *Who is to Blame?* and *What is to Be Done?* (see also **Герцен**, 7.2).

Illustration:

   (a)   A cartoon in the newspaper *Изве́стия*, 1997, depicts a bookstore as a metaphor for modern Russia: all the copies of *Who is to Blame?* are sold out, while the copies of *What is to Be Done?* collect dust on overcrowded shelves.

Рис. Н.КИНЧАРОВА (Волгоград).

Fig. 3-19.

◀)) 3-77 (b) **«Что де́лать?» или как расши́рить и укрепи́ть свой би́знес»** "'What is to be done,' or how to improve and increase your business." An advertisement for a food-packing machine in *Аргуме́нты и фа́кты*, 1996.

◀)) 3-78 **12.1.1. Разу́мный эгои́зм** "Rational egotism/selfishness." A belief of "the new people," heroes of *What is to be Done?*, according to which acting in one's own best interests guarantees the flourishing of society.

◀)) 3-78 *Illustration:* A headline in *Но́вое вре́мя*, March 1997: **«На поро́ге доктри́ны Кли́нтона? Экономи́ческий эгои́зм как осно́ва разу́много эгои́зма».** "On the threshold of Clinton's doctrine? Economical selfishness as the foundation for rational selfishness."

◀)) 3-79 **12.1.2. Ве́ра Па́вловна** Vera Pavlovna. The female protagonist in *What is to Be Done?* seeking emancipation for women. Several chapters describe her dreams, revealing her utopian hopes of a happy future based on Equality, Fraternity and Freedom.

◀)) 3-80 ## 13. KOZ'MA PRUTKOV (mid-19th century)

КОЗЬМА́ ПРУТКО́В

Koz'ma Prutkov is a satirical character created by the writers A.K. Tolstoy **Алексе́й Константи́нович Толсто́й** (1817–75), A.M. Zhemchuzhnikov **Алексе́й Миха́йлович Жемчу́жников** (1821–1908) and V.M. Zhemchuzhnikov **Влади́мир Миха́йлович Жемчу́жников** (1830–84). Assuming the name and identity of Koz'ma Prutkov (a bombastic petty bureaucrat, greatly pleased with himself), they entertained Russia with Prutkov's hilarious poems, dramas, and diaries, especially his *Thoughts and Maxims*: "**Мы́сли и афори́змы**," many of which became part of spoken Russian.

Fig. 3-20.

◀)) 3-81 **13.1. Бди!** "Be vigilant (beware)!"

◀)) 3-82 **13.1.2. Е́сли хо́чешь быть счастли́вым, будь им.** "If you wish to be happy, then do."

◀)) 3-83 **13.1.3. Никто́ не обни́мет необъя́тного.** "No one can embrace the unembraceable [the infinite]."

13.1.4. Смотри́ в ко́рень! "Look into the root." [Look into the heart of the  🔊 3-84 matter].

13.1.5. Éсли у тебя́ есть фонта́н, заткни́ его́: дай отдохну́ть и фонта́ну.. "If 🔊 3-85 you have a fountain, plug it up: let the fountain, too, have its rest."

13.1.6. Мно́гие лю́ди подо́бны колба́сам: чем их начи́нят, то и но́сят в себе́. 🔊 3-86 "Many people resemble sausages: they carry in them whatever someone stuffed them with."

13.1.7. Специали́ст подо́бен флю́су: полнота́ его́ односторо́нняя. "An 🔊 3-87 expert resembles a swollen cheek: its fullness is one-sided."

14. LEV NIKOLAEVICH TOLSTOY, LEO TOLSTOY (1828–1910)

ЛЕВ НИКОЛА́ЕВИЧ ТОЛСТО́Й

Tolstoy was
 born into one of the oldest of aristocratic families: he was a count, an officer, and a rich man with a splendid education. An estate-owner in Yasnaya Polyana **Я́сная По ля́на** (now a museum), Tolstoy worked throughout his long life like a man condemned to penal servitude: there are 90 volumes in the most complete collection of his work. Russians are familiar with several aspects of Tolstoy's life, including that Sofia Andreevna, Tolstoy's wife, copied by hand all his

Fig. 3-21.

Fig. 3-22.   Tolstoy's estate Yasnaya Polyana

Fig. 3-23.   Tolstoy leaving home in his last days

drafts, took care of his health, and bore him 13 children. Theirs was not a happy marriage. While Tolstoy was for his contemporaries the highest moral authority, he was excommunicated from the Russian Orthodox Church for his non-Orthodox interpretation of the New Testament. Tolstoy advocated a simple way of living, did not eat meat, wore peasant clothes and did all kinds of physical work from farming to shoemaking. He believed that one can change the world for the best by improving oneself and that evil cannot be fought by violence. The followers of his teaching were called толсто́вцы, "Tolstoyans." At the age of 82, he secretly left home intending to live the life of a pilgrim, but soon fell ill and died of heart failure in the house of the station-master at the railroad station Astapovo.

A giant in everything he did, he was a fearless seeker of truth and the meaning of life, art and religion, a fighter for social justice, an educator and one of the greatest writers in world literature. No other writer in Russian literature has captured the joy of life so fully or was so optimistic as Tolstoy.

Lenin's article about the significance of Tolstoy, "Leo Tolstoy as a Mirror of the Russian Revolution" «Лев Толсто́й как зе́ркало ру́сской револю́ции», was part of the school program during the Soviet years. According to Lenin, Tolstoy was ideologically retarded, since he misunderstood the role of the proletariat, but his criticism of tsarist Russia was valuable. The title of the article is often used as a source for ironic statements:

◀))) 3-88

(a)   A headline in *Но́вое вре́мя*, November 1996: «Анато́лий Чуба́йс как зе́ркало росси́йской госуда́рственности». Anatoly Chubais as a Mirror of the Russian State System."

· (b)   In *Но́вое вре́мя*, December 1996: «Мир в Чечне́ как зе́ркало ру́сского капитали́зма». "Peace in Chechnia as a Mirror of Russian Capitalism."

Fig. 3-24.   Tolstoy's wife outside the house in which he died

14.1. *War and Peace* (1869)   «Война́ и мир»

The novel describes Russia during its war with Napoleon. There are about 600 characters and two principal families: the Rostovs, with young Natasha and her brother Nikolai, and the Bolkonskys (Prince Andrei and his sister Princess Maria). Pierre Bezukhov is a friend to both families.

14.1.1. **Пе́рвая коло́нна марширу́ет ... Втора́я коло́нна марширу́ет ...** "The ◀))) 3-89 first column marches to.., The second column marches to ..." A plan for military action read at the council by a German General and in the German language; Tolstoy shows that no one listens to him through the list of unfinished sentences. The quotation is often used humorously when planning some event.

14.1.2. **Всё пусто́е, всё обма́н, кро́ме э́того бесконе́чного не́ба** "Everything ◀))) 3-90 is empty [void of meaning], everything is a deceit, everything but this limitless sky."(Thoughts of Prince Andrei lying wounded on the battlefield.)

14.1.3. **Она́ не удоста́ивает быть у́мною** "She does not condescend to be ◀))) 3-91 intelligent." Pierre's answer to Princess Maria's question whether Natasha is intelligent.

14.1.4.

3-92

… дуби́на наро́дной войны́ подняла́сь со все́ею свое́ю гро́зною и вели́чественною си́лой и, не спра́шивая ничьи́х вку́сов и пра́вил, с глу́пою простото́й, но с целесообра́зностью, не разбира́я ничего́, поднима́лась, опуска́лась и гвозди́ла францу́зов до тех пор, пока́ не поги́бло всё наше́ствие.

И бла́го тому́ наро́ду, кото́рый не как францу́зы в 1813 году́, отсалютова́в по всем пра́вилам иску́сства и переверну́в шпа́гу эфе́-сом, грацио́зно и учти́во передаёт её великоду́шному победи́телю, а бла́го тому́ наро́ду, кото́рый в мину́ту испыта́ния, не спра́шивая, как по пра́вилам поступа́ли други́е в подо́бных слу́чаях, с просто-то́ю и лёгкостью поднима́ет пе́рвую попа́вшуюся дуби́ну и гвозди́т е́ю до тех пор, пока́ в душе́ его́ чу́вство оскорбле́ния и ме́сти не заме́нится презре́нием и жа́лостью.

The club of the people's war rose with all its fierce might and majestic power; and not asking for anyone's opinion or rules, with complete simplicity, but purposefully, not looking either way, rose and fell, rose and fell, pounding the French until the whole invasion had perished.

And blessed are those nations who did not do as the French in 1813: saluting according to all of the rules of war and turning their sword hilt first, graciously and with civility handing it over to the magnanimous victor; but blessed are those nations who, in a trying time, did not ask what rules others had followed in similar cases, but with ease and simplicity picked up the first club available and pounded it until in their hearts the feeling of injustice, affront and revenge were substituted by contempt and pity.

3-93 14.1.5. **Éжели бы я был не я, а краси́вейший, умне́йший и лу́чший челове́к в ми́ре, и был бы свобо́ден, я бы сию́ мину́ту на коле́нях проси́л руки́ и любви́ ва́шей.** "If I were not I, but the most handsome, intelligent man and the best person in the world, and were free, I would this instant, on my knees, beg for your hand in marriage and for your love." Pierre's words to Natasha.

14.2. *Anna Karenina* (1877)   «А́нна Каре́нина»

Tolstoy wrote to his friend, N.N. Strakhov:

3-94

Éсли же бы я хоте́л сказа́ть слова́ми всё то, что име́л в виду́ вы́-разить рома́ном, то я до́лжен бы был написа́ть рома́н тот са́мый, кото́рый я написа́л, снача́ла.

"If I wanted to say in words all I wanted to express by this novel, I would have to write again that same novel which I have written."

Fig. 3-25.   "The Two Tsars of Russia"

14.2.1. Все счастли́вые се́мьи похо́жи друг на дру́га, ка́ждая несчастли́вая 🔊 **3-95** **семья́ несча́стлива по-сво́ему.** "All happy families are similar to one another, but all unhappy families are unhappy in their own way."

14.2.2. Всё смеша́лось в до́ме Обло́нских. "Everything was mixed up in the 🔊 **3-96** Oblonskys' house."

Illustration: **«Всё смеша́лось в до́ме Обло́нских»** is a subheading to the article **«Ма́ленькое сраже́ние за большу́ю нефть».** "A small battle for big oil." *Но́вое вре́мя,* June 1997.

14.2.3. Образу́ется. "Things will settle themselves/shape themselves up."   🔊 **3-97**

15. NIKOLAI LESKOV (1831–95)   НИКОЛА́Й ЛЕСКО́В

15.1. "Lefty" (1881)   «Левша́»

Leskov wrote short stories and novels, and, while he largely failed as a novelist, his stories remain some of the most dazzling in the Russian language. He also wrote **«Ле́ди Ма́кбет Мце́нского уе́зда»** "Lady Macbeth of the Mtsensk 🔊 **3-98** District," which was later the source for an opera by Shostakovich. "Lefty" is about a left-handed Russian master craftsman who bests the English masters who created a life-sized steel flea: Lefty provides the flea with golden shoes.

16. ANTON PAVLOVICH CHEKHOV (1860–1904)

АНТÓН ПÁВЛОВИЧ ЧÉХОВ

Fig. 3-26.

Chekhov, a medical doctor by education, a master of the short story and one of the world's greatest playwrights, is also remembered as a model representative of the Russian intelligentsia. He was the grandson of a serf and the son of a small shopkeeper who ruled over his family with a heavy hand. Chekhov had bitter memories of the early years of his life, which he described in the aphoristic form: **В дéтстве у меня нé было дéтства** "In my childhood I had no childhood." He began to write his humorous stories, usually using the pen-name **Антóша Чехонтé**, Antosha Chekhonte, exclusively for money, and for a long time did not take his talent seriously. A gentle, tactful person with iron discipline and principles, Chekhov did a tremendous amount of social work, from organizing immediate help to famished peasants to his thorough investigation of the penitentiary system on the island of Sakhalin. Chekhov died at 44, of tuberculosis. His last words were: "Ich sterbe," "I am dying"—in German.

🔊 3-99 16.1. Aphoristic sayings from Chekhov's notebooks and letters. Chekhov hated physical, mental and moral sloppiness; some lines from his letters to his brother with admonitions to this effect entered the popular stock of quotations: **Я всю жúзнь выдáвливал из себя по кáпле рабá** "All my life, I squeezed out the slave in me, drop by drop."

Illustration: A joke in the humorous section of ***Нóвое врéмя***, Feb. 1995, based on a mixture of Chekhov's line with the proverb «**кáпля кáмень тóчит**»
🔊 3-99 "constant dripping wears away the stone": «**Мóжно ли тóчить кáплей кáмень, выдáвливая из себя по кáпле рабá?**» "Can one wear away a stone while squeezing out the slave in oneself, drop by drop?"

🔊 3-100 16.2. "The Plaintive Book" **Жáлобная кнúга** (1884) (colloquial distortion of "the book of complaints" **Кнúга жáлоб**). A series of funny entries in the book of complaints at a provincial railroad station includes various observations of bored passengers (silly scribbles, declarations of love, pompous statements with grammatical mistakes, and so on).

🔊 3-101 16.2.1. **Подъезжáя к сиéй стáнции и глядя на прирóду в окнó, с меня слетéла шляпа. И. Ярмóнкин.** "Approaching this station and looking at nature through the window, my hat flew off my head. I. Yarmonkin." Cited in all school grammar-textbooks as an example of a dangling participle.

16.2.2. Проезжа́я через ста́нцию и бу́дучи го́лоден, в рассужде́нии, чего́ бы 🔊 **3-102**
покýшать, я не мог найти́ по́стной пи́щи. Дья́кон Ду́хов. "Passing through
this station and being in contemplation as to what should I eat, I could not find
lenten food here. Deacon Dukhov."

Illustration: In his famous autobiography, *I Myself* **«Я сам»**, Mayakovsky explains the reason for his collaboration with the magazine *The New Satiricon*:

В рассужде́нии, чего́ бы покýшать, стал писа́ть в «Но́вом Сатирико́не». 🔊 **3-102**
"Being in contemplation as to what should I eat, I began to write in *The New
Satiricon*."

16.3. "Letter to a Learned Neighbor" **«Письмо́ к учёному сосе́ду»** (1880). One
of the funniest of Chekhov's stories. The letter of an idle and ignorant old man
inviting his educated neighbor to debate scientific matters.

16.3.1. Э́того не мо́жет быть, потому́ что э́того не мо́жет быть никогда́. 🔊 **3-103**
"This can't be, because it never can be."

16.4. "Van′ka" **«Ва́нька».** The diminutive of Ivan is Vanya, and Van′ka is its
pejorative form. A 9-year-old boy, Vanya Zhukov, an abused shoemaker's
apprentice, secretly writes to his grandfather, complaining of his cruel masters
and begging the grandfather to take him back home.

16.4.1. На дере́вню де́душке "To my Grandfather, to the village" (the standard form would be **в дере́вню**). Having very vague ideas of how mail works,
this is the only address Van′ka writes on the envelope. The reader knows that
the poor boy will never get help. [See also Chapter 4.]

Ми́лый де́душка, сде́лай бо́жецкую ми́лость, возьми́ меня́ отсю́да 🔊 **3-104**
домо́й, на дере́вню, не́ту никако́й мое́й возмо́жности ... [...] Поду́-
мав немно́го, он умакну́л перо́ и написа́л а́дрес: На дере́вню
де́душке.
    Пото́м почеса́лся, поду́мал и приба́вил: "Константи́ну
Мака́рычу." (Van′ka's spelling: **божецкую** should be **божескую**).

Dear Granddaddy, have God's mercy on me, take me home to the village from here. [...] He thought a little, then dipped the pen in the ink-
pot and wrote the address: "To my Grandfather, to the village." Then
he scratched himself, gave it another thought, and added: "To
Konstantin Makarovich."

Use:

    (a)   A frequent joke whenever a lack of address or a wrong address is
           discussed.

    (b)   When asking for help or a favor, one can say: **Ми́лый де́душка**
           Константи́н Мака́рович, сде́лай бо́жецкую мило́сть ... (a direc-
           tive follows).

🔊 **3-105** 16.5. From the story "Kashtanka" **«Кашта́нка»** (1887), written from the point of view of a dog: **Ты, Кашта́нка, насеко́мое суще́ство и бо́льше ничего́. Супроти́в челове́ка ты всё равно́, что пло́тник супроти́в столяра́.** "You, Kashtanka, you are just an insect creature and nothing more. In comparison to a man you are nothing, the same as a carpenter in comparison to a cabinet maker." (Literally: against a man; **супроти́в** is a dialectal form of **про́тив**.) These are the words of a drunken cabinet maker addressed to his faithful dog, Kashtanka. (The dog's name comes from the color of its coat; **кашта́новые во́лосы** is light brown hair in Russian.) [See also Chapter 4.]

16.6. "A Defenseless Creature" **«Беззащи́тное существо»** (1887). The wife of a petty official intimidates his superiors with her irrelevant but persistent complaints and manages to get a pension.

🔊 **3-106** 16.6.1. **Я же́нщина сла́бая, беззащи́тная.** "I am a weak, defenseless woman."

🔊 **3-106** 16.6.2. **Ко́фий сего́дня пила́, и без вся́кого удово́льствия.** "Today I drank my coffee and did not get any pleasure from it." One of Shchukina's complaints, especially frequently quoted.

16.7. "The Man in a Case" **«Челове́к в футля́ре»** (1898) is one of the most famous of Chekhov's stories. The main character, Belikov, is a schoolteacher scared of life and thought. He protects himself from life by wearing in any weather his galoshes, thick coat, glasses and umbrella. His thoughts never deviate from official instructions.

🔊 **3-107** 16.7.1. **Как бы чего́ не вы́шло** "I fear something bad will come of it." These words were the only reaction Belikov had to any innovation. The quotation is used to describe bureaucrats.

🔊 **3-108** 16.8. Another story about a schoolteacher, "The Teacher of Literature" **«Учи́тель слове́сности»** (1894), yields this quote: **Во́лга впада́ет в Каспи́йское мо́ре. Ло́шади ку́шают овёс и се́но.** "The Volga flows into the Caspian sea. Horses eat oats and hay." A colleague of the protagonist was famous for saying nothing but trivialities.

🔊 **3-109** 16.9. **Пострада́вший отде́лался лёгким испу́гом** "The victim escaped with nothing but a slight scare." From the story "Joy" **«Ра́дость»** (1883). The joy is that of Mitya Kuldarov, who was hit by a horse and cab and felt honored to read a report about this event in a local newspaper. The quotation is a line from this report. Mitya shows it to all his relatives and friends.

Illustration: In a satirical novel by Il'f and Petrov [see 20] a note mimicking Chekhov's is published:

🔊 **3-109** **ПОПА́Л ПОД ЛО́ШАДЬ**
    Вчера́ на пло́щади Свердло́ва попа́л под ло́шадь изво́зчика № 8974 гр. О. Бе́ндер. Пострада́вший отде́лался лёгким испу́гом.

HIT BY A HORSE
Yesterday on Sverdlov square Mr. O. Bender was hit by the horse of cab-driver #8974. The victim escaped with nothing but a slight scare.

16.10. "Horse's Last Name" **«Лошади́ная фами́лия»** (1885). Trying to think of ◀)) **3-110** the name of a healer who can help the General with a severe toothache, the protagonist remembers only that the last name had something to do with horses; for two days he goes on trying out horselike surnames: Mr. Stallion? No. Mr. Mare? Doesn't sound right. Only when someone asks him to sell a bag of oats, does it dawn on him that the last name is Ovsov, Mr. Oats. By then, of course, it is too late.

16.11. "Sleepy" **«Спать хо́чется»** (1888). One of the darkest of Chekhov's sto- ◀)) **3-111** ries, in which a young girl is mistreated by her masters: during the day she runs errands without a moment's rest, and at night takes care of a crying baby. Losing her reason from tiredness and lack of sleep, she smothers the baby and finally falls asleep.

16.12. "The Fat One and the Thin One" **«То́лстый и то́нкий»** (1883). The ◀)) **3-112** story describes two officials, former classmates, who meet by chance on the street. As soon as the thin one learns that the fat one has achieved the higher rank, his manner drastically changes from friendly to sycophantic.

Illustration: The quotation heads an advertisement for tea in *Аргуме́нты и фа́кты,* May 1997: **«То́лстым и то́нким на заме́тку»** "To the attention of the ◀)) **3-112** fat and the thin ones."

16.13. "The Lady with the Lap-Dog" **«Да́ма с соба́чкой»** (1899) is a story of two married people who meet at the resort in Yalta and fall in love.

Illustration:
(a) *Огонёк*, April 1996, informs its readers that Elizabeth Taylor presented a new perfume from her collection, called Black Pearl. According to the actress, who had just been through her latest divorce, this perfume perfectly suits the lonely "ladies with lap-dogs."

Элизабе́т Тэ́йлор предста́вила но́вые духи́ из свое́й колле́кции. ◀)) **3-113** **Называ́ются «Чёрный же́мчуг». По мне́нию актри́сы, неда́вно в очередно́й раз разве́дшейся, они́ о́чень подхо́дят одино́ким «да́мам с соба́чками».**

(b) An article in *Комсомо́льская пра́вда,* 1997, discusses casual relationships at the southern resorts under the heading **«Тут у ка́ждого своя́ да́ма с соба́чкой»** "Here, everyone has his own lady with a lap-dog."

(c) A cartoon in *Крестья́нка* shows a man in bed, embracing a huge book with the title *Lady with a Lap-Dog.* The balloon over his head says: "Finally I too have a family …"

Fig. 3-27.

17. ALEKSEI MAXIMOVICH GORKY (known popularly as Maksim Gorky Макси́м Го́рький) (1868–1936)

АЛЕКСЕ́Й МАКСИ́МОВИЧ ГО́РЬКИЙ

Maksim Gorky was born into a poor family in the city of Nizhny Novgorod. He was orphaned at 11, and had to earn his daily bread while still a small child. Gorky described the hardships of his childhood and what he called **«свинцо́вые ме́рзости жи́зни»**, "leaden abominations of life," in the autobiographic trilogy *Childhood*, *In the World* and *My Universities* **«Де́тство», «В лю́дях», «Мои́ университе́ты»**. Gorky **Го́рький** ("bitter") was his pen-name; his real surname is **Пе́шков** Peshkov. His early stories, full of lower-class romantic rebellion, fascinated the younger generation. Gorky himself became a legend of the Revolution, yet in 1921 he left for Italy and stayed outside the Soviet Union for a good ten years.

A founder of socialist realism, a personal friend of Lenin and other revolutionaries who later came to power, in the Soviet period Gorky was officially proclaimed the best writer of the 20th century. He used his influence with the Bolsheviks to save the lives of many ideologically suspect writers.

17.1. "The Song of Storm-Petrel" (1901)   «Песнь о Буреве́стнике»

3-114 The word **буревестник** literally means "foretelling the storm/storm-harbinger." Written in a solemn elevated romantic chant, this "Song" gained Gorky a new name: **«буреве́стник револю́ции»** "Harbinger of Revolution."

3-115 17.1.1. **Вот он но́сится над мо́рем, го́рдый, чёрный де́мон бу́ри.** "Here he is, flashing over the sea, like a proud black demon of the storm."

Use: When one is very busy and running around like mad, one might say: **Я**
3-115 **ношу́сь, как го́рдый чёрный де́мон бу́ри!** I heard a mother saying about her little boy: **Он носи́лся по коридо́ру как го́рдый чёрный де́мон бу́ри.** "He was running in the hallway like a proud black demon of the storm."

17.1.2. Глу́пый пи́нгвин ро́бко пря́чет те́ло жи́рное в утёсах. "The silly penguin timidly hides his fat body in the cliffs."  3-116

Use: **Глу́пый Ми́шка ро́бко пря́чет те́ло жи́рное в руба́шку.** "Silly Michael timidly hides his fat body in his shirt." (From an overheard conversation). 3-116

17.1.3. Пусть сильне́е гря́нет бу́ря! "Let the storm break out stronger!" 3-117

17.2. "The Song of the Falcon" (1895)   «Песнь о Со́коле»

Written in the same romantic chant, this "Song" has a plot: a wounded falcon lies on the top of a cliff and dreams of flying at least one more time. He is overheard by a fat, self-satisfied grass snake (**уж**), clearly a cowardly bourgeois, who begins questioning the brave bird, but cannot understand falcon's aspirations: **«Мне здесь прекра́сно: тепло́ и сы́ро».** "I love it here: it's warm and humid." 3-118

17.2.1. Рождённый по́лзать — лета́ть не мо́жет. "He who was born to crawl, cannot fly." 3-119

17.2.2. Безу́мство хра́брых — вот му́дрость жи́зни! Безу́мству хра́брых поём мы пе́сню. The madness of the brave ones — that's the wisdom of life! We sing to the madness of the brave." 3-120

Illustration:

(a) A joke in ***Но́вое вре́мя***, February, 1996: **«Безу́мству хра́брых ну́жен психиа́тр!»** "The madness of the brave ones requires a psychiatrist!"

(b) **«Безу́мству Жа́нны поём мы пе́сню»** "We sing to the madness of Joan." Headline in an article about Joan of Arc as a psychopath and about the thin line between disease and superhuman achievement; in the newspaper ***На гра́ни невозмо́жного*** *On the Borderline of the Impossible*, 1997.

3-120

БЕЗУМСТВУ ЖАННЫ
ПОЕМ МЫ ПЕСНЮ

Fig. 3-28.

17.3. "The Old Woman Izergil" (1894)   **«Стару́ха Изерги́ль»**

🔊 3-121 **В жи́зни всегда́ есть ме́сто по́двигу.** "There is always room in life for heroic deeds."

Illustration:

🔊 3-121   (a) A headline in ***Огонёк***, November 1996: **«В жи́зни всегда́ есть ме́сто га́дости?»** "There is always room in life for foulness, is there?"

          (b) Headline in ***Аргуме́нты и фа́кты***, 1996: **«В жи́зни всегда́ есть ме́сто по́длости»** "There is always room in life for baseness."

          (c) Humorous story by **П. Блужда́йцев** in ***Но́вое вре́мя***, August 1995, entitled: **«Практи́ческий патриоти́зм. В жи́зни всегда́ есть ме́сто всему́»** "Practical patriotism: there is always room in life for everything."

17.4. *Mother* (1906)   **«Мать»**

This novel is dedicated to the first Russian revolution of 1905. Nilovna, mother of the worker Pavel, gradually comes to understand her son's revolutionary activity and becomes an active member of a revolutionary movement. The novel was the model for socialist-realist literature.

🔊 3-122 **17.4.1. О́чень своевре́менная кни́га** "An exceptionally well-timed book." This is how Lenin (according to Gorky's essay "V.I. Lenin," 1924, 1930) evaluated *Mother*.

Illustration: The use of Lenin's words as a headline in ***Но́вое вре́мя***, May 1997: **«О́чень своевре́менная кни́га»** is highly ironic, since the article refers to memoirs by Sergei Kovalev **Ковалёв**, a famous dissident, who devoted his entire life to the destruction of Lenin's ideology.

17.5. "Vladimir Il'ich Lenin" (1924, 1930)   **«Влади́мир Ильи́ч Ле́нин»**

Gorky's essay about his encounters with Lenin and conversations with him.

🔊 3-123 **17.5.1. Кака́я глы́ба, а? Како́й матёрый челове́чище!** "What a mountain, eh? What a full-grown giant of a man!" Lenin's words about Leo Tolstoy.

          17.5.2.

🔊 3-124   **Ничего́ не зна́ю лу́чше «Аппассиона́ты», гото́в слу́шать её ка́ждый день. Изуми́тельная, нечелове́ческая му́зыка ....Но ча́сто слу́шать му́зыку не могу́, де́йствует на не́рвы, хо́чется ми́лые глу́пости говори́ть и гла́дить по голо́вкам люде́й, кото́рые, живя́ в гря́зном аду́, мо́гут создава́ть таку́ю красоту́. А сего́дня гла́дить по голо́вкам никого́ нельзя́—ру́ку отку́сят, и на́добно бить по голо́вкам, бить безжа́лостно, хотя́ мы, в идеа́ле, про́тив наси́лия над людьми́.**

"I don't know anything better than *The Appassionata*, I am ready to listen to it every day. Astounding, superhuman music … But I can't listen to this music often, it bothers me: while listening to it I want to say silly sweet things and pat people on the head—people who live in a dirty hell and are still able to create such beauty. But today one shouldn't stroke people's heads, or else they bite your hand off; one has to hit people on those heads, hit mercilessly, although we, ideally, object to the use of violence against people."

17.6. "The Maiden and Death" (1892)   «Де́вушка и смерть»

No one remembers any part of this weak, sentimental imitation of a romantic ballad; the title, however, is quoted often, especially in conjunction with Stalin's praise of it: «Э́та шту́ка посильне́е «Фа́уста» Гёте». "This stuff surpasses Goethe's *Faust*." These words are usually quoted when the speaker wishes to point to someone's ignorance and/or lack of literary taste. ◀)) 3-125

Illustration: A headline in the magazine *Ито́ги*, June 1997, uses the quotation as a matrix for expressing the skeptical point of view on enlarging the European Union: «Э́та шту́ка мо́жет быть посильне́е расшире́ния НА́ТО!» ◀)) 3-125 "This stuff might surpass the enlargement of NATO!"

17.7. *The Life of Klim Samgin*   «Жизнь Кли́ма Самгина́»
(begun in 1925)

This four-volume historical novel was unfinished. Klim, though intelligent and gifted, observes life completely from the sidelines.

17.7.1. **А был ли ма́льчик?** "But was there a boy?" This is the only line ◀)) 3-126 remembered from this huge novel. It refers to the episode in which little Klim watches his friend fall through the ice without making any attempt to help him. After the boy disappears under the ice and from Klim's life, Klim tries to convince himself that he didn't do anything bad. After all, maybe the whole scene was just in his imagination. The thought "But was there a boy?" comes to Klim's mind throughout his life.

Illustration:
    (a) A headline in the newspaper *Сове́тская Росси́я*, June, 1997: «А ◀)) 3-126 был ли шпио́н?» "But was there a spy?"
    (b) A headline in *Комсомо́льская пра́вда*, Aug., 1997: «А бы́ли ли ма́льчики? Но́вый фильм про Гео́рга О́тса отве́тит на э́тот щекотли́вый вопро́с биогра́фии вели́кого певца́». "But were there boys? A new film about George Ots will answer this delicate question about the biography of the great singer."

(c) «А был ли ма́льчик?» Inscription under a photo of Petr Tchai-
      kovsky, next to an article mocking the officials who claimed that
      Tchaikovsky Street was named after the namesake of the great
      composer, the revolutionary N.V. Tchaikovsky (*Но́вое вре́мя*,
      April 1997).

🔊 **3-127** **17.8. "The City of the Yellow Devil" (1906)**   «Го́род Жёлтого Дья́вола»

In Gorky's essay, the Yellow Devil is gold, that is, money, and the city is New
York.

18. ISAAK BABEL′ (1894–1941)   ИСАА́К БА́БЕЛЬ

18.1 *Red Cavalry*   «Кона́рмия»

🔊 **3-128** Babel′ was a master of the short story, and wrote three cycles: a series of stories
about his growing up in Odessa; Odessa tales about the Jewish gangster Benya
Krik; and *Red Cavalry* **«Конармия»**. Babel′, a Jew, enlisted in the Red Army
right after the revolution and served with Budenny in the war against the Poles.
Red Cavalry depicts the brutality of war and army life in clean, almost imper-
sonal prose, and it is this juxtaposition that stays in the mind of most readers.
Many of his childhood stories combine a child's innocent view of the word with
ominous reminders of the anti-semitism rampant in Russia.

19. NIKOLAI ALEKSEEVICH OSTROVSKY (1904–36)

НИКОЛА́Й АЛЕКСЕ́ЕВИЧ ОСТРО́ВСКИЙ

The son of a worker, at the age of fifteen Ostrovsky
joined the Red Army to fight for the beautiful future
promised by the Bolsheviks. Wounded, handicapped
and blind, he turned to writing to continue to serve
the cause of Revolution.

Fig. 3-29.

19.1. *How Steel Was Tempered*   «Как закаля́лась сталь»

Autobiographical novel with the protagonist Pavel Korchagin; together with
Gorky's *Mother* was considered the best example of socialist realism and widely
used for Communist propaganda. For writing the novel Ostrovsky received
assistance from the Soviet authorities: a house (now a museum) in Sochi, a
resort town near the Black Sea, a secretary, and, as rumored, ghost-writers to
smooth his style.

19.1.1.

Са́мое дорого́е у челове́ка—это жизнь. Она́ даётся ему́ оди́н раз, и прожи́ть её на́до так, *что́бы не́ было мучи́тельно бо́льно за бесце́льно про́житые го́ды,* что́бы не жёг позо́р за по́дленькое и ме́лочное про́шлое, и что́бы, умира́я, мог сказа́ть: вся жизнь и все си́лы бы́ли о́тданы са́мому прекра́сному в ми́ре—борьбе́ за освобожде́ние челове́чества. ◀)) 3-129

Man's dearest possession is life. It is given to him only once and he must live through it so as to feel no torturous regrets for wasted years, so as not to be ashamed of the base and petty past, to live so that, dying, he could say to himself: all my life and all my strength were given to the most beautiful cause in the world: to the struggle for the liberation of mankind.

These lines had to be memorized in schools and usually were remembered verbatim.

Illustration: Огонёк, March, 1997 published an article on the physiology of sleep under irreverent heading: **«Со́нное ца́рство. Жизнь даётся челове́ку** ◀)) 3-130 **оди́н раз, и проспа́ть её на́до уме́ючи».** "The sleepy kingdom. Live is given to a man only once and one has to sleep through it skillfully."

20. ILIA ILF (1897–1937) AND EVGENII PETROV (1903–42)

ИЛЬЯ́ ИЛЬФ И ЕВГЕ́НИЙ ПЕТРО́В

These two co-authors are remembered exclusively by their last names, pronounced in one breath: **Ильф-и-Петро́в** Il'fandPetrov. They were the creators of two hilarious satirical novels about the

Fig. 3-30.

same character, Ostap Bender, a witty con man. Both novels describe the early twenties, the period of NEP (Lenin's New Economic Policy, allowing private property).

20.1. *The Twelve Chairs* (1927)   «Двена́дцать сту́льев»

Ostap chases after diamonds hidden from the authorities in one of twelve chairs sold to different people.

🔊 **3-131** 20.1.1. **Остáп Бéндер**. The name of the protagonist became synonymous with (a) a clever schemer, a cheat, and (b) humor and satire:

(a) The supplement to the newspaper *Аргумéнты и фáкты*, «Золотóе кольцó» has a regular column about cheaters called *O. Bender's Corner*, «Уголóк О. Бéндера».

(b) A headline in *Огонёк*, March 1996: «"Остáп"—это "Оскáр", но в фурáжке». *"Ostap"—that's "Oscar" in a cap* (reference to the American "Oscar" prize). The sub-heading explains: «В Сáнкт-Петербýрге прошёл V Междунарóдный фестивáль юмора и сатúры 'Золотóй Остáп-97'». In Saint Petersburg the Fifth International Festival of Satire and Humor, *Golden Ostap-97,* was held.

🔊 **3-132** 20.1.2. **Кúса Воробьянинов**. Kisa Vorobianinov (Vorobianinov the Pussycat), the childhood nickname Bender used to address his associate **Ипполúт Матвéевич Воробьянинов** because of his whiskers. ("Kisa!" «Кúса!» is used to call a cat in Russian, and **воробéй** is a sparrow.)

🔊 **3-132** *Illustration:* Headline in *Огонёк*, April, 1997: «Как и слéдовало ожидáть, после относúтельного рассáсывания албáнского крúзиса, на Балкáнах, как на щекé Кúсы Воробьянинова, нáчал вспухáть нóвый вулканúческий прыщ». "As expected, after the tumor of the Albanian crisis has been more or less resolved, in the Balkans, as on the cheek of Kisa Vorobianinov, a new volcanic carbuncle has begun to swell."

🔊 **3-133** 20.1.3. **Велúкий Комбинáтор**. "The Great Schemer." The title of the chapter introducing Ostap Bender, repeated later as his regular epithet.

20.1.4. The answer Ostap gives to a boy running after him asking for money,

🔊 **3-134** «Ключ от квартúры, где дéньги лежáт» "The key to the apartment where my money is" is now a well-used expression in Russian. The exchange goes as follows:

> —Дядя, —вéсело кричáл он, —дай дéсять копéек! […]
> —Мóжет быть, тебé дать ещё ключ от квартúры, где дéньги лежáт?

> "Could you spare ten kopecks, sir?" "Shall I also give you the key to the apartment where the money is?"

🔊 **3-134** *Illustration:* Headline in *Аргумéнты и фáкты*, May 1997: «Ключ от сéйфа, где дéньги лежáт» "The key to the safe where the money is."

🔊 **3-135** 20.1.5. **Лёд трóнулся, господá присяжные заседáтели!** "The ice is breaking, ladies and gentlemen of the jury." A phrase repeated by Ostap whenever things go according to his plans.

🔊 **3-135** *Illustration:* A headline in the newspaper *Труд*, 1997: «Лёд трóнулся?» "Has the ice broken?" (an article about the first visit of the Abkhazian leader to Georgia).

20.1.6. Голубо́й вори́шка "Innocent little crook." [Literally: blue little thief]. ◀))) **3-136**
The corrupt manager of a nursing home, stealing right and left and always
keenly ashamed of his deeds. The word **голубо́й** stands for "innocent"; in those
days it did not have the meaning it has acquired in modern slang: "a homosexual male."

20.1.7. Зно́йная же́нщина, мечта́ поэ́та "A sultry woman, a poet's dream." ◀))) **3-137**
Bender's reference to a plump widow, Madame Gritsatsueva, whom he marries
to get possession of her chair, and then immediately abandons.

Illustration: A lengthy sub-heading in the magazine **Огонёк**, May 1996. runs:

> «Одна́жды мне повезло́. Подо́бно одному́ из че́ховских геро́ев, а   ◀))) **3-137**
> та́кже не́коему Оста́пу Бе́ндеру, разы́скиваемому безуте́шной
> вдово́й, я попа́л на страни́цы пре́ссы». (see also 12.7)

> "Once I got lucky. Similar to one of Chekhov's characters, and also to
> a certain Ostap Bender who was chased by an inconsolable widow, I
> got into the printed pages of the media."

20.1.8. Людое́дка Э́ллочка "Ellochka the cannibal." She is described in the
following way:

> Слова́рь Ви́льяма Шекспи́ра, по подсчёту иссле́дователей, со-   ◀))) **3-138**
> ставля́ет двена́дцать ты́сяч слов. Слова́рь не́гра из людое́дского
> пле́мени "Му́мбо-Ю́мбо" составля́ет три́ста слов. Э́ллочка Щу́-
> кина легко́ и свобо́дно обходи́лась тридцатью́. Вот слова́ и фра́зы,
> приди́рчиво вы́бранные е́ю из всего́ *вели́кого, многосло́вного и*
> *могу́чего ру́сского языка́* ....

> "According to the calculations of researchers, the vocabulary of
> William Shakespeare consists of twelve thousand words. The vocabu-
> lary of an African from the Mumbo-Jumbo tribe of cannibals consists
> of three hundred words. Ellochka Shchukina managed to make do with
> thirty words, which she wielded with ease and fluency. Here are the
> words which she hand-picked from the entire great, many-worded and
> powerful Russian language: ... [See 8.6.].

> Ellochka's most famous and oft-repeated phrase is **«Не учи́те меня́**   ◀))) **3-139**
> **жить».** "Don't teach me how to live my life."

20.1.9. Пода́йте что́-нибудь бы́вшему депута́ту Госуда́рственной ду́мы. ◀))) **3-140**
"Give alms to the former Deputy of the State Council." In his hunt for the
chairs, Ostap runs out of money and makes Kisa Vorobianinov beg money
from passers-by, using this phrase.

Illustration: A headline in **Огонёк**, April, 1996, cleverly combines quotes 16.1.4. ◀))) **3-140**
and this one: **«Пода́йте бы́вшему депута́ту ключи́ от кварти́ры»** "Give the
keys to an apartment as alms to the former Deputy."

◀))) **3-141** 20.1.10. **Мне моя́ жизнь дорога́ как па́мять.** "My life is as precious to me as memory."

20.2. *The Golden Calf* (1931)   «Золото́й телёнок»

The second book of Ostap's adventures. This time he is planning to blackmail a millionaire into parting with some of his illegal millions. In this story, his accomplices are young **Шу́ра Балага́нов** Shura Balaganov, a light-hearted simpleton, a driver, **Ада́м Кази́мирович Козле́вич** Kozlevich, devoted to his lemon of a car, which by Ostap's orders is painted yellow and renamed **Антило́па-Гну** (Antelope-Gnu), and **Михаи́л Самуэ́левич Паника́вский** Panikovskii, who makes his living by begging in the streets or picking pockets.

◀))) **3-142** 20.2.1. **Де́ти лейтена́нта Шми́дта.** "Children of Lieutenant Schmidt." Having run completely out of money, Ostap goes to the local executive committee and claims to be a son of Lieutenant Schmidt [a revolutionary hero] who has been robbed on a train. Just when the secretary is about to hand over some money to help out the son of a hero, yet another con-artist appears, Shura Balaganov— and with a similar claim. Later it turns out that a total of thirty swindlers have been working under this pretext.

◀))) **3-142** *Illustration:* An article about the election campaign in *Аргуме́нты и фа́кты*, 1996, is entitled «Нет дете́й у лейтена́нта Шми́дта» "Lieutenant Schmidt has no children."

◀))) **3-143** 20.2.2. **Узнаёшь бра́та Ко́лю?** "Do you recognize your brother Kolya?" [dim. of Nikolai]. These are the words Ostap uses to save the situation in the office, addressing Shura Balaganov, the second "son of Lieutenant Schmidt."

Illustration: The caption under a photo of two playful baby monkeys, taken in the zoo, reads: «Узнаю́ бра́та Ко́лю!» —*Росси́йская газета*, 1997.

Fig. 3-31.

20.2.3. Ostap sees this sign in a cafeteria: **«Пи́во отпуска́ется то́лько чле́нам** 🔊 **3-144**
профсою́за». "Beer is sold only to members of the trade-union."

20.2.4. **... на блю́дечке с голубо́й каёмочкой** "... on a plate [literally saucer] 🔊 **3-145**
with a blue rim." Ostap's expression referring to the ease with which he can
make a millionaire part with his money: **«Ах, е́сли бы то́лько найти́ инди-**
ви́да! Уж я так устро́ю, что он свои́ де́ньги мне сам принесёт, на блю́дечке
с голубо́й каёмкой». "Oh, if only I could find such an individual! I would fix it
so that he would bring me his money himself, on a plate with a blue rim."

Illustration: From an article about the disastrous state of prisons in **О́бщая**
газе́та, 1997: **«Степа́шин в пе́рвом своём выступле́нии то́лько заикну́лся —** 🔊 **3-145**
и все зо́ны, все тю́рьмы Росси́и бы́ли по́даны ему́ на блю́дечке с голубо́й
каёмочкой». "No sooner had Stepashin mentioned it than all the zones, all the
prisons of Russia were handed over to him on a plate with a blue rim."

20.2.5. **Кома́ндовать пара́дом бу́ду я.** "I am the one who will run the show" 🔊 **3-146**
[literally: will control the parade].

20.2.6. **Эх, прокачу́!** "Hey, I'll give you a great ride!" The inscription Koz- 🔊 **3-147**
levich decorated his taxi cab with in an attempt to procure passengers in a tiny
town where a taxi was an unheard of luxury.

Illustration: Headline in an article about the slow speed of trains, **Огонёк**, Feb.,
1997: **«Эх, прокачу́! Како́й же ру́сский не лю́бит бы́строй езды́?»** "Hey, I'll 🔊 **3-147**
give you a great ride! What Russian does not love fast driving?" [see also 7.8.6].

20.2.7. **Автомоби́ль — не ро́скошь, а сре́дство передвиже́ния!** "An automo- 🔊 **3-148**
bile is not a luxury, it is a means of transportation."

Illustration:

   (a)   Advertisement in **Кура́нты**, 1996: **«Ягуа́р, маши́на, безусло́вно,** 🔊 **3-148**
       экзоти́ческая. Это ро́скошь, а не сре́дство передвиже́ния». "No
       doubt a Jaguar is an exotic car. It is a luxury rather than a means of
       transportation."

   (b)   Headline in the magazine **Семья́**, 1997: **«Телефо́н — не ро́скошь, а**
       сре́дство обще́ния» "A telephone is not a luxury, it is a means of
       communication."

20.2.8. **Не де́лайте из еды́ ку́льта.** "Do not make a fetish out of food." Said by 🔊 **3-149**
Ostap in the following episode:

> **Панико́вский, пригну́вшись, убежа́л в по́ле и верну́лся, держа́ в**
> **руке́ тёплый криво́й огуре́ц. Оста́п бы́стро вы́рвал его́ из рук**
> **Панико́вского, говоря́: не де́лайте из еды́ ку́льта. По́сле э́того он**
> **съел огуре́ц сам.**

"Panikovskii ducked down, dashed into a nearby field, and returned
with a warm, bent cucumber. Ostap snatched it from Panikovskii's

hands, saying 'Do not make a fetish out of food,' after which he ate the cucumber himself."

🔊 **3-150** **20.2.9. Уда́рим автопробе́гом по бездоро́жью и разгильдя́йству!** "Let us combat bad roads and slovenliness with a motor tour!" Famous slogan from Ostap's speech. After learning from the newspapers that a caravan of automobiles is being sent through provincial towns as a part of the official campaign for some propaganda cause, Ostap and his companions pretend that their car has gotten ahead of the caravan. They drive through the towns, collecting gasoline, food, and so on, and giving in return some vague, fiery political speeches.

🔊 **3-150** *Illustration:* Article in **Огонёк**, February 1996, about selling a Russian car, the Zaporozhets, to Finland: **«Уда́рили "Запоро́жцем" по бездоро́жью и Финля́ндии».** "We battled bad roads and Finland with the Zaporozhets."

🔊 **3-151** **20.2.10. Жа́лкая, ничто́жная ли́чность.** "(You are) a pathetic, wretched person." Favorite insult used in any quarrel by Panikovskii.

🔊 **3-152** **20.2.11. Графи́ня измени́вшимся лицо́м бежи́т пруду́.** "The countess, her face altered, runs to the pond." A telegram mimicking the style of cheap novels sent by Ostap to the millionaire as part of his psychological attack. The comical effect is increased by omitted prepositions, a common practice, since the cost of a telegram depends on the number of words. Here the preposition omitted is **к**, and it should go right before the word **пруду**.

🔊 **3-153** **20.2.12. Грузи́те апельси́ны бо́чках бра́тья Карама́зовы.** "Load the barrels of oranges. —The Brothers Karamazov." Another "psychological" telegram to the millionaire, usually quoted in the form: **Грузи́те апельси́ны бо́чками** (by the barrelful).

🔊 **3-153** *Illustration:*

    (a) Advertisement for a shampoo which protects hair against radioactive particles in **Аргуме́нты и фа́кты,** 1997: **«Противоа́томный шампу́нь. Грузи́те бо́чками …»** "Anti-radioactive shampoo. Load it by the barrelful."

    (b) **«Грузи́те кита́йцев … чемода́нами»** "Load the Chinese by the suitcaseful." Article about Chinese people trying to cross the Russian border illegally. Customs officials discovered fifty-seven Chinese inside suitcases.

    (c) **«Грузи́те ба́ксы коро́бками тчк Бра́тья Карама́зовы»** "Load bucks by boxes. Stop. The Brothers Karamazov." An article in **Но́вое вре́мя,** December 1996, in response to the newspaper **Моско́вский комсомо́лец,** which published an article against using US dollars in the Russian economy.

🔊 **3-154** **20.2.13. Васисуа́лий Лоха́нкин** Vasisualii Lokhankin. A person in the novel from whom O. Bender was trying to rent a room. His first name is a fancy form of ordinary **Васи́лий** and his last name means "a wash-tub." He is a wicked parody on the intelligentsia (unlike workers and peasants), an ideologically suspicious social group; the authors doubtless aimed at pleasing the Soviet authorities.

20.2.14. **Волчи́ца ты. Тебя́ я презира́ю. К любо́внику ухо́дишь от меня́, к Птибурдуко́ву от меня́ ухо́дишь. Так вот к кому́ ты от меня́ ухо́дишь! Ты по́хоти преда́ться хо́чешь с ним. Волчи́ца ста́рая и ме́рзкая прито́м!** ◀)) **3-155** "You are a she-wolf. I despise you. You are leaving me for your lover, you are leaving me for Ptiburdukov [Little Slops]. That's who you are leaving me for! You want to indulge in lust with him. Old she-wolf, and abominable at that!" Chanting in iambic pentameter, Vasisualii Lokhankin is trying to stop his wife from leaving him.

20.2.15. **Воро́нья слобо́дка** "Crowsville." Ironic name of a huge communal ◀)) **3-156** apartment notorious for the noisy squabbling of its numerous inhabitants, Vasisualii Lokhankin among them. It is there that the neighbors subjected him to a flogging for his chronic failure to switch off the electricity in the communal bathroom.

Illustration: In **Огонёк**, June, 1996, we find:

> **«… и если Диа́не уда́стся сохрани́ть за собо́й ти́тул "Её Коро-** ◀)) **3-156**
> **ле́вское Высо́чество," то её роль в "Воро́ньей слобо́дке" Букин-**
> **ге́мского дворца́ бу́дет сравни́ма с ро́лью "короле́вы-ма́тери».**

"… and if Diana manages to keep the title 'Her Royal Highness,' her role in the Crowsville of Buckingham Palace will be comparable with that of the Queen Mother."

20.2.16. **Мо́жет быть, и́менно в э́том вели́кая сермя́жная пра́вда. (Сер-** ◀)) **3-157** **мя́жный** is an adjective describing a coarse, heavy fabric from which peasants made their clothes, and is applied to peasants in general). "Maybe that's where the great harsh truth lies." This philosophical statement is produced by Lokhankin whenever there is a cause for suffering.

20.2.17. **Вы не в це́ркви, вас не обма́нут.** "You are not in church, no one is ◀)) **3-158** going to deceive you." (Bender says these words to Lokhankin to avoid paying a deposit.)

20.2.18. **Я год не́ был в ба́не. Я ста́рый. Меня́ де́вушки не лю́бят.** "I have ◀)) **3-159** not been in a bathhouse for a year. I am old. Girls do not love me." Panikovskii says these words in an attempt to evoke sympathy.

20.2.19. **«Рога́ и копы́та»** "Horns and hooves." The name of the sham com- ◀)) **3-160** pany opened by Bender.

🔊 **3-161** 20.2.20. **А ты кто тако́й?** "And who are you?" These words usually precede a fist fight between Balaganov and Panikovskii.

🔊 **3-162** 20.2.21. **Я к вам пришёл наве́ки посели́ться.** "I have come to live with you forever." With these words Lokhankin appears in the new home of his former wife and her husband after a fire destroys his room in Crowsville.

🔊 **3-163** 20.2.22. **Сбыла́сь мечта́ идио́та.** "The dream of an idiot has come true." This is what Ostap Bender says after finally receiving his million.

🔊 **3-164** 20.2.23. **Придётся переквалифици́роваться в управдо́мы** (**управдом** is an abbreviation for **управля́ющий домом**, "apartment building manager"). "I will have to train for another profession, that of apartment building manager." Bitter words of Ostap at the very end of the novel, after he discovers that Soviet Russia is not a good place for millionaires and then gets beaten and robbed while trying to cross the Romanian border.

Illustration: See the use of this line in the article about the film **«Кавка́зский пле́нник»** *The Captive of Caucasus* in **Ито́ги**, Nov. 1996:

🔊 **3-164** **Éсли бы все на́ши режиссёры (за исключе́нием бра́тьев Михалко́вых, кото́рые счита́ются звёздами не росси́йскими, а общеевро-пе́йскими) переквалифици́ровались в управдо́мов, никто́ бы ни в Ка́ннах, ни в Голливу́де сего́ печа́льного фа́кта и не заме́тил.**

"If all our film directors (except for the brothers Mikhalkov, considered stars not just in Russia, but all over Europe) were retrained to be building managers, nobody would notice this sad fact either in Cannes or in Hollywood."

21. MIKHAIL ZOSHCHENKO (1895–1958)   МИХАЙЛ ЗО́ЩЕНКО

Mikhail Zoshchenko was the author of numerous satirical short stories. Zoshchenko's stories were, and remain, popular because they cheerfully and matter-of-factly make fun of Soviet reality. The language is simple, a good example of the "skaz" **сказ** technique (writing in stylized prose that imitates someone else's voice). The situations are absurd, but all the more delightful because based in fact. Zoshchenko's brand of humor was immensely popular in the 1920s, but by 1933 he was forced to write works that fit with the official literary line. Despite these attempts, Zoshchenko, along with Anna Akhmatova, was denounced in 1946 by Andrei Zhdanov as an "anti-Soviet element." Am-

🔊 **3-165** ong the popular stories are **«Аристокра́тка»** "The Aristocratic Lady," **«Ба́ня»** "The Bathhouse," and **«Кочерга́»** "The Fireplace Poker."

21.1. **«Аристокра́тка»** "The Aristocratic Lady"

🔊 **3-166** **Доку́шивайте, доку́шивайте!** "Eat up! Eat up!" The narrator urges his companion to finish her eclair in the theater since he's the one who paid for it.

22. MIKHAIL AFANASIEVICH BULGAKOV (1891–1940)

МИХАИ́Л АФАНА́СЬЕВИЧ БУЛГА́КОВ

One of the best prose writers and dramatists of the post-Revolution era, Bulgakov was always "ideologically suspicious"; his works were accepted for publication with great reluctance or they were rejected outright. Finding himself near starvation, he had the courage to write Stalin a bold letter requesting him either to allow his works to be published or to let him live abroad; the result was a telephone call from Stalin, who enabled Bulgakov to find work in the Khudozhestvennyi (Art) Theater.

22.1. *The Master and Margarita*

«Ма́стер и Маргари́та»

This novel is the favorite and most quoted book in contemporary Russia, despite the fact that it has only recently become part of the school program. Finished in 1940, the novel was published only in 1966 in a severely censored version in the journal *Москва́ Moscow* (the Ginsburg translation is of this censored version); the full text appeared in 1973 and immediately acquired the status of a gold standard (sold and resold on the black market for 70 rubles, the store price at the time was a little over four rubles).The plot interweaves two stories. In one, the devil (Voland) and his cohorts appear in the Moscow of the 1930s, causing commotion and punishing bureaucrats, liars and cheaters. The other plot takes place in ancient times and contains the story of the last days of Jesus Christ.

22.1.1. Voland (referred to here as "the stranger"), speaking with Berlioz, the editor of an anti-religious journal, claims that a person cannot predict his own future, can't even tell in the morning what will happen in the evening. The most famous words of this exchange are given in italics below:

> —Сего́дняшний ве́чер мне изве́стен бо́лее или ме́нее то́чно. Само́ собо́ю разуме́ется, что, е́сли на Бро́нной мне сва́лится на го́лову кирпи́ч ... —*Кирпи́ч ни с того́, ни с сего́* —внуши́тельно переби́л неизве́стный, —*никому́ и никогда́ на го́лову не сва́лится.* В ча́стности же, уверя́ю вас, ва́м он ни в како́м слу́чае не угрожа́ет. Вы умрёте друго́й сме́ртью.

🔊 3-167

"This evening I can predict more or less precisely. That is, if only a brick does not fall on my head on Bronnaia street ..." "A brick," interrupted the stranger gravely, "would never fall on anyone's head out of the blue. Thus, for you, let me assure you, there is no danger of being hit by a brick. You will die from another cause."

22.1.2. **Áннушка уже́ разлила́ ма́сло.** "Annushka has already spilt the oil." Annushka (dim. of Anna) is a nosy old lady. This is a continuation of the same conversation; after Berlioz ironically inquires whether the stranger by any chance knows what Berlioz will die of, the stranger announces that Berlioz's head will be cut off. Berlioz says that this is very unlikely. And as for tonight—tonight he will chair a literary meeting. At this point the stranger (called "the foreigner" here) says:

◀)) 3-168   **Нет, э́того быть ника́к не мо́жет,—твёрдо возрази́л иностра́нец.**
              —Э́то почему́?
              —Потому́,—отве́тил иностра́нец и прищу́ренными глаза́ми посмотре́л в не́бо, где, предчу́вствуя вече́рнюю прохла́ду, бесшу́мно черти́ли чёрные пти́цы,—что А́ннушка уже́ купи́ла подсо́лнечное ма́сло, и не то́лько купи́ла, но да́же и разлила́. Так что заседа́ние не состои́тся.

"No, this cannot happen," said the foreigner firmly.
"And why not?"
"Because," said the foreigner, and looked with his squinting eyes at the sky, where in anticipation of the coolness of the night the black birds soared in silent circles, "because Annushka has already bought the sunflower oil, and not only bought it but already spilt it. So there will be no meeting."

[Though it sounds like pure nonsense, what happens afterwards follows this scenario: Berlioz slips on the oil spilt by Annushka, falls under a streetcar, and ends up with his head cut off, as was predicted.]

◀)) 3-169 *Illustration:* This quotation is used to show that everything is set for some planned event. For example, I heard a teenage girl say while setting the table: **А́ннушка уже́ разлила́ ма́сло, а их всё нет!** "Annushka has already spilt the oil, and they are still not here!" (meaning: the dinner is ready and they still are not here).

◀)) 3-170 22.1.3. **Пра́вду говори́ть легко́ и прия́тно.** "Telling the truth is easy and pleasant." The response of **Иешуа Га-Ноцри** (Yeshua Ha-Notsri) to Pontius Pilate.

22.1.4. Voland and his associates put on a show of Black Magic in the Variety Theater, during which real money descends on the public from the ceiling. The official master-of-ceremonies, Bengalsky, tries to keep things under control, saying that the money is not real. Voland's assistant, Fagot, announces:

◀)) 3-171   *—Это опя́ть-таки слу́чай так называ́емого вранья́,* —объяви́л он гро́мким козли́ным те́нором, —бума́жки, гра́ждане, настоя́щие.

"This, again, is a case of what they call lies," he announced in his loud, goat-like tenor. "The money, citizens, is real."

22.1.5. Part of Voland's speech about the Muscovites:

Ну, легкомы́сленны … ну, что ж … и милосе́рдие иногда́ стучи́тся 🔊 3-172
в их сердца́ … обыкнове́нные лю́ди … в о́бщем, напомина́ют
пре́жних … *кварти́рный вопро́с то́лько испо́ртил их …*

Sure, they are thoughtless … well … they can open their hearts to
compassion at times.. they are ordinary people … much like those before them … only the housing problem messed them up.

Illustration:

    (a) Headline in ***Росси́йская газе́та***, 1997: «**Кварти́рный вопро́с** 🔊 3-172
        продолжа́ет по́ртить жизнь» "The housing problem continues to
        mess up life."

    (b) Similar headline in ***Коммерса́нтъ***, 1991 «**Отноше́ния ГУВД и**
        мэ́рии: кварти́рный вопро́с испо́ртил их» "Relationship between
        the State Bureau of Internal Affairs and the Office of the Mayor:
        The housing problem messed it up."

22.1.6. Кати́тесь отсю́да! Без вас веселе́й. "Get out of here, we will have 🔊 3-173
more fun without you." With these words Voland's assistant gets rid of
Bengalsky during the show in the Variety Theater.

22.1.7. Нехоро́шая кварти́ра "The haunted apartment." Apartment #50 had a 🔊 3-174
bad reputation because people who lived in it at different times kept
disappearing (Bulgakov's hint at the years of Stalin's arrests). After Voland
settled in it, various supernatural events increased that reputation.

Illustration: An article in ***Черномо́рская здра́вница***, August 1997, about
"squatters" illegally occupying empty apartments with the headline: «**Нехоро́-**
шие кварти́ры».

22.1.8. During the episode in which the buffet manager comes to Voland with
complaints about the public using fake money from Voland's show in his buffet.
Voland begins reproaching him for the quality of food in his buffet. The following dialogue ensues:

    —**Осетри́ну присла́ли второ́й све́жести, —сообщи́л буфе́тчик.** 🔊 3-175
      —**Голу́бчик, э́то вздор!**
      —**Чего́ вздор?**
      —**Втора́я све́жесть—во́т что вздор! Све́жесть быва́ет то́лько**
одна́—пе́рвая, она́ же и после́дняя. А е́сли осетри́на второ́й
све́жести, э́то означа́ет, что она́ ту́хлая!

"They sent me sturgeon of second-degree freshness," the buffet manager informed him. "My dear fellow, this is nonsense!" "What is nonsense?" "Second-degree freshness, that's what is nonsense! Freshness
exists only in the first degree, which is also its last. And if a sturgeon is
of second-degree freshness, it can only mean that it's rotten!"

◀))) **3-175** *Illustration:* From an overheard conversation: «**Понима́ешь, дру́жба, как осетри́на, не быва́ет второ́й све́жести**». "You know, friendship, like sturgeon, does not exist in the second degree of freshness."

◀))) **3-176** 22.1.9. **Вино́ како́й страны́ вы предпочита́ете в э́то вре́мя дня?** "Which country's wine do you prefer at this time of day?" So Voland inquires of the Variety's buffet manager, with exaggerated elegance..

◀))) **3-177** 22.1.10. **Ру́кописи не горя́т!** "Manuscripts do not burn!" With these words Voland restores to the Master his burned manuscript, a novel about Pontius Pilate.

Illustration:

    (a)   The magazine ***Но́вое вре́мя*** has a regular column entitled «**Ру́кописи не горя́т**».

◀))) **3-177**   (b)   Headline of an article about robbery from the Russian National Library in ***Но́вое вре́мя***, Nov. 1996: «**Ру́кописи не горя́т. Их краду́т**» "Manuscripts do not burn. They get stolen."

22.1.11. Voland was supposed to fulfill Margarita's request that he return the Master, her lover, to her after she acted as hostess-queen at his satanic ball, but since he did not mention the reward, she did not ask for it. The following exchange takes place:

◀))) **3-178**   —**Вы соверше́нно пра́вы!** —гу́лко и стра́шно прокрича́л Во́ланд, —**так и на́до!** <..> **Мы вас испы́тывали**, —продолжа́л Во́ланд, —*никогда́ и ничего́ не проси́те!* Никогда́ и ничего́, в осо́бенности у тех, кто сильне́е вас. *Са́ми предло́жат и са́ми всё даду́т.*

"You are absolutely right!" cried Voland in a resounding, frightening voice. "Never ask for anything! Never and for nothing, and especially of those who are more powerful than you are. They will offer everything themselves and give you all you need themselves."

Illustration: Headline in ***Изве́стия***, 1993: «**Никогда́ и ничего́ не проси́те**».

◀))) **3-179** 22.1.12. **За мно́й, чита́тель!** "Follow me, reader!"

22.2. *The Heart of a Dog* (1925)   «Соба́чье се́рдце»

Social science fiction. In the course of his experiments with rejuvenation, a scientist inadvertently creates a human being out of a live dog and parts of the corpse of a drunkard. This new Frankenstein, named Sharikov, has all the features of the Soviet "masses": he is rude, ignorant, stuffed full of current political slogans and wants to govern the universe.

◀))) **3-180** 22.2.1. **В о́чередь, су́кины де́ти, в о́чередь!** "Get in line, you sons of bitches, get in line!"

Illustration: The magazine **Огонёк**, November 1996, contained the following ◀)) **3-180** headline: «**В óчередь, сýкины дéти, в óчередь! Именно такóй отвéт в дýхе Шáрикова в совéтские временá давáло госудáрство желáющим улýчшить свой жилúщные услóвия**». "Get in line, you sons of bitches, get in line! This is precisely the answer, in the spirit of Sharikov, that the government would give people wishing to improve their housing situation during Soviet times."

23. ARKADY NATANOVICH STRUGATSKY (b. 1925) AND BORIS NATANOVICH STRUGATSKY (b. 1933)

СТРУГÁЦКИЕ АРКÁДИЙ НАТÁНОВИЧ И БОРИ́С НАТÁНОВИЧ

These writers used the genre of science fiction for social satire. Their most popular works are «**Понедéльник начинáется в суббóту**» *Monday Begins on* ◀)) **3-181** *Saturday* (1965); «**Трýдно быть бóгом**» *It is Difficult to be God* (1964), and «**Гáдкие лéбеди**» *Ugly Swans* (1967).

23.1. Суетá вокрýг дивáна "The hustle and bustle around the couch." Title of ◀)) **3-182** a chapter in «**Понедéльник начинáется в суббóту**».

23.2. «**Пикник на обóчине**» *The Picnic at the Side of the Road* (1972, basis of ◀)) **3-183** A. Tarkovsky's film "**Стáлкер**").

Illustration: An article about an unsuccessful performance of the rock group «**Пикни́к**» in *Аргумéнты и фáкты*, 1996, had the headline: «**Пикни́к на обóчине**».

24. ALEXANDER ISAEVICH SOLZHENITSYN (b. 1918)

Алексáндр Исáевич Солжени́цын

An important political figure and writer, Solzhenitsyn fought in the Soviet Army during World War II, and was arrested at the end of the war after his letters, containing criticism of Stalin, were intercepted by the military equivalent of the KGB, the **спецслýжбы** special forces. His monumental account of the forced labor system, «**Архипелáг ГУЛáг**» *GULag Archipelago* (1953–57), is a literary memorial to the victims of the Soviet regime. It includes, apart from his personal recollections, the memoirs of other survivors and a wealth of historic documents. His novels «**В крýге пéрвом**» *The First Circle* (1955–64) and «**Рáковый кóрпус**» *Cancer Ward* (1963–66) are dedicated to the same topic. In 1970, Solzhenitsyn was awarded the Nobel Prize for literature. After 20 years in the United States, Solzhenitsyn returned to Russia in 1994 and now lives in Moscow.

24.1. *One Day in the Life of Ivan Denisovich* (1962)

«**Оди́н день Ивáна Дени́совича**»

A detailed account of one day in a concentration camp in Siberia.

◀)) **3-184** *Illustration:* Headline in *Аргуме́нты и фа́кты,* 1997: «Оди́н день из жи́зни "ста́рой ру́сской"» "One day in the life of 'a Russian woman, old style'" (a play on the terms "New Russians" vs. "Old Russians").

24.2. *GULag Archipelago*   «Архипела́г ГУЛаг»

An abbreviation for **Госуда́рственное Управле́ние Лагере́й**, State [labor] Camp Network.

Illustration:

◀)) **3-185**
(a) «**Здра́вствуй, ГУЛаг! Судьба́ диссиде́нтов в КНР остаётся тяжёлой**» (headline in *Но́вое вре́мя*, February 1996). "Hello, 'GULag'! The fate of dissidents in the People's Republic of China remains difficult."

(b) An old pre-perestroika joke:

Леони́д Ильи́ч Бре́жнев отправля́ется с визи́том в Казахста́н. Чтобы произвести́ прия́тное впечатле́ние на каза́хов, он предвари́тельно це́лый ме́сяц у́чит каза́хское приве́тствие: «Саля́м але́йкум!» и отве́т на него́: «Але́йкум саля́м!» По прибы́тии в Казахста́н Бре́жнев ока́зывается окружённым полити́ческими заключёнными.
—Архипела́г ГУЛаг! —гне́вно крича́т заключённые.
—Гула́г архипела́г, —благоду́шно улыба́ясь, отвеча́ет Леони́д Ильи́ч.

Leonid Brezhnev is preparing to visit Kazakhstan. In order to favorably impress the Kazakhs, before his trip he diligently studies the Kazakh greeting, "Salaam alaykum" and the response to it, "Alaykum salaam." Upon arriving he finds himself surrounded by political prisoners, who chant angrily: "Archipelago GULag!" "Gulag archipelago" replies Brezhnev with a benevolent smile.

24.3. "Reorganizing Russia"   «Как нам обустро́ить Росси́ю?»

A 1990 article by Solzhenitsyn with suggestions about the future of Russia.

Illustration:

◀)) **3-186**
(a) Headline in *Но́вое вре́мя,* December 1996: «**Как нам обустро́ить грани́цу?**» "How shall we reorganize the border?"

(b) *Огонёк*, June 1997: «**Каза́хский акы́н Джамбу́л Джамба́ев проводи́л дни на кошме́ в специа́льно для него́ обустро́енной ю́рте**». "Kazakh folksinger Jambul Jambaev spent his days in a yurt (an equivalent of a tepee) specially fixed up [= reorganized] for him" [Jambul Jambaev was famous for his flowery songs dedicated to Stalin].

<table>
<tr><td>

Children's Literature

</td><td>

4

</td><td>

Де́тская литерату́ра

</td></tr>
</table>

Robert A. Rothstein and Halina Weiss

For D.K. Ozlatičko

This chapter is an attempt to provide clues to the literary imagination of Russian children as formed in their earliest exposure to folk and literary sources. It tries to show the lasting effect of childhood exposure to literature through the recollections of different generations represented by people in their 20s to 50s. The sample was small but, it is hoped, representative. Informants were asked what they remembered best from childhood stories either told or read to them in early childhood and from reading on their own through adolescence, age 12 to 14. The goal was not to test their knowledge of Russian and Soviet literature, but to elicit an emotional response: what came to their mind first, what they could recall most vividly and perhaps recite from memory.

The linguistic, cognitive and imaginative development of the Russian child is nourished with elements of Russian folklore, of nineteenth- and twentieth-century Russian literature and of foreign literature (especially French, English and American). The starting-point in this process is easy enough to define: the lullabies and verbal games **поте́шки** through which parents and other adults interact with infants. The end-point is much more problematic. In the Soviet period books published by **«Де́тская кни́га»** (earlier: **«Детги́з»**) or **«Малы́ш»** bore such age-related labels as "for preschoolers" **«для дошко́льного во́зраста»**, "for young schoolchildren" **«для мла́дшего шко́льного во́зраста»**, "for young children" **«для мла́дшего во́зраста»**, "for children in middle grades or older children" **«для сре́днего (ог: сре́днего и ста́ршего) во́зраста»**, and so on.[1] But school children's reading—whether assigned or extracurricular—is not limited to "children's literature." The books that Russians remember from childhood often belong to what one might consider to be part of the "adult canon."

---

[1] "Children's Literature" **«Де́тская литерату́ра»** and "Child" **«Малы́ш»**, both with headquarters in Moscow, were the two main publishing houses specializing in children's literature in the RSFSR. Until 1963 the former was known as "the State Publishing House for Children's Literature" **«Госуда́рственное изда́тельство де́тской литерату́ры»**, or **«Детги́з»** (cf. the corresponding publishers of military, musical, physical-mathematical literature—**«Военги́з»**, **«Музги́з»**, **«Физматги́з»**—and many others).

There is another problem area, that of generational differences. The cultural baggage of today's Russian twenty-five-year-olds differs to some extent from that of their compatriots who are ten or twenty years older. Not only did the different generational cohorts read different books, but they also saw different films and stage adaptations and watched different cartoons on television. A case in point are the translations or retellings by Boris Zakhoder **Борис Заходер** of such English children's classics as *Winnie the Pooh* **«Ви́нни–Пу́х и все–все–все́»** (1964), *Mary Poppins* **«Мэ́ри По́ппинс»** (1968) and *Alice in Wonderland* **«Приключе́ния Али́сы в Стране́ Чуде́с»** (1974). These books (and the associated films and cartoons) are now part of growing up Russian, but as recently as 25–35 years ago did not exist, or—in the case of *Alice*—existed only in weaker translations that did not have a great effect on Russian children.

Let us try, despite these difficulties, to sketch out a body of material that would constitute a "shared children's culture" for many people who grew up speaking Russian in the Soviet Union, especially in the decades since World War II.[2] The material can be divided for ease of reference into three categories: folklore, Russian literature, and foreign literature. The distinction between the first two is arbitrary in part since some items that are folkloric in origin are best known in reworkings by Russian authors.

FOLKLORE   ФОЛЬКЛО́Р

Perhaps the first folklore that the Russian child encounters are lullabies **колыбе́льные пе́сни** (lit., cradle songs), such as:

◀)) 4-1 Ба́ю, ба́юшки-баю́,	Lulla, lulla, lullabye,
♫ 4-2 Не ложи́ся на краю́.—	Don't lie down at the edge [of the bed].
Придёт се́ренький волчо́к,	A gray wolf will come along.
Он ухва́тит за бочо́к,	He will grab you by your side,
Он ухва́тит за бочо́к	He will grab you by your side
И пота́щит во лесо́к,	And will drag you into the forest,
И пота́щит во лесо́к,	And will drag you into the forest
Под раки́товый кусто́к.	Under a broom bush.
К нам, волчо́к, не ходи́,	Wolf, don't come to us.
На́шу Ка́тю не буди́.	Don't wake our Katya up.

Also part of earliest childhood are parents' wordplay to accompany massaging or simple exercising with the infant, such as:

---

[2] Our sources included a wide range of publications of and about Russian children's literature (both individual works and anthologies) and the invaluable comments of Irina and Roman Yakub, Taissia and Dmitri Rumynin, and Snejana Tempest, to all of whom we are most grateful.

Потягу́нюшки, порасту́нюшки,	Stretch, grow,	🔊 4-3
В но́жки—ходу́нюшки,	May your legs gain speed.	
В рото́к—говоро́к,	May your mouth gain speech.	
В го́лову—разумо́к.	May your head gain intellect.	

"Poteshki" поте́шки are the verbal accompaniment to mild tickling or to little games played with the infant's or child's fingers or hands. Extending the index finger and little finger of one hand in imitation of a goat's horns, the adult pretends to butt the child while reciting:

Идёт коза́ рога́тая,	A horned goat is on its way.	🔊 4-4
Идёт коза́ бода́тая,	An angry goat is on its way.	
Но́жками топ-топ,	It goes stomp, stomp with its feet.	
Гла́зками хлоп-хлоп.	It goes flop, flop with its eyes.	
Кто ка́шу не ест,	If you don't eat your porridge,	
Молока́ не пьёт,	If you don't drink your milk,	
Забода́ет, забода́ет, забода́ет.	It will butt you with its horns.	

To accompany something like patty-cake the child hears:

Ла́душки, ла́душки!	Patty-cake, patty-cake!	🔊 4-5
Где бы́ли? —У ба́бушки.	Where have you been?—We visited grandma.	
Что е́ли? —Ка́шку.	What did you eat?—We had some porridge.	
Что пи́ли? —Бра́жку.	What did you drink?—We had some ale.	
Ка́шка ма́сленька,	The porridge was buttery,	
Бра́жка сла́денька.	The ale was sweet,	
Ба́бушка до́бренька.	Grandma was kind.	
Попи́ли, пое́ли,	We drank some, we ate some	
Домо́й полете́ли,	And we flew away home.	
На голо́вку се́ли,	We sat on your [the child's] head.	
Ла́душки запе́ли.	And began singing patty-cake.	

Finally, while playing with the child's palm and fingers the adult recites:

Соро́ка-воро́на	Magpie-the-crow	🔊 4-6
Ка́шу вари́ла,	Cooked some porridge,	
Де́ток корми́ла,	Fed the children,	
На поро́г скака́ла,	Hopped to the threshhold,	
Госте́й созыва́ла.	And invited guests.	
Го́сти не быва́ли,	The guests didn't come	
Ка́ши не еда́ли.	And didn't eat the porridge,	
Всю свою́ ка́шу	So magpie-the crow	
Соро́ка-воро́на	Gave all the porridge away	
Де́ткам отда́ла.	To the children.	
Э́тому дала́,	This one [touching thumb] got some.	
Э́тому дала́,	This one [touching index finger] got some.	

Э́тому дала́,	This one [touching middle finger] got some.
Э́тому дала́,	This one [touching fourth finger] got some.
А э́тому не дала́.	But this one [touching little finger] didn't get any.
Заче́м дров не пили́л,	Why didn't you cut any firewood?
Заче́м во́ду не носи́л!	Why didn't you bring the water?

Early in life the Russian child hears short tales in verse **ска́зки в стиха́х** or **прибау́тки**, sometimes sung. Among the most widespread are the following:

🔊 **4-7**

Жи́л-был у ба́бушки	Once upon a time, there was an old woman,
Се́ренький ко́злик.	And she had a little gray billy-goat.
Во́т как! Во́т как!	Indeed, indeed,
Се́ренький ко́злик.	A little gray billy-goat.
Ба́бушка ко́злика	The old woman loved the little billy-goat
О́чень люби́ла.	Very dearly.
Во́т как! Во́т как!	Indeed, indeed,
О́чень люби́ла.	She loved it very dearly.
Взду́малось ко́злику	One day the little billy-goat got the idea
В лес погуля́ти.	Of taking a walk in the woods.
Во́т как! Во́т как!	Indeed, indeed,
В лес погуля́ти.	Taking a walk in the woods.
Напа́ли на ко́злика	Gray wolves fell upon
Се́рые во́лки.	The little billy-goat.
Во́т как! Во́т как!	Indeed, indeed,
Се́рые во́лки.	Gray wolves.
Оста́лись от ко́злика	All that was left of the little billy-goat
Ро́жки да но́жки.	Were horns and hoofs.
Во́т как! Во́т как!	Indeed, indeed,
Ро́жки да но́жки.	Horns and hoofs.

🔊 **4-8**

Жи́ли себе́ (or Жи́ли-бы́ли)	Once upon a time, there was an old
дед да ба́ба.	man and an old woman.
Была́ у них ку́рочка Ря́ба.	They had a spotted hen.
Снесла́ ку́рочка яи́чко.	The hen laid an egg.
Яи́чко не просто́е—	The egg was not an ordinary one—
Золото́е.	It was golden.
Дед бил, бил—	The old man tried to break it
Не разби́л.	And couldn't.
Ба́ба би́ла, би́ла—	The old woman tried to break it
Не разби́ла.	And couldn't.
Мы́шка бежа́ла,	A small mouse ran by,
Хво́стиком махну́ла,	Swung its tail,
Яи́чко упа́ло	The egg fell down
И разби́лось.	And broke.
Дед и ба́ба пла́чут,	The old man and old woman cried,

Ку́рочка куда́хчет:	But the hen clucked:
«Не плачь, дед, не плачь, ба́ба!	"Don't cry, old man, don't cry, old woman.
Я снесу́ вам яи́чко друго́е,	I'll lay another egg for you,
Не золото́е—просто́е».	An ordinary egg, not a golden one."

Ти́ли-ти́ли-ти́ли-бом!	Tili-tili-tili-bom!	4-9
Загоре́лся ко́шкин дом.	The cat's house went up in flames.	
Ко́шка вы́скочила,	The cat jumped out	
Глаза́ вы́пучила.	And looked on with its eyes bulging.	
Бежи́т ку́рочка с ведро́м,	A hen ran up with a pail	
Залива́ет ко́шкин дом.	And doused the cat's house.	

(There is also a longer version by Samuel Marshak **Самуи́л Марша́к**; see below.)

Из-за ле́са, из-за гор	Old Egor	4-10
Е́дет де́душка Его́р:	Is coming from afar.	
Сам на лоша́дке,	He is riding on a horse.	
Жена́ на коро́вке,	His wife is on a cow.	
Де́ти на теля́тках,	His children are riding on calves.	
Вну́ки на соба́чках.	His grandchildren are on dogs.	

Как у на́шего сосе́да	Our neighbor	4-11
Весела́ была́ бесе́да:	had such a merry conversation going on:	
Гу́си—в гу́сли,	The geese played psalteries,[3]	
У́тки—в ду́дки,	The ducks played the pipes,	
О́вцы—в до́нцы,	The sheep beat on boards,	
Тарака́ны—в бараба́ны.	The cockroaches beat the drums.	

We might also include here the first verses of a well-known narrative song (based on a 1903 poem by a much less known poet, Raisa Kudasheva **Раи́са Куда́шева**):

В лесу́ роди́лась ёлочка,	A little spruce tree was born in the woods.	4-12
В лесу́ она́ росла́,	It grew up in the woods.	
Зимо́й и ле́том стро́йная,	Winter and summer it stayed graceful	
Зелёная была́.	And green.	

Мете́ль ей пе́ла пе́сенку:	The snowstorm would sing it a song:
«Спи, ёлочка, ба́й-ба́й!»	"Sleep, my little tree, lullaby."
Моро́з снежко́м уку́тывал:	Frost would wrap it in snow:
«Смотри́, не замерза́й!»	"Take care you don't freeze."

There are also short, incantation-like verses dealing with nature, such as

---

[3] See "gusli" in Chapter 7.

◀)) **4-13** Улита, улита,   Snail, snail,
     Высунь рога,   Stick out your horns.
     Дам тебе пирога,   I'll give you some pie,
     Дам тебе лепёшки,   I'll give you some flatbread.
     Поползи по дорожке. Crawl along the path.

◀)) **4-14** Божья коровка,   Lady-bug,
     Улети на небо,   Fly away into the sky.
     Принеси нам хлеба,   Bring us some bread,
     Чёрного и белого,   Black and white,
     Только не горелого.   But not burnt.

◀)) **4-15** Радуга-дуга,   Rainbow-bow,
     Не давай дождя,   Don't bring us rain.
     Давай солнышка—   Bring us some sun—
     Колоколнышка.   The bell.

Children's folklore, of course, includes both folklore *for* children (such as the preceding items) and folklore *of* children, such as the following counting-out[4] rhymes and game songs:

◀)) **4-16** Между нами дураками Among us fools
     Есть один большой дурак. There's one (great) big one.
     Раз, два, три,   One, two, three,
     Это, верно, ты!   It must be you!

◀)) **4-17** Аты-баты—шли солдаты, Aty-baty, soldiers were marching.
     Аты-баты—на базар.   Aty-baty, they marched to the marketplace.
     Аты-баты—что купили? Aty-baty, what did they buy there?
     Аты-баты—самовар.   Aty-baty, a samovar.
     Аты-баты—сколько стоит? Aty-baty, how much did they pay?
     Аты-баты—три рубля.   Aty-baty, three rubles.
     Аты-баты—кто выходит? Aty-baty, who's out?
     Аты-баты—ты и я.   Aty-baty, you and me.

◀)) **4-18** Раз, два, три, четыре, пять, One, two, three, four, five,
     Вышел зайчик погулять. A hare went for a walk.
     Вдруг охотник выбегает— Suddenly a hunter ran out
     Прямо в зайчика стреляет: And took a shot at the hare.
     Пиф, паф! ой, ой, ой!   Bang, bang! My, oh my!
     Умирает зайчик мой.   My hare is dead.

---

[4] In counting rhymes the stress on each syllable is very strong.

—Кто укра́л?	"Who did the stealing?"	◀))) **4-19**
—За́яц бе́лый.	"A white hare."	
—Куда́ бе́гал?	"Where did he run?"	
—В лес дубо́вый!	"To the oak forest!"	
—Что там де́лал?	"What did he do there?"	
—Лы́ки драл!	"He stripped bark from the trees."	
—Куда́ клал?	"Where did he put it?"	
—Под коло́ду!	"Under a log!"	
—Родио́н!	"Rodion!"	
—Вы́йди вон!	"You are out!"	

—Гу́си, гу́си!	"Geese, geese!"	◀))) **4-20**
—Га-га-га!	"Honk, honk, honk!"	
—Есть хоти́те?	"Do you want to eat?"	
—Да, да, да.	"Yes, yes, yes."	
—Так лети́те же домо́й.	"Then fly home."	
—Нам нельзя́ лете́ть домо́й:	"We can't go home.	
Се́рый волк под горо́й—	The gray wolf at the foot of the mountain	
Зу́бы то́чит,	Is sharpening his teeth.	
Нас съесть хо́чет.	He wants to eat us."	
—Ну лети́те,	"Then fly	
Как хоти́те!	As you like."	

У попа́ была́ соба́ка,	A priest had a dog	◀))) **4-21**
Он её люби́л.	And he loved it.	
Она́ съе́ла кусо́к мя́са—	The dog ate a piece of meat	
Он её уби́л.	And the priest killed it.	
И в зе́млю закопа́л,	And buried it	
И на ка́мне написа́л:	And inscribed on the headstone:	
У попа́ была́ соба́ка,	A priest had a dog	
Он её люби́л …	And he loved it …	

Чи́жик-пы́жик, где ты был?	"Fat little siskin [a bird], where have you been?"	◀))) **4-22**
На Фонта́нке во́дку пил.	"I had some vodka on Fontanka Street.	
Вы́пил рю́мку, вы́пил две—	I emptied one or two shot glasses,	
Закружи́лось в голове́.[5]	And my head began to spin."	
Ста́ла му́зыка игра́ть,	A band struck up music,	
Стал чи́жик танцева́ть.	And the siskin began to dance.	
Танцева́л, танцева́л	He danced and danced	
И штани́шки потеря́л.	And lost his pants.	

---

[5] In his **"Петербургский фолклор"** (**СПб.: Изд-во Максима**, 1994) Naum Sindalovskii quotes only the first four lines as a bit of St. Petersburg folklore, noting that ***чи́жики-пы́жики*** was the nickname given to students of the St. Petersburg Law School because of their yellow-green uniforms.

Some children's folklore is better known in parody versions than in the original.
The following, for example, was sung by children in the 50s:

🔊 4-23 **Заинька, попрыгаинька,**   A little hare, a jumping hare
некуда заиньке выпрыгнуть.   Has no place to go.
Там стоят города все турецкие,   Turkish towns are all around
а на них замочки советские.   With Soviet locks on them.

(This version alludes to a Soviet slogan: "The border is locked." **Граница на замке**, from a 1938 film of the same name.)

Tongue-twisters are on the border of folklore of and for children. Two well-known examples are the following:

🔊 4-24 **На дворе—трава,**   Grass grows in the yard.
На траве—дрова.   Firewood is on the grass.

🔊 4-25 **Четыре чёрненьких**   Four black
Чернявеньких чертёнка   Blackish little devils
Чертили чёрными чернилами   Drew a blueprint [*lit.* "blackprint"]
Чертёж.   In black ink.

The inheritance of early childhood also includes folktales in prose. Although they can all be found in the classic collection *Russian Folktales* **«Народные русские сказки»** edited by **Александр Афанасьев**, they are usually told in adapted versions. Like early nursery rhymes, they can often be reproduced quite accurately by Russians, who can recite whole chunks of them. One of the earliest stories a child learns is "The Spotted Hen" **«Курочка Ряба»**, quoted above as a tale in verse, although it can be read as poetic prose. In any case Russians remember the opening line(s) for the rest of their lives:

Жили–были дед да баба, была у них курочка Ряба.

Once upon a time there was an old man and an old woman, and they had a spotted hen.

"The Turnip" **«Репка»** is another story of an old man and an old woman. The old man planted a turnip, and it grew so big that he could not pull it out. He tries again and again, first with the help of his wife and then with additional helpers, recruited one by one by the previous helper after the latest unsuccessful try: his granddaughter, the dog, the cat. The refrain summarizing the unsuccessful attempts can be used jokingly to describe an inept person:

Тянет-потянет (Тянут-потянут), вытянуть не может (могут).

He (They) pulls and pulls, but can't pull it out.

Finally a mouse joins in the queue and helps to pull the turnip out.

Not all tales of grandma and grandpa are so sentimental. Somewhere along the line, older children pick up a rhyme that was not normally reproduced in Soviet anthologies of children's folklore:

Жи́ли-бы́ли дед да ба́ба,	Once upon a time there was an old man and an old woman	🔊 4-26
Е́ли ка́шу с молоко́м,	and they were eating a porridge with milk.	
Рассерди́лся дед на ба́бу,	The old man got angry with the old woman	
Трах по пу́зу кулако́м.	and punched her in the belly.	
Ба́ба в о́бморок упа́ла,	The old woman fainted;	
Дед за до́ктором бежи́т.	the old man ran out to get a doctor.	
Е́дет до́ктор на свинье́,	The doctor is riding on a pig.	
Балала́йка на спине́	He has a balalaika on his back	
И гита́ра на носу́,	and a guitar on his nose.	
До́ктор лю́бит колбасу́.	The doctor likes to eat sausage.	

In "Kolobok" **«Колобо́к»**, a Russian version of the gingerbread man story, a small round loaf **колобо́к** escapes from the oven and goes on a journey of discovery, encountering various animals (a hare, a wolf, a bear and a fox) that want to make a meal of it. Each one announces:

Колобо́к, колобо́к, я тебя́ съем!   🔊 4-27

Kolobok, Kolobok, I'm going to eat you!

But **колобо́к** rolls on, singing:

... Я от де́душки ушёл,	I got away from the old man,
Я от ба́бушки ушёл,	I got away from the old woman,
Я от (во́лка) ушёл,	I got away from (the wolf).
От тебя́, (медведь), не хитро́ уйти́.	It's a cinch to get away from you, (bear).

It finally meets its end, tricked by the cunning fox.

"Masha and the Bear" **«Ма́ша и медве́дь»** is a tale about a little girl who gets lost in the woods and happens upon the house of a bear. The bear forces her to stay and cook for him. He finally agrees to deliver some treats to Masha's grandparents, and Masha hides in the basket with the pies. Along the way he is periodically tempted to sit down and sample the tasty morsels:

Ся́ду на пенёк,	I'll sit down on the stump	🔊 4-28
Съем пирожо́к.	And eat a pie.	

Masha, however, admonishes him from inside the basket:

Ви́жу, ви́жу!	I can see you, I can see you!
Не сади́сь на пенёк,	Don't sit down on the stump,
Не ешь пирожо́к!	Don't eat a pie.

The bear is amazed that she can see from so far away.

Other favorite tales frequently mentioned are "The Little Tower" **«Те-ремо́к»**, a story about a house in the woods that keeps getting additional tenants: first a fly, then a flea, followed by a mosquito, a mouse, a frog, a hare, a fox, a wolf, until a bear tries to join them and destroys the house; "The Rooster and the Bean Seed" **«Петушо́к и бобо́вое зёрнышко»**, a cumulative story in which the hen tries to get help for the rooster, who is choking on a bean seed, and succeeds in getting the blacksmith to help the master who helps the cow who helps the mistress who gives the hen butter to lubricate the rooster's throat; "The Fox with a Rolling-pin" **«Лиси́чка со ска́лочкой»**, about a fox who tricks people into giving her a chicken and a goose before being tricked herself; "The Fox, the Hare and the Rooster" **«Лиса́, за́яц и пету́х»**, a tale of friendship among three unlikely friends, very similar to the Grimm Brothers' "Bremen Town Musicians" **«Бре́менские музыка́нты»**, which is also popular among older children.

As the child's attention span grows, the tales get longer (and in some cases more unsettling). "The Wolf and the Seven Kids" **«Волк и се́меро козля́т»** is about a goat who leaves her seven children alone at home, where a wolf tricks them into letting him in. "Sister Fox and the Wolf" **«Лиси́чка-сестри́чка и волк»** tells of a fox who fools a peasant and a wolf. **«Моро́зко»** is one Russian version of the international tale type about an evil stepmother whose plan to get rid of her stepdaughter is foiled when the stepdaughter is rewarded for her good behavior while her stepsister is punished for her nastiness. The heroine of "Geese-Swans" **«Гу́си–ле́беди»** is able to rescue her brother, who has been spirited away, when she learns to be polite to potential helpers.

In "The Dark-Gray Chestnut Horse," **«Си́вка-бу́рка»** a magic horse helps foolish Ivan **Ива́нушка-дурачо́к** win the tsar's daughter, Elena the Beautiful **Еле́на Прекра́сная**. Part of the formula that Ivanushka uses to call the horse has entered the language as a way of demanding that someone or something appear: "Stand before me like a leaf before grass!" **Встань передо мной, как лист перед траво́й**! Ivanushka-durachok, the proverbial Russian simpleton, is lazy and seemingly slow-witted (the traditional image of the Russian peasant), and yet wins out through cunning in numerous tales. "Sister Alenushka and Brother Ivanushka" **«Сестри́ца Алёнушка и бра́тец Ива́нушка»** is a tale of love and devotion between sister and brother, who triumph over the evil witch.

In "The Frog Princess" **«Царе́вна-лягу́шка»** Prince Ivan **царе́вич Ива́н** marries a frog, who turns out to be the beautiful Vasilisa the Wise **Васили́са Прему́драя**. Ivan, however, spoils everything when he burns the frog skin so that Vasilisa will not turn back into a frog. She disappears, telling Ivan that he will have to find her "beyond the twenty-seventh land, in the thirtieth king-dom" **«за три́девять земе́ль, в тридеся́том ца́рстве»**. After many travails he finds his way there and rescues her from the evil Immortal Koshchei **Коще́й** (*or* **Каще́й**) **Бессме́ртный**. Both the "geographical" formula and the character of Koshchei occur in various tales and have become proverbial, with the name Koshchei Bessmertnyi also used to refer to an anorexic-looking man. In this story (as in some others) the hero is helped along the way by bony-legged Baba-Iaga **Ба́ба-яга́, костяна́я нога́**, who is more often an evil figure with an appetite for human flesh. Her name has become a proverbial way of referring to a mean old woman. (See also Chapter 3, "Folklore.")

Like Baba-Iaga herself, her residence, a hut standing on chicken legs **избу́шка на ку́рьих но́жках**, is a staple of Russian folktales and can be used in non-folkloric contexts to refer to any hovel. The formula that she uses when she notes the arrival of a possible victim, "I smell a Russian" **«ру́сским ду́хом па́хнет»** (or Pushkin's variant, from **«Русла́н и Людми́ла»**, **«там ру́сский дух, там Ру́сью па́хнет»**—cf. "Fi-fi-fo-fum, I smell the blood of an Englishman") has become a proverbial reference to things or situations that are typically Russian. The title of another folktale, "Go I Don't Know Where and Bring I Don't Know What" **«Поди́ туда́—не зна́ю куда́, принеси́ то—не зна́ю что»**, has also entered the language as a way of referring to an unreasonable request. (In the folktale it is the assignment given the hero by the king, who wants to get rid of him and marry his wife.)

To refer to something that happens miraculously, as if in a fairy tale, Russians use the formula "by order of the pike, by my wish" **«по щу́чьему веле́нию, по моему́ хоте́нию»**, the first half of which is the title of a folktale. It tells the story of a poor man who catches a pike, but releases it in return for the magic formula "by order of the pike …," which will make his every wish come true. (In the version first published by Afanas'ev around 1863, the second half of the formula is "by God's blessing" **«по бо́жьему благослове́нью».**)

In addition to the formulas already mentioned, some other fairy-tale commonplaces have entered the language and are readily recognized by children and adults. Among them are the traditional Russian version of "once upon a time," **«жи́ли-бы́ли»**, or, in the singular, **«жил(а́)-был(а́)»**. One of the traditional closing formulas is:

И я там был, мёд, пи́во пил, по уса́м текло́, да в рот не попа́ло.   🔊 4-30

I was also there, I drank mead and beer. It ran down my mustache, but missed my mouth.

The second half of this formula is also used proverbially to mean that a desired thing was not obtained or result not achieved.

Yet another fairy-tale formula that has become proverbial is:

Ско́ро ска́зка ска́зывается, да не ско́ро де́ло де́лается.   🔊 4-31

It takes no time to tell a story, but it takes a long time to accomplish a deed.

The works cited above come from prerevolutionary folklore sources; some of the tales exist in retellings by Soviet authors, but the basic structure and content remained intact. It is primarily through retellings in prose that Russian children become familiar with the heroes and plots of the Old Russian epic **были́на**. Particularly well-known is the troika of epic heroes, **«Три богатыря́»**: Il'ia Muromets **Илья́ Му́ромец**, Dobrynia Nikitich **Добры́ня Ники́тич**, and Alesha Popovich **Алёша Попо́вич**.

| PREREVOLUTIONARY LITERATURE FOR YOUNGER CHILDREN | ДОРЕВОЛЮЦИО́ННАЯ ЛИТЕРАТУ́РА ДЛЯ МЛА́ДШЕГО ВО́ЗРАСТА |

Also part of the canon are original works by both pre-revolutionary and Soviet authors. We will first look at works for children of preschool and early elementary-school age.

Soviet children were introduced to Ivan Krylov **Ива́н Крыло́в**, the Russian La Fontaine, very early. Even before beginning school they were read such fables **ба́сни** as "The Dragonfly and the Ant" **«Стрекоза́ и муравей»** and "The Quartet" **«Кварте́т»**, while "The Crow and the Fox" **«Воро́на и лиси́ца»** is so well-known that it is cited in its entirety in Chapter 2. Krylov is the undisputed master of Russian aphorism; his works are a treasure trove of quotations that have entered the language. One example from "The Quartet" **«Кварте́т»**:

🔊 4-32 **А вы, друзья́, как ни сади́тесь,**
Всё в музыка́нты не годи́тесь.

And you, my friends, no matter how you arrange yourselves
Still you won't do as musicians.

Other oft-cited works by Krylov include: "The Wolf and the Crane" **«Волк и жура́вль»**, "The Wolf and the Lamb" **«Волк и ягнёнок»**, "The Wolf in the Kennel" **«Волк на пса́рне»**, "Two Dogs" **«Две соба́ки»**, "Dem'ian's Fish Soup" **«Демья́нова уха́»**, "The Mirror and the Monkey" **«Зе́ркало и обезья́на»**, "The Cuckoo and the Rooster" **«Куку́шка и пету́х»**, "The Fox and the Grapes" **«Лиси́ца и виногра́д»**, "The Monkey and the Eye-Glasses" **«Марты́шка и очки́»**, "The Pig under the Oak" **«Свинья́ под ду́бом»**, "The Elephant and Mos'ka the Dog" **«Слон и Мо́ська»**, "Trishka's Caftan" **«Три́шкин кафта́н»**.

Generations of Russian and Soviet children were raised on *The Little Hunchbacked Horse* **«Конёк–горбуно́к»**. Published in 1834, it is a much-beloved fairy tale in verse by Petr Ershov **Пётр Ершо́в** about the youngest son **Ива́н-дура́к**. With the help of the talking horse, Ivan captures a Firebird **Жа́р-пти́ца**, and a princess **Царь-деви́ца**, visits her mother, the Moon, and saves a stranded whale **Чу́до-ю́до ры́ба-кит**, who helps him retrieve a ring from the bottom of the sea. The story ends with Ivan, magically transformed into a handsome prince, marrying the princess and replacing the elderly tsar who wanted to make her his bride. Both **Конёк-горбуно́к** and **Си́вка-бу́рка**, the name of the horse in the folktale of the same name, have become proverbial ways of referring to a horse.

Some of the best-remembered tales belong to the pen of Alexander Pushkin **Алекса́ндр Пу́шкин**: *The Tale of Tsar Saltan* **«Ска́зка о царе́ Салта́не»**, *The Tale of the Tsar's Dead Daughter and the Seven Knights* **«Ска́зка о мёртвой царе́вне и о семи́ богатыря́х»**, *The Tale of the Fisherman and the Fish* **«Ска́зка о рыбаке́ и ры́бке»** (the story of a poor fisherman, his greedy old wife and a golden fish that grants them their wishes). Most Russians can recite from memory the opening lines of Pushkin's *Ruslan and Liudmila* «Русла́н и Людми́ла»:

У лукомо́рья дуб зелёный;	A green-leaf oak tree grows by the cove.	🔊 4-33
Злата́я цепь на ду́бе том:	A gold chain is attached to the oak tree.	
И днём и но́чью кот учёный	Day and night a learned cat	
Все хо́дит по́ цепи круго́м ...	Walks around on the chain.	

An older generation is likely to remember a piece of children's revenge from school folklore:

У лукомо́рья дуб сруби́ли,	The oak tree by the cove was cut down.	🔊 4-34
Злату́ю цепь в ути́ль снесли́,	The gold chain was taken to be sold for scrap.	
Кота́ на мя́со поруби́ли,	The cat was cut up for meat.	
Руса́лку на ветвя́х сожгли́.	The mermaid sitting in the branches was cremated.	

Like those of Krylov, the contributions of Pushkin are so extensive that it would be impossible to provide sufficient examples here. See Chapter 2.

The rugged life of peasant children as well as the simple pleasures of the Russian countryside are recalled in the sweetly sentimental poems about the Russian village by Nikolai Nekrasov **Никола́й Некра́сов**. A section of *Peasant Children* «**Крестья́нские де́ти**», for example, was a staple in Soviet readings for school-children; it begins with the well-known lines:

Одна́жды, в студёную зи́мнюю по́ру,	🔊 4-35
Я и́з лесу вы́шел; был си́льный моро́з.[6]	

One day, in the freezing winter-time,
I came out of the forest; it was very cold.

It portrays a six-year-old walking alongside of a cart loaded with firewood, helping his father cut wood. In *Grandfather Mazai and the Hares* «**Де́душка Маза́й и за́йцы**» an image of kindness and wisdom is created in the person of the title character, who goes hunting and saves bunnies from drowning. «**Генера́л Топты́гин**» is a merry tale about a bear mistaken for a general. Lev Tolstoy **Лев Толсто́й** wrote many tales to teach literacy and morality to peasant children. His retelling of "Goldilocks" «**Три медве́дя**», also became a staple of Soviet childhood, and the following lines are as familiar to Russian children as they are in different languages to children around the world.

Кто хлеба́л из мое́й ча́шки?	Who has been eating from my bowl?	🔊 4-36
Кто сиде́л на моём сту́ле ...?	Who has been sitting on my chair?	
Кто ложи́лся в мою́ посте́ль?	Who has been lying on my bed?	

---

[6] These lines are widely parodied among schoolchildren.

The Town in the Snuff-Box «**Городо́к в табаке́рке**» is a story by Vladimir Odoevskii **Влади́мир Одо́евский** about a boy who visits the little people living inside a music-box. They tell him that a life of all play is no fun. Misha learns how the music-box works, but when he touches the spring, it snaps, waking him up from his dream. Odoevskii's «**Моро́з Ива́нович**» is a morality tale about a diligent sister and a lazy sister.

SOVIET LITERATURE	**СОВЕ́ТСКАЯ ЛИТЕРАТУ́РА**
FOR YOUNGER CHILDREN	**ДЛЯ МЛА́ДШЕГО ВО́ЗРАСТА**

The contributions of Soviet authors to the heritage of Russian children's literature are vast and rich. Some of them, notably Kornei Chukovskii **Корне́й Чуко́вский**, Samuil Marshak **Самуи́л Марша́к** and Vladimir Mayakovsky **Влади́мир Маяко́вский**, are in a class by themselves and had a profound effect on the esthetic development of Soviet children.

It would be difficult to overstate the significance of Chukovskii, who wrote volumes of inimitable verse for children and penetrating studies about children. As in the case of Krylov and Pushkin, snippets of his poetry have been indelibly imprinted in the minds of those who grew up in the Soviet Union. *The Chattering Fly* «**Му́ха–Цокоту́ха**» (1924) is a story about a fly, an evil spider and a brave mosquito; it also served as a libretto for a 1956 opera. Its opening lines are well-known:

🔊 4-37

Му́ха, Му́ха, Цокоту́ха,	The fly, the chattering fly,
Позоло́ченое брю́хо!	The fly with a gilded belly!
Му́ха по́ полю пошла́,	The fly walked across the field.
Му́ха де́нежку нашла́.	The fly found a coin.
Пошла́ Му́ха на база́р	The fly went to the market
И купи́ла самова́р:	And bought a samovar:
—Приходи́те, тарака́ны,	"Cockroaches, please come over.
Я вас ча́ем угощу́!	I will treat you to some tea!"

Also well-known are the lines of the mosquito who has triumphed over the spider:

Я злоде́я заруби́л,	I've killed the villain
Я тебя́ освободи́л	And freed you,
И тепе́рь, душа́-деви́ца,	And now, my lovely maiden,
На тебе́ хочу́ жени́ться!	I want to marry you!

Another Chukovskii hero is a sparrow **воробе́й** who saves all the frightened animals from a huge cockroach, «**Тарака́нище**» (1923). The poem begins peacefully with the well-known lines:

Éхали медвéди	Bears were riding
На велосипéде.	On a bicycle.
А за нúми кот	And behind them, a cat
Зáдом наперёд. …	Was riding backwards …
Вóлки на кобы́ле.	Wolves were riding on a mare.
Львы в автомобúле.	Lions were in a car.
Зáйчики	Little hares
В трамвáйчике.	Were riding in a little trolley car.
Жáба на метлé.	A toad was on a broom.

🔊 4-38

But soon a monster appears:

Таракáн, Таракáн, Таракáнище!	Cockroach, Cockroach, a Monster-Cockroach!

The monster demands sacrifices from the frightened animals:

Да и какáя же мать	But what kind of a mother
Согласúтся отдáть	Would agree to give up
Своегó дорогóго ребёнка—	Her dear child—
Медвежóнка, волчóнка, слонёнка,—	Her little bear cub, or wolfcub or her baby elephant,—
Чтóбы несы́тое чýчело	So that the insatiable monster
Бéдную крóшку замýчило!	Could torment the poor little thing!

«Мойдоды́р»[7] (1923) is a personified washbasin:

Я—Велúкий Умывáльник,	I am the Great Washbasin,
Знаменúтый Мойдоды́р,	The famous Moidodyr,
Умывáльников Начáльник	The Boss of all washbasins
И мочáлок Командúр!	And the Commander of all washrags!

🔊 4-39

The washbasin shames children who are too lazy to wash:

Ты одúн не умывáлся	You're the only one who hasn't gotten washed
И грязнýлею остáлся ….	And who has remained a slob.

It also teaches them the virtue of cleanliness, which makes everyone and everything love you:

Нáдо, нáдо умывáться	You must, you must get washed
По утрáм и вечерáм,	In the morning and the evening.
А нечúстым	Shame, shame
Трубочúстам—	Shame, shame
Стыд и срам!	On all dirty
Стыд и срам!	Chimneysweeps!

---

[7] «Мойдоды́р» literally means "wash to [the point of making] holes."

Another large, and initially frightening, creature is the main protagonist (if not exactly the hero) of *The Crocodile* **«Крокоди́л»** (1917), which begins with the famous lines:

🔊 **4-40**

> **Жил да был**
> **Крокоди́л.**
> **Он по у́лицам ходи́л,**
> **Папиро́сы кури́л,**
> **по-туре́цки говори́л,—**
> **Крокоди́л, Крокоди́л Крокоди́лович!**

> There once was
> A crocodile.
> He would walk down the street,
> Smoking cigarettes
> And speaking Turkish,—
> Crocodile, Crocodile the son of Crocodile!

Among the myriad of unforgettable characters Chukovskii created, one of the most beloved is Doctor Ouchithurts **до́ктор Айболи́т**, who appears both in a novel based on Hugh Lofting's books about Dr. Dolittle (**«До́ктор Айболи́т»**, 1936), and a narrative poem, **«Айболи́т»** (1929). The opening lines of the latter are familiar to many Russians:

🔊 **4-41**

> **До́брый до́ктор Айболи́т!**
> **Он под де́ревом сиди́т.**
> **Приходи́ к нему́ лечи́ться**
> **И коро́ва, и волчи́ца,**
> **И жучо́к, и червячо́к,**
> **И медве́дица!**

> Kind doctor Ouchithurts!
> He sits under a tree.
> Everybody, come to him for treatment:
> The cow and the mama-wolf
> And the little bug and the worm
> And the mama-bear!

Fig. 4-1.   Doctor Ouchithurts
до́ктор Айболи́т

Also familiar are the lines announcing an urgent invitation to Africa:

Вот вам телегра́мма	Here's a telegram for you
От Гиппопота́ма!	From the Hippopotamus!

And the explanation:

Мы живём на Занзиба́ре,	We live on [the island of] Zanzibar,
В Калаха́ри и Саха́ре,	In the Kalahari and Sahara [deserts],
На горе́Ферна́ндо-По́,	On the mountain of Fernando Po,
Где гуля́ет Ги́ппо-по́	Where the Hippo-po takes his walks
По широ́кой Лимпопо́.	Along the wide Limpopo River.

Africa is also the setting for **«Бармале́й»** (1926), the tale of a pirate tamed by two children, which begins with the famous warning:

Ма́ленькие де́ти!	Little children!	🔊 4-42
Ни за что на све́те	Do not go to Africa,	
Не ходи́те в А́фрику,	Do not go to visit Africa,	
В А́фрику гуля́ть! ...	Not for anything in the world! ...	
В А́фрике разбо́йник,	A villain lives in Africa,	
В А́фрике злоде́й,	An evil-doer lives in Africa,	
В А́фрике ужа́сный	In Africa lives the horrible	
Бар-ма-ле́й!	Bar-ma-lei!	

Lines from Chukovskii even entered children's games, for example, the opening lines from his *Telephone* **«Телефо́н»** (1926):

(У меня́ зазвони́л телефо́н.)	(My telephone rang.)	🔊 4-43
—Кто говори́т?	"Who is it?"	
—Слон.	"The Elephant."	
—Отку́да?	"Where are you calling from?"	
—От верблю́да.	"From the Camel's house."	
—Что вам на́до?	"What do you want?"	
—Шокола́да.	"Some chocolate."	
—Для кого́?	"For whom?"	
—Для сы́на моего́.	"For my son."	

The last two lines of **«Телефо́н»** also became proverbial:

Ох, нелёгкая э́то рабо́та—	Oh, it's not such an easy job
Из боло́та тащи́ть бегемо́та!	To pull a hippopotamus out of a swamp!

Also proverbial are some lines from the middle:

Неуже́ли	Is it possible?
В са́мом де́ле	Is it really true?
Все сгоре́ли	That all the merry-go-rounds
Карусе́ли?	Have burned down?

Many children learned the alphabet from Marshak's *About Everything in the World* «Про всё на све́те», which has a couplet for each letter, beginning with:

4-44 **А́ист с на́ми про́жил ле́то,**   The stork spent the summer with us,
      А зимо́й гости́л он где́-то.   But in the winter it went to visit some
                                              place else.

Marshak's poetry is a treasure-house of familiar expressions and quotations. Americans have their "absent-minded professor"; Russians have "the absent-minded man from Basseinaia St." «рассе́янный с у́лицы Бассе́йной» from Marshak's poem «Вот како́й рассе́янный» (1928), who even mixes up forms of address:

4-45 **Глубо́коуважа́емый**   Most venerable
      Ваго́ноуважа́тый!   Trolley-driver!
      Ваго́ноуважа́емый   Trolley-venerable
      Глубо́коуважа́тый!   most-driver!

There is the famous railroad passenger who checks a large quantity of baggage in *Baggage* «Бага́ж»:

4-46 **Да́ма сдава́ла в бага́ж**   A lady checked as baggage
          Дива́н,   A sofa,
          Чемода́н,   A suitcase,
          Саквоя́ж,   A traveling bag,
          Карти́ну,   A picture,
          Корзи́ну,   A basket,
          Карто́нку   A carton,
      И ма́ленькую собачо́нку.   And a tiny little dog.

(The little dog runs away, and the railroad employees replace it with a large dog, explaining to the protesting passenger that her dog could have grown during the journey.)

Marshak's retelling of the internationally known folktale about an old man, a boy and a donkey who are criticized by onlookers no matter who is walking and who is riding, "The Miller, the Boy and the Donkey" «Ме́льник, ма́льчик и осёл», contributed the lines:

4-47 **Где э́то**   Who has ever
      Ви́дано?   Seen such a thing?
      Где э́то   Who has ever
      Слы́хано? —   Heard such a thing?
      Ма́ленький   The young one
      Е́дет,   Is riding,
      А ста́рый   While the old one
      Идёт!   Is walking.

His song of praise to the postal service, *Mail* **«Пóчта»** (1927), which tells about a registered letter chasing his colleague Boris Zhitkov **Борúс Житкóв** around the world, begins with the famous lines:

Кто стучúтся в дверь ко мне	Who is knocking at my door	🔊 4-48
С тóлстой сýмкой на ремнé? ...	With a bulging shoulder bag? ...	
Это он,	It's him	
Это он,	It's him,	
Ленингрáдский почтальóн.	The Leningrad postman.	

Marshak's 1940 play, *The Little Tower* **«Теремóк»**, based on the folk-tale cited above, contributed the lines:

В чúстом пóле теремóк,	There's a little tower in the open field,	🔊 4-49
Теремóк.	A little tower.	
Он не нúзок, не высóк,	It's neither too low nor too high,	
Не высóк.	Not too high.	

His *Tale about a Stupid Little Mouse* **«Скáзка о глýпом мышóнке»** (1923) tells the story of a little mouse who doesn't like his mother's voice when she sings him a lullaby and is equally critical of the substitutes that his mother recruits (a duck, a toad, a horse, a pig, a hen, a pike); only the cat's voice appeals to him, which leads to an unhappy ending and explains the title of the poem. The mouse criticizes each singer with a variant of these lines:

Нет, твой гóлос нехорóш.	No, your voice isn't nice.	🔊 4-50
Слúшком грóмко ты поёшь!	You sing too loudly.	

Marshak's anticapitalist poem of 1933, *Mister Twister* **«Мúстер Твúстер»**, introduced a cigar-chomping, paunchy character destined to become famous:

Мúстер	Mister	🔊 4-51
Твúстер,	Twister,	
Бывший минúстр	The former minister,	
Мúстер	Mister	
Твúстер,	Twister,	
Миллионéр,	The millionaire,	
Владéлец завóдов,	The owner of factories,	
Газéт, парохóдов ...	Of newspapers, steamships ...	

Finally, the titles of several of his poems or of collections have become proverbial: *Little Children in a Cage* **«Дéтки в клéтке»** (a book of poems about animals); "If You're Polite" **«Ежели вы вéжливы»** (a poem about politeness, kindness and proper behavior in general); "The Master Breaker" **«Мáстер-ломáстер»** (about a would-be carpenter who starts out to make a piece of furniture and winds up producing only kindling for the stove); and "Mustached and Striped" **«Усáтый-полосáтый»** (a story in prose and verse about a cat).

Vladimir Mayakovsky **Влади́мир Маяко́вский**, the poet of the Russian revolution, believed that children should be treated as equals. His books for children were written with passion; they present serious and challenging topics and were beautifully designed and illustrated. In *What Shall I Be* «**Кем быть**» (1928) he explored the dilemma of what profession to choose:

◀))) 4-52

У меня́ расту́т года́,	I am getting on in years;
бу́дет и семна́дцать.	I'll soon be seventeen.
Где рабо́тать мне тогда́,	Where should I go to work?
чем занима́ться?	What should I take up?

The poem ends with the famous lines:

все рабо́ты хороши́,	All jobs are good
выбира́й	Choose
на вкус!	what you like best!

What's Good and What's Bad «**Что тако́е хорошо́ и что тако́е пло́хо?**» (1925) was the original politically correct book on civic and personal virtue (parodied in a saying popular in Soviet Odessa: "what's good and how to fight it" «**что тако́е хорошо́ и как с ним боро́ться**»).

◀))) 4-53

Кро́шка сын	A small son
к отцу́ пришёл,	came to his father,
и спроси́ла кро́ха:	and the little one asked:
—Что тако́е	—What is the meaning of
хорошо́	"good"
и что тако́е	and what does "bad"
пло́хо?	mean?

Mayakovsky illustrates the good and the bad, and of course there are no gray areas:

По́мни	Every son
э́то	Should keep this
ка́ждый сын,	in mind,
Знай	Every child
любо́й ребёнок:	Should know this:
вы́растет	A son
из сы́на	will grow up to be
свин,	a swine
е́сли сын—	if the son is
свинёнок.	a little pig.

What I Saw «**Что я ви́дел**» by Boris Zhitkov **Бори́с Житко́в** (1939) is a unique encyclopedia for four-year-olds, a book of why's, but also a story filled with the emotions, fears, joys and apprehensions of the first-person narrator, a little boy experiencing the world around him as he travels with his mother and spends time with his grandmother in the provinces. The book was meant to be read aloud to preschoolers over a period of one year. An example of "popular science" on a much smaller scale, a 1936 song about the escalator by Elizaveta Tarakhovskaia **Елизавéта Тарахóвская**, introduced the phrase "the magic staircase" **«лéстница-чудéсница»** (the title of the song) into the language. (Tarakhovskaia actually used the phrase first in a longer 1930 poem about the Moscow subway, **«Метрополитéн».**)

Sergei Mikhalkov **Сергéй Михалкóв** (the coauthor of the Soviet national anthem) created the character of Uncle Stepa, the hero of his **«Дя́дя Стёпа»** (1936) and of *Uncle Stepa the Policeman* **«Дя́дя Стёпа милиционéр»** (1954). The address "apartment house 8/1 near the Il'ich Gate" **«дом вóсемь дробь оди́н у застáвы Ильичá»**, along with Marshak's Basseinaia Street, became one of the best-known addresses in Soviet literature:

В дóме вóсемь дробь оди́н	In apartment house 8 slash 1	🔊 4-54
У застáвы Ильичá	Near the Il'ich Gate	
Жил высóкий граждани́н,	There lived a tall citizen	
По прозвáнью «Каланчá» ...	Nicknamed "Fire (Lookout) Tower."	

Mikhalkov's *And What's New with You?* **«А что у вас?»** depicts a group of children standing around and discussing the news of the day:

Дéло бы́ло вéчером,	It was evening-time	🔊 4-55
Дéлать бы́ло нéчего.	And there was nothing to do.	

Well-known are such lines as:

—А у нас в кварти́ре газ.	"We've got gas in our kitchen,
А у вас?	And what about you?"
—А у нас водопровóд.	"Well, we have running water.
Вот.	So there."
—А из нáшего окнá	"We can see Red Square
Плóщадь Крáсная виднá.	From our window,
А из вáшего окóшка	But from your window
Тóлько у́лица немнóжко.	All you can see is a little bit of the street."

As well as:

Мáмы рáзные нужны́	We need all kinds of mothers,
Мáмы вся́кие важны́.	And all kinds of mothers are important.

Mikhalkov also wrote the immensely popular **«Три поросёнка»**, his prose adaptation of Walt Disney's film *Three Little Pigs*, and the refrain "Who's afraid of the big, bad wolf?" **«Нам не стрáшен сéрый волк»** and its tune are as familiar to Russian children as to Americans. His fable "Two Girlfriends" **«Двe подру́ги»** (1945), about a mouse and a rat who are only interested in imported things, concludes with a line that has become proverbial:

🔊 **4-56** **А са́ло ру́сское едя́т!**

And yet they continue to eat Russian bacon (fat[8])!

Another fable, "The Rams" **«Бара́ны»** (1937), about two stubborn rams, neither of which would allow the other to cross a narrow bridge first, ends with the lines (popularized in a children's song):

🔊 **4-57** **В э́той ре́чке у́тром ра́но**   Two rams drowned
        Утону́ли два бара́на.   In this river early in the morning.

Another Mikhalkov poem, "A Song of Friends" **«Пе́сенка друзе́й»**, also set to music (and used in a film), starts with the well-known lines:

🔊 **4-58** **Мы е́дем, е́дем, е́дем**   We are going, going, going
        В далёкие края́,   Far away.
        Хоро́шие сосе́ди,   We are all good neighbors
        Счастли́вые друзья́.   And happy friends.

The second stanza also became popular:

Красота́! Красота́!   It's wonderful! It's wonderful!
Мы везём с собо́й кота́,   We have a cat with us,
Чи́жика, соба́ку,   A siskin, a dog,
Пе́тьку-забия́ку,   Peter, the trouble-making rooster,
Обезья́ну, попуга́я—   A monkey, a parrot.
Вот компа́ния кака́я!   What a company we have!

Although Mikhalkov was best-known for his poetic works for children, he also wrote the popular story *Holiday from Obedience* **«Пра́здник непослуша́ния»** (1972), about what happens when all the parents and grandparents in town, disgusted with their misbehaving children and grandchildren, sneak off and leave the children to their own devices for three days.

Generations of Soviet children grew up reciting poems by Agniia Barto **А́гния Барто́** from her collection *Toys* **«Игру́шки»**, for example, "Teddy Bear" **«Ми́шка»**:

🔊 **4-59** **Урони́ли ми́шку на́ пол,**   They dropped the teddy bear on the floor.
        Оторва́ли ми́шке ла́пу.   They tore teddy's paw off.
        Всё равно́ его́ не бро́шу—   No matter, I won't forsake him
        Потому́ что он хоро́ший.   Because he's nice.

or "The Ball" **«Мя́чик»**:

🔊 **4-60** **На́ша Та́ня гро́мко пла́чет:**   Our Tania is crying loudly.
        Урони́ла в ре́чку мя́чик.   Her ball fell into the river.
        —Ти́ше, Та́нечка, не плачь: "Hush, Tania, don't cry,
        Не уто́нет в ре́чке мяч.   Your ball won't drown in the river."

---

[8] See *Russian's World*, 2nd edition, 116.

The latter is perhaps the best-remembered of her poems. It was parodied in a садюшка:[9]

На́ша Та́ня гро́мко пла́чет,	Our Tania is crying loudly.	🔊 4-61
По голо́вке ска́чет мя́чик.	A ball bounces off her head.	
Э́то вы́думка отца́—	It's her father's idea:	
Мя́чик сде́лан из свинца́!	The ball is made of lead.	

New fairy tales were written by such Soviet writers as Pavel Bazhov **Па́вел Бажо́в**. The heroes of his *Malachite Box* **«Малахи́товая шкату́лка»** (1939) are the stone-cutters who toil in the Ural Mountains, as well as the mountains themselves. (The skill of Russian craftsmen is also the topic of the older, pre-revolutionary humorous tale of Russian cunning and cleverness, *The Lefty* **«Левша́»** by Nikolai Leskov **Никола́й Леско́в**.)

In 1936 Aleksei Tolstoy **Алексе́й Толсто́й** published his reworking of Carlo Collodi's *Pinocchio, The Little Golden Key or The Adventures of Buratino* **«Золото́й клю́чик, или Приключе́ния Бурати́но»**, which became a staple of Russian children's litererature. (It was also made into a play [1938] and a television film [1975], both called **Приключе́ния Бурати́но**.) Such phrases as "the little golden key" **«золото́й клю́чик»**, "the Land of Fools" **«Страна́ Дурако́в»** and "the Field of Wonders" **«По́ле Чуде́с»** have entered the language (the last also as the name of a television game show of the 90s), as have the lines:

Я бу́ду у́мненький, благоразу́мненький. 🔊 4-62

I will be smart and sensible.

and

Э́то о́чень хорошо́!	This is very good!
Да́же о́чень хорошо́!	Even very good!

In *Old Khottabych* **«Стари́к Хотта́быч»** by Lazar' Lagin **Ла́зарь Ла́гин** (1938) twelve-year-old **Во́лька Костылько́в** finds an ancient amphora while swimming and releases a genie, **Гасса́н Абдуррахма́н ибн Хотта́б**. Like all other genies, Khottabych tries to serve his new master with magic incantations, which sometimes work and sometimes fail. One of the best-known incantations, **«Трах-тибидо́х-тох-тох»**, is actually not in Lagin's book but from its 1956 film version.

The 1928 fantastic novel, *Three Fat Men* **«Три толстяка́»** by Yuri Olesha **Ю́рий Оле́ша**, starts with the well-known line:

---

[9] **Садю́шки** (also known as **страши́лки**) are the bawdy and bloody verses deriding the existing order within family and society that became popular in school folklore in the 70s and 80s. Our example comes from **«Ма́льчик в овра́ге нашёл пулемёт. Страши́лки — антоло́гия чёрного ю́мора», сбор и составле́ние А.П. Яро́ся и А.Н. Нау́мова— Минск: Реда́кция журна́ла «Па́рус», 1993.**

Вре́мя волше́бников прошло́.

The age of wonder-workers has come and gone.

and goes on to tell the story of a revolution against the oppressive rule of the Three Fat Men, led by the acrobat **Тибу́л** and the gunsmith **Проспе́ро**, aided by the actress and dancer **Суо́к**, whose kidnapped brother **Ту́тти** had been brought up by the despots to be heir to their throne. Olesha's novel was made into a film in 1966 and even into a ballet.

A more recent addition to the canon was *The Merry Family* «**Весёлая семе́йка**» (1949) by Nikolai Nosov **Никола́й Но́сов**, a very popular tale about a pair of boys constructing an incubator and raising chicks. His *Adventures of Know-Nothing and His Friends* «**Приключе́ния Незна́йки и его́ друзе́й**» (1954), a story about the lives of little people in a magical land, unfolds through the adventures of **Незна́йка**, a mischievous know-nothing. It was followed by *Know-Nothing in Sun City* «**Незна́йка в со́лнечном го́роде**», 1958, and *Know-Nothing on the Moon* «**Незна́йка на Луне́**», 1964–66 (see also Physics section in Chapter 12 Appendix).

Gena the Crocodile and His Friends «**Крокоди́л Ге́на и его́ друзья́**» by Eduard Uspenskii **Эдуа́рд Успе́нский** is well-known to younger Russians; it was popularized by film and television versions, including the animated film «**Чебура́шка**» (1971), which included "Gena's Song" «**Пе́сенка крокоди́ла Ге́ны**» by Alexander Timofeevskii **Алекса́ндр Тимофе́евский** with the lines:

🔊 4-63 **К сожале́нию, день рожде́ния**   Unfortunately, one's birthday
         То́лько раз в году́.   Only comes once a year.[10]

Fig. 4-2.   **Чебура́шка и крокоди́л Ге́на**

---

[10] One verse of this song appears in Chapter 7.

The line "You just wait!" «**Ну, погоди́!**» was also popularized in a series of animated films by that title (1969 and later with screenplays by Feliks Kamov **Фе́ликс Ка́мов** et al.), in which the wolf kept saying to the hare, "You just wait, Hare!" «**Ну, За́яц, погоди́!**»

And finally, a single poem by Stepan Shchipachev **Степа́н Щипачёв** stands out not for esthetic reasons, but because it became associated with the institution of young pioneers. Shchipachev was the author of "The Red Tie" «**Кра́сный га́лстук**», a poem about the triangular red scarf that every Soviet child wore around the neck after being inducted into the Pioneers:

Как повя́жешь га́лстук,	When you tie your tie,	🔊 4-64
Береги́ его́:	Take good care of it,	
Он ведь с кра́сным зна́менем	For it is the same color	
Цве́та одного́.	As the red flag.	

How persistent this image is can be judged from the fact that in late Soviet period this poem was still being parodied:

Как наде́нешь га́лстук,	When you put on your tie,	🔊 4-65
Береги́ его́—	Take good care of it,	
Он ведь с кра́сным зна́менем	For it is the same color	
Цве́та одного́!	As the red flag.	
Пересы́пкин Во́ва	Vova Peresypkin	
Га́лстук свой сберёг:	Took good care of his tie:	
Вме́сте с кра́сным зна́менем	He went to his grave	
Он в моги́лу лёг.	With the red flag.	

PREREVOLUTIONARY LITERATURE FOR OLDER CHILDREN / ДОРЕВОЛЮЦИО́ННАЯ ЛИТЕРАТУ́РА ДЛЯ СТА́РШЕГО ВО́ЗРАСТА

Among books favored by older children are many well-known prerevolutionary classics. Often what is remembered most vividly are scraps from the works of classical authors which were force-fed to generations of schoolchildren through rote memorization. Pushkin's *Song of Oleg the Seer* «**Песнь о Ве́щем Оле́ге**», for example, is remembered largely for the opening lines:

Как ны́не сбира́ется ве́щий Оле́г   🔊 4-66
Отмсти́ть неразу́мным хоза́рам …

It seems like only yesterday that Oleg the Seer was getting his troops ready
To wreak vengeance on the foolhardy Khazars ….

Similarly, what is recalled from Mikhail Lermontov **Михаи́л Ле́рмонтов** are such things as the first line of "The Sail" «**Па́рус**»:

Беле́ет па́рус одино́кий …	There is a lonely white sail …

and the opening lines from "[The Battle of] Borodino" «Бородино́»:

🔊 4-67

—Скажи́-ка, дя́дя, ведь не да́ром	Tell me, uncle, wasn't there a reason
Москва́, спалённая пожа́ром,	That Moscow, consumed by fire,
Францу́зу отдана́?	Was handed over to the French?

as well as part of the answer to that question, which has become a proverbial deprecatory description of contemporary youth:

—Да, бы́ли лю́ди в на́ше вре́мя,	Yes, there were [real] people in our day,
Не то, что ны́нешнее пле́мя:	Not like today's breed.
Богатыри́—не вы!	Heroes, not you people!

Magical literature for older children (and for adults) is indebted to the legacy of Nikolai Gogol **Никола́й Го́голь**, especially his two collections of fantastic tales set in Ukraine, *Evenings on a Farm near Dikanka* «Вечера́ на ху́торе близ Дика́ньки» (1831–32) and «Ми́ргород» (1835).

Among prerevolutionary works there are also those that deal with the bleakness of childhood. *The Guttapercha Boy* «Гуттапе́рчевый ма́льчик» by Dmitri Grigorovich **Дми́трий Григоро́вич** (1883), for example, is a story about an exploited young circus performer who plunges to his death. In "Sleepy" «Спать хо́чется» by Anton Chekhov **Анто́н Че́хов** (1888) a young girl in the service of an abusive couple is falling asleep by the cradle of a small child, who keeps crying. Unable either to fall asleep or to stay awake, the half-dazed girl puts a pillow over the face of the child and finally is able to sleep.

In another Chekhov story of childhood misfortune, «Ва́нька», an orphan sent off to learn the shoemaker's trade writes a heart-wrenching letter to his grandfather, begging to be saved from the cruel master. Van′ka addresses his letter "to grandfather in the country" «на дере́вню де́душке», a very touching phrase that has entered the language. Finally, it is difficult to imagine a Russian child who has not read «Кашта́нка» (1887), Chekhov's story of a dog's loyalty and love, despite its miserable life at the hands of its drunkard-master.

| **SOVIET LITERATURE** | **СОВЕ́ТСКАЯ ЛИТЕРАТУ́РА** |
| **FOR OLDER CHILDREN** | **ДЛЯ СТА́РШЕГО ВО́ЗРАСТА** |

Soviet literature for adolescents includes many autobiographical works. *Nikita's Childhood* «Де́тство Ники́ты» by Aleksei Tolstoy **Алексе́й Толсто́й** (1922), set in the 1890s, recounts one year in the life of eighteen-year-old Nikita. A more difficult childhood, frequently filled with deprivation and struggle, is recounted in the trilogy by **Макси́м Го́рький** *Childhood* «Де́тство» (1913), *In the World* «В лю́дях» (1916) and *My Universities* «Мои́ университе́ты» (1923). *Konduit and Shvambraniia* «Кондуи́т и Швамбра́ния» by Lev Kassil′ **Лев Касси́ль** is an autobiographical novel, the first parts of which were published by Mayakovsky in «Но́вый Леф» in 1928. It tells how two brothers invent a fantastic country (**Швамбра́ния**), choosing the illustration of a tooth from the library of their physician father for the map of their kingdom. ("Кондуит" refers to the journal in which teachers recorded children's misbehavior.) Kassil' was also the author of one of the first books about Soviet sports, *Goalkeeper of the Republic* «Вратáрь респýблики», which he wrote in parallel with the screenplay for the 1936 film «Вратáрь». A sports march written for the film, «Спортúвный марш» (words by Vasilii Lebedev-Kumach **Васúлий Лéбедев-Кумáч**, music by Isaak Dunaevskii **Исаáк Дунаéвский**), became the most popular Soviet sports song. Its refrain is especially well-known:

Физкульт-урá!   🔊⟩ 4-68
Физкульт-урá! Урá! Ура! Будь готóв!
Когдá настáнет час бить врагóв,
От всех грани́ц ты их отбивáй!
Лéвый край! Прáвый край! Не зевáй!

Phys Ed, hurray!
Phys Ed, hurray! Hurray, hurray! Be prepared!
When the time comes to crush our enemies,
You drive them away from all our borders.
Left end! Right end! Be alert!

A difficult coming of age during the Civil War is recalled in *The ShKID Republic* «Респýблика ШКИД» (1927), the story of a special school for orphaned street children in Petrograd during those hunger-filled years. Grigorii Belykh **Григóрий Белы́х** and Aleksei Panteleev **Алексéй Пантелéев**, two former inmates of the Dostoevsky School for Social and Individual Education **Шкóла социáльно-индивидуáльного воспитáния и́мени Достоéвского**, were barely out of their teens at the time of publication of their novel.

The events that convulsed Russia — the revolutions of 1905 and 1917, the Civil War — and that transformed it into the Soviet Union are the topic of a trilogy of adventure books by Vladimir Beliaev **Владúмир Беля́ев**, *The Old Fortress* «Стáрая крéпость» (1935–50). *The Lonely White Sail* «Белéет пáрус одинóкий» by Valentin Kataev **Валентúн Катáев** (1936) explores the revolution of 1905 through the experiences of two young boys (eight and nine) growing up in Odessa. *RVS* «РВС» by Arkadii Gaidar **Аркáдий Гайдáр** (1926) is the story of two boys caught up in the events of the Civil War.

A number of Soviet classics dealing with the early post-revolutionary period crossed over from adult literature. They are most likely to be remembered by older generations, but the titles and the names of the heroes are recognizable by much younger people raised in the Soviet Union. Two novels by Mikhail Sholokhov **Михаúл Шóлохов**, *Virgin Soil Upturned* «Пóднятая целинá» (1931) and the monumental *The Quiet Don* «Тúхий Дон» (1928–40) are perhaps the best-known. Both of them were popularized in a version for the radio in the 50s and later in a film. *Cement* «Цемéнт» by Fedor Gladkov **Фёдор Гладкóв** (1925) is a work about the painful transformations taking place in the private lives of a young couple in the wake of the Civil War. It shows the emergence of an independent woman who can no longer return to the old ways, and it is also one of the first books to treat sexual relations in a strikingly frank manner, exploring the clash between the old and emerging mores. **Па́вел Корча́гин**, the romantic hero of *How the Steel Was Tempered* **«Как закаля́лась сталь»** by Nikolai Ostrovsky **Никола́й Остро́вский** (1932–34), dedicated his life to the Revolution. The novel was modelled after the immensely popular book *The Gadfly*, by the English novelist and translator Ethel Voynich (published in 1897 and translated into Russian as **«Óвод»** in 1898). *The Young Guard* **«Молода́я гва́рдия»** by Alexander Fadeev **Алекса́ндр Фаде́ев** (1945) also belongs to this category of cross-over works; it deals, however, with World War II.

Of all the heroes and martyrs of the Revolution and Civil War, real or fictional, none is more controversial than Pavlik Morozov **Па́влик Моро́зов**, a real-life boy who informed on his father, testified against him in court, and who was later murdered along with a younger brother by his grandfather and others identified as kulaks. Pavlik was memorialized in stories, novels and epic poems. The tale of betrayal and murder is also parodied in the **садю́шка**:

🔊 **4-69**

Бе́дный Во́вочка лежа́л	Poor dear Vova lay
В лу́же кро́ви ро́зовой—	In a pool of pink blood.
Э́то па́па с ним игра́л	His father was playing
В Па́влика Моро́зова.	The game of Pavlik Morozov with him.

As could be expected, World War II constitutes a special chapter in Soviet literature for children and adolescents. Many stories are modern hagiographies, based on the lives of real people. Perhaps the best-known of them is "Tania" **Та́ня**, the nom de guerre of Zoya Kosmodem'ianskaia **Зо́я Космодемья́нская**, an eighteen-year-old partisan who was captured and executed by the Nazis in 1941. Her brief life was recounted in articles in Pravda **«Пра́вда»** in 1941 and in the film *Zoya* **«Зо́я»** (1944), as well as in *The Story of Zoya and Shura* **«По́весть о Зо́е и Шу́ре»** by her mother, L.T. Kosmodem'ianskaia **Л.Т. Космодемья́нская**. Two statements attributed to Zoya entered the language. When her Nazi interrogators asked her where **Ста́лин** was, Zoya is said to have replied, "Stalin is at his post" **«Ста́лин на посту́»**, and before her execution she defiantly told the Germans, "There are two hundred million of us; you can't hang us all" **«Нас две́сти миллио́нов, всех не переве́шаете»**.

The Fourth Height **«Четвёртая высота́»** by Elena Il'ina **Еле́на Ильина́** (1945) is a story based on another real-life heroine, Gulia Koroleva **Гу́ля Королёва**, who died heroically during the war, leaving her mother to raise her little son **Ёжик**. *The Tale of a Real Man* **«По́весть о настоя́щем челове́ке»** by Boris Polevoi **Бори́с Полево́й** (1946) is also based on a real-life hero, Aleksei Mares'ev **Алексе́й Маре́сьев**, a legendary World War II pilot who flies again despite having had both legs amputated. In *Son of the Regiment* **«Сын полка́»** by Valentin Kataev **Валенти́н Ката́ев** (1945) orphaned **Ва́ня** fights with the

Fig. 4-3.   Timur and his crew **Тиму́р и его́ кома́нда**

partisans against the fascists in occupied Ukraine. No character, however, real
or fictional, was as influential as the hero of *Timur and His Crew* **«Тиму́р и его́
кома́нда»** by Arkadii Gaidar **Арка́дий Гайда́р**, which had a long-lasting effect
on Soviet society. It first appeared in the children's newspaper **«Пионе́рская
пра́вда»** in installments in late 1940 and was turned into a film in 1941. Filled
with the foreboding of war, it is the story of a group of children led by Timur
who were dedicated to performing good deeds, especially for families whose
menfolk had been drafted into the army. The story spawned a nationwide
movement of "timurites" **тиму́ровцы**, who collected firewood, scrap metal, and
so on; the movement persisted into the post-war period. Both Gaidar's and
Polevoi's titles have become proverbial expressions.

In the trilogy by Valentina Oseeva **Валенти́на Осе́ева**, *Vasek Trubachev
and His Buddies* **«Васёк Трубачёв и его́ това́рищи»** (1947–52), fourth-graders
wind up in occupied Ukraine and led by their leader Vasek, fight against the
fascists. In the rear they continue their activities like *timurovtsy*, through good
deeds. In her three volumes Oseeva describes the lives of Soviet children just
before, during and after the war. Oseeva also wrote the well-known story "The
Magic Word" **«Волше́бное сло́во»** (1944) about the magic accomplished by
the word "please" **пожа́луйста**.

Not all of the best-remembered Soviet stories were set in wartime or dealt
exclusively with historical events. Gaidar's **«Чук и Гек»** (1939) is the story of a
long journey from Moscow undertaken by a young mother with her two small
boys to rejoin her geologist husband, who is stationed in Siberia. With a nod to
the opening line of Tolstoy's **«А́нна Каре́нина»**, Gaidar ends his story:

Что тако́е сча́стье — э́то ка́ждый понима́л по-сво́ему.

Happiness meant different things to different people.

Feelings of love and hurt are explored in another favorite by Gaidar, "The Blue Cup" **«Голуба́я ча́шка»** (1936), an unusual tale of family discord. When **Мару́ся** unjustly accuses her husband and six-year-old daughter of breaking her blue cup, they leave the house, hurt by this latest in a series of indignities. While walking, the father tells his daughter what Marusia was like when they were both young, and she convinces her father that her mother still loves him. They return to the eagerly waiting Marusia.

Dingo the Wild Dog, or a Story about a First Love **«Ди́кая соба́ка Ди́нго, и́ли по́весть о пе́рвой любви́»**, by Ruvim Fraerman **Руви́м Фраерма́н** (1939) is another complicated story of a family. When her father with his new wife and adopted son moves back to the town where she lives with her mother, fifteen-year-old **Та́ня** is torn: she loves her parents but is full of jealousy and resentment. Her feelings are complicated by the realization that she is in love with **Ко́ля**, her father's adopted son, and has hurt the feelings of the local boy who is in love with her. And so she begins to understand how complicated love can be.

Two Captains **«Два капита́на»** by Veniamin Kaverin **Вениами́н Каве́рин** (1938–44) is an adventure story about the search by a young boy, **Са́ня Григо́рьев**, to discover the fate of an explorer-captain. Sanya himself grows up to become a sea captain. His motto (a paraphrase of the concluding line of Alfred Lord Tennyson's poem "Ulysses": "To strive, to seek, to find, and not to yield") has become proverbial: **«Боро́ться и иска́ть, найти́ и не сдава́ться».** Another tale of adventure is *The Dagger* **«Ко́ртик»** by Anatolii Rybakov **Анато́лий Рыбако́в** (1948), a detective story in which the dagger of the title is a key that unlocks a clock where documents are hidden.

The works of two Soviet authors of science fiction have entered the canon of children's literature. *The Human Amphibian* **«Челове́к-амфи́бия»** by Alexander Beliaev **Алекса́ндр Беля́ев** (1928) is a novel about an Indian child in Argentina who is surgically transformed into a human amphibian. Beliaev's 1937 novel, *Professor Dowell's Head* **«Голова́ профе́ссора До́уэля»**, was a reworking of his 1925 story about cloning. *The Girl from Earth* **«Де́вочка с Земли́»**, by Kir Bulychev **Кир Булычёв** is the story of a girl from the future who shows up in our time.

WORLD LITERATURE　　　　　Мирова́я литерату́ра

Finally, reading world literature in translation is an important part of growing up Russian. Russian children read the fairy tales of Hans Christian Andersen **Ганс** (or **Ханс**) **Христиа́н А́ндерсен**, Charles Perrault **Шарль Перро́** and the Brothers Grimm **бра́тья Гримм**; Greek myths; the *Arabian Nights* **«Ты́сяча и одна́ ночь»** and collections of tales ranging from the Br'er Rabbit stories to Armenian and Georgian folktales and beyond. Among the individual foreign works domesticated by Russia's outstanding literary translators are the following, with authors' names given in their original form in a footnote and their Cyrillic version, and the names of their works given in their Russian translation:

4-70

1. Фрэнк Баум,[11]«Волше́бник Изумру́дного го́рода» (Alexander Volkov's retelling of *The Wizard of Oz*).

2. А́ртур Ко́нан Дойль, «Соба́ка Баскерви́лей и други́е расска́зы о Шерло́ке Хо́лмсе».

3. Джеймс Фенимо́р Ку́пер, «Зверобо́й, и́ли Пе́рвая тропа́ войны́; После́дний из могика́н»; «Следопы́т, и́ли О́зеро-Мо́ре; Пионе́ры; Пре́рия».

4. Альфо́нс Доде́, «Тартаре́н из Тараско́на».

5. Даниэ́ль Дефо́, «Робинзо́н Кру́зо».

6. Алекса́ндр Дюма́, «Три мушкете́ра»; «Граф Мо́нте-Кри́сто».

7. Э.Т.А. Го́фман, «Щелку́нчик и мыши́ный коро́ль».

8. А́стрид Ли́ндгрен, «Малы́ш и Ка́рлсон, кото́рый живёт на кры́ше». (The line «Я мужчи́на в са́мом расцве́те сил» was popularized in the 1968 animated film «Малы́ш и Ка́рлсон».)

9. Джек Ло́ндон, «Зов пре́дков»; «Бе́лый клык»; «Морско́й волк»; «Ма́ртин И́ден».

10. То́мас Майн Рид, «Вса́дник без головы́».

11. А.А. Милн, «Ви́нни-Пу́х и все-все-все́».

12. Рудо́льф Э́рих Ра́спе, «Приключе́ния баро́на Мюнха́узена».

13. Джа́нни Рода́ри, «Приключе́ния Чиполли́но».

14. Антуа́н де Сент-Экзюпери́, «Ма́ленький принц». (This is the source of such well-known lines as «Ка́ждое у́тро приводи́ в поря́док свою́ плане́ту» and «Мы в отве́те за тех, кого́ приручи́ли» as well as «Зо́рко одно́ лишь се́рдце. Са́мого гла́вного глаза́ми не уви́дишь».)

15. Ро́берт Лью́ис Сти́венсон, «О́стров сокро́вищ».

16. Га́рриет Би́чер-Сто́у, «Хи́жина дя́ди То́ма».

17. Джоната́н Свифт, «Путеше́ствия Гулливе́ра».

18. Па́мела Тре́верс, «Мэ́ри По́ппинс».

19. Марк Твен, «Приключе́ния То́ма Со́йера»; «Приключе́ния Ге́кльберри Фи́нна».

20. Жюль Верн, «Пятнадцатиле́тний капита́н»; «Таи́нственный о́стров»; «Два́дцать ты́сяч лье под водо́й»; «Де́ти капита́на Гра́нта». The film version of the last of these included the song «Пе́сня о капита́не» (words by Lebedev-Kumach, music by Dunaevskii) with the well-known refrain:

---

[11] 1. L. Frank Baum, 2. Arthur Conan Doyle, 3. James Fenimore Cooper, 4. Alfonse Daudet, 5. Daniel Defoe, 6. Alexandre Dumas, 7. E.T.A. Hoffmann, 8. Astrid Lindgren, 9. Jack London, 10. Thomas Mayne Reid, 11. A.A. Milne, 12. Rudolf Erich Raspe, 13. Gianni (Giovanni) Rodari, 14. Antoine de Saint-Exupéry, 15. Robert Louis Stevenson, 16. Harriet Beecher Stowe, 17. Jonathan Swift, 18. P.L. Travers, 19. Mark Twain, 20. Jules Verne.

Капита́н, капита́н, улыбни́тесь,
Ведь улы́бка—э́то флаг корабля́!
Капита́н, капита́н, подтяни́тесь,
То́лько сме́лым покоря́ются моря́!

◀)) 4-71

Captain, oh captain, please smile,
For a smile is like a ship's banner!
Captain, oh captain, pull yourself together.
Only the brave can be masters of the seas!

The enormous changes of the last decade have had a profound effect on the publishing life of Russia. On the one hand, the removal of censorship freed writers to explore any subject they chose, but another effect it may have is to lure talented writers away from children's literature, which in the past provided a relatively safe haven from politics and ideology. On the other hand, the disappearance of heavy state subsidies that in the past insured wide dissemination of inexpensive and often beautifully produced books for children has already led to great increases in prices.

With the dissolution of the Soviet Union into Russia and the other successor states, there are presumably fewer children being raised on Mayakovsky, Gorky and Ostrovsky's *How the Steel Was Tempered*. It is too soon to tell how many other authors and works of children's literature may lose their place in the canon of Russian cultural literacy, and which ones will regain their position in calmer times.

<table>
<tr><td>**Proverbs and
Sayings**</td><td>**5**</td><td>**Посло́вицы и
погово́рки***</td></tr>
</table>

Olga T. Yokoyama

"Out of sight, out of mind"—the phrase can be used in many different situations and it sounds neat. It also somehow seems to be true and indisputable, in a way the plain statement, "Once you stop seeing something or someone, you forget about it or them" is not. Phrases such as "Out of sight, out of mind" apparently have a certain truth status in our community. Their neatness comes partly from the way they are shaped. Even though the same idea could be expressed in many different ways, it would be not just less authoritative but also much clumsier to use the long version.

More or less fixed sentences like this one—called proverbs or sayings—exist in any language. They usually cannot be traced to a particular author. This is why proverbs are considered to be part of folklore **фолькло́р**. Most commonly, they declare some generalities about life, people, or the world, and they are usually striking in ways that make them memorable and more attractive than their plain literal alternatives.

But how would you go about, then, finding a way to say "Out of sight, out of mind" in Russian? Would you try to translate the English proverb word for word, something like (the wrong) **«Из ви́да, из ума́»**? And when that does not get across (and it wouldn't), would you try the literal **«Когда́ вы перестаёте ви́деть что́-либо и́ли кого́-либо, вы забыва́ете об э́той ве́щи и́ли об э́том челове́ке»**? This would probably work. Even so, chances are that you would be only partially satisfied. This translation is not nearly so short and sweet, nor nearly so eloquent as the original English proverb. And the response of your Russian partner will surely be somewhat tentative and not entirely convincing—that is, unless that person comes up with the established Russian equivalent: **«С глаз доло́й—из се́рдца вон».** (Approximately: "Away from the eye, out of the heart.")

Just as in English, Russian proverbs declare some general truths about life, people or the world. Knowing at least some of them will also lead you to discover some not-so-general truths about life, people or the world that nevertheless are accepted as truths in Russian culture. And since proverbs are often creatively used as a point of reference for irony or humor, being able to decipher these references will make Russian easier to understand.

---

* To my parents, who taught me to love proverbs.

Russian proverbs on record are actually quite numerous. The number of entries in the proverb collection[1] by Dal′ **Даль**, a well-known 19th-century philologist and folklorist (a naval officer and later a physician by training), was over 30,000, though most of these proverbs are not used by, or even known to educated Russians today. A comparable number of proverbs and sayings collected in the second half of the 20th century by V.I. Zimin and A.S. Spirin was published in 1996.[2] In the Appendix to this chapter, we will consider only the most frequent or traditional Russian proverbs. We will also include some sayings imported from other languages, as well as some recent native formations. When reading this material, keep in mind that proverbs often exist in several versions, and that there may be differences in how people understand and use them. All existing variants and all possible interpretations even of the versions presented here could not be included in this survey.

| HOW EDUCATED RUSSIANS USE PROBERBS AND SAYINGS | КАК ПОСЛÓВИЦЫ И ПОГОВÓРКИ ИСПÓЛЬЗУЮТСЯ В РÉЧИ ОБРАЗÓВАННОГО НОСЍТЕЛЯ РÝССКОГО ЯЗЫКÁ |

Proverbs and sayings are used to spice up speech. They make a neat and esthetically pleasing, or at least a striking, generalization. They enable us to relate a specific situation to a generic one, making us feel secure about our judgment. They also often serve to show off a command of the language and familiarity with the culture, very much the same way citing a line from Shakespeare or from a recent popular film would do. Inserting a proverb, of course, has a different effect from a literary allusion. Literary allusions imply the speaker's participation in high culture. Proverbs and sayings imply primarily a knowledge of folk tradition or of popular culture. The Russian educated urban population has generally been more exposed to modern and Western culture rather than to traditional Russian culture, so that frequent usage of proverbs in a Russian's speech may suggest a special philological background, a penchant for things Russian, or simply a certain folksiness of the speaker, possibly rural roots. Younger people tend to use fewer traditional proverbs. They indicate their ties to popular culture by means of more recent slangy sayings, some of which, as we shall see below, may nevertheless be built on older prototypes.

Notice that proverbs or sayings are not necessarily used just because they happen to fit the context. They are generally avoided in formal speech, or when talking to someone who is socially superior. When the relationship is informal, on the other hand, people not only freely allow themselves to make all sorts of value judgments, but they also enjoy playing with the language. So-called collo-

---

[1] For those interested in the original collection of his proverbs, see Vladimir Dal′. **«Пословицы русского народа».** The collection has been repeatedly republished.

[2] **«Пословицы и поговорки русского народа. Объяснительный словарь». Москва: Сюта.**

quial Russian **ру́сская разгово́рная речь**[3]—spoken among those educated Russians who feel close to one another—is known for all sorts of linguistic play. Mixing speech levels is a typical way of having fun in colloquial Russian, so that archaisms, slang, bureaucratese, and other marked features can all be mixed into a single sentence.

An implication, if not an outright purpose, of using a proverb, a literary allusion, or a reference to pop culture is to establish solidarity with the addressee. It is as if the speaker says, "See how I chose to package this idea? I knew that you would recognize this and would enjoy it, too!" Reliance on recognition is greater, of course, when proverbs and sayings are not used in their fully fixed "dictionary" form. Actually, more often than not speakers alter them. One common way of varying a saying is to say only one part of it, and to assume that the addressee will supply the other half (if only mentally). For example, the speaker may say **«Челове́к предполага́ет ...»** [Man proposes ...] and assume that the rest—**«а Бог располага́ет»** [but God disposes]—will be supplied by the addressee. Another popular device is to substitute parts of the saying to fit the situation. For example, instead of the usual **«Се́меро одного́ не ждут»** [Seven don't wait for one] (cf. B48 below), the speaker may say **«Пя́теро одного́ не ждут»** [Five don't wait for one], if it happens that there are five people waiting for the sixth. To adapt to reality, proverbs may be altered even more drastically. For example, one may say **«Ты про́сто обжёгся на молоке́ и тепе́рь ду́ешь на во́ду»**, alluding to the proverb **«Обжёгся на молоке́—ду́ет на во́ду»** [He got burned on hot milk, so he blows on water, or "The scalded cat fears cold water"]. The speaker's assumption invariably is that the interlocutor is able to reconstruct the original saying. With partial substitution, the speaker also expects the interlocutor to appreciate the speaker's wit.

Another way to use a proverb is to keep some of the packaging but to change the meaning altogether. It is the same kind of linguistic creativity you may have observed in English, for example, the mock modern variants "A penny saved isn't worth the trouble" or "Early to bed and early to rise makes a man healthy, wealthy and boring." One of the dominant functions of traditional proverbs in Russia today is to serve as the basis for this kind of new creation. Using an old proverb or an official slogan and altering it in an irreverent or cynical way has in fact been the pattern for Russian folkloristic activity of the past several decades. Among alterations are many obscene ones, which would never be used by most educated people, at least not in mixed company. As a relatively tame example, here are some risqué variations on the traditional proverb **«Своя́ руба́шка бли́же к те́лу»** [One's own shirt is closer to one's body] (meaning that one's own interests supersede those of others, cf. C58 below): **«Без руба́шки бли́же к те́лу»** [Without a shirt—closer to the body], **«Без руба́шки бли́же к Ма́шке»** [Without a shirt—closer to Mashka], and

---

[3] The most comprehensive description for specialists to date appeared in 1973, edited by E.A. Zemskaia, as **«Русская разговорная речь»**.

«**Сними́ руба́шку—бли́же к те́лу**» [Take off (your) shirt (so) it is closer to your body], which all allude to intimate situations. Perhaps the epitome of proverb-based creativity may be combining two unrelated proverbs into an absurd sequence such as: «**Что с во́зу упа́ло, не вы́рубишь топоро́м**» [What fell off the cart you can't cut out with an axe], which is a nonsensical combination of two proverbs «**Что с во́зу упа́ло, то пропа́ло**» [What fell off the cart is lost] (cf. B56) and «**Что напи́сано перо́м, того́ не вы́рубишь топоро́м**» [What is written with the pen can't be cut out with an axe] (cf. A93 below). Semantically incoherent sequences such as «**Что с во́зу упа́ло, не вы́рубишь топоро́м**» don't have a discernible message. Their only function is the joy that comes from the mutual recognition of sources; it amounts to an assertion of a shared cultural base.

Speakers who are more verbal and closer emotionally to their addressees will sprinkle their speech with sayings, puns, and/or literary allusions. It should be flattering to students of Russian as a foreign language when native speakers embellish their speech in this way when talking to them. Such linguistic play implies that the Russians think quite highly of your command of both the Russian language and culture. It also means that they feel no alienation towards you as a person. As with any linguistic play, it is an embarrassment to miss the point and to have to ask what the saying means. It also underscores alienness, so an advanced non-native speaker of Russian would probably feel better recognizing as many sayings as are likely to turn up in colloquial Russian.

Recognition, in fact, is the extent to which most people may want to "master" Russian sayings. Producing them actively is actually dangerous. Like all other instances of linguistic play in a foreign language, it is always risky to be creative. A poetic license is not granted to aliens lightly, and native speakers, especially Russian native speakers, are rather stingy about granting one to those who still occasionally make mistakes in aspect, word order, or pronunciation. And even if minor mistakes are no longer made, it is very important to keep in mind the interpersonal factor. Linguistic play and humor is permitted only when the speaker and the addressee are close enough, and gauging the proper social and psychological distance correctly is one of the greatest challenges of intercultural communication. Misguided assumptions baffle, annoy, or even anger the speech partner. It is a safe rule for this reason *never to engage in colorful language* with a member of the intelligentsia unless your partner initiates it with you first.

Proverbs are used, of course, not only by Russian intelligentsia and not only in oral communication. When they are used in written communication between educated speakers, proverbs and sayings serve to show off a command of the language and cultural heritage and imply the same sense of closeness and solidarity as they do in oral communication. In the uneducated speech of those with a strong rural cultural background, on the other hand, traditional proverbs may be used quite in earnest. In traditional proverbs, such a speaker seeks serious support for an argument and justification for actions, attitudes, and emotions. They are considered to be words of wisdom shared and accepted by all members of the community. The number of speakers who do this, however, is rapidly dwindling even in rural areas.

Sayings are frequently used in the media, where they usually help create a catchy headline or caption. They are supposed to impress readers with their wit, and are often meant to be humorous or ironic. Sometimes, by appealing to widely accepted traditional wisdom, they are used for persuasion as well. Proverbs rarely appear in headlines in their full original form. Most often, they are altered or cut short, with the reader expected to recognize the allusion. They tend to appear in headings of a less objective and less serious nature, mostly in contexts equivalent to the American "Sports," "Living," or "People" sections. A 1992 newspaper article on bus tourism in **Независимая (газе́та)** [The Independent (Newspaper)], for example, was entitled «**Ти́ше е́дешь — да́льше бу́дешь**»; this is a complete proverb as is. A 1995 article in **Сего́дня** ["Today"] on basketball, entitled «**Попро́буем пры́гнуть вы́ше головы́**», on the other hand, only alludes to a proverb. The original proverb «**Вы́ше головы́ не пры́гнешь**» (cf. B10 of the appendix below) points to the limits of human capacity. When a caption reading «**Что напи́сано перо́м ...**» [What is written by the pen ...] appeared under a photo of Clinton and Yeltsin signing an agreement in Yeltsin's 1996 election campaign album, the intent was to appeal to the common knowledge of the whole proverb discussed above (cf. A93), implying both the strength and the folksiness of Yeltsin's government.

Proverbs appear, of course, in Russian literature as well. There they serve several functions. When put into the speech of the narrator or the characters, they help create the kinds of characters and suggest the kinds of interpersonal relationship that admit proverbs in real life. The occurrence of proverbs in literature is more frequent than in the spoken language, and it would be good to be able at least to recognize allusions to them when you read the classics.[4] Some authors, like Shakespeare, use proverbs in the titles of their works. Particularly known for this in Russia was the 19th-century playwright Alexander Ostrovsky **Алекса́ндр Остро́вский**.

As with many words of wisdom, proverbs with opposite meanings are not a rarity. This inevitably makes one think of the multiplicity of philosophies that exist in every culture. Take the pair «**Бережёного (и) Бог бережёт**» ("God takes care of those who take care of themselves") and «**Во́лка боя́ться — в лес не ходи́ть**» ("Nothing ventured, nothing gained," cf. C7). These two pairs advocate opposing attitudes. Still, both are good advice in both cultures.

---

[4] A reasonable reference is S.S. Kuz'min and N.P. Shadrin's 1989 *Russian-English Dictionary of Proverbs and Sayings*, with 500 entries of proverbs and idioms.

Proverbs and Generality   ПОСЛО́ВИЦЫ И ОБОБЩЕ́НИЕ

General truths are usually abstract. They are meant to apply to many situations and many people. One way to attain generality is through expressing the idea not literally but metaphorically. For example, the proverb "All that glitters is not gold" **«Не всё то зо́лото, что блести́т»** in either English or Russian is not a statement about precious metals or glittering substances. What it really means is that appearances are deceiving.

The literal meaning of any pair of essentially equivalent proverbs sharing the same general meaning can be very different between languages. This is so because metaphors, similes, and other devices for "packaging" the main messages conveyed in proverbs are far less universal than the generalities packaged in them. Packaging the message "Appearances are deceiving" into the words "All that glitters is not gold" can be effective only in an economy where gold is known, valued and coveted, and in a culture where the shine of gold is considered to be pleasing. The English and Russian cultures and economies happen to be similar in this respect, and it makes the two packages almost exactly the same and equally suitable in this case.

Fig. 5-1.

It is safer not to assume that the packaging of English and Russian proverbs coincide. A speaker of English may say "It never rains but it pours." In approximately the same circumstances, a Russian might say **«Беда́ не прихо́дит одна́»** [Misfortune doesn't come alone]. Since the Russian counterpart in this case does not resort to any metaphors, its meaning is quite transparent even though its form is completely different from the English counterpart. In a case like this, Russians would have more difficulty understanding the English counterpart than English speakers would have with the Russian one.

This is not the case with the Russian proverb **«Назва́лся гру́з-дем — полеза́й в ку́зов»**, whose closest English equivalent is "In for a penny, in for a pound" (cf. C6). Both proverbs mean: "Once you begin doing something or promise to do it, there is no backing out." The Russian package for this general meaning literally says "If you called yourself a **груздь** (mushroom), get into the basket." The metaphors make sense in a mushroom-picking culture, where **груздь** *Lactarius resimus* is widely considered to be a choice pickling mushroom, and where people go mushrooming equipped with baskets referred to as **кузов**.[5] Understanding the metaphors of the English equivalent, on the other hand, heavily depends on knowledge of the British monetary system, in which *penny* is one of the smallest and *pound* one of the largest denominations. A literal translation of either the Russian or the English proverb into the other language would accomplish very little in cases like these.

OLD PROVERBS AND ANTIQUITY   СТА́РЫЕ ПОСЛО́ВИЦЫ И ДРЕ́ВНОСТИ

The ways in which the general messages of proverbs are packaged often reveal many things about older culture. There is, for example, a Russian proverb **«Гром не гря́нет, мужи́к не перекре́стится»** [Unless it thunders, a peasant won't cross himself]. The proverb refers to the human failure to anticipate problems and plan ahead judiciously, until it's too late. Many speakers of Russian will get only this much out of it, although for some, the proverb will evoke associations with earlier times. The packaging of this proverb refers to the old custom of crossing oneself, lighting candles and performing other rituals when thunder is heard to prevent the lightning from striking the household. The custom goes back to the pre-Christian worship of the Thunder and Lightning god **Перу́н** (Thor's counterpart in Slavic culture), who may strike those who are disobedient. With Christianity, Perun's place was taken over in the folk imagination by the Prophet Elijah (**Илья́**), as well as other Judeo-Christian holy figures. This is how crossing oneself came to be associated with thunder. A devout man was supposed to pray and cross himself regularly, and not only when divine wrath was already in the air. The peasant who does not cross himself until it thunders is for this reason not a judicious character. The packaging of this proverb reflects the complex relationship between Christianity and the older pagan beliefs of the Slavic people called **двоеве́рие** "double faith." You would not expect the English packaging to be similar to that of the Russian proverb, if only because the English were christianized much earlier and their pagan past has fallen deeper into oblivion than is the case among the Eastern Slavs, to which Russians belong. In fact, a somewhat similar idea is rendered in English as "A stitch in time saves nine." The packaging, as you can see, can tell us a lot about peculiarities of the culture.

    If you like antiquities, proverbs can be revealing. Here is another case of a Russian proverb that is heavily culture-specific: **«Не красна́ изба́ угла́ми, а**

---

[5] For a discussion of mushrooms in Russian culture, see Genevra Gerhart's *The Russian's World*, 2nd ed., 121–23.

красна́ пирога́ми». It literally says that a house is good not because its corners look beautiful but because its pies taste good. For this idea, too, there happens to exist no equivalent proverb in English, but the idea itself is quite understandable. Obviously, most people would agree that it is nicer to visit a house that serves good food than a house that is just pretty but does not serve any good food. This is how most Russians would understand this proverb now. A minority, however, would appreciate it much better, because they understand the historical allusions of its "packaging" beyond the plain meaning of its words. The "beautiful corner" **кра́сный у́гол** (formerly, **кра́сный** meant "beautiful") is an interior, and not an exterior corner of a peasant house **изба́**. Moreover, it is not just any interior corner, but the corner that is farthest from the entry door and the stove **печь**; it is up in this corner that icons were placed before the revolution and where they have begun to reappear after the fall of the Soviet Union. During the Soviet era, the **кра́сный у́гол** usually displayed Lenin's portrait (although behind it an icon may often have been hidden), giving credence to the very old proverb **Свя́то ме́сто пу́сто не быва́ет** [A holy place is never empty]. Perhaps a thousand years ago newly baptized Russians in just the same way removed their "retired" idols and put Christian icons in their place (possibly hiding the old idols behind them for the first few centuries after christianization). The big table at which guests are seated is put in the **кра́сный у́гол**.[6] The image evoked by the metaphor is distinctly based on traditional peasant culture. It may even be possible to read a certain woman-centered idea into it. **Кра́сный у́гол** is where originally the male host entertained his male guests, while the women served them. (In various social strata and at various times in Russian history, the segregation between the sexes was even more severe: women and children ate separately from the man of the house in a different room, and they even occupied the "women's half" of the house.) The pies are baked by women in the stove **печь** across the room, and **печь** is the women's realm. (Compare another proverb that mentions **печь** as one of the end points delimiting a woman's space: «**Ба́бья доро́га от печи́ до поро́га**» [A wench's (= peasant woman's) path is between the stove and the threshold].) When these distinctions between the male and female spheres in a traditional peasant house are taken into consideration, the proverb begins to seem to imply the importance of the woman's activity in the well-being of a home.

Metaphors used in proverbs can evoke pictures of nature familiar to the Russian heart, as in «**В ти́хом о́муте че́рти во́дятся**». At first glance, this proverb's closest English correspondence seems to be "Still waters run deep," but the values expressed are actually just the opposite. The Russian proverb literally says: "In quiet deep water, devils abide." The image is that of a pleasing but deceptive peace, which is spooky and treacherous. Imagine a still, sleepy, seemingly bottomless spot in a river or lake, the kind that abound in the forests

---

[6] For an extensive illustrated description of **изба́**, see Genevra Gerhart's *The Russian's World,* 96–105.

where Russia, Ukraine, and Belarus meet, with waterlilies, cattails, and with old willows reaching down to the dark water; imagine **чёрт**, the wiry and skinny impish Russian devil, the tricky evil spirit who is waiting there in the depths of the still waters. The proverb is used to warn against trusting a closed and quiet person, who withholds an opinion and does not show emotions. Characterizing a person by this proverb indicates an alienating and hostile attitude on the part of the speaker. Russians value openness and disapprove of a closed and reserved style of socialization. Note that **душа́ нараспа́шку** "an open soul" is a description of a likable person (usually a male), no matter how many other weaknesses he might have. A closed or reserved person is called **скры́тный** "secretive," and this is never a positive characterization. Somehow the metaphor about devils in a quiet deep water-hole is more likely to be used when speaking about women, perhaps because waters are generally a woman's thing: in ancient Slavic culture women were associated with nocturnal moisture and waters, and the earth, as opposed to men's association with fire, day and sun. Women brought water from the river and did the wash, and women stood around the town well and chatted. It is also women who, to this day, are thought to possess uncanny powers, who are incomprehensible, at least from men's point of view, and who can harbor strong negative emotions beneath a quiet and pleasant veneer. Now the English "Still waters run deep" seems to share with the Russian only the metaphor of still waters.

PROVERBS IN TIME AND SPACE   ПОСЛО́ВИЦЫ, ВРЕ́МЯ И МЕ́СТО

The degree to which an educated Russian person today can relate to a proverb rooted in Russian antiquity is proportionate to the degree of interest in things Russian. As mentioned above, for most Russians today who hear or use **«Гром не гря́нет, мужи́к не перекре́стится»**, only a vague sense of the awe of thunder may be present in the associations aroused by the proverb.

The post-perestroika era has witnessed intensive re-writing of Russian history. The past that seemed to have been forgotten is now being revived. It would be interesting to see if the packaging of some proverbs can regain its transparency to native speakers as this cultural revival takes place in post-communist Russia. Take the Russian proverb **«В чужо́й монасты́рь со свои́м уста́вом не хо́дят»** [One does not go to someone else's monastery (or convent) with one's own statute (= rules)]. Hardly any monasteries or convents survived the seven decades of the militantly atheist Soviet regime, and the generation of adults born after the 1970s is not likely to use this proverb in their speech, although most educated adults of the same generation would still recognize it. (See Fig. 5-2 on the following page.)

A proverb with the timeless metaphor of the animal kingdom is more likely to be used in somewhat similar situations: **«С волка́ми жить — по во́лчьи выть»** [To live with wolves is to howl like wolves]. Can you think of the English equivalents? "When in Rome, do as the Romans do" is more or less equivalent

Как и положено, в ваш монастырь – не со своим уставом

Fig. 5-2.

to the convent and statute proverb. Both recommend adjusting one's customs to those of the surroundings. The wolf proverb, however, goes far beyond custom. It's a rather depressing message about survival. It speaks of the inevitability of losing one's human voice in order to survive among beast-like humans. It would be interesting to see if the less value-laden metaphor of monastic statutes is restored to frequent usage in the next generation of Russians, provided the recent dramatic increase in the number of functioning monasteries and convents in Russia continues and life gets less harsh politically and economically. And in that case, would the wolf proverb become obsolete?

New sayings constantly enter the language. Some of them arise through popularization of phrases found in literary sources. As time goes by and the memory of the original author is lost to speakers, it becomes more and more legitimate to consider such sayings folklore. Nowadays, for example, you would have to look very hard to find a Russian who knows that one of the more frequent sayings **«С ми́лым рай и в шалаше́»** [With a beloved one, even a lean-to is paradise] is not an authentic proverb. It is actually a line from a song by the **5-4** minor poet Ibragimov **Ибраги́мов** published in 1815 and very popular for a while. The line (which is sometimes also paraphrased as **«С ми́лым сча́стье в шалаше́»** [With a beloved one, even a lean-to is happiness]) acquired a circulation far beyond its author's name. The result was that the author was forgotten and speakers of Russian came to perceive the sentence to be folklore, and to call it a proverb (cf. B 45).

A similar loss of association with the original source is often found with sayings that originate in the Old or New Testament. There was a time when even such expressions as "My Heavens!" **Бо́же мой!** Or "Swear to God" **Ей-Бо́гу!** were disallowed in public speech. The ideas expressed in the Bible—if used at all—were often reassigned to a more acceptable source. **Ле́нин** used quotes from the Old or New Testament quite often, and in the context of Lenin's writings these quotes sounded like proverbs. For all practical purposes—and the purposes were certainly practical!—the original source was forgotten and new quotable "proverbs" were born. It was in this way, for example, that the original source of **«Кто не рабо́тает, (тот) не ест»** [Who does not work does not eat] was lost for modern speakers of Russian. This phrase from the apostle Paul's letters, "If any would not work, neither should he eat" was the origin of one of the slogans of the October Revolution, used to help justify the destruction of the former gentry, clergy, intelligentsia, and other "enemies of the people."

During the Soviet era, the government encouraged the coinage of new sayings to suit its ideology. Visible but not very convincing attempts were made to keep the packaging traditional. Such formations sounded fake and remained alien to the linguistic sensibilities of the people. Here are some examples of such Soviet "proverbs": **«Ле́нина заве́т на ты́сячи лет»** [Lenin's testament is for thousands of years], **«Что Ста́лин напи́шет—вся́кий услы́шит»** [What Stalin writes every man hears], **«Хоро́шая ни́ва то́лько у коллекти́ва»** [A good field is only that of a collective farm]. Not surprisingly, most such "proverbs" were never much used in speech. Those which were not ideological have a better chance to be remembered today, such as **«Кури́ть—здоро́вью вреди́ть»** [To smoke is to harm health].

True proverbs are constantly born naturally, and the 20th century was no exception. In fact, it gave rise to many spontaneous proverbs. What is remarkable about these modern formations is that very few of them are self-sufficient and have a positive message. Most of them take issue with other, better-established proverbs and sayings, as well as with official slogans. Even in their form, many of them enter the language as mock variants of phrases found in other widely known sources. In fact, the recognizability of the source is the critical ingredient of the fun of such sayings. In response to the official slogan **«Кури́ть—здоро́вью вреди́ть»** one can, for example, defiantly say: **«Куре́нье—вред, а некуря́щих нет»** [Smoking is harmful yet there are no non-smokers], or **«Кто не ку́рит и не пьёт, тот здоро́веньким помрёт»** [Who does not smoke or drink shall die nice 'n' healthy] (see also C49). In response to the traditional **«Ти́ше е́дешь, да́льше бу́дешь»** [The slower you go, the farther you'll be]

("Slow and steady wins the race") drivers today would mockingly add: **«от того́ ме́ста, к кото́рому е́дешь»** [from the place where you're going to], or retort with: **«Бо́льше ско́рость—ме́ньше ям»** [The higher the speed the fewer the potholes]. Sayings like these can be called "living folklore," as opposed to the more traditional, "fossilized" proverbs. While the old proverbs are becoming more and more opaque to speakers of modern Russian, "living" sayings acquire wide currency and enjoy the tremendous benefit of being conceptually and linguistically *au courant*. Their ideas appeal to modern people and they often contain elements of slang and other features of youth culture. Perhaps because their form and language betray their youth, they may seem somehow less authoritative, and many culturally more conservative speakers are reluctant to consider them on a par with traditional proverbs.

There is also another source for proverbs and sayings. Just as with words and phrases, proverbs can be borrowed from other languages. Such borrowings may replace existing proverbs or coexist with them. For example, **«Игра́ не сто́ит свеч»** ("The game is not worth the candle") was probably borrowed into Russian from France at the time when card-playing came to Russia (the French have the same proverb in exactly the same package: "Le jeu ne vaut pas la chandelle"). Russia borrowed proverbs mostly, but not exclusively, from Western Europe. Borrowed proverbs that coexist with native ones convey the same general meaning but have a different packaging. The idea expressed by the French proverb just mentioned had in fact already been packaged in Russia into a different metaphor, based on an authentic Russian experience: **«Овчи́нка/шку́рка вы́делки не сто́ит»** [The sheep-/skin is not worth the manufacturing labor]. This older proverb is still widely used today, competing with the borrowed one about card-playing. The difference is that of orientation: the borrowed proverb shows off one's familiarity with Europe-inspired 19th century culture, when card playing was in vogue, while the native one implies familiarity with indigenous tradition—the familiar Westerners **за́падники** vs. Slavophiles **славянофи́лы** contrast in a mild subconscious form. You will immediately recognize a few "Russian" proverbs and sayings in section A of the Appendix, since you probably have heard them in English.

The Packaging of Proverbs   **Как посло́вицы оформля́ются**

Traditional proverbs are quite sophisticated in their form. Some of the compositional poetic rules they follow are very archaic. Traditional proverbs often have alliteration (the poetic figure according to which words begin with the same sound, **аллитера́ция**) and other fancy arrangements of sounds (for example, paronomasia **парономáзия**). They may have rhyme **ри́фма** and meter **разме́р**, for example, iambic (based on the iamb **ямб**) or trochaic (based on the trochee **хоре́й**), among other patterns. Their phrasing (syntax **си́нтаксис**) is often quite striking, too. Old proverbs often consist of two parts that are in some way structurally parallel. These formal devices, together with the imagery proverbs employ, are what make them both striking and remarkably easy to memorize.

Since many proverbs have been around for centuries, their language may contain old words, old forms, or old meanings of words. In «Бодли́вой коро́ве Бог рог не даёт» for example, the form **рог** (gen. pl. of "horn") would be considered a mistake if anyone were to use it today. The proverb literally says: "To a butting cow God gives no horns." The genitive plural form required for *horn* in this construction would be **рого́в** in modern Russian, and it has been **рого́в** for the past eight centuries or so, at least in the literary language. So why has the old form survived in this phrase? Besides the power of habit, there is another reason, which has to do with poetics. If the form **рог** in this proverb were replaced with the modern **рого́в**, the nice amphibrachic **амфибра́хий** meter of the proverb would be destroyed.

To see how delightful the details of the packaging of traditional proverbs can be, let's look at the formal poetic characteristics of some of them:

Без труда́ не вы́тащишь и ры́бку из пруда́. No pain, no gain. This proverb has rhyme: **труда́** and **пруда́**. The frequency of [r] is also conspicuous, and the rhythmic pattern can be interpreted as essentially iambic. The literal meaning is: "Without work you won't even pull a small fish out of a pond."

Бережёного (и) Бог бережёт. Better safe than sorry. / God helps him who helps himself. This proverb has alliteration of the [b] sound. The repetition of forms based on the same root **бере́чь** "save" also results in the striking occurrence of the same sounds twice in this short sequence: **бережёного** and **бережёт.** Finally, the stressed vowel in all three words is [o]. The proverb literally says: "God (also) protects the one who is well protected." There is a modern indecent addition to this proverb that clearly illustrates the difference between older and more modern ways of making a proverb: «сказа́ла мона́хиня, надева́я презервати́в на све́чку» [said a nun while putting a condom on a candle]. Notice that the addition displays no poetic devices like rhyme or sound orchestration. It derives its "fun" from the specific meaning of "safe," reinterpreting it narrowly as sexual hygiene, and from the unexpected associations of God-nun-candle-condom-penis, which lead from piety to sin. The packaging of modern sayings is discussed shortly below.

Ку́рица не пти́ца, ба́ба не челове́к. This proverb apparently has no parallel in English. It does not resort to metaphors but rather uses a straight comparison. It literally says "A hen is not a bird, a wench (= peasant woman) is not a human." The syntactic and semantic parallelism of the two clauses is striking. The first clause makes reference to a hen, which is clearly less than a prototypical bird; it is also a domestically useful bird which is not considered particularly poetic or beautiful. This reference to an indisputable and familiar case of deviation from the avian prototype eloquently evokes the Russian male's traditional view of women. A modern and subtler version of the same idea is «Же́нщина—друг челове́ка» [Woman is human's (best) friend]. This variant capitalizes on the association with the official saying «Соба́ка—друг челове́ка» [Dog is man's (best) friend] and also exploits the idea that a woman is not a member of the set that includes humans. Note the recent political variations using the hen/bird relationship: «Ку́рица не пти́ца, Болга́рия (Ве́нгрия, По́льша, etc.) не заграни́ца» [A hen is not a bird, Bulgaria (Hungary, Poland etc.) is not abroad]. Before Perestroika, the only trips "abroad" most citizens were allowed to take, if at all, were to the "brotherly republics" of the Soviet bloc.

Ма́гко сте́лет, да жёстко спать. A honey tongue, a heart of gall. Here note the syntactic parallelism of "adverb + verb" repeated in both clauses: **ма́гко сте́лет** and **жёстко спать.** The adverbs are antonyms (*soft* and *hard*), and the verbs show alliteration. Note also the trochaic meter. The proverb literally says: "(S/he) makes the bed soft (but) it's hard to sleep (in)." (To some, the immediate association of this proverb is female, although it is also used to refer to a man. In this respect it is like **«В ти́хом о́муте че́рти во́дятся»** discussed above.)

These proverbs are not just authoritative statements of folk wisdom; they are also a form of art—mini-poems, like *haiku* plus a philosophical message. Their form is just as important for their effectiveness as the cleverness and power of their imagery and the significance of their general idea. The packaging features of old proverbs that have survived the test of time are much more elaborate than those of proverbs more recently translated from other languages, such as «Не откла́дывай на за́втра то́, что мо́жешь сде́лать сего́дня» [Don't put off till tomorrow what you can do today] (cf. C42 below). Most borrowed proverbs sound more like regular sentences. Equally unremarkable are the fake sayings artificially created during the Soviet era. «Ле́нина заве́т на ты́сячи лет», for example, has a rhyme (заве́т—лет), but that's about it. No grammatical parallelism, no orchestration of vowel and consonant sounds, and no striking imagery, to say nothing of the generality or the truth value of the idea itself.

Of the non-traditional sayings, it is clearly the spontaneously created new "living" sayings that are poetically the richest. Most of their fun, however, usually comes from irony, from a cynical twist, and from a sharp denial of both traditional wisdom and official government values. The wording of the recent formation «Кто не ку́рит и не пьёт, тот здоро́веньким помрёт», for example, is not metaphorical, but the proverb rhymes, there is syntactic parallelism, and the meter is clearly trochaic. The diminutive form of the adjective **здоро́веньким** "nice 'n' healthy" is dripping with irony. This succinct pro-smoking and pro-drinking message, which polemicizes against the official anti-smoking slogan, is packaged so effectively that even a non-drinking non-smoking Californian might pause momentarily (if such a person could appreciate the packaging of the Russian proverb) to question a health-conscious life style, in contrast to the fatalistic and pleasure-affirming Russian stance. An even more elaborate mock proverb is based on the party slogan **«Во́дка—пережи́ток про́шлого»** [Vodka is a holdover from the past]. To this anti-drinking official Soviet slogan, the people responded with a clever pro-drinking saying: **«Во́дка—пережи́ток про́шлого, настоя́щего и бу́дущего»** [Vodka is a holdover from the past, present and future]. This is a particularly biting and complex allusion, because it also mocks Soviet triplet clichés such as **«Ле́нин жил, Ле́нин жив, Ле́нин бу́дет жить»** [Lenin lived, Lenin lives, Lenin will live] (this triplet actually comes from a 1924 eulogy to Lenin by the poet Mayakovsky **Маяко́вский**), which in turn capitalized on the Orthodox prayer ending **и ны́не, и при́сно, и во ве́ки веко́в** "now, and always, and for ages of ages."

There are also spontaneous sayings of the 20th century which are quite simple in form, and their meaning often is not expressed metaphorically but literally. They may sound just like a plain sentence, with a minimal amount of poetics, if any. The meaning of some of them may be transparent, as in **«Что есте́ственно, то не сты́дно/безобра́зно»** [What is natural is not shameful/ugly], referring to bodily functions. More often, though, it depends on implications and requires a certain amount of deciphering, as in **«Хоте́ть не вре́дно»** [It's not harmful to wish = you can wish as much as you want, but you won't get it / it won't happen] or **«Чего́ не дано́, в магази́не не ку́пишь»** [What was not given (to you by Mother Nature) you can't buy in a store], meaning intelligence, talent, or abilities. Play with associations is an important part of the "fun" in modern sayings. The associations may be simply those of the meanings of the words, as the string of associations "God-nun-candle-" etc. in the case of the modern addition to **«Бережёного (и) Бог бережёт»**, or those of the cultural background, as in the case of **«Во́дка—пережи́ток про́шлого, настоя́щего и бу́дущего»**.

Appendix: Frequent
Proverbs and Sayings

Приложе́ние: Ча́сто повторя́емые
посло́вицы и погово́рки

Here you will find the proverbs that educated Russians are more likely to use actively in their speech. The entries are arranged alphabetically by first word. The Russian proverbs are followed by an English equivalent when there is one. Unless the English equivalent is exactly the same, a literal translation is given in square brackets [ ]. Near-equivalents within one or another of the languages are separated by "/." Any cultural comments that seem interesting are given after the literal translation, and where possible, modern variations are provided, whether similar or opposite in meaning. Keep in mind that archaic and otherwise unusual words or forms may be used in proverbs, so your knowledge of standard language rules may not be sufficient to understand them even as sentences. Proverbs are often elliptical (that is, one or more words may be missing), and one needs constantly to try to reconstruct the full sentence. The word order in proverbs may also surprise you. If proverbs involve metaphors, then of course you need to exercise your metaphorical thinking. No comments on the sound or the syntax of the proverbs are given below, but you can easily explore that realm yourself. In actual communication you will, of course, hear adaptations and fragments of these proverbs. Slightly different variants exist, too, but as a rule they are not given here unless they are interesting in some way. Modern mock "proverbs" are provided in the commentaries to the well-established proverbs. For practicality, the Russian proverbs in this Appendix are divided into three groups A-C, with a list of certain common English proverbs following in D; the groups are characterized at the beginning of each list.

A. Easy Proverbs   Лёгкие посло́вицы

These are proverbs immediately recognizable by English speakers, such as: **«Лу́чше оди́н раз уви́деть, чем сто раз услы́шать».** Seeing is believing. [It's better to see once than to hear a hundred times.]

Many proverbs in this section are essentially the same as their English counterparts. Most were originally borrowed into both English and Russian from their shared European heritage; some have been borrowed into Russian from English. For speakers of American English who know these sayings in English, it will be gratifying to recognize the Russian equivalents. For other proverbs in this section, there is no equivalent in English but they are still immediately recognizable, either because they can be understood literally, or because their universal message is packaged by means of equally universal metaphors.

◀)) 5-5 A1.   **Аппети́т прихо́дит во вре́мя еды́.** [Appetite comes with the meal.]

◀)) 5-6 A2.   **Береги́ пла́тье сно́ву, а честь смо́лоду.** A good name is sooner lost than won. [Care for clothes while new, and for honor while young.]

A3. **Благи́ми наме́рениями и ад вы́мощен.** The road to hell is paved with ◀))) **5-7** good intentions. [Even hell is paved with good intentions.]

A4. **В гостя́х хорошо́, а до́ма лу́чше.** East or West, home is best. / There's ◀))) **5-8** no place like home. [It's nice visiting (others), but it's better at home.]

A5. **В здоро́вом те́ле здоро́вый дух.** [A sound mind in a sound body.] ◀))) **5-9**

A6. **В семье́ не без уро́да.** There is a black sheep in every family. [There's ◀))) **5-10** no family without a freak.]

A7. **В чужо́м глазу́ сучо́к/сори́нку ви́дим, а в своём бревна́ не замеча́ем.** ◀))) **5-11** [We see a twig/dust in another's eye but don't see a log in our own.]

A8. **Век живи́, век учи́сь (а дурако́м умрёшь).** Live and learn. [Live a life- ◀))) **5-12** time, learn a lifetime (yet you'll die a fool).]

A9. **Вре́мя — де́ньги.** Time is money. A more recent version is: **В ре́мя** ◀))) **5-13** **доро́же де́нег.** [Time is dearer than money.]

A10. **Вре́мя ле́чит / — лу́чший врач.** [Time cures / is the best physician.] ◀))) **5-14**

A11. **Вре́мя не ждёт.** Time and tide wait for no man. [Time does not wait.] ◀))) **5-15**

A12. **Все мы лю́ди (все мы челове́ки).** We are all only human. ◀))) **5-16**

A13. **Все там бу́дем.** We'll all be there (= die) some day. [We will all be ◀))) **5-17** there.]

A14. **Всё поня́ть — всё прости́ть.** [To understand all is to forgive all.] ◀))) **5-18**

A15. **Всё хорошо́, что хорошо́ конча́ется.** All's well that ends well. ◀))) **5-19**

A16. **Где хоте́нье, там и уме́нье.** Where there's a will, there's a way. ◀))) **5-20**

A17. **Го́лод — лу́чший по́вар.** Hunger is the best sauce [cook]. ◀))) **5-21**

A18. **Дарёному коню́ в зу́бы не смо́трят.** Don't look a gift horse in the ◀))) **5-22** mouth. [They don't look into the gift horse's teeth.]

A19. **До́брая сла́ва лежи́т, а худа́я (по доро́жке) бежи́т.** [A good reputa- ◀))) **5-23** tion lies (holds still), but a bad one runs (ahead on the road).] This proverb explains the big sales of tabloid gossip papers.

A20. **До́брое сло́во и ко́шке прия́тно.** [A kind word comforts even a cat.] ◀))) **5-24**

A21. **Друзья́ познаю́тся в беде́.** A friend in need is a friend indeed. [Friends ◀))) **5-25** are recognized (found out) in misfortune.]

A22. **Живи́ и жить дава́й други́м.** Live and let [others] live. ◀))) **5-26**

A23. **За двумя́ за́йцами пого́нишься, ни одного́ не пойма́ешь.** [If you chase ◀))) **5-27** two rabbits, you won't catch either one.]

A24. **Инициати́ва должна́ быть наказу́ема. / Ни одно́ до́брое де́ло не** ◀))) **5-28** **остаётся безнака́занным.** No good deed goes unpunished. [Initiative must be punished. / Not a single good deed remains unpunished.] These are all recent borrowings.

🔊 **5-29** A25. **Ка́ждому своё. / Кому́ как. / Ту хум ха́у.** To each his own. The first version is standard; the third Russian variant is a modern mistranslation into English of the second, «**Кому́ как**», that is, "To whom how."

🔊 **5-30** A26. **Как ау́кнется, так и откли́кнется.** [As the call, so the echo.] (You'll be treated as you treat others.)

🔊 **5-31** A27. **Како́в поп, тако́в и прихо́д.** [As the priest, so his parish.]

🔊 **5-32** A28. **Ка́пля ка́мень то́чит. / Ка́пля по ка́пле и ка́мень до́лбит.** [A drop erodes a stone. / Drop by drop dents even a stone.]

🔊 **5-33** A29. **Коне́ц—де́лу вене́ц.** The end crowns the work. [The end is the crown to the work.] An indecent modern variant is: **Коне́ц—те́лу вене́ц.** [The tip (penis) is the crown of (to) the body.]

🔊 **5-34** A30. **Ко́нчил де́ло, гуля́й сме́ло. / Де́лу вре́мя, поте́хе час.** [If you have finished the work, have a good time boldly (= without reservations).] / [There is time for work, (and) time for play.] After you have spent your weekend having fun, however, nowadays you might say: **Понеде́льник—день тяжёлый.** [Monday is a hard day.]

🔊 **5-35** A31. **Копе́йка рубль бережёт.** A penny saved is a penny earned. [A kopek saves a ruble.] (See Fig. 5-3 below.)

🔊 **5-36** A32. **Ку́рочка по зёрнышку (клюёт, да сыта́ быва́ет).** [A hen (pecks) a grain at a time (but always gets full).]

🔊 **5-37** A33. **Лу́чше по́здно, чем никогда́.** Better late than never. This pattern is very productive, for example, **Лу́чше что́-нибудь, чем ничего́.** [Better something than nothing.]

🔊 **5-38** A34. **Мал золотни́к, да до́рог.** [A gold piece is small but expensive.] This proverb claims just the opposite of the American "Big is beautiful."

ДЕЛО

Марка евро бережет

К январю 1998 года обеспечить условия Маастрихтского договора о создании валютного союза явно не удастся. Теперь у лидеров ЕС вся надежда на май

ОБОРОТНЫЕ СТОРОНЫ МОНЕТ ЕВРО РЕШЕНО СДЕЛАТЬ НАЦИОНАЛЬНЫМИ (СПРАВА – НЕМЕЦКИЙ ВАРИАНТ), ХОТЯ ВСЕ МОНЕТЫ БУДУТ ИМЕТЬ ХОЖДЕНИЕ ВО ВСЕХ СТРАНАХ ЕВРОСОЮЗА

Алексей Портанский

Fig. 5-3.

A35. **Молча́ние—знак согла́сия.** [Silence gives (is a sign of) consent.] 🔊 5-39

A36. **На Бо́га наде́йся, да сам не плоша́й.** God helps those who help them- 🔊 5-40
selves. [Trust in God, but don't foul it up yourself.]

A37. **На всех не угоди́шь.** You can't please everyone. 🔊 5-41

A38. **Наси́льно мил не бу́дешь. / Се́рдцу не прика́жешь.** [You will not be 🔊 5-42
forcibly loved/liked.] / [You cannot order (your) heart.]

A39. **Не говори́ "Гоп!", пока́ не переско́чишь. / Цыпля́т по о́сени** 🔊 5-43
счита́ют. [Don't say "hup" until you have made the jump.] Don't count 🔲 5-44
your chickens before they are hatched. [Chickens are counted after
autumn.]

A40. **Не гора́ к Магоме́ту, так Магоме́т к горе́.** If the mountain won't 🔊 5-45
come to Mohammed, then Mohammed will go to the mountain. [If not
the mountain to Mohammed, then Mohammed to the mountain.]

A41. **Не да́вши сло́ва, крепи́сь, а да́вши, держи́сь.** [Not having given your 🔊 5-46
word, hold back (from giving one), but having given it, hang on.]

A42. **Не зна́я бро́ду, не су́йся в во́ду.** Look before you leap. [Not knowing 🔊 5-47
the ford, don't get in the water.] A jocular literal recent formation is: **Не**
зна́я бро́ду, не су́йся в мо́ду. [Not knowing the ford, don't get into
fashion.]

A43. **Не мечи́те би́сера перед сви́ньями.** Cast not pearls [beads] before 🔊 5-48
swine.

A44. **Не по хоро́шу мил, а по ми́лу хоро́ш.** [It/he isn't dear (to our hearts) 🔊 5-49
because it/he is good (or good looking), but it/he is good (good looking)
because it/he is dear (to our hearts).]

A45. **Не рой я́му друго́му, сам в неё попадёшь.** [Don't dig a pit (lay a trap) 🔊 5-50
for another, you'll fall into it yourself.]

A46. **Не хле́бом еди́ным (жив бу́дет челове́к).** Not by bread alone (shall a 🔊 5-51
man live).

A47. **Нельзя́ служи́ть двум господа́м.** No man can serve two masters. 🔊 5-52

A48. **Нет ды́ма без огня́.** Where there's smoke there's fire. [There's no 🔊 5-53
smoke without fire.]

A49. **Нет ничего́ та́йного, что не ста́ло бы я́вным.** There is nothing that is 🔊 5-54
secret that would not become evident.

A50. **Нет/несть проро́ка в оте́честве своём.** A prophet is not without ho- 🔊 5-55
nor, save in his own country. [There is no prophet in one's birthplace.]

A51. **Нет ху́да без добра́. / Не́ было бы сча́стья, да несча́стье помогло́. /** 🔊 5-56
Никогда́ не зна́ешь, где найдёшь, где потеря́ешь. / Всё к лу́чшему.
Every cloud has a silver lining. [There is no evil without good. / There
would have been no luck, but the misfortune helped. / You never know
where you'll find (and) where you'll lose. / All is for the better.]

🔊 **5-57** A52. **Ничто́ не возника́ет из ничего́.** [Nothing arises from nothing.]

🔊 **5-58** A53. **Ничто́ не но́во/ве́чно под луно́й.** There is nothing new under the sun. [Nothing is new/eternal under the moon.] The second variant is a secondary development.

🔊 **5-59** A54. **Но́чью все ко́шки се́ры.** All cats are gray at night.

🔊 **5-60** A55. **О мёртвых и́ли хорошо́, и́ли ничего́.** [Of the dead (one speaks) either well or (says) nothing.]

🔊 **5-61** A56. **Одна́ ла́сточка весны́ не де́лает.** One swallow does not make a summer [spring].

🔊 **5-62** A57. **О́ко за о́ко, зуб за́ зуб.** An eye for an eye, a tooth for a tooth.

🔊 **5-63** A58. **От вели́кого до смешно́го то́лько оди́н шаг.** There is but one step between the sublime and the ridiculous. This frame can be applied to other pairs of opposites: **От любви́ до не́нависти / от гениа́льности до безу́мия то́лько оди́н шаг.** There is but one step between love and hatred / genius and madness.

🔊 **5-64** A59. **Пле́тью о́буха не перешибёшь.** Might is right. [You can't break an axe with a whip.]

🔊 **5-65** A60. **Плох тот солда́т, кото́рый не хо́чет стать генера́лом.** [Bad is that soldier who does not want to become a general.]

🔊 **5-66** A61. **Победи́телей не су́дят.** [Victors are not judged.] Even though it is claimed that these words were first said by Catherine the Great in the 18th century, the proverb has repeatedly been confirmed in the 20th century: only the sides that capitulated are usually prosecuted for war crimes.

🔊 **5-67** A62. **Пови́нную го́лову меч не сечёт.** [A sword does not sever a contrite head.]

🔊 **5-68** A63. **Под лежа́чий ка́мень вода́ не течёт.** A rolling stone gathers no moss. [No water flows under a lying stone.]

🔊 **5-69** A64. **Попы́тка—не пы́тка, а спрос не беда́. / За спрос де́нег не беру́т.** There's no harm in trying/asking. [Trying is no torture, and asking is no grief.] / [They don't charge money for a question.]

🔊 **5-70** A65. **По́сле нас хоть пото́п.** After us let there be a deluge.

🔊 **5-71** A66. **Поспеши́шь—люде́й насмеши́шь.** Haste makes waste. [If you hurry, you'll make people laugh (at you).]

🔊 **5-72** A67. **Пра́вда глаза́ ко́лет.** The truth hurts. [Truth pokes eyes.]

🔊 **5-73** A68. **Привы́чка—втора́я нату́ра.** Custom [habit] is second nature.

🔊 **5-74** A69. **Путь к се́рдцу мужчи́ны лежи́т че́рез желу́док.** The way to a man's
🔲 **5-75** heart is [lies] through (his) stomach.

A70. **Сапо́жник без сапо́г.** The cobbler's wife is the worst shod. / The cobbler's children go barefoot. [The shoemaker (is) without shoes.] ◀)) 5-76

A71. **Сде́ланного не воро́тишь.** What's done cannot be undone. [You cannot reverse what's been done.] ◀)) 5-77

A72. **Семь раз отме́рь, оди́н раз отре́жь.** Look before you leap. / Measure three [seven] times, cut once. ◀)) 5-78

A73. **Скажи́ мне, кто твой друг, и я скажу́, кто ты.** A man is known by his friends. [Tell me who is your friend and I will tell (you) who you are.] A native Russian version is: **С кем поведёшься, от того́ и набере́шься.** [With whom you keep company, from him you learn.] Its risqué slangy version is: **С кем поведёшься, от того́ и залети́шь.** [With whom you keep company, from him you get pregnant.] ◀)) 5-79

A74. **Ско́ро ска́зка ска́зывается, да не ско́ро де́ло де́лается.** Easier said than done. [A tale is told quickly, but a deed is not done quickly.] ◀)) 5-80 / 📷 5-81

A75. **Слеза́ми го́рю не помо́жешь.** It's no use crying over spilt milk. [One can't help a misfortune with tears.] In any case it is useful to keep in mind that, as the title of a 1979 film says, **Москва́ слеза́м не ве́рит** Moscow does not believe/trust tears (and not *Moscow Does Not Believe in Tears*, as the movie title is usually translated!)]. "Moscow" here stands for any urban and hence, presumably, jaded community and not just the Russian capital, of course. ◀)) 5-82

A76. **Ста́рость—не ра́дость.** [Old age is no joy.] A modern addition makes it even more pessimistic: **и мо́лодость га́дость** [and youth is disgusting.] ◀)) 5-83

A77. **Ста́рый друг лу́чше но́вых двух.** [An old friend is better than two new ones.] ◀)) 5-84

A78. **Ста́рый, что ма́лый.** [An old person is like a child.] This is a kind rather than a condescending statement. It calls for patience and gentleness in treating the old. ◀)) 5-85

A79. **Терпе́ние и труд всё перетру́т.** Diligence is the mother of success. / Everything comes to him who waits. [Patience and effort will rub through anything.] ◀)) 5-86

A80. **У ба́бы во́лос до́лог, да ум коро́ток.** Long hair and short wit. [A woman's hair is long but (her) mind is short.] ◀)) 5-87

A81. **У кого́ что боли́т, тот о том и говори́т.** The tongue ever turns to the aching tooth. [Whoever aches with something talks about it.] ◀)) 5-88

A82. **У семи́ ня́нек дитя́ без гла́зу.** Too many cooks spoil the broth. [With seven nannies the child is without an eye (that is, without a watchful eye, or without supervision).] Some people today forget that the word **глаз** has an archaic meaning of "supervision," and take the proverb more literally, namely that a child who has too many nannies gets hurt, for example, loses an eye in an accident. ◀)) 5-89

—Одна голова хорошо,
а две—лучше...

Рис. В.ШИЛОВА (Санкт-Петербург).

Fig. 5-4.

5-80 A83. **Ум хорошо́, а два—лу́чше.** Two heads are better than one. [One mind
5-91   is good, but two is better.

5-92 A84. **Утопа́ющий хвата́ется за соло́минку.** A drowning man snatches at a
5-93   straw.

5-94 A85. **Учи́ться никогда́ не по́здно.** It's never too late to learn.

5-95 A86. **Хоро́шего понемно́жку.** Moderation in all things. [Good things
                 (should come) in small quantities.]

5-96 A87. **Хорошо́ смеётся тот, кто смеётся после́дним.** He who laughs last
                 laughs best.

5-97 A88. **Худо́й мир лу́чше до́брой ссо́ры.** Better a bad peace than a good
5-98   quarrel.

5-99 A89. **Цель опра́вдывает сре́дства.** The end justifies the means.

5-100 A90. **Челове́ку сво́йственно ошиба́ться. / Не ошиба́ется тот, кто ничего́
                 не де́лает.** To err is human. [It is natural for a person to err.] / [He does
                 not err who does nothing.]

5-101 A91. **Что бы́ло, то прошло́.** Let bygones be bygones. [What was has gone
                 by.]

5-102 A92. **Что име́ем, не храни́м, потеря́вши, пла́чем.** [We don't take care of
                 what we have, having lost it we weep.]

5-103 A93. **Что напи́сано перо́м, того́ не вы́рубишь топоро́м.** [What is written by
                 the pen can't be cut out with an axe.] The importance of "hard copies"
                 and of "having it in writing" obviously did not begin with Americans
                 and did not begin today. (See **5-3**)

5-104 A94. **Что посе́ешь, то и пожнёшь.** As you sow, so you shall reap. [What you
5-105   sow, that you shall reap.]

5-106 A95. **Я́блочко от я́блони недалеко́ па́дает.** As the tree, so the fruit. / The
                 apple doesn't fall far from the [apple] tree.

B. Proverbs of Medium Difficulty   Посло́вицы сре́дней
                                              сте́пени тру́дности

These proverbs can be interpreted more or less safely based on common sense notions shared by both cultures. They may involve minimal culture-specific background, as in: «**Обжёгся на молоке́, ду́ет на во́ду**». The scalded cat fears cold water. [Burnt on milk, blows on water.] Remember that milk boils at a higher temperature than water, so one can burn oneself pretty badly when drinking hot milk (milk is regularly boiled in Russia). Additional packagings for the same idea are: «**Пу́ганая воро́на куста́ бои́тся**» [A scared crow fears (even) a bush] and «**У стра́ха глаза́ велики́**» [Fear has big eyes].

Proverbs in section B may have English equivalents that are packaged differently, or there may be no equivalent proverbs in English.

B1.   **Без бума́жки ты бука́шка, а с бума́жкой—челове́к.** [Without (a piece ◀)) 5-107
      of) paper, you are a bug, but with (a piece of) paper (you are) a person.]
      This modern saying, originally from **Ле́бедев-Кума́ч** Lebedev-
      Kumach's 1931 humorous song, expresses sentiments not so alien to
      those who live in America today: it is difficult to be anything without an
      ID or some other document; in a subverted version, **бука́шка** "bug" is
      replaced with **кака́шка** "poo poo." Another way to put the same idea is:
      Спра́вка—бо́льше, чем жизнь. [A certificate is bigger than life.] (This
      saying is based on the film title «**Ста́вка бо́льше, чем жизнь**» *A Stake
      Bigger than Life*, based on a Polish TV serial from the mid 60s.) There
      also exists a humorous modern proverb that alters the meaning but imi-
      tates the structure of the first proverb of this entry. It stresses the impor-
      tance of showing up at social occasions with a bottle of alcohol: «**Без
      буты́лки ты Мурзи́лка, а с буты́лкой—челове́к**» [Without a bottle
      (of vodka), you are Murzilka (a character in a children's magazine), but
      with a bottle (of vodka) (you are) a person].[7]

B2.   **Без ка́йфа нет ла́йфа.** [Without fun there's no life.] A very new and ◀)) 5-108
      slangy saying popular among the young. **Кайф** is a multipurpose posi-
      tive (and hip) slang term meaning "pleasure, luck, the good things in
      life," and **лайф**, of course, is taken directly from English. Borrowing
      words from English is very widespread in youth culture.

B3.   **Бли́зок ло́коть, да не уку́сишь.** How near, and yet so far! [Close is ◀)) 5-109
      (your) elbow, but you can't bite (it).] The ring of the Russian proverb is
      not at all as elegant as that of its English equivalent. It is said almost vi-
      ciously when someone's desires are frustrated, despite the apparent
      availability of the prize.

---

[7] I am grateful to Robert Rothstein for several pieces of information in this entry.

🔊 **5-110** B4. **Большóму кораблю́—большóе плáванье.** A great ship asks for deep waters. [To a big ship, a big journey.] The saying would apply, for example, to an outstanding young man from a small village who deserves to be sent away to the big city to pursue his dreams.

🔊 **5-111** B5. **Брань на ворóту не вúснет.** Sticks and stones will break your bones, but names will never hurt you. [Swearing does not hang off (one's) collar.]

🔊 **5-112** B6. **Бумáга всё тéрпит.** Pens may blot, but they cannot blush. [Paper endures all.] Although this saying is attributed to Cicero, for a modern day Russian the proverb summarizes a cynical view of the printed word (contrary to the older proverb A93). This cynicism arose from the "Newspeak" of the totalitarian era, but continues to linger.

🔊 **5-113** B7. **В теснотé, да не в обúде.** There is always room for one more. [In a crowded space, but not abused.] This proverb stresses the importance of human relationship over the physical environment. The proverb is often said to a newcomer to crowded quarters as an indirect apology for the lack of space. An opposite (and nasty) modern saying does not welcome newcomers: **Бóльше нарóду—мéньше кислорóду. / Мéньше нарóду— бóльше кислорóду.** [More people, less oxygen.] / [Fewer people, more oxygen.]

Fig. 5-5.

B8. **Внýки—нáши мстúтели.** [(Our) grandchildren are our avengers.] A 🔊 **5-114**
modern begrudging saying used by embittered parents who wish their
grandchildren to give their parents as hard a time as their children gave
them (don't get lost in the pronouns: there are only three generations
involved here!). This is a sentiment that became possible when the older
culture of obeying one's parents disappeared.

B9. **Всяк сверчóк знай свой шестóк.** Let the cobbler stick to his last. [Let 🔊 **5-115**
each cricket know his hearth-nook.] **Шестóк** is the area before the
opening of the big Russian stove **рýсская печь** in the peasant house.
Most of the **шесток** is flat and horizontal, but it also includes the nooks
around it where crickets find cracks to hide in. Another place they live
in is said to be behind the stove **за пéчкой**. These places are comfortably warm in winter and references to a cricket singing behind the stove
evoke a cozy and somewhat melancholy feeling of a long winter night.
Don't be surprised if the Russians you speak to tell you that **шесток** is a
grass stem, since this is how most people these days understand the
proverb: they know nothing about the structure of **рýсская печь** but do
know that the word **шест** means "a pole" or "a stick."

B10. **Вы́ше головы́ не пры́гнешь.** A man can do no more than he can. [One 🔊 **5-116**
cannot jump higher than one's head.] This is actually true, because no
matter how high you may jump, your head is still higher than the hurdle
you jump over. (See 📖 **5-2**)

B11. **Горá с горóй не схóдятся, а человéк с человéком сойдётся.** Men may 🔊 **5-117**
meet but mountains never. [A mountain and a mountain never meet,
but a man and a man will meet.] This is said usually when one runs into
someone one did not expect to meet ever again, or when people are
parting without any concrete hopes of seeing each other again. There is
a distinct ring of fate **судьбá** in this proverb.

B12. **Горбáтого могúла испрáвит.** Can the leopard change his spots? [A 🔊 **5-118**
hunchback will be cured by (his) grave.] Another fatalistic proverb used
when commenting on a person's negative characteristics.

B13. **Для мúлого дружкá и серёжку из ушкá.** A friend who shares is a 🔊 **5-119**
friend who cares. [For a dear friend (one will take) even an earring out
of (one's) ear.] This proverb describes the traditional code of friendship,
but it is mostly used humorously in response to thanks for having gone
out of one's way for the sake of a friend.

B14. **Долг платежóм крáсен.** One good turn deserves another. [A debt is 🔊 **5-120**
beautiful because of repayment.] Aside from advocating that debts literally be paid, this piece of traditional wisdom may encourage a gracious
return for a kindness, as well as the notorious corruption attested to in
Russian literature since the 18th century. Note that the modern cynical
saying **«Берёшь чужúе, а отдаёшь свой»** [You take somebody else's

(money), but you return your own (money)] justifies just the opposite sentiment: human unwillingness to return borrowed money.

5-121 B15. **Дурна́я голова́ нога́м поко́я не даёт.** [A stupid head does not let legs rest.] When the head is stupid, one ends up doing a lot of running around with no result. This sounds much more literal in Russia, where people use their legs to get places much more than in the United States. If you don't plan your day well and don't find out things first, you, too, will end up going to the same place several times to finish your task in Russia.

5-122 B16. **Жизнь прожи́ть — не по́ле перейти́.** Life is not a bed of roses. [To live a life is not to cross a field.] A path or road is a common metaphor of life. This proverb evokes the vision of an open field on a vast terrain; crossing it takes time, but is not particularly eventful or challenging, unlike going through life.

5-123 B17. **За «спаси́бо» некраси́во, на́до де́нежки плати́ть.** [For a "Thank you" doesn't look good, you must pay money.] This is used primarily as a rude response to a "Thank you," to indicate that monetary compensation is expected. This modern saying has many variants, and all of them sound quite rude: **Из «спаси́бо» пла́тья не сошьёшь** [From a "Thank you" you can't sew a dress], **«Спаси́бо» на хлеб не нама́жешь** [You can't spread a "Thank you" on your bread (like butter)], **За «спаси́бо» и прыщ не вско́чит** [For a "Thank you" even a pimple won't appear], **За «спаси́бо» и в лицо́ не плю́нут** [For a "Thank you" they won't even spit in your face]. **За «спаси́бо» и чи́рей на жо́пе не вско́чит** [For a "Thank you" even a zit won't appear on one's ass] is an "unprintable" member of the set. The old Russian spirit of generosity expressed, for example, in **«С ми́ру по ни́тке — го́лому руба́ха»** (see C56 below) seems in this century to have met with an array of new formulations of folk wisdom that flatly contradict it.

5-124 B18. **Зара́за к зара́зе не пристаёт.** [Infection does not stick to infection (= bad person).] This is a modern pessimistic saying that expresses belief in a lack of justice in the world. Bad things do not happen to bad people, it says; conversely, they happen to good people. It can also be used jokingly by someone in response to a warning not to come close to a sick person.

5-125 B19. **Из пе́сни сло́ва не вы́кинешь.** [One can't throw a word out of a song.] This is used apologetically when the whole gory truth needs to be told once the topic has been touched upon.

5-126 B20. **Клин кли́ном (вышиба́ют).** One nail drives out another. [A wedge (is driven out) by a wedge.] Strong actions require strong counteractions. This proverb would apply, for example, when you want to say that to forget one's unhappy love one must fall in love again. The saying is also a common justification for a glass of vodka for a hangover, the equivalent of "hair of the dog that bit you."

B21. **Ла́сковый телёнок двух ма́ток сосёт.** [A cuddly calf sucks two mothers.] This is often offered as a piece of advice to children and young women to be genuinely nice and gentle. ◀))) 5-127

B22. **Лежа́чего не бьют.** Don't hit a man when he is down. [They don't strike one who is lying (on the ground).] The striking, of course, is usually not physical but figurative: you don't get someone who's down and who can't get you back. This used to be a measure of human decency in Russia, accounting for the notable magnanimity of Russians towards the defeated and the fallen. The experience of the 20th century seems to have limited the application of the proverb, as it was violated all too often. ◀))) 5-128

B23. **Лиха́ беда́ нача́ло.** The first step is always the hardest. [Beginning is bad trouble.] This can be used to encourage a procrastinator to begin action. It can also mean that having done something once, whether an act of courage or a crime, one overcomes one's initial reluctance and is likely to repeat the act again. ◀))) 5-129

B24. **Лю́бишь ката́ться, люби́ и са́ночки вози́ть.** He that would eat the fruit must climb the tree. [If you like to ride (a sled), you ought to like to pull it (for others or for yourself up the hill), too.] Picture the kind of sled that children pull each other in on a snowy day. ◀))) 5-130

B25. **Ми́лые браня́тся—то́лько те́шатся.** The course of true love never runs smooth. [(When) lovers fight, they're only having fun.] This proverb implies that a marital argument must not be taken seriously—an unlikely piece of advice in American culture today. Another rather teasing characterization of a close (but not necessarily intimate) relationship is: **Вме́сте те́сно, а врозь ску́чно** [Together it's too cramped, but apart it's lonely.] The difficulty of defining one's territory even between those who care for each other is universal. ◀))) 5-131

B26. **Мир те́сен.** It's a small world. This proverb has a new variant: **Не мир те́сен, а просло́йка тонка́.** [It's not that the world is small, but that the (intelligentsia) layer is thin (that is, there are few of us).] In Marxism, **просло́йка** "a layer sandwiched between two other layers" refers to the intelligentsia, the layer between the two major classes of the exploiters and the exploited. The new variant reflects the fact that in intelligentsia circles, everybody knows everybody else. A simpler version is: **Не мир те́сен, а круг у́зок.** [It's not that the world is small, but that the (intelligentsia) circle is small.] ◀))) 5-132

B27. **Мно́го бу́дешь знать, ско́ро соста́ришься / пло́хо бу́дешь спать.** Curiosity killed the cat. / Too much knowledge makes the head bald. [If you know much, you'll age quick / you'll sleep poorly.] This is often said ◀))) 5-133 to children as a response to their inquisitiveness. It can also be said humorously to adults. In either case, the real answer is withheld.

🔊 **5-134** B28. **На «нет» и суда́ нет.** [To "none" there is nothing to make a judgment about.] Another fatalistic proverb that helps one come to terms with shortage and denial.

🔊 **5-135** B29. **На серди́тых во́ду во́зят.** [On angry (animals/people) they haul water.] This is advice not to get sticky and not to be overly principled. There is something comical in the image of a stubborn person who ends up being hitched to a cart and used as a draft animal.

🔊 **5-136** B30. **На́ тебе́, Бо́же, что нам него́же.** [Here, take it, God, what is not good for us!] This is said sarcastically when someone else gives away an undesirable thing as a gift or pretending to do you a favor. We all know several people who love to give away as gifts things that are somehow defective. This would be just the proverb to say about their gift-giving practices. The original proverb used until a century or two ago addressed not God but a pauper **убо́же**, but the word got shortened by one vowel, leaving **бо́же**.

🔊 **5-137** B31. **На чужо́й рото́к не наки́нешь плато́к.** [One can't throw a kerchief to cover somebody else's mouth.] This is a Russian folk version of the First Amendment. The fundamental difference is that it states the impossibility of stopping any speech, including speech unpleasant to others. In fact, it is often said in response to complaints about false and unpleasant rumors.

🔊 **5-138** B32. **Нача́льство не опа́здывает, оно́ заде́рживается.** [Management is never late, (instead) it gets tied up.] The phenomenon commented on in this apt modern saying is not entirely alien to our culture. When you are late for your appointment with an important person, you will never say: "Sorry, I was tied up." This phrase is reserved for those in a position of power. To be sure, in America the VIP is more likely to say "Sorry, I'm late" than is his counterpart in Russia.

🔊 **5-139** B33. **Не по́йман—не вор.** [If not caught, not a criminal.] This is a Russian folk version of "Innocent until proven guilty." The word **вор** now means a "thief," but the proverb dates back to olden times when **вор** had the more general meaning "cheater, traitor, criminal." (Most speakers today would not recognize the old meaning.)

🔊 **5-140** B34. **Не сра́зу Москва́ стро́илась.** Rome was not built in a day. [Not at once was Moscow built.] Recall that when Constantinople fell, Moscow began to identify itself with Rome.

🔊 **5-141** B35. **Недосо́л на столе́, а пересо́л на спине́.** [A shortage of salt is (adjusted) at the table (that is, one can always add salt directly into one's plate), but a surplus of salt is (adjusted) on the (wife's) back.] In older days it literally meant that if a wife put too much salt into a dish, she was to be beaten. Such a frank wife-beating message is felt to be too embarrassing today, so the second half is often omitted, and the first one is used as an invitation to add salt to taste from the salt container **солóнка** on the table.

B36. **Обéщанного три гóда ждут.** [They wait for what has been promised 🔊 **5-142** (to them) for three years.] This proverb helps one to be patient when one says this proverb to oneself, but it is maddening when the person who promised something puts you off with it.

B37. **Одúн в пóле не вóин.** One man, no man. [One on the battlefield is no 🔊 **5-143** warrior.] This proverb evokes the image of the vast Kulikovo Field **Куликóво пóле** where 14th-century Russian warriors **вóины** faced the Mongols, who were as numerous as locusts **саранчá**. Note a Soviet reformulation: **И одúн в пóле вóин, если он совéтский вóин.** [Even one on the battlefield is a warrior, if he is a Soviet soldier.]

B38. **От добрá добрá не úщут.** Let/Leave well enough alone. / If it ain't 🔊 **5-144** broke, don't fix it. [One does not seek good from good (situation).] A modern paraphrase is: **Лýчшее—враг хорóшего.** [Better is the enemy of good.]

B39. **Охóта пýще невóли.** [Will is stronger than force.] This is used when 🔊 **5-145** someone volunteers to undertake something difficult and challenging that a normal person, presumably, would not want to do even if forced, ▢ **5-146** such as becoming a(n eventually starving) musician, artist, or teacher, or a Slavic linguist, for that matter. It's accompanied with a mental, if not actual, shrug of the shoulders or shake of the head.

B40. **Пар костéй не лóмит.** [Steam causes no bone ache.] This is a very spe- 🔊 **5-147** cific straightforward saying, used simply to justify excessive warmth. Imagine a situation when your mother insists that you put on that extra ▢ **5-148** scarf and you are trying to get away from it. A Russian mother would surely say to you: «**Пар костéй не лóмит**», and a Russian child is surely likely to comply. Russians in general hate cold and find the idea of saving money on heating bills unappealing. This is true even now, when they must pay for heat in their homes. Let's watch what happens to this proverb and to this love for warm houses in the next decade.

B41. **Перемéлется, мукá бýдет.** Time works wonders. [It'll go through the 🔊 **5-149** mill (and) there will be flour.] Thus eventually everything works out.

B42. **По одёжке встречáют, по умý провожáют.** [They meet you according 🔊 **5-150** to your clothes, they see you off according to your brain.] Two apparently contradictory conclusions follow from this: (1) it's important to make a good first impression, and (2) you can't fool people with your facade. When (1) is intended, only the first clause of the proverb is said.

B43. **Поднявший меч от мечá да погúбнет.** He who takes the sword shall 🔊 **5-151** perish by the sword. [He who raised a sword from a sword shall perish.]

Though originally this is a sentence from the New Testament, many Russians attribute it to **Алекса́ндр Не́вский** who is given a similar line in the classic 1938 film by **Эйзенште́йн**. The home team may say about the visiting team: **Подня́вший мяч от мяча́ да поги́бнет.** [He who raised a ball from a ball shall perish.]

🔊 **5-152 B44.   Ры́ба и́щет, где глу́бже, а челове́к, где лу́чше.** [Fish seek where it's deeper, and man seeks where it's better.] This Russian proverb justifies one's right to the pursuit of happiness, as stated in the American Declaration of Independence. A modern saying provides a somewhat cynical twist: **Ры́ба и́щет, где глу́бже, а челове́к, где ры́ба.** [Fish seek where it's deeper, and man seeks where the fish is.]

🔊 **5-153 B45.   С ми́лым рай и в шалаше́.** [With a beloved one, even a lean-to is paradise]. A cynical recent addition is: **«е́сли ми́лый—атташе́»** [if the beloved one is an attaché]. Attachés are, of course, among the most eligible bachelors, especially if they are attached to a Western embassy.

🔊 **5-154 B46.   Свет кли́ном не сошёлся.** [The world does not end in a wedge.] The image is that of one being caught in a narrow wedge-shaped dead end, with no way out or back. The proverb denies such a pessimistic view of life, insisting that there is more than one option available at all times. It's an effective proverb for consoling those who are desperate, especially those suffering from unrequited love. A similar proverb is: **Свет не без до́брых люде́й.** [It's not that the world is without good people.]

🔊 **5-155 B47.   Седина́ в бо́роду, бес в ребро́.** [Grey into the beard, devil into the rib.] A succinct and funny description of what happens to some men in middle age: a sudden lust for younger women.

🔊 **5-156 B48.   Се́меро одного́ не ждут.** [Seven don't wait for one.] This is a rule for group behavior that urges someone to keep up with the rest of the group.

🔊 **5-157 B49.   Сло́во—серебро́, а молча́нье—зо́лото.** Speech is silver, silence is golden. [A word is silver but silence is gold.] A more dynamic way of putting this idea is: **Сло́во не воробе́й, вы́летит—не пойма́ешь.** Think before you speak. [A word is not a sparrow: once it's flown out you can't catch it.] And those who know the Church Slavonic version may show off and say: **Во многосло́вии несть (= нет) спасе́ния.** [There is no salvation in wordiness.]

🔊 **5-158 B50.   Сня́вши го́лову, по волоса́м не пла́чут.** [Having cut off the head, one does not weep over the (lost) hair.] Although beautiful hair is valued in Russia both in men and women, the head is after all more valuable than the hair. The proverb tells us that it's stupid to lament a lesser loss that is a direct consequence of a bigger loss.

🔊 **5-159 B51.   Соловья́ ба́снями не ко́рмят.** [You can't feed a nightingale with tales.] This means that "real," practical values like food, money, and action are more important than fancy talk. The proverb is sometimes used as the transition from a nice pre-meal conversation to the meal.

B52. **Сы́тый голо́дного не разуме́ет.** [A sated one does not understand a 🔊 **5-160** hungry one.] The limits of all abstract notions are established by this saying: man cannot really understand anything unless he experiences it. It implies that the well-fed congressmen should not decide the fate of the homeless.

B53. **То́чность—ве́жливость короле́й.** Punctuality is the politeness of kings. 🔊 **5-161** This is clearly a borrowing from a culture that had kings—in fact, France. Punctuality is hardly a national trait of Russians, although it is also true to this day that in Russia—what with standing in lines or running into lunch-breaks—one often does not have control over one's own time. Educated people of the westernized type, on the other hand, take pride in being punctual.

B54. **Уче́нье—свет, неуче́нье—тьма.** Learning is the eye of the mind. 🔊 **5-162** [Learning is light, no learning is darkness.] Among modern mock variations are: **Уче́нье—свет, а неучёных тьма.** [Learning is light, but there's a host (**тьма** = many) of ignorant ones.] and **Уче́нье—свет, учёных—тьма.** [Learning is light, (and) there's a host of learned ones.] The two variants mean opposite things. The first one points out that despite the old truth about learning there are many ignorant people, and the second one laments the inflation of academic degrees.

B55. **Что до́рого, то ми́ло, что дёшево, то гни́ло.** [What is expensive is 🔊 **5-163** dear, what is cheap is rotten.] This is a motto of the material culture of the days that predated consumer culture. A preference for better quality even if the price was higher seems to have been the norm before the October Revolution. This principle remained intact throughout the Soviet era, despite the fact that there was little choice of merchandise available. It would be interesting to see what happens to this proverb in another half century, as consumerism and cheap imports take over Russia.

B56. **Что с во́зу упа́ло, то пропа́ло.** There's no use crying over spilt milk. 🔊 **5-164** [What fell off the cart is lost.] It was a medieval law that what fell on the ground in passing another man's land belonged to that land. So there's no use lamenting the loss. In contrast with **«Слеза́ми го́рю не помо́жешь»** this saying simply calls for resignation.

B57. **«Чуть-чуть» не счита́ется.** A miss is as good as a mile. ["Almost" does 🔊 **5-165** not count.] This is said not only to refuse praising someone for a near-success, but also to avoid the blame for causing a near-mishap.

B58. **Ши́ла в мешке́ не утаи́шь.** Murder will out. [You can't hide an awl in a 🔊 **5-166** sack.] **Ши́ло** "awl" is not a weapon but it is long, sharp and conspicuous, and a **мешо́к** "sack" is made of rough sackcloth, easily pierced by a sharp long object like an awl. The proverb discourages one from trying to hide a significant (and not nice) act.

5-167 B59. **Я нача́льник—ты дура́к, ты нача́льник—я дура́к.** [(When) I'm the boss, you are a fool, (when) you're the boss, I'm a fool.] This is a cynical modern saying, implying that the superior always has the last word.

B60. **«Я»—после́дняя бу́ква алфави́та.** [«Я» is the last letter of the alpha-
5-168 bet.] This saying tells one to put oneself last, not first.

C. Difficult Proverbs   Тру́дные посло́вицы

These proverbs require much culture-specific context to be appreciated or sometimes even to be understood at all. They are the most difficult for non-native speakers. Many of them make reference to older culture, involving Slavic mythology, folklore, and history. To understand them you must not only know the original point of reference, but also, often, the associations they evoke in native speakers. Included here are also sayings which do not allude to specific cultural/historical facts, but that are still hard to grasp because they reflect cultural experience and values alien to those of the English-speaking world.

5-169 C1. **Ба́бушка на́двое сказа́ла (гада́ла).** We'll see. [Grandma said it both ways.] The association here is with a wise old woman who makes prophetic statements about the future that can be interpreted in more than one way. Old women in Russia are often powerful figures considered to be in touch with magic. The saying is used to counter somebody else's remark about what will happen, and to make the point that one never knows what will actually happen, as if blaming it on the ambiguity of all oracular pronouncements.

5-170 C2. **Без меня́ меня́ жени́ли.** [They married me off without me.] (See also C59 below.) This sort of situation is hardly imaginable in our day and in our culture. But it was in fact the custom all over Europe that sons and daughters were married off or betrothed without their consent or even knowledge. The custom of marriage by matchmaking, without consulting the would-be bride and groom, lasted in Russia until the 20th century, and the memory is still relatively fresh. The proverb is used metaphorically when important decisions or judgments about oneself are made in one's absence.

5-171 C3. **Бу́дет и на на́шей у́лице пра́здник.** [On our street, too, there will be a celebration.] This proverb may reveal a begrudging, even threatening attitude on the part of those who are having a hard time and who look forward to a reversal of luck or power. People who consider envy and bearing grudges morally inferior may hesitate to use it (even when the proverb reflects their genuine feelings). It evokes a slogan of the Proletarian Revolution of 1917: «Кто был ниче́м, тот ста́нет всем»

[Who was nothing will become everything], originally from the French "Internationale." On the slangy side, there is a contemporary mock English paraphrase: «Бу́дет и на на́шем стри́те селебре́йшн».

C4. **Бы́ло бы боло́то/коры́то, а че́рти/сви́ньи найду́тся.** [As long as there ◀)) 5-172 is a swamp/trough, there will always be devils/pigs (to live in it/to eat from it).] A very pessimistic outlook here. This means that if a bad system is created, or a shady opportunity presents itself, there will always be those who will want to benefit from it. Since any power is perceived by most Russians as basically evil and corrupt, the proverb can mean that any system is subject to abuse. A new capitalistic saying builds on the same syntactic pattern: **Бы́ло бы здоро́вье, а остально́е ку́пим** [As long as there is health, we'll buy the rest].

C5. **Быль мо́лодцу не уко́р.** [A fine young man is not to be reproached for ◀)) 5-173 (his) past.] Unlike a maiden **де́вица**, a young man **мо́лодец** can have past affairs and still be considered fine and desirable. This is an old proverb and in olden days it probably referred primarily to sexual mores. Now it can mean more generally that if someone is really good, old sins should not matter. Many would have loved it if English had an equivalent proverb.

C6. **Взя́лся за гуж, не говори́, что не дюж. / Назва́лся гру́здем—полеза́й** ◀)) 5-174 **в ку́зов.** In for a penny, in for a pound. [If you grabbed the tug, don't say you're not strong (enough).] / [If you called yourself a **груздь** (name of a choice mushroom), get into the basket]. A "tug" **гуж** is a leather loop that is used to attach the horse to the cart. This procedure preceded any horse cart trip and required a lot of physical strength. The proverb discourages quitters and advises us to stick things out. A more restricted meaning, teasingly encouraging one to finish saying what one has started to say, is packaged into a modern saying that closely copies the first of the proverbs above: **Взя́лся за грудь, говори́ что́-нибудь** [If you grabbed your chest, say something]. The image of grabbing one's chest as if in an emotional sincere gesture is jocular. This saying also has an obscene literal interpretation: If you grabbed her/my chest …

C7. **Во́лка[8] боя́ться—в лес не ходи́ть.** Nothing ventured, nothing gained. ◀)) 5-175 [To fear a wolf is not to go to the woods.] This proverb was much more dramatic in times past than it may seem now. If a Russian peasant never went to the woods he could not survive. A typical village was surrounded by woods, and everybody went there regularly to pick berries, nuts and mushrooms, to cut firewood for winter, to strip the trees for the bark to make bark shoes **ла́пти**, or to hunt or to set up animal traps. Yet forests were dangerous, and not only because of wolves. For a Russian peasant, they were inhabited by supernatural forces like **руса́лки** (tree

---

[8] Many people use the plural form **волко́в** here but the stress change destroys the meter.

and river maiden spirits) and **ле́ший** (forest spirit). One should stay away from woods and forests as much as one can, yet survival was impossible without going there. A lighter modern variant is: **Кто не риску́ет, тот не пьёт шампа́нского.** [He who does not take risks does not drink champagne.] A risqué modern twist is: **Дете́й боя́ться—в лес не ходи́ть.** [To fear (begetting) children is not to go to the woods.]

5-176 C8. **Во́льному—во́ля, спасённому—рай.** [To the free man—freedom, and to the saved man—paradise.] **Во́ля** is that Russian word for *freedom* which, unlike **свобо́да** has no legal, sociological or philosophical associations. It is a typically Russian freedom from constraints, freedom to be dissolved in nature and the elements, and freedom to dream; it is the frivolous type of freedom. And he who prefers that kind of freedom shall have it, the proverb says. But he is also going to pay for it, for the one who instead listens to good advice and is saved goes to heaven. This proverb is used following a negative reaction to advice one has just offered: "All right, it's your choice, I've warned you."

5-177 C9. **Всему́ своё вре́мя.** There is a time for everything. [To everything (there is) a time.] A more traditional proverb is: **Вся́кому о́вощу своё вре́мя.** Everything is good in its season. [To each vegetable (there is) its time.] A modern rendering with a cynical twist is: **Гла́вное—во́время останови́ться/подсуети́ться/смы́ться.** [The most important thing is to stop/bustle/disappear in time (= to know when it's time to).] Knowing when to **смы́ться** "disappear" is an important survival skill that enables one to avoid undesirable developments. Knowing when to **подсуети́ться** "bustle," however, was a particularly hypocritical skill cultivated by would-be good citizens and social climbers in Soviet society. A younger person now is likely to use different packaging for the old idea of an appropriate time for everything: **В два́дцать лет ума́ нет—и не бу́дет; в три́дцать лет жены́ нет—и не бу́дет; в со́рок лет де́нег нет—и не бу́дет.** [If (one has) no smarts at twenty, there won't be any; if (one has) no wife at thirty, there won't be one; if (one has) no money at forty, there won't be any.]

5-178 C10. **Всяк кули́к своё боло́то хва́лит.** [Every snipe praises his own swamp.] Boasting about one's village, town, or even country was apparently not uncommon for Russians. But around the Age of Enlightenment, the Russian intelligentsia developed just the opposite feeling, the longing to go abroad. It was never easy for Russians until the last decade to obtain the permit to go abroad. Among the famous early "refuseniks" was **Пу́шкин**, who applied for a permit to travel and was rejected. Ironically, most Russians who managed to get out never felt at home in alien lands **на чужби́не, за грани́цей**. This is how the insight was born that there is no place on earth where a Russian *intelligent* is happy: **Там хорошо́, где нас нет.** [It is good wherever we are not.] This proverb originated as a line in Griboedov's play, *Woe from Wit,* but is often used today as a proverb, without association with its origins. It is a high frequency saying nowadays, especially among the first generation immigrants (to America) who are unhappy, and long to go back to "where they are not" any longer.

C11. **Го́лод—не тётка.** [Hunger is not an aunt.] An aunt, no matter what a 🔊 **5-179** nuisance she may be sometimes, will give you something to eat when you are hungry. Hunger, however, is relentless and forces you to do something about it. Hunger does force one to respond to it, and Russians have had enough famines in their collective memory to know this.

C12. **Голь на вы́думки хитра́.** Necessity is the mother of invention. [The 🔊 **5-180** poor are crafty at inventions.] Though essentially the same as its English counterpart, the Russian proverb has a slighting self-deprecating nuance. This comes from the words **голь**, **вы́думки** and **хитра́**, which are all slightly negative. **Голь** means the naked ones, that is, those without possessions, **вы́думки** is a light, even an irresponsible act of invention, and **хитра́** is not a positive description either, implying virtuosity to the point of craftiness.

C13. **Гото́вь са́ни ле́том, а теле́гу зимо́й.** [Prepare a sled in the summer, 🔊 **5-181** and a horsecart in the winter.] A good moral for procrastinators all over the world (provided they live in a climate with four seasons). It tries to educate those very peasants who don't cross themselves until it thunders (see the section on proverbs and antiquity above). On the other hand, to instruct those gentlemen hunters, who don't plan well, they put it differently: **На охо́ту е́хать—соба́к корми́ть.** [When it's time to go hunting, they start feeding the dogs.] As you may guess, dogs need to be fed well before the hunt, otherwise the temptation to chase those wolves and deer is either too high or too low. A truly farsighted man of the 20th century with a well developed traditional sense of the unpredictability of "fate" **судьба́** would say: **Е́дешь на́ день, бери́ хле́ба на неде́лю.** [When you're going away for a day, pack a week's portion of bread.]

C14. **Даю́т—бери́ (а бьют—беги́).** [When they give (you something), take 🔊 **5-182** (it) (and when they are beating (you), run).] Usually only the first part of the proverb is used, encouraging one to accept a gift. The second half is omitted, perhaps because it's felt to be a strange continuation. The survival wisdom the two halves teach is too passive and may be too unheroic to accept for a modern man. The modern version of the Russian proverb reverses the advice in the second half: **Даю́т—бери́, бьют— сда́чи дава́й.** [When they give (you something), take (it), and when they hit (you), hit back.]

C15. **Двум смертя́м не быва́ть, а одно́й не минова́ть.** One can only die 🔊 **5-183** once. [Two deaths don't happen, but one is not to be avoided.] A fatalistic proverb. It is used to justify taking relatively serious risks. In similar situations, where "Come what may" is roughly appropriate, other proverbs can be used, too, such as **«Или пан, или пропа́л»** [(I will be) either lord or destroyed], which is probably an intra-Slavic borrowing, judging from the Polish and Ukrainian word **пан** "lord." There is also **«Была́, не была́»** ("Come what may," [was or was not]), **«Ра́ньше сме́рти не умрёшь»** [One cannot die before death], and **«Умира́ть/ погиба́ть, так с му́зыкой»** [If one is to die/perish, then (one should die) with music], which is the most modern and the most ostentatious version of them all. Note that, on the whole, Russians have a more intimate relationship with death than do Americans. Death is not as unmentionable in Russian as it is in American English, and there is even the endearing **сме́ртушка** alongside **смерть,** the usual word for death. (Compare the similarly endearing **судьби́нушка** for **судьба́** "fate" and **го́рюшко** for **го́ре** "grief.")

5-184 C16. Де́ньги счёт лю́бят. [Money likes being counted.] This is often said to encourage someone who is reluctant to count the bills received in the

5-185

presence of the giver. This encouragement is often needed because of the Russian reluctance to deal squarely with money, including salary, debts, loans, honoraria, and other compensation. Reservations, if not actually guilt associated with the pursuit of money, are expressed plainly

5-186

in: **Не в де́ньгах сча́стье.** [Happiness is not in money.] Note that the modern saying **«Всех де́нег не зарабо́таешь»** [One can't earn all the money (in the world)] shows that the passive attitude towards money (and, consequently, towards hard work) remains alive. A cynical modern twist, however, is also available: **Не в де́ньгах сча́стье, а в их нали́чии/коли́честве.** [Happiness is not in money, but in its availability/quantity.]

5-187 C17. До́ма и сте́ны помога́ют/ле́чат. There is no place like home. [At home even walls help/cure.] This is another proverb that underscores the security of home. Unlike **«В гостя́х хорошо́, а до́ма лу́чше»**, which compares a good experience at someone else's place to home (and finds home to be still better), this proverb assumes some difficult or bad experience out there and states that at home help emanates even from such seemingly irrelevant and trivial objects as walls. The proverb conveys the intense longing for the security of home that is so familiar to a nation with a powerful collective memory of arrests and labor camps. Unfortunately, even homes were bugged, and that fact, too, found its way into a proverb: **И у стен есть у́ши.** [Even walls have ears.]

5-188 C18. Дру́жба дру́жбой, а слу́жба слу́жбой. [Friendship is friendship, but a job is a job.] The opposition between the personal and the official is hard to balance in any culture. This proverb addresses this issue and makes it easier to stipulate that the job be done even when the rela tionship between the subordinate and the superordinate happens to be personal and close. Such closeness seems to be more common in Russian rather than in Anglo-Saxon culture, where "Familiarity breeds contempt." There is a different variant that stresses the limits of friendship, very much in the spirit of "going Dutch": **Дру́жба дру́жбой, а табачо́к/де́нежки врозь.** [Friendship is friendship, but tobacco/money is apart.] Note that the diminutive for "tobacco" is an example of a food-related word like **во́дочка** "vodka" and **чаёк** "tea" to which even men attach diminutive suffixes (otherwise generally used by women), especially when they ask for these objects.

C19. **Е́сли бы да кабы́, да во рту́ росли́ грибы́, да/то был бы не рот, а** 🔊 5-189
це́лый огоро́д. [If mushrooms grew in one's mouth, and if/then there was/would be not a mouthful but a whole garden.] Here is a very folksy way to tell someone that it's time to stop nonsensical wishful thinking. Mushrooms are good, and finding plenty of mushrooms is the dream of every mushroom picker, who, like hunters, are known to tell stories about how they came across a patch of king boletes that was Oh so big! So a garden full of mushrooms is something really nice to fantasize about. But fantasies won't feed you.

C20. **За би́того двух неби́тых даю́т.** [They give two unbeaten (men) for a 🔊 5-190
beaten (one).] The old wisdom insists that by learning it the hard way man gets wiser and becomes more valuable. There are more recent mock sayings that build on the same faith in the effectiveness of negative reinforcement in the learning process. A mock version of Marx's dictum **«Бытие́ определя́ет созна́ние»** [Being determines cognition] is **«Битиё определя́ет созна́ние»** [Beating determines cognition]. Even children chant: **«Глу́по, ту́по, неразви́то, потому́ что ма́ло би́то»** [Stupid, dense, undeveloped, because not beaten enough]. The idea may not be that alien to the Western world after all, since apparently a small business owner who has experienced bankruptcy (hence, is **би́тый**) usually has no difficulty finding a job in big business because his experience is considered to be very valuable.

C21. **И во́лки сы́ты, и о́вцы це́лы.** [The wolves are satisfied and the sheep 🔊 5-191
are unharmed.] This characterizes a logically impossible situation created at the expense of reason and principles. It is used mostly critically, but a positive usage also occurs to indicate the possibility of a compromise **компроми́сс**. The word, by the way, is a negative concept in Russian that borders on lack of principles **беспринци́пность** (compare **идти́ на компроми́сс = де́лать сде́лку с со́вестью** "make a deal with one's conscience"). Still, there are many proverbs that advocate against rigid principles. It will be interesting to see how the attitude towards compromise changes as the political experience of Russians increases in the 21st century.

5-192 C22. **И на стару́ху быва́ет пору́ха.** To err is human. [Even to an old woman an error may happen.] The interesting part here is the "even," which presupposes that old women are least likely to err. As in some other sayings, it is implied that old women are particularly wise (if not witches altogether). There are, of course, many Russian proverbs that deny women any intelligence, yet it is also women who are likely to be at home with the supernatural and need to be reckoned with. Another proverb saying that even an expert may err is: **Конь о четырёх нога́х, да спотыка́ется.** [A stallion has four legs but he still stumbles.]

5-193 C23. **Как во́лка ни корми́, он всё в лес смо́трит.** Can the leopard change his spots? [No matter how long you feed a wolf, he keeps looking toward the forest.] The implication of the Russian version is more value-laden than its English counterpart. Recall that the forest is an essentially alien and hostile place for humans, and that that's where wolves belong. The proverb implies a lack of gratitude and a lack of willingness to reciprocate trust and good will. This is an alienating thing to say about a person you have helped and who nevertheless cannot change loyalties and become your friend or ally. (See Fig. 5-6 below.)

5-194 C24. **Ка́шу ма́слом не испо́ртишь.** Never too much of a good thing. [A (hot) cereal cannot be spoiled by butter.] Hot cereal **ка́ша** is a good thing in Russia, and **ка́ша с ма́слом** "hot cereal with butter" is even better. Try adding extra butter to your hot buckwheat cereal and you will agree. Buckwheat is supposed to be so good as to boast about it itself: **Гре́чневая ка́ша сама́ себя́ хва́лит.** "Buckwheat cereal praises itself," just as braggarts do. And butter, too, is supposed to be very good for you (don't even think of cholesterol!). The point of the proverb is that one good thing cannot spoil another good thing.

5-195 C25. **Кто ста́рое помянёт, тому́ глаз вон.** Let bygones be bygones. [Who mentions old (injuries), he loses (his) eye.] This is used to stop someone from raising old issues and wrongs, and to redirect the conversation to

Сколько нерезидента ни корми...

ДМИТРИЙ ЛАДЫГИН

Рынок госбумаг наконец достиг равновесия, к которому стремился несколько месяцев. Колебания доходности облигаций в пределах от 31–32% до 34–35% годовых вполне устраивают и участников рынка, и денежные власти. Однако уже в ближайшее время с трудом достигнутое равновесие может быть утрачено.

Fig. 5-6.

the present. It's an expression of the traditional Russian willingness not to pursue old grudges and retribution. **Мсти́тельный** "vengeful" and **злопа́мятный** "rancorous" are clearly negative characteristics. There is a modern continuation, however, that mocks the traditional values by adding «**а кто забу́дет, тому́ о́ба**» [but who forgets (them) loses both (eyes)].

C26. **Куда́ конь с копы́том, туда́ и рак с клешнёй.** [Where the stallion ◀🔊 5-196 (goes) with (his) hoof, there (goes) the crayfish with his claw.] This proverb ridicules the weak and untalented who try to keep up with the strong and able. The strong, noble, and swift one is a stallion and the weak, clumsy, ignoble, and slow one is a crayfish, who is also known to every Russian for moving backwards rather than forwards. The contrast between them is as great as it can be, which makes the ridiculousness all the more biting. This is a real put-down for the one who corresponds to the crayfish.

C27. **Куй желе́зо, пока́ горячо́.** Make hay while the sun shines. / Strike ◀🔊 5-187 while the iron is hot. [Strike iron while hot.] In the playful modern variant the second clause is replaced with «**не отходя́ от ка́ссы**» [before you leave the (store cashier's) window], the expression **не отходя́ от ка́ссы** is used as a slangy synonym of "immediately," copying the notices displayed at cashiers encouraging the customers to double check the money before they leave the window. Note also these variations of the 1980s and 1990s: **Куй желе́зо, пока́ Горбачёв. Де́лай де́льце, пока́ Ельцин.** [Strike iron while (there is) Gorbachev. Do business while (there is) Yeltsin.]

C28. **Лес/дрова́ ру́бят—ще́пки летя́т.** One cannot make an omelet without ◀🔊 5-198 breaking eggs. [When they chop wood, chips fall.] This permissive and forgiving proverb acquired a special irony in the Soviet era, when it was used to justify the victimization of the innocent. The reasoning was that the government undertook the monumental task of building a new society, that it needed to destroy real internal enemies, and that even if the innocent were punished, these were, after all, negligible errors. Poignantly, even the victims themselves used this proverb to excuse the government that was responsible for their personal tragedies.

C29. **Любо́вь зла—полю́бишь и козла́.** Love is blind. [Love is nasty: you ◀🔊 5-199 could fall in love with a goat.] Besides being a metaphor for stubbornness, **козёл** (he-goat) is also associated with uncouth masculinity, so one may say about an unaired room inhabited by a man that it **па́хнет козло́м** "smells like a he-goat." There is, however, a folk tale "The Snotty Goat" **Сопли́вый козёл** about a girl who married a goat, and who for a while had to endure the unpleasantness of wiping his snot and slobber off for him and being ridiculed by her family; but in the end he turned into a handsome young man and they lived happily ever after.

Evoked by the association with this "goat" proverb is the pretty awful picture of the sexes painted by the modern saying: **Мужчи́на до́лжен быть зол, воню́ч и волоса́т, а же́нщина боса́я, бере́менная и на ку́хне / как поликли́ника: чи́стая, беспла́тная и общедосту́пная.** [A man must be angry, stinky and hairy, and a woman (must be) barefoot, pregnant and in the kitchen / (must be) like a health clinic: clean, free and generally accessible.] Note that until recently, people in Russia didn't have to pay for medical care. The reference to the kitchen connects this modern Russian man's ideal of a woman to another old saying which delimits the woman's realm in the area of the threshold and the stove (see "Old Proverbs and Antiquity" above).[9]

◀») 5-200 C30. **Мужи́к за́дним умо́м кре́пок.** [A peasant is good at back-wisdom (at being smart in retrospect).] So ignorant peasants **мужики́** not only do not plan ahead (crossing themselves only after it thunders, as the proverb discussed above says), but they are also known for being smart after the fact. The same idea is phrased even more derogatorily as: **Хоро́шая мысля́ прихо́дит опосля́.** [A good thought comes afterwards.] In this packaging, the language of peasants is satirized through the dialectal forms **мысля́** and **опосля́**. A plain modern rendering of a similar idea tells us to stop talking tough after the fight is over: **По́сле дра́ки кулака́ми не ма́шут.** [They don't swing their fists after the fight.]

◀») 5-201 C31. **На безры́бье и рак—ры́ба (на беспти́чье и жо́па солове́й).** [When there's no fish (in the river), then even a crayfish counts as fish (when there are no birds, then even an arse is a nightingale).] Another expression of practical compromise. Crayfish are considered to be the scavengers of the river, and not the most desirable kind of food. The lesson is that we all should not be too demanding and take advantage of what there is. Note, by the way, that **ра́ковый суп** "crayfish soup" tastes very good. The second part is obscene.

◀») 5-202 C32. **На брю́хе шёлк, а в брю́хе щёлк.** [On the belly is silk, and in the belly is "click!" (= empty sound).] The metaphor of silk in this proverb evokes an association of a young Westernized aristocrat, who follows the latest Parisian fashion at the expense of his family estate. The saying criticizes vanity, prodigality, and lack of substance.

◀») 5-203 C33. **На вкус и цвет това́рищей нет. / О вку́сах не спо́рят.** Each to his own taste. [For taste and color there are no confederates./They don't argue about tastes.] A somewhat risqué variant jocularly talks about two types of men with different, possibly major attractions in life (at least in older Russia), religion and women: **Кто лю́бит попа́, а кто попадью́ (а кто**

---

[9] Robert Rothstein brought to my attention a similar English expression about keeping one's wife "pregnant in summer and barefoot in winter": some attitudes towards women may be more universal than one might expect!

поповну). [Some like the priest, and some like his wife (and some like his daughter).] Making indecent jokes about priests' wives and daughters, incidentally, was not uncommon in the 19th century. A modern playful variant opposes food and love: **У каждого свой вкус, своя манера: папа любил арбуз, а мама—офицера.** [Each has his own taste, his own manner: papa loved watermelons and mama (loved) an officer.] (See Fig. 5-7 below.)

C34. **На ловца и зверь бежит.** [To a (skilled) catcher, even (wild) animals come.]. One wonders why animals should run towards their catcher rather than away from him. It's because catchers and trappers are thought of as knowing the secret of attracting them. Perhaps rooted in the prehistoric experience of hunters and gatherers, those who went out into the woods to hunt and trap animals were felt to have a deep knowledge of wildlife and an uncanny sense of nature that bordered on the supernatural. Traditionally, they were not part of the farming community in their own village, but tended to be loners and not good family men. And they knew what charms to say when they looked for their wild animals. In the original meaning, the proverb means something like "Nothing succeeds like success," and it is still used in this meaning. It is, however, more often said today in a sense similar to "Speaking of the devil," to the person one has been looking for. Impolite variants for this modern usage are: **Вспомнишь чёрта/дурака, он и появится.** These are not words to be spoken so as to be heard by the one referred to. Russians do not want to be called **чёрт** even though the word "devil" is allowable in the English equivalent.

🔊 5-204

C35. **На миру/людях и смерть красна.** [With company, even death is fine.] **Мир** is not the world at large, but rather the village community of pre-

🔊 5-205

У кого какой вкус: один любит
дыню, а другой — арбуз.

Fig. 5-7.

revolutionary Russia, which had some power to make decisions about the welfare of its members and in which peasants saw a source of authority, as well as of support and comfort. It is used, of course, in the more general sense of the importance of community and company. (See also C56.)

🔊 5-206   C36.   **На чужо́й карава́й рта не разева́й.** [Don't open your mouth to somebody else's loaf.] Used to rebuke someone who wants to join in on a benefit that was produced by somebody else. A modern mock risque version that warns against coveting a neighbor's wife is: **На чужу́ю крова́ть рот не разева́й.** The word **чужо́й** is particularly telling in this context. While Russia has a culture of hospitality and sharing, there is also a strong resistance to the presumption of generosity on the part of those who don't belong, that is, who are **чужи́е.** A continuation of the proverb about loaves that plays out the opposition between one's own and what is alien (**свой** vs. **чужо́й**) may be added: **а пора́ньше встава́й, да свой затева́й** [but get up early and start your own.] **Свой** is a relationship of entitlement and security in Russia. They even say: **Свой своему́ понево́ле друг/брат.** [Want it or not, one's own is a friend/brother to one's own.] Even you—a member of a culture that is not so dependent on the concept of **свой**—probably have experienced something like this when you ran into a fellow American abroad when you were feeling particularly homesick. The word **свой** occurs in such phrases as **свой челове́к** "one of ours, a trustworthy person" and **среди́ свои́х** "among friends." There are quite a few proverbs in this chapter that refer to the concepts of **свой** and **чужо́й** (see C38, C57, C58, C67–69).

🔊 5-207   C37.   **Не бо́ги горшки́ обжига́ют.** [It's not gods who fire clay pots.] The assumption is, of course, that firing clay pots requires special skills: that is, even such a special job as pottery need not be done by gods but can very well be done by mere mortals. The proverb sounds a bit strange today; but earlier, the potter's work was thought of as challenging. The metaphor testifies to the proverb's age. It is said in response to timidity in undertaking some challenging task.

🔊 5-208   C38.   **Не в свои́ са́ни не сади́сь.** [Don't sit in somebody else's sled.] The sled used to be a very important means of transportation in a country with long winters. The message is for people not to intrude on others' possessions or territory (one's own = **свой**, see also C36, C57, C58, C67–69). You may still see or hear it used as a rebuke to those who behave in a manner not befitting their modest status, but these days the proverb is used mostly to tell people to mind their own business. A modern crude mock variant tells men to mind their own women: **Не на свою́ Са́ню не ложи́сь.** [Don't lie on somebody else's Sanya (female name).]

🔊 5-209   C39.   **Не всё коту́ ма́сленица, бу́дет и вели́кий пост.** Every day is not Sunday. [It is not forever Mardi Gras for a cat, there will be Great Lent,

too.] The pagan holiday of Mardi Gras **ма́сленица** falls on the week be- 🔲 **5-210**
fore the beginning of the Great Lent that precedes Easter. During
ма́сленица, people traditionally feast on pancakes **блины́** served with
lots of butter, sour cream, caviar and other good things.[10] Tom cats
коты́ are considered Epicurean and hedonistic in nature, as well as wise
and/or tricky. The prediction is that a pleasure-loving Falstaffian trick-
ster cannot expect to get away with that sort of behavior forever.

C40.   **Не вся́кое лы́ко в стро́ку.** [Not every strip of bark gets to be used in a ◀)) **5-211**
row (in weaving).] Another forgiving proverb that advises one not to
take every (usually stupid or negative) word seriously and not to react
to it in earnest. The metaphor is that of shoe weaving. Peasant's bark
shoes **ла́пти** were woven with strips from the bark of the linden tree;
obviously, not every strip was nice enough to be used. So, folks, don't
pay attention to every stupid word you hear!

C41.   **Не име́й сто рубле́й, а име́й сто друзе́й.** [Do not have a hundred ◀)) **5-212**
rubles, but do have a hundred friends.] This saying stresses the importance of friends over riches. Actually, **«сто друзе́й»** is not all that realistic in Russia because the word **друг** "friend" in Russian is taken very seriously. There can really be only two or three of them in the course of
one's life, the remaining "friends" being **знако́мые** "acquaintances,"
однокла́ссники/одноку́рсники "classmates at school/in college,"
прия́тели "buddies, pals" and many other similar designations. Note
also the recent cynical variant: **Не име́й сто рубле́й, а име́й ты́сячу.**
[Do not have a hundred rubles, but do have a thousand rubles.]

C42.   **Не откла́дывай на за́втра то, что мо́жешь сде́лать сего́дня.** Never ◀)) **5-213**
[don't] put off till tomorrow what you can do today. A modern Russian
mock variant challenges Ben Franklin's work ethic and tells us otherwise: **Не откла́дывай на за́втра то, что мо́жно сде́лать послеза́втра.**
[Don't put off till tomorrow what can be done the day after tomorrow.]
The same modern idea appears in the wolf-forest packaging: **Рабо́та/
де́ло не волк/медве́дь, в лес не убежи́т.** [Work is not a wolf/bear, it
won't run away to the forest.] An indecent modern variant is: **Рабо́та не
член: постои́т.** [Work is not a member (= penis), it will wait / stay up.]
There is also a more restricted, gastronomic mock version of Franklin's
aphorism: **Не откла́дывай на за́втра то, что мо́жно съесть сего́дня.**
[Don't set aside till tomorrow what can be eaten today.]

C43.   **Не плюй в коло́дец: пригоди́тся воды́ напи́ться.** [Don't spit into a ◀)) **5-214**
well, (for) it may be useful (to you) to get a drink of water.] A cynical
modern version reverses the message: **Не пей из коло́дца: пригоди́тся
плю́нуть.** [Don't drink from a well, (for) it may be useful (to you) to

---

[10] For more on pancakes and other good Mardi Gras food, see Genevra Gerhart's *The
Russian's World,* 2nd ed., 139–40 and 332–33.

spit in.] A Soviet version with a less general meaning is: «Éсли ты плю́нешь на коллекти́в, коллекти́в утрётся. Éсли коллекти́в плю́нет на тебя́, ты уто́нешь». [If you spit at the collective, the collective will wipe it off. If the collective spits at you, you will sink.] Indeed, being subjected to a critique by a collective used to be an ominous matter, often preceding an official (and lethal) sanction. A modern combination of this proverb with **Сло́во не воробе́й, вы́летит—не пойма́ешь.** Think before you speak. [A word is not a sparrow: once it's flown out you can't catch it.] gives the playful **Не плюй в коло́дец: вы́летит—не пойма́ешь.**

◀)) 5-215 C44. **Не так стра́шен чёрт, как его́ малю́ют.** [The devil is not as scary as they paint him.] The proverb says that the official images of the devil are not that reliable. Perhaps the devil is not as scary as, for example, in the frescoes of the Last Judgment, perhaps he is rather foolish, more like the folktale imps, and the imps of **Пу́шкин**'s tale about the priest and the worker, or **Го́голь**'s devil in the story about Christmas eve. All these imps were tricked by men and made to serve them. The proverb implies that it may be worth any brave man's effort trying to saddle the devil, after all. A modern mock version shifts the meaning to express reservations about children: **Не так стра́шен чёрт, как его́ малю́тки.** [The devil is not as scary as are his little ones.]

◀)) 5-216 C45. **Незва́ный гость ху́же тата́рина.** [An uninvited guest is worse than a Tartar.] This is usually used by those who drop in uninvited as a way of showing that they realize the inappropriateness of their unexpected arrival. The hosts are of course expected to reassure them that they are most welcome. (A famous joke describes how the Tartars went to Stalin to complain about this saying. He took the matter under advisement, consulted with the Supreme Soviet, and later came back with: "You are right, the old saying was unfair. The new saying is «Незва́ный гость лу́чше тата́рина» [An uninvited guest is better than a Tartar].") Recall, by the way, that it is recorded in the collective memory of Russians that during the Tartar Yoke (between the 13th and the 15th century) Tartars (= Mongols) felt free to arrive uninvited to rape and pillage. Proverbs like this one continue to reenforce centuries-old hostilities and contribute to ethnic prejudices. (See Fig. 5-8 on the next page.)

◀)) 5-217 C46. **Но́вая метла́ чи́сто метёт.** A new broom sweeps clean. This is a critical, grudging statement about the excesses of those newly appointed to positions of responsibility. The phenomenon is a high-powered variant of "administrative euphoria" **административный восто́рг**, the intoxication with petty power described by **Достое́вский**. Clean jobs are obviously not a very positive thing in the value system that underlies this proverb. But more than that, it's the Russian distaste towards power structure and bureaucracy that comes through in this proverb.

Налоговый полицейский
хуже монголо-татарина

9 декабря Черёмушкинский суд Москвы впервые довёл до логического завершения уголовный процесс по делу о неуплате налогов и отправил за решётку гражданина Анисимова Алексея. Если учесть, что, по данным налоговой полиции, Анисимов задолжал казне около 150 млн рублей, эта история превращается в фарс, напоминающий разгон бравыми ребятами в бронежилетах и с автоматами старушек, приторговывающих спичками.

Fig. 5-8.

C47. **Нужда́ научит калачи́ есть.** Necessity is the mother of invention. ◀)) 5-218
      [Need will teach one to eat white bread.] This proverb is based on a his-
      torical fact. When in the 18th century some northerners migrated south
      fleeing from financial hardship, they ended up in Southern Russia
      eating fancier white bread, whereas the North had only dark rye bread.

C48. **От судьбы́ не уйдёшь.** [You shall not escape from fate.] The word ◀)) 5-219
      судьба́ is much more frequent in Russian than "fate" is in American
      English and the concept of fate судьба́, до́ля figures large in Russian
      culture. It is usually personified as a woman. The same idea of one's
      powerlessness in the face of fate can be expressed more concretely as:
      От сумы́ да от тюрьмы́ не зарека́йся [Don't say you'll never carry a
      сума́ (bag, that is, be a beggar) or be in jail]. Russian history has not of-
      fered its people much reassurance that they are the masters of their own
      fate. Simpler and more recent versions are: **Что бу́дет, то бу́дет. / Чему́
      быть, того́ не минова́ть.** What will be will be. / [What is to be shall not
      pass/be by-passed.] Notice that most Russians find the American ten-
      dency to make appointments several weeks in advance ridiculous. They
      normally tell you to call again later, a day or so before the day you are
      ready to come. Planning ahead in Russia is almost like testing fate. But
      then, some American grandmothers, too, will tell you not to buy baby
      clothes before the baby is born.

C49. **Пей, да де́ло разуме́й.** [Drink, but know your job.] Strictly speaking, ◀)) 5-220
      this saying has an author, the famous fable-writer **Крыло́в.** Most
      Russians, however, think that this is an authentic proverb, rather than a
      well-cited line from Krylov. As you can see from this saying, drinking is
      not considered much of a problem as long as the drinker does his job
      well—something that would justify the election of Yeltsin as president
      despite his heavy drinking problems. The same pro-drinking message
      appears in the more recent: «Кто не ку́рит и не пьёт, тот здоро́вень-
      ким умрёт» and «Во́дка—си́ла, спорт—моги́ла» [Vodka is strength,
      sports is a grave (= death)]

🔊 **5-221** C50. **Пе́рвый блин ко́мом.** If at first you don't succeed, try, try again. [The
first crepe comes out a lump.] **Блины́** are supposed to be thin, even and

📷 **5-222** tender to the palate. The temperature of the grill or pan is one of the
keys to success but it is also hard to get it right in the beginning, so the
first **блин** is often a failure. This is of course a metaphor for any undertaking in life, and it usually serves as a consolation.

🔊 **5-223** C51. **Посади́ свинью́ за стол, она́ и но́ги на стол.** [Seat a pig at the table
and it will put its feet on the table as well.] The metaphors of swine in
Russian and in English are similar: swine are ill-mannered, ignoble, and
crude. They are not normally creatures you want to invite to your
dinner table. And if you do, don't expect anything good: the swine
would misbehave even further. It will put its feet on the table, the
epitome of obnoxiousness. Remember that to Russians, putting one's
feet on the table is an obvious proof that Americans lack manners in the
most shocking way.

🔊 **5-224** C52. **Пришла́ беда́—отворя́й воро́та.** When sorrows come, they come not
single spies, but in battalions. [Grief has come, open the gates!] This is

📷 **5-225** another one of the fatalistic Russian proverbs. **Беда́**, like its synonym
го́ре and like **судьба́** "fate" and **смерть** "death" are often personified.
Воро́та (normally, the stress is on the second syllable) are wide double
gates, wide enough for a carriage to pass through. They separate the security of home from the outside world. The image evoked by the saying
is that of a hostile takeover against which there is no resisting.

🔊 **5-226** C53. **Простота́ ху́же воровства́.** [Simple-mindedness is worse than theft/
trickiness.] This is a somewhat surprising idea for a traditional proverb.
It flatly contradicts the moral view that honesty is the best policy, and
frankly gives preference to clever dishonesty over naive honesty—just
the opposite of what **Толсто́й** would have recommended. **Простота́** is
in fact not a straightforwardly positive quality in Russian. Notice that
«Он просто́й» (with the long form adjective) tells us that he is a nice
unpretentious person, but **«Он прост»** (with the short form adjective)
is not exactly a complimentary thing to say about somebody. It may
be more like a euphemism for "stupid." It is this meaning that figures in
the proverb used by Ostrovsky as the title for his play **«На вся́кого
мудреца́ дово́льно простоты́»** [There is enough simple-mindedness
for every wise man]. A more explicit paraphrase for **Простота́ ху́же
воровства́** is: Лу́чше име́ть де́ло с у́мным моше́нником, чем с
че́стным дурако́м. [It's better to deal with a smart rascal than with an
honest fool.]

🔊 **5-227** C54. **Пья́ному мо́ре по коле́но.** [To a drunk man, the sea is up to (his)
knees.] Among many proverbs about drinking, this one expresses the
megalomaniac perception of the intoxicated man. It may have been the
lure of this power trip that made drinking into a serious problem in Rus-

sia. Note also a reference to the sensation of power experienced through vodka in the modern «**Во́дка—си́ла, спорт—моги́ла**» [Vodka is strength, sports is a grave (= death)].

C55. **Рыба́к рыбака́ ви́дит издалека́.** It takes one to know one. [A fisher- 🔊 **5-228** man sees another fisherman from far away.] Fishermen, like hunters, (see C34 above) are felt by peasants to have an uncanny nature sense that borders on the supernatural. They are also known to find particular pleasure in the company of those like themselves. The proverb implies that they spot one another from far away because of the unusual powers they possess in common. The idea can of course be generalized to any situation in which those who share some special quality or interest (more often than not, a negative one) identify each other easily and are attracted to one another.

Рыбак рыбака видит издалека.
Рис. Юлии ОРЛОВОЙ

Fig. 5-9.

5-229 **C56.** **С ми́ру по ни́тке — го́лому руба́ха.** [A thread from each in the community (makes) a shirt for a naked one.] This is a Russian version of the March of Dimes idea. A cynical modern version is: **С ми́ру по ни́тке — го́лому верёвка.** [A thread from each in the community (is) a rope for a naked one.] (See also C35.)

5-230

5-231 **C57.** **Свой глаз — алма́з.** If you want a thing well done, do it yourself. [One's own eye is a diamond.] This serves as a justification for those who don't know how to delegate. One may add: **а чужо́й — стекло́** [and someone else's is glass], with the typical opposition of **свой** vs. **чужо́й** (cf. C36, C38, C58, C67–69). There is a sinister ring to the similar but modern **Доверя́й, но проверя́й** [Delegate, but check], which really means "Don't trust, and do check," and was on occasion used to help justify witch hunts and purges.

5-232 **C58.** **Своя́ но́ша не тя́нет / тяжела́.** [One's own baggage is not heavy.] And similarly, **Своя́ руба́шка бли́же к те́лу** [One's own shirt is closer to (one's) body]. Both proverbs proclaim the special psychological status of things that are **свой** "one's own" (cf. C36, C38, C57, C67–69). A physiologically more immediate significance of things **свой** shows in a modern "unprintable" variant **Своё говно́ не па́хнет** [One's own shit does not smell]. The recent cynical saying **«Берёшь чужи́е, а отдаёшь свои́»** [You take somebody else's (money), but you return your own (money)] capitalizes on this ancient opposition, too, quite aptly explaining why some people are not too enthusiastic when they have to return borrowed money.

5-233

5-234

5-235 **C59.** **Сте́рпится — слю́бится.** You can get used to anything. [Once (it's) endured long enough, it becomes likable.] Although the power and the benefit of habit is recognized in all cultures, this proverb is somewhat frightening. Imagine being told this when you object to your despotic father, who wants you to marry someone he chose for you and someone you don't happen to love, or maybe even never met. You say: **«Но я не люблю́ его́/её!»**, and your father responds: **«Сте́рпится — слю́бится».** Then you are taken to church and wed for life. And remember, those were the good old days when divorce was not possible.

5-236 **C60.** **Терпи́, каза́к, атама́ном бу́дешь.** Never say die. [Endure, cossack, and you shall be a chieftain.] Adults quote this proverb to children when they want them to stop whining, and children usually resent it. This is yet another proverb that commends **терпе́ние** "patience, endurance," one of the centuries-old Russian virtues. **«Пой ему́ пе́сню о ве́чном терпе́нии, пой, терпели́вая мать»** (Sing him a song about eternal patience, sing, o patient mother), the 19th-century poet **Некра́сов** tells a Russian peasant woman standing over her baby. A modern variant is: **Терпи́, каза́к, с автома́том бу́дешь.** [Endure, cossack, and you shall have a machine gun.] There is also a cute but risqué variant based on a child's misunderstanding of the original proverb: **Терпи́, коза́, а то ма́мой бу́дешь.** [Endure, she-goat, or you shall be a mama.] This variant was recorded by **Чуко́вский** in his famous book «**От двух до пяти́**». The poet was fascinated by the way Russian children learn to speak Russian, and left this remarkable record of what is called "child language acquisition." The variant with the she-goat is an interesting example of how children introduce linguistic change. The child was too young to know what the words **каза́к** and **атама́н** mean, and reinterpreted the proverb using words accessible to a child's vocabulary: the famous she-goat of Russian fairy tales and, of course, mama. The child obviously made some kind of sense out of this *non sequitur*, however little sense it seems to make—but then children often put up with not understanding what is said around them. The risqué interpretation came later, attached by the intelligentsia, among which **Чуко́вский**'s book was quite popular. Adults know more about how one becomes a mother than the "author" of the mock saying did, and the old proverb in its child-created new garb came to be used as friendly advice.

C61.   **У́тро ве́чера мудрене́е.** Tomorrow is another day. [Morning is wiser 🔊 **5-237** than evening.] This is a suggestion to postpone a difficult discussion or decision until the next morning. As a matter of fact, you will find this ancient wisdom to be very useful advice. Exactly this advice was given by wise old magicians to youths and maidens on their way to heroic exploits, and it is still given by mothers and fathers to the young and the excited who are ready to spend the night arguing about the fate of Russia. There is of course a simple physiological reason for this advice, and tired people often take it without protesting. Few know that there is also an ancient pagan belief connected to this advice, according to which one should mistrust night and darkness, and value sunlight. Night is unreliable since it is the time when evil forces are released.

C62.   **Челове́к челове́ку волк.** [Man is wolf to (another) man.] This pes- 🔊 **5-238** simistic saying is a direct translation of a phrase by the ancient Roman playwright Plautus, but Russian speakers usually treat it as a true proverb. Because the philosopher Thomas Hobbes is known among the Russian intelligentsia to have professed similar pessimistic views of mankind, there exists also a modern mock variant: **Челове́к челове́ку Го́ббс.** [Man is Hobbes to (another) man]. During the Soviet period, the proverb was used to illustrate the inhumane nature of the Western world. By contrast, the official slogan of the XXII Communist Party Congress (1961) proclaimed that in the happy land of the Soviets: **Челове́к челове́ку—друг, това́рищ и брат.** [Man is friend, comrade and brother to (another) man.]

C63.   **Чем бы дитя́ ни те́шилось, лишь бы не пла́кало.** [Whatever the child 🔊 **5-239** is amused by, as long as it does not cry (anything is all right).] This proverb says that it is sometimes important to overlook minor problems for the benefit of other more important things. It may be used as a patronizing statement about a person who, like the child in the proverb, is attached to some useless idea or project, which causes no problems as long as the person is occupied with it. It's like saying: "Let the person have his/her pacifier, as long as s/he does not give us any trouble." A very recent obscene variation is not metaphorical: **Чем бы дитя ни тешилось, лишь бы не фа́калось.** [Whatever the child is amused by, as long as it does not fuck around (anything is all right).] For Russians, **фа́калось** sounds much tamer, of course, than its source word sounds for English speakers.

◀))) 5-240 C64. **Чем да́льше в лес, тем бо́льше дров.** [The deeper into the woods, the more firewood.] Despite the literal meaning, the proverb does not say anything positive about the woods. It is used to describe a situation or a conversation that becomes entangled as it develops, and/or to warn against getting too involved in complicated matters. The reason, of course, is that forests are an alien and unfriendly realm for mortals: the deeper in you go the greater the chances that you'll never find your way home.

◀))) 5-241 C65. **Что бы ни де́лать, лишь бы ничего́ не де́лать.** [No matter what to do, as long as one does not have to do anything (one is happy).] This describes well what came to be known as **халту́ра** "hackwork," caused by a lack of interest in work due to the way the Soviet economy worked (or didn't work). A similar variant: **Где бы ни рабо́тать, лишь бы не рабо́тать.** [No matter where to work, as long as one does not have to work (one is happy).] Another succinct way to put it is: **Ешь—поте́й, рабо́таешь—мёрзни.** [When you eat, sweat, when you work, chill.] This means that you should work hard when you are eating, but take it easy when you are working. This must have been especially true for those trying to survive in labor camps.

◀))) 5-242 C66. **Что у тре́звого на уме́, то у пья́ного на языке́.** [What is on a sober man's mind is on a drunk man's tongue.] A universal truth, although particularly relevant in Russia, with its drinking problem. There is even a concept of **спа́ивать кого́-либо** "to make someone become drunk or an alcoholic" just so that person can be taken advantage of. It is considered to be particularly disastrous when a woman takes to drinking, as another one of the numerous proverbs about drinking says: **Муж пьёт—полдо́ма[11] гори́т, жена́ пьёт—весь дом гори́т** [When the husband drinks it's (like) half the house is on fire, (but) when the wife drinks it's (like) the whole house is on fire].

---

[11] **полдо́ма**: the first "o" is also pronounced as "o"

C67. **Чтóбы человéка узнáть, нáдо пуд сóли съесть.** [To get to know a per- 🔊 **5-243** son, one must eat a pood of salt.] A pood is equivalent to 36 pounds. To consume that much salt, you need to know the person for no less than half a century. Be prepared to feel bitter in the process, since too much salt can taste bitter. The philosophy is very cautious about, if not out-right suspicious of, mankind. There is also a folk belief that salt has magic powers to protect one from evil. Another way to put this idea is: **Чужáя душá—потёмки/лес дремýчий/тёмный** [Another person's soul is darkness/ thick/dark forest]. Recall again that the dark of night and the still and dreamy thickness of the forest **лес**[12] seemed treacherous to the ancient Slavs, and that security lies in **свой** rather than **чужóй**. This proverb makes one feel enclosed within oneself, cautious and mistrust-ful of stepping out and dealing with the people out there. (Cf. also C36, C38, C57, C58, C67–69)

C68. **Чужóй хлеб/мёд гóрек.** [Someone else's bread/honey is bitter.] This is 🔊 **5-244** a sentiment that would lead one to decline food coupons and social security checks. But the reason is not so much because one should earn one's living as because it's not pleasant to receive someone else's cha-rity. What comes from **чужóй** is not lovable no matter how good it may be; it is also hard to accept and often has strings attached to it. Those referred to as **чужúе** are usually someone you have no choice but to live with, whether in order to hold your job, or to be apprenticed to, or be-cause you have no other means of support. In the 19th century such poor adult relatives and neighbors were called **приживáлы**, and there were also orphan children **сирóты** in a similar position. Pushkin credits Dante for this proverb when he describes, in his "Queen of Spades," the sad lot of a young live-in companion of this sort. The lovely girl must have said this many times. It was also probably said by laborers import-ed from Russia by the Germans during World War II (they were called **óстовцы** "Easterners"). It may also be said today by the Russian abroad who is a migrant worker, like many who come to "visit their relatives" in New York and work as live-in nannies or elderly caretakers earning below minimum wage. (Cf. also C36, C38, C57, C58, C67–69)

C69. **Чужýю бедý рукáми разведý, а к своéй умá не приложý.** [I can handle 🔊 **5-245** someone else's grief easily, but I can't even begin to deal with my own grief.] One says this after giving advice to someone in trouble, self-dep-recatingly, to mean "Of course, it's easy for me to give advice to you, but I probably would be at a loss myself if I were in your shoes." The speakers are often women, perhaps because it's a woman's thing to share complaints with another woman, as it is to give advice, even when

---

[12] **дремýчий** is a beautiful and eerie, fairy-tale-like adjective used almost exclusively with **лес**; it is derived from **дремáть** 'sleep, doze off.'

no one has asked for it. And finally, it is also a woman's thing to bond by minimizing one's contribution, and by giving credit to the other, if only as a polite gesture. The proverb can also be used to refer to a third person who volunteers unwelcome advice. (Cf. also C36, C38, C57, C58, C67–69)

◀) 5-246 C70. **Язы́к до Ки́ева доведёт.** [The tongue will lead (you) to Kiev.] "Tongue" here means language and communication. Why Kiev? Because between the 8th and 12th centuries Kiev was the capital of Kievan Rus', the cradle of Eastern Slavic culture and a medieval international metropolis. In that part of the world, all roads led to Kiev, where the language spoken was one of the mutually intelligible Eastern Slavic dialects, which later developed into three distinct languages: Belorussian, Russian and Ukrainian. You can guess the age of this proverb. (See Fig. 5-9 below.)

◀)) 5-247 C71. **Я́йца ку́рицу не у́чат.** Don't teach your granny to suck eggs. [Eggs don't teach the hen.] This is a typically Russian message, as elders **ста́ршие** have assumed authority over their juniors **мла́дшие** in this culture from ancient times to this day. The image of eggs, those silent rounded ovals, trying to teach a hen, is very funny. It is also eloquent, making those juniors who may have tried to teach an elderly person look and feel ridiculous. A plainer saying is: **Не учи́ учёного** [Don't teach a taught one], and an "unprintable" version is: **Не учи́ отца́ еба́ться** [Don't teach (your) father how to fuck].

**Общий язык
до Киева
доведет**

Fig. 5-10.

**D. ENGLISH PROVERBS WITHOUT
IMMEDIATE RUSSIAN
EQUIVALENTS**

**АНГЛИ́ЙСКИЕ ПОСЛО́ВИЦЫ, НЕ
ИМЕ́ЮЩИЕ РУ́ССКИХ
СООТВЕ́ТСТВИЙ**

There may be times when you like a certain English proverb and cannot think of its Russian equivalent. It may be that there simply is none. To save you time trying to remember it to no avail, you will find in D1 to D18 a list of some common English proverbs that do not have obvious Russian equivalents. Sample translations are given after the English proverbs in double brackets [[ ]]. A few of these proverbs have similar proverbs in Russian, which are given after the translations in parentheses.

There are also cases when Russian equivalents do exist but are not very much in use, either because they are not yet quite established, or because they are becoming archaic and at this point belong more to literature than to life. (If you want to impress, you may try to use the archaic-sounding ones.) Proverbs that have such low-frequency equivalents are given here in D19 to D25.

And if you don't find your favorite proverb in this chapter, you simply have to say: «По-англи́йски есть така́я посло́вица: ...», that is, "There is a proverb in English, which goes: ..." Then you will have to try to translate it literally and explain what it means.

D1. A chain is no stronger than its weakest link. [[**Цепь не быва́ет кре́пче своего́ са́мого сла́бого звена́; т.е. си́ла, про́чность систе́мы или гру́ппы определя́ется её са́мым сла́бым чле́ном.**]] (**Где то́нко, там и рвётся** [It's the thin spots that tear] says that if there is a weak spot it always lets you down. It is not used when one talks about the strength of a system or a team.)

D2. A watched pot never boils. [[**Горшо́к, над кото́рым ждут, никогда́ не закипа́ет; е́сли ждёшь, когда́ же закипи́т горшо́к, то ка́жется, что он до́лго не закипа́ет, что вре́мя тя́нется бесконе́чно до́лго.**]]

D3. Art is long, life is short. [[**Иску́сство — ве́чно, жизнь — коротка́.**]]

D4. Don't cry wolf. [[**Не кричи́ "Волк!"; т.е. не поднима́й ло́жную трево́гу, а не то тебе́ переста́нут ве́рить.**]]

D5. Don't put all your eggs in one basket. [[**Не клади́ всех яи́ц в одну́ корзи́нку; т.е. не ставь всё на одну́ ка́рту.**]]

D6. Every tub must stand on its own bottom. [[**Ка́ждая каду́шка должна́ стоя́ть сама́ по себе́; т.е. ка́ждая часть предприя́тия должна́ себя́ окупа́ть.**]]

D7. Familiarity breeds contempt. [[**Бли́зость порожда́ет презре́ние.**]] (**Нет проро́ка в оте́честве своём** [There is no prophet in one's birthplace] talks about a similar human psychology, but its gist has to do with the lack of recognition accorded to great ones by their immediate surroundings.)

D8. Forewarned is forearmed. [[**Заблаговре́менно предупреждённый э́тим уже́ вооружён.**]]

D9. Handsome is as handsome does. [[**Краси́в тот, кто краси́во поступа́ет; т.е. суди́ть сле́дует по дела́м.**]]

D10. Let sleeping dogs lie. [[**Пусть спя́щие соба́ки лежа́т.**]] (**Не дразни́ гусе́й** [Don't tease geese] is similar but focuses more on not initiating a confrontation than on not raising a potentially controversial issue.)

D11. Love me, love my dog. [[**Е́сли лю́бишь меня́, люби́ мою́ соба́ку; т.е. принима́й мои́ осо́бенности и недоста́тки.**]]

D12. No news is good news. [[**Нет новосте́й—всё равно́ что хоро́шая но́вость; т.е. когда́ лю́дям нужна́ по́мощь или когда́ есть на что пожа́ловаться, лю́ди даю́т о себе́ знать; зна́чит, если ничего́ не слы́шно, то всё хорошо́.**]]

D13. One man's meat is another man's poison. [[**Что мя́со одному́, то яд друго́му.**]] (This English proverb refers to a more drastic contrast between individual differences than does "To each his own" (**Кому́ что / Ка́ждому своё / Кому́ как**). A modern "unprintable" saying has an opposition similar to "meat/poison" but it is used only when the addressee has laughed: **Тебе́ смешно́, а мне оби́дно, тебе́ говно́, а мне пови́дло.** [To you it's funny, but to me it's offensive, to you it's shit and to me it's jam.] The second half of this modern saying is, of course, unacceptable in polite society.

D14. People who live in glass houses should not throw stones. [[**Тем, кто живёт в стекля́нных дома́х, не сле́дует броса́ться камня́ми; т.е. тому́, у кого́ со́весть нечиста́, не сле́дует напада́ть на други́х, так как те мо́гут сде́лать ему́ большу́ю неприя́тность.**]]

D15. The proof of the pudding is in the eating. [[**Пу́динг познаётся в еде́; т.е. всё проверя́ется пра́ктикой.**]]

D16. Truth is stranger than fiction. [[**Пра́вда дико́виннее вы́мысла.**]]

D17. You can't have your cake and eat it, too. [[**Нельзя́ и сохрани́ть свой пиро́г це́лым, и съесть его́; т.е. прихо́дится выбира́ть ме́жду двумя́ хоро́шими веща́ми.**]] (**Хо́чется и ры́бку съесть, и по мо́рде не получи́ть.** [One feels like both eating the fish and not getting (a punch) in the face.] refers to a similar situation, but is purely descriptive and does not have a moral. The language of the second part of this saying is quite crude.)

D18. A bird in the hand is worth two in the bush. **Лу́чше сини́ца в рука́х, чем жура́вль в не́бе.** [A titmouse in hands is better than a crane in the sky.]

D19. Don't put the cart before the horse. **Каре́ту впереди́ ло́шади не запряга́ют.** [They don't put the coach before the horse].

D20. Great minds think alike. **Вели́кие умы́ схо́дятся.** [Great minds converge.] (**У дурако́в мы́сли схо́дятся.** [Fools' thoughts converge.])

D21. Nothing succeeds like success. **Кому́ поведётся, у того́ и пету́х несётся.** [If someone is lucky, then even his rooster lays eggs.]

D22. One rotten apple spoils the barrel. **Одна́ парши́вая овца́ всё ста́до по́ртит.** [One mangy sheep spoils the whole herd.]

D23. The early bird catches the worm. / Early to bed and early to rise makes a man healthy, wealthy and wise. **Ра́нняя пта́шка носо́к прочища́ет, а по́здняя гла́зки продира́ет. / Кто ра́но встаёт, тому́ Бог даёт.** [An early bird is cleaning its beak, but a late one is rubbing its eyes.] / [God gives to him who gets up early.]

D24. Well begun is half done. **Хоро́шее нача́ло — полови́на де́ла. / Хоро́шее нача́ло полде́ла откача́ло.** [A good beginning is half the job. / A good beginning accomplished a half.]

D25. When the cat is away, the mice will play. **Чем чёрт не шу́тит, когда Бог спит.** [When God is asleep, there are no tricks devil won't play.] (**На то и щу́ка в мо́ре, что́бы кара́сь не дрема́л.** [The pike lives in the sea so that the (European small) carp does not slumber (that is, remains alert)] is similar in logic, but the message of the Russian proverb is completely different. It says that danger and other unpleasant things in life are good for teaching those who are naive.)

Fig. 5-11.

Part 3. Contexts of Spectacle

Нина: *В вашей пьесе трудно играть. В ней нет живых лиц.*

Треплев: *Живые лица! Надо изображать жизнь не такою, как она есть, и не такою, как должна быть, а такою, как она представляется в мечтах.*

Антон Чехов

Nina: *Your play's hard to act. There are no living people in it.*

Treplev: *Living people! We should show life neither as it is nor as it ought to be, but as we see it in our dreams.*

Anton Chekhov

<table>
<tr><td>

Theater in Language

</td><td>

6

</td><td>

Теа́тр

</td></tr>
</table>

Eloise M. Boyle

<table>
<tr><td>

</td><td>

</td></tr>
</table>

«Теа́тр начина́ется с ве́шалки» "Theater begins in the cloakroom" (in other words, the theatrical experience begins the moment one enters the theater)—the words are attributed to Stanislavsky, the sentiment is understood by all theater-loving Russians. The rather dry definition of the word "theater" **теа́тр** in the standard Russian dictionary by Ozhegov: "the art of representing theatrical works on stage" **иску́сство изображе́ния драмати́ческих произведе́ний на сце́не** does very little to convey the importance of theater in Russian life and imagination. *Anything* going on in a theater (and the word **теа́тр** never refers to movie theaters) is **теа́тр:** plays, ballet, opera, operetta, spectacles of all kinds are theater. The theater is a place of transformation where a child can delight in the adventures of Puss in Boots **«Ко́т в сапога́х»**, an adolescent can suffer along with the lovers of "Valentin and Valentina" **«Валенти́н и Валенти́на»**, and where an adult could once see the Soviet reality he knew metamorphosed into Galileo's Italy—all at ticket prices well below those in any major American city. (Foreigners find these tickets an unbelieveable bargain, while the average Russian has a harder time affording a night out at the theater.)

Fig. 6-1.   Photo of a theater interior

Fig. 6-2.   Griboedov Canal

Going to the theater is one of the most cherished benefits of being a Russian city-dweller. Indeed, the buildings that are home to theatrical troupes are often the architectural focus of the main urban squares. Many Moscow and St. Petersburg theater buildings were declared architectural monuments at the moment of their completion. But even those that were hidden away in the cities' side streets or housed in spaces dedicated to mercantile enterprises were sought out by theatergoers of both cities. Although the theaters that stood on them have, in some cases, long vanished, many streets retain "stage names:" one of the side streets leading to Dynamo stadium in Moscow is **Театра́льная аллея**; in both Moscow and St. Petersburg one finds a Theater Square **Театра́льная пло́щадь;** one of St. Petersburg's bridges is Theater Bridge **Театра́льный мост**, which, appropriately, crosses Griboedov Canal **кана́л Грибое́дова.** Art Theater Passage **Прое́зд Худо́жественного теа́тра** and Theater Passage **Театра́льный прое́зд** are well-known downtown Moscow streets.

The history of professional theater in Russia is not long when compared to that of Europe: while the plays of Shakespeare, Lope de Vega and Moliere were being produced on the stages of the continent, in Russia the only forms of theater that existed were folk theater (based on holiday and festival traditions or folk tales), mystery plays **мисте́рии** performed on religious themes, and with the approval of the Orthodox church, and school plays (staged at the Cadet Academy of Petersburg, and the Slavonic-Greek-Latin Academy **Славя́но-гре́ко-лати́нская акаде́мия** in Moscow).

Fig. 6-3.   Petrushka

The most famous Russian folk play is a puppet show, "Petrushka" **Петрýшка,** which was a favorite at town fairs during the Butter Festival (Maslenitsa) **Мácленица.** Maslenitsa was a carnival based on pagan celebrations, and occurred the week immediately preceding Lent. Large quantities of food were consumed during this week, with the emphasis on blini (Russian pancakes) and meat and dairy products. The blini symbolized the sun, and meat and dairy products were forbidden during Lent. Petrushka is a cheerful, brave, resourceful hero who always manages to get the upper hand over his foes. (Stravinsky and Diaghilev produced a sumptuous ballet of the same name, first performed in 1911 by the Ballets Russes.)

The very first actors in Russia were the skomorokhi **скоморóхи**: itinerant singers, musicians and comedians who wandered ancient Rus'. True professional theater came to Russia from the outside, that is, from Europe. But in the minds of the modern Russians, theater is as home-grown as the beets in borshch. The titles of favorite plays are often taken from well-worn proverbs, and many of the expressions used by people every day are from Russian drama. The speakers of the language may have forgotten the specifics, but the frequency with which these titles and citations are encountered indicates that theater is viewed by Russians as their own.

Affordable ticket prices and subsidized theatrical ventures in the former Soviet Union did much to promote theatergoing in major Russian cities, and one may be astonished at how much more frequently cultured Russians attend the theater than their Western counterparts. For this reason it is useful to know something about the theaters of Moscow and Petersburg, and the playwrights, directors and actors referred to in everyday speech. The language of theater is also used metaphorically (we have the same thing in English when we say, for instance, something happens "behind the scenes" or that a politician is waiting "in the wings"). But first, a little history.

In 1664 the first professional comedy was put on at the home of the English ambassador in Moscow, with a troupe invited from the West. It was a modest spectacle, with boyars sitting right on the stage and the tsar and his attendants in uncomfortable proximity to the actors. In 1672, in the Moscow palace

Fig. 6-4.   A. Sumarokov

пала́ты of the boyar Miloslavskii, the first space specifically designated for
theatrical productions (где быть коме́дии) was created. In 1702 the performance venue was moved to the public sector: a poorly located comedy hall
комеди́йная храми́на was established on Red Square by order of Peter the
Great. Attendance was poor much of the year, chiefly because the spectators
did not wish to slog through the muck to get to the theater, especially in mud
season распу́тица, and the church opposed it. Boyars and titled gentry took up
the running of theatrical enterprises until Alexander Petrovich Sumarokov
Сумаро́ков (the father of modern Russian drama) was named the first director
of the Russian Theater in 1756.

    Early productions on the Russian stage were (often very poor) translations
of foreign plays, plays centering on Russian history and military triumphs, or
those based on Biblical stories—not an auspicious beginning. Moreover, actors
and actresses were seen as little more than scoundrels and prostitutes (as they
often were in the West until recently), and the evil influence of the western secular tradition was at once a titillating inducement to attend a production and a
cautionary tale of what could happen to Russian youth if allowed too much access to outside trends. Soon, though, Lomonosov, Trediakovsky and Sumarokov all began to write original works for the stage, and it was during the 18th
century that Russian drama began to develop. The following two centuries saw
the establishment of professional theaters and the emergence of great
dramatists, many of whom are discussed below.

THE THEATERS OF MOSCOW AND ST. PETERSBURG	МОСКО́ВСКИЕ И ПЕТЕРБУ́РГСКИЕ ТЕА́ТРЫ
«А что идёт в … ?»	"What's on at the …?"

When making plans for an evening out, the question one most frequently hears is "What's playing at …?" «А что идёт в …»? with the name of the theater dropped into the end of the question. Reading the newspaper "Leisure Time in Moscow" «Досу́г в Москве́» is one way to find out, and the reply might start "At the Mossovet there's …" «В Моссове́те идёт …».

1. Moscow

Of the 35 or so professional dramatic, comedic and musical theaters in Moscow, most can be named by any educated Russian familiar with theater, but a few of them stand out as the chief attractions in a city known for the breadth and depth of its theatrical traditions. They are the Bolshoi **Большо́й**, the Maly **Ма́лый**, the Moscow Art Theater **Моско́вский Худо́жественный академи́ческий теа́тр им. Че́хова (МХАТ)**, the Taganka **Тага́нка,** the Mossoviet **Моссове́т (Госуда́рственный академи́ческий теа́тр им. Моссове́та),** the Lenkom **Ленко́м (Моско́вский теа́тр им. Ле́нинского комсомо́ла),** the Sovremennik (The Contemporary) **Совреме́нник**, the Theater of Satire **Теа́тр сати́ры**, the Yermolova Theater **Теа́тр им. Ермо́ловой**, The Mayakovsky Theater **Теа́тр им. Маяко́вского,** and the Theater of Miniatures **Теа́тр миниатю́р** (just what this is will be explained below**).** Among the theaters dedicated to younger viewers, three are remembered with affection by adults: the Theater for the Young Spectator **Моско́вский теа́тр ю́ного зри́теля** (universally simply known as **ТЮЗ**), the Puppet Theater **Центра́льный академи́ческий теа́тр ку́кол (Ку́кольный теа́тр)** and the Children's Musical Theater **Моско́вский госуда́рственный де́тский музыка́льный теа́тр.** There are many smaller theaters making a name for themselves in post-Soviet Moscow thanks to the talents of their artistic directors: the Theater on Malaia Bronnaia **Теа́тр на Ма́лой Бро́нной** (a well-established Moscow institution)**,** the Theater at the Nikitskii Gate **Теа́тр у Ники́тских воро́т** and the Theater of Roman Viktiuk **Теа́тр Рома́на Виктюка́** (recently called "passé" by one Moscow critic). Until recently, some of the most widely-discussed theatrical events took place in the theater-studios **теа́тры-сту́дии** of Moscow and St. Petersburg.

The Bolshoi Theater is discussed in Chapter 7.

In the same way as the Bolshoi is known for spectacular opera and ballet performances, the Maly is universally recognized for its dramatic art. Located just across from the Bolshoi, the Maly opened its doors in 1824, three months earlier than its famous neighbor. The unofficial name for the Maly is "The House of Ostrovsky" («Дом Остро́вского»), so called because of the playwright's long and fruitful relationship with the theater. Alexander Nikolaevich Ostrovsky wrote around 40 plays, realistic examinations of the injustices and

Fig. 6-5.   Maly Theater

hardships of merchant and middle-class life. When someone suggests going to the Maly, you can be sure you will see a classic Russian play, performed in the tradition of Russian realistic acting.

The Moscow Art Theater began in 1898, when Konstantin Stanislavsky and Vladimir Nemirovich-Danchenko produced their first play in the Hermitage theater in Moscow. Most older Russians also know that the idea for the theater was born in a marathon 18-hour meeting at the Slavic Bazaar **Славя́нский База́р**, a great old Russian restaurant. The two playwrights most immediately associated with the first days of MKhAT (originally **МХТ**, later **МХАТ**) are Anton Chekhov **Че́хов** and Maksim Gorky **Го́рький**.

Fig. 6-6.   MKhAT (original building)

The repertoire consists mainly of Russian works, classic and contemporary, but European and American authors have also been produced at the Moscow Art Theater. The theater currently is housed in two buildings; the new one was built in 1973. In fact, the Moscow Art Theater is now two "art theaters:" the Gorky Art Theater, which broke away in 1987, and the Chekhov Art Theater. Oleg Efremov **Ефрéмов** took the reins of the theater in 1970, and tried to broaden the theater's repertoire by championing young playwrights at the same time that he established a permanent playbill of classic works. Efremov's tenure at MKhAT has not been trouble-free, but he and the professionals of MKhAT **мхáтовцы** struggle to find new means of expression in this era of belt-tightening.

Founded in 1964, the Taganka **Тагáнка** has been the setting for remarkable creativity and stormy controversy its entire life. Yuri Liubimov **Любúмов** was appointed director in 1964, and was stripped of his Soviet citizenship and exiled in 1984. In the intervening years the Taganka was one of the most innovative, electric performance venues in Russia. The Taganka came to be known as the place for "prose theater:" many of its stagings were theatrical adaptations of classic and contemporary prose works.

Among the best-known of the plays based on novels and short stories transformed for the stage by Liubimov and his collaborators are *Hero of Our Time* **«Герóй нáшего врéмени»** (Lermontov), *Crime and Punishment* **«Преступлéние и наказáние»** (Dostoevsky), *Master and Margarita* **«Мáстер и Маргарúта»** (Bulgakov), *Wooden Horses* **«Деревя́нные кóни»** (Abramov), *Ten Days that Shook the World* **«Дéсять дней, котóрые потряслú мир»** (based on the book by John Reed; adapted by Liubimov) and *The Exchange* **«Обмéн»** (Trifonov). Liubimov as director sought to break away from the stagnation, as he saw it, of the realistic tradition of Russian theater. His productions

Fig. 6-7.   The Taganka (new building)

were known for their unflinching examination of contemporary Soviet life, yet they were graced with a lyricism and creativity unknown since Meyerhold (see below): in Liubimov's theater actors did not merely recite words: they often danced, sang, and played musical instruments. By far the most well-known and

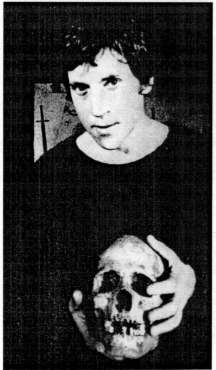

beloved actor of the Taganka troupe was Vladimir Vysotsky, a hard-living bard of the 60s and 70s who died prematurely in 1980. He is best remembered for the captivating charisma of his Hamlet, Galileo and Svidrigailov (from Dostoevsky's *Crime and Punishment* «Преступле́ние и наказа́ние»), and for his talent as a poet, singer, and musician. (See Chapter 7 for more information on Vysotsky). The most well-known actress of the Taganka troupe was Alla Demidova, famed for her fiercely intellectual and graceful performances. Liubimov returned from exile in 1989, and since then the Taganka has endured many critical attacks for not being the daring, innovative theater laboratory it used to be. In fact, just about everyone who loves this theater bemoans the deterioration of the troupe into warring camps, which began when Liubimov was ousted. Still, tickets are hard to get.

Fig. 6-8.   Vysotsky as Hamlet

Founded in 1923, the Mossovet **Теа́тр им. Моссове́та** now has two stages, a small studio theater where interesting contemporary works are produced, and the larger auditorium, in which extremely popular costume dramas can be seen. Boris Milgram **Ми́льграм** is the director most closely associated today with the Mossovet.

The Theater of the Lenin Komsomol, under the leadership of Mark Zakharov **Заха́ров** since 1973, is universally known as the Lenkom **Ленко́м.** Zakharov and the Lenkom produced the first Russian rock-operas (*The Star and Death of Joaquin Mureta* «**Звезда́ и смерть Хоаки́на Мурье́ты»**, *Iunona and Avos* «**Юно́на и Аво́сь»**). Its themes reflect the most pressing concerns of young people in contemporary Russia. Some of the actors who play at the Lenkom are also very well known because of their movie roles: Oleg Yankovskii **Янко́вский**, Inna Churikova **Чу́рикова**, Alexander Abdulov **Абду́лов**, Nikolai Karachentsev **Кара́ченцев**.

Fig. 6-9.   The Sovremennik

The Sovremennik **Современник** began life as a studio theater in 1956. Founded by a group of graduates of MKhAT, among them "the Olegs **Олеги**" (the director Oleg Efremov and actor Oleg Tabakov), the theater made its debut with a bold production of V. Rozov's *Eternally Living* **«Вéчно живы́е»**. Currently under the dynamic leadership of Galina Volchek (a long-time director at the theater, she took over in 1972), the Sovremennik continues to satisfy theatergoers with its productions of previously forbidden works such as Evgeniia Ginzburg's *Into the Whirlwind* **«Крутóй маршру́т»**. The lead actress of the theater, Marina Neelova **Неёлова** is famous for her portrayal of Ginzburg. It is well-worth attending the Sovremennik, whose troupe in the mid-1990s completed a triumphant tour in New York, to view the building itself, which used to be the movie theater "Coliseum" **Колизéй**.

Founded as a studio theater in 1925, the current Yermolova theater **Теáтр им. Ермóловой** dates from 1937. The Yermolova Theater has a mixed repertoire: Russian and Western classics as well as contemporary plays by native and foreign authors. The theater is located right in the center of town (Tverskaia St. **ул. Тверскáя, 5**, next door to the enormous Hotel Intourist) and may be thought of as much for its location as for what goes on inside on the stage.

The Moscow Theater for the Young Spectator **ТЮЗ** is hailed for its original staging of children's classics. The beloved actress Lidiia Kniazeva **Кня́зева** strode the boards here for many years. Nowadays the theater provides space for the innovative staging of Kama Ginkas **Гúнкас**, a very well-known director.

Fig. 6-10.   The Clock outside the Puppet Theater

The brainchild of S.V. Obraztsov, who founded the theater in 1931, the Puppet Theater **Центра́льный теа́тр ку́кол** produces plays for adults and children alike. The shows are witty, lyrical and often satirical (the long-running *Unusual Concert* **«Необыкнове́нный конце́рт»** continues to delight audiences). The joy of this theater experience begins before one has even set foot inside: the facade is graced by an enormous clock and at 12 noon wild animals and birds come to life to toll the hours.

The Children's Musical Theater **Де́тский музыка́льный теа́тр** was established in 1965. In 1979 a new building was erected and its foyer is beautiful: artists from Palekh **Па́лех** decorated the panels with operatic and fairy tale scenes.

Several other Moscow theaters deserve mention: the dramatic theaters named for Yevgenii Vakhtangov **Вахта́нгов** and Vladimir Mayakovsky **Маяко́вский**; and one musical theater, known simply as The Operetta Theater **Теа́тр опере́тты.** Finally, there is what claims to be the only gypsy theater in the world: The "Romaine" Theater **Теа́тр «Ромэ́н».**

2. St. Petersburg

Fig. 6-11.   The BDT

The Bolshoi Drama (Tovstonogov) Theater **Рýсский академи́ческий Большо́й драмати́ческий теáтр им. Товстоно́гова (БДТ**; BDT) was formerly the Gorky theater. This venerable St. Petersburg establishment recently was renamed in honor of its late director, Georgii Tovstonogov, probably the most well-known name in Petersburg theater for decades. Tovstonogov was instrumental in forming one of the most talented acting troupes in all of Russian theater. The theater is known for, and came under governmental scrutiny because of, its unorthodox interpretations of the classic plays of Griboedov, Chekhov, and Gorky. Many actors who later became popular in films started their careers at the BDT: Innokenty Smoktunovskii, **Смоктуно́вский**, who died in 1994, Sergei Iurskii, **Ю́рский,** the late Yefim Kopelian **Копеля́н,** and Alisa Freindlikh **Али́са Фре́йндлих**.

The Aleksandrinskii Theater **Александри́нский** (formerly the Pushkin Drama Theater **Теáтр дрáмы им. А.С. Пýшкина)** is a monumental building and home to productions of the Russian classics, as well as plays by contemporary Russian playwrights.

At the Open Theater on Vladimirskii Prospekt **Откры́тый теáтр на Влади́мирском проспéкте** (the former Lensovet Theater **Т еáтр им. Ленсовéта**) you will see interesting productions of Russian plays, and while the classics are featured in the repertoire, the Lensovet is committed to staging works by contemporary Russian and world authors.

Baltic House **Балти́йский дом** used to be called the Lenin Komsomol Theater **Ленингра́дский теа́тр им. Ле́нинского Комсомо́ла (Ленком)**, and it offers a varied repertoire, the legacy of the late director Gennadii Oporkov, who favored psychological drama with much conflict. His leading lady for many years was the actress Larisa Malevannaia, who also performed at the Sovremennik in Moscow.

The word miniature **миниатю́ра** in the theatrical sense refers to sketches, and the Leningrad Miniature Theater (The Raikin Theater of Miniatures) **Теа́тр миниатю́р Арка́дия Ра́йкина (Ленингра́дский)** was famous for its variety shows. Arkadii Raikin did not formally found this theater, but his name has been associated with it since his debut there in the late 1930s, and he became its artistic director in 1942. (The theater moved to Moscow in 1981, but is now known as the Hermitage Theater **Теа́тр Эрмита́ж**.) While the older generation remembers his stage work, more recent generations know Raikin from his numerous television appearances. (See Chapter 9 for more information on Raikin.)

3. Studio Theaters   Теа́тры-сту́дии

During the 1970s and 1980s, those who loved the theater tried to get a ticket to one of the studio theaters, and the experience of sitting almost nose to nose with the actors in a cramped, dark apartment-house basement is still a vibrant memory for many Moscow and St. Petersburg intellectuals.

The studio theaters **теа́тры-сту́дии** of Moscow and Leningrad began to appear as early as the 1950s, but peaked in popularity and creativity in the late 1970s and early 1980s. They are significant in Russian theatrical history for their staging of officially banned (or at least frowned-upon) texts such as Evgenii Shvarts's *The Dragon* **«Драко́н»**, Eugene Ionesco's *Rhinoceros* **«Носоро́г»**, and Liudmila Petrushevskaia's plays (among them *Music Lessons* **«Уро́ки му́зыки»**). Because the theaters were so small and their audience sizes so limited, the studio theaters were often able to elude the censors. The directors of these theaters had to settle for converting basements, libraries, and corners of Houses of Culture **Дома́ культу́ры** into intimate stages that reflected their lack of funds and were maintained in defiant contrast to the lavish interiors of the official state theaters, but the intimacy of the performance space tore down the barriers between performer and spectator. Despite the many technical inadequacies of the productions, audiences flocked to them, and the studio theaters gained a reputation for their courage in striving to create in the face of financial hardship and bureaucratic bullying. The Russian word for this type of theater is **самоде́ятельный**, and it actually means "amateur," and, in fact, this form of theater served as a vital workshop for future professional actors who studied under the many veteran actors and directors who dedicated years to these theaters. Studios like Leningrad's Blue Bridge **Си́ний мост**, Saturday **Суббо́та** or Four Little Windows **Четы́ре око́шка**, Moscow's Man **Челове́к**,

Studio-Theater at Iugo-Zapad **Теа́тр-сту́дия на Юго-За́паде**, and The Krasnaia Presnia Studio-theater **Теа́тр-сту́дия на Кра́сной Пре́сне** are all examples of this "amateur" theater. Participants of these theaters, known as **студи́йцы,** often performed many jobs around the theater, one night making tea, another cleaning up after the audience had gone home. Many now-famous directors, among them the late Roman Bykov (later a film director), Mark Zakharov (of the Lenkom), Mark Rozovskii (Theater at the Nikitskii Gate) and Roman Viktiuk (The Viktiuk Theater) got their start in the studio theater movement that emerged from the Moscow University Student Theater club. The loosening, and eventual collapse of cultural controls first in the USSR, then in Russia, led to the decline or extinction of many studios, as previously banned works were taken over by the mainstream, more financially solvent theaters. Actors and directors were lured away to other, more profitable venues. But the studio theaters persevere and remain in the Russian mind a courageous, creative, collective effort.

Certainly Moscow and St. Petersburg do not have exclusive ownership of good theater. The theater carries on in many other Russian cities such as Novosibirsk, Omsk, Nizhny Novgorod, but Moscow and St. Petersburg are its heart. Theater companies from the former Republics of Ukraine, Uzbekistan, and Georgia, among others, frequently perform acclaimed productions in the Russian capital.

ТЕАТР НА ЮГО-ЗАПАДЕ

Ад – это другие («Недоразумение» А.Камю, «Взаперти» Ж.-П.Сартра). Режиссер В.Белякович (3'10'', 1 антракт). 60 р.
пт 3 марта, 19.00

ПРЕМЬЕРА **Братья** С.Мрожека. Режиссер В.Белякович (2'00'', 1 антракт). 100 р.
чт 9 марта, 19.00

ПРЕМЬЕРА **Калигула** А.Камю. Режиссер В.Белякович (2'00'', 1 антракт). 100 р.
вс 12 марта, 19.00

Макбет У.Шекспира. Режиссер В.Белякович (3'00'', 1 антракт). 70 р.
вт 29 февраля, 19.00

Мастер и Маргарита М.Булгакова. Режиссер В.Белякович (3'30'', 1 антракт). 100 р.
пн 6 марта, 19.00

Слуга двух господ К.Гольдони. Режиссер В.Белякович (2'30'', 1 антракт). 70 р.
ср 1 марта, 19.00

Собаки К.Сергиенко. Режиссер В.Белякович (2'00'', 1 антракт). 60 р.
сб 11 марта, 14.00

Сон в летнюю ночь У.Шекспира. Режиссер В.Белякович (3'00'', 1 антракт). 100 р.
сб 4, вт 7 марта, 19.00

Трактирщица К.Гольдони. Режиссер В.Белякович (1'45'', 1 антракт). 60 р.
ср 8 марта, 19.00

ПРЕМЬЕРА **Три сестры** А.Чехова. Режиссер В.Белякович (2'00'', 1 антракт). 70 р.
пт 10 марта, 19.00

Щи В.Сорокина. Режиссер В.Белякович (2'00'', 1 антракт). 70 р.
чт 2 марта, 19.00

ПРЕМЬЕРА **Dostoevsky-Trip** В.Сорокина. Режиссер В.Белякович (2'00'', 1 антракт). 70 р.
вс 5 марта, 19.00

Fig. 6-12. Listing from Iugo-zapad

DIRECTORS AND ACTORS   РЕЖИССЁРЫ И АКТЁРЫ

In the Russian theater, there are certain names everyone knows. Directors, especially, have left their imprint on the Russian memory: Russians know stage and screen directors as well as they do actors and actresses. Konstantin Stanislavsky **Константи́н Станисла́вский** and Vsevolod Meyerhold **Все́волод Мейерхо́льд** are the best-known Russian directors. Although both men broke with the theatrical traditions of the 19th century, which were based on the "star system," **актёрский теа́тр** their philosophies and methods completely diverged from one another.

Stanislavsky strove above all for authenticity in the theater, and trained his actors to experience true emotions on stage, to *live* the character. The term "emotional realism" best sums up Stanislavsky's system (not to be confused with the "Stanislavsky method" which was formulated by pupils of Stanislavsky only later).

If Stanislavsky's theater was one of internals, then Meyerhold can be said to have been interested in all the external aspects of the theatrical experience. The director emphasized spectacle over historical accuracy, he blurred, and even destroyed the boundaries between the stage and the auditorium by bringing the performance space right out into the hall, and he concentrated on training his actors. Meyerhold was more interested in the development of the actor's ability to control his voice and body through gymnastic-like movement than he was in emotional verisimilitude.

Fig. 6-13.   K. Stanislavsky

Fig. 6-14.   V. Meyerhold

Fig. 6-15.   Meyerhold's production of *The Forest*, 1924

Often Meyerhold resorted to the techniques of the commedia dell'arte (a type of comedy that relies on improvisation from a plot outline and stock characters), or the puppet show in staging his spectacles. Therefore, if a director is hailed as the "new Stanislavsky," one can be sure his productions will be true-to-life and intensely emotional. If someone is called a student of Meyerhold, visual and physical elements of the play will stand out.

Another figure, the actor and director Evgenii Bagrationovich Vakhtangov **Вахта́нгов** is the best-known and by most accounts most brilliant director of MKhAT early this century. He was committed to modern works, contemporary stagings of classic works, and tried to forge a unity between the artists and the spectators. A theater on the Arbat (in Moscow), which he founded (in 1921), is named for him and perpetuates his fame.

Fig. 6-16.   The Vakhtangov Theater

Many of today's most popular directors deserve credit for weathering the stagnation of the 1970s and 1980s and emerging as theater managers on their own. Among the most widely discussed are "the Marks" «Ма́рки»: Mark Zakharov at the Lenkom, who tapped into the youth market with his rock operas, and Mark Rozovskii of the Theater at the Nikitskii Gate, whose eccentric, often gifted reworkings of classic literature are often discussed by theater-going Muscovites. Oleg Yefremov had a stormy tenure at MKhAT. Boris Milgram at the Mossovet and Kama Ginkas at The Theater for Young Spectators are critically acclaimed. Roman Viktiuk is credited for bringing the sexual revolution and overt homosexual themes to Russian theater.

In the history of Russian theater, many actors and actresses left indelible impressions. The first great Russian actor was Mikhail Shchepkin **Щéпкин** (1788–1863), who began his career as a serf actor. His popularity was so enormous that when his owner, Count Volkenstein, did not want to grant Shchepkin his freedom, a special performance was organized in Poltava to raise the money to buy the actor's liberty. Shchepkin is considered the father of Russian realistic acting.

Mariia Yermolova **Ермóлова** (1853–1928) began acting at 13 years of age, and ended her career as a distinguished Grande Dame of the Maly Theater.

Fig. 6-17. M. Shchepkin

Fig. 6-18. V. Serov, *Portrait of M. Yermolova*

В. Ф. Комиссаржевская в ролях: 1. Роза. 2. Клерхен. 3. Лариса. 4. Нина Заречная. 5. Варя. 6. Беатриса.

Fig. 6-19.   V. Komissarzhevskaia

Vera Komissarzhevskaia **Комиссарже́вская** (1864–1910) was an extremely talented actress who captivated audiences. She began her own theater in 1904, and worked for a time with Meyerhold. Mikhail Chekhov **Че́хов** (1891–1955), nephew of the great writer, was one of the most popular of all Russian actors. He's been called an actor of the grotesque, and a "lyric comic," and in general is known for the eccentricity of his acting art.

1. М. А. Чехов. 2—3. М. А. Чехов в ролях: 2. Эрик XIV. 3. Мальволио.

Fig. 6-20.   M. Chekhov

В. И. Качалов в ролях: 1. Тузенбах. 2. Вершинин. 3. Захар Бардин. 4. Барон.

В. И. Качалов в ролях: 1. Юлий Цезарь. 2. Иоганн Фокерат. 3. Чтец от автора «Воскресение».

Fig. 6-21.　V. Kachalov

In the 20th century Vasilii Ivanovich Kachalov **Кача́лов**, who played over 55 roles at the Moscow Art Theater, stands out among stage stars. He was known for his enormous presence and charm, the musicality of his voice, and his exceptional artistry. He combined emotion and intellect, and conveyed the psychological and moral conflicts of the characters he played. In addition to his performances at MKhAT, Kachalov wrote and starred in his own literary-musical evenings.

Whereas in the past actors and directors often spent their entire careers at one theater, today's economic and artistic situation, with few exceptions, has led to a generation of nomadic theater professionals. Pinpointing today's favorites, then, becomes a more difficult task. Among the actors and actresses singled out by the public are Konstantin Raikin and Natalia Vdovina of the Satirikon, Mikhail Kozakov and Marina Zudina (who acted at various theaters), Inna Churikova and Leonid Bronevoi of the Lenkom, Tatiana Peltser, Mikhail Shirvindt and the late Andrei Mironov of the Satire Theater, and Alexander Lazarev and Svetlana Nemoliaeva of the Mayakovsky. Several stage actors have gone on to fame in films, among them Oleg Tabakov and Margarita Terekhova, who made a splash in the film **«Зе́ркало»** *The Mirror* and is hugely popular among both stage and film fans.

PLAYS AND CHARACTERS   ПЬÉСЫ И ГЕРÓИ

"What are you laughing at? You're laughing at yourselves!" **Чемý смеётесь? Над собóю смеётесь!»**

Seeing themselves on the stage has always had an unsettling effect on Russians and the Russian establishment: from the delayed and censored publication of *Woe From Wit* **«Гóре от умá»** to the scandalized protests against *The Inspector General* **«Ревизóр»** to the repression of Yuri Liubimov's Taganka Theater, Russian authorities have had an uncertain relationship with theater. Yet always and everywhere the Russian audience has recognized truths being revealed by the greatest playwrights on the stage, and these pronouncements on human nature lie at the heart of many of the theatrical quotes found in common Russian parlance.

The question of which plays the average well-educated Russian is likely to know well enough to quote is at once an easy and very difficult one to answer. Certainly those Russians educated under the Soviet system would know plays from the required reading list in school: **Прогрáмма по литератýре—едíная для всех школ.** But the recent dissolution of the Soviet Union has plunged the educational system into uncertainty and even chaos, therefore one must state that the educated Russians interviewed for this project were without exception those who received their schooling under the Soviet regime.

Griboedov's *Woe from Wit*   «Гóре от умá»

Fig. 6-22.   Playbill from a recent production of *Woe from Wit*

Far and away, the play Russians quote most often is *Woe From Wit,* begun in 1820 and completed in 1824. It was first staged at the Maly in 1831, but the publication of the text of the play was permitted by the censor only in 1860. *Woe from Wit* is a scathing satire on the morals of Moscow society during the first quarter of the 19th century. The title of the play itself, **«Го́ре от ума́»**, implies both noble suffering as a result of following one's intellect and conscience, and a slight wariness of all things intellectual. The hero is Aleksander Andreevich Chatskii **Ча́цкий**. Chatskii's impassioned rhetoric is the best feature of the play, and his speeches have produced the most common citations (22 in all). *Woe from Wit* is written in iambic lines of varying length, but, far from sounding like stuffy poetry, the language is lively and natural.

The action takes place in a single day in the house of the wealthy, powerful Pavel Afanasievich Famusov **Фа́мусов** (Famusovs are bureaucrats through and through). The main characters are Famusov, his daughter Sofia **Со́фия**, his secretary Molchalin **Молча́лин** (the "silent one" [from **молча́ть,** "to be silent"]), an old friend of the family, Chatskii **Чацкий**, one of Sofia's suitors, Colonel Skalozub **Скалозу́б** (**ска́лить зу́бы** means "to bare one's teeth," "to smile"; if you hear someone referred to as a real Skalozub, you know you are dealing with an ignoramus, a crude, loud-mouthed soldier), and Repetilov **Репети́лов** (from the Latin *repetitio,* "repetition or rehearsal"; a Repetilov is a layabout, a liar and a braggart, one who repeats other's words). The hero, Chatskii, returns home from an extended trip abroad to announce that he loves Sofia. He finds, to his chagrin, that she loves Molchalin. Sofia's father, Famusov, would like Sofia to marry well, and although he feels some loyalty to Chatskii as an old friend of the family, he is alarmed by Chatskii's contempt for the aristocracy, the government, and hypocrisy of any kind. The action of the play follows two lines: Sofia tries to hide her relationship with Molchalin, and the cast of characters behaves in a manner that bears out all Chatskii's criticism of Russian society. This blend of bedroom farce and social satire quickly became and remains a favorite of Russians, so much so that the following list of quotations from the play are known and used by Russian speakers in their everyday speech.

Act I

🔊 **6-1**   I.1   "Lord, spare us the worst of disasters, the master's wrath and, just as much, his love." The maid, Liza, after fending off one of Famusov's clumsy attempts to seduce her. **Мину́й нас пу́ще всех печа́лей/ И ба́рский гнев, и ба́рская любо́вь.**

🔊 **6-2**   I.2   "My friend, couldn't you possibly stroll in some different direction?" Famusov, upon catching Molchalin near Sofia's bedroom. **Мой друг, нельзя́ ли для прогу́лок/Пода́льше вы́брать закоу́лок?**

🔊 **6-3**   I.3   "He headed for one room, ended up in another." (Russians say this upon finding themselves in the wrong place.) Sofia to her father as an explanation of what Molchalin was doing near her room early in the morning. ” **Шёл в ко́мнату, попа́л в другу́ю.**

I.4 “The way I do things is: I sign things and they’re out of my mind. 🔊 **6-4** Famusov’s unwitting revelation of the feeble workings of his intellect. ” **Обы́чай мой тако́й:/ Подпи́сано, так с плеч доло́й.**

I.5 “Blessed is he who believes that life is easy!” Chatskii, upon seeing 🔊 **6-5** Sofia again after their long separation. **Блаже́н, кто ве́рует, тепло́ ему́ на све́те!**

I.6 “Where is it better?” “Wherever we’re not.” One of the most fa- 🔊 **6-6** mous exchanges of the play: Chatskii condemns Moscow for its obsession with balls and European fads, so that when Sofia asks, “Where is it better?” Chatskii gives this sarcastic reply. —**Где ж лу́чше? —Где нас нет.**

I.7 “Even the very smoke of home is sweet and pleasant!” Chatskii, 🔊 **6-7** explaining the pull of his native land. **И дым оте́чества нам сла́док и прия́тен!**

I.8 “In more volume, but with a cheaper price tag.” Chatskii’s con- 🔊 **6-8** demnation of cheaply hired at-home tutors. **Число́м побо́лее, цено́ю подеше́вле.**

I.9 “A mix of French and Nizhnii Novgorod.” Chatskii’s ironic 🔊 **6-9** characterization of the Francomania that swept Russian high so- ciety, to the extent that Russian aristocrats could not even speak their own language. (Today this phrase describes uncouth or clumsy speech.) **Смеше́нье языко́в францу́зского с нижегоро́дским.**

I.10 “Bound for important places/He’ll go far.” Chatskii’s reluctant 🔊 **6-10** prediction about Molchalin’s future success. **А впро́чем, он дойдёт до степене́й изве́стных**

I.11 “O Lord Almighty, what a burden it is to have a grown-up 🔊 **6-11** daughter!” Famusov. **Что за коми́ссия, Созда́тель,/Быть взро́слой до́чери отцо́м!**

Act II

II.1 “With feeling, expression and vigor.” Famusov asking his servant, 🔊 **6-12** Petrushka **Петру́шка,** to read aloud what’s on the week’s calendar. **[С] чу́вством, с то́лком, с расстано́вкой.**

II.2 “Just try to philosophize—it’ll turn your head!” Famusov’s reaction 🔊 **6-13** to his social duties. **Пофилосо́фствуй—ум вскружи́тся!**

II.3 “I’d gladly serve, but subservience makes me sick.” Chatskii’s 🔊 **6-14** reaction to Famusov’s suggestion that he get himself a civil service job. **Служи́ть бы рад, прислу́живаться то́шно.**

II.4 “The tradition is recent but I can hardly believe it!” Chatskii is 🔊 **6-15** appalled at Famusov’s explanation that fawning and obsequiousness gets one ahead in life. **Свежо́ преда́ние, а ве́рится с трудо́м!**

🔊 **6-16**   II.5   "Oh! The things he says! And he talks like he writes!" Famusov. He is alarmed at Chatskii's speeches. **Что говори́т! И говори́т, как пи́шет!**

🔊 **6-17**   II.6   "Hardly anyone in my department is not related to me: they're all nephews and second cousins." Famusov, trying to flatter Skalozub by insisting they are related. **При мне служа́щие чужи́е очень ре́дки / Всё бо́льше сёстрины, своя́ченицы де́тки.**

🔊 **6-18**   II.7   "One must help one's relatives." Famusov, on employing relatives. **Ну как не пораде́ть родно́му челове́чку?**

🔊 **6-19**   II.8   "Pretty far." Skalozub, explaining that one would have to travel far to find Moscow's equal. (This phrase now carries the meaning of something difficult to achieve.) **Диста́нции огро́много разме́ра.**

🔊 **6-20**   II.9,   "The door is always open to the invited and those who are not." **Дверь отперта́ для зва́ных и незва́ных.**

🔊 **6-21**   II.10   "Every word they utter is unnaturally made fancy." Famusov, continuing to try to flatter Skalozub, praises Muscovites. **Слове́чка в простоте́ не ска́жут, всё с ужи́мкой.**

🔊 **6-22**   II.11   "The houses and everything are brand-new" **Дома́ и всё на но́вый лад.** Famusov furthers extolls Moscow, to which Chatskii replies:

🔊 **6-23**   II.12   "Yes, the houses are new, but the prejudices are old." **Дома́ новы́, но предрассу́дки ста́ры.**

🔊 **6-24**   II.13   "And just who are my judges?" This is Chatskii's reply when Famusov tries to explain away the young man's scorn. **А су́дьи кто?**

🔊 **6-25**   II. 14   "Sharp tongues are more terrible than a pistol." Molchalin urges Sofia to guard her reputation against gossip. **Ах! Злы́е языки́ страшне́е пистоле́та!**

Act III

🔊 **6-26**   III.1   "He is not the hero of my novel." Sofia, explaining to Chatskii that she does not fancy Col. Skalozub. **Геро́й не моего́ рома́на.**

🔊 **6-27**   III.2   "One doesn't need intelligence to produce children." Chatskii, musing on Molchalin's obvious idiocy. **Чтоб име́ть дете́й, кому́ ума́ недостава́ло?**

🔊 **6-28**   III.3   "Moderation and punctuality" (This line was frequently cited by V.I. Lenin.) Molchalin enumerating his best qualities. He boasts that these two traits have repeatedly brought him rewards: **Уме́ренность и аккура́тность.**

🔊 **6-29**   III.4   "To mix these two crafts is the secret of master craftsmen; I am not one of their number." A moment of self-revelation by Chatskii: he is a proud, clever, but haughty and humorless young man, one perhaps too serious in all endeavors. **А сме́шивать два э́ти ремесла́ / Есть тьма иску́сников; я не из их числа́.**

III.5 "I do not read stupidities, least of all exemplary ones." Chatskii and 🔊 **6-30** Molchalin disagree on the merits of the work of a certain department head. **Я глу́постей не чтец / А пу́ще образцо́вых.**

III.6 "I dare not allow any independent thought at this stage in my ca- 🔊 **6-31** reer." Molchalin explains his way of getting ahead in his career. **В мои́ лета́ не до́лжно сметь / Своё сужде́ние име́ть.**

III.7 "If we are to cut down evil, we must gather up all books and burn 🔊 **6-32** them." Famusov's famous line (nowadays addressed to reaction- aries) is a reaction to the chaos caused by Sofia's malicious rumor that Chatskii is mad: **Уж ко́ли зло пресе́чь / Забра́ть все кни́ги бы да сжечь.**

III.8 Madame Khlestova **Хлёстова** (хлеста́ть "to whip"; **хлёсткий** 🔊 **6-33** "scathing, trenchant") and Famusov then argue over how many serfs Chatskii held: 400 by Famusov's "count" **в моём календаре́;** Khlestova counters with 300 and tells Famusov that "such accounts lie all the time" **Всё врут календари́.** (Nowadays the word **календа́рь** means "calendar" and this phrase is quoted in joking reference to someone's age.)

III.9 Famusov notes how awful Chatskii looks, to which the latter replies 🔊 **6-34** that he's suffered "a million torments" **мильо́н терза́ний.**

III.10 "A little Frenchy from Bordeaux" (a phrase now used to charac- 🔊 **6-35** terize arrogant foreigners) is Chatskii's condemnation of the Russian mania for all things French. **Францу́зик из Бордо́.**

III.11 Chatskii accuses the French of polluting Russian culture, of turning 🔊 **6-36** Russians into clowns who dress "against all reason and in defiance of the season" **рассу́дку вопреки́, напереко́р стихи́ям.**

Act IV

IV.1 "My devotion to you is a sort of illness." Repetilov tries to reassure 🔊 **6-37** Chatskii of his devotion to him. **А у меня́ к тебе́ влече́нье, род неду́га.**

IV.2 "Byron and, well, other important matters." Repetilov continues his 🔊 **6-38** ravings by telling Chatskii about his "English Club" and what they discuss there. **О Ба́йроне, ну об мате́рьях ва́жных.**

IV.3 "A sketch, a view and something or other." Repetilov quotes the 🔊 **6-39** poets who read for the club. **Отры́вок, взгляд и не́что.**

IV.4 "[He] speaks of the highest honesty." Repetilov continues his praise 🔊 **6-40** of the idiotic club members. These turns of phrase, all quite well- known to Russians, mark the buffoon of the piece. **Об че́стности высо́кой говори́т.**

IV.5 At Skalozub's entrance Repetilov immediately shifts his fawning to 🔊 **6-41** the Colonel, who says, threateningly, "I'll send the sergeant-major for your Voltaires" **... и вам фельдфе́беля в Волте́ры дам.**

◀))) 6-42   IV.6   Repetilov, deferring to the Colonel, reveals his base tastes: "Now vaudeville, there's something for you; all the rest is just nonsense." Despite this he continues to defend Chatskii. **Да, водеви́ль есть вещь, а про́чее всё гниль;**

◀))) 6-43   IV.7   "There's society's opinion for you!" This is one of Chatskii's most famous lines, reflecting our hero's complete contempt for the idiocy, hypocrisy and emptiness of Moscow society. **И вот обще́ственное мне́нье!**

◀))) 6-44   IV.8   "I am going to seek out a place in the world where an injured man can nurse his wounds" **Пойду́ иска́ть по све́ту, где оскорблённому есть чу́вству уголо́к.** Chatskii's disillusion is complete when he overhears Sofia declare her love for Molchalin, and learns that she, whom he had loved ardently and devotedly, is the very person who started the rumor of his madness.

◀))) 6-45   IV.9   "What will Princess Maria Alekseevna say!?" This line brings down the curtain, and is an unmistakable indictment of Russian society. Despite all Chatskii's preaching about hypocrisy, deceit and slavishness to fashion, all Famusov can worry about upon Chatskii's departure is what the nobles will say. **Ах! Бо́же мой! Что ста́нет говори́ть / Княги́ня Ма́рья Алексе́евна!**

Other Commonly Quoted Plays

Other playwrights commonly quoted in normal Russian speech include Pushkin, Fonvizin, Gogol', Ostrovsky, Chekhov, and Gorky. Pushkin's *Boris Godunov* **«Бори́с Годуно́в»** yields a quote about responsibility weighing heavily on one's shoulders: "Oh, how heavy you are, crown [lit. "cap"] of Monomakh!" **Ох, тяжела́ ты, ша́пка Монома́ха!** The final scene in the play contains the stage direction "The people are silent" **Наро́д безмо́лвствует** and this expression today is used when someone refuses to enter into a discussion. Fonvizin's *The Minor* **«Не́доросль»** yielded "I don't want to study, I want to get married" **Не хочу́ учи́ться, хочу́ жени́ться** and "Why does one need to know geography when there are coachmen?" **Заче́м геогра́фию знать, когда́ изво́зчики есть?** and the character who utters these empty-headed words, Mitrofanushka **Митрофа́нушка,** is a spoiled, imbecilic offspring—as is anyone now referred to by that name. "Skotinin" **Скоти́нин** (from **скоти́на** "cattle") is instantly recognizable as one in a long line of ignorant, crude landowners found in Russian literature.

Gogol's *The Inspector General* **«Реви́зо́р»,** produced in 1836 at the Aleksandrinskii **Александри́нский** Imperial Theater in St. Petersburg, is the second most-often quoted play by Russians. In fact, the title can be used humorously: "The Inspector General is coming" **К нам е́дет реви́зо́р** is said when one is expecting an official guest, or in jest when one is speaking of impending visitors. The action takes place in the course of a few days in a dusty, seedy little provincial town far from the capital of St. Petersburg. The corrupt officials of the town get word that an inspector is coming, incognito, to evaluate the workings of the municipality.

The mayor **городни́чий** announces this to the others, and tells them that he knew this was going to happen: he had a dream about unusually large rats who "arrived, sniffed around, and left again" **Пришли́, поню́хали и пошли́ прочь.** They decide to get the town ready for the inspector; the postmaster **почт-мейстер** suggests the reading of all letters that arrive in town (something he already does with relish). He relates the contents of one letter, from a young lieutenant to his friend, in which the officer describes how there are many young ladies, "music plays, and the standards [regimental banners] gallop off" **Му́зыка игра́ет, штанда́рт ска́чет.** This phrase is now used when someone is jokingly or ironically describing a solemn occasion or large official gathering. The mayor orders the coaches to be ready to take the important officials around town; he tells Petr Ivanovich Bobchinskii **Бо́бчинский** (one of two buffoons, the other is Petr Ivanovich Dobchinskii **До́бчинский**) that there will be no room in the coach for him, but Bobchinskii is not dismayed. He states his intention to "trot along behind the carriages" **петушко́м, петушко́м побегу́ за дро́жками** and **петушко́м, петушко́м** now describes the actions of someone fawning after those in power. The mayor, along with his bureaucratic cohort mistakes a penniless young rascal for the inspector and procedes to flatter, wine and dine, and ultimately bribe him into writing a favorable report of the town. The scoundrel, Khlestakov **Хлестако́в**, quickly recognizes what is going on, and takes full advantage of the situation. He flirts with the mayor's wife (who

Fig. 6-23.   Still from film **«Ревизо́р»**

tells him, "I am, in a way, married" **Я, нéкоторым óбразом, зáмужем**) and daughter, plays the officials for fools, and leaves with their money in his pocket. Throughout the play he reveals his complete lack of intelligence: he wants nothing more than to "pick the flowers of satisfaction" [partake of life's pleasures] **срывáть цветы́ удовóльствия** [the phrase now carries connotations of irresponsibility], and he thinks he is being particularly poetic when he admits that, "I have an unusual lightness of thought" **У меня лёгкость необыкновéнная в мы́слях.** Khlestakov pretends to be well-acquainted with the literary set, and name-drops shamelessly ("So, brother Pushkin!" **Ну что, брат Пушкин?** "I am on friendly terms with Pushkin" **С Пу́шкиным на дру́жеской ногé**), and he makes wild claims about his career. One of his phrases "35,000 couriers" **тридцать пять ты́сяч курьéров** (he is referring to the department he once headed) is used in conversation whenever one wishes to point out extreme exaggeration. Interestingly, this line is often misquoted: it has been contaminated by yet another theatrical allusion, Hamlet's "40,000 brothers" **сóрок ты́сяч брáтьев**, and comes out **40 ты́сяч курьéров.** Yet he is more savvy than any of the provincial bureaucrats. Khlestakov must perform some of the duties of a real inspector, including receiving the petitions of the town's merchants, who rail against the corrupt mayor. They complain of his pocketing resources meant for the town, and their phrase "for Anton and for Honufrii" **на Антóна и на Ону́фрия** is now quoted when someone gets double pay for doing something. But the mayor consistently denies any wrongdoing: "God bless you, but I am not guilty" **Да благословúт вас Бог, а я не виновáт** (now also quoted when trying to avoid being drawn into something). When news reaches the town that the real inspector has arrived, the officials' horror turns them mute, and the final pantomime **немáя сцéна** is one of the most famous scenes in Russian theater. Just before this scene, the mayor turns to the audience and asks "What are you laughing at? You're laughing at yourselves!" **Чему́ смеётесь? Над собóю смеётесь!**

The Inspector General is a full of symbolic names: Luka Lukich **Лукá Лукúч**—from **лукáвый** sly; Liapkin-Tiapkin **Ля́пкин-Тя́пкин**—a bungler **ля́пать**; to work poorly, sloppily **тя́пать; ляп-тяп** means "any old way" (today a Liapkin-Tiapkin is a person who is just about to be called on the carpet, from the mayor's line "Get Liapkin-Tiapkin in here!" **А подáть сюдá Ля́пкина-Тя́пкина!**); Khlestakov **Хлестакóв** [**хлестáть** means 'to flog']. Many of the most often quoted lines from the play are those upon which the plot hinges, or those that characterize the utterly corrupt and contemptible main characters. The Inspector General is a satire not merely on corruption in high places; it is a satire on mankind itself, summed up in the above-cited famous last line. All the characters are skewered by Gogol, and only Khlestakov, it seems, escapes unscathed (though not from the author's criticism!)

Alexander Ostrovsky's **Острóвский** plays—over 40 of them in all—often have as their titles Russian proverbs. Here are just a few that are commonly known:

- *Poverty is No Vice* **«Бе́дность не поро́к»**
- *It Could Happen to You* **«Грех да беда́ на кого́ не живёт»** (Lit: Sin and misery can happen to anyone.)
- *Every Day is Not Sunday* **«Не всё коту́ ма́сленица»** (Lit: It is not Mardi gras forever for a cat.)
- *Truth is Good, But Happiness is Better* **«Пра́вда хорошо́, а сча́стье лу́чше»**
- *Mind Your Own Business* **«Свои́ соба́ки грызу́тся, чужа́я не приставай»** (Lit: Our own dogs are fighting here, foreign ones should not interfere.)

Ostrovsky's majestic play *The Forest* **«Лес»** provides two characters known to Russians for their embodiment of opposing sides of the Russian character: Schastlivtsev **Счастли́вцев** ('the Lucky One') and Neschastlivtsev **Несчастли́вцев** ('the Unfortunate'). Schastlivtsev is a cunning character, hardened by life, and has some of the plays most biting lines. Neschastlivtsev, the preeminent example of the generous Russian giant, is full of warmth and deep humanity. This pair comes to life in the minds of many Russians in the Maly Theater's productions of the 1970s, in which Igor' Il'inskii as Schastlivtsev and Roman Filippov as Neschastlivtsev stole the show.

Fig. 6-24.   A. Ostrovsky

Another great actor of the Maly, Boris Babochkin, embodied for many Russians the well-known Ostrovsky character Kuligin **Кули́гин**—a philosopher, a dreamer, above all an eccentric—in the Maly's production of *The Storm* **«Гроза́»**.

Anton Pavlovich Chekhov **Че́хов,** too, makes frequent appearances in common speech.

Fig. 6-25.   A. Chekhov and MKhAT actors

His *Three Sisters* «**Три сестры́**» long to go "To Moscow! To Moscow! To Moscow!" **В Москву́! В Москву́! В Москву́**!, a phrase that now characterizes unrealizable dreams, as does the "sky full of diamonds" **не́бо в алма́зах** of Sonya in *Uncle Vanya* «**Дя́дя Ва́ня**». In Act II of that same play, Astrov utters these famous words: «**В челове́ке всё должно́ быть прекра́сно: и лицо́, и оде́жда, и душа́, и мы́сли**» "Everything about a person should be beautiful: his face, clothes, soul and thoughts."

Fig. 6-26.   An advertisement in «**База́р**», September 1997, exemplifies the popularity of these lines: «**На ва́шем рабо́чем столе́ всё должно́ быть прекра́сно: и дыроко́л, и черни́льница, и сте́плер, и скре́пки**». "Everything has to be its finest on your work desk: the hole-puncher, the ink-pot, the stapler and the paper clips."

Chekhov quotes from Gogol (see Chapter 3, 7.6) in *Three Sisters* when Masha says in Act II "Gogol said, 'This world is dreary, Gentlemen!'" **У Го́голя ска́зано: ску́чно жить на э́том све́те, господа́!** Those down on their luck may find themselves the victims of "22 misfortunes" **два́дцать два несча́стья**, a line from *The Cherry Orchard* **«Вишнёвый сад»**. The very title of this play conjures images of a life long vanished, yet not forgotten, and this is echoed in the words "Our orchard is all of Russia" **Вся Росси́я наш сад.** The original tenor of the line "We will plant a new orchard" **Мы наса́дим но́вый сад!** indicated hope for the future, but it now expresses cynicism. *The Seagull* yields the famous lines "I am a seagull" **Я — ча́йка** and "If you ever need my life, come and take it" **Если тебе́ когда́-нибудь пона́добится моя́ жизнь, то приди́ и возьми́ её.** A non-human character, and another symbol, is the seagull **ча́йка** from the play of the same name. The seagull appears on the curtain at MKhAT, and is forever associated with that theater. Yearning for exotic worlds is found in Chekhov's *Wedding* **«Сва́дьба»** "Greece has everything" **В Гре́ции всё есть.**

One of Chekhov's most memorable characters is the ancient butler Firs **Фирс** in *The Cherry Orchard*: he symbolizes loyalty and resignation to fate.

As we move from the refined world of Chekhov to the seamy cityscapes of Maksim Gorky **Го́рький**, we still do not lose sight of the most important subject matter of all: the human being.

Gorky's most famous citation, one in use today, but even more popular in the Soviet era is Satin's line from *The Lower Depths* **«На дне»:** "Man—that has a proud sound to it" **Челове́к—это звучи́т го́рдо.**

Fig. 6-27.   M. Gorky

Foreign Playwrights   **Иностра́нные драмату́рги**

Certainly, educated Russians are familiar with the works of William Shakespeare, and can quote them. Boris Pasternak produced some of the finest, if not most exact, translations of Shakespeare into Russian, and many Russians know Shakespeare through Pasternak's artistic renderings. The best-known plays are *Hamlet* **«Га́млет, принц да́тский»**, *Romeo and Juliette* **«Роме́о и Джулье́тта»**, *Othello* **«Оте́лло»**, *King Lear* **«Коро́ль Лир»**, and *Macbeth* **«Макбе́т»**. In addition, many famous quotes from *Julius Caesar* **«Ю́лий Це́зарь»**, *The Tempest* **«Бу́ря»**, and *Richard III* **«Коро́ль Ри́чард III»** can be heard in Russian conversations. Well-known characters include Caliban **Калиба́н**, Falstaff **Фальста́ф**, Iago **Я́го**, and King Lear **Коро́ль Лир**. The most famous Shakespearean quotes are listed below:

- "Et tu, Brute?" **И ты, Брут?** (*Julius Caesar* **«Ю́лий Це́зарь»**)
- "A horse! A horse! My kingdom for a horse!" **Коня́! Коня́! полца́рства за коня́!** (*Richard III* **«Коро́ль Ри́чард III»**) (Note how, in order to preserve the original meter, the translator has Richard III give "half a kingdom" for a horse in the Russian version.)
- "For never was a story of more woe, Than this of Juliette and her Romeo." **Нет по́вести печа́льнее на све́те, чем по́весть о Роме́о и Джулье́тте.** (*Romeo and Juliette* **«Роме́о и Джулье́тта»**)
- "Words, words, words." **Слова́, слова́, слова́.** (*Hamlet* **«Га́млет»**)
- "To be or not to be, that is the question." **Быть, иль не быть, вот в чём вопро́с.** (*Hamlet* **«Га́млет»**)
- "Get thee to a nunnery!" **Иди́ в монасты́рь!** (*Hamlet* **«Га́млет»**)
- "Something is rotten in the state of Denmark." **Подгни́ло что-то в да́тском короле́встве** (*Hamlet* **«Га́млет»**)
- "Poor Yorick!" **Бе́дный Йо́рик!** (*Hamlet* **«Га́млет»**)
- "40 thousand brothers" **40 ты́сяч бра́тьев.** (*Hamlet* **«Га́млет»**)
- [Shylock's] "pound of flesh." **(Ше́йлоков) фунт мя́са** (*The Merchant of Venice* **«Венециа́нский купе́ц»**)
- "She loved me for the dangers I had pass'd, And I loved her that she did pity them." **Она́ меня́ за му́ки полюби́ла, А я её за сострада́нье к ним.** (*Othello* **«Оте́лло, венециа́нский мавр»**)
- "Did you pray last night, Desdemona?" **А ты моли́лась на́ ночь, Дездемо́на?** (*Othello* **«Оте́лло, венециа́нский мавр»**)

Other western playwrights are not as well known, though many Russians can quote from Schiller, Goethe, Moliere, Lope de Vega, and some of the classical Greek plays. Certain characters such as Falstaff **Фальста́ф** (refers to jolly, fat, drunken layabouts), Tartuffe **Тартю́ф** (a sanctimonious hypocrite), and Alphonse **Альфо́нс** (a man who lives on his lover's money) have entered the Russian language.

The Language of Theater   Говоря́ о теа́тре

There are common words and expressions that apply to all theater. Dramatic theaters, as well as ballet and opera troupes, go on tour **на гастро́ли**. (But even when not on tour, your favorite company might be performing in another venue. This is known as **выездно́й спекта́кль**.) The company is referred to either as troupe **тру́ппа** or an ensemble **анса́мбль**. This group is further subdivided into the main cast **пе́рвый соста́в** and secondary cast **второ́й соста́в**. The stars of such casts are called leading performers **веду́щие исполни́тели**, though in the ballet you also find the prima ballerina **при́ма-балери́на** and in ballet and the opera theater (**о́перный теа́тр**) an assortment of soloists **соли́сты/соли́стки**.

Certain theatrical traditions are well worth knowing: performers, male and female, are presented numerous bouquets of flowers after the show as they are taking their curtain calls. When the audience wants more, they clamor for an encore **вызыва́ть на бис**: «Бра́во!, Бис!». To give an encore is **биси́ровать**.

In everyday speech one may encounter terms and images from the theater, even in rather untheatrical situations. Such expressions may come from stage components [see also illustration below]: behind the scenes; in the wings **за кули́сами** (**кули́сы** refers to the area to the sides of the stage, hidden from the spectators) carries the same meaning as it does in English. One can encounter a behind-the-scenes struggle **закули́сная борьба́,** or backstage intrigues **закули́сные интри́ги**. The boards **подмо́стки** refers to the stage itself. Before the curtain falls **под за́навес** means right before the conclusion of something. It also means to save the best for last. Traditionally actors step onto the boards from the side and the phrase **выходи́ть на сце́ну** means to appear, arrive on the scene, and reflects the stepping out of the wings.

A hidden but often indispensable part of the stage is the box in which the prompter **суфлёр** stands. If you have learned your lines, you speak without a prompter **без суфлёра**—without any prompting or help; on one's own.

One's position in life, one's role **роль,** figures prominently in a number of expressions: **игра́ть роль**—literally, to play a part in a production; also to have meaning, influence; **игра́ть пе́рвую роль** to be the most important; **на вторы́х роля́х** to be in a supporting role; and **поменя́ться роля́ми** to change places (note the plural in these phrases). A person's behavior can be straightforward, or he can be said to **разы́грывать роль** to put on an act, pretend to be what he is not. A related phrase, **лома́ть (игра́ть, разы́грывать) коме́дию,** means to play-act, to pretend, to be insincere. The situation in which this may occur can be characterized as a "puppet comedy" **ку́кольная коме́дия**—play-acting, or a farce.

When you see a situation as more dire than it really is, you "make a tragedy" in Russian: **де́лать [разводи́ть] траге́дию**. This may lead you to make a scene, **устра́ивать сце́ну**, and in turn you may find yourself losing credibility or influence: **сходи́ть со сце́ны**. This last phrase also means to end one's career.

CONCLUSION

What looms ahead in the future of the Russian theater? With fewer and fewer government subsidies, theaters in Russia are struggling to support themselves, and ticket prices, though not quite as astronomical as those in major American cities, are rising alarmingly. More and more Russians find their leisure time dwindling as they take on second or even third jobs to make ends meet. Yet for many middle and upper-class Russians, the theater remains a place to forget about everyday woes, to relax, and to explore their past and present. The Russian theater, accustomed to long and bitter struggles for expression, survives, for now, at least, because of its ability to adapt to the changing times. In fact, of all the fine or performing arts in Russia, theater is recuperating most quickly from the loss of state support. As life beyond the proscenium takes on new forms and dimensions, so, too, do the theaters of Russia.

Among contemporary Russian playwrights, critics and the public praise Olga Mukhina **Му́хина**, Nikita Voronov **Во́ронов**, Leonid Zorin **Зо́рин**, Viktor Slavkin **Сла́вкин**, Elena Gremina **Греми́на**, and Nadezhda Ptushkina **Пту́шкина.**

Music and Dance[1] # 7 # О му́зыке и та́нце

Thomas J. Garza

«Из наслажде́ний жи́зни
Одно́й любви́ музы́ка уступа́ет;
Но и любо́вь—мело́дия ...»[2]

А. Пу́шкин, «Ка́менный гость»

The Russian musical tradition is oral and singing **пе́ние** comes naturally. You will notice this most often at the dinner table when some event is being celebrated. People sing, often in harmony **в лад** and unselfconsciously; those who are tone deaf **у кото́рых плохо́й слух** often sing, too. (**Слон/медве́дь ему́ на́ ухо наступи́л.** "An elephant/bear stepped on his ear.") The oral tradition has been reinforced in church where no musical instruments are used. Through history, long winter nights combined the literary and musical tradition with the recitation of epic poems **были́ны** which were sung, or at least chanted. Today there are more or less formal competitions for singers of chastushki **часту́шки**.[3] And today, musical instruments are also popular; the possessor of a guitar will (sometimes) bring it to the party, without invitation; and even very small apartments often include an upright piano **пиани́но**.[4] That is to say, music lessons are standard high culture.

For those learning Russian, the time spent memorizing words to songs familiar to Russians will not be wasted. Russians are delighted to find foreigners who enjoy what they enjoy; and also the songs will stay for your pleasure while verb forms may be more tenuous.

Singing **пе́ние** (that is, music) is taught early—the first grade music book includes not just do-re-mi but also where whole-tones **то́ны** and half-tones

---

[1] If English has an accepted spelling of a musician's or a composer's name as affirmed by a biographical dictionary, then that spelling is used. Otherwise, we refer you to the usual Library of Congress system.

[2] "Of life's pleasures, music gives way only to love, but even love is a melody." Pushkin.

[3] See *The Russian's World*, 2/e, 353.

[4] The only large apartment room I ever saw included a grand piano **роя́ль** among the furniture.

Fig. 7-1.

полутóны appear in the scale **гáмма** (**звукоря́д** is less frequent and can refer to any sequence of sounds). The sixth grade music book introduces all the instruments of the orchestra, among other things. And then there are music schools that can be attended for several hours after regular school for seven years; they include lessons in sight reading **сольфéджио**, music history, chorus, orchestra, piano, smaller ensembles each week *in addition to* lessons on a chosen instrument. Future musicians, however, attend a music academy **учи́лище** after the ninth grade.

BASIC TERMINOLOGY   **ОСНОВНА́Я ТЕРМИНОЛО́ГИЯ**

With few exceptions, the written music **нóты** will look much the same in Russian and English: the staff **нóтный стан** consists of five parallel lines **линéйки**, that begin with a key signature **ключевы́е знáки** (**ключи́**) which might be either a treble clef **скрипи́чный ключ**[5] or a bass clef **басóвый ключ** followed by the sharps **диéз** or flats **бемóль**[6] required to show the key **тонáльность** the music is written in: the major key **мажóр** or minor key **минóр**. "Time" **размéр**, **метр** is indicated by a fraction where the top number shows the number of beats to the measure **такт**, and the bottom number indicates what size note (often a quarter note **однá четвертнáя**) gets one beat. ("This is written in 3/4 time." **Это напи́сано на три чéтверти … на две чéтверти, на шесть восьмы́х.** Also one can ask: **На какóй счёт?—На четы́ре чéтверти** or [less often] **Какóв размéр тáкта?—Четы́ре чéтверти.**)

Fig. 7-2.

---

[5] This use of the word "key" **ключ** has led to the expression **В какóм ключé?** which means "How," or "In what range?" (should something be done), or "What sort of thing do you want?"

[6] In reading music, "B natural" would be **си бекáр**.

Fig. 7-3.

The notes themselves are equally straightforward, with the whole note **це́лая**, the half note **полови́нная (полови́нка)**, the quarter note **четвертна́я/че́тверть (четверту́шка)**, eighth note **восьма́я (восьму́шка)**, and the sixteenth note **шестна́дцатая**. These notes are arranged in measures **в та́ктах** separated by bars **та́ктовые черты́** according to the time indicator. Even dynamics look the same with *ff*—**форти́ссимо**, *f*—**фо́рте**, *mf*—**ме́ццо-фо́рте**, *p*—**пиа́но**, *pp*—**пиани́ссимо**.

However, reading the music and talking about it are two different things. In Russian, music is usually described as written not in the key of C, D or E,[7] for example, but rather in the key **тона́льность, ключ** of "do, re, mi …," instead, that is, they use a fixed "do" at middle C, and then continue to use their version of re, mi, fa, sol, la, ti, (do) instead of our D, E, F, G, A, B. The C major scale **га́мма до мажо́р, домажо́рная гамма: до ре ми фа соль ля си до** (one octave **окта́ва** of the scale). So Bach's Mass in B minor comes out as **Ме́сса Ба́ха си мино́р**, and Melody in F is **Мело́дия фа мажо́р** (except that the Russian title for the song is just **Мело́дия**). In reading music, D♯ is **ре дие́з**, D♭ is **ре бемо́ль**, and D♮ is **ре бека́р**. Middle C = "**до**" **пе́рвой окта́вы**.

Musical Groups   Музыка́льные анса́мбли

A chorus **хор** often includes four groups of singers **певцы́**: sopranos **сопра́но**[8], altos **альты́**, tenors **тенора́**, and basses **басы́**. Operas also employ contraltos **контра́льто**, mezzo-sopranos **ме́ццо-сопра́но**, and baritones **барито́ны**.

Chamber music **ка́мерная му́зыка** is most often played by a string quartet **стру́нный кварте́т (две скри́пки, альт, виолонче́ль)** though there are also duets **дуэ́ты**, and trios **три́о**, not to mention the chamber orchestra **ка́мерный орке́стр** which is nothing but a small orchestra.

A band **духово́й орке́стр** employs woodwinds **деревя́нные духовы́е инструме́нты**, brass **ме́дные инструме́нты** and percussion **уда́рные инструменты**.

Popular music groups are discussed under that heading.

---

[7] A similar "letter designation" system **бу́квенное обозначе́ние зву́ков** is used in Germany and sometimes on (printed) music or on programs in Russia where "B" corresponds to American B-flat, and our B-flat is "H." The other letter/notes, C, D, E, etc., are the same as ours.

[8] Singular is also **сопра́но** which is neuter when referring to a voice, feminine when its a person.

Instruments of the Orchestra   Инструме́нты орке́стра

The strings **стру́нные инструме́нты** are the singers in the orchestra. All of them require a bow **смычо́к** and therefore sometimes are called bowed instruments **смычко́вые инструме́нты**. The violin **скри́пка** (**скрипе́ть** to squeak!) is played by a violinist **скрипа́ч** (**О́йстрах**). The viola **альт** is played by a violist **альти́ст** (**Башме́т**), the cello **виолонче́ль** by a cellist **виолончели́ст** (**Ростропо́вич**), and the double bass **контраба́с** by a bassist **контрабаси́ст**. String players find a tuning fork **камерто́н** a convenience; strings and others require a mute **сурди́на** (with a mute **под сурди́нку**). The harp **а́рфа** is also considered to be part of the strings.

The woodwinds **деревя́нные духовы́е инструменты** start at the top with the piccolo **пи́кколо** played by the same person who plays the flute **фле́йта**, then the instruments requiring reeds **тро́сти** are the clarinet **кларне́т**, the oboe **гобо́й**, the English horn **англи́йский рожо́к**, and the bassoon **фаго́т**. (The saxophone **саксофо́н** is usually confined to popular music, especially jazz **джаз**.)

The brass **ме́дные инструме́нты** have a trumpet **труба́** at the top, then a trombone **тромбо́н**, a French horn **валто́рна** and the tuba **ту́ба**.

The percussion **уда́рные инструме́нты** most relied upon are the snare drum **ма́лый бараба́н/бараба́н со стру́нами**, the bass drum **большо́й бараба́н**, the kettle drum **лита́вра**, and the cymbals **таре́лки**; special effects sometimes require the gong **гонг/тамта́м**, the triangle **треуго́льник**, the tambourine **тамбури́н/бу́бен**, the celesta **челе́ста**, castanets **кастанье́ты**, big bells **колокола́**, little bells **колоко́льчики** and the xylophone **ксилофо́н**.

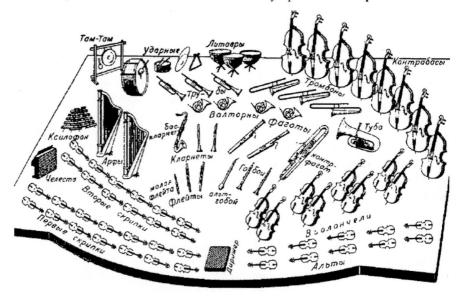

Fig. 7-4.   Instruments of the orchestra

The grand piano **роя́ль** mostly appears at concerts while the upright **пиани́но** is surprisingly common even in what seem like miniscule apartments. (A harpsichord: **клавеси́н**.) The organ **орга́н** may appear in concert but never in the Russian Orthodox church. Since they have a keyboard **клавиату́ра** (key: **кла́виша** or **кла́виш**) these are also called keyboard instruments **кла́вишные инструме́нты**.

- The orchestra is tuning up. **Орке́стр настра́ивается/настра́ивает инструме́нты.**
- "She tuned her violin." **Она́ настро́ила скри́пку.**
- "This piano is out of tune!" **Э́тот роя́ль не настро́ен.**

What People Play   На каки́х инструме́нтах игра́ют

The contemporary common domestic instrument is surely the guitar **гита́ра**. The Russian seven-stringed guitar **семистру́нная гита́ра** is required by parties, campfires and bards **ба́рды** who also have been aptly named "guitar poets" in English. The guitarists are city boys and girls. (Our six-stringed guitar is also popular among those who consider westerness more desirable, that is, any younger person.)

THE BEGINNINGS: НАРО́ДНАЯ И ЦЕРКО́ВНАЯ МУ́ЗЫКА
FOLK AND CHURCH MUSIC

The first formal music came to Kievan Russia in the form of Byzantine liturgi- ♫ 7-1
cal chants the earliest of which was the "znamenny" chant **зна́менный распе́в**, which, to our ears, resembles a Gregorian chant with only a melody (no harmony, nothing we would call rhythm).

Early secular music of which there is some record includes byliny **были́ны** which were very long verse tales of folk heroes and their exploits. They were sung and sometimes accompanied by musicians playing their instruments such as "gusli" **гу́сли** and "dudki" **ду́дки** (see below). One of the most frequently encountered characters of the byliny is the hero **богаты́рь** Mikula Selianinovich, whose exploits are recounted in "About Vol'ga and Mikula" **О Вольге́ и Мику́ле**:

Жил Святосла́в девяно́сто лет,	Sviatoslav lived 90 years,
Жил Святосла́в, да перестáвился,	Sviatoslav lived, and died,
Оставáлось от него́ чáдо мáлое,	He left a small child,
Молодо́й Вольгá Святослáвович.	The young Vol'ga Sviatoslavovich.

Also common in the folk song tradition were the ritual songs associated with the seasons and the calendar, among them the "vesnyanki" **весня́нки**. These songs were most common during the (pagan) spring festival of maslenitsa **мáсленица**, invoking images of renewal and rebirth in the calling in of a new season. An obligatory feature of these songs was the repetition of key nature motifs:

Ле́то, ле́то, выла́зь из-под кле́та! А ты, зима́, иди́ туда́!

Summer, summer, come out from under the shed! And you, winter, go there!

or

Весна́ красна́, что ты нам принесла́?

Beautiful spring, what did you bring us?

These ritual songs were usually accompained by round dances **хорово́ды**, and music played on folk instruments.

Folk Instruments   **Наро́дные инструме́нты**

The balalaika and the "garmon" in this group are the only two instruments still to be seen, if rarely heard, to this day. Though probably the most familiar of the Russian folk instruments, the balalaika appeared in Russia only in the early 18th century. The sound of this three-stringed instrument quickly found its place in many established folk songs and dances, and new compositions soon followed. The domra **до́мра** is a similar but older instrument, with a round face rather than a triangular one.

Fig. 7-5.   Balalaika **балала́йка**

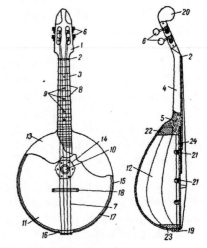

Fig. 7-6.   Domra **до́мра**

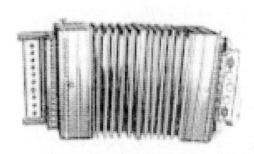

Fig. 7-7.   Garmon/garmoshka
            гармóнь/гармóшка

Fig. 7-8.   Bayan **баян**

Associated with the country and/or the past is a simplified accordion-like instrument **гармóнь** or even **гармóшка** (formally, **гармóния** or **гармóника**[9]) with a limited[10] keyboard. Larger and more complicated[11] and refined is the bayan **баян**, a Russian invention using knobs rather than a keyboard on the right side and chords on the left. Of course, the accordion **аккордеóн** is also found, usually among professional players.

Gusli are mentioned in the byliny, folk tales, songs and folk sayings of old Russia as a favorite instrument of the skomorokhi **скоморóхи**—the strolling minstrel/clowns of medieval Russia. Byliny were accompanied on the gusli. **Под гýсли пéлись былúны.** The player plucks the strings of the instrument which rests on his lap.

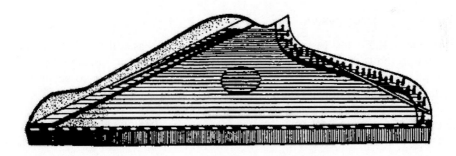

Fig. 7-9.   Gusli **гýсли**

---

[9] **Губнáя гармонúка** is a harmonica.

[10] With a diatonic scale.

[11] With a chromatic scale, for instance.

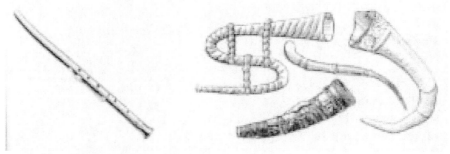

Fig. 7-10. Dudka **дýдка**   Fig. 7-11   Horn **рог**

Also called "svireli" **свирéли**, "sopeli" **сопéли** and "dudochki" **дýдочки**, dudki are attested in Ukrainian, Belorussian and Russian folk music traditions. These flute-like instruments create the birdsong melodies in many of the older folk songs and chants. **Скоморóхи игрáли на дýдках.**

Common to almost all ancient musical traditions, the horn figures prominently in Russian musical history from its earliest days to the late 18th century. At that time, the art of horn playing peaked with the creation of horn orchestras **«роговы́е оркéстры».**

Fig. 7-12. Rozhok **рожóк**

One of the oldest instruments found in central Russia, the *rozhok* is made of wood—and is associated with a shepherd's flute for herding livestock (shepherd **пастýх**). Later the instrument was used extensively to accompany folk songs, dances and choruses. **Рýсский пастушóк игрáет на рожкé.**

RUSSIAN CLASSICAL MUSIC   РÝССКАЯ КЛАССИ́ЧЕСКАЯ
TO THE 1917 REVOLUTION   МÝЗЫКА ДО РЕВОЛЮ́ЦИИ

In what follows, we discuss the Russian contribution to Western classical music. The reader should assume, however, that the educated Russian will also be familiar with, for example, Bach **Бах**, Haydn **Гáйдн**, Mozart **Мóцарт**, Beethoven **Бетхóвен**, Brahms **Брамс**, and Verdi **Вéрди**.

By the beginning of the 19th century, Western classical music had found its way into Russia, especially through its use in drama and opera. Many composers had gone to Italy and Germany to study music, and Russia was preparing for the birth of a truly Russian school of classical music.

Mikhail Ivanovich Glinka (1804–57)

Михаи́л Ива́нович Гли́нка

Often considered the founder of Russian classical music, Glinka studied composition in Italy and Germany. When he returned to Petersburg in 1833, he made friends with the poet Zhukovsky, who had been writing literary versions of popular folk and fairy tales. On Zhukovsky's suggestion, Glinka wrote an opera based on the life of the Russian patriot Ivan Susanin who sacrificed his own life to save Tsar Mikhail Alekseevich, the founder of the Romanov dynasty in 1613. *Ivan*

Fig. 7-13. M. Glinka

Susanin, or A Life for the Tsar «Ива́н Суса́нин, или Жизнь за царя́» (1836) was a great success throughout Russia. Originally titled simply *Ivan Susanin*, this four-act opera was renamed after Tsar Nicolas I attended its rehearsal at the Bolshoi Theater and noticed that the work had been dedicated to him. After the 1917 Revolution, the original title was restored. Following Zhukovsky's advice about adapting folktale themes to his work, Glinka's next opera was *Ruslan and Liudmila* «Русла́н и Людми́ла» (1842), based on Pushkin's tale that tells the story of two lovers who persevere to be together against all odds.

Aleksander Sergeevich Dargomyzhsky (1813–69)

Алекса́ндр Серге́евич Даргомы́жский

A student of Glinka's, he is best known for his operas based on Russian folk themes. *Rusalka* «Руса́лка» (1856) was a four-act opera based on Pushkin's literary fairy tale about a mermaid, for which he took inspiration from the young nationalist composers, the "Five" (see below). He also was one of the founders of the Russian Musical Society Ру́сское музыка́льное о́бщество (РМО). In 1860 he began the opera *The Stone Guest* «Ка́менный гость», based on Pushkin's play of the same name.

The Golden Age of Russian Music

Золото́й век ру́сской му́зыки

In the second half of the 19th century, Russian literature and the arts were beginning their "Golden Age"—a late renaissance marked by creative maturity and prolific production. In tandem with this literary movement, Russian musicians entered their own Golden Age, producing major orchestral compositions, operas, and ballets that placed Russian music and musicians among the ranks of the best in the world.

"The Five"   *«Могу́чая ку́чка»*

(Also translated as "The Mighty Five" or "The Mighty Handful.") The Russian music critic Vladimir Stasov coined this term for a newspaper article in 1867 to denote five composers—Balakirev, Borodin, Cui, Mussorgsky and Rimsky-Korsakov—who shared a particularly nationalist perspective on their music. Many of their compositions draw extensively from source materials in Russian literature, history, and folk music.

Milii Alekseevich Balakirev (1837–1910)   Ми́лий Алексе́евич Бала́кирев

Balakirev was the leader of the Five. He also founded the Free School of Music **Беспла́тная музыка́льная шко́ла**, which served as the performance platform for many of the early compositions of The Five's nationalist **патриоти́ческая** school. He also served as concert director for the Russian Musical Society. His oriental fantasy for piano, *Islamei* **«Исламе́й»** (1869), was composed after visiting the Caucasus; it demonstrated Balakirev's own virtuosity at the instrument.

Aleksander Porfir′evich Borodin (1833–87)

Алекса́ндр Порфи́рьевич Бороди́н

Both a doctor/chemist and a musician, he completed his medical education in Petersburg and Heidelberg in 1862 and was appointed to the teaching faculty of the Academy of Medicine. In that same year, Borodin also met with Balakirev, who convinced him to pursue music while continuing his scientific work. He began his opera *Prince Igor* **«Князь И́горь»**, but was never able to finish it. Rimsky-Korsakov and Glazunov

Fig. 7-14.   A. Borodin

completed the work after Borodin's death in 1887, securing his place in Russian music. He brought the string quartet form to Russia, and also wrote a number of art songs **рома́нсы**. The *Second Symphony* **«Втора́я (Богаты́рская) симфо́ния»**, and a symphonic poem *In the Steppes of Central Asia* **«В Сре́дней А́зии»** (1880) are also among his best-known works.

- *Prince Igor* **«Князь И́горь»** (1890). This opera is based on the life and battles of the 12th-century Russian hero described in the Russian epic **«Сло́во о полку́ И́гореве»** that had been recently discovered. (See: Chapters 1 and 3.) Borodin wrote both the music and the libretto of the opera, which was still unfinished when he died. It is best known for the Polovetsian Dances **Полове́цкие пля́ски** in the second act.

Fig. 7-15.   Poster art for *Prince Igor*

- *In the Steppes of Central Asia* «В Сре́дней А́зии» (1880) was composed as an "orchestral picture" of a passing caravan to accompany a *tableau vivant* commemorating the 25th anniversary of Tsar Alexander II's reign.

Tsezar Antonovich Cui (1835–1918)   Це́зарь Анто́нович Кюй

Cui was most influential as a music critic and writer of pieces that promoted the new Russian music and musicians in Russia and abroad, a role he maintained for more than fifty years. He was one of the Five.

Anton Grigor'evich Rubinstein (1829–94)   Анто́н Григо́рьевич Рубинште́йн

By the age of twelve Rubinstein had already performed as a pianist in Moscow and in Paris, attracting the attention of Liszt and Chopin. He became concert director of the Russian Musical Society and in 1862 he co-founded the Petersburg Conservatory. He is best known in America for his piano piece "Melody in F" «Мело́дия (фа мажо́р)», and in Russia for his three-act opera with prologue and epilogue, *Demon* «Де́мон» (1871), based on Lermontov's romantic poem set in Georgia. Widely known in Russia for commanding more performances than any other opera in the 19th century with the exception of *Life for the Tsar*.

Modest Petrovich Mussorgsky (1839–81)

Моде́ст Петро́вич Му́соргский

Mussorgsky's birth into modest estate life near Pskov in 1839 and close contact with the folk songs and tales he heard from the peasants almost certainly provided some Russian themes for his music. Enrolled by his parents into a military academy at age ten, Mussorgsky continued his musical educa-

Fig. 7-16. M. Mussorgsky

tion simultaneously, and by 1859 formally resigned from the army to try to pursue a musical career while in the government service. Health and financial problems through the 1860s made writing difficult, but in 1868 he began the opera *Boris Godunov* **«Бори́с Годуно́в»**, based on Pushkin's play. The overtly Russian historical and national themes of this and a second opera, *Khovanshchina* **«Хова́нщина»** (1873) secured Mussorgsky's place among the "Five." During this time, he also revised his composition *Night on Bald Mountain* **«Ночь на Лы́сой горе́»** (1867), which, like *Boris Godunov*, Rimsky-Korsakov would later "correct" to the accepted norm of nineteenth century Russian phrasing. He also finished the cycle for the piano *Pictures at an Exhibition* **«Карти́нки с вы́ставки»** (1874). Most of his compositions after *Boris Godunov* were cycles of songs, including "Songs and Dances of Death" **«Пе́сни и пля́ски сме́рти»** (1877) and "Without the Sun" or "Sunless" **«Без со́лнца»** (1874). By the late 1870s his health steadily declined, exacerbated by years of heavy drinking, until his death in a military hospital in 1881.

- *Boris Godunov* **«Бори́с Годуно́в»** (1874). This opera is based on Pushkin's tragedy about the life of the 16th-century Russian ruler. Rimsky-Korsakov revised and re-orchestrated the opera, significantly cutting the original and adding material, such as the St. Basil scene. For Russians, the title role of the opera is identified almost exclusively with the bass Chaliapin **Фёдор Шаля́пин**.

Fig. 7-17. Poster for *Boris Godunov*

- *Khovanshchina* **«Хова́нщина»** (1873). This opera about the Khovansky princes at the time of Peter the Great was never finished during Mussorgsky's life. Rimsky-Korsakov completed the piece based on Mussorgsky's and Vladimir Stasov's libretto.

- *Night on Bald Mountain* **«Ночь на Лы́сой горе́»** (1876). Introduced as an orchestral work about a witches' sabbath described in a story by Gogol **(«Ночь накану́не Ива́на Купа́лы»)**, this piece ultimately became the opening of Act III of *Sorochinsk Fair* **«Соро́чинская я́рмарка»**. Rimsky-Korsakov reworked and revised the composition, sometimes called *St. John's Night on Bald Mountain* from the original Russian title.

- *Pictures at an Exhibition* **«Карти́нки с вы́ставки»** (1874). This composition for piano represents ten pieces by the Russian artist Viktor Hartmann, who had died in 1873, with a linking "promenade" **прогу́лка** passage creating the movement through the "exhibition." The pictures include: "The Gnome" **«Гном»**, "The Old Castle" **«Ста́рый за́мок»**, "Tuileries" **«Сад Тюильри́ (с со́ра дете́й по́сле игр)»**, "Cattle" **«Бы́дло»**, "Unhatched Chickens" **«Бале́т невы́лупившихся птенцо́в»**, "Samuel Goldenberg and Shmuyle" **«Два евре́я, бога́тый и бе́дный»**,

"Marketplace at Limoges" **«Лимо́ж. Ры́нок (Больша́я но́вость)»**, "Catacombs" **«Катако́мбы (Ри́мская усыпа́льница). С мёртвыми на мёртвом языке́»**, "The Hut on Chicken Legs. Baba Iaga" **«Избу́шка на ку́рьих но́жках. Ба́ба Яга́»**, and "The Great Gate of Kiev" **«Богаты́рские воро́та Ки́ева»**.

Pëtr Il'ich Tchaikovsky (1840–93)

Пётр Ильи́ч Чайко́вский

Tchaikovsky studied music as a child but his formal musical training began when he was twenty-two at the Petersburg Conservatory of Music; from 1866–78 he taught at the Moscow Conservatory where he began composing; before long he would distance himself from "The Five." Late in this early period, Tchaikovsky also briefly married, separated, attempted suicide and became seriously ill. He never remarried. His travel to Europe to recuperate proved to be the necessary catalyst for his creativity. During

Fig. 7-18. Portrait of Tchaikovsky by Kuznetsov

the following years, Tchaikovsky was able to devote himself to his music thanks to an annuity from Nadezhda von Meck, whom he never met, but with whom he corresponded for 14 years. He settled not far from Moscow in the village of Klin in 1885, where he lived in near-isolation and wrote prolifically. In his last years Tchaikovsky worked on his *Symphony No. 6 in B minor,* Op. 74, or *Pathetique* **«Шеста́я, или Патети́ческая, симфо́ния»**, which he considered to be his best, and died just nine days after its first performance in 1893. While it was reported for years that Tchaikovsky died of cholera, recent evidence strongly suggests that his death was arsenic-induced suicide, prompted by rumors of a scandalous affair with the nephew of a Russian nobleman. Since 1938 his name, still much beloved in Russia, has been attached to the Tchaikovsky Concert Hall **Конце́ртный зал и́мени Чайко́вского** in Moscow and, every four years since 1958, to the Tchaikovsky International Music Competition **Междунаро́дный ко́нкурс музыка́нтов и́мени П.И. Чайко́вского**.

- *Symphony No. 4 in F minor,* **«Четвёртая симфо́ния»**, Op. 36 (1877)
- *Symphony No. 5 in E minor,* **«Пя́тая симфо́ния»**, Op. 64 (1888)
- *Symphony No. 6 in B minor* **«Шеста́я, или Патети́ческая, симфо́ния»**, Op. 74 (1893). The subtitle "Pathetique" [**«патети́ческий»** = "passionate" or "emotional," not "pathetic"] was assigned by Tchaikovsky himself after rejecting "Tragic" **«Траги́ческая симфо́ния»**. Perhaps the

most popular of his symphonies among Russians, the piece is often associated with and used at funeral ceremonies.

- *Piano Concerto No. 1 in B flat minor* «**Пе́рвый концéрт для фортепиáно с оркéстром**», Op. 23 (1874–75)
- *Piano Concerto No. 2* «**Вторóй концерт для фортепиáно с оркестром**»
- *Piano Concerto No. 3 in G* «**Трéтий концерт для фортепиано с оркестром**», Op.44 (1879–80)
- *Violin Concerto in D major* «**Концéрт для скри́пки ре мажóр**», Op. 35 (1878)
- *The Sleeping Beauty* «**Спя́щая красáвица**», Op. 66 (1889). Regarded by most Russians as Tchaikovsky's ballet masterpiece, this work in three acts and a prologue was first choreographed by Petipa. Based on the Perrault fairy tale "La belle au bois dormant" and later brought to Russia by Zhukovsky, Sergei Diaghilev took the ballet to London with his Ballets Russes in 1921 and used Zhukovsky's title, *The Sleeping Princess* «**Спя́щая царéвна**».
- *Swan Lake* «**Лебеди́ное óзеро**», Op. 20 (1876). It was not until 1895 — after the death of the composer — that audiences saw Petipa's version of what Russian audiences would make one of their country's treasures. Based on a German fairy tale, this piece, like *Sleeping Beauty* and *The Nutcracker*, uses elements of magic and the supernatural to create its artistic effect.

Fig. 7-19.   *Swan Lake* performed by the Bolshoi Ballet

- *The Queen of Spades* «**Пи́ковая дáма**», Op. 68 (1890). This opera in three acts is based on the famous eponymous novella by Pushkin with the scenario written by Tchaikovsky's brother. The original production revealed a story which deviated significantly from its famous source, an evil that was "corrected" by Meyerhold during the Soviet period to make for a more Pushkinian opera. In both cases, though, the real masterpiece of the opera is Tchaikovsky's creation of a dream world merging the musical and the surreal.

- *The Nutcracker* «Щелку́нчик», Op. 71 (1892). L.I. Ivanov choreographed and Petipa wrote the scenario for this ballet in two acts and three scenes based on E.T.A. Hoffman's *Der Nussknäcker und der Mäusekönig*. Though the piece became a Christmastime standard in the West by the mid-twentieth century, it was slow to "catch fire" in Russia though today Russians almost unanimously praise the music of the ballet.

- *Eugene Onegin* «Евге́ний О не́гин» (1879). One of the most beloved and well-known pieces of literature in the Russian language, Pushkin's novel in verse was the source material for this three-act opera. Russians are particularly fond of the way Tchaikovsky's music "reads" the way Pushkin's famous lines do. Most notable in this respect is the scene depicting the reading of Tatiana's letter.

- *1812 Overture* (**Торже́ственная увертю́ра**) **«1812-й год»** (1880)

- *Francesca da Rimini* **«Франче́ска да Ри́мини»** (1876)

- *Romeo and Juliet* **«Роме́о и Джулье́тта»** (1869)

- *Variations on a Rococo Theme* **«Вариа́ции на те́му рококо́»** (1876)

- *Capriccio italien* **«Италья́нское капри́ччио»** (1880)

- Essentially all Russian piano students learn to play *The Seasons* **«Времена́ го́да»** (1876), a collection of 12 piano pieces.

Nikolai Andreevich Rimsky-Korsakov (1844–1908)

Никола́й Андре́евич Ри́мский-Ко́рсаков

Rimsky-Korsakov began piano study at the age of six, though his parents planned a career in the Russian navy. Still, he also pursued his study of music and in 1865, upon his return from his tour of duty, his first symphony was performed—the first symphony composed by a Russian. Rimsky-Korsakov began a lifelong friendship with Modest Mussorgsky in 1866, which marked the beginning of "The Five"—Russian composers who consciously employed

Fig. 7-20.   Potrait of Rimsky-Korsakov by Serov

Russian themes in their compositions. He wrote the symphonic poem *Sadko* «**Садко́**» in 1867, which would become the basis for his opera of the same name. In the early 1870s, Rimsky-Korsakov left the navy and turned his attention fully to music, completing Dargomyzhsky's opera *The Stone Guest* «**Ка́менный гость**» in 1896, and writing his own first opera *The Maid of Pskov* «**Псковитя́нка**» in 1872. With the publication of his collection of "100 Russian Folk Songs," Rimsky-Korsakov pursued the folk theme in his work, especially in operas such as *The Snow Maiden and the Tsar's Bride* «**Снегу́рочка и Ца́рская неве́ста**» (1881), to his last piece *The Golden Cockerel* «**Золото́й петушо́к**» (1907). After Borodin died, Rimsky-Korsakov completed his compatriot's opera *Prince Igor* «**Князь Йгорь**»in 1887, and composed the vibrant orchestral pieces *Capriccio Espagnol* «**Испа́нское капри́ччио**» (1887) and *Sheherazade* «**Шехераза́да**» (1888). His later years were marked by government censorship and bans due to his sympathy for revolutionary students, leaving him to revise and "correct" works such as Mussorgsky's *Boris Godunov* «**Бори́с Годуно́в**»(1906). After Rimsky-Korsakov's death in 1908, the influence of his school of composition and orchestration extends to more than two hundred musicians, including Stravinsky, Prokofiev, and Glazunov.

- *Sadko* «**Садко́**» (1898). Building on an early symphonic tone poem also called *Sadko* «**Садко́**» from 1867, this opera-bylina in seven scenes was first performed in Moscow. Rimsky-Korsakov wrote the libretto for the piece, telling the story of the historical folk figure from the 10th century, who embodies the roots of Russian mercantilism. It includes the Song of India «**Пе́сня инди́йского го́стя**».

♪ 7-2

- *The Golden Cockerel* (*Le Coq d'or*) «**Золото́й петушо́к**» (1907). His last opera, called a "dramatized fable" **небыли́ца в листа́х** in three acts and an epilogue, is based on Pushkin's literary fairy tale of the same title (Pushkin's tale is based on two stories by Washington Irving). To accentuate the folk themes, the production designer for the first performance was Ivan Bilibin **Ива́н Били́бин**, well-known for his illustrations of Russian literary fairy tales.

- *Capriccio espagnol* «**Испа́нское капри́ччио**», Op. 34 (1887). Rimsky-Korsakov's orchestral piece shows his penchant for national themes, even when they are Spanish, not Russian. He liked color, wherever it came from.

- *Sheherazade* «**Шехераза́да**», Op. 35 (1888). This symphonic suite for orchestra is named for and thematically based on *The Thousand and One Nights* heroine who, by telling entertaining stories is able to keep from being executed by the Sultan Shahriar.

The Silver Age of Russian Music   Серебряный век русской музыки

The beginning of the 20th century brought major changes to the face of Russia and ushered in a new period of creativity in the arts as the country was transformed by war and revolution. This Silver Age kept Russian composers, musicians, performers and their works in the full view of the world.

Aleksander Konstantinovich Glazunov (1865–1936)

Алекса́ндр Константи́нович Глазуно́в

Born in St. Petersburg, Glazunov's first formal musical instruction was—at least briefly—under the tutelage of Rimsky-Korsakov. His first symphony, completed in 1881, was conducted by Balakirev and was well-received by the critics. Glazunov was the inheritor of the compositional tradition of "The Five" **Могу́чая ку́чка**, as well as of Tchaikovsky. By the time he was made director of the St. Petersburg Conservatory in 1905, Glazunov had completed eight symphonies and written a popular concerto for violin, but is best known as a composer of ballet scores, most notably *Raymonda* **«Раймо́нда»** (1897) and *The Seasons*, Op. 67 **«Времена́ го́да»** (1899). He remained at the Conservatory until 1928 when he emigrated to Paris, where he remained until his death in 1936.

Fig. 7-21. Repin's painting of Glazunov

- *Raymonda* **«Раймо́нда»** (1897). This ballet in three acts and four scenes is based on a chivalric tale. The original production choreographed by Petipa opened at the Mariinskiy Theater in St. Petersburg in 1898.
- *The Seasons* **«Времена́ го́да»**, Op. 67 (1899). With a libretto and choreography by Petipa, this allegorical ballet in one act and four scenes contains, as the title suggests, portraits of the four Russian seasons, including the remarkable autumn "Bacchanale." It was first performed at the Hermitage Theater in St. Petersburg in 1900.

Aleksander Nikolaevich Scriabin (1872–1915)

Алекса́ндр Никола́евич Скря́бин

Of the Russian musicians and composers of the late
nineteenth century, the Moscow-born Scriabin
stands out as a true prodigy of the piano. After finishing at the Moscow Conservatory, he was briefly
employed as a professor there, but found much more
satisfaction touring and performing. His early compositions carry a decided flavor of Chopin, while his

Fig. 7-22.   A. Skriabin

later pieces show daring innovation in combining chords, creating an
"impressionist atonality," notably in his *Poem of Ecstasy,* Op. 54 **«Поэ́ма
экста́за»** (1908). For his late works, he developed the so-called "mystic" chord,
built on a series of ascending fourths: C, F$\sharp$, B$^\flat$, E, A, and D. This pattern is
most visible, literally, as Scriabin was experimenting in the play of color and
music (**цветому́зыка**), in his symphonic poem *Prometheus: Poem of Fire,* Op.
60 **«Промете́й: Поэ́ма огня́»** (1910).

Sergei Vasil′evich Rakhmaninov (1873–1943)

Серге́й Васи́льевич Рахма́нинов

Rakhmaninov studied first at the Petersburg, then at the
Moscow Conservatory of Music, where he began and
continued a career equally divided between composition
and performance as a virtuoso pianist. Before his twentieth birthday, he had written the opera *Aleko* **«Але́ко»**
and the *Prelude in C# minor* **«Прелю́дия до дие́з ми-
но́р»**, for which he gained immediate fame throughout

Fig. 7-23.   S. Rach-
maninov

Russia. In the early 1900s, he composed prolifically, completing two operas,
including *The Miserly Knight,* Op. 24 **«Скупо́й ры́царь»** (1905), the *Second
Symphony* **«Втора́я симфо́ния»** (1908), the symphonic poem *The Isle of the
Dead,* Op. 29 **«О́стров мёртвых»** (1909), and the choral composition *The Bells*,
Op. 35 **«Колокола́»** (1913)—often considered his most brilliant piece. In 1917
with the beginning of the Russian Revolution, Rakhmaninov emigrated to the
U.S., and devoted the bulk of his time to touring as a concert pianist and
conducting. In 1934 he completed and performed *Rhapsody on a Theme of
Paganini,* Op. 43 **«Рапсо́дия на те́му Пагани́ни»**, followed in 1936 by his *Third
Symphony* **«Тре́тья симфо́ния»**. His compositions include four piano concertos. His last piece, *Symphonic Dances,* Op. 45 **«Симфони́ческие та́нцы»**, was
completed in 1940, just three years before his death in Beverly Hills.

Igor Fedorovich Stravinsky (1882–1971)

Йгорь Фёдорович Стравинский

Born near Petersburg, Stravinsky became a star pupil of composer Rimsky-Korsakov, though the two shared little in the style or interpretation of music. The older composer was reported to have stopped Stravinsky during his playing of an early ballet, saying, "Stop playing that terrible thing or I might begin to enjoy it!" Shortly after the death of Rimsky-Korsakov in 1908, Stravinsky began a prolific period begin-

Fig. 7-24.   I. Stravinsky

ning with *The Nightingale* «Соловей» in 1909,which combined elements of opera and ballet. In 1910, Stravinsky met Sergei Diaghilev, the director of the Russian Ballet, with whom he became a close friend. Stravinsky was commissioned that same year to write a ballet based on the Russian folktale *The Firebird* «Жар-птица». This piece established Stravinsky's reputation as a composer both in Russia and France, where the ballet was first performed. His

second ballet, *Petrushka* «Петрушка», was completed in 1911 and was also based on Russian folk themes. The production of the ballet *The Rite of Spring* (from the French version of its title "Le sacre du printemps") «Весна священная» was danced by Vaslav Nijinsky and actually caused a riot in Paris between its supporters and detractors. In 1917, his continuing association with Diaghilev produced *The Soldier's Tale* «История солдата», a vocal ensemble piece which embraced his love of Russian folk and American jazz. Stravinsky emigrated first to Switzerland, then to France where he became a citizen in 1934. Still, Russians held Stravinsky as a native son, inviting him to tour Russia in 1962, including a command performance in the Kremlin for Nikita Khrushchev. He died in New York in 1971, but was buried in Venice near the grave of Diaghilev.

Fig. 7-25.   Karsavina in *The Firebird* (1910)

| THE SOVIET PERIOD | СОВЕ́ТСКИЙ ПЕРИ́ОД |
| IN RUSSIAN MUSIC | В РУ́ССКОЙ МУ́ЗЫКЕ |

The era following the Revolution in 1917—though tumultuous and difficult in political and social terms—was nonetheless rich and productive in the further development of Russian music in composition and performance. The new Soviet State placed a premium on the arts as part of the socialist order. Like their achievements in science and technology, Soviet leaders placed their composers and musicians before the world as a demonstration of the superiority of the state. The individuals and works which emerged from this period were, indeed, some of the finest in the world.

Sergei Sergeevich Prokofiev (1891–1953)

Серге́й Серге́евич Проко́фьев

Prokofiev received his formal instruction at the Petersburg Conservatory from several of the masters, including Rimsky-Korsakov. In 1917 he completed his *First*, or *Classical Symphony in D major, Op. 25,* **«Пе́рвая, или Класси́ческая, симфо́ния ре мажо́р»** and immediately after began his first tour of the U.S., during which the Chicago Opera commissioned the opera *Love for Three Oranges* **«Любо́вь к трём апельси́нам»** (1919). After moving to Paris

Fig. 7-26.   S. Prokofiev

in 1920, he wrote three ballets for Diaghilev and another opera, *The Fiery Angel* **«О́гненный а́нгел»** (1923), which was never performed during his life. He returned to live in Russia in 1933, just as the doctrine of "socialist realism" was taking control of the arts. So Prokofiev turned instead to film scores as a creative outlet, producing some of the most memorable soundtracks in Russian film, most notably for two of Sergei Eisenstein's films *Alexander Nevsky* **«Алекса́ндр Не́вский»** (1938) and *Ivan the Terrible* **«Ива́н Гро́зный»** (1942). During this period he also wrote two popular ballets: *Romeo and Juliet* **«Роме́о и Джулье́тта»** (1936) and *Cinderella* **«Зо́лушка»** (1944), as well as his extremely popular narrative orchestral piece to introduce children to the orchestra *Peter and the Wolf* **«Пе́тя и Волк»** (1936). His opera *War and Peace* **«Война́ и мир»** (1943) was also first performed, and he completed what is perhaps his most famous symphony, the *Fifth Symphony in B flat major*, Op. 100 **«Пя́тая симфо́ния си бемо́ль мажо́р»** (1944). By 1948, Prokofiev again came under fire from the Soviet government for writing "formalist" compositions, a crime to which he was compelled to confess in an open letter. Ironically, he died on the same day Stalin did in 1953.

Dmitri Dmitrievich Shostakovich (1906–75)

Дми́трий Дми́триевич Шостако́вич

Shostakovich was born in St. Petersburg and began his musical education with his mother. His formal musical education began at the Petrograd Conservatory, where he received instruction and encouragement from Glazunov. He gained world recognition with the performance of his diploma project, the *First Symphony in F minor*, Op. 10 «**Пе́рвая симфо́ния фа мино́р**», when only twenty years of age. In the late 1920s and early 1930s Shostakovich broad-

Fig. 7-27. D. Shostakovich

ened his creative projects to include ballets, such as *The Golden Age* «**Золото́й век**» (1930), and operas, such as the avant-garde *The Nose,* Op. 15 «**Нос**» (1928), and *Lady Macbeth of the Mtsensk District* «**Ле́ди Ма́кбет Мце́нского уе́зда**» (1932). The opera was revived in 1953 and renamed *Katerina Izmailova* «**Катери́на Изма́йлова**», after the opera's heroine. The original title was finally restored in 1964. The 1932 production caused strong reaction in the press against its "formalism," a term of abuse in the system of Socialist Realism. His response to such criticism was to compose the *Fifth Symphony in D minor,* Op. 47 «**Пя́тая симфо́ния ре мино́р**» (1937). During World War II, Shostakovich served as a firefighter through the seige of Leningrad and portrayed this experience in his *Seventh Symphony in C major,* Op. 60 «**Седьма́я симфо́ния до мажо́р**» (1941), widely known as the *Leningrad Symphony*. During the years of Socialist Realism, Shostakovich—like his contemporary Prokofiev—worked on film scores, and on new orchestrations of works, such as Mussorgsky's *Boris Godunov* «**Бори́с Годуно́в**» (1940). It is during the last twenty years of his life, after Stalin's death, that Shostakovich composes prolifically and brilliantly. He also returned to film scores late in his life, writing the music for *Hamlet* «**Га́млет**» (1964) and *King Lear* «**Коро́ль Лир**» (1970), before his death in 1975.

Fig. 7-28.   Scene from *The Golden Age*

Aram Il'ich Khachaturian (1903–78)

Ара́м Ильи́ч Хачатуря́н

Khachaturian brought to his compositions the distinctive influence of Armenian folk melodies and instrumentation. After studying science and biology, Khachaturian turned to the cello at the Moscow Conservatory, where he was noticed by Prokofiev. His *First Symphony* «Пе́рвая симфо́ния» (1938) was well-received, but it was his ballet productions that brought him fame.

Fig. 7-29.   A. Khachaturian

Gayane «Гаянэ́» (1942) featured the frenetic "Sabre Dance" **Та́нец с са́блями** and enjoyed a long run. When his *Second Symphony* «Втора́я симфо́ния» (1948) brought official criticism from the State, Khachaturian turned to scoring films including *Lenin* (1949) and *Othello* (1955). 1954 brought the composer his greatest triumph with his compositions for the ballet *Spartacus* «Спарта́к».

Alfred Garrievich Schnittke (1934–98)

Альфре́д Га́рриевич Шни́тке

Russian-born Schnittke received his early music education in Vienna, but returned to Russia to the Moscow Conservatory to finish his formal training. From 1962–72 he taught music composition at the Conservatory, promoting his radical, dramatic use of quotations from other works in his compositions. During the Soviet period, Schnittke's music was best known to Rus-

Fig. 7-30.   A. Schnittke

sians from his compositions for films, such as Romm's *And still I believe* «И всё-таки я ве́рю» and Klimov's *Agony* «Аго́ния». He is best known for his operas, such as *Life with an Idiot* «Жизнь с идио́том» (1991), and ballets, such as *Peer Gynt* «Пер Гюнт» (1987). From 1990 Schnittke lived and worked in Germany.

RUSSIAN BALLET AND OPERA

In the Theater

РУ́ССКИЙ БАЛЕ́Т И О́ПЕРА

В теа́тре

Fig. 7-31.

1)	curtain	за́навес	11)	box seat	ме́сто в ло́же
2)	scenery	декора́ция	12)	orchestra seats	парте́р
3)	dancer	балери́на; танцо́р	13)	mezzanine	бельэта́ж
4)	spotlight	прожéктор	14)	balcony	балко́н
5)	stage	сце́на	15)	audience	зри́тели
6)	orchestra	орке́стр	16)	ticket-taker	билетёр(ша)
7)	podium	дирижёрский пу́льт	17)	program	програ́мма
8)	conductor	дирижёр	18)	music stand	пульт
9)	baton	па́лочка	19)	wings, behind the scenes	кули́сы, за кули́сами
10)	musician	музыка́нт	20)	topmost balcony	галёрка

Founded in Moscow in 1776, the Bolshoi is one of the oldest and certainly the best known of Russia's theaters. Presenting the musical talents of Russia's best composers and performers, the theater quickly gained the reputation as a world class stage for opera and ballet. The original theater burned down in 1853 and was rebuilt into the form in which it remains today. The opera and ballet companies of the Bolshoi have toured the theaters of the world, bringing Russia's classical musical tradition to millions.

Fig. 7-32.   Bolshoi Theater **Большо́й теа́тр Р о с си́ и, Госуда́рственный академи́ческий Большо́й теа́тр (ГАБТ)**

The ballet company of the Mariinsky Theater (below) in Petersburg is the oldest in Russia and surely one of the best in the world. After the Revolution, the theater was renamed the Kirov State Academic Theater **Госуда́рственный академи́ческий теа́тр о́перы и бале́та им. Ки́рова**, which it remained until 1991, when it was renamed the Mariinsky Theater.

Fig. 7-33.   Mariinsky Theater **Марии́нский теа́тр**

Opened in 1785, the Hermitage Theater in Petersburg was used to stage operas, ballets and balls for the Imperial family and their guests. After the October Revolution, the theater building was used to house the first Worker's University, and then served as a musical museum until 1935. Today ballets and plays as well as conferences are held in the theater.

Fig. 7-34.   Hermitage Theater **Эрмита́жный теа́тр**

The Artists   **Исполни́тели**

Most of the artists—musicians, singers, dancers shown here—have parentheses around their patronymics. That was done to emphasize that performers are usually known only by their last names, or last names plus first names. Exceptions might be the case of Ulanova or Plisetskaya, whose patronymics became common in the press only in their later years.

Musicians and Singers   *Музыка́нты и певцы́*

Fedor Ivanovich Chaliapin (1873–1938)

Фёдор (Ива́нович) Шаля́пин

Russia's most famous opera singer, Chaliapin is closely identified with his role as Boris Godunov. Diaghilev first brought the singer to Paris in 1913, which brought immediate fame to Chaliapin. In 1922 he emigrated to Paris where he remained and continued to perform. (On the accompanying CD-ROM, Chaliapin may be heard singing a portion of the Volga Boatmen's song, link 7-8 on p. 425.)

Fig. 7-35. Chaliapin as Boris Godunov

David Fedorovich Oistrakh (1908–74)

Дави́д (Фёдорович) О́йстрах

Born in Odessa, Oistrakh became one of the twentieth century's greatest violinists and one of the best-known Russian musicians in the West. He toured and performed around the world for more than forty years. Shostakovich dedicated his violin concertos to Oistrakh, who took up conducting during his last decade, often performing in an ensemble with Richter.

Fig. 7-36.   D. Oistrakh

Emil′ Grigor′evich Gilels (1916–85)

Эми́ль (Григо́рьевич) Ги́лельс

Born in Odessa, Gilels began his study of piano at the age of five and made his debut at the Odessa Conservatory in 1929. He continued his music education at the Moscow Conservatory and soon after began a performing career on an international scale, winning competitions in

Fig. 7-37.   E. Gilels

Belgium, France, Austria and the US. Considered one of the best piano performers of the twentieth century, Gilels was known to listeners around the world.

Sviatoslav Teofilovich Richter (1915–97)

Святосла́в (Теофи́лович) Ри́хтер

Child prodigy of the piano, Richter was born in Zhitomir. After finishing his musical education at the Moscow Conservatory, he made his debut in Odessa in 1934, gaining immediate international acclaim. He specialized in performing the works of Prokofiev, who dedicated his *Piano Sonata No. 9* to Richter.

Fig. 7-38.   S. Richter

Irina Konstantinovna Arkhipova (b. 1925)   Ири́на (Константи́новна) Архи́пова

Arkhipova is a mezzo-soprano **ме́ццо-сопра́но** who made her debut at the Bolshoi in the role of **в па́ртии** Carmen which made her famous. She sang there from 1956 until 1988.

Mstislav Leopoldovich Rostropovich (b. 1927)

Мстисла́в (Леопо́льдович) Ростропо́вич

Born in Baku, Azerbaijan, Rostropovich began his study of music early with his talented musician parents. He studied formally at the Moscow Conservatory under Shostakovich and graduated with high honors. In 1955 he married Galina Vishnevskaya, soloist with the Bolshoi opera. He gained fame as cellist with the Moscow Philharmonic thoughout the 1950s and 1960s. In 1974, however, he and his wife left the Soviet Union and were subsequently stripped of their Soviet citizenship,

Fig. 7-39. M. Rostropovich

largely for their outspoken support of Alexander Solzhenitsyn. For a number of years he was the director of the National Symphony Orchestra in Washington, DC. Russian citizenship was returned to Rostropovich and Vishnevskaya in 1990. In August 1991, Rostropovich returned to Moscow without a visa during the historic coup and received a hero's welcome.

Galina Pavlovna Vishnevskaya (b. 1926)

Гали́на (Па́вловна) Вишне́вская

Born in Leningrad, Vishnevskaya began her singing career in the operetta and with the philharmonic. In 1944 she became a soloist with the Bolshoi Theater in Moscow, performing roles such as Liza in *Queen of Spades*, Tatiana in *Eugene Onegin*, and Natasha in *War and Peace*. Vishnevskaya married the cellist Mstislav Rostropovich.

Fig. 7-40. G. Vishnevskaya

Elena Vasil′evna Obraztsova (b. 1930)   **Еле́на (Васи́льевна) Образцо́ва**

Perhaps the best known female opera singer, Obraztsova began at the Bolshoi in 1964. Her roles **па́ртии** included: Marfa in *Khovanshchina* (Mussorgsky), Liubasha in *The Tsar's Bride* (Rimsky-Korsakov), the countess in *The Queen of Spades* (Tchaikovsky), *Carmen* (Bizet), and others.

Mikhail Vasil′evich Pletnev (b. 1957)   **Михаи́л (Васи́льевич) Плетнёв**

Winner of the Sixth Tchaikovsky International Piano Competition in 1978, Pletnev is the founder and conductor of the Russian National Orchestra. Since the 1980s he has toured internationally both as a performer and conductor.

Evgenii Kissin (b. 1971)   **Евге́ний Ки́син**

At age twelve Kissin debuted with Moscow Symphony Orchestra and then with the BBC Proms, playing both Chopin concertos. By 1990 with his American debut, Kissin had made his repertoire primarily Russian composers.

Ballet   *Бале́т*

Ballet is not just an art form in Russia but also one of the sports, that is, it is often shown on television and there are active fans: pro-Ulanova or pro-Plisetskaya in the old days, those who root for Pavlova, or Ananiashvili or Chenchikova these days. When the Bolshoi broke up, everybody watched it like an athletic competiton, which side would win, Grigorovich or Vasil′ev, and so on. Ballet matters. What follows is the Hall of Fame for ballet.

Marius Ivanovich Petipa (1818–1910)

Ма́риус (Ива́нович) Петипа́

French-born Petipa began his long relationship with Russian ballet in 1847, when he was invited to Petersburg as a dancer, but quickly discovered his own passion for choreography and production. Petipa has been credited with bringing European technique to the Petersburg Imperial Theater. His innovative versions of *The Sleeping Beauty* and *Raymonda* are still regarded as superior. He worked on dozens of ballets in his lifetime, adding to each his unique sense of movement and composition on the stage.

Fig. 7-41.   M. Petipa

Sergey Pavlovich Diaghilev (1872–1929)

Сергéй (Пáвлович) Дя́гилев

Diaghilev finished law school while simultaeously studying the arts in Petersburg. In 1899 he became artistic adviser to the Mariinsky Theater, but the turning point in his career came in 1908 when he organized with Chaliapin a series of Russian concerts, including *Boris Godunov*, in Paris. The following year he presented a season of Russian ballet and opera, which became the basis for his Ballets Russes. Founded by Diaghilev in 1910 following his brilliant presentation in Paris of a season of Russian opera and ballet, the Ballets Russes included Fokin as artistic director, Nijinsky as lead dancer, Karsavina

Fig. 7-42.   S. Diaghilev

as prima ballerina, S.L. Grigoriev as director, plus an 85-member troupe from Petersburg, Moscow and Warsaw. The creative foresight of Diaghilev brought the immeasurable talent of avant-garde choreographers (Nijinsky, Fokin, Balanchine) and artists (Bakst, Benois, Picasso, Matisse) to Russian dance. Despite numerous financial and creative setbacks, the ballet company performed throughout Europe and in the United States for twenty years, bringing a new aesthetic of dance to the West.

Mathilde Feliksovna Kshesinskaia (1872–1971)

Матú́льда (Марú́я) (Фéликсовна) Кшесú́нская (Кржесú́нская)

Prima ballerina of the Mariinsky Theater, Kshesinskaya danced almost all of the great classical roles from Odette in *Swan Lake* to Aurora in *The Sleeping Beauty*. Beyond her dancing, she was known also for many and varied lovers, including the future tsar, Nicolas II. She emigrated to France shortly after the October Revolution, where she opened a studio, attracting students such as Margot Fonteyn.

Fig. 7-43.   M. Kshesinskaia

Mikhail Mikhailovich Fokin (1880–1942)

Михаи́л (Миха́йлович) Фо́кин

Fokin studied theater and dance at the Mariinsky Theater in his native Petersburg from 1898 to 1902, when he began a teaching appointment there. He worked with the best dancers in the troupe, choreographing for Pavlova and Karsavina. He was especially influential and active in reforming ballet methods from academic to more aesthetic. Diaghilev saw Fokin's tremendous talent and recruited him for his Ballets Russes. His genius is most prominent in his ballets such as *The Firebird*, *Les Sylphides*, and *Petrushka*. He moved to New York after leaving the Ballets Russes, breaking with Diaghilev over artistic differences.

Fig. 7-44. Fokin in *La Halte de Cavalerie*

Anna Pavlovna Pavlova (1881–1931)

А́нна (Па́вловна) Па́влова

At the turn of the century, Pavlova was in the troupe of the Mariinsky Theater, and in 1906 she became a featured ballerina. By 1910 she was Russia's prima ballerina with a worldwide reputation. She was best known for her interpretations of Giselle and of Odette in *Swan Lake*, focusing her immense talent on indigenous Russian ballets. Her performances became legendary; there is even a film of her dancing the *Dying Swan* by St. Säens.

Fig. 7-45. A. Pavlova in *Paquita*, 1908

Tamara Platonovna Karsavina (1885–1978)

Тама́ра (Плато́новна) Карса́вина

A Petersburg native, Karsavina completed her education and began her dance career there. In the midst of the artistic debates over the "academicism" of the ballet at the turn of the century, Karsavina found her ideal environment in the choreography of Mikhail Fokin, who had been focusing his efforts on Anna Pavlova. Karsavina turned out to be the ideal interpreter of his "intellectual art" of ballet, which was exemplified in works such as *Chopiniana*, *The Firebird*, and *Petrushka*. From 1918 to 1929 she danced in Diaghilev's Ballets Russes before becoming vice president of the Royal Academy of Dance in Britain.

Fig. 7-46.   Karsavina in *Le Pavillon d'Armide*

Vaslav Fomich Nijinsky (1889–1950)

Ва́цлав (Фоми́ч) Нижи́нский

Born in Kiev to ballet dancer parents, Nijinsky received his training and early dance experience in Petersburg, joining the Mariinsky troupe in 1907. There he was paired with Russia's leading ballerinas, including Anna Pavlova and Tamara Karsavina. He was fired from the Mariinsky in 1911 for deciding to wear a controversial costume for his role in *Giselle*. In the following years, he joined Diaghilev's Ballets Russes as both master of the ballet and principal dancer. His unique style of interpretation made roles in ballets such as *L'après-midi d'un faune* and *Sacre du printemps* exclusively his. In 1917, at the peak of his creativity, Nijinsky developed a mental dysfunction which caused him to be institutionalized for the remainder of his life. The homoerotic nature of the ambiguous relationship between Nijinsky and Diaghilev was documented by the dancer in his diary, published in Russia in 1995.

Fig. 7-47.   Nijinsky in *Jeux*

George Melitonovich Balanchine (1904–83)

Гео́ргий (Мелито́нович) Баланчи́н

Born in Petersburg into a Georgian family (Balan-
chivadze), Balanchine was classically trained in the
Petrograd Imperial School of Ballet and, in 1921, became a dancer in the Petrograd Theater of Opera
and Ballet. He emigrated from Russia in 1924, and
joined Diaghilev's Ballets Russes as a choreographer
during the last years of the company. His choreography of Stravinsky's *Apollo Musagetes* and *Orpheus*

Fig. 7-48.   G.
Balanchine

are still considered standards. In 1934 he moved to New York, where he
created the American Ballet Company and became the major force and inno-
vator of American dance for the next fifty years.

Konstantin Mikhailovich Sergeev (b. 1910)

Константи́н (Миха́йлович) Серге́ев

Born in Petersburg, Sergeev danced with the Kirov
Theater from 1931 to 1961, bringing classical interpretations of principal roles in works such as *Swan
Lake, The Sleeping Beauty*, and *Romeo and Juliet*,
for which he was paired with Ulanova—his principal
partner throughout the 1930s and early 1940s. He
turned to teaching and lecturing later in his career.

Fig. 7-49.Sergeev as
the prince in *Cinderella*

Galina Sergeevna Ulanova (1910–98)

Гали́на Серге́евна Ула́нова

A native of Petersburg, Ulanova was born into
a family of dancers. In her very first performances, critics noted how seamlessly and expres-
sively she danced, without violating the para-
meters of classical requirements. She brought
this portrait of classicism to many of her most
notable performances at the Kirov Theater,
such as Odette in *Swan Lake*, Masha in *The
Nutcracker*, and the title role in *Giselle*. From

Fig. 7-50. Ulanova as Ju-
liet in *Romeo and Juliet*

1944 to 1960 she was prima ballerina at the Bolshoi Theater in Moscow, where her most memorable characterizations included Maria in *The Fountain of Bakhchisarai*, and Juliet in *Romeo and Juliet*. In her lifetime she was honored with festivals, prizes and exhibitions all over the world.

Maya Mikhailovna Plisetskaya (b. 1925)

Ма́йя (Миха́йловна) Плисе́цкая

Plisetskaya received early training in dance in her native Moscow, and immediately became famous for her style—an unusual expressiveness of every gesture and pose in her dances. These elements, combined with her phenomenal leaps and athleticism, gained her entry into the Bolshoi Theater in 1943, where she remained until 1990. Her first role as the Autumn fairy in *Cinderella* in 1945 distinguished her as a major talent in ballet. Among

Fig. 7-51.   Plisetskaya in *Swan Lake*

her most famous roles were in the ballets *The Carmen Suite*, *Anna Karenina* and *The Firebird*, but her signature role was in *Dying Swan* by Saint-Säens. Later in her career Plisetskaya danced in several films and, since 1990, has conducted master dance classes all over the world.

Maris (-Rudolf Eduardovich) Liepa (1936–89)

Ма́рис(-Рудо́льф Эдуа́рдович)[12] **Лие́па**

Riga-born Liepa was an accomplished dancer, choreographer and ballet master over three decades. Dancing a wide range of leading roles, such as Albert in *Giselle* and Krass in *Spartak*, Liepa's interpretations were marked by their physicality and strength.

Fig. 7-52. Liepa in *Walpurgis Night*

---

[12] Usually known as **Ма́рис Лие́па**.

Rudolf Hametovich Nureyev (1938–93)

Рудо́льф (Хаме́тович) Нуре́ев

A Siberian, Nureyev became a member of the Kirov Ballet in 1958, attracting world attention for his athletic and expressive artistic interpretations of roles such as Albert in *Giselle*, and Desirée in *The Sleeping Beauty*. While on tour in Paris in 1961 Nureyev defected to the West and is therefore better known as an expatriate than as a dancer in Russia.

Fig. 7-53. Nureyev as James in *La Sylphide*

Ekaterina Sergeevna Maksimova (b. 1939)

Екатери́на (Серге́евна) Макси́мова

Born in Moscow, Maksimova completed her dance training in 1958 and immediately joined the troupe of the Bolshoi Theater, where she continued to perform until 1988. Even while still a dance student, she danced the role of Masha in *The Nutcracker* at the Bolshoi before becoming a lead dancer there. She married Vladimir Vasil'ev while at the Bolshoi, and the pair became one of the most famous dancing couples in the history of the theater, performing

Fig. 7-54.   Maksimova and Vasil'ev in *The Nutcracker*

together in ballets such as *Romeo and Juliet*, *The Nutcracker*, and *Carmen*. She was the designated "heiress" of Ulanova. Later in her career she turned her attention to directing ballet and since 1990 has been the ballet master and trainer at the Theater of the Kremlin Palace of Congresses.

Natal′ia Romanovna Makarova (b. 1940)

Ната́лья (Рома́новна) Мака́рова

Makarova began performing with the Kirov
ballet in her native Leningrad in 1959 and remained as their prima ballerina until 1970.
During her remarkable time with the Kirov, she
interpreted such roles as Aurora in *The
Sleeping Beauty*, Odette in *Swan Lake*, and the
title role in *Giselle*. Since 1970 she has lived and
worked abroad, dancing in creative partner-
ships with Nureyev, Balanchine and
Baryshnikov.

Fig. 7-55. Makarova in
A Distant Planet

Vladimir Viktorovich Vasil′ev (b. 1940)

Влади́мир (Ви́кторович) Васи́льев

Moscow-born Vasil′ev burst onto the Russian ballet
scene at the Bolshoi Theater in 1958 with remarkably physical and energetic new interpretations of
Daniel in *The Stone Flower* «Ка́менный цвето́к»
and Ivanushka in *The Humpback Horse* «Конёк-
горбуно́к». In his thirty years at the Bolshoi he
masterfully played a variety of leading roles, but is
best known for his portrayal of Spartacus in 1964.
His regular partner throughout his career was
Ekaterina Maksimova, with whom he performed in
The Nutcracker and many other works. He continues to dance and teach; from 1995 to 2000 he was
the artistic director of the Bolshoi.

Fig. 7-56. Vasil′ev in
Don Quixote

Natal′ia Igorevna Bessmertnova (b. 1941)

Ната́лья (И́горевна) Бессме́ртнова

Immediately following her formal training in Moscow, Bessmertnova joined the Bolshoi Theater in 1961. From her very first performances in *Chopiniana*, she exhibited an unusual romanticism and artistry which would mark all of her interpretations for the next 34 years. Her ability to transform even the most frequently performed roles into new character portraits all her own made her one of the most popular ballerinas among Russian audiences. Some of her most famous performances were in *The Nutcracker*, *Swan Lake*, *Don Quixote* «Дон Кихо́т», *Romeo and Juliet*, and especially *Giselle* «Жизе́ль».

Fig. 7-57. Bessmertnova in *Giselle*

Mikhail Nikolaevich Baryshnikov (b. 1948)

Михаи́л (Никола́евич) Бары́шников

A product of the Riga school of ballet, Baryshnikov showed extraordinary talent as a young dancer and, after winning all of the major prizes for graduates, became a member of the Kirov troupe in Leningrad in 1967. In the early 1970s he caught the attention of the world with his brilliant interpretations in *Giselle*, *Swan Lake*, and *Romeo and Juliet*. In 1974, while on tour in the United States, Baryshnikov defected and joined the American Ballet Theater. Later Baryshnikov would become first a dancer for and then director of the New York City Ballet.

Fig. 7-58. Baryshnikov in *The Four Temperaments*

Viacheslav Mikhailovich Gordeev (b. 1948)

Вячесла́в (Миха́йлович) Горде́ев

After dancing for twenty-one years with the Bolshoi Theater ballet in memorable roles such as Romeo, Albert, Desiree, and the Prince in "The Nutcracker," Gordeev became more involved in the productions themselves as ballet master. Since 1995, Gordeev has served as the artistic director of the Bolshoi Ballet.

Fig. 7-59. Gordeev as Romeo

Nadezhda Vasil'evna Pavlova (b. 1956)

Надéжда (Васи́льевна) Па́влова

First appeared with the Perm' Ballet, where she gained fame as a dancer of roles such as Juliet and Giselle in the early 1970s. From 1975, she danced with the Bolshoi Theater Ballet, reprising her role as Juliet with Gordeev dancing the part of Romeo. Her repertoire expanded to include the roles of Odette in *Swan Lake* «Лебеди́ное óзеро», Kitri in *Don Quixote* «Дон Кихóт», Aurora in *Sleeping Beauty* «Спя́щая краса́вица», and Masha in *The Nutcracker* «Щелку́нчик».

Fig. 7-60. Pavlova in *Don Quixote*

Nina Gedevanovna Ananiashvili (b. 1963)

Ни́на (Гедевáновна) Ананиашви́ли

Georgian-born and trained Ananiashvili joined the Bolshoi Theater ballet in 1981. She became world famous in the Bolshoi dancing the roles of Giselle, Raymonda, Juliet and Aurora among others. Since 1988 she has danced with various international troupes, including the New York City Ballet, the Danish Royal Ballet, and the Royal Ballet in London.

Fig. 7-61. Ananiashvili in *Raymonda*

Andris Marisovich Liepa (b. 1962)   А́ндрис (Ма́рисович) Лиéпа

Son of Maris-Rudolf Liepa, Andris began his ballet career in the Bolshoi Theater from 1981 to 1990. Since 1990, he has danced with the Kirov Ballet at the Mariinsky Theater, the New York City Ballet and the American Ballet Theater under the direction of Baryshnikov. Some of his most famous roles include the Prince in *Cinderella* and Romeo in *Romeo and Juliet.*

Ilze Marisovna Liepa (b. 1963)   Й́лзе (Ма́рисовна) Лиéпа

Daughter of Maris-Rudolf Liepa, Ilze danced with Bolshoi Theater in roles such as Mercedes in *Don Quixote* and Odette-Odile in *Swan Lake*. Her performances are marked by their classical form and style.

Opera   Óпера

The first major difference between opera here and opera there can be expected: they play many more Russian operas than do we: *Eugene Onegin* «Евгéний Онéгин» and the *Queen of Spades* «Пúковая дáма» by Tchaikovsky, *Boris Godunov* «Борúс Годунóв» and «Ховáнщина», by Mussorgsky, *Prince Igor* «Князь Úгорь» by Borodin, *Sadko* «Садкó» and the *Tsar's Bride* «Цáрская невéста» (and several others) by Rimsky-Korsakov, *Ruslan and Liudmila* «Руслáн и Людмúла», and *Ivan Susanin* «Ивáн Сусáнин/Жизнь за царя́» by Glinka.

The other difference is that the variety and number of operas more familiar to us is different from ours. Especially in Soviet days it was easier to replay or redo an accepted opera rather than attempt a new one. As a result, popular operas were *Carmen* «Кармéн», *La Traviata* «Травиáта», *Rigoletto* «Риголéтто», *Il Trovatore* «Трубадýр», *Marriage of Figaro* «Свáдьба Фúгаро», *Barber of Seville* «Севúльский цирю́льник», *Tosca* Тóска», *Madame Butterfly* «Чúо-Чúо-сáн», *Don Carlos* «Дон Кáрлос», *Pagliacci* «Пая́цы», while much less frequently *La Forza del Destino* «Сúла судьбы́», and especially *Aida* «Аúда», and *La Bohème* «Богéма» which have dominated in the United States.

Though exceptions were occasionally made for some foreign singers, the practice has been to sing operas in Russian (thus conforming to the quaint European custom of singing opera in the language of the country). As a result some lines from famous arias have gone into the language: from *The Barber of Seville* « Фúгаро тут, Фúгаро там»; from *Boris Godunov* « И м áльчики кровáвые в глазáх» and «Обúдели юрóдивого, óтняли копéечку»; from *La Traviata* «Поднúмем, поднúмем бокáлы»; from *Rigoletto* «Сéрдце красáвицы склóнно к измéне, и к перемéне, как вéтер мáя»; from *Carmen* «Тореадóр, смелéе в бой»; and from *Pagliacci* «Смейся, пая́ц!»

Contemporary Popular Music   Совремéнная популя́рная   мýзыка

If classical music unites us (any us), then popular music often separates us. In any country popular music is a means of expression; the Soviet government watched such things closely, controlled them, and over time, often spoiled (that is, rendered sickening) many otherwise lovely, even inspiring melodies by merely overplaying them and thus condemning them to the category of "Soviet."

As much as politics, time separates us: grandma knows songs you have never heard, you have heard your mother's songs but you don't know the words, and some parents have difficulty listening to the productions of the youngest age group. But some songs are staples ("Yankee Doodle"), are unavoidable (the "Wedding March"), or have strong associations with events, singers, or musical groups. Most of the musical selections here reflect the opinions of educated city Russians in their thirties in the year 2000. Samples of most of the following songs can be heard on the CD-ROM, with an accompanying text of the song lyrics and the names of the lyricist and composer of the music given in that order. The selections should be thought of as representative rather than complete since we must confine ourselves to the possible.

Folk Songs   Народные песни

Folk songs here, are (more or less technically) those from the past without a known composer **композитор** or lyricist. Still usually familiar are the following where first lines are often the title:

- «Во́ поле берёза стоя́ла»   🗎 7-3
- «Дуби́нушка»   🗎 7-4
- «Ой, полны́м-полна́ коро́бушка»   🗎 7-5
- «Пойду́ ль, вы́йду ль я» (This is a round **кано́н**.)   🗎 7-6
- «Се́ни, мои́ сени»   🗎 7-7
- «Эй, у́хнем, эй, ух-нем!»   🗎 7-8

The "Romance"   Рома́нс

Very popular in certain groups (mostly middle class) and at certain times (especially at the turns of the centuries), is a particularly Russian phenomenon, the "romance." These are a high-toned late 19th century love song, often a sad one ("cruel" romance **жесто́кий рома́нс**) or a lament, **«Отцвели́ уж давно́ хризанте́мы в саду́»** ("The Chrysanthemums in the Garden Faded Long Ago"). They are often sung to the accompaniment of a guitar **под гита́ру** by trained singers, even some opera singers. Still famous are: **П. Ле́щенко, С. Ле́мешев, И. Архи́пова, Е. Образцо́ва, И. Козло́вский, А. Верти́нский, В. Агафо́нов.** The romance is responsible for making many a poet's words more familiar than they might have been otherwise. The romance is currently rising in popularity.

Actually, a large number of what are thought of as classic and old songs began as romances. For example, "Dark Eyes" **«О́чи чёрные»** and "The Long Road" **«Доро́гой дли́нною»** (1926) started out life as romances in the gypsy style, and therefore Russian thought places them with violinists in restaurants.

- «Доро́гой дли́нною»   🗎 7-9
- «О́чи чёрные»   🗎 7-10
- «Пе́сня цыга́нки (Мой костёр)»   🗎 7-11

Classic (Old) Songs   **Старинные песни**

Some of the old, classic songs began life as romances, or folk songs, or just old songs. They are known by older people and familiar to younger people since their elders often sing them at celebrations.

7-12 • «Калинка»

7-13 • «Однозвучно гремит колокольчик»

7-14 • «Метелица»

7-15 • «Вечерний звон»

7-16 • «Позарастали стёжки-дорожки». Now familiar only to denote something long gone.

7-17 • «Раскинулось море широко»

7-18 • «Славное море, священный Байкал» (See Chapter 10, Lake Baikal)

7-19 • «Степь да степь кругом»

7-20 • «Тройка»

7-21 • «Вдоль по Питерской»

7-22 • «Крутится, вертится шар голубой»

In this same general category are drinking songs where usage does not parallel ours: we have drinking songs from operas and we have songs drunks sing ("How dry …") with nothing in between. Drinking and singing is done at the table in Russia so that songs associated with drinking are "seated at table songs" **застольные песни**, for example:

 7-23 • «Из-за острова на стрежень» (Стенька Разин) (See Ch. 1 for words)

7-24 • «Шумел камыш»

7-25 • «Ой, цветёт калина» (из кинофильма «Кубанские казаки»)

War Songs   **Военные песни**

The Russo-Japanese war supplied "On Manchurian Mountains" **«На сопках Маньчжурии»**. And the revolution popularized "Boldly, Comrades, All Together" **«Смело, товарищи, в ногу»**. World War II was the background for some glorious songs, and some less so. In the latter category is "Katiusha" **«Катюша»** (1938).

Other songs are also associated with World War II. Many are remembered from recordings of the Soviet Army Chorus.

7-28 • «Полюшко, поле»

7-29 • «Синий платочек» A song made famous and still associated with Shul'zhenko **Клавдия Шульженко** (the Russian version of Marlene Dietrich).

7-30 • «Священная война»

7-31 • «На безымянной высоте» (из кинофильма «Тишина»)

- «День Побе́ды»   🗎 **7-32**
- «Тёмная ночь»   🗎 **7-33**
- «В земля́нке»   🗎 **7-34**
- «В лесу́ прифронтово́м»   🗎 **7-35**
- «Эх, доро́ги»   🗎 **7-36**

"Soviet" Songs   Сове́тские пе́сни

These are the songs that are perfectly good, and sometimes even glorious songs acceptable to the older population (and also, therefore, to the establishment) and as a result were also regarded as over-played by the younger generation. Most war songs could be in this category, as were songs strongly associated with movies.

- "Moscow Evenings" «Подмоско́вные вечера́». The song won the 1957 🗎 **7-37** International Song Competition in Moscow, and is known to every citizen from radio "Mayak" **Мая́к** signal every hour.
- «Шко́льный вальс»
- «Я люблю́ тебя́, жизнь»   🗎 **7-38**
- «Пе́сня о дру́ге»
- «Дорога́я моя́ столи́ца» (= Моя́ Москва́)   🗎 **7-39**
- «Гла́вное, ребя́та, се́рдцем не старе́ть»   🗎 **7-40**
- «Течёт Во́лга»   🗎 **7-41**

Songs from Films   Пе́сни из фи́льмов

Many songs are strongly associated with motion pictures (see Chapter 9):

«Широка́ страна́ моя́ родна́я»	from «Цирк»
«Легко́ на се́рдце от пе́сни весёлой»	from «Весёлые ребя́та»
«Всё ста́ло вокру́г голубы́м и зелёным»	from «Весна́»
«Когда́ весна́ придёт»	from «Весна́ на Заре́чной у́лице»
«Мгнове́ние»,	from «Семна́дцать мгнове́ний
«С чего́ начина́ется ро́дина?»	весны́»
«Где́-то на бе́лом све́те»	from «Кавка́зская пле́нница»
«В тёмно-си́нем лесу́»	from «Бриллиа́нтовая рука́»
«У приро́ды нет плохо́й пого́ды»	from «Служе́бный рома́н»
«Ва́ше благоро́дие, госпожа́ разлу́ка»	from «Бе́лое со́лнце пусты́ни» 🗎 **7-42**
«Пе́сня о дру́ге»	from «Я шага́ю по Москве́»
«Капита́н, капита́н, улыбни́тесь»	from «Де́ти капита́на Гра́нта» 🗎 **7-43**
(Пе́сня Паганéля)	
«Пе́сня о Москве́»	from «Свина́рка и пасту́х»
«Ста́рый клён»	from «Девча́та»

Singers   **Певцы́**

Liudmila Georgievna Zykina (b. 1929)   **Людми́ла Гео́ргиевна Зы́кина**

Zykina completed her musical training in Moscow and in 1947 became a soloist
for the Pyatnitsky Russian Folk chorus. In 1951 she became the voice of
Russian folk music through the All-Union Radio. Currently, Zykina is conductor and soloist for the State Republic Russian Folk Ensemble "Russia" **Росси́я**.

Iosif Davydovich Kobzon (b. 1937)   **Ио́сиф (Давы́дович) Кобзо́н**

Born in Ukraine, Kobzon began his musical career in the army, performing in a
musical ensemble. He continued to develop his natural singing talent at a musical institute, when he also began performing on Soviet radio. In 1963 he began
a twenty-six year stint as a soloist for Moskonsert. At that time, Kobzon was
elected to a four-year term as a people's deputy of the USSR. He continued
performing during his tenure and after, until 1997, when he was elected to the
State Duma of Russia, in spite of a variety of allegations of mafia connections.
That year he completed a farewell tour of Russia, performing in dozens of cities
and towns. (He was still singing in 2000. His constancy was doggerel-described:
**Как нельзя́ останови́ть бегу́щего бизо́на, так нельзя́ останови́ть пою́щего
Кобзо́на.** Just as you can't stop a running bison [**бизо́н**], you can't stop a
singing Kobzon.)

The Russian Bards   *Ру́сские ба́рды*

With the period of the so-called post-Stalin "Thaw" **«о́ттепель»** in Khrushchev's Soviet Union of the late 1950s and early 1960s, a new direction in
Russian music developed which exploited the literary and folk traditions of native songwriters. As many of Russia's poets turned to songwriting and performance to reach larger audiences with their works, these authors' songs
«а́вторские пе́сни» or bards' songs **«ба́рдовские пе́сни»** became a genre of
their own. Though the period of the Russian bards lasted only through the
1980s, a new generation of young fans of these songs is now emerging with the
inclusion of the bards' works in the 1993 revised Russian high school curriculum. Above the rest and in a class by themselves are Okudzhava and Vysotsky.

Alexander Arkad′evich Galich (1918–77)

Алекса́ндр (Арка́дьевич) Га́лич

Born Alexander Ginzburg in Moscow, Galich was educated in the theatrical schools of the Moscow Art
Theater under the direction of Stanislavsky. His acting
skills served him well in World War II where he
performed in the theater at the front. After the war, he
gained considerable fame as a playwright and screen
writer. But it was his vocal interpretation of his own lyrics that made Galich
most famous by the end of the 1950s. Several of his songs contained anti-
Stalinist lyrics—not uncommon for writers in the period of the "Thaw," and he
was severely censured by Soviet authorities. He was driven into exile in Paris in
1974 where he continued to write and record until his death by accidental
electrocution in the recording studio. His plays, including **«Матро́сская
тишина́»**, were published in Russia after 1991. In the end he was better known
as a dissident than as a singer in Russia.

Fig. 7-62.   A. Galich

- "Clouds" **«Облака́»**
- "When I Return" **«Когда́ я верну́сь»**

 7-44

Bulat Shalvovich Okudzhava (1924–97)

Була́т (Ша́лвович) Окуджа́ва

A native Muscovite of Georgian and Armenian
parentage, Okudzhava used the Arbat region
where he lived, as well as other Moscow environs,
as the backdrop for many of his popular poems,
lyrics and songs. After serving in World War II
(1941–45) and teaching in a village school in the
early 1950s, he returned to Moscow and became editor of the poetry section
of the popular   weekly newspaper **Литерату́рная газе́та**. As early as 1961,
"Melodiia" took an interest in the many songs circulating in taped form written,
composed and performed by Okudzhava; however, not until some 15 years later did the first official recording of the bard's songs appear. Okudzhava continued to write poetry and songs and perform in public until his death in 1997.

Fig. 7-63.   B. Okudzhava

 7-45   • "The Midnight Trolley" **«Полно́чный тролле́йбус»**
 7-46   • "Song of the Arbat" **«Пе́сенка об Арба́те»**
         • "A Wish to My Friends" **«Пожела́ние друзья́м»**
 7-47   • "The Paper Soldier" **«Бума́жный солда́т»**

Vladimir Vysotsky (1938–80)

Влади́мир (Семёнович) Высо́цкий

Remembered by Russians as "the bard's bard," Vysotsky wrote more than 600 original songs in his short life. The general themes of his cycles of songs included war (though he never served in active combat), prison life (though he never was incarcerated), the creation of art, and human relations. Though few of his songs were officially recorded by "Melodiia" during his lifetime, almost every

Fig. 7-64.   V. Vysotsky

Russian had one or more of Vysotsky's recordings at home on bootleg reel-to-reel recordings, a fact for which he is often credited with beginning "magnitiz-dat" **магнитизда́т** in the Soviet Union. Since many of the songs he sang used the style of the so-called forbidden "songs about the underworld" **блатны́е пе́сни** which dealt with prison camps and army boot camps, they were often censored by Soviet authorities. Besides his singing career, Vysotsky was at least as well known in the Soviet Union for his acting on both stage and screen. His many and diverse roles at Moscow's Taganka Theater, such as Hamlet, Pugachev, and Svidrigailov, are still remembered today. He appeared in more than 20 films, many of which he sang in, such as *The Vertical Line* **«Верти-ка́ль»**. And, as if that were not enough, he married a famous French film actress of Russian descent, Marina Vlady. His death in 1980, though given only minor notice in the offical Soviet press, was followed by a massive funeral procession to the Vagan'kovskoe Cemetery **Вага́ньковское кла́дбище**.

 7-48
- "Restive Horses" **«Ко́ни привере́дливые»**
- "Song about a Friend" **«Пе́сня о дру́ге»**
- "I Do Not Like" **«Я не люблю́»**
- "He Didn't Return from Battle" **«Он не верну́лся из бо́я»**

Zhanna Vladimirovna Bichevskaya (b. 1944)

Жа́нна (Влади́мировна) Биче́вская

Bichevskaya began formal study of voice and guitar early in her life. She was greatly influenced by the work of **Vysotsky** and **Okudzhava** and styled her musical interpretation after theirs. In 1971, on the suggestion of Okudzhava, she added an old Russian folk song called "Mother Dear" **«Ма́тушка»** to her performance list and began her career of collecting and performing folk stan-

Fig. 7-65.   Zh.
Bichevskaya

dards. She has performed all over the world, often called the Russian Joan Baez because of her skill at playing the guitar and her expressive voice.

- •"I Was in a Little Garden" «Я в садо́чке была́»
- •"Mother Dear" «Ма́тушка»

Alexander Yakovlevich Rozenbaum (b. 1950)

Алекса́ндр (Я́ковлевич) Розенба́ум

During his student years Rozenbaum began singing and studying jazz arrangement in night school. In the late 1970s he played with the group "The Argonauts" «Аргона́вты» and began writing his own songs. By the 1980s he was recording cycles of songs dealing with subjects dear to him: Leningrad, the war in Afghanistan, Jewish ethnicity, and childhood. Throughout the 1990s Rozenbaum has concentrated on the writing and performing of his own material.

Fig. 7-66. A. Rozenbaum

- •"Babii Yar" «Ба́бий Яр»
- •"Draw Me a House" «Нарису́йте мне дом»
- •"Duck Hunt" «Ути́ная охо́та»

Veronica Arkad′evna Dolina (b. 1956)

Верони́ка (Арка́дьевна) До́лина

Dolina was born and educated in Moscow. While a student there, she began writing and performing her own songs in 1971 and gained the attention of fans and critics alike. Her lyrics were full of themes politically charged in the pre-glasnost era, and Dolina performed them before countless live audiences. She continues to write and perform her songs in Russia and abroad today.

Fig. 7-67. V. Dolina

- •"When Will We Live Simply" «Когда́ б мы жи́ли без зате́й»
- •"Don't Let the Poet Go to Paris" «Не пуска́йте поэ́та в Пари́ж»

Other bards are Sergei Nikitin, Aleksandr Gorodnitskii, Yurii Vizbor, Aleksandr Sukhanov, Evgenii Bachurin, Aleksandr Dol′skii, and Yulii Kim.

Popular and Rock Music	**Популя́рная и рок-му́зыка**
Stage and Cabaret Music	*Эстра́дная му́зыка*

Often called "light" music **лёгкая му́зыка**, Russian stage music was more acceptable to the authorities, who saw jazz as decadent and too Western. Musicians and singers tried to soften jazz riffs in favor of a lighter sound. Later, when jazz was rehabilitated and a Soviet school of jazz was formed, Russian stage music evolved into dance music with vocals, although elements of jazz remain. Some of the best known performers of Russian stage music include Alla Pugacheva, Sofia Rotaru and Valerii Leont'ev. (Other singers are Muslim Magomaev **Мусли́м Магома́ев,** Lev Leshchenko **Лев Ле́щенко,** and Eduard Khil' **Эдуа́рд Хиль.**)

VIA: Vocal-instrumental Ensemble	*ВИА: вока́льно-инструмента́льный анса́мбль*

This term was coined in the mid 1960s to describe the performing groups—predominantly rock—which began appearing at that time. Though a VIA can in principle be any musical group, the term most frequently describes bands using electric instruments, especially guitar, and drums and percussion. Usually these groups have no fewer than four members, a number modeled most famously by the Beatles **Битлы́, Битлз**. The first Russian VIA was called "The Singing Guitars" **Пою́щие гита́ры** and was formed in 1966. Other notable VIAs include "DDT" **ДДТ**, "Aquarium" **Аква́риум**, "Time Machine" **Маши́на вре́мени**, "Nautilus Pompilius" **Наути́лус Помпи́лиус**, "The Singers" **Песняры́,** and "Bravo" **Бра́во**.

A contemporary musical assemblage can also be almost stunningly obvious: **Э́та гру́ппа игра́ет рок/ди́ско/рейв/рэп/джаз.**

Alla Borisovna Pugacheva (b. 1949)

А́лла (Бори́совна) Пугачёва

Cabaret diva of Russian stage music and concerts, Alla Pugacheva has found success in recording, film, and producing. Her first recording for the Soviet firm "Melodiia" **«Мело́дия»** was called "Harlequin" **«Арлеки́но»** in 1975. It immediately established her as a recording star of the Soviet Union. She took her fame to the Soviet screen in films such as *The Woman Who Sings* **«Же́нщина, кото́рая поёт»** (1978), but unlike Vysotsky, played roles that closely paralleled her real life. She also lent her voice to the soundtracks

Fig. 7-68. A. Pugacheva

of some of the most popular films of the seventies, such as *The Irony of Fate* «Ирóния судьбы, и́ли с лёгким пáром». After the Chernobyl disaster in 1986 she organized an All-Union relief concert for the victims and their families. More recently, she has promoted the careers of other cabaret and stage artists, such as Filip Kirkorov (whom she married in 1994), and the duet «Акадéмия», while continuing to make her own records.

- "Harlequin" «Арлеки́но»
- "A Million Dark Red Roses" «Миллиóн áлых роз»   📄 **7-49**
- "Kings Can Do Everything" «Всё мóгут королú»   📄 **7-50**

Sofia Mikhailovna Rotaru (b. 1947)

Софи́я (Михáйловна) (Евдокимéнко-) Ротáру

Born and educated in Moldavia, Rotaru began singing in student groups while still in university. In 1971 she and her husband formed a musical ensemble VIA called Chervona Ruta ("Red Rue") **Червóна рýта** with the Chernovtsy philharmonic orchestra. In 1977 she became a soloist for the Crimean philharmonic and began recording solo albums.

Fig. 7-69.   S. Rotaru

- "Where Are You, Love" «Где ты, любóвь»
- "My Homeland" «Рóдина моя́»

Valerii Iakovlevich Leont'ev (b. 1949)

Валéрий (Я́ковлевич) Леóнтьев

Leont'ev was born in a provincial town in the Komi Autonomous Republic. After working at many different jobs, Leont'ev finally began study at the All-Russia Creative Workshop for Stage Arts «Всероссúйская твóрческая мастерскáя эстрáдного искýсства» in 1970. As a performer,

Fig. 7-70.   V. Leont'ev

he began singing songs of prominent Russian composers Raymond Pauls, Dmitri Tukhmanov and others who were working with other contemporary artists such as Alla Pugacheva. After several prizes at international song festivals, Leont'ev found his musical stride in the mid-1980s and began his lucrative solo career as a performer of cabaret stage music **эстра́дная му́зыка**. Like Pugacheva, Leont'ev has also made a career of acting in films such as *The Colonel's Daughter* **«Дочь полко́вника** and *ESP* **«Экстрасе́нс»**. He continues to record, make videos, and perform live. His most recent project was a 1997 full-stage show called "On the Road to Hollywood" **«По доро́ге в Голливу́д»**.

- "The Velvet Season" **«Ба́рхатный сезо́н»**
- "Alone with Everyone" **«Наедине́ со все́ми»**

Boris Borisovich Grebenshchikov (b. 1953)

Бори́с (Бори́сович) Гребенщико́в

The very popular and enigmatic leader of the premier Russian rock band of the late 1970s and 1980s was born and educated in Leningrad. While a student of applied mathematics at Leningrad State University, Grebenshchikov and a young drama student formed the band "Aquarium" **Аква́риум** in 1972. This

Fig. 7-71.   B. Grebenshchikov

avant-garde and underground band became quite popular in the early eighties by unofficial circulation of cassette tapes. Not until Gorbachev and glasnost was "Aquarium" released on the official "Melodiia" record label in 1987.

- "Empty Places" **«Пусты́е места́»**
- "Rock and Roll is Dead" **«Рок-н-ролл мёртв»**
- "Sitting on a Beautiful Hill" **«Си́дя на краси́вом холме́»**
- "The City" **«Го́род (золото́й)»**

7-51

Andrei Vadimovich Makarevich (b. 1954)

Андре́й (Вади́мович) Макаре́вич

Together with his schoolmates from School #19 in Moscow, Makarevich formed the pop-rock group, "Time Machine" **Маши́на вре́мени** in 1969. With their longish hair and upbeat tunes, the group quickly became known as the Russian "Beatles." Throughout the 1970s the group was

Fig. 7-72.   A. Makarevich

featured as the Soviet Union's premier rock band—a dubious honor, given the government's official negative stance on decadent Western rock music. Still, with "Melodiia" pressing all of the group's records and a solid touring schedule around the Soviet Union, the group enjoyed massive popularity through the 1980s. Today **«Маши́на вре́мени»** continues to perform, though mostly in smaller venues, and make records and videos. Makarevich also now hosts a popular television cooking and talk show called *Smak* **Смак** (a play on his name and the word for "tasty") and publishes the magazine *Russkii Smak* **Ру́сский Смак**.

- "Cardboard Wings of Love" **«Карто́нные кры́лья любви́»**
- "A Turn" **«Поворо́т»**   7-52
- "To Those at Sea" **«За тех, кто в мо́ре»**   7-53

Viktor Valentinovich Tsoi (1962–90)

Ви́ктор (Валенти́нович) Цой

Tsoi became the charismatic lead singer and songwriter for the Leningrad rock band "Kino" **«Кино́»** in 1981. Together with "Aquarium" and other avant garde Leningrad rock bands in the late 1980s, "Kino" created a new independent movement of Russian rock apart from the

Fig. 7-73.   V. Tsoi

tamer bands being recorded on "Melodiia" records. As Kino's popularity increased, Tsoi extended his career to include films, such as the fantastic *ASSA* and the controversial *The Needle* **«Игла́»** from 1990. Tsoi was killed August 15, 1990 in a car accident. In Russia today Tsoi is still revered as a rock icon in posthumous recordings, posters, T-shirts and unofficial memorials in most cities.

- "Change!" **«Переме́н!»**   7-54
- "A Star Called The Sun" **«Звезда́ по и́мени Со́лнце»**   7-55

MUSIC IN EVERYDAY LIFE   МУ́ЗЫКА В БЫТУ́

Soviet and Russian National Anthems   Сове́тский и Росси́йский Ги́мны

Written in 1871 and 1887, the music and words of "The International" became the anthem for the *Commune de Paris* in France. Just after the October Socialist Revolution in 1917, a Russian-language version of "The International"
7-56 «Интернациона́л» became the offical anthem of the new Soviet nation, replacing the tsarist anthem "God Save the Tsar" **Бо́же, царя́ храни́**,[13] a melody
7-57 familiar to those who hear Tchaikovsky's 1812 Overture. Lenin decreed in 1919 that the International be played from the Spasskii Tower of the Kremlin. Some people remember it because it was sung after every Komsomol meeting.

In 1944, a new National Anthem[14] of the Soviet Union was adopted, which
7-58 remained until the collapse of the Soviet Union in 1991. (An amended version in 1977 eliminated the reference to Stalin.) Between 1991 and 1998, Russia adopted Glinka's "Patriotic Song" **«Патриоти́ческая пе́сня»**, for which A. Mashistov's words were eventually adopted; however, in early 1998 the State Duma soundly rejected the Glinka anthem and narrowly failed to reinstate the old Soviet Anthem. In 2000, the earlier anthem by Aleksandrov was reinstated
7-59 and S. Mihalkov wrote new words.

Lullaby   Колыбе́льная пе́сня

Lullabies can usually be identified by their repetition of "by": **бай, бай-бай, ба́ю, ба́юшки.** Except perhaps in this, the best known one:

7-60   • «Спи, моя́ ра́дость»

7-61   And yet another version: «Спи, моя́ ра́дость»

If mother isn't singing, then those listening to the children's program **Споко́йной но́чи, малыши́!** will hear:

7-62   • «Спят уста́лые игру́шки»

Music for Children   Му́зыка для дете́й

The unquestionable master of the genre of Russian children's music is Vladimir Iakovlevich Shainsky **Влади́мир Я́ковлевич Шаи́нский** (b. 1925). In addition to his birthday tune "Gena the Crocodile's Song," Shainsky has composed some of the most popular children's songs in Russia, including "A Smile"

---

[13] Which in turn was preceded by **Коль сла́вен**, whose melody can be found in Protestant Hymnals.

[14] The lyrics were written by Sergei Mikhalkov, famous as a children's poet and father of filmmakers Nikita Mikhalkov and Andrei Konchalovskii, and Garol′d El′-Registan.

Fig. 7-74.   Cheburashka and Gena the Crocodile

«Улы́бка» and "The Blue Traincar" «Голубо́й ваго́н». These popular tunes permeate Russian popular culture through films, jokes, literature and even other songs. All of them first appeared in cartoon films мультфи́льмы (му́льтики). (See Chapter 9).

- «Улы́бка»   7-63
- «Чу́нга-ча́нга»   7-64
- «Голубо́й ваго́н»   7-65
- «Пе́сенка Чебура́шки»   7-66
- «Пе́сня друзе́й»   7-67
- «Пусть всегда́ бу́дет со́лнце» According to Chukovsky, the refrain to   7-68
  this song was written by a 4-year old in 1928:

Пусть всегда́ бу́дет со́лнце,
Пусть всегда́ бу́дет не́бо,
Пусть всегда́ бу́дет ма́ма,
Пусть всегда́ бу́ду я!

Birthday Music   **День рожде́ния**

Though Russian does not have an occasion-specific birthday song like "Happy Birthday to You," since 1971, Shainsky's "Gena the Crocodile's Song" «Пе́сенка крокоди́ла Ге́ны», words by Alexander Pavlovich Timofeevskii, has been the popular unofficial Russian birthday song, which was taken from a popular children's cartoon film "Cheburashka" «Чебура́шка», 1971.

- "Gena the Crocodile's Song" «Пе́сенка Крокоди́ла Ге́ны»   7-69
- "The Names Day Game/song" «Карава́й, Каравай»

70 years was not enough to erase the custom of the children's game хорово́дная игра́ and the song that went with it. When a child's names-day имени́ны is being celebrated the following game is traditional:

The children all join hands except the celebrator **имени́нник** who is "it" in the center of the circle. The circle rotates and the children sing, holding hands *all the way through*:

Как на Ва́нины (Та́нины и т.д.) имени́ны испекли́ мы карава́й[15] (How on Vania's names-day we baked a Karavai (a large loaf of bread)

Вот тако́й вышины́! (This tall!) All hands are raised as high as they can go.

Вот тако́й нижины́! (This low!) All hands are lowered to floor.

Вот тако́й ширины́! (This wide!) Participants spread apart as far as they can.

Вот тако́й ужины́! (This narrow!) Circle becomes very small and Vanya is squeezed.

Карава́й, карава́й, кого́ лю́бишь, выбира́й! (Karavai, Karavai, choose the one you love!) Said by those in the circle.

Я люблю́, призна́ться, всех. А вот Ма́шу бо́льше всех. (I of course like everybody, but Masha most of all.) Said by "it" in the center. Masha joins Vanya and is the next one to make a choice. The process repeats until there are too many people in the center and the circle can no longer circle.

New Year/Christmas   **Но́вый Год/Рождество́**

Though Russian Orthodox Christmas has only recently once again been recognized officially in Russia, even during the Soviet regime it was "celebrated" under the guise of the New Year's holiday. In addition to the religious ecclesiastical music associated with Christmas, there are many popular secular songs that are favorites of Russian children.

 7-70
- "A Christmas Tree was Born in the Forest" **«В лесу́ роди́лась ёлочка»** This song is based on a poem by Raisa Kudasheva (see Chapter 4), with music by L. Bekman.

---

[15] See *Russian's World*, 2/e, 111.

<table>
<tr>
<td>

Art and the Language of Russian Culture*

</td>
<td>

8

</td>
<td>

Худóжественные произведéния в языкé рýсской культýры

</td>
</tr>
</table>

James D. West

The language of a culture is not confined to words. The members of any society also communicate through a variety of visual images, many of which do not operate on their own, but associate with verbal communication and extend it. It goes without saying that the student of a foreign language will not advance very far before encountering expressions that are meaningful only by reference to some visible emblem, which can be anything from a national flag to a building, a garment, an implement or a musical instrument, a plant, a landscape feature or a celebrated work or art. Some of these are international, disseminated among many cultures by the spread of education: few people in the Western world, including Russia, do not associate the Mona Lisa **Мóна Лúза**[1] with a sardonic smile or the Taj Mahal **Тадж Махáл** with a fabulously opulent monument to love. However, the most interesting and revealing examples, and of course the most challenging for the language-learner, are those that are peculiar to a given culture. Here again, they may be quite widely shared as the cliché attributes of particular nations or peoples—edelweiss and the cuckoo-clock, the Russian samovar, the baseball cap, the turban or the distinctive headgear of countless priesthoods, Mount Fujiyama **Фудзия́ма** or the Leaning Tower of Pisa **Пизáнская бáшня**. These images constitute in their own right a semi-conscious "metalanguage" which plays a more pervasive role in our daily lives than most of us realize. In particular, there is a lot to be learned from the way in which a nation incorporates its art into its extended language. When Grant Wood won a prize in 1930 for his painting *American Gothic*, depicting a Midwest farmer and his spinster daughter standing with implements in hand in front of a wooden house, critics debated whether his deliberately naive treatment of his subject was a serious tribute to the simple rural origins of many Americans, or a parody. In all likelihood it was both, and ironically *American Gothic* has since become a commonplace image, even to those with no interest in art, through the use made of it in both advertising and political or social cartoons. Whether the reference made to it is verbal or visual, it has become a "byword," and a somewhat ambivalent one at that. What follows is a brief exploration of the equivalent phenomenon in Russia.

---

* All illustrations in this chapter may be viewed in color on the CD-ROM.

[1] Pronounced: **Мóнна Лúза**; also possible: **Джокóнда**.

Cartoons **карикату́ры** provide a good way to illustrate the visual language of a culture, since cartoonists develop a shorthand that invokes the familiar emblems of their society to highlight its characteristics, whether cherished values or national idiosyncracies. The satirical weekly *Krokodil* **Крокоди́л**, published from 1923 to the present, has been the closest thing to the *New Yorker* in Russia, and throughout the decades of Soviet rule it seemed to enjoy a special license to poke fun at everything from social foibles to serious misbehavior by public servants — as long as they were not too close to the Kremlin. A strikingly high proportion of the cartoons in *Krokodil* have made their point by reference to works of art. The English-speaking world is certainly no stranger to this form of humor, but it has been consistently more frequent over the last few decades in the pages of *Krokodil*. This has been possible because the magazine's readers were familiar, and sometimes all too familiar, with the heritage of nineteenth-century Russian painting and sculpture. Aside from the fact that the Russians have always taken their cultural heritage seriously, the school curriculum has generally contained a component of art appreciation, in which pride of place has been given to nineteenth-century Russian paintings selected for their historical importance or their socially and politically edifying content. As a result, educated Russians bring away from their school years not just the visual images of the nation's best-known paintings, but the classroom teacher's or museum guide's version of what they are "about" — in other words, a body of associated verbal information that hooks deeply into the fabric of their society. The familiarity of Russians with a substantial number of paintings, along with a more or less official account of their significance, provides Russian cartoonists with a ready-made language, ripe for exploitation in the serious business of poking fun. And they have been encouraged to regard it as serious business.

The cartoon on the left launches a line of official party criticism promulgated from Moscow: "The local press makes too little use of that sharp political weapon, caricature" **«Ме́стная печа́ть сла́бо испо́льзует о́строе полити́ческое ору́жие—карикату́ру»**, and the card held out by the hand that pokes through the newspaper reads: "Laughter is a serious business" **«А смех—де́ло серьёзное»**.

Fig. 8-1.

A relatively small group of paintings, sculptures and architectural monuments features repeatedly in the work of Russia's cartoonists. Some are clearly historical emblems, such as Etienne Falconet's **Фальконе́** celebrated equestrian statue of Peter the Great in the Senate Square of St. Petersburg, erected to his memory by Catherine II in 1782.

In the cartoon below, which is a tongue-in-cheek centenary tribute to the Russian life-saving society, **ОСВОД, «О́бщество спасе́ния на вода́х»**, the statue is incongruously surrounded by water. This will immediately put an educated Russian in mind of Alexander Pushkin's narrative poem "The Bronze Horseman" **«Ме́дный вса́дник»** (1837), which tells of a flood that threatens Peter's city, rises around the base of his sta-

Fig. 8-2. Falconet's statue of Peter the Great

tue and tests his defiance of the laws of nature. Founded in 1703 following the rebuff of Swedish forces invading Russia from the North, St. Petersburg was sited for military and political reasons on the extremely flood-prone estuary of the river Neva **Нева́**. In Pushkin's poem, an ordinary Russian dares to reproach Peter for the havoc wrought by the flood on the lives of the common people. The statue comes to life, and the mounted monarch gallops in vengeful pursuit of the protester. In the cartoon the statue is again alive, and Peter, true to his character, points sternly down from his perch, but this time he is directing a life-boat crew to a drowning victim's hat floating on the river, while a couple in casual garb perch irreverently on the rock beneath the rearing horse. The rostral column **ростра́льная коло́нна** in the background places the scene just across the Neva from the Palace Embankment—today the site of the Hermitage—quite a way from where the statue belongs, and on the wrong side of the river!

Fig. 8-3.

8-4

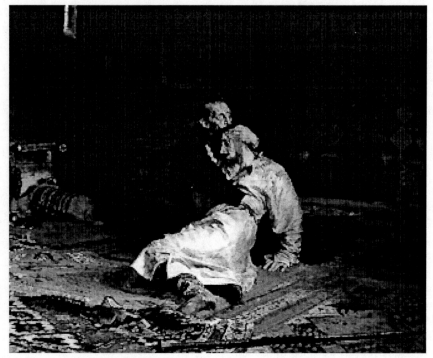

Fig. 8-4.   Il'ia Repin, *Ivan the Terrible and his Son Ivan on November 16, 1581*
«**Ива́н Гро́зный и сын его́ Ива́н 16 ноября́ 1581 го́да**» (1885)

Historical paintings are of course liable to be used in the classroom, and the best-known of them, those whose message is particularly meaningful or forcefully expressed, will find their way into every adult's storehouse of images. Once seen, there is no forgetting the 1885 canvas by Il'ia Repin **Илья́ Ре́пин** (1844–1930) of Ivan the Terrible **Ива́н Гро́зный** on 16 November 1581, in the moments after he has fatally wounded his son in a fit of rage.[2]

In the great painter's epitome of all that Russia's most notorious monarch stood for, Ivan's face reflects stark horror at what he has done, and as he clutches the young man's head, blood oozes between his fingers and down across the victim's face. The pointed stick that inflicted the fatal blow lies in the foreground on the rumpled carpet. As if to lighten the weight of Russia's often violent history, cartoonists have used this painting to inject some black humor into their comments on more ordinary violence closer to home. In the cartoon in Fig. 8-5, a citizen bent on minding his own business and avoiding trouble scurries furtively past Repin's painting, and the caption is a fine example of the compactness of colloquial Russian: "Next thing you know, you'll be involved as a witness!" «**Ещё в свиде́тели попадёшь!**»

---

[2] Formally: «**Ива́н Грозный и сын его Ива́н**». Informally: «**Ива́н Гро́зный убива́ет сы́на**».

8-5

— Еще в свидетели попадешы!

Fig. 8-5.

Ice-hockey, next to soccer, is Russia's national sport, and in Fig. 8-6, the cartoonist (who adds Il'ia Repin's name to the credits) takes a dig at the all-too-frequent tendency for ice-hockey matches to degenerate into a brawl: "Ivan the Terrible (Number 4) is sent to the bench for two minutes for striking an opponent's head with his stick." **«Ива́н Гро́зный (но́мер 4) за уда́р клю́шкой по голове́ проти́вника удаля́ется на две мину́ты».**

8-6

И. РЕПИН, Е. МИГУНОВ. «Иван Грозный [номер четыре] за удар клюшкой по голове протианика удаляется на две минуты...»

Fig. 8-6.

8-7

Fig. 8-7.

At least as often as their American counterparts, Russian parents have traditionally disciplined their children with the time-honored leather strap реме́нь, and feel the same ambivalence about corporal punishment. Fig. 8-7 shows a remorseful father and his tearful son in an instantly familiar pose. The reproduction of Repin's painting on the back wall is not necessary for recognition: it is reduced to a few pictorial hints, recognizable only to those who already know the painting, and it is there just for ironic effect. On the floor in place of the stick lie the tell-tale strap and a report book that shows nothing but twos on the Russian five-point grade scale—"straight D's" сплошны́е дво́й-ки—that will doom the boy's chances in a world of strongly competitive access

8-8 to higher education. This may seem an oddly melodramatic treatment of something as banal as bad grades, but it reflects deep-seated anxieties felt by many Russians about a good education and the opportunities it opens.

The theme was lodged firmly in post-war Russian visual culture by F.P. Reshetnikov's *A Two Again* «Опя́ть дво́йка», a comic-but-serious genre painting with the same kind of appeal that Norman Rockwell has for Americans. The tousle-headed schoolboy in Reshetnikov's painting stands shamefacedly in front of his pained mother and embarrassed siblings, his book-bag dangling from his hand, unable to respond to the affectionate attentions of his dog.

Fig. 8-8. F.P. Reshetnikov, *A Two Again*
«Опя́ть дво́йка» (1952)

This image has entered the cartoonist's language in its own right. Fig. 8-9 rebukes the Soviet Union's soccer team for a lackluster performance in the European Championships, where it is trailing in fourth place behind Greece, Hungary and Finland. The tousled hair of the player, the string bag of soccer balls dangling from his hand and the dog jumping up combine with the three coaches sitting glumly in the background to provide an unmistakable prompt, and the familiar theme of the painting delivers the message.

🗖 8-9

Fig. 8-9.

Some paintings are Russian favorites because they resonate in a particular way with the everyday world of the cartoonists and their audience. The landscape painter Ivan Shishkin **Ива́н Ши́шкин** (1832–98), celebrated for his highly realistic but magically evocative paintings of Russia's fields and forests, secured a special place in the popular imagination with his *Morning in a Pine Forest* **«У́тро в сосно́вом лесу́»**, portraying a family of bears playing on a fallen tree in the early morning sunlight.

🗖 8-10

Fig. 8-10.   Ivan Shishkin, *Morning in a Pine Forest* **«У́тро в сосно́вом лесу́»** (1889)

Fig. 8-11.   I.V. Nikolaev, (1987)

This is an endearing scene in any culture, but Russians have a particularly affectionate relationship with the bear, especially the toy variety—«**Ми́шка**». In Russian folklore, the bear may be a human transformed by magic into a wild beast, and therefore unwilling to attack humans, or the offspring of a union between a human and forest animal, who has gained acceptance among humans by helping them. The bear was regarded as a powerful spirit, always named separately from other spirits and able to ward them off, for which purpose a captive bear might be walked around a household or a bear's head attached to a stable. To this day a teddy-bear **мишка**[3] is often attached for good luck to the hood of the bride and groom's car at weddings, as in the 1987 painting by I.V. Nikolaev **И.В. Никола́ев**, a playful essay in neo-primitivism from the era of *glasnost'* (Fig. 8-11).

Cartoonists, not surprisingly, have zeroed in on Shishkin's family of bears, and Fig. 8-12 is an example of the genre. It is after hours at the art museum, and the mother bear and her three cubs, looking much more like toy bears than the real thing, have escaped and are warming their furry backsides on a radiator. The janitor is remonstrating with them, vacuum-cleaner in one hand, as she points the way back into Shishkin's painting.

Fig. 8-12.

---

[3] Or a wedding doll **сва́дебная ку́кла**, or both.

In the last decades of the nineteenth century a renewed interest in the folk tradition, both oral and visual, found expression in Russian art. This represented a conscious effort on the part of a handful of painters to bring studio art closer to the culture of the people. The leader in this effort was Victor Vasnetsov **Ви́ктор Васнецо́в** (1848–1926), who became known for his pictorial realizations ("illustrations" does not adequately describe them) of Russia's folk-epics and fairy-tales. One painting in particular, **«Ви́тязь на распу́тье»** *Warrior at the Parting of the Ways* (1878, 1882) shows the warrior-knight of legend, helmet on head and lance in hand, paused on his white steed before a stone marker whose inscription warns of the fate that awaits him if he ventures beyond it.

8-13

Fig. 8-13. Victor Vasnetsov, *Warrior at the Parting of the Ways* **«Ви́тязь на распу́тье»** (1878, 1882)

At the foot of the stone are the whitened bones of the last horse and rider who dared to pass that way, while hungry ravens perch expectantly nearby. The image has obvious psychological significance as the fairy-tale emblem of life's fateful choices. The larger 1882 version of it is on permanent display in the Russian Museum in St. Petersburg, and has always been one of the most popular exhibits with school-children, who love to decipher the Old Russian letters of the inscription. In the pages of *Krokodil*, this painting has probably prompted more cartoons than any other over the years. The target of the humor is the things that Russians watch out of habit, or are obliged to look at but would rather not. In Fig. 8-14 on the next page the warrior's gaze is riveted by a television announcer who is urging viewers to watch a film with a title reminiscent of all the world's soap-operas: "The Paths we Choose" **«Доро́ги, кото́рые мы выбира́ем»**.

Fig. 8-14.

The attraction in Fig. 8-15 is the factory or office notice-board in the paternalistic Soviet workplace. The warrior is reading a notice posted by the Trade Union Committee **профко́м** announcing the availability of vacation travel vouchers: **«Име́ются тури́стские путёвки»** and the arrows beneath point to three favorite vacation destinations: the Caucasus, the Baltic region and the Crimea.

Fig. 8-15.

8-16

Fig. 8-16.

The warrior in Fig. 8-16. stares in disbelief at a sign appealing to the workers on a collective farm: «**Засе́ем уго́дья в срок**» (literally, "Let's sow our fields in time").

Fig. 8-17 enlists Vasnetsov's painting to take a deeper dig at contemporary values. Here the warrior is an ordinary Russian, the lance is replaced with a **ёлка**, the equivalent of the Christmas tree for the Russian celebration of the New Year, and the hero's back is loaded with provisions for the New Year's table. In the distance is a stylized urban utopia, and the stone, with a raven perched mockingly on top of it, reads: «**Почему́? Где? Куда́? Как?**» "Why? Where? Whither? How?"

8-17

Fig. 8-17.

Fig. 8-18.

Finally, Fig. 8-18 is an excellent example of the language of visual emblems delivering a covert message. The warrior is now an overweight Russian male in a sweat-suit, his steed a vaulting-horse, while the lance on close inspection turns out to be a billiard cue. The stone does no more than list three kinds of sports facility: «Спортза́л. Стадио́н. Дворе́ц спо́рта» (An indoor sports facility, a stadium and a "Palace of Sport"). Only familiarity with Vasnetsov's painting unlocks the point of the cartoon—that the necessity of engaging in some kind of exercise confronts the sedentary Russian male with only unpleasant, fateful, and indeed potentially fatal choices.

A particularly striking example of the absorption of famous paintings into the language of humorous social commentary is a complex cartoon by I. Semenov **И. Семёнов** that appeared in *Krokodil* in 1971, entitled **«Ночь в карти́нной галере́е»** *The Art Museum at Night*. (Fig. 8-19). It provides in fact a short glossary of the "metalanguage" of Russian painting in the sense described above, that is, the images that are widely enough known to make them available to poets, parodists, and anyone else who would use them. With the public gone and the guardians off duty, the figures from seventeen well-known paintings are leaving their frames and gathering to watch an ice-hockey game on television. In the paintings in which they belong, most of the figures are portrayed looking at something in particular, and in these cases the cartoonist has retained their postures, with the museum television substituted for the original object of their attention. The humor depends not just on recognition of the figures, but on the reader's knowledge of their context, which is comically inappropriate to the activity of watching a sports event, in some cases grotesquely so. Most of the paintings are from the work of the **Передви́жники**, known in English sometimes as "The Wanderers," sometimes as "The Society of Traveling Exhibitions," a group of painters who broke away in the 1860s from the stylistic and thematic tyranny of the St. Petersburg Academy of Arts, with its near monopoly on major exhibitions and competitions, and its marked aversion to distinctively Russian subjects.

Fig. 8-19. Semenov's *The Art Museum at Night* «**Ночь в карти́нной галере́е**» (1971)

Over the next half-century the Peredvizhniki and their followers spearheaded a rich and colorful national revival in Russian art, exploring their country's characteristic landscape and its peoples, its architecture and its history, imbuing their paintings with social and political content and the spirit of Russian folklore. Technically proficient, ideologically progressive and intensely national, the Peredvizhniki as a group had pride of place in the curriculum of art education in the Soviet period, and it is as a group that they are installed in the popular imagination.

Seated on the floor immediately below the television set is the familiar pair of Ivan the Terrible and his wounded son, but Ivan's hand rests affectionately round the shoulders of the young man, who is looking up at the TV. By morning, we know, they will be back in their usual horrifying pose. Is there a message here?

8-20

At the extreme right a peasant boy in ragged clothes stands leaning on a stick as he watches the television set from one of the best positions. In Nikolai Bogdanov-Bel'skii's *At the School Door* «**У дверéй шкóлы**», 1897, the boy stands in the schoolroom doorway gazing wistfully at the more fortunate children studying inside, a symbol of unjust exclusion.

Vasilii Maksimov's 1889 painting «**Всё в прóшлом**» *Everything is in the Past* (see Fig. 8-21) depicts an old lady in a lace cap, seated by the steps of her modest house in the country, staring into the distance as she recalls better days now past, the epitome of lonely and forlorn old age. She is flanked by her only companion, her servant, who wears a headscarf and stares glumly down at her knitting. Here they are seated immediately in front of the screen, above Ivan the Terrible, and the servant is looking up at the match with rapt attention.

Fig. 8-20.   N. Bogdanov-Bel'skii, *At the School Door* «**У дверéй шкóлы**» (1897)

Fig. 8-21.   Vasilii Maksimov, *Everything is in the Past* «Всё в прошлом» (1889)

Behind them two children crane their necks at the TV with startled expressions that derive from Repin's highly-charged painting, **«Не ждáли»** *They Did not Expect Him*, 1884–88, in which their father has just entered the room, returning unannounced from banishment or prison.

Fig. 8-22.   Il'ia Repin, *They Did Not Expect Him* **«Не ждáли»** (1884–88)

Fig. 8-23. Vasilii Surikov, *Menshikov at Berezovo* «Méншиков в Берёзове» (1883)

Behind the startled children sits Prince Menshikov with one of his daughters. Menshikov's claim to fame was his role in the dubious succession to Peter the Great, who had raised him from humble origins to high office in recognition of his abilities. On Peter's death in 1725, Menshikov secured the succession to the throne of Peter's second wife, his own former mistress, who became the Empress Catherine I. This made Menshikov in effect Russia's ruler, but his attempt to secure his position by marrying one of his daughters to the future Peter II failed, and in 1827 he was exiled to Siberia. In Vasilii Surikov's **Васи́лий Су́риков** celebrated painting «Ме́ншиков в Берёзове» *Menshikov at Berezovo* (1883) the banished statesman and his daughter, emblems of the fickleness of political favor, sit huddled in misery, staring obliquely downward out of the picture. Here they are looking up just enough to take a grudging interest in the match.

Behind Menshikov stands a lame boy on a crutch, clutching his cap in his right hand. He is the center of attention in Repin's **«Кре́стный ход в Ку́рской губе́рнии»** (see Fig. 8-24), where he is being roughly driven out of the way of respectable citizens taking part in a religious procession in the Kursk Province. Injustice and rough treatment are now forgotten in the excitement of the ice-hockey game.

8-24

Fig. 8-24. Il′ia Repin, *Religious Procession in Kursk Province* «Кре́стный ход в Ку́рской губе́рнии» (1880–83)

Two figures in the bottom left corner, an old man leaning on a staff and a younger figure rising from a crouching position, have retained their expressions of surprise from their source: they are staring at nothing less than the distant figure of the risen Christ in Alexander Ivanov's **Алекса́ндр Ива́нов** monumental *Appearance of Christ to the People* «Явле́ние Христа́[4] наро́ду» (1837–57) This is one of the best-known masterpieces of Russian art, partly because the twenty years of its composition left a multitude of studies and sketches for it that are now distributed among art museums throughout Russia. The position of the two figures in the cartoon and their distance from the television make the original easy to recognize.

8-25

Fig. 8-25. Alexander Ivanov, *Appearance of Christ to the People* «Явле́ние Христа́ наро́ду» (1837–57)

---

[4] Also **Явле́ние Месси́и наро́ду**, the Appearance of the Messiah to the People.

8-26

Fig. 8-26.   Il'ia Repin, *The Zaporozh'e Cossacks Write a Letter to the Sultan of Turkey* «Запоро́жцы пи́шут письмо́ туре́цкому султа́ну» (1880–91)

On the middle level at the far right, six burly Cossacks appear highly amused by what they are seeing on the screen. They are in fact from Repin's *The Zaporozh'e Cossacks Write a Letter to the Sultan of Turkey* «Запоро́жцы пи́шут письмо́ туре́цкому султа́ну», 1880–91, in which their mirth is directed at the Turkish Sultan, soon to receive a strongly-worded rejection of his bid for their allegiance.

 8-27 In front of the Cossacks, above Menshikov's head, a stout figure of indeterminate gender stands with arms crossed, glowering at the screen. This is in fact the Tsarevna Sofia Alekseevna **Царе́вна Со́фья Алексе́евна**, the older half-sister of Peter the Great, confined to the Novodevichii Monastery **Новоде́вичий монасты́рь** in 1698 for her part in a plot of the Streltsy to depose Peter and restore her regency. She is the subject of a painting by Repin dating from 1879, and her conversion to a television-watcher represents almost the blackest humor in the whole cartoon, given what motivates her numb stare in Repin's portrayal: she is contemplating not just the horror of her circumstances, but the rotting corpse of a Strelets hanging outside her window.

Fig. 8-27.   Il'ia Repin, *Tsarevna Sofia Alekseevna at Novodevichii Monastery in 1698* «Царе́вна Со́фья Алексе́евна в Новоде́вичьем монастыре́ в 1698 году́» (1879)

Fig. 8-28.   Il'ia Repin, *Barge-Haulers on the Volga* «Бурлакѝ на Вóлге»
              (1870–73)

At the center of the cartoon are the barge-haulers from Repin's *Barge-Haulers on the Volga* «Бурлакѝ на Вóлге» (1870–73), their bodies straining against their chest-harnesses like pack-animals. These are the "Volga boatmen" of the celebrated song, long-standing symbols of back-breaking physical labor and exploitation, and their painful forward straining has been made into an effort to see the television better.

Close to the left edge of the television screen stands Henrietta Hirschmann, the subject of a 1907 society portrait by Valentin Serov **Валентѝн Серóв**, with a fur stole across her shoulders, taking a quizzical sideways look at the television screen (see Fig. 8-29). The humor here is that sideways look, which is in fact a witty "recycling" of the coquettish sideways tilt of the head that is the characteristic feature of Serov's portrait.

Fig. 8-29.   Valentin Serov, *Portrait of H.L. Hirschmann* «**Портрет Г.Л. Гиршман**» (1907)

Across the top of the cartoon a number of figures are hurrying along a gallery on their way to join the television audience. In the top right corner the purposefully striding figure in a frock-coat, his retainers struggling to keep up with him, is of course Peter the Great **Пётр Пéрвый**, that monarch of legendary energy and ship-building prowess who strides along a wharf in Serov's *Peter I* (1907).

Fig. 8-30. Valentin Serov, *Peter I* «**Пётр I**» (1907)

8-31

Fig. 8-31.   Vasilii Polenov, *Grandmother's Garden* «Ба́бушкин сад» (1878)

In front of Peter an old lady is helped along by a younger woman; they are the figures taking a garden walk in Vasilii Polenov's **Василий Поле́нов** *Grandmother's Garden* «Ба́бушкин сад», 1878.

Next, a matronly woman clutches at the dress of the young lady racing ahead of her. In the picture that is her home—Pavel Fedotov's «Сватовство́ майо́ра» *The Major's Courtship* (1848)—she is fleeing the suitor her parents have invited to meet her, while her mother angrily restrains her.

8-32

Fig. 8-32.   Fedotov's *The Major's Courtship*

8-33

8-34

Fig. 8-33.   Konstantin Makovsky,
             Alekseich **«Алексе́ич»**
             (1882)

Fig. 8-34.   Konstantin Savitskii, *The
             Stevedore* **«Крю́чник»**
             (1884)

The last two figures in the upper gallery are Konstantin Makovsky's **Кон-
станти́н Мако́вский** *Alekseich* **«Алексе́ич»**[5] standing benignly behind his
samovar, and the muscular stevedore from Konstantin Savitskii's **Константи́н
Сави́цкий** *The Stevedore* **«Крю́чник»** (1884).

    Finally, in the top left corner of the cartoon is a train, and a small group of
young men is being hustled up the gallery steps to board it. One of the young
men has his head turned back for a last look at the hockey game. In Savitskii's
«На войну́» *Off to War*, 1888, he is a recruit bound for the front, turning for a
last longing look at his sweetheart who stands behind him, weeping as she
reaches towards him in vain.

8-35

Fig. 8-35.   Konstantin Savitskii, *Off to War* **«На войну́»** (1888)

---

[5] A common reduction of **Алексе́евич**.

What Semenov's inspired cartoon demonstrates to perfection is the repertoire of Russian paintings whose fame, aided by the diligence of several generations of teachers and critics, has added them to the storehouse of phrase and fable that is one of the cultural dimensions of the Russian language. It also demonstrates what might be called the "visual grammar" by which they operate. These images are neither purely visual nor purely verbal. They exist as a package, so to speak, with a commonplace moral or political message attached to the lowest common denominator of the elements that give them their visual impact. It is in fact an interesting exercise to compare the caricatures to the original paintings and see what elements the cartoonist has selected as the minimum that will guarantee identification, even where three sets of figures have been rotated to face in the opposite direction from their originals. The reduction is particularly challenging for larger and more complex paintings, and the solutions are particularly interesting. Alexander Ivanov's *Appearance of Christ to the People* is a panoramic canvas crowded with figures: which one or two will be enough to identify the painting? With the sure instinct of an artist, Semenov has chosen the two figures that Ivanov has placed to lead the viewer into his painting from its lower left corner, and, with their gaze fixed on the distant figure of Christ, to lead the eye to the focal point of the composition. Semenov has reproduced this trick of composition in his cartoon, and the result is instantly recognizable.

8-36

One last example makes the point that features of composition are sometimes an important part of the images that make their way into the popular imagination. The icon of the Virgin Mary has for centuries been close to the hearts of Russians, particularly one form of it: the «Богома́терь умиле́ния» the "Virgin of Tenderness," in which the head of the Virgin bows over in tender love towards the upturned face of the Christ-child in her arms, giving the resulting composition a circular dynamic.

This image is so deeply embedded in the popular imagination that it has even shown up in tattoos on the chests of prison camp inmates. The cartoon in Fig. 8-37 targets young women who would emulate the lifestyle of Madonna—what better image to put to work than the Virgin herself?

Fig. 8-36. "Virgin of Tenderness"

8-37

The denim jacket over a tank-top, the hair-cut, the stereo headset, the lipstick and the cigarette all belong in Madonna's world, but the composition is unmistakably that of *the* Madonna: the head leans forward, the cradling arms reach up, but where the Christ-child should complete the circle, the composition is fulfilled by a scroll held up by the young woman and the cigarette hanging down from her lips to meet it. The scroll reads: **«Заявле́ние: от ребёнка отка́зываюсь»** "Declaration: I renounce the child." The arches in the background identify this particular Madonna as Western—Leonardo da Vinci's *Madonna Litta*, which has long been familiar to visitors to the Hermitage Museum in St. Petersburg. Anchored by the pun on the stage name of America's own "material girl," both the verbal-visual humor and the scathing social commentary come full circle.

Fig. 8-37.

8-38

Fig. 8-38.   Leonardo da Vinci's *Madonna Litta*

Appendix   Приложе́ние

Michael Ivanov

[In the article below, (adapted from "Painting in Bedroom Tones" by Michael Ivanov[6] and published in the January 2000 issue of *Russian Life*), the language of art involves some particular terminology.]

For example, those who revere the splendid colors of Ivan Aivazovsky's canvases (*Russian Life,* July 1997) will understand the idiom "worthy of Aivazovsky's hand" **досто́йно ки́сти Айвазо́вского** [brush **кисть**]. The phrase is widely applied to picturesque scenes **ви́ды** or landscapes **пейза́жи**. But recently, it has also been used to express admiration or amazement over almost anything, often in an ironic sense. At the other end of the spectrum a mediocre or poor painting might be called a daub **мазня́** or smear **пачкотня́** — terms used often by socialist realists to denigrate the work of abstract painters.

If you roam the halls of the Tretyakov[7] or the Hermitage[8] long enough, you are bound to overhear useful expressions to help you sound like a true lover of the arts: "the play of light and shadow" **игра́ светоте́ни**, "this canvas was painted by ..." **э́то полотно́ принадлежи́т** ..., pastel tones **пасте́льные тона́**, portrait artist **портрети́ст**, landscape artist **пейзажи́ст**, painter of battle

🔲 **8-39**

Fig. 8-39.   Ivan Aivazovsky, *View of Odessa at Night*

---

[6] Michael V. Ivanov is executive editor of *Russian Life,* 89 Main Street, Suite 2, Montpelier, VT 05602.

[7] **Третьяко́вская галере́я**, perhaps Moscow's best known art gallery.

[8] **Эрмита́ж**, St. Petersburg's best known museum and art gallery.

Fig. 8-40.   Ivan Aivazovsky, *Ninth Wave*

scenes **баталист**, seascape painter **маринист**, animal painter **анималист**. The feminine and masculine for "model" is **нату́рщица, нату́рщик**, and without a carefully chosen model, the world's art would be short of many a world's masterpiece **шеде́вр**.

More terminology includes sketch **этю́д**, still life **натюрмо́рт**, panorama **панора́ма**, diorama **диора́ма** and triptych **три́птих**, but don't translate "nude" (*f*) as naked **го́лая**. The proper translation is **обнажённая** or rarely **нага́я**. The term **передви́жники** has caused nothing but trouble for translators, who sometimes call this group of 19th century realists "ambulants" or "itinerants," while the most common usage is "wanderers."

Misinformed and misanthropic museum guides who slip on terms such as these are good grist for the humor mills. Comedian Efim Shifrin (see *Russian Life*, April 1996) made his comic debut with his now famous stand-up sketch *Repentant Magdalena* «**Ка́ющаяся Магдали́на**». In the sketch, Shifrin mimics a museum guide who points out the contradictory character of Magdalena's repentance. (El Greco painted her nude ...) and keeps repeating that the canvas was executed in "bedroom tones" (**посте́льные/пасте́льные** are homonyms).

There are a number of Russian artists whose styles are so distinctive they have acquired adjectival status. For instance, there is something we have come to call "a forest like those in the paintings of Ivan Shishkin" **ши́шкинский лес**,

8-41

Fig. 8-41.   Ivan Shishkin, *Rye* «**Рожь**» (1878)

and there is the incomparable beauty of "an autumn landscape in the style of painter Isaac Levitan" **левита́новская о́сень**. But there also is the cliché of "Kustodiev-like women" **кусто́диевские же́нщины**. This refers to the buxom subjects of Boris Kustodiev who liked to portray Russian women as creatures of flesh and blood (see Fig. 8-43), enjoying all the pleasures of life, be it a gorgeous meal or a steam bath.

8-42

Fig. 8-42. Levitan's *Golden Autumn*

Fig. 8-43.   A "Kustodiev woman"

Some, however, have criticized Kustodiev for what we call **лубóк** or **лу-бóчность** which derives from the word for "bast," but which can be approximately translated as "exaggerated, at times *kitschy* Russianness." And there are a lot of samovars, *bliny*, and "typical Russian colors" in Kustodiev's work.

Interestingly, Nikita Mikhalkov's recent film *Siberian Barber* **Сибúрский цирю́льник** has been criticized for such **лубóчность**. Indeed, Mikhalkov confessed in television interviews that he told his cameraman to think of Kustodiev paintings when shooting the film. The promotional trailers for the film are reminiscent of Kustodiev's bright paintings. They dissuaded this writer from attending the three-hour long canvas because, as they say in the world of art, a copy is always worse than the original **кóпия всегдá ху́же оригинáла** and throwing in the **лубóк** is not enough to create a **шедéвр**.

<table>
<tr><td>**Entertainment**</td><td style="font-size:2em">**9**</td><td>**Развлека́тельные
жа́нры**</td></tr>
</table>

Ludmila Pruner

Four major entertainment genres are discussed in this chapter: cinema **кино́,** television **телеви́дение**, variety shows **эстра́да**, including stand-up comedy, and the circus **цирк.**

FILM	КИНО́
Introduction	**Введе́ние**

The cinema is as much a part of high Russian culture as are paintings, monuments, novels, plays, and poetry. A Russian who has Chekhov, Dostoevsky, Tolstoy and Sholokhov on his bookshelves will also have seen the movies of Tarkovskii, Mikhalkov and Riazanov. Sadly, film production has fallen drastically in the recent past: many Russians today lament the disintegration of the Russian film industry after the 70-year era of government subsidies.

The films discussed here are those with plots, musical scores, and scripts well-known to educated Russians. Not all are of the same quality: some are true artistic achievements, others are propaganda showpieces, and still others are simply light entertainment. One thing unites them: for one reason or another they have entered the Russian language and remain there as cultural referents.

Studios	*Сту́дии*

The film establishment under the Soviets was tightly controlled, and becoming a film director required yet another academic pursuit. One went to a film institute, learned the skills of the trade, and toiled for many years making documentary or educational films. Among the best-known of the higher learning and research cinema institutions are the State (former All-Union) Institute of Cinematography **Всесою́зный госуда́рственный институ́т кинематогра́фии (ВГИК)** (VGIK) (established 1919), and the State (former All-Union) Research Institute of Cinema **Всесою́зный нау́чный госуда́рственный институ́т кинематогра́фии (ВНИИК).**

All Soviet film studios shared state-provided resources to support script development and to finance film production. In addition to the mandatory imposition of state censorship rules, non-Russian films produced in the Soviet Union had to be dubbed into Russian prior to being distributed throughout the country. The rule was imposed in order to maintain the image of a harmonious Union of nationalities that was communicating in the "great and powerful

Russian language." Foreign films previewed at Dom Kino or distributed in the Soviet Union could be shown with subtitles. In fact, Soviet filmmakers enjoyed elite cinema status and never had to worry about financial failure, as long as they contributed to the Party mission: to educate the population, and to teach people how to be humane, patient and unselfish. Filmmakers who wished to circumvent such strict dogma mainly made comedies and detective thrillers. Films that normally make no money at all, avant-garde or experimental films, were not a part of the Soviet cinematic machine.

During most of its existence, the rigid structure of the Soviet Russian film industry was confined to three major film studios **кру́пные киносту́дии**, under the control of the State Cinematography Kommittee **Комите́т по кинемато-гра́фии, Госкино́**: Mosfilm **Мосфи́льм** and the Gorky Studio **Центра́льная сту́дия де́тских и ю́ношеских фи́льмов им. М. Го́рького** located in Moscow, and Lenfilm **Ленфи́льм** in Leningrad, now St. Petersburg. Among the most productive national film studios were Dovzhenko Film studio **Киносту́дия им. А. Довже́нко** in Kiev and Gruziiafilm **Гру́зияфильм** in Tbilisi. Other national film studios included Uzbekfilm **Узбекфи́льм**, Kazakhfilm **Казахфи́льм**, and Belorussianfilm **Беларусьфи́льм**. The Baltic film industry was also prolific.

Russian viewers were always skeptical of the cultural idiosyncrasies of non-Russian cultures, yet in the 1970s and 1980s the so-called "national" film studios played a notable role in Soviet film. One of the early popular national cinemas was Kirgizfilm. The studio's popularity coincided with the cultural thaw of the 1960s when Kirgizfilm served as a launching pad for new Russian directors. Among them was Andrei (Andron) Mikhalkov-Konchalovsky **Андре́й Михалко́в-Кончало́вский** (*The First Teacher* «**Пе́рвый учи́тель**», 1966), the brother of the director Nikita Mikhalkov. The Kirgizfilm Studio also allowed Larisa Shepitko **Лари́са Шепитько́** to produce *Heat* «**Зной**», 1963, and her second film, *Wings* «**Кры́лья**», 1966. Tragically, Shepitko died in a car accident in 1979 at the age of 40. Had she lived, many feel she would have been a major figure on the international film scene today. Ironically, none of the efforts involved in launching the careers of the above-mentioned directors benefited Kirgiz filmmakers.

Film Festivals   *Кинофестива́ли*

Throughout the Cold War, film festivals **кинофестива́ли** served as an important means of communication between the Western free societies and countries behind the Iron Curtain. Thanks to these festivals, and to the special showings at the cinema clubs, Russian film audiences became familiar with such foreign directors as Charlie Chaplin, Michelangelo Antonioni, Federico Fellini, Alfred Hitchcock, Vittorio DeSica, Ingmar Bergman, Akira Kurosawa, Milos Forman, and Andrzej Wajda.

Contemporary film festivals in Russia include the Moscow International Film Festival **Моско́вский Междунаро́дный кинофестива́ль**, White Nights

Documentary Film Festival **Фестива́ль документа́льного кино Бе́лые но́чи**, and Kinotavr National and International Film Festival (held in the resort town of Sochi) **Междунаро́дный Откры́тый кинофестива́ль Кинота́вр**. Today's film festivals inside and outside Russia serve as the main means of film distribution, so that most of the films produced in post-Soviet Russia are made exclusively to be shown at them. Besides recognition, prestigious prizes received by the films assure further film production for their directors.

It should not be thought, though, that film festivals were the sole means by which the Soviet audience got a glimpse at the Western world. Also very popular were the so-called "foreign film weeks" **неде́ли зарубе́жного кино**. Foreign films were shown even in regular movie theaters, affording large audiences the chance to see, among others, Antonioni, Bergman, and Fellini. French films were especially popular, and some viewers would go to each Gallic release without bothering to check what the film was about. Films made by Eastern European filmakers were also widely distributed in the Soviet Union.

Cinema centers, **киноце́нтры,** commonly called Houses of Cinema **Дома́ кино́**, provided a place for socializing for those in the trade (members of the Union of Cinematographers, for instance). Non-members found gaining entrance to showings at a house of cinema very difficult. On special occasions one could view foreign film productions. Many of the films were from Eastern Europe, but Western directors were also represented at these showings. Interestingly, there were practically no Hollywood films shown in Russia until the 1990s: the USSR refused to join the international agreement on copyright protection until 1974, and continued to have a serious problem with pirating, so the United States refused to sell Russia any of its films. The most prestigious cinema center was the Central House of Cinema **Центра́льный Дом Кино́**. Another large cinema center was Moscow's Cinema Center **Киноце́нтр**.

Film publications **кинопре́сса** range from the glossy to the academic. *Soviet Screen* **«Сове́тский экра́н»** used to be the most popular magazine about cinema, and had a large subscription base. *Eye on Cinema* **«Киногла́з»** and *Movie Park* **«Кинопа́рк»** document and illustrate post-Soviet cinema and are widely available at kiosks. The most informative as well as entertaining articles on Russian cinema of the nineties appeared in *Performance* **«Сеа́нс»**, published in St. Petersburg. Unfortunately, the restricted budget of the magazine has limited its distribution and popularity. *The Art of Cinema* **«Иску́сство кино́»** is the more scholarly journal for serious readers, moviegoers, cinema scholars and students. *Cinema Critics' Notes* **«Кинове́дческие запи́ски»** publishes scholarly articles on diverse cinematic issues.

Directors   *Режиссёры*

Russian movie directors have been a strong cultural force since the founding of the film industry in the Soviet Union, and their names are practically household words among Russian intellectuals. The most famous directors are Sergei

Eisenstein **Серге́й Эйзенште́йн**, Alexander Dovzhenko **Алекса́ндр Довже́н-ко**, Vsevolod Pudovkin **Все́волод Пудо́вкин**, Grigorii Aleksandrov **Григо́рий Алекса́ндров**, the Brothers Vasil'ev **Бра́тья Васи́льевы** (two non-related directors with the same name), and Ivan Pyr'ev **Ива́н Пы́рьев**. Eldar Riazanov **Эльда́р Ряза́нов**, Grigorii Chukhrai **Григо́рий Чухра́й**, Leonid Gaidai **Леони́д Гайда́й**, and Vladimir Motyl' **Влади́мир Моты́ль** joined their ranks after World War II. Mikhalkov-Konchalovsky and Shepitko, along with Andrei Tarkovskii **Андре́й Тарко́вский** were among the very talented directors who graduated from VGIK in the mid-1960s. The younger generation of Soviet filmmakers studied with such renowned directors as Eisenstein and Dovzhenko, and as a result are seen as the direct continuation of the early glory days of Soviet cinema. The directors of serious dramas, such as Chukhrai, who tried to tear away the myths of the past and replace them with new views of the individual and society, hold a special place in Russian culture. No less important are directors of "light" comedies such as Gaidai and Riazanov, who teach Russians about themselves and their society through the veneer of absurdity and humor. They are the humorists who added so much to the Russian language.

The Language of Film

Movies generally start with a script **сцена́рий**, written by a screenwriter **сценари́ст**. The scenes and dialogues **сце́ны и диало́ги** are brought to life by a director **режиссёр (кинорежиссёр, постано́вщик)**, who is assisted by a cameraman **опера́тор**, lighting artist **освети́тель**, sound engineer **звукоопера́тор,** and editor **монтажёр**. Music is created by the composer **компози́тор**. The money comes from the producer **продю́сер,** who used to be known as the **дире́ктор карти́ны.** Since the breakup of the Soviet Union, the radical changes in the Russian economy have brought Russian filmmaking at least somewhat closer to the western way of doing film business. The producer and director now try together to raise the funds necessary to make a movie. Under the Soviets, the director was given a salary and was in charge of the film's budget.

Russian films are produced in a studio **киносту́дия**, on a sound stage **съёмочный павильо́н,** where the entire production crew **съёмочная гру́ппа,** including actors and actresses **актёры и актри́сы,** labor throughout the shooting of the film **съёмочный пери́од** until the release **вы́пуск**. The film is designed by a number of people. Sets **декора́ции** and costumes **костю́мы** are created by artists **худо́жники**. The person in charge of wardrobe is the **костюме́р,** and the make-up artist is the **гримёр.** "Starring" does not occur in Russian film vocabulary; instead you will find "in the (main) roles:" **в (гла́вных) роля́х.**

After the filming **съёмка,** the audience **зри́тели** can see the film on screen **на экра́не** in a number of places: a movie theater **кинотеа́тр,** a House of Cinema **Дом кино́,** or at a film festival **кинофестива́ль.** Foreign films are dubbed into Russian **дубли́руются на ру́сский язы́к** or are shown with (sub)titles **с (суб)ти́трами.**

Russian film categories include:

Feature Film	игрово́е кино (худо́жественный фильм)
Full-length	полнометра́жный
Short	короткометра́жный
Musical	музыка́льная кинокоме́дия
Detective story	детекти́в
Action film	боеви́к
Drama	дра́ма
Comedy	кинокоме́дия
Melodrama	мелодра́ма
Horror film	фильм у́жасов
Historical Film	истори́ческий фильм
Popular science	нау́чно-популя́рный
Documentary	документа́льный (документа́лка)
Newsreel	(кино)хро́ника
Animated	мультипликацио́нный фильм (му́льтик)
Serial	сериа́л

How to Read This Chapter

Soviet film (that term is used here to include the film industries not only of Russia, but of other Soviet republics) clearly reflected Soviet reality. Thus the divisions found in this chapter were made not strictly chronologically, but rather in terms of the significant events facing the Soviet citizen: the 1920s era of experimentation; the 1930s, enthusiasm and industrialization; 1940s–50s, war and reconstruction; the 1960s, thaw and new directions; 1970s–80s, stagnation and scepticism.

All films are listed this way: title in English followed by title in Russian, then the name of the director (given in English and Russian), then the year of production. Quotes from the films are listed if they have been assimilated into everyday conversation. Most of them were quoted by A. Khaniutin in an article in «Кинове́дческие запи́ски» in 1993. Others were included on the advice of Russian friends and acquaintances.

Early Popular Genres   Ра́нние популя́рные жа́нры

The earliest genres were the newsreel хро́ника and the literary adaptation экраниза́ция. The sensational 1896 newsreel of the coronation of the last Russian tsar Nicholas II filmed in the Kremlin Palace on Red Square in Moscow was among the first popular attractions. *The Defense of Sevastopol* «Оборо́на Севасто́поля», by Goncharov and Khanzhonkov (1911), though actually a mix of documentary footage and fictional filmmaking, and the funeral of Vera Kholodnaia **Ве́ра Холо́дная** (newsreel, 1919), are remembered as examples of remarkable early documentaries. Early literary adaptations экраниза́ции of Tolstoy's *Anna Karenina* **«А́нна Каре́нина»** (1915) by Alexander Khanzhonkov and two films by Yakov Protazanov **Я́ков Прота-за́нов**, Pushkin's *Queen of Spades* **«Пи́ковая да́ма»** (1915) and Tolstoy's *Father Sergii* **«Оте́ц Се́ргий»** (1917) were very popular at the time.

The first real Russian movie stars appeared in the 1910s. The most revered among them were Ivan Mozzhukhin **Ива́н Мозжу́хин** and Vera Kholodnaia. Kholodnaia's untimely death at the age of 26 was an occasion of national mourning. In his 1975 film *Slave of Love* **«Раба́ любви́»,** Soviet filmmaker Nikita Mikhalkov **Ники́та Михалко́в** paid tribute to this legendary Russian actress. Ivan Mozzhukhin left the country following the October Revolution.

V.I. Lenin saw in film a powerful tool for the Soviet state: **«Из всех иску́сств для нас важне́йшим явля́ется кино́».** "For us [that is, the new Soviet state] the most important of all the arts is cinema." The first didactic use of film, developed shortly after the 1917 October Revolution, was a propaganda short film **агитфи́льм, аги́тка** depicting a political issue or event.

The 1920s: Era of Experimentation   Э́ра экспериме́нта

The most famous experimental film of the 1920s is *The Extraordinary Adventures of Mr. West in the Land of the Bolsheviks* **«Необыча́йные приключе́ния ми́стера Ве́ста в стране́ большевико́в»** (1924). It depicts the adventures of a Yankee in communist Moscow of the 1920s.

Film greats who emerged in the 1920s were Dziga Vertov **Дзи́га Ве́ртов** (the pseudonym of Denis Kaufman) and Sergei Eisenstein **Серге́й Эйзен-ште́йн** who, in *The Battleship Potemkin* **«Бронено́сец Потёмкин»** (1925), earned world-wide recognition. It is still considered one of the best films of all times. It depicts the insurrection on board a battleship on the Black Sea in June 1905. The montage depicting the massacre on the city steps made Odessa itself famous. The marching and shooting soldiers, the lion heads, a baby carriage heading down the steps, a fallen woman with her mouth open in a desperate cry have become oft-used references to Eisenstein in world cinema and art. (The 1990s Hollywood production of *The Untouchables* and Francis Bacon's *Study for a Pope* [1952] and his *Study for the Nurse in the Film* Battleship Potemkin (1957) are among numerous examples.)

Among other revered masterpieces of early Soviet cinema is Vsevolod Pudovkin's **Все́волод Пудо́вкин** *Mother* **«Мать»** (1926). *Mother* is the story of an illiterate and abused woman who embraces the Russian Revolution. The film, based on Maxim Gorky's novel, is known to generations of Russians, and served as a strong ideological and educational tool for young Soviet women.

The other notable filmmaker of the 1920s and 1930s is Alexander Dovzhenko **Алекса́ндр Довже́нко**. His film *Earth* **«Земля́»** (1930) is a romanticized chronicle of the formation of the first Soviet collective farms in Ukraine, and the film is remembered for its cinematography rather than for its ideological content.

The 1930s: Enthusiasm and Industrialization

Энтузиа́зм и индустриализа́ция

The sound cinema of the 1930s brought forth new experimentation with sound effects and a new social assignment: the portrayal of a new hero. *The Road to Life* «Путёвка в жизнь» Nikolai Ekk **Никола́й Экк** (1931) was the first Russian sound film, which gained international recognition. It depicts the life of homeless children in a correction community during the first decades of Soviet Russia. The best-remembered scene is the famous shot at the train station. The jubilant cries of the awaiting crowd change into sorrowful silence as the train approaches. The viewer recognizes the body of Mustafa, the young hero murdered by criminals from his past. The expression "sleight of hand and no cheating" **ло́вкость рук и никако́го моше́нства** is used when someone is surprised at how deftly or adroitly someone did something.

The 1930s also saw the development of Russian musicals. The film director Grigorii Aleksandrov **Григо́рий Алекса́ндров** and the actress Liubov' Orlova **Любо́вь Орло́ва** were legends of the Russian cinema.

The Happy Guys «Весёлые ребя́та» (1934) was Aleksandrov's first production. Leonid Utyosov **Леони́д Утёсов**, the famous jazz band director and singer, co-starred with Orlova. In the film, a Soviet shepherd Kostia (Utyosov) became a jazz band director, and a Soviet house servant Aniuta (Orlova) was transformed into a great singer. The film is full of Hollywood-style singing and dancing. The new genre earned the instant acceptance and admiration of the mass audience. Two popular expressions from the film are:

- **А плати́ть кто бу́дет, Пу́шкин?** Who is going to pay, Pushkin? Used whenever you want to establish who is responsible for something.
- **Игра́й-игра́й, а рука́м во́ли не дава́й!** You may play, but keep your hands to yourself! Often used in its abbreviated form as «Ты рука́м во́ли не дава́й!» Similar to «То́лько без рук!» (see under *The Diamond Arm*) the expression is used to stop a fight, or an act of transgression. It also means "Please don't touch."

Fig. 9-1.   L. Orlova in *The Circus*

The musicals that followed asserted the popularity of the new genre and its creators. *The Circus* «Цирк» of Aleksandrov (1936) was a story of the American circus performer Marion Dixon (Orlova) who escaped racist America and found love and friendship in a hospitable Russia.

Aleksandrov's *Volga-Volga* «Во́лга-Во́лга» (1938) portrayed two provincial non-professional artistic groups participating in a national competition in Moscow. It is interesting to note that the film made a laughingstock of Soviet bureaucracy, yet was not banned. In spite of or, perhaps, thanks to their naive simplicity, these musicals continue to amuse viewers. Copies of these films in video format are readily available in Russia and abroad. These quotes are the best-known from *Volga Volga*:

- **Бу́дучи ли́чно знако́м с това́рищем Шу́льбертом ...** Personally knowing Comrade Shulbert ... This expression is used with a strong note of sarcasm: the name of the composer Schubert is mispronounced, indicating the lack of education typical among Soviet bureaucrats. The use of the word "Comrade" applied to Schubert as well as "personally knowing" further the comic/sarcastic effect.
- **Хо́чется рвать и мета́ть.** I want to rip and rage. This familiar quote is used to underscore the feeling of anger and frustration.

An important aspect of Soviet cinema in general and the musicals of the 1930s in particular was the popularization of diverse musical genres. First and foremost was the dissemination of Soviet songs: "My Motherland is Broad" **«Широка́ страна́ моя́ родна́я»** by Isaak Dunaevskii **Исаа́к Дуна́евский** from the film *The Circus* is a case in point. Russian cinema also popularized opera singers and modern classical composers. The educated Russian speaker may not instantly recall the title of the films but would be able to comment on opera singers' performances in films by Sergei Lemeshev **Серге́й Ле́мешев** and Ivan Kozlovskii **Ива́н Козло́вский**, on the appearances in films of jazz performers such as Leonid Utyosov, and on the use of modern classical works by such composers as Dmitri Shostakovich **Дми́трий Шостако́вич**.

Many early Soviet films portrayed historical figures that the regime had a special interest in glorifying. Two films in particular stand out among many: *Chapaev* **«Чапа́ев»** and *Alexander Nevsky* **«Алекса́ндр Не́вский»**. Georgii and Sergei Vasil'ev (The Brothers Vasil'ev, **Бра́тья Васи́льевы**) were not related in real life, but their collaboration, *Chapaev* **«Чапа́ев»**, (1934) was a masterpiece of popular cinema. The performance in the title role immortalized Boris Babochkin **Бори́с Ба́бочкин**. Despite its strong ideology the film enjoys some popularity even today. Partly the success is due to the title character himself. The film is based on the illiterate peasant Vasilii Chapaev, whose military genius brought glory to the Red Army and contributed to the victory against the Whites in the Civil War of 1918–20. Songs, legends and a thousand jokes have created a mythological figure out of this historical character. Selected expressions from the film:

- **Наплева́ть и забы́ть.** Forget about it!
- **Ти́хо, гра́ждане, Чапа́й ду́мать бу́дет!** Silence, Chapai is about to think! Used any time you want silence for any reason.

Fig. 9-2.   Cherkassov (standing, right) in the role of Ivan the Terrible

The Russian cinematic masterpiece of the 1930s may be *Alexander Nevsky* «Алекса́ндр Не́вский» by Sergei Eisenstein (1938). The role of Alexander Nevsky was played by the actor Nikolai Cherkassov **Никола́й Черка́сов**. There are many scenes and lines that Russians know from this film, including the biblical:

- **А е́сли кто с мечо́м к нам войдёт — от меча́ и поги́бнет. На том стои́т и стоя́ть бу́дет ру́сская земля́.** He who enters our land with a sword will perish by the sword. The Russian land stands and will stay by that rule.

The 1940s and 50s: War and Peace   **Война́ и мир**

Anton Ivanovich is Angry «**Анто́н Ива́нович се́рдится**», Alexander Ivanovskii **Алекса́ндр Ивано́вский** (1941).

- **Пу́блика бу́дет визжа́ть и пла́кать.** The public will howl and cry. Everybody will be delighted with it (a cake, for instance).

The Wedding «**Сва́дьба**», Isidor Annenskii **Исидо́р А́нненский** (1944) Based on Chekhov's play by the same title.

- **В Гре́ции всё есть.** They have everything in Greece.
- **Позво́льте вам вы́йти вон!** Be so kind as to get out!

Spring «**Весна́**», G. Aleksandrov (1947). The film is cited as the source of the expression which became the motto of cynical post-war Soviet generations:

- **Где бы ни рабо́тать, лишь бы не рабо́тать.** It doesn't matter where you work, as long as you don't work.

Some war films are still popular. The best-known include the following:

The Deed of a Secret Agent «Подвиг разведчика» (1947) was a huge hit. An experienced Soviet intelligence officer played by Pavel Kadochnikov **Павел Кадочников** defeats the Nazi command in occupied Soviet territory. This role was among his most popular portrayals of a regular **обычный** Soviet hero, a simple **простой** Soviet citizen who demonstrates uncommon strength, loyalty, and cleverness under extreme duress. Kadochnikov created the image of a smart and cool-headed Soviet spy leading the Russians to victory. He is also remembered for his role in *Story About a Real Man* «Повесть о настоящем человеке» (1948). The book and script by Boris Polevoi **Борис Полевой** was based on the life of a famous Soviet war pilot Aleksei Mares′ev **Алексей Маресьев**. Generations of Soviet children grew up admiring this man who returned to flying after losing both legs in a plane crash.

In the 1930s and 1940s, Soviet filmmaker Ivan Pyr′ev **Иван Пырьев** created memorable rural comedies that provided entertainment for generations, including *The Tractor Drivers* «Трактористы» (1939). What starts out as a competition becomes a love story between a young soldier who serves in the Soviet Army as a tank driver and a distinguished collective farm tractor driver—a woman. Marina Ladynina **Марина Ладынина** and Nikolai Kriuchkov **Николай Крючков** played the leading roles.

Ladynina, Vera Maretskaia **Вера Марецкая** and Tamara Makarova **Тамара Макарова** were among the popular actresses of the 1930s and 1940s who forged the new ideal of a Soviet woman on screen. Actively involved in the structuring of the new Soviet society, these actresses earned respect for their partnership in the industrial and political development of Soviet Russia.

Fig. 9-3.　M. Ladynina and N. Kriuchkov

Below is a list of the popular films of the 1940s recognized by the educated viewer today and not mentioned above:

The Hearts of the Four «**Сердца́ четырёх**», Konstantin Iudin **Константи́н Ю́дин** (1941). The film was released in 1944. The recent restoration of the film in 1988 attests to its historical value as well as its current popularity. It is a musical based on a comedy of errors that takes place near a military location. The stars Ludmila Tselikovskaia **Людми́ла Целико́вская** and Evgenii Samoilov **Евге́ний Само́йлов** were among the most popular actors in Russian cinema.

Slow Sky Rider «**Небе́сный тихохо́д**», Semen Timoshenko **Семён Тимоше́нко** (1945). This film is a heroic comedy. Three pilot friends decide not to fall in love till the war is over. But then they meet the pilots from an all-female flying squadron. It is one of the most memorable roles of Nikolai Kriuchkov, who played one of the pilots. The film is one among very few that pay tribute to women pilots during war time. A popular song, "In the Evening, Evening, Evening" «**Ве́чером, ве́чером, ве́чером**» is from this movie.

At Six O'Clock in the Evening After the War Is Over «**В 6 часо́в ве́чера по́сле войны́**», Pyr'ev (1944). An artillery soldier (E. Samoilov) and his sweetheart (M. Ladynina), promise to meet at six o'clock after the war is over. They keep their promise. The popularity of the leading actors makes the film interesting even for today's viewers.

The World War II generation was more tolerant of Soviet propaganda and films romanticizing the heroic in wartime. The music of Dunaevskii **Дунае́вский** and Shostakovich **Шостако́вич** contributed significantly to the mood of films dedicated to patriotism.

Fig. 9-4.   Dunaevskii

The post-World War II generation grew up under the strong influence of the prolific genre of war films.

Gerasimov's *The Young Guard* «Молодáя гвáрдия» was the most popular movie of 1948. The film was used as propaganda material in the education of Soviet youth. The film was restored in 1964. Tamara Makarova, Viacheslav Tikhonov **Вячеслáв Тúхонов**, Inna Makarova **Úнна Макáрова**, Nonna Mordiukova **Нóнна Мордюкóва**, and Sergei Bondarchuk **Сергéй Бондарчýк** became popular in the roles of young heroes who gave their lives for the liberation of the Motherland from the Nazis.

In the early 1950s, mass arrests, severe repression and the increased scrutiny of Soviet censorship paralyzed the livelihood of the country including the Soviet film industry. According to the statistics, in 1950 13 films were completed. By 1951 the production dropped to nine films. Significant improvement in film production began after the death of Stalin in 1953, when 51 films were made. By 1956 production was restored to its usual average of over 100 films per year.

The search for sincerity **úскренность,** as it was called in literary circles, raised new issues in the cinema. The film industry responded with films that addressed the issue of the rehabilitation of societal consciousness. The rebirth of the Soviet cinema brought in a new "humanized" hero: an intimate portrayal of a person, his inner world and his private relationships with other people. Although the concept of a "simple Soviet hero" remained, the increased production led to a diversity of films and genres. The expansion of the film industry opened the door to young filmmakers.

Fig. 9-5.   N. Mordiukova in the film *The Russian Field*

Fig. 9-6.   V. Lanovoi

Pavel Korchagin «Па́вел Корча́-гин», Aleksander Alov and Vladimir Naumov **Алекса́ндр Алов и Влади́мир Нау́мов** (1956). A biographical sketch of a man and his devotion to the revolutionary cause. The film was based on *How Steel Was Tempered* «**Как закаля́лась сталь**», a famous novel by Nikolai Ostrovsky **Никола́й Остро́вский**. Soviet youth used to memorize part of the text for school assignments. Vasilii Lanovoi **Васи́лий Лано́вой**, a popular actor for decades (televised plays contributed to his popularity), played the main character. By the 1970s the film had lost its relevance.

The Communist «**Коммуни́ст**», Yuri Raizman **Ю́рий Ра́йзман** (1957), told the tale of an ordinary party member participating in one of the first construction sites of the young Soviet republic. Evgenii Urbanskii **Евге́ний Урба́нский** became famous in the role of the hero who gives his life to get bread to the starving.

New directors focused on ordinary people and their lives in communal apartments and the post-war landscape. These films often took place at train stations. Some films of this period can be compared with Italian neorealism. Others focused on the so-called "village theme," a theme that depicted the rural population or described the idiosyncrasies of life in a rural area.

Spring on Zarechnaia Street «**Весна́ на Заре́чной у́лице**», Felix Mironer and Marlen Khutsiev **Фе́ликс Миро́нер** and **Марле́н Хуци́ев**, was a hit in 1956. It is a complex love story between a young night school instructor and a construction worker (Nikolai Rybnikov **Никола́й Ры́бников**). The life of young Soviet workers in a small town is explored. Rybnikov remains among the most popular film actors of Soviet cinema.

Fig. 9-7.   E. Urbanskii in
The Communist

♪ 9-1

The Heights «**Высота́**», Alexander Zarkhi **Алекса́ндр За́рхи** (1957). The modern method of blast furnace construction is introduced with the help of a love story between construction workers (Nikolai Rybnikov and Inna Makarova). It was one of Makarova's best roles. The song «**Не кочега́ры мы, не пло́тники**» "We Are Neither Stokers Nor Carpenters" by Rodion Shchedrin **Родио́н Щедри́н**, sung by Nikolai Rybnikov, is known even today, forty years later.

With the end of World War II, comedy reclaimed its popularity. Arkadii Raikin **Арка́дий Ра́йкин** soon became a legend. His stand-up comedy routines were recorded on film and enjoyed by generations.

Fig. 9-8.   I. Makarova in
              Three Soldiers

We Met Somewhere «**Мы с ва́ми где́-то встреча́лись**», Nikolai Dostal′ **Никола́й До́сталь** and Andrei Tutyshkin **Андре́й Туты́шкин** (1954). It wasn't the film itself, but rather Raikin's name and his stand-up routines that made the film popular. Popular expressions from the film:

• **Во́дку?! По утра́м?! Стака́нами??!! —Хорошо́-о-о!...** Vodka?! In the morning? Glass after glass? Goo-o-od! Often used whenever one drinks at unusual times (say, in the morning) or anticipates a lot of drinking. It is always used in pleasurable anticipation!

• **Ка́ждому о́вощу свой фрукт.** To each vegetable his own fruit. This expression is a play on the phrase «**Ка́ждому о́вощу своё вре́мя**» "Everything has its own season."

• **Ру́ки и но́ги на́до облом́ать э́тому коллекти́ву.** That collective should have its arms and legs broken off. The word "collective" was a buzz word used throughout the Soviet era. Everyone was supposed to be a part of a collective group, farm, opinion, and so on. Here, the comic effect consists of the treatment of the word "collective" as it were an *individual* with *individual* arms and legs.

• **Скус спесфи́ский ...** Speshl tase ... Drunken version of "special taste." See also the next comment.

• **Тако́й дифси́т.** Such a shortage. "Speshl tase" and "such a shortage" are not exclusively or necessarily drunk expressions making fun of drunkenness. Rather, they make fun of uneducated people who use big words such as "specific" and "deficit"—words that belong to business rather than conversational Russian. Again, the reference is made to poorly educated bureaucrats.

• **В гре́ческом за́ле, в гре́ческом за́ле ...** In the Greek room ... This is used in reference to a great location. Most frequently in Russian, Greece symbolized ancient times of opulence and high standards of living.

• **Кто́-то в лесу́ ау́кнулся, а я, дура́к, откли́кнулся и вот уже́ 18 лет алиме́нты плачу́.** Like a fool I answered somebody's call in the forest, and I've been paying alimony for 18 years now. (Why did I get myself into this mess?)

• **Пить, кури́ть, ходи́ть и говори́ть я научи́лся одновре́менно.** I learned to drink, smoke, walk, and talk simultaneously.

The next expression is used to let a petitioner know that the request will involve considerable difficulty (though the speaker will do it):

• **Е́сли меня́ в тёмном ме́сте прижа́ть к тёплой сте́нке ...** If I'm pushed to a warm wall in a dark place ...

Carnival Night «**Карна-ва́льная ночь**», Eldar Riazanov **Эльда́р Ряза́нов** (1956), was an instant success. From early on, Riazanov was among the best feature comedy film directors. The actors and comedy theater stars Igor Il'inskii **Игорь Ильи́нский** and Sergei Filippov **Серге́й Фили́ппов** contributed to the success of the film, but the star was Liudmila Gurchenko **Людми́ла Гурче́нко**, who sang the enormously popular "Five Minutes, Five Minutes" «**Пять мину́т, пять мину́т ...**».

In the film, a group of young factory workers decide to outwit their boss, a bureaucrat, and organize in their House of Culture a truly happy celebration of the New Year. It gently criticized Soviet bureaucracy.

Fig. 9-9. L. Gurchenko in the 1980s

Below are the humorous expressions from the film still remembered today:

- **Есть ли жизнь на Ма́рсе, нет ли жи́зни на Ма́рсе, э́то нау́ке неизве́стно.** Whether there is life on Mars or there is no life on Mars—Science knows nothing about it. This expression means either "I have no idea" or refers to drunkenness.

- **Короте́нько, мину́т на со́рок.** Very briefly, for no more than forty minutes. Refers to any job that might take a little time, but which must be completed (in the movie it refers to a speech, the end of which matters).

- **Одна́ звёздочка, две звёздочки … лу́чше всего́ пять звёздочек!** One star, two stars … five stars is best of all! The stars refer to the system of rating the quality of cognac or drunkenness.

- **Я и сам шути́ть не люблю́, и людя́м не дам.** I don't like jokes myself and won't allow others to make jokes either. The stress on **лю́дям** is placed on the wrong syllable, thus revealing the director's poor education.

Soviet post-war cinema begins to differentiate between individuals and masses. Screen characters are allowed to make mistakes and possess negative characteristics.

The Cranes Are Flying «Летя́т журавли́», Mikhail Kalatozov **Михаи́л Калато́зов** (1957). A young woman (Tatiana Samoilova **Татья́на Само́йлова**) betrays her fiance (Aleksei Batalov **Алексе́й Бата́лов**) after he leaves for the front. The film earned national and international recognition.

Fig. 9-10.   T. Samoilova in the role of Anna Karenina (1968)

Fig. 9-11.   A. Batalov in the 1980s

The Ballad of a Soldier «Балла́да о солда́те», Grigorii Chukhrai **Григо́рий Чухра́й** (1959). A young enlisted soldier (played by Vladimir Ivashov **Влади́мир Иваше́в**) becomes a hero after he stops an enemy tank. He didn't struggle to win nor did he intend to commit a heroic act in defense of his Mother Russia. He was running away to save his life. This was the first portrayal of a new type of hero, a sincere and naive character who commits heroic acts in "self-defense" or because it seems the only logical thing to do under the circumstances. In the film, he is proclaimed a hero and granted a leave of absence to visit his mother. On his way home he meets a young woman (Zhanna Prokhorenko **Жа́нна Прохоре́нко**) and falls in love. The innocence and sincerity of the lead actors captivated viewers.

Fate of a Man «Судьба́ челове́ка», Sergei Bondarchuk **Серге́й Бондарчу́к** (1959). Based on a short novel by Mikhail Sholokhov **Михаи́л Шо́лохов**, the film describes the return of a soldier from the destruction of a war to the emptiness of a "new" life where he has yet to find his place. The film contains a moving performance by Bondarchuk in the lead role.

The 1960s: The Thaw and   **О́ттепель и но́вые направле́ния**
New Directions

Comedy was the most popular genre of the 1960s.

Striped Voyage «Полоса́тый рейс», Vladimir Fetin **Влади́мир Фе́тин** (1961). Funny situations develop when a monkey traveling aboard a ship transporting tigers to a zoo opens their cages. Famous expression:

* **Краси́во плыву́т—та гру́ппа в полоса́тых купа́льниках.** They swim beautifully—that group in striped bathing suits. Used at the sight of anything good-looking.

The Girls «Девча́та», Yuri Chuliukin **Ю́рий Чулю́кин** (1961), was a romantic comedy idealizing the hard life and hard labor of young people conquering the Russian wilderness. The theme song of the film («**Хоро́шие девча́та, весёлые подру́ги**» "Good Gals, Happy-Go-Lucky Girlfriends") became a hit. It is shown regularly on television.

♪ 9-2 *I Walk Around Moscow* «Я шага́ю по Москве́», Georgii Daneliia **Гео́ргий Дане́лия** (1963). This film portrays the Soviet capital city and the young generation of the 1960s, centering around a young man from Russian provinces visiting Moscow and his new friends. Nikita Mikhalkov played the lead.

Welcome, Or No Admittance «Добро́ пожа́ловать, и́ли посторо́нним вход запрещён», Elem Klimov **Эле́м Кли́мов** (1964), is a story of a rebellious teen who survives underground at a pioneer summer camp. Evgenii Evstigneev's **Евге́ний Евстигне́ев** popularity grew from his playing the Soviet bureaucrat in charge of the children's education and well-being. The best known expression from the film:

- **А чо́й-то вы тут де́лаете?** What are you doing here?

Leonid Gaidai **Леони́д Гайда́й** is a household name in Russia. His brilliant comedies are as popular today as they were when they first appeared. They are broadcast regularly on Russian television. The expressions from his films are as alive as they were in the 1960s.

Operation "Y" «Опера́ция "Ы" и други́е приключе́ния Шу́рика» (1965). A three-part comedy about events in the life of a Soviet college student Shurik:

- **Бабу́ля, закури́ть есть?** Hey, Grandma, got a cigarette? Can be used when asking *anyone* for a cigarette.

- **Вы не ска́жете, как пройти́ в библиоте́ку?** Be so good as to tell me how to get to the library. Any absurd situation (in the movie he asks for a library in the middle of the night).

- **Е́сли я вста́ну, ты у меня́ ля́жешь.** If I get up, you'll get knocked down. This is a coarse and threatening expression used to warn, "if I have to do such and such, then you are sure going to get it from me!"

- **На́до, Фе́дя, на́до.** We have to, Fedya, we have to. When someone questions the necessity of doing something.

- **Послу́шай, у вас несча́стные слу́чаи бы́ли? Бу́дут.** Listen, did you have any accidents? You will. A hidden threat.

The (Woman) Prisoner of the Caucasus «Кавка́зская пле́нница или но́вые приключе́ния Шу́рика» (1966), a humorous allusion to famous literary works by Pushkin and Tolstoy with the same title. The film continues the story of Shurik's summer adventures in the Caucasus mountains region. This popular theme of Russian classic literature surfaces again in the 1996 cinematic production *The Prisoner of the Caucasus* by Sergei Bodrov **Серге́й Бодро́в**. The title is translated into English as *The Prisoner of the Mountains* (see page 494).

- **Бе́лая горя́чка. Да, бе́лый, горя́чий, совсе́м больно́й.** White fever. Yes, white, hot, and totally sick. This ailment is what is known in English as a blackout, namely, the person is so drunk he does not know what he is doing, and cannot remember, even the next day.

- **Да здра́вствует сове́тский суд—са́мый гума́нный в ми́ре!** Hail the Soviet court, the most humane in the world! Used anytime one is making fun of bureaucrats.

- **Же́нщина—друг челове́ка.** Woman is man's best friend. The allusion is to dogs as "man's best friend."

- **Жить, как говори́тся, хорошо́! А хорошо́ жить—ещё лу́чше.** To live, as they say, is good. And living well is even better. It alludes to a famous verse from Mayakovsky's poem "Good!" **«Хорошо́!»** Often memorized in Soviet schools: "Life is good, and to live is good!"

- **Коро́че, Слихасо́вский!** Shorter, Slikhasovskii! For this to be funny, one has to know that Sklifosovskii was a famous surgeon. The E.R. section of the famous Sklifosovskii City Hospital in downtown Moscow is well known for saving lives of the critically injured (alcoholics among them), especially during Soviet times when medicine was free for all. Obviously the character from the film does not get the name right in referring to him. Is used to interrupt someone's pointless argument or a long didactic speech. Is it as humorous as it is sarcastic.

- **Пти́чку жа́лко!** I feel sorry for the bird! It is used as an excuse for sudden tears and overwhelming sadness. It might be said about a sobbing drunk person.

- **Спортсме́нка, комсомо́лка, краса́вица.** An athlete, a Komsomol member, a beauty. Used to describe anyone both able and good-looking. Associated with the popular Soviet slogan **«В здоро́вом те́ле здоро́вый дух»** ("In a healthy body [dwells] a healthy mind"); the expression is used with sarcastic overtones.

The following saying mixes up all three genders in Russian:

- **Чей ту́фля? Моё, спаси́бо.** Whose is it? Mine, thanks.

- **Я не пью. —А я пью? Что́ тут пить?** I don't drink. Do I drink? What is there to drink here? This humorous remark may allude to the amount of alcohol served. The unofficial ratio used at gatherings in "the good old days" in Soviet Russia was a minimum of a liter of vodka and a liter of cognac per man and half a bottle to one bottle of sweet wine per woman.

The Diamond Arm «**Бриллиа́нтовая рука́**» (1968) is a comedy of errors. A modest accountant traveling abroad (this itself was droll under the Soviets) is mistaken for a diamond smuggler. During his walk around town, he falls and loses consciousness. When he comes to, his arm is in a cast. Hidden in the cast are diamonds. The accountant is played by the very popular comedian Yuri Nikulin **Ю́рий Нику́лин**.

Fig. 9-12.   Yuri Nikulin in the 1970s

Expressions from the film:

• **Бу́ду бить аккура́тно, но си́льно.** I'm going to hit neatly, but hard.

• **Е́сли челове́к идио́т, то э́то надо́лго.** If a person is an idiot, then it's for a long time

• **Клие́нт дозрева́ет.** The client is ripening. Someone will be ready soon.

• **Кто возьмёт биле́тов па́чку, тот полу́чит водока́чку.** He who takes a packet of tickets is the one who'll get a water tower. Very few people believed in the possibility of winning the lottery in the Soviet Union. The encouragement to purchase lottery tickets seems as absurd as the lottery itself. When purchasing tickets to the theater, circus, or cinema, for every popular *good* show one bought, one often was obligated to purchase «**нагру́зка**» (an additional load) for unpopular or poorly attended performances.

The following phrase combines two rather incongruous things: the proverb «**Ку́й желе́зо пока́ горячо́**» "Strike while the iron is hot," and the admonition seen in all stores, «**Счита́йте де́ньги, не отходя́ от ка́ссы**» "Count your change before leaving the cashier's window."

• **Куй желе́зо не отходя́ от ка́ссы.** Strike the iron before leaving the cashier.

• **На чужо́й счёт пьют да́же тре́звенники и я́звенники.** Even sobersides and dyspeptics will drink when someone else pays.

• **На́ши лю́ди в бу́лочную на такси́ не е́здят.** Our people don't take a taxi to the bakery. It is a tradition to use the word **на́ши** (ours) or **на́ши лю́ди** (our people) to differentiate them against **нена́ши** (not-ours), Westerners or decadent society. In Soviet society, where children would often walk to and from school on roadways closed to buses, taking a taxi to a bakery—or anywhere for that matter—was the height of decadence.

• **Не бу́дут брать—отклю́чим газ!** If they don't take [it]—we'll cut off the gas! Used to force someone to do something.

• **Не винова́та я, он сам пришёл.** I'm not to blame, he came himself. Used to proclaim one's innocence.

• **Не зна́ю, как за грани́цей, а у нас управдо́м—друг челове́ка.** I don't know what it's like abroad, but in Russia the "super" is man's best friend. The house administrator or superintendent of the house literally runs the house. This person determines who gets what and when, and doles out (often unfair) disciplinary measures such as cutting off the gas, as in the previous expression. Corruption and abuse of power were typical among those administrators.

• **Поскользну́лся, упа́л, потеря́л созна́ние, очну́лся—гипс.** I slipped, fell, lost consciousness, came to—a cast. Used to express "I have no idea how this happened."

• —**Ребя́та, ведь на его́ ме́сте до́лжен был быть я.** —**Напьёшься—бу́дешь!** —Guys, I was supposed to be in his place. —Get drunk and you will be!

• **Смотри́ не перепу́тай, Куту́зов! Детя́м** [wrong stress again] **моро́женое, ба́бе—цветы́.** Careful, don't mix [them] up, Kutuzov! The children get the ice cream, the dame gets the flowers. Said when someone mixes things up.

• **То́лько без рук.** Only without hands. Don't fight, don't get emotional.

• **Туале́т, ти́па сорти́р (обозна́ченный бу́квами "Мэ" и "Жо").** A rest room, like an outhouse, with the letters M and W. The comic effect stems from a mixture of conversational «**туале́т**» with its more vulgar equivalent «**сорти́р**», and a business word «**тип**»—type, or class. In addition, instead of the correct name of the letter «**Ж**» the character uses «**Жо**» which alludes to «**жо́па**» arse, a popular slang word that in conversational Russian may imply a reprimand or an insult.

• **Челове́ку на́до ве́рить то́лько в са́мом кра́йнем слу́чае.** One must believe a person, but only when absolutely necessary.

• **Чтоб ты сдох, чтоб я ви́дел тебя́ в гробу́ в бе́лых та́пках.** Drop dead, I want to see you in your coffin in your white slippers. Equivalent to "Drop dead!" or "Damn you!"

• **Чтоб ты жил на одну́ зарпла́ту!** May you have to live on one paycheck. A nearly impossible feat in the former Soviet Union. The joke makes fun of the puny salaries provided by the state for its workers. It was well known that illegal income, "under the table" pay **подрабáтывать налéво** or the so-called "shadow economy" **теневáя эконóмика** provided much better sources of income than the salary paid by the state.

- **Шампáнское по утрáм пьют úли аристокрáты, или дегенерáты.** Only aristocrats and degenerates drink champagne in the morning. Might be used as a joke when people drink at unusual times which, among Russians, is often!

- **Я дóлжен принять вáнну, выпить чáшечку кóфэ ...** I must take a bath, drink a cup of coffee ... **«Кóфэ»** "coffee" is pronounced with a particularly French twist, thus making the phrase funnier, since the hero is pretending to be an intellectual.

- **Я не трус, но я боюсь.** I'm no coward but I am afraid.

Watch Out For the Car **«Берегúсь автомобúля»**, Riazanov (1966), is the story of Yuri Detochkin **Дéточкин** (played by Innokentii Smoktunovskii **Иннокéнтий Смоктунóвский,**) who during the day works as an insurance agent and by night steals cars. His victims are bureaucrats who take advantage of their positions to bribe others, and to whom the law doesn't seem to apply. After selling the cars, Detochkin donates all the money to orphanages. Smoktunovskii's earlier success in *Hamlet* **«Гáмлет»** (Grigorii Kozintsev **Григóрий Козинцев**, 1964) was eclipsed by his convincing performance as this hero-thief. Expressions from the film include:

- **—Кто свидéтель? —Я! А что случúлось?** —Who's the witness? —Me! What happened?

- **Ничегó, ничегó! В тюрьмé тебя перевоспитáют. ...Вернёшься другúм человéком.** It's all right. You'll be retrained in prison ...You'll come back a different man. Same as "Hail the Soviet court, the most humane in the world!" (see: *The (Woman) Prisoner of the Caucasus*), the expression makes fun of the naive trust of the educational and rehabilitating powers of the Soviet judiciary system and Soviet prisons in particular.

♪ 9-3   *White Sun of the Desert* **«Бéлое сóлнце пустыни»**, Vladimir Motyl' **Владúмир Мотыль** (1969). The popularity of this comedy can be compared with or surpassed only by Gaidai's comedies. It was recently named "Russians' Most Beloved Movie" at a Russian TV festival. Many Russian theater and film professionals consider it one of the most well-made Russian movies. The public agrees. During the Civil War, a Red Army soldier Sukhov (played by Anatolii Kuznetsov **Анатóлий Кузнецóв**) is ordered to accompany a group of women, former members of a harem, to safety and freedom.

- **Восто́к—де́ло то́нкое.** The Orient is a very subtle thing.

- **Грана́ты не той систе́мы.** Grenades of a different type. Refers to anything that doesn't fit.

- **Гюльчета́й! Откро́й ли́чико.** Giulchetai! Open your face! (Don't be embarrassed.)

- **За держа́ву оби́дно.** I feel sorry for the country. This is now a very popular expression to use when talking about the fall of the USSR. It's also used when your group makes you ashamed.

- **Опя́ть икра́, хоть бы хле́ба купи́ла.** Caviar again! You could have at least bought bread.

- **Тамо́жня даёт добро́.** Customs (office) approves. Used when something is allowed by the authorities.

- **Я вот (то́же сейча́с) э́то допью́ и бро́шу!** And now I'll drink this up and then not drink any more. Said about anything that will be completed.

We'll Survive Till Monday «Доживём до понеде́льника», Stanislav Rostotskii **Станисла́в Росто́цкий** (1968), was a revelation. The film serves as a condemnation of dogmatic teaching in Soviet schools. No one will wonder after viewing this film why Soviet teenagers abandon attempts at developing critical thinking in their early teens. Viacheslav Tikhonov **Вячесла́в Ти́хонов** played the role of a teacher opposed to dogma.

The 1970s and 80s: Stagnation and Scepticism   Засто́й и скептици́зм

The so-called political stagnation period of the 1970s demonstrated that the film industry was very active. The era of confessional films by Chukhrai and others of the 1960s passed. The 1970s developed the genres of everyday **быто-во́й** and office-centered **делово́й** films. (Office-centered films are sometimes called industrial cinema **произво́дственнное кино́** since the action may take place at a factory. An example of this type of film is *The Prize*, «Пре́мия»). New directors introduced documentary materials to feature films, as in Tarkovskii's *The Mirror* «Зе́ркало». War films and comedies remained popular.

The Belorussian Station «Белору́сский вокза́л», Andrei Smirnov **Андре́й Смирно́в** (1970). Friends get together thirty years after the war to bid farewell to one of their company. Songs by famous bard Bulat Okudzhava **Була́т Окуджа́ва** accompany the film.

The Twelve Chairs «Двена́дцать сту́льев», Leonid Gaidai **Леони́д Гайда́й** (1971), is based on the novel by Il'f and Petrov. Famous expression from the film:

- **Бензи́н ваш—иде́и на́ши.** The gas is yours, the ideas are ours.

(Other expressions from this work are found in the Chapter 3)

Gentlemen of Luck «**Джентльме́ны уда́чи**», Alexander Seryi **Алекса́ндр Се́рый** (1971). The story of how a gentle and good-natured director of a kindergarten joins a group of dangerous criminals in order to catch their ringleader.

- **Туда́ не ходи́! Сюда́ ходи́!** Don't go there! Come here! Do it this way, not that way.

- **Де́ньги ва́ши, бу́дут на́ши.** The money is yours but will be ours.

- **Де́точка, а вам не ка́жется, что ва́ше ме́сто во́зле пара́ши?** Baby, don't you think your place is next to the toilet bucket? Meaning: You come last!

- **Ку́шать по́дано! Сади́тесь жрать, пожа́луйста!** Dinner is served! Sit down and pig out, please.

- **Нехоро́ший челове́к, реди́ска!** He's not a good man, he's a radish. "Radish" is slang for a petty thief or swindler. This humorous expression is used in conversational Russian especially among friends as **Реди́ска ты!** (What a radish you are!) to say "you don't get it!" or "you're wrong again."

- **Укра́л, вы́пил — в тюрьму́. Рома́нтика!** (You) stole, drank — went to prison. How romantic!

- **Ходи́ ло́шадью, ло́шадью ходи́, дура́к!** Make your move, you fool! [Literally, in chess: Move your knight, you fool!] This is a pun on the genders and meanings associated with steed **конь** (masculine), and horse **ло́шадь** (feminine). **Конь** is also the Russian word for the knight chess piece, and means a stallion, a stud. **Ло́шадь** implies a work horse and has never been used as a term in chess. So when in the movie, one of the characters tells his friend to move his **ло́шадь**, it creates a comic effect. The expression may be used in a situation when both parties are wrong.

- **Чем бо́льше сдади́м, тем лу́чше!** The more [people] we turn in, the better.

- **Я не прокуро́р, чтоб с тобо́й по душа́м разгова́ривать.** I'm not a prosecutor, I can't have a heart to heart talk with you.

Snowball Berry Red «**Кали́на кра́сная**», Vasilii Shukshin **Васи́лий Шукши́н** (1973). The film was named the best film of 1974 and Shukshin, who played the main character, best actor. Shukshin's character is a former criminal who attempts to break away from his criminal friends and change his destiny. Shukshin was a writer as well as a director and actor, and this film is among the most well-loved "village prose" films. As in literature, the village films described life outside the city. The narrative makes the viewer feel and see the profound differences between city and countryside.

Fig. 9-13.   V. Shukshin in the 1970s

The Irony of Fate **«Иро́ния судьбы́, и́ли с лёгким па́ром»**, Eldar ♪ **9-4**
Riazanov (1975), is both the story of a New Year's celebration gone terribly
wrong and a satire on the uniformity of Soviet life: the same street names, the ♪ **9-5**
same anonymous apartment blocks, the same stores with the same goods on
the shelves were found in every major Soviet city. The film is still shown on
Russian television every New Year's Eve.

- **Заче́м вы меня́ всё вре́мя роня́ете**?! Why do you keep dropping
me?

- **Кака́я га́дость эта ва́ша заливна́я ры́ба**. How awful your fish in
aspic is. Said about *anything* you don't like.

Autumn Marathon **«Осе́нний марафо́н»**, G. Daneliia **Гео́ргий Дане́лия**
(1979), is about a gifted and good-natured translator and college professor
Buzykin, played by the popular Oleg Basilashvili **Оле́г Басилашви́ли**, who
tries to please everyone around him. His inability to say "no" leads to serious
personal and professional conflicts. Evgenii Leonov **Евге́ний Лео́нов** plays the
house manager **управдо́м**, one of his most popular roles. Expressions from the
film include:

- **Про меня́ трёп был?** Was there any noise about me?

- **Тосту́емый пьёт до дна!** Bottoms up! The person being toasted
must finish the glass.

- **Хорошо́ сиди́м.** We're having a good time. Usually said at a party.
Сиде́ть, to sit, in this context means "to have a good time at a party"
which may imply eating, drinking, chatting, singing, and dancing. In the
movie, three characters are totally silent and solemn. So, the expression may also be used with a hint of humor.

Garage «Гара́ж», Riazanov (1979). The members of a Soviet scientific research institute **нау́чно-иссле́довательский институ́т (НИИ)**, in cooperation with the State, are building a garage for their own private cars. The space is limited and the members of the cooperative are very protective of their property. A general meeting is held to decide who will have to be evicted from the garage when space is cut.

♫ 9-6 *Moscow Does Not Believe in Tears* «Москва́ слеза́м не ве́рит», Vladimir Men′shov **Влади́мир Меньшо́в** (1979), earned an Oscar for Best Foreign Film. Three Soviet women work hard to make a better life. Although sentimental and overly simplified, the film offers a glimpse of the everyday life of postwar Muscovites. The most well-known expression from the film is:

- **Не учи́ меня́ жить, лу́чше помоги́ материа́льно.** Don't teach me how to live—help me with money instead. The first part of this phrase, "Don't teach me how to live," comes from *The Twelve Chairs* by Il′f and Petrov. (See Chapter 3, 16.1.)

Hello, I Am Your Aunt! «Здра́вствуйте, я ва́ша тётя!», Viktor Titov **Ви́ктор Тито́в** (1975). Russians use this expression when something unexpected occurs.

The films of the 1980s are diverse. Among the most popular were:

The Pokrovskii Gate «Покро́вские воро́та», Mikhail Kozakov **Михаи́л Козако́в** (1982). A nostalgic film about the inhabitants of communal apartments in Moscow of the 1950s.

Train Station for Two «Вокза́л для двои́х», Riazanov (1982). A melodrama about two adults who meet under unusual circumstances at a train station. Soviet Russia through the prism of a train station where all roads meet.

A Cruel Romance «Жесто́кий рома́нс», Riazanov (1984). Another Best Film of the Year by Riazanov based on the Ostrovsky play *Without Dowry*. Nikita Mikhalkov played one of the lead characters in the film.

My Friend Ivan Lapshin «Мой друг Ива́н Лапши́н», Aleksei German **Алексе́й Ге́рман** (1984), is among the best movies made by the director. The story of a secret police detective is loosely based on Yuri German's writings.

Repentance «Покая́ние», Tengiz Abuladze **Тенги́з Абула́дзе** (1980). A philosophical and symbolic drama of guilt and innocence with allusions to Stalinism. The release of this internationally known film in 1984 signaled perestroika in Soviet cinema.

Plumbum or a Dangerous Game «Плю́мбум, и́ли опа́сная игра́», Vadim Abdrashitov **Вади́м Абдраши́тов** (1986), is about a teenager from a Russian provincial town who leads a double life. Cruel, eccentric, and unpredictable, the film captivated viewers.

Little Vera «Ма́ленькая Ве́ра», Vasilii Pichul **Васи́лий Пичу́л** (1988). The story of a young woman (Natalia Negoda **Ната́лья Него́да**) living in a small provincial town surrounded by the misery of Russian daily existence with hard work and low pay. It was the first Soviet film to contain extended sexual scenes and nudity. Following the successful release of the film in the U.S., Playboy Magazine devoted an entire issue to Russian women.

The Needle «Игла́», Rashid Nugmanov **Раши́д Нугма́нов** (1989). This hit was seen by millions in the first three months of its release. The film tackled the taboos of narcotics, sex, and rock-n-roll. It was the last role of Victor Tsoi **Ви́ктор Цой**, the Russian rock superstar of the 1980s.

Tsoi was also in the film *Assa* «А́сса», Sergei Solov'ev **Серге́й Соловьёв** (1987), the story of a young woman who gets mixed up with a band of criminals, with predictably tragic results. The film's musical score is especially well known.

Formerly banned films attracted mass viewers during the Glasnost period of the mid-1980s. Soviet filmmaker Elem Klimov created a committee that previewed and made public knowledge the films "shelved" by the State censors from the 1960s on.

Beginning in 1988, ideological, societal, moral, and sexual taboos were lifted. But freedom in art translated into a cult of unprecedented hopelessness. Violence, including sexual violence, appeared in 82% of films between 1989 and 1990. In 35% of those films the heroes die a violent death or slowly deteriorate as human beings. Russian society is perceived as without rules or morals. Unhappy sexually, morally, and psychologically, the population becomes more aggressive.

In an attempt to reach new levels of free artistic expression, the filmmakers overplayed the role of drugs, sex and pseudo-western life style. "Chernukha" «черну́ха» films became the accepted means of portraying the past, present, and future. The term "chernukha" is from **чёрный** "black" and stands for a total void of purpose and lack of any sense of direction in life. The 1980s witnessed the fall of socialist propaganda and the rise of chernukha-pornukha **черну́ха-порну́ха** ("pornukha" is from the Russian for pornography **порногра́фия**) style, a chaotic attempt to gain freedom of expression in the time of Glasnost. One film remembered from this time is *The Intergirl* «Интерде́вочка», Petr Todorovskii **Пётр Тодоро́вский** (1989). It caused a furor upon release: it's the story of a nurse who is a model daughter and Komsomol member by day and a hard-currency prostitute at night. Many feel it contributed to the growth of prostitution in Russia.

The shock produced by *chernukha* films slowly destroyed Russian viewers' interest in Russian film productions. However, up until 1994, Russia was the largest filmmaking country in Europe.

Among the most frequently mentioned films of the 1990s are:

We Cannot Live This Way Anymore «Так жить нельзя́», Stanislav Govorukhin **Станисла́в Говору́хин** (1990). A gloomy account of Soviet reality on the threshold of the 1990s: alcoholism, crime, and a future without hope.

Adam's Rib «Ребро́ Ада́ма», Viacheslav Krishtofovich **Вячесла́в Криштофо́вич** (1990), is a story of three generations of Russian women.

Taxi Blues «**Такси́-Блюз**», Pavel Lungin **Па́вел Лунги́н** (1990), is a co-production, a form of cinematic cooperation that became popular in Russia in the early 1990s. Petr Mamonov **Пётр Мамо́нов** plays a homeless saxophone player.

Encore, Again Encore «**Анко́р, ещё анко́р**», Petr Todorovskii **Пётр Тодоро́вский** (1992), depicts Soviet military families on a military base right after World War II.

Little Angel, Make Me Happy «**Ангело́чек, сде́лай ра́дость**», L. Papilova and Usman Saparov **Л. Папи́лова** and **Усма́н Сапа́ров** (1992), explores the Stalinist deportations. Six-year-old Georg **Гео́рг** faces a grim life alone after he escapes deportation.

Burnt by the Sun «**Утомлённые со́лнцем**» (1994) won the director, Nikita Mikhalkov, an Oscar. It is the story of a high commanding officer who is destroyed by the Stalinist system he helped to build. It was filmed entirely on the estate Stalin gave to the director's father for having written the words to the national anthem.

The Particularities of National Hunting «**Осо́бенности национа́льной охо́ты**», Alexander Rogozhkin **Алекса́ндр Рого́жкин** (1995). A highly popular story, especially among men, of a young Finn visiting Russia with the dream of participating in a Russian hunt as he imagined it to be from his reading of Russian classics. Reality, of course, proves to be different.

Prisoner of the Caucasus «**Кавка́зский пле́нник**», Sergei Bodrov **Серге́й Бодро́в** (1996). This compelling cinematic narrative was nominated for an Oscar. In spite of the fact that Bodrov started working on his film prior to the Chechen war, his film is often associated with the military events in the Chechen region. In the film, two Russian soldiers are captured by a man from the Caucasus mountains (in the film he spoke Georgian) who wants only to exchange these soldiers for his son imprisoned by Russians. This film provoked a lot of controversy at the International Film Festival Kinotavr in Sochi. Though many critics in Russia accused Bodrov of exploiting the war in the Caucasus, Bodrov's work transcends the political boundaries of Russian military conflicts within or outside of Russia.

By 1994, no films by Russian directors sold even half a million tickets (in Russia). In spite of the talented work of post-Soviet filmmakers, the generation of the mid-1990s seemed to ignore cinema completely. The new generation turns for entertainment to cable television and foreign films recorded on video.

TELEVISION   ТЕЛЕВИ́ДЕНИЕ

Television entered everyday Soviet life in the 1950s. The limited production of television sets and their high production cost made them accessible to only a limited number of viewers. Even in the 1960s neighbors would gather together at one television set in the communal apartments and enjoy a film, a concert or a figure skating competition. Watching television became a social event, as depicted in the film *Five Evenings* **«Пять вечеро́в»**, Nikita Mikhalkov (1978).

The segregation between movies and television was not as pronounced as it is in the United States. Both old and new films were shown on television, since both the television networks and the film studios were organs of the state entertainment monopoly. Several of the films mentioned in this chapter are as popular as they are precisely because they were shown so often on television.

Each city had at least one channel. Moscow always had at least two or three channels with programs starting in the afternoon and ending at about midnight. There are still channels that follow a similar timetable in the Russian provinces.

Sports programming is enormously popular, especially soccer games between national and international teams. Hockey, figure skating, and international sports competitions also rate very highly.

Popular Television Shows   Популя́рное телеви́дение

The programs listed below are those known to a wide television viewing audience from the Soviet through the post-Soviet era. Some of the shows may no longer be broadcast. They are listed here because they continue to be referred to by Russians in everyday speech.

Time **«Вре́мя»** (National and International News)

The News **«Ве́сти»** (National and International News)

International Panorama **«Междунаро́дная панора́ма»** (International News)

View Point **«Взгляд»**. Program with sections on diverse topics, including history, crime, law, domestic and foreign affairs, art and daily life.

Cinema Travelers' Club **«Клуб кинопутеше́ственников»** was particularly popular among Soviet viewers of all ages. Unable to travel abroad, viewers enjoyed this opportunity to explore far-off lands.

The World of Animals **«В ми́ре живо́тных»**. "Wild Kingdom" for the Russian-speaking world.

Topic (of the Day) **«Те́ма»**. A dialogue between two panelists who debate current affairs. The audience participates with questions and suggestions. The anchorman Viacheslav List'ev **Вячесла́в Ли́стьев** managed to create an open forum for diverse opinions on controversial issues and taboo topics. His growing popularity and influence brought on his brutal assassination in 1994. He was seen as a hero-martyr in the struggle against the demands of Russian mafia.

The Wick **«Фити́ль».** A mild satire criticizing diverse aspects of Soviet society. Performed in skits featuring well-known actors and documentary film, the discussion tackles such issues as the lack of discipline in the work place, alcoholism, and insubordination.

KVN (Club of Funny and Smart People) **«КВН» (Клуб весёлых и нахо́дчивых).** Students organized and conducted competitions testing each team's sense of humor and ability to answer questions in the funniest and most clever way.

Field of Miracles **«По́ле чуде́с».** A television game largely based on the American program "Wheel of Fortune." Participants solve a word puzzle by guessing the correct letters, and receive prizes. The expressions "The word does contain that letter" and "A commercial break" **«Есть така́я бу́ква в э́том сло́ве»** and **«Рекла́мная па́уза»** were the tag lines of the program's anchorman Leonid Yakubovich **Леони́д Якубо́вич.** The phrase **«Есть така́я бу́ква»** is a play on Lenin's **«Есть така́я па́ртия»** about the Communist Party and its ability to lead the nation.

The Blue Light **«Голубо́й огонёк».** A concert show attracting major stage stars, musicians, actors and stand-up comedians. **Голубо́й экра́н** "the blue screen" is a common way of referring to the television.

Television Series Films   **Телефи́льмы**

Seventeen Moments of Spring **«Семна́дцать мгнове́ний весны́»,** 1973, Tatiana Lioznova **Татья́на Лио́знова.** Twelve 70-minute episodes make up the series, whose popularity lasted for years. The legendary star of Soviet film, Viacheslav Tikhonov **Вячесла́в Ти́хонов** as the Soviet spy Shtirlits **Шти́рлиц,** achieved even greater fame on television. After the show ended, the popularity of Shtirlits continued in the telling of jokes. Among the popular expressions from the film are:

- **Информа́ция к размышле́нию** Information to think about.

- **Хара́ктер норди́ческий (Беспоща́ден к врага́м ре́йха).** Nordic character (Merciless to enemies of the Reich). Said of a hard character.

- **Шти́рлиц знал …** Shtirlits knew … Said about a man who is well informed, or when one is sure of one's information.

The Meeting Place Cannot be Changed **«Ме́сто встре́чи измени́ть нельзя́»** Stanislav Govorukhin (1979). This five-part, 350-minute series engaged television viewers in a story about the Soviet military investigating criminal activity in postwar Russia.

Other popular television films were *Little Tragedies* **«Ма́ленькие траге́дии»;** and *The Great Patriotic* **«Вели́кая Оте́чественная».** Television keeps older feature films such as *The Siberiad* **«Сибириа́да»;** and *The Twelve Chairs* **«12 сту́льев»** alive for new generations of viewers.

Shows for Children   Де́тские переда́чи

Good Night, Little Ones! «Споко́йной но́чи, малыши́!» An educational children's show before bed time. The show features two endearing puppets, the piglet Khriusha **Хрю́ша** and the bunny rabbit Stepashka **Степа́шка.** They help a human tell a bed time story, sing songs, and show cartoons. The program, shown nightly, remains very popular.

Cartoons   Мультфи́льмы

The Russian cartoon[1] **мультфи́льм** is a medium, even an art form, whose appeal is not confined to children. Indeed, some were designed for their elders and therefore are of special interest to the student of Russian. The visual and audible material is authentic, phrases are often repeated, and many of the cartoons mentioned here have entered the language, since they are all classics in the popular sense. These films are all blessedly short, usually 10–20 minutes long, so that their repetition can be contemplated. The Soyuzmultfilm studio was founded in 1936, but the genre was at its height in the 1970s and 1980s. Yuri Norstein **Ю́рий Норште́йн** earned international recognition with his animated films produced in the 1970s.

The cartoons are often in series: for example, one of the most popular, *Just You Wait!* «Ну, погоди́!» has some 18 different versions featuring a small defenseless hare who always eludes the big scary wolf chasing him. The popular actor Anatolii Papanov **Анато́лий Папа́нов** was the voice of the wolf and his phrase "Just you wait, Hare!" «Ну, За́яц, погоди́!» was the trademark, and frequently the only line, of the show.

There were several *Vacations in Prostokvashino* «Кани́кулы в Простоква́шине»; they supplied the line "I know how to cross-stitch!" **Я и вышива́ть кре́стиком уме́ю!** (used generally to express the satisfaction of righteousness). Another very popular series was *The Adventures of Leopold the Cat* «Приключе́ния кота́ Леопо́льда», which produced "Leopold, you scaredy-cat, get out here!" **Леопо́льд, по́длый трус, выходи́!** (used to urge anyone to come forward or out of hiding); and "Guys, let us live together peacefully!" **Ребя́та, дава́йте жить дру́жно!** (used as it sounds). There were 10 versions of *38 Parrots* «38 попуга́ев», and perhaps 12 of *The Adventures of Captain Vrungel'* «Приключе́ния капита́на Вру́нгеля», 3 *Crocodile Gena* «Крокоди́л Ге́на», 2 *Musicians of Bremen* «Бре́менские музыка́нты», and 2 *The Kid and Carlson who Lives on the Roof* «Малы́ш и Ка́рлсон, кото́рый живёт на кры́ше».

Russian friends insist that their version of *Winnie the Pooh* «Ви́нни Пух и все все все» is much better than the English cartoon. The translation by Boris Zakhoder **Бори́с Заходе́р** is also a famous example of the art of translation. Other classic "cartoons" of course include Pushkin's fairy tales and various folk tales.

---

[1] A cartoon in the sense of a drawing with a comedic point to it is a **карикату́ра.**

Advertisements   Рекла́мы

Television ads appeared now and then on Russian television before the disintegration of the Soviet Union in 1991, but became a regular feature only in the 1990s. Among the most popular ads were:
Oil of Olay, 1990s:

- **Как не повезло́ я́блоку, а как повезло́ вам.** How unlucky for the apple, how lucky for you.

Bank Imperial ads. The series showed world history encapsulated in sixty-second visual stories. The creators of the advertisement (former members of the Kazakh New Wave of the late 1980s) presented television viewers with glorious moments from the life of Nicholas II, Suvorov and Catherine the Great among other personalities. **«Ждём-с»**! "We await you!" attracted particular attention. In the episode, Suvorov refuses to eat at Catherine II's banquet until she bestows on him a long overdue military award: **«до пе́рвой звезды́»** "not until [you bestow] the first star."

VARIETY SHOWS AND STAND-UP COMEDY   ЭСТРА́ДА И КОМЕ́ДИЯ

The variety stage **эстра́да** (the term originated from French and Spanish "small stage") offers a rich choice of entertainment. The most popular traditional shows were folk groups with the emphasis on folksiness, and were based on the 18th-century balagan **балага́н** and lubok **лубо́к** (from **луб** the inner bark of a lime tree. It had many uses in the country. A **лубо́к** is any unschooled presentation or object). More urbane entertainment was found in typically Russian song styles such as salon romance, cruel **жесто́кий** romance, song, dance and instrumental folk ensembles. Gypsy songs **цыга́нские пе́сни** such as "Those Were the Days" **«Доро́гой дли́нною»**, "Dark Eyes" **«О́чи чёрные»** and "Two Guitars" **«Две гита́ры»** are still immensely popular. The performers Anastasiia Vialtseva **Анастаси́я Вя́льцева**, Nadezhda Plevitskaia **Наде́жда Плеви́цкая**, Vera Panina **Ве́ра Па́нина** and Alexander Vertinskii **Алекса́ндр Верти́нский** (who sang his own songs) became legends.

Western-minded youth kept current on American jazz **джаз** (via the BBC and Voice of America radio broadcasts) and tape recordings of rock **рок** and pop **поп** groups whose music came to be as popular in Russia as it was in the West. Russian youth who do not know English sing songs by the Beatles **Битлз, Битлы́**.

The appearance of the Russian bards Bulat Okudzhava **Була́т Окуджа́ва,** Vladimir Vysotsky **Влади́мир Высо́цкий** and Alexander Galich **Алекса́ндр Га́лич** opened new opportunities for self-expression. Their concerts always sold out. All three were known as "guitar poets," and Vysotsky and Galich also delved into the criminal world for inspiration for their songs. At the same time there was a rebirth of old stars such as Alexander Vertinskii.

Fig. 9-14.   Arkadii Raikin

Russia's comedians have added as much to life as to language. The greatest was Arkadii Raikin **Аркáдий Рáйкин,** whose performances never failed to attract people with their fresh humor and lack of didacticism. Today's superstar is Mikhail Zhvanetskii **Михаи́л Жване́цкий**, who is given credit for, "Yesterday they cost five apiece but they were bigger. Today they cost three, but they are small" **Вчерá бы́ли по пять, но больши́е, а сегóдня по три, но мáленькие** (used when a comparison is treated as a juxtaposition, and it is not).

The comedian Gennadii Khazanov **Геннáдий Хазáнов** (who emigrated to Israel) came up with **Пóлный хоккéй**, meaning completely/totally all right, that is, "OK" (even though "hockey" is what he says).

The classic comedians also include Mikhail Zadornov **Михаи́л Задóрнов**, and Clara Novikova **Клáра Нóвикова**. You will know you have reached the heights of understanding Russian when you laugh at their jokes when the Russians do.

THE CIRCUS   ЦИРК

The circus **цирк** was established in 1853 by non-Russian performers: the Salomanskii family of Berlin (in Moscow) and the Italian Cinizelli family (in St. Petersburg). The early 20th century brought popularity to Russian performers like the Nikitin Brothers and the animal circus of the Durov Brothers. The latter was a dynasty in the Russian circus tradition.

The circus **цирк** is deep within the Russian psyche. Watch children's cartoons to see how often the circus is part of the plot. Show Russians the silhouettes of famous clowns and they will identify them. The circus is frequently shown on television, and the Moscow Circus has a demanding touring schedule, both at home and abroad. By far the most popular circus performers are the clowns: the names and routines of Durov **Ду́ров**, Karandash **Каранда́ш**, Oleg Popov **Оле́г Попо́в,** Yuri Kuklachev **Ю́рий Куклачёв**, and, especially, the late Yuri Nikulin **Ю́рий Нику́лин** are simply known to or remembered fondly by all.

Fig. 9-15.   Yuri Nikulin

APPENDIX: A List of Films Every Student of Russian Should See

I. Classic Films

In this group you will find films you ought to see at least once. Most of them contributed to the development of the art of film, and all of them are considered by Russians to be classics.

- *The Battleship Potemkin* «Бронено́сец Потёмкин» (1925)
- *Chapayev* «Чапа́ев» (1934)
- *Volga-Volga* «Во́лга-Во́лга» (1938)
- *Alexander Nevsky* «Алекса́ндр Не́вский» (1938)
- *The Communist* «Коммуни́ст» (1957)
- *The Mirror* «Зе́ркало» (1960s)

II. Changing Lifestyles

These films reflect life or ways of thinking about it in the Soviet Union and Russia in the 20th century. Some are included because their very release onto public movie screens signalled a change in the Russian way of life.

- *The Happy Guys* «Весёлые ребя́та» (1934)
- *The Cranes are Flying* «Летя́т журавли́» (1957)
- *The Heights* «Высота́» (1957)
- *Autumn Marathon* «Осе́нний марафо́н» (1979)
- *Garage* «Гара́ж» (1979)
- *Moscow Does Not Believe in Tears* «Москва́ слеза́м не ве́рит» (1979)
- *Repentance* «Покая́ние» (1980)
- *The Pokrov Gate* «Покро́вские воро́та»(1982)
- *Little Vera* «Ма́ленькая Ве́ра» (1988)
- *The Needle* «Игла́» (1989)
- *Burnt by the Sun* «Утомлённые со́лнцем» (1994)
- *The Particularities of National Hunting* «Осо́бенности национа́льной охо́ты» (1995)

III. Russian Favorites

The following movies are those that Russians see again and again or remember with great fondness. They are the films that have contributed the most to the Russian language.

- *Operation Y and Other Adventures of Shurik* «Опера́ция Ы и други́е приключе́ния Шу́рика» (1965)

- *(Woman) Prisoner of the Caucasus* **«Кавка́зская пле́нница, или но́вые приключе́ния Шу́рика»** (1966)
- *The Diamond Arm* **«Бриллиа́нтовая рука́»** (1968)
- *White Sun of the Desert* **«Бе́лое со́лнце пусты́ни»** (1969)
- *Snowball Berry Red* **«Кали́на кра́сная»** (1973)
- *The Irony of Fate* **«Иро́ния судьбы́, или с лёгким па́ром»** (1975)

Part 4. Contexts in Reality

В России нет дорог-только направления.

Russia has no roads, only directions.

Anonymous

Genevra Gerhart

Fig. 10-1. Russia, in troubled times

The object of this chapter is to describe what the educated Russian knows about Russian geography, and to present what images and associations go with that knowledge. Russia has been divided into eleven economic regions **регио́ны** which are commonly used by geographers, economists and politicians in Russia and in the United States, so those divisions are described and used here. School textbooks have been a great help for background, but nothing would have been possible without my friends: Julia Tolmacheva, Andrey Yusov, Vera Brekhovskikh, Vera Khokhlova, Oleg Sapozhnikov, Sergey Drozdov, Tatiana Zolotareva.

In this chapter we use the transliteration system established by the U.S. Board of Geographic Names (BGN), and conventional name spellings supplied by the Merriam Webster Geographical Dictionary, Third Edition.

Location is part of real estate, and language. We identify with a place *and* with its name, so that getting it right matters. (And so does everyone. Say, "Ore-ee-gone" and the inhabitants will let you know.) Views and opinions about places are uncommonly strong and often closely held. The Russians tend to be suspicious of foreign views of them: sometimes hurt that the outside world does not know of such-and-such a wonder, sometimes derisive of foreign misinformation about Russia or Russians. This insecurity is epitomized by the story of the Frenchman who returned to his homeland and told of sitting under a "spreading cranberry tree"[1] **развéсистая клю́ква**. According to **Крыла́тые слова́**[2] (Ashukiny) the expression originated in a 1910 *Russian* play that parodied foreign ignorance of Russia: two French playwrights, *Romaine* and *Lettuce*, propose to a French director a play that takes place somewhere in central Russia near Sankt-Muscovy[3] on the shores of the Volga.[4] The heroine, Aksyona,[5] is threatened with force to marry a Cossack, but she pines for her Ivan, remembering their time together under the spreading cranberry tree. The phrase entered the language and originally meant *any collection of misapprehensions about Russia indulged in by a foreigner*, and now means any ridiculously improbable story about anything.

POLITICAL DIVISIONS　　　　　　АДМИНИСТРАТИ́ВНЫЕ ДЕЛÉНИЯ

Russia **Росси́я** was Muscovy **Моско́вия** 500 years ago, and before that "Rus" **Русь**, a now poetic name for Russia and sometimes Russians. The usual adjective to denote the Russian nationality is **ру́сский**, while **росси́йский** and **россия́не** are used where Russian ethnicity itself is not involved, for example in the titles of government offices and organizations.[6]

The lists of political divisions in Appendix 2 are given to show the current structure of political naming, and to serve as a reference, since names do matter, now that other nationalities are demanding, and getting, recognition. It should be stressed that some republics and autonomous okrugs[7] are only hazily represented in the Russian mind. Such an area might be correctly located as being in the Caucasus, in Siberia, or the Far East, but exactly where is something else. Russians are more familiar with the names of individual cities, however, a great help for us since most oblasts are named after their major city. (See Appendix 2, which includes the Library of Congress translation and transliteration of political names.)

---

[1] Cranberries grow on low bushes in bogs.

[2] Literally entitled "Winged Words," this standard reference gives the origin or background of many frequently used phrases, from clichés to literary references.

[3] An obvious combination of *St. Petersburg* and *Moscow*.

[4] Neither city is on the Volga.

[5] **Аксёна** is a very unheroic name, which fact adds to the humor.

[6] For example, the Russian Academy of Sciences **Росси́йская акадéмия нау́к** (**РАН**).

[7] To avoid confusion, political subdivisions below the republic level will be transliterated: thus, **край** will be kray, **о́круг** will be okrug, **о́бласть** will be oblast (no soft sign, since *oblast* is in the English dictionary), **райо́н** will be rayon.

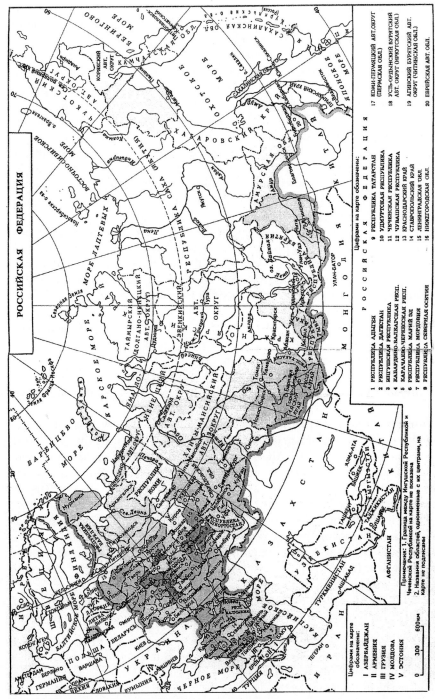

Fig. 10-2. Political Map of Russia

The former Soviet Union (FSU) **бы́вший Сове́тский Сою́з** or USSR **СССР** (Union of Soviet Socialist Republics **Сою́з Сове́тских Социалисти́ческих Респу́блик**, often in the past referred to incorrectly as "Russia") was made up of 15 Republics (Ukrainian SSR, Latvian SSR, Kazakh SSR ... and so forth) among which was the Russian Republic RSFSR **РСФСР** (Russian Soviet Federated Socialist Republic **Росси́йская Сове́тская Федерати́вная Социалисти́ческая Респу́блика**). Article 1 of the 1993 Constitution states that the current "Russian Federation," **Росси́йская Федера́ция** or just "Russia," **Росси́я** are equivalent titles.

Before the Revolution, Russia was divided into provinces **губе́рнии**, and after the Revolution most of these became oblasts **о́бласти**, some retaining their original titles. Today Russia has a different set of divisions: republics, krays, oblasts, "federal cities" (that is Moscow and St. Petersburg), autonomous okrugs, and one autonomous oblast.

The titles in Appendix 2 are used for areas where nationality differences[8] require recognition and as a result the units have been granted some local autonomy: republics, autonomous okrugs and the autonomous oblast. Most current republics are former ASSRs (Autonomous Soviet Socialist Republic **Автоно́мная Сове́тская Социалисти́ческая Респу́блика**).

21 Republics   21 респу́блика

A list of the 21 republics may be found in Appendix 2.

Autonomous Okrugs   Автоно́мные округа́

The former *national* okrug **национа́льный о́круг** has now become an *autonomous* okrug **автоно́мный о́круг** (**АО**, *also* **ао**[9]) [see Appendix 2]. (A few were promoted to republics.) All okrugs are a subdivision of an oblast or kray. The use of a nationality title gives no indication of the actual ratio of natives to Russians in that area. (Some of these subdivisions are vague in the Russian mind. They are given in Appendix 2 for reference.)

There is one autonomous oblast, the Jewish autonomous oblast **Евре́йская автоно́мная о́бласть** or **Биробиджа́н** (Birobidzhan in English is used both for the oblast and city name); the population there is 83 percent Russian and only 4 percent Jewish. (Note that the terms are mutually exclusive: Jews are felt to comprise a separate nationality.)

The oblast is the current standard subdivision of Russia. A complete list of their names is found in the appendix. A kray may be regarded as a large oblast.

---

[8] In Russia the word "nationality" **национа́льность** refers to ethnicity (as understood by a Russian), not to citizenship **гражда́нство**.

[9] **АО, ао** can be distinguished by the gender of the modifier: "о" can refer to **о́бласть** or **о́круг**. The first is feminine, the second is masculine.

(Earlier the kray differed from the oblast by containing an autonomous oblast. These autonomous areas are no longer under kray administration; the title "kray" remains, and its obligations are the same as those of the oblast.) The smallest territorial subdivision is the rayon **райо́н**, so if Russia were the United States, then oblasts and krays would be states and rayons would be counties. (Some cities also have subdivisions called rayon **райо́н**, but Moscow, for example, now instead has larger jurisdictions called "okrug" **о́круг**, *pl.* **округа́**.)

In May, 2000, President Putin divided Russia into seven federal districts **федера́льные округа́** (some resembling those regional divisions already used in school texts) and to each assigned a representative to report to him on whether their zone adhered to federal laws. A list of those districts is on the ⬚ **10-2** CD and an outline map of the districts is in Chapter 11.

NEW AND OLD PLACE NAMES · НО́ВЫЕ И СТА́РЫЕ НАЗВА́НИЯ

In the last ten years, the names for some republics have gone from (1) the original name in Russian, to (2) the name as the locals want it, to (3) the name Russians insist is the name if you are speaking Russian, that is, the original name in Russian. Item (3) indicates that the Russians have concluded that the Russian term is acceptable if one is speaking Russian to Russians in Russia. The alternate forms are shown in Appendix 2 as formal and informal names. (For a while, guilt kept the liberals saying **Кыргызста́н** even though **Кирги́зия** was much easier on the Russian ear. Thus it is that a reporter might describe events in **Кыргызста́н** in the newspaper, but talk to friends about the same event in **Кирги́зия**.)

Geographical names change relatively frequently in Russia; new city street names can be found in the front pages of the telephone book for that city. Below are some major cities with the date they acquired the preceding name.

- **Вели́кий Но́вгород** 1999, **Новгород** ?, **Великий Новгород** 10th century?
- **Владикавка́з** 1990, **Орджоники́дзе** 1931, **Владикавказ** 1784
- **Волгогра́д** 1961, **Сталингра́д**[10] 1925, **Цари́цын** 1555
- **Вя́тка** 1991, **Ки́ров** 1934, **Вятка** 1781
- **Екатеринбу́рг** 1991, **Свердло́вск** 1924, **Екатеринбу́рг** 1723
- **Калинингра́д** 1945, **Ке́нигсберг** 1255
- **На́бережные Челны́** 1988, **Бре́жнев** 1982, **На́бережные Челны́** 1930
- **Нижний Но́вгород** 1990, **Го́рький** 1932, **Нижний Новгород** 1221
- **Оренбу́рг** 1957, **Чка́лов** 1938, **Оренбург** 1735
- **Ры́бинск** 1989, **Андро́пов** 1984, **Щербако́в** 1946–57

---

[10] Old folks who remember the Battle of Stalingrad find "Volgograd" to be namby-pamby.

- **Сама́ра** 1991, **Ку́йбышев** 1935, **Самара** 1586
- **Санкт-Петербу́рг** 1991, **Ленингра́д** 1924, **Петрогра́д** 1914, **Санкт-Петербург** 1703, 1706
- **Се́ргиев Поса́д** 1991, **Заго́рск** 1930, **Се́ргиев Поса́д** 1345
- **Тверь** 1990, **Кали́нин** 1931, **Тверь** 1164 (упомина́ется)

The military-industrial complex **вое́нно-промы́шленный ко́мплекс (ВПК)** in communist times involved some ten percent of the populace in production and research, not only of obvious military equipment but also technical products for the civilian market, from refrigerators to computers. One characteristic of this complex was that its enterprises were located in "closed" cities **закры́тые города́** which didn't exist according to the maps, though they did have names followed by numbers that one could use for mail.[11] For example, the former **Свердло́вск-44** is now **Новоура́льск**, **Арзама́с-16** is either **Кремлёв** or **Са́ров**, and **Красноя́рск-26** is now **Железного́рск**. There are, and were, many, many others.

PHYSICAL GEOGRAPHY   **ФИЗИ́ЧЕСКАЯ ГЕОГРА́ФИЯ**

Physical geography requires maps in color and many charts, pictures, and graphs, so this section is treated on the CD alone.

10-5 A physical map of Russia   **10-7** Peoples and cities
10-6 Rivers and seas

A Short Course in Junior Physical Geography

10-8 Determining altitude	**10-16** Earthquakes
10-9 Using noonday sun for directions	**10-17** Mountains and their parts
10-10 The shape and size of the earth	**10-18** Lower elevations
10-11 Latitude	**10-19** Atmosphere
10-12 Longitude	**10-20** Average temperatures in Moscow
10-13 What geography is about	**10-21** Design of barometer
10-14 Several outside layers of Earth	**10-22** Summer and winter winds
10-15 Structure of a volcano	**10-23** Different clouds at differing altitudes

---

[11] Closed places of work were often called "mail boxes" **почто́вые я́щики – п/я**. Now the term refers to post office box numbers used by those who fear thievery from their mail delivery boxes at home.

History

☐ **10-64** Expansion from 11th–15th centuries

☐ **10-65** Major migration 16th–20th centuries

☐ **10-66** Russians abroad

Nature

☐ **10-67** Map of nature zones, USSR

☐ **10-68** Map of nature regions outlines

☐ **10-69** Nature zones in western USSR

☐ **10-70** Found in the ground

☐ **10-71** Where the ore is

☐ **10-72** Map of USSR land use

☐ **10-73** Earthquakes and volcanoes

☐ **10-74** Depths, temperatures, salinity of Black Sea

☐ **10-75** Table of largest rivers

☐ **10-76** Table of largest lakes

☐ **10-77** Table of highest mountains

Plants

☐ **10-78** Relation of soils, vegetation types and climate

☐ **10-79** Vegetation changes with latitude

☐ **10-80** World forests

☐ **10-81** Forest renewal after fire, in years

☐ **10-82** Locations of ecological disasters

☐ **10-83** Map of which trees grow where

☐ **10-84** Food production in various countries

☐ **10-85** U.S. agricultural labor productivity compared to other countries

Animals

☐ **10-86** Map showing where wild animals grow

☐ **10-87** Fur-bearing animals

☐ **10-88** Tundra inhabitants

☐ **10-89** Forest residents

☐ **10-90** Animals of the steppe

☐ **10-91** Animals adapt to heat and drought

RUSSIA DIVIDED   По региóнам[12]

Russia has a North **сéвер**, a South **юг**, and a Far East **Дáльний Востóк**, but no West **зáпад**. (The West is another world altogether.) Central Russia **Центрáльная Россúя** extends from the Gulf of Finland **Фúнский залúв** to Ukraine in the popular mind, but Russia also has her unique Volga region **Повóлжье**, the Urals **Урáл**, and her very own Siberia **Сибúрь**.

Of course there are other ways to divide the country. This map, for ▦ **10-92** example, is a division into "Nature Zones."

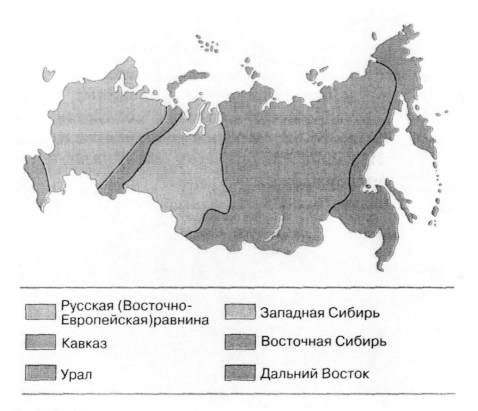

▦ Русская (Восточно-Европейская)равнина	▦ Западная Сибирь
▦ Кавказ	▦ Восточная Сибирь
▦ Урал	▦ Дальний Восток

Fig. 10-3.   Nature zones

---

[12] Literally, "By regions," but meaning major divisions of the country such as "The South" in the US. **Региóны** is also used to mean "the provinces" (as opposed to the capital). The word **райóн** is also sometimes used this way.

10-93

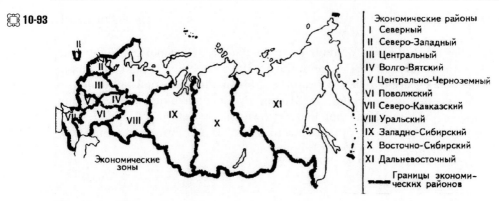

Fig. 10-4.   Economic zones

An economic text suggests the possibility of two major divisions: one is the West, including the Ural mountains, and the other is everything East of there. **10-94** The same text also proposes a possible north/south division, mostly in fact based on population. The regions as we describe them below correspond to those made by geographers, economists and government planners.

Central Russia   **Центра́льный райо́н**

10-95 (Including: Bryansk, Vladimir, Ivanovo, Kaluga, Kostroma, Moscow [city], Moscow, Orel, Ryazan′, Smolensk, Tver′, Tula and Yaroslavl′ oblasts.)

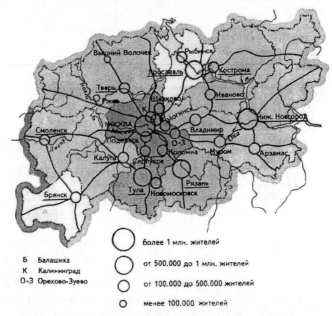

Fig. 10-5.   Outline of Central Russia

"Central Russia" to the non-technical mind means the space from St. Petersburg in the north to Ukraine in the south and Nizhniy Novgorod in the east. Our divisions here have different boundaries because geographers, economists and politicians, both Russian and non-Russian, use these specific subdivisions.

Moscow and its oblast is at the center of the region which includes all the contiguous oblasts plus Bryansk oblast and Orel oblast to the south and Kostroma oblast to the north. This is Russia's heart. If the north is gloomy and gray, then central Russia is lighter, with evergreen forests giving way to mixed forest **смéшанные лесá** with birches **берёзы** and meadows **лугá** mixed in. And in the south the fields **поля** open to the light from above. The country houses are notably smaller than in the north since larger cattle can survive in adjacent buildings, this is the land of the "five-walls" **пятистéнки** or two-room houses in which one room has a Russian stove and the other is kept in neater condition, with only a small "Dutch stove" **голлáндка** for heating. Root vegetables, cabbage and grains are the staples. With more cattle, the food is richer with more milk and sour cream so this land allows a richer diet: Tula cookie-cakes **тýльские прáники** are famous. If rye **рожь** is the grain of the north, then wheat **пшенúца** attends the south.

Moscow and   **Москвá и Московская**
Moscow oblast   **óбласть/Подмосковье**

Fig. 10-6.   Moscow oblast

Moscow is to Russia what New York was to the United States 50 years ago, with its concentration of government administrations, business activities, artistic endeavors, educational facilities, not to mention its concentration of people and now, cars. The pace is brisk, noisy (and felt to be less safe than it used to be). It has the feel of a village that just grew, as opposed to St. Petersburg, which has an air of formal majesty to it.

10-96   At its heart is the Kremlin **Кремль** (see Fig. 10-7 on the facing page) or, more accurately, "a" kremlin since this word means "fortification surrounding the city," and many other old Russian cities have their own "kremlins" (**Но́вгород, А́страхань, Ни́жний Но́вгород, Росто́в, Псков, Смоле́нск, Ту́ла, Коло́мна, Каза́нь, У́глич, Тобо́льск**). The Kremlin wall **Кремлёвская стена́** is roughly a triangle with the Moscow river **Москва́-река́** on one side, Red Square **Кра́сная пло́щадь** on another and Manezhnaya St. **Манéжная ул.** on the third. One of the official entrances is through the Savior's Gates **Спа́сские воро́та** at the base of Savior's Tower **Спа́сская ба́шня**. (It is this tower that appears on the television screen on New Year's eve at the stroke of midnight when the Kremlin bells ring **бой кремлёвских кура́нтов** and in the news program **«Вре́мя».**) Two other entrances are: Borovitskiye Gates **Борови́цкие воро́та** (for government vehicles **для спецмаши́н**), and Trinity Gates **Тро́ицкие воро́та** (for visitors and tourists **для посети́телей и тури́стов**). Inside today's Kremlin, among the familiar landmarks, the Russian may not necessarily know the names of three ancient cathedrals **собо́ры** (**Арха́нгельский** Archangel, **Успе́нский**[13] Assumption, **Благове́щенский** Annunciation) which are now operating churches, but everyone could name the giant Tsar Bell **Царь-ко́локол**, a large Tsar Cannon **Царь-пу́шка**, the Palace of Congresses **Дворе́ц съе́здов** (familiar because concerts are held there), the Armory **Оруже́йная пала́та**, the Arsenal **Арсена́л**, and Ivan the Great's Bell-Tower **Колоко́льня Ива́на Вели́кого**. (**Звони́ть "во всю Ива́новскую"** means to ring all the bells in this tower at once; with other verbs the phrase indicates using full force.)

10-97   When asked where they live, or where something in Moscow is located, Muscovites **москвичи́** are more likely to name a nearby monument, or edifice, or subway stop. Be sure to ask for the latter to add to any address you may be given. Away from downtown **Центр**, people might refer to an area, often a former village: **в Черта́нове, в Черёмушках**.

Key to Fig. 10-7 on opposite page:

1.	Борови́цкая ба́шня	6.	Сте́ны Кремля́ **10-99**
2.	Спа́сская ба́шня	7.	Собо́рная пло́щадь **10-100**
3.	Тро́ицкая ба́шня **10-98**	8.	Успе́нский собо́р **10-101**
4.	Тро́ицкий мост	9.	Благове́щенский собо́р **10-102**
5.	Ба́шня Кутафья	10.	Це́рковь Ризположения **10-103**

---

[13] Of the three cathedrals, this is the most important. Coronations took place here.

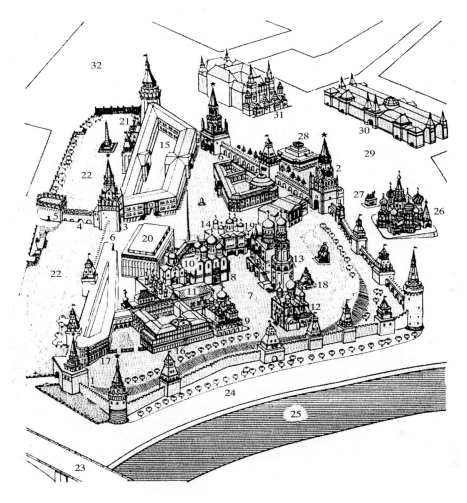

Fig. 10-7. Drawing of the Kremlin

11.	Грановѝтая палáта	10-104	22.	Александровский сад	10-114
12.	Архáнгельский собóр	10-105	23.	Большóй Кáменный мост	
13.	Колокóльня Ивáна Велѝкого	10-106	24.	Кремлёвская нáбережная	10-115
14.	Собóр «Двенáдцать апóсто-лов» и Патриáршие палáты	10-107	25.	Москвá-рекá	10-116
			26.	Храм Васѝлия Блажéнного	10-117
15.	Здáние Арсенáла	10-108	27.	Пáмятник К. Минину и	10-118
16.	Большóй Кремлёвский дворéц	10-109		Д. Пожáрскому	
17.	Оружéйная палáта		28.	Мавзолéй В.И. Лéнина	10-119
18.	Царь-кóлокол	10-110	29.	Крáсная плóщадь	10-120
19.	Царь-пушка	10-111	30.	ГУМ и Лóбное мéсто	10-121
20.	Кремлёвский Дворéц съéздов	10-112	31.	Исторический музéй	10-122
21.	Могѝла Неизвéстного солдáта	10-113	32.	Манéжная плóщадь	10-123

(The following Moscow place names have English translations, examples of usage, and many pictures on the CD-ROM accompanying this book.)

Moscow Place Names	*Достопримеча́тельности Москвы́*
Squares	*Пло́щади*

10-124
10-125
10-126
10-127
10-128

- **Кра́сная пло́щадь** Red Square: **Храм Васи́лия Блаже́нного** St. Basil's (= **Покро́вский собо́р** Cathedral of the Protection); **па́мятник Ми́нину и Пожа́рскому** a Memorial to Minin and Pozharskiy; **Ло́бное ме́сто** Execution Place; **ГУМ** GUM department store; **Истори́ческий музе́й** the Historical Museum; **Кремлёвская стена́** the Kremlin wall and **Мавзоле́й Ле́нина** Lenin's Mausoleum; **Каза́нский собо́р** Kazan Cathedral.
- **Театра́льная пло́щадь** Theatre Square: **Большо́й теа́тр, Ма́лый теа́тр** the Bol'shoy and Malyy Theatres; **Центра́льный де́тский теа́тр** Central Children's Theater; **Метропо́ль** Metropol' Hotel.

Streets	*У́лицы*

10-129

- **Садо́вое кольцо́** The "Garden Ring" is not one street but a series of streets that together encircle a large portion of central downtown Moscow **центр**. The US embassy is on one such street.

10-130

- **Бульва́рное кольцо́** An inner ring in a horseshoe shape formed from assorted "Boulevards"—the Russian term means a broad street with a walkway and trees down the middle—**Го́голевский бульва́р, Страстно́й бульва́р, Тверско́й бульвар, Цветно́й бульва́р.**
- **Арба́т (пешехо́дная ул. в Це́нтре)** The Arbat is now for pedestrians and artists, musicians.
- **Но́вый Арба́т (бы́вший Проспе́кт Кали́нина)** "New" Arbat (formerly, Prospekt Kalinina).

10-131
10-132

- **Тверска́я ул.** Tverskaya (formerly, Gorky) Street is a major downtown commercial site. The main post office **главпочта́мт** is located there.

10-133

- **Ле́нинский проспе́кт** Leninskiy prospekt is famous for being very long, and is also associated with the University and the Russian Academy of Sciences **Росси́йская акаде́мия нау́к (РАН).**
- **Ленингра́дский проспект** Leningradskiy Prospekt leads (eventually) to Leningrad (St. Petersburg)
- **Кузне́цкий мост** Kuznetskiy Bridge. There's no bridge now (although once there was); a winding street in the center of town.
- **Моско́вская кольцева́я (автомоби́льная) доро́га (МКАД)** The Moscow Ring Road.

Moscow's Familiar Sites   *Знамени́тые места́ в Москве́*
(not otherwise classified)

- **Бе́лый дом** The White House (wherefrom government affairs are conducted).   🔲 **10-134**
- **Мане́ж** The Manege is a major downtown exhibition hall; formerly, it   🔲 **10-135**
  was the tsar's riding school.   🔲 **10-136**
- **Лужники́** Luzhniki is a sports arena for soccer and other sports.   🔲 **10-137**
- **Стадио́н «Дина́мо»** Dinamo stadium is only for soccer.   🔲 **10-138**
- **Новоде́вичий монасты́рь** Novodevichiy Monastery. Many famous peo-   🔲 **10-139**
  ple are buried in the neighboring cemetery, called **Новоде́вичье**   🔲 **10-140**
  кла́дбище: Chaliapin, Khrushchev, Chekhov, Mayakovsky and many   🔲 **10-141**
  others.   🔲 **10-142**
- **Оста́нкинская телеба́шня** Ostankino television tower is a symbol of
  television.
- **МГУ Моско́вский госуда́рственный университе́т и́мени Ломоно́сова**   🔲 **10-143**
  Moscow State University (named after Lomonosov) is on Sparrow
  (formerly, Lenin) Hills **на Воробьёвых (бы́вших Ле́нинских) гора́х**
  and is the largest and oldest university in the country.
- **Киносту́дия Мосфи́льм** *Mosfilm* studio produces most of the movies in
  Russia.
- **РГБ (эр-гэ-бэ) Росси́йская госуда́рственная библиоте́ка (бы́вшая**
  Библиоте́ка им. Ле́нина), «Ле́нинка» The Russian State Library
  (formerly, the Lenin State Library) is the largest in the country.
- **Храм Христа́ Спаси́теля** The Church of Christ the Savior has been re-   🔲 **10-144**
  built on (its original) site—an outdoor pool in Stalinist times. It was a
  pet project of Luzhkov, Moscow's mayor.
- **Луба́нка (зда́ние МВД)** The Lubyanka is a building of the Ministry of
  Internal Affairs **Министе́рство вну́тренних дел.** (Also see Prisons.)
- **«Дом на на́бережной»** The House on the Embankment was famous as   🔲 **10-145**
  the residence of many well-known Soviets who were arrested in the
  purges. A close-up view shows panels memorializing them. (See story of
  the same name by Yuri Trifonov.)
- **Консервато́рия** The Conservatory is the oldest music school. The
  International Tchaikovsky Music Competition **Междунаро́дный музы-**
  ка́льный ко́нкурс имени Чайко́вского takes place at **Конце́ртный зал**   🔲 **10-146**
  имени Чайко́вского The Tchaikovskiy Concert Theater.
- **Триумфа́льная а́рка (Куту́зовский проспе́кт)** The Triumphal Arch on
  Kutuzov Prospect was built to commemorate the victory over
  Napoleon.
- **Бороди́нская панора́ма** The Borodinskaya Panorama is a three-
  dimensional representation of the Battle of Borodino in the war with
  Napoleon.

- **Акаде́мия нау́к (на Ле́нинском проспе́кте)** The Academy of Science (on Leninskiy prospekt) is a new building for the Presidium of the Academy of Sciences; it is very noticeable, rising above the city in this part of town.

10-147
- **ВДНХ (вэ-дэ-эн-ха́)—бы́вшая Вы́ставка достиже́ний наро́дного хозя́йства** The VDNKh, the former Exhibition of Economic Achievements now is a trade center **ВВЦ Всеросси́йский вы́ставочный центр.**
- **Донско́й монасты́рь** is the residence of the Moscow patriarchate.
- **Дани́ловский монасты́рь** Danilov monastery.

Tall "Stalin" Buildings   Высо́тные «ста́линские» дома́

10-148
- **Высо́тный дом на пло́щади Восста́ния** the tall building on Insurrection Square. The first residents were famous actors, high military and government officials.

10-149
- **Зда́ние МИД (Министе́рство иностра́нных дел)** The Ministry of Foreign Affairs building.

10-150
- **Гости́ница Украи́на** The Hotel Ukraina.
- **Высо́тный дом на Коте́льнической на́бережной** The tall building on Kotel'nicheskaya (Boilermaker) embankment is an apartment house **жило́й дом.**

10-151
- **Зда́ние МГУ** The Moscow University building.
- **Жило́й дом на пло́щади Ле́рмонтова** The apartment house on Lermontov Square.
- **Гости́ница Ленингра́дская** The Leningrad Hotel near Leningrad station.

Theaters are shown in Chapter 6.

Moscow's Museums   Музе́и

10-152
- **Третьяко́вская галере́я (Третьяко́вка)** The Tret'yakov Gallery has pictures by many Russian artists. The icon collection is superb.
- **Пу́шкинский музе́й** The Pushkin Museum has not only Russian rooms **ру́сские за́лы**, but also Western exhibits, for example, it has a good collection of the Impressionists. They often exhibit collections from other museums in the world.
- **Моско́вский дом худо́жника** The Moscow House of the Artist is an exhibition hall on Krymskaya embankment **на Кры́мской на́бережной.**
- **Оруже́йная пала́та в Кремле́** The Armory (Tsars' collections of treasures from 12th century onward).
- **Политехни́ческий музе́й** The Polytechnic Museum.
- **Истори́ческий музей** The Historical Museum is on Red Square.

- **Музей-усáдьба «Кускóво»** The Museum and former Country Estate at Kuskovo once belonged to the Sheremet'yevs (of salt mine fame); it contains original or restored interiors and art objects.
- **Андрóников монастырь** Andronikov Monastery has a collection of Rublyov icons, including the well-known Trinity (See Chapter 8).

Parks   *Парки*

- **Парк культуры (и óтдыха) им. Гóрького** Gorky Park.
- **Измáйловский парк** Izmaylov Park has a large outdoor art market.
- **Лосíный óстров** Moose Island.
- **Сокóльники** Sokol'niki.
- **Филёвский парк** Filyovskiy park.
- **Серéбряный Бор** Silver Glade is a recreation area and has the best-known beaches on the Moscow River within the city limits.
- **Колóменское** Kolomenskoye has monuments of ancient architecture, is the destination of holiday trips and serves as a background to groups of folk singers.
- **Парк Побéды** Victory Park is a recently built monumental complex [] **10-153** dedicated to the 50th anniversary of the Victory in the "Great Patriotic War" (World War II). [] **10-154**
- **Крылáтское (зáпад, у Москвы-рекú)** Krylatskoye (in western Moscow, near the river) is a very large sports center and recreation area with a canal for rowing, a bicycle track and a downhill skiing area.
- **Зоопáрк** The zoo. [] **10-155**
- **Ботанúческий сад** The botanical garden.
- **Ипподрóм** The horse racing pavilion. [] **10-156**

Monuments to … (Statues of …)   *Пáмятники*

- **Юрию Долгорýкому, основáтелю Москвы** To Yuri Dolgorukiy, the [] **10-157** founder of Moscow.
- **Пýшкину** To Pushkin (poet). [] **10-158**
- **Мúнину и Пожáрскому** To Minin and Pozharskiy (who organized opposition to the false Dmitri).
- **Скульптýрный ансáмбль «Рабóчий и колхóзница» рядом с ВВЦ** [] **10-159** **(скýльптор Мýхина)** *The Worker and the Kolkhoz Woman*, by the sculptor Mukhina, is near the VVTs (All-Russian Exhibition Center, but people still use the old initials **ВДНХ**).
- **Маякóвскому** to Mayakovsky (the poet).
- **Петрý Пéрвому на Крымской нáбережной** The Statue of Peter the Great on Krymskaya Embankment (by the Georgian sculptor Tsereteli **Церетéли**) has come in for considerable criticism.
- **Юрию Гагáрину** To Yuri Gagarin (the first cosmonaut), on a pedestal. [] **10-160**

Stores   *Магази́ны*

- **ГУМ (Госуда́рственный универса́льный магази́н), о́коло Кра́сной пло́щади** GUM (State Department Store), on Red Square.
- **ЦУМ (Центра́льный универса́льный магази́н), о́коло Большо́го теа́тра** TsUM (Central Department Store), near the Bolshoy Theater.
- **Москва́, на Ле́нинском проспе́кте** Moscow (department store), on Leninskiy Prospekt.
- **Де́тский мир** Children's World (not far from where a statue of Dzerzhinskiy used to be and the Lubyanka still is).
- **Моско́вский, о́коло трёх вокза́лов** The Moscovian is near the three terminal stations (on Komsomolskaya Square).
- **Новоарба́тский гастроно́м** The New Arbat Delicatessen.
- **Дом о́буви, Дом тка́ни, Дом фарфо́ра — все на Ле́нинском проспе́кте** The House of Shoes, House of Fabrics, and House of China are all on Leninskiy prospekt.

Markets   *Ры́нки*

There are major covered markets, those with roofs, among which the best known are **Центра́льный, Дани́ловский и Черёмушкинский ры́нки**. There are many other outdoor or sometimes impromptu markets that indulge particular tastes, for example, the art market at **Изма́йловский парк**, the pet (actually called "Bird") market **«Пти́чий ры́нок»** at Taganka, and the technology market **Горбу́шка**, (i. e., near **Дом культу́ры и́мени Горбуно́ва**). The largest market is at the Luzhniki stadium.

Hotels   *Гости́ницы*

⬚ **10-161**
- **«Национа́ль», «Метропо́ль»** The National and the Metropol are old downtown hotels associated with cold war intrigue.
- **«Росси́я»** The Rossiya Hotel is not far from the Kremlin (and is notable for its incredible size).
- **«Ко́смос», о́коло ВВЦ (ВДНХ), «Украи́на»** The Cosmos, near the VVTs, and the Ukraine are both very large.
- **«Славя́нская» (или «Рэ́диссон-Славя́нская»)** Slavyanskaya (or Radisson-Slavyanskaya) is a symbol of American luxury.
- **«Саво́й» (бы́вший «Берли́н»)** The Savoy (formerly, the Berlin).

Railway Terminal Stations   *Вокза́лы*

Non-Muscovites tend to be familiar with the railway stations since most people go to Moscow at one time or another and the stations are the gateway. (They are also home to many pickpockets, petty thieves, and con men/women.)

Komsomol'skaya ploshchad' alone has three terminal stations, Leningrad, Yaroslavl, and Kazan stations **Ленингра́дский**, **Яросла́вский**, **Каза́нский**.

Other terminal stations are: the Kiev **Ки́евский**, Kursk **Ку́рский**, Paveletskiy **Павеле́цкий**, Riga **Ри́жский**, Belorussian **Белору́сский** and Savelovskiy **Савёловский** stations. 🔲 **10-162**

Restaurants   *Рестора́ны*

The Aragvi (Georgian) **Ара́гви**, the Prague (Czech) **Пра́га (чешкий)**, the Pekin (Chinese) **Пеки́н (кита́йский)**, the Budapest (Hungarian) **Будапе́шт** 🔲 **10-163** **(венге́рский)** and Slavic Bazaar (Russian) **Славя́нский База́р (русский)** are old and famous restaurants, while the new world brings us Mc Donald's and **Ёлки-па́лки** not to mention a myriad of others.

Prisons   *Тю́рьмы*

- **Буты́рская**, **Буты́рки** Butyrki (informal). 🔲 **10-164**
- **Лефо́ртово** Lefortovo (this is where the organizers of the 1991 putsch stayed, as did the opponents in 1993).
- **Матро́сская Тишина́** Sailor's Quiet.
- (The Lubyanka **Лубя́нка** houses the offices of the MVD, Ministry of 🔲 **10-165** Internal Affairs; though many people remember the underground floors that were used as a prison, and worse).

Moscow Oblast   *Моско́вская о́бласть, Подмоско́вье[14]:*

(See Figure 10-6; and Chapter 7 for the song "Moscow Nights" **«Под-моско́вные вечера́»**) These are places one should know about in Moscow oblast:

- **Музей-уса́дьба «Арха́нгельское».** Arkhangel'skoye is a museum and country estate.
- **Се́ргиев Поса́д (бы́вший Заго́рск)—наибо́лее посеща́емый тури́стами город в Моско́вской о́бласти; знамени́тая ла́вра (духо́вная семина́рия) и мно́жество церкве́й.** Sergiyev Posad (formerly Zagorsk) is the city most often visited by tourists in Moscow oblast; it has a famous monastery, a seminary and a multitude of churches.
- **Дубна́—го́род, где нахо́дится изве́стный институ́т я́дерных иссле́дований.** Dubna (is the site of) a famous nuclear research institute.
- **Клин (клинча́не)—го́род, где нахо́дятся Дом-музей Чайко́вского и большо́й пивно́й заво́д.** Tchaikovsky's house in Klin is a museum; the city is also famous for a beer factory.

---

[14] Moskovskaya oblast is the specific formal term, while **Подмоско́вье** is the land around Moscow.

- **В уса́дьбе «Абра́мцево» гости́ли мно́гие знамени́тые лю́ди.** Many famous people were guests at the Abramtsevo estate (now a museum).
- **Красного́рск—здесь ката́ются на лы́жах.** Krasnogorsk is famous for skiing.
- **Коло́мна (коло́менцы)—краси́вый ста́рый ру́сский городо́к.** Kolomna is a beautiful old Russian town.
- **Се́рпухов—го́род, где нахо́дится а́томный ускори́тель.** Serpukhov is known for its atom accelerator.
- **Пу́щино—ме́сто жи́тельства мно́гих нау́чных рабо́тников.** Pushchino is where many scientists live.
- **Бородино́ (Бороди́нское поле)—ме́сто истори́ческого сраже́ния с Наполео́ном в 1812 году́: "… Неда́ром по́мнит вся Россия про день Бородина́.» (Ле́рмонтов).** The field at Borodino is the site of a famous battle with Napoleon in 1812: "… For very good reason, all Russia remembers the day of Borodino." (Lermontov)

⟠ 10-166
- **Жуко́вский—го́род авиаконстру́кторов.** Zhukovskiy is a city of airplane designers.

Around Moscow Oblast   *Вокру́г Моско́вской о́бласти*

Just north of Moscow oblast (see Fig. 10-5) is the upper Volga region, which includes Tver′ oblast **Тверска́я о́бласть**, Yaroslavl′ oblast **Яросла́вская о́бласть**, and Kostroma oblast **Костромска́я о́бласть**, all names at the heart of Russian history. Small and large industries are associated with particular places.

Tver′ **Тверь (тверяки́)**, formerly Kalinin **Кали́нин**, a large and old city north and west of Moscow on the Volga with its own kremlin, a pleasant shoreline, and famous for Tver merchants **тверски́е купцы́**.

Ostashkov **Оста́шков** is a small place on Lake Seliger **о́зеро Селиге́р** in the Valday Hills **Валда́й**, famous as a resort area.

Kimry **Ки́мры (кимряки́)** is one of a number of smaller towns that concentrate on one kind of production. Here, the specialty is footwear; earlier it was boots and now it is "Keds" **ке́ды**.

Bologoye **Бологое** is famous as a train stop between Moscow and St. Petersburg. A popular song: **«Бологое, Бологое, Бологое. Это ме́жду Ленингра́дом и Москво́й».**

Rybinsk **Ры́бинск** is a very old town now directly associated with a huge reservoir **Ры́бинское водохрани́лище**. It is also a stop on the Volga boat trip between Moscow and St. Petersburg. This is a popular vacation area.

Pereslavl′-Zalesskiy **Пересла́вль-Зале́сский** is a beautiful old town near Moscow on the Golden Ring **Золото́е кольцо́**, which is itself a set of particularly beautiful and interesting sites with old churches, monasteries and forts.[15]

---

[15] Other cities on the Golden Ring: **Росто́в Великий, У́глич, Яросла́вль, Кострома́, Ива́ново, Су́здаль, Влади́мир, Ю́рьев-По́льский**.

Uglich **У́глич (углича́не)** is known to Russians as another very old small town on the Volga with monasteries and churches, and its kremlin.

Rostov the Great **Росто́в Вели́кий (росто́вцы[16])** is small, old, beautiful, and formerly famous for its bells **росто́вские зво́ны**.

Kostroma **Кострома́ (костромичи́)** is a major city, very old, on the Volga; manufacturing: textiles.

There are eight oblasts to the west and south of Moscow oblast (see Fig. 10-5); from north to south they are:

On the Dniepr **Днепр**, Smolensk **Смоле́нск (смоля́не)** is the oblast capital **Смоле́нская о́бласть**. On major trade routes from ancient times both north-south and east-west, its strongest associations are with wars and battles against the Tartars, against the Poles and Lithuanians, the French, and against the Germans in World War II (The Great Patriotic War **Вели́кая Оте́чественная война́**). Both Smolensk and Vyazma **Вя́зьма (вя́зьмичи)** are very old and were virtually totally destroyed during the war, now rebuilt.

Kaluga **Калу́га (калужа́не)** is the oblast capital **Калу́жская о́бласть**. It is a large and old Russian city on the Oka River **на Оке́**, one of the major train directions from Moscow. There are many dachas in the area. For a description of the land and the people, see Turgenev's story, "Khor and Kalinich" **«Хорь и Кали́ныч»** in *A Hunter's Notebook* **Запи́ски охо́тника**.

Tula **Ту́ла (туляки́)**, the capital of the oblast **Ту́льская о́бласть**, is another large old city with its own kremlin and is well known for Tula cookie-cakes **ту́льские пря́ники**, the manufacturing of samovars,[17] and for major weapons factories. Not far to the south is Yasnaya Polyana **Я́сная Поля́на**, Tolstoy's country estate and the object of visits from natives, foreigners, and wedding parties.

Bryansk oblast **Бря́нская о́бласть** has the capital Bryansk **Брянск (бря́нцы)** a medium size old Russian city. Songs and novels of World War II refer to partisan activities in the area.

Orel **Орёл (орло́вцы)** is the capital of Orel oblast **Орло́вская о́бласть** on the Oka **Ока́** river. A medium sized city that goes back to the middle of the 16th century, it was mightily damaged during the war. The natives use a soft southern "g." Turgenev is from this area. **«Орло́вские рысаки́»—знамени́тая поро́да лошаде́й.** Orel trotters are a famous breed of horses.

We are still in central Russia (see Fig. 10-5), but the following are the three remaining oblasts in the area just east of Moscow oblast in, around and between the Volga and the Oka rivers. This is the heart of ancient Russia, the

---

[16] Note that people living in Rostov-on-the-Don (a much larger, southern city) are called **ростовча́не**.

[17] Just as one does not carry coal to Newcastle in English, one does not take one's samovar to Tula in Russian. **В Ту́лу со свои́м самова́ром не е́здят.**

Vladimir-Suzdal kingdom that once held sway over all of central and north Russia. (See Chapter 1.) Many of the names evoke images of ancient warriors **богатыри** and fairy tales **ска́зки**. From north to the south we have:

Ivanovo oblast **Ива́новская о́бласть** has its capital at Ivanovo **Ива́ново**, a large old city renowned especially for weaving **город ткаче́й/ткачи́х**. Since weaving factories employ quantities of women, it is also therefore famous as a good place to look for wives: it is known as a city of brides **го́род неве́ст**.

In this same oblast is the village Palekh **Па́лех (палеша́не)** which is known for its carefully painted and wildly expensive lacquered boxes. (Earlier the same people painted icons.) Not far away (but in Vladimir oblast) Mstera **Мстёра (мстерча́не)** uses a different style to do a similar thing at a lower price.

Vladimir **Влади́мир (влади́мирцы)**, the venerable capital of Vladimir oblast **Влади́мирская о́бласть**, has now grown into a major factory town but is nevertheless the site of many ancient and beautiful churches. It was founded by Vladimir Monomakh in 1108. On the Golden Ring **Золото́е кольцо́**.

Suzdal′ **Су́здаль (су́здальцы)** is a small town of stunning medieval Russian architecture, a major jewel on the Golden Ring.

Gus′-Khrustal′nyy **Гусь-Хруста́льный** is a small town renowned for its crystal.

Murom **Му́ром** is the ancient small town where the mythical warrior **богаты́рь** Il′ia Muromets **Илья́ Му́ромец** came from.

Ryazan′ **Ряза́нь (ряза́нцы)** is a very old Russian city and the capital of Ryazan oblast **Ряза́нская о́бласть**.

The Northwest Region   **Се́веро-За́падный райо́н**

Many economic and geography books separate this region from Central Russia, but the Russian mind includes it as central to Russia. The discussion involves Leningrad oblast,[18] Kaliningrad oblast, Pskov oblast, Novgorod oblast, and St. Petersburg. It is famous as a forested region of lakes and rivers and the Valday Hills **Валда́йская возвы́шенность**, and is associated with Russia's earliest history as Vladimir-Suzdal′ and wars with Sweden, the Livonian knights and the Lithuanians in mid-thirteenth century. (See Alexander Nevsky in Chapter 1.)

Kaliningrad **Калинингра́д** is a city and oblast totally separated from Russia by the intervening Baltic countries of Lithuania **Литва́**, Latvia **Ла́твия**, and Estonia **Эсто́ния**. Formerly called Königsberg and very Germanic in demeanor, it is retained for its position as an ice-free military port and for access to the west. (It was acquired from Germany at the end of World War II; resident Germans were removed to Siberia.)

Velikiye Luki **Вели́кие Лу́ки (великолуча́не)** is an old Russian town.

---

[18] The name of the oblast remains "Leningradskaya" because those who lived outside of the city of St. Petersburg voted to keep that name.

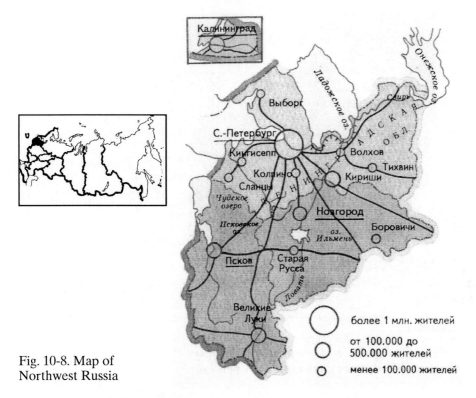

Fig. 10-8. Map of
Northwest Russia

Pskov **Псков (псковичи́)** is an old border city not far from the beautiful and connecting lakes **Пско́вское озеро**, **Чудско́е о́зеро**; associated with medieval merchants (or **го́сти**, as in **Гости́ный Двор**, the name of the large department store in St. Petersburg); near the Baltic Sea.

Lake Peipus **Чудско́е озеро** has Estonia on one side and Russia on the other, thus the two names. The lake is very large, navigable, and known to Russians as the site of a battle where Alexander Nevsky defeated the Livonian knights in 1242. **Би́тва на Чудско́м о́зере с крестоно́сцами**.

Lake Il'men **о́зеро Ильме́нь** appears in Russian fairy tales; the name has an eastern sound to Russians.

Novgorod **Но́вгород**. **«Господи́н Вели́кий Новгород» (новгоро́дцы)**. The (medieval) city assembly **городско́е ве́че** was given credit for maintaining Russia's independence even during the time of Tartars. Alexander Nevsky **Алекса́ндр Невский** is associated with the city. It was also a member of the Hanseatic League **Ганзе́йский сою́з**. In 1999 its name was officially changed back to **Вели́кий Но́вгород** Great Novgorod.

Gatchina **Га́тчина (га́тчинцы)** is on the outskirts of St. Petersburg, and is the site of an 18th century palace and park.

Vyborg **Вы́борг (выборжа́не)** is an old city on the Gulf of Finland and on the road between Helsinki and St. Petersburg.

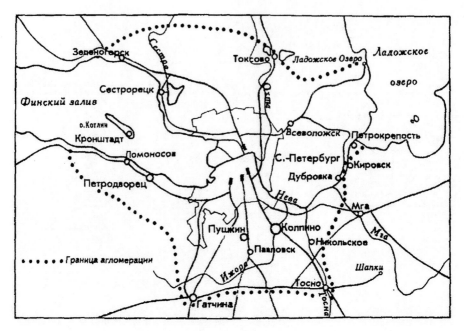

Fig. 10-9.   Map of St.Petersburg environs

St.Petersburg   **Санкт-Петербу́рг**

St. Petersburg **Санкт-Петербу́рг** (in conversation: **Петербу́рг**, **Пи́тер**) is, of
course, in a class by itself; along with Moscow, it is a "federal city." Peter the
Great's city is yet another major world capital built on a swamp and designed
by a French architect (cf. Washington D.C.). This one is on the Gulf of Finland
Фи́нский зали́в and therefore provides a window of access («**В Евро́пу
проруби́ть окно́**») to the West where Peter thought Russia could find progress.
He is Pushkin's "Bronze Horseman" **Ме́дный вса́дник**. (A debate about whether that was progress has raged ever since.) It is a large and graceful city,
proud of its massive cultural heritage. Great universities, libraries, theaters,
ballet, museums and galleries. (Currently culture is not seen as an economic
necessity, so that the city noticeably lags behind Moscow in upkeep.) Peters-
burgers **петербу́ржцы** are not in such a hurry as their Muscovite relatives; they
give the impression of being more polite, more dignified, as if a film of former
nobility had actually rubbed off on them.

    The river running through it is the Neva **Нева́**, a mere 75 kilometers long,
from Lake Ladoga **Ла́дожское о́зеро** to the Gulf of Finland **Фи́нский зали́в**.
The river supplies one of the major themes of the city: recurring floods. Another theme is the "white" nights **бе́лые но́чи** that accompany the summer sol-
stice in northern latitudes: the atmosphere is hazily light, not a time to sleep. It
is a city particularly associated with Pushkin because he lived there, went to

school nearby at Tsarskoye Selo **в Ца́рском Селе́**, died there, and set the action of many of his works there (especially the poem The Bronze Horseman **«Ме́дный вса́дник»**, which describes Peter and his city). Also see: Bely, Gogol, Dostoevsky, Chukovsky.

During World War II the city was blockaded for 900 days, which itself amounted to a monument to its fierce resistance; and was also time enough for some 800,000 to starve to death. (See Leningrad in Chapter 1.)

Sights of St. Petersburg	*Достопримеча́тельности С.-Петербу́рга*

Central St. Petersburg is divided into regions two of which are sometimes 🛈 **10-167** called "sides" **сто́роны** (where the similar origin of the word for country **страна́** can be seen): **Вы́боргская сторона́, Петрогра́дская сторона**. Both 🛈 **10-168** are on the right bank as is "Basil's" Island **Васи́льевский о́стров**, another major city area.

Vyborg Region	*Вы́боргская сторона́*

- **Финля́ндский вокза́л** The Finland Station is where Lenin arrived from 🛈 **10-169** abroad and made a famous speech from an armored car.
- **Кресты́** The "Crosses" is the most famous prison.   🛈 **10-170**
- **Пискарёвское мемориа́льное кла́дбище** The Piskarevskoye Memorial 🛈 **10-171** Cemetery is the burial site of victims of the blockade.   🛈 **10-172**

The Petrograd Region	*Петрогра́дская сторона́*

- **Кре́йсер «Авро́ра»** The Cruiser Aurora—a shot from the Aurora was a signal to storm the Winter Palace in 1917
- **Петропа́вловская кре́пость** The Peter and Paul Fortress was a poli- 🛈 **10-173** tical prison in tsarist times used to imprison Decembrists and many 🛈 **10-174** others. Cannons are fired at this fortress every day at noon. Also see 🛈 **10-175** **Пётр Пе́рвый Шемя́кина, Моне́тный двор, Бо́тный до́мик Петра́ I.** 🛈 **10-176**
- **Петропа́вловский собо́р** The Cathedral of Peter and Paul is located on 🛈 **10-177** the grounds of the fortress and is the burial site of Peter I, Catherine II, 🛈 **10-178** and now Nicholas II and Alexandra.

Basil's Island	*Васи́льевский о́стров*

- **Стре́лка** "Strelka" (spit) is where the Neva divides into the Lesser 🛈 **10-179** Neva **Ма́лая Нева́** and the Greater Neva **Больша́я Нева́**. This is the 🛈 **10-180** location of the former Stock Market building **Би́ржа**, and in front of it 🛈 **10-181** are the rostral columns **ростра́льные коло́нны. Кунстка́мера** Kunst- 🛈 **10-182** kamera, founded by Peter the Great, was the first museum in Russia,

10-183
    and the Academy (of Sciences) **Акаде́мия** are both along the shoreline between the Strelka and the university.
- **Ли́нии** "Lines": On Vasil'evskiy Island the north-south streets are called "Lines" (one side of the street will be one Line and the other side *of the same street* will be the next Line).

10-184
- **БАН (Библиоте́ка акаде́мии нау́к)** The Academy of Sciences Library is not far from the university.

Other islands in the Neva delta supplied dacha sites to the rich before the revolution, became parks after it, and are now being reconverted to contruction sites for "cottages" **котте́джи** of the *nouveaux riches*, that is, **но́вых ру́сских**. The best known is "Stone Island" **Ка́менный о́стров**.

Downtown   *Центр*

We will cover downtown **центр** St. Petersburg in two long walks. The first one will start at the Astoria Hotel and then go northeast, mostly paralleling the Neva River, and the second one will start at the Arch of the General Staff and continue southeast along Nevsky Prospect to its end at Alexander Nevskaya Lavra.

The first walk:

10-185
- **Гости́ница Асто́рия** The Astoria is a famous old hotel (recently renovated).

10-186
- **Исаа́киевский собо́р** St. Isaac's Cathedral is famous for its immense cupola.

10-187
- **Сена́тская пло́щадь (бы́вшая пло́щадь Декабри́стов)** Senate Square: this is where the statue of Peter — the Bronze Horseman **Ме́дный вса́дник** — is located and where the Decembrists' uprising took place.

10-188
- **Адмиралте́йство и шпиль — «Адмиралте́йская игла́»** The Admiralty is topped by a spire called the Admiralty Needle.

10-189
- **Дворцо́вая пло́щадь** Palace Square includes the **Алекса́ндровская коло́нна («Александри́йский столп» Пу́шкина)** Alexander column in the center, **а́рка Генера́льного шта́ба** the Arch of the General Staff

10-190
toward the south and **Зи́мний дворе́ц** the Winter Palace on the north.
- **Зи́мний-ца́рский дворе́ц** The Winter Palace was the tsar's palace; the

10-191
capture of the Winter Palace marked the October Revolution.
- **Эрмита́ж** The Hermitage, a huge art museum, is part of the Winter

10-192
Palace complex. **Атла́нты** Atlantes help support the entrance.

10-193
- **Мо́йка** Moyka Canal, **Большо́й Коню́шенный мост**.

10-194
- **Музе́й-кварти́ра Пу́шкина на Мо́йке** Pushkin's apartment on the Moika is a museum.

- **Ма́рсово по́ле** The Field of Mars has an eternal flame **ве́чный ого́нь** 🔲 **10-195** and a memorial cemetery **мемориа́льное кла́дбище**.
- **Ле́тний сад** The Summer Garden is famous for sculptures, most of 🔲 **10-196** which are copies of Greek and Roman originals.
- **Ле́тний дворе́ц** The Summer Palace is Peter the Great's comparatively 🔲 **10-197** small house in the Summer Garden.

The second walk:

- **А́рка Генера́льного шта́ба** The Arch of the General Staff. 🔲 **10-198**
- **Не́вский проспе́кт** Nevsky Prospect is the main street of the city and 🔲 **10-199** appears in many works of literature by Dostoevsky and Gogol, for example.
- **Каза́нский собо́р** Kazan Cathedral is an architectural monument on 🔲 **10-200** Nevsky Prospekt, and formerly the Museum of Religion and Atheism, now the Museum of Religion.
- **«Спас на крови́»** "The Savior on Spilt Blood" is the church opposite 🔲 **10-201** the Kazan Cathedral on the quay at the end of Griboedov canal. The site of the assasination of Alexander II in 1881, it is now a museum of mosaics.
- **Гости́ница Европе́йская** The European Hotel is old, famous, elegant 🔲 **10-202** and recently rebuilt.
- **Ру́сский музе́й** The Russian Museum houses an enormous collection of 🔲 **10-203** Russian pictorial art.
- **Гости́ный Двор** The Merchant's Hall is a very large department store 🔲 **10-204** on Nevsky Prospekt.
- **Библиоте́ка им. Салтыко́ва-Щедрина́ («публи́чка»)**, The Saltykov- 🔲 **10-205** Shchedrin Library is called the public (library). 🔲 **10-206**
- **Александри́нская пло́щадь** The Alexandrian Square. The oldest dra- 🔲 **10-207** ma theater in Russia **«Александри́нский»** is located here, together with 🔲 **10-208** a monument to Catherine the Great.
- **Фонта́нка** The Fontanka is a river parallel to the Moyka river.
- **А́ничков мост**. At the four corners of Anichkov Bridge over the Fon- 🔲 **10-209** tanka is a sculpture by Klodt of horses and their trainers.
- **Алекса́ндро-Не́вская Ла́вра** The Aleksander-Nevskaya Lavra is a 🔲 **10-210** large and famous monastery at the end of Nevsky Prospekt. 🔲 **10-211** Lomonosov, Suvorov, and Glinka are buried at the monastery. 🔲 **10-212**

To the East of Downtown: *К восто́ку от це́нтра:*

- **Музе́й-кварти́ра Достое́вского** Dostoevsky's apartment is a museum. The writer is associated with St. Petersburg, as in *White Nights, Crime and Punishment, The Idiot.*

- **Лите́йный проспе́кт** Liteynyy Prospekt is another major street of Petersburg associated with the cultural life of the 19th century.
- 📷 10-213 • **Таври́ческий дворе́ц** The Tauride Palace is a tsar's palace, built on orders of Catherine II.
- 📷 10-214 • **Смо́льный институ́т — бы́вший Институ́т благоро́дных деви́ц** Smol'nyy Institute is the former Institute for Noble Maidens; later it was bolshevik headquarters; a famous painting is entitled *Lenin in Smol'nyy*. On the grounds there remains a building with a famous slogan. Right alongside is Smol'nyy Cathedral.

To the West of Downtown: *К за́паду от це́нтра:*

- 📷 10-217 • **Садо́вая у́лица, Сенна́я пло́щадь** "Garden" Street and "Hay" Square appear in **Мойдоды́р** "Wash until there are holes" by Chukovskiy (See Chapter 4).
- 📷 10-218 • **Мари́инский теа́тр (бы́вший Теа́тр о́перы и бале́та и́мени Ки́рова)** The Mariinsky Theater (formerly the Kirov) is famous all over the world.

Outside St.Petersburg   *За́ городом*

- **Па́вловск** Pavlovsk is a small palace and a park that was presented as a gift to her son Paul from Catherine II.
- **Петерго́ф (бы́вший Петродворе́ц)** Peterhof (formerly Peter's Palace) is famous for its cascading water fountains.
- **Пу́шкин (бы́вшее Ца́рское Село́ и Де́тское Село́)** Pushkin, the former Tsarskoye selo (the Tsar's village) and Children's village, is closely associated with Pushkin who studied here; it is also the location of Catherine's Palace (rebuilt) and park.

  The palaces and parks of Pushkin, Pavlovsk and Peterhof were totally destroyed during World War II, and then restored just as they had been in tsarist times.
- **Ора́ниенбаум** Oranienbaum is the location of Menshikov's Palace; he died in exile in Siberia. A famous painting on the subject is *Menshikov in Berezovo* «**Ме́ншиков в Берёзове**» (see Chapter 8).
- **Чёрная ре́чка** "Black" Stream is where the duel between Pushkin and D'Antés took place. (Pushkin was badly wounded, and died young a few days later. The place is currently well within the boundaries of St. Petersburg.)

Central Black Earth Region   Центра́льно-Чернозёмный район

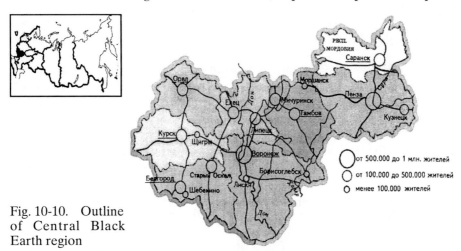

Fig. 10-10. Outline of Central Black Earth region

The Central Black Earth Region includes Belgorod **Белгоро́дская**, Voronezh **Воро́нежская**, Kursk **Ку́рская**, Lipetsk **Ли́пецкая** and Tambov **Тамбо́вская** oblasts **о́бласти**. This is a large wedge of rich, black land in Russia's southwest where temperatures are also conducive to the growth of grains, sugar beets, hemp and sunflower, and where huge deposits of iron ore have assured the development of heavy industry.

The capital Lipetsk **Ли́пецк (липча́не)** of the oblast **Ли́пецкая о́бласть** was founded in the 13th century, destroyed by the Tartars, and rebuilt when Peter I required iron to conduct his wars. Metallurgy, machine building, tractors are the major industry.

Kursk oblast **Ку́рская о́бласть** naturally has its capital at Kursk **Курск (куря́не)**, again very old and Russian, metallurgical, and associated with World War II battles. The oblast is also the site of the KMA **Ку́рская магни́тная анома́лия** (Kursk magnetic anomaly) where there is so much iron ore in the ground that compass arrows point to it, rather than to the north. The area (including south Orel and Belgorod oblasts) has a higher concentration of iron ore than any other place on earth.

Belgorod oblast **Белгоро́дская о́бласть** has its capital at Belgorod **Бе́лгород (белгоро́дцы)**, another old medium sized Russian town originally built for defense against the Tartars and now more devoted to construction materials.

Along the Don River **на Дону́** is the southern extension of the Eastern European (Russian) Plain **Восто́чно-Европе́йская (Ру́сская) равни́на** which includes, from the north to south, Tambov oblast **Тамбо́вская о́бласть** (capital **Тамбо́в**[19]), and Voronezh oblast **Воро́нежская о́бласть** where the capital,

---

[19] The expression **Тамбо́вский волк тебе́ това́рищ**! started out as prison slang and means, "You're no friend of mine! Go keep company with a Tambov wolf."

Voronezh **Воро́неж**,[20] was founded (1586) as an outpost against the Tartars, and later against the Turks.

The Volga-Vyatskiy Region   Во́лго-Вя́тский райо́н

Including the Republic of Mari El **Респу́блика Ма́рий Эл**, the Republic of Mordovia **Респу́блика Мордо́вия**, the Chuvash Republic **Чува́шская рес-пу́блика**, and the Kirov **Ки́ровская** and Nizhniy Novgorod **Нижегоро́дская** oblasts. (The upper Volga, a region just north of Moscow, was discussed as part of central Russia.) The Volga-Vyatskiy Region centers on the middle Volga and includes the land due east of Central Russia (our first region **регио́н**).

10-219   This region is characterized by a variety of nationalities many of which tend to be ignored by the Russians. The non-Slavic populations were the first to arrive: the Ugro-Finnic antecedents of the Mari and Mordva arrived in the millenium BC, then the Tartars and Chuvash, speaking a Turkic language, came in the third and fourth centuries AD, while the Slavs in the 13th century founded Nizhniy Novgorod. The Volga Germans **не́мцы Пово́лжья** were originally Swabian (Southern German) farmers who had been invited by Catherine II (the Great) to come in the second half of the 18th century; they were removed to Kazakhstan during World War II for fear they would collaborate with Nazi Germans. (Now they remove themselves in large numbers back to Germany where they become Russians.)

Vyatka **Вя́тка (вятча́не)**, formerly Kirov **Ки́ров**, is the capital of the oblast **Ки́ровская о́бласть** and a very old Russian city on the Vyatka river, a tributary of the Kama.

Nizhniy Novgorod **Ни́жний Но́вгород (нижегоро́дцы)**, formerly Gorky, is Russia's third largest city famous for its remarkable hillside location at the confluence of the Oka **Ока́** and Volga rivers, famous historically for its imposing kremlin and its market **Нижегоро́дская я́рмарка** or **Мака́рьевская я́рмарка**,[21] and famous economically for its automobile factory (**ГАЗ Го́рьковский автомоби́льный заво́д**), not to mention highly secret cold-war submarine factories, famous politically as Sakharov's place of exile, and now, the place where Boris Nemtsov began a major political career as governor of the oblast. It is also capital of the Nizhniy Novgorod oblast **Нижегоро́дская о́бласть**. The same oblast enfolds the village of Khokhloma **Хохлома́** where the brightly colored lacquered bowls and tableware come from; and south of Nizhniy is Boldino **Бо́лдино**, Pushkin's estate, where he wrote so much one autumn that the period became known as **«Бо́лдинская о́сень»**. (See Chapters

---

[20] **Ме́сто ссы́лки Мандельшта́ма** The poet Osip Mandelshtam (see Chapter 2) was exiled to Voronezh. See the poem **«Воро́неж, ты меня́ хоро́нишь»** from **«Воро́нежские тетра́ди»**.

[21] So called because the market originated at the magnificent Makar'yevskiy monastery a few kilometers downstream from Nizhniy on the Volga.

2 and 3.) And south of that is Arzamas **Арзама́с** which is associated with nuclear power stations and secret research as well as the background for Gorky's *Childhood* «**Де́тство**».

Yoshkar-Ola **Йошка́р-Ола́** (before 1919, **Царевококша́йск**) is the capital of the Mari Republic **Мари́йская респу́блика**.

The Chuvash republic **Чува́шия** has its capital at Cheboksary **Чебокса́ры**, a port on the Volga.

The Mordovian **Мордва́**, **Мордо́вия** capital is at Saransk **Сара́нск**. (The Mari, Chuvash, and Mordva are Russian Orthodox and relatively few in number, so that they and their problems tend to get lost in the Russian mind.)

The European Russian North   Европе́йский Се́вер

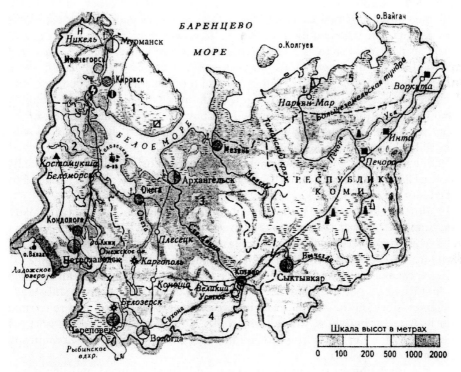

Fig. 10-11. Map of Russian North

The European Russian North includes the Republic of Karelia **Респу́блика Каре́лия** and the Komi Republic **Респу́блика Ко́ми**, and Archangel **Арха́нгельская**, Vologda **Волого́дская** and Murmansk **Му́рманская** oblasts. (Farther East, the Siberian North is sometimes called the "Far North" **Кра́йний Се́вер**.)

Associations include the Polar Circle **Поля́рный круг**, permafrost **ве́чная мерзлота́**, and swamps **боло́та**, which are the home for numerous mosquitoes **комары́**, cloudberries **моро́шка** (*Rubus chamaemorus*), and for northern bog berries (*Vaccinium sp.*) such as cranberries **клю́ква**, bog huckleberries **голуби́ка**, and lingonberries **брусни́ка**. The farthest north is the tundra **ту́ндра** which can only support scraggly bushes at most, while conifer forests **хво́йные леса́**, especially pine trees **со́сны** and spruce **ели**, abound in the taiga **тайга́**. As a result northerners are famous for their woodworking, a major demonstration of which is surely the centuries-old wooden churches and other buildings assembled at Kizhi **Кижи́** on Lake Onega **Оне́жское о́зеро** (Finns or Karelians say **Ки́жи**). The cold and the forests are also good suppliers of fur-bearing animals so hunting **охо́та** is a major pastime and industry. In the North the peasant houses are large, so also to enclose the livestock that might otherwise freeze; windows are small, since they release too much heat. The people themselves have the reputation of being quieter, more dignified, often taller, blonde and blue-eyed since their ancestors did not have to submit, shall we say, to the Tartar yoke. Lake Ladoga **Ла́дожское о́зеро** (**Ла́дога**) is also associated with the north, these expanses of water are the object of delight for many who enjoy paddling in their kayaks **на байда́рках**, a popular sport in this area, especially in Karelia **Каре́лия**, the land of lakes, and people **каре́лы** who are related to the Finns.

Northerners have the reputation of pronouncing all their "o"s. (Muscovite or "standard" Russian pronounces unstressed "o" as "a.")

Murmansk **Му́рманск (мурманча́не)** is famous as a major military port with ice-free access to Western waters; its climate is notoriously unpleasant.

Árkhangel'sk **Арха́нгельск (архангелогоро́дцы)** is felt to be an epitome of old Russia, a port (shipping lumber and fish) and named after its still-standing monastery on the Northern Dvina River **Се́верная Двина́**, and renowned for its wooden buildings, wooden sidewalks. Tourists are taken on a short expedition to the nearby village of Kholmogory **Холмого́ры**, where Lomonosov **Ломоно́сов**[22] was born.

Kirovsk **Ки́ровск (кировча́не)** is large, industrial, polluted, and a producer of nickel.

🔲 **10-220**   Syktyvkar **Сыктывка́р**, capital of the Komi Republic, in the severe north is associated with the gulag **ГУЛаг**.[23]

---

[22] The scientific equivalent of Ben Franklin (the literary equivalent of Chaucer?).

[23] From **Гла́вное управле́ние лагере́й** The Main Administration of [here: Labor] Camps.

Vologda **Вóлогда (вологжáне)**, associated with old Russia, pretty, with woodcarving on houses, famed in popular song, gave its name to a kind of lace **вологóдское крýжево**, and the most famous butter **вологóдское мáсло**.

Вóлогда	Vologda
Где ты, моя черноглáзая, где?	Where are you, my dark-eyed girl, where?
В Вóлогде, где, где, где,	In Vologda, gda, gda gda,
В Вологде, где,	In Vologda, (that's) where
В дóме, где резнóй палисáд.	In the house with the carved fence.
Что б ни случи́лось, я к ми́лой приду́,	No matter what happens, I will go to my dear one,
В Вóлогду, гду, гду, гду,	To Vologda, gda, gda, gda
В Вологду, гду,	To Vologda
К дóму, где резной палисáд.	To the house with the carved (palisade) fence.

Petrozavodsk **Петрозавóдск**, industrial city famous for two statues, one of Peter the Great, and the other of Lenin who is shown with a fur cap in his hands and one on his head. It is also the capital of Karelia **Карéлия**.

Пéсня о Карéлии	Song of Karelia
Дóлго бýдет Карéлия сни́ться,	Karelia will long be dreamt of,
Бýдут сниться с э́тих пор	From that time will long be dreamt of
Остроконéчных éлей ресни́цы	The sharp-pointed spruce, like eyelashes
Над голубы́ми глазáми озёр.	Over the blue eyes of the lakes.

The inhospitable North was used by earlier refugees, among them the Old Believers **старовéры**, and earlier and later by governments as a store- and work-house **гулáг** for undesirables, from the merely politically suspect, to the criminal. Notorious are such names as Vorkuta **Воркутá**, **Нарья́н-мáр**, **Печóра,**[24] and both famous and infamous are the Solovetskiy Islands **Соловéцкие островá**, **Соловки́** in the White Sea. They are famous for hunting and fishing, and infamous for a monastery **Соловéцкий монасты́рь** that was used as a prison.[25] The White Sea **Бéлое мóре** in turn lent its name to the 🔲 **10-221** infamous White Sea Canal **Беломоро-Балти́йский канáл** (and to the cigarettes **папирóсы**[26] of the same name **Беломорканáл**) that extends north from Lake Onega **Онéжское óзеро (Онéга)** and south via Lake Ladoga **Лáдожское óзеро (Лáдога)** and then west to St. Petersburg.

---

[24] **У Пýшкина герóй—Онéгин. А у Лéрмонтова герой—Печóрин.**

[25] **Лихачёв сидéл на Соловкáх.** Dmitriy Likhachev (a renowned historian, scholar) was imprisoned at Solovki.

[26] These cigarettes ("papyrus") consist of a long paper holder, often kinked by the smoker, and with only a small bit of tobacco at one end.

The Russian South/Northern Caucasus   Юг/Се́верный Кавка́з

Fig. 10-12.   The Russian
          South plus Kalmykia

Including the republics: Adygeya **Респу́блика Адыге́я**, Dagestan **Респу́блика Дагеста́н**, Kabardino-Balkaria **Кабарди́но-Балка́рская респу́блика**, Chechnya **Чече́нская респу́блика**, Karachay-Cherkessia **Карача́ево-Черке́сская респу́блика**, North Ossetia **Респу́блика Се́верная Осе́тия**, Ingushetia **Ингу́шская респу́блика**; and Krasnodar Kray **Краснода́рский край**, Stavropol Kray **Ставропо́льский край** and Rostov oblast **Росто́вская о́бласть**.

When a Russian says he's going south **на юг**, he has in mind most likely vacation time either at the Black Sea beaches **на Чёрном мо́ре** or in the Caucasus mountains **на Кавка́зе**. In the past, if one inquired about the Russian south, the answer would often indicate somewhere in the Ukraine or the Crimea. These days, such an answer is not politic or correct, especially in Ukraine. Serious problems are involved here: before 1991 the demarcation between "us" (the Russians) and "them" (the Ukrainians) was very blurry in the *Russian* mind, and surely did not hinder travel; the Russians did not feel they were in another country. The locals could speak Ukrainian if they wanted to, just as long as they also could use some form of Russian. The foreigner could speak Russian and be understood almost everywhere. For those reasons Khrushchev could give the Crimea over to the Ukraine without making waves (he was just changing names, after all), and millions of Russians could settle especially in eastern Ukraine. Currently Russians traveling to the Crimea, for example, are subject to the caprice of border clerks of a poor country; and more than twenty percent of the Ukrainian population (1989) is Russian, most of whom live in eastern Ukraine, especially Kharkov **Ха́рьков**; the fact can be troublesome for the Ukrainians.

Rostov oblast **Росто́вская о́бласть** is the farthest north in this group. Its capital, **Росто́в-на-Дону́**, is a colorful port city with colorful people (**ростов-ча́не**) of many backgrounds. The area is southern and it is Russian—long straight flat roads along grain fields, corn fields, and sunflower fields ... former Cossack **каза́к** grasslands.) Novocherkassk **Новочерка́сск** was a center for the (Don) Cossacks **каза́ки**. Country houses are not large and often made of clay, or clay and straw, since wood is at a premium. Gardens include the southern luxuries: fruit trees, melons, squashes, tomatoes and the like.

The South **юг** brings several strong associations to the Russian mind, the first of which might be vacation land: the Black Sea beaches at Anapa **Ана́па** and Tuapse **Туапсе́ (туапси́нцы)** are the site of large summer camps and Sochi **Со́чи (со́чинцы)** is a warm and glitzy resort.

A familiar song:

Наде́ну я бе́лую шля́пу,	I'll put on my white hat,
Пое́ду я в го́род Ана́пу,	I'll go to the city of Anapa
И там це́лый день пролежу́,	And I'll lie down there all day
На солёном, как слёзы, пляжу́.	On the beach salty as tears.

Novorossiysk **Новоросси́йск** is better known as a military port that figured in both world wars and was also the site of Brezhnev's youth. Of course, the Crimea **Крым** has been Russian vacationland ever since they wrested control of it from the Tartars. Yalta is **Я́лта**. Tartars were deported from the Crimea during World War II and many have now returned; however the population is still mostly Russian despite the fact that in 1997 Russia acknowledged Ukraine's hegemony over the Crimea in exchange for a significant portion of the Black Sea fleet and a temporary base at Sevastopol **Севасто́поль** (an exchange guaranteed to rankle a Russian).

The approaches to and the foothills of the Caucasus **Предкавка́зье**[27] is the land of fruit, tea, summer squash, eggplant, tomatoes, and melons of all sorts. The lowlands are thought of as a granary (breadbasket) **жи́тница**. Long, low corn and grain fields in the north slowly rise toward the majestic towers of the Caucasus in the south. Meat supplies come mostly from sheep (as does wool and sheepskin), which supply a major industry in the mountains, where farming is very difficult.

Krasnodar kray **Краснода́рский край** borders on the Black Sea and is therefore the location of our aforementioned beaches. Its capital is of course Krasnodar **Краснода́р**, whose name is associated with tea **краснода́рский чай** and watermelons **краснода́рские арбу́зы**. The Kuban' **Куба́нь** river flows through it and the area is renowned for its Cossacks.

---

[27] Thus, Transcaucasia is **Закавка́зье**.

Stavropol Kray **Ставропо́льский край** has its capital at Stavropol **Ста́врополь**, the birthplace of Mikhail Gorbachev, and now, associated with the defenses against Chechnya. Nevinnomyssk **Невинномы́сск** is also now known for its proximity to Chechnya, and also has the largest wool processing plant in all of Russia. Many of the resorts whose specialty is salubrious waters are in mountainous parts of this kray.

Rest and recreation also take place in the foothills of the Caucasus where mineral waters reign and the sheep roam. Place names become mineral water names: **Ессентуки́**, **Минера́льные Во́ды (Минво́ды)**, **Кислово́дск**. Pyatigorsk **Пятиго́рск** is both a major health resort and a major city; it is strongly associated with the poet Mikhail Lermontov **Ле́рмонтов** whose tomb is there. Hikers or mountain climbers **тури́сты** and skiers **лы́жники**, both of them the hardy kind, also find resort in the high mountains, but their activities are not well supplied with "infrastructure" and tend to bring them closer to troubled areas than is reasonable. (Both the hotel supply and the danger problems are of course amenable to change.)

Russia's southernmost border, the one shared with Azerbaijan **Азербайджа́н** and Georgia **Гру́зия**, mostly follows the crest **хребе́т**[28] of the main Caucasian range **Большо́й Кавка́з** which extends from a few miles south of Sochi on the Black Sea **Чёрное море**, south and east to a few miles south of Derbent on the Caspian Sea **Каспи́йское мо́ре**. The high central part of this range extends from Mt Elbrus **Эльбру́с** (5642 m), the highest mountain in Europe, to Kazbek **Казбе́к**[29] in Georgia, a majestic and more visible peak not far from the Georgian Military Road **Вое́нно-Грузи́нская доро́га**. (The "Lesser Caucasus" **Ма́лый Кавка́з** is a less imposing range in Georgia.)

The many republics in the region, each with a variety of nationalities, become confused in the Russian mind, except perhaps for the first three below, which follow the crest **хребе́т** of the main Caucasus from east to west.

Dagestan **Дагеста́н**, is right on the Caspian sea, its capital is Makhachkala **Махачкала́**, a major port. Also on the Caspian, Derbent **Дербе́нт** is Russia's southernmost city, and surely among its oldest. Dagestan is renowned for the large variety of nationalities within its borders.

Слова́ популя́рной в 60–70 гг. пе́сни:	Words to a song popular in the 60s and 70s:
От Махачкалы́ до Баку́	From Makhachkala to Baku
Во́лны ка́тятся на боку́.	Waves roll on their side
И, кача́ясь, бегу́т валы́	And, rocking, run the swells
От Баку́ до Махачкалы́.	From Baku to Makhachkala.

---

[28] **(Большо́й Кавка́зский хребе́т)**

[29] Also a brand name for cigarettes **папиро́сы**.

Chechnya **Чечня́** has its capital at Groznyy **Гро́зный**, which suffered considerable damage during the war with Russia. The enmity between Chechnya and Russia is ancient and practiced.

This is the second verse of Lermontov's *Cossack Lullaby* (1840):

По камня́м струи́тся Те́рек,	The Terek river flows over stones,
Пле́щет му́тный вал;	A cloudy wave splashes,
Злой чече́н ползёт на бе́рег,	An evil Chechen crawls onto the shore,
То́чит свой кинжа́л;	And sharpens his dagger.
Но оте́ц твой ста́рый во́ин,	But your father is an old fighter,
Закалён в бою́;	Hardened in battle
Спи, малю́тка, будь споко́ен;	Sleep baby, be quiet
Ба́юшки-баю́.	Lullaby, lullaby.

The Chechen trump card is the oil pipeline that crosses it. (Chechens are charged with (illegally) tapping it to get all the oil they need.)

Ingushetia **Ингуше́тия** separated from Chechnya some time in the early 1990s. It is a thin strip along the eastern border of Chechnya; its new capital is at Nazran' **Назра́нь** (a new capital has been proposed at Magas **Мага́с**).

North Ossetia **Се́верная Осе́тия** has its capital at **Владикавка́з** (formerly **Орджоники́дзе**), a resort city **куро́ртный го́род**, and one of the major stops on the Georgian Military Road **Вое́нно-Грузи́нская доро́га**, the passageway through the Caucasus to Georgia's capital at Tbilisi.

Kabardino-Balkaria **Кабарди́но-Балка́рия** is the next republic along the crest. Its capital, Nal'chik **На́льчик**, is probably most familiar to mountain climbers and those seeking the water cure. The twin peaks of Mt. Elbrus **Эльбру́с**, the highest mountain in Europe, are much more familiar than is its location. Dombay **Домба́й** is the most popular downhill skiing resort in Russia.

Karachay-Cherkessia **Карача́ево-Черке́сская республика** is a mountainous republic formerly a part of Krasnodar Kray and the next along the main Caucasus crest. Its capital is at Cherkessk **Черке́сск**.

Adygey Republic **Респу́блика Адыге́я** is the last along the main Caucasus crest **Большо́й Кавка́з**, and has its capital at Maykop **Майко́п**.

It must be repeated that the word "Caucasian" **кавка́зский** and its derivatives refers to any of the people from the Caucasus, and specifically is not used to denote someone of the white race, as we use the word. The Caucasian is often felt to be untrustworthy, and Russians suspect they may have other, more serious, character defects.

The Volga Basin   Пово́лжье

This region includes: the Republic of Kalmykia/Khal'mg Tangch **Калмы́кия/Ха́льмг Тангч**, the Republic of Tatarstan **Татарста́н**, and Astrakhan **Астраха́нская**, Volgograd **Волгогра́дская**, Penza **Пе́нзенская**, Samara **Са́марская**, Saratov **Сара́товская** and Ul'yanovsk **Улья́новская** oblasts **о́бласти**.

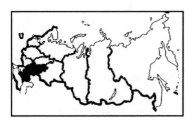

О Во́лга!.. колыбе́ль моя!
Люби́л ли кто тебя́, как я?
Некра́сов, *На Во́лге*

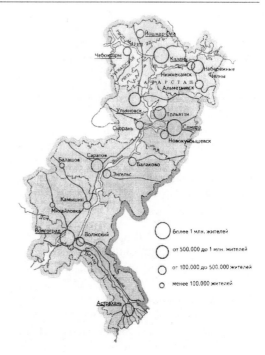

Fig. 10-13. Map of the Volga
           basin

From north to south the mixed and deciduous forest zone gradually gives way to grasslands and finally semi-desert at the Caspian Sea. Two large tributaries, the Oka **Ока́** and then the Kama **Ка́ма** rivers contribute as much water as the Volga itself did before them. Let us start where Kirov oblast leaves off in the north and progress southward.

The Volga is the Russian Mississippi, with many similar romantic associations (especially for Nekrasov), and many man-made disasters and accomplishments that a major watery arterial makes possible: Volga boatmen **бурлаки́**,[30] barges, grain, heavy industry, settlements, trading, sturgeon, the delta, nature itself. The Volga **Во́лга** is not only the largest river in Europe (but only the fifth largest in Russia), but is a major shipping traffic route, a major tourist ship route, and a source of electric energy from the many dams[31] built not only to facilitate the traffic but to control flooding downstream. This "control" has had the unhappy effect of also reducing the population of the sturgeon **осетро́вые ры́бы** who make the caviar **икра́**, a symbol of wealth for Russians as well as foreigners. Poachers **браконье́ры** are also effective in reducing the fish population.

Kazan **Каза́нь** on the Volga has a beautiful kremlin and prodigious history, as well as a thriving local economy. It is now the capital of Tatarstan **Тата́рия**,

---

[30] Volga boatmen were men, and sometimes women, who were used instead of horses for pulling barges upstream in the good old days. See Repin in Chapter 1 and Chapter 8.

[31] **ГЭС ги́дроэле́ктроста́нция**; reservoir **водохрани́лище**.

Татарста́н, though it was built as a defense against the Tartars in the thirteenth century. Tatarstan has managed to attain some independence partly because of the number and ratio of Tartars in the population. Naberezhnyye Chelny **На́бережные Челны́** is the site of major factories.

Ul'yanovsk **Улья́новск**, formerly Simbirsk **Симби́рск**, is the birthplace of Lenin (**Ленин**, a pseudonym of **Влади́мир Ильи́ч Улья́нов**) and the capital of Ul'yanovsk oblast. It is also known as the place where the jeeplike "UAZiki" **уа́зики (Улья́новский автомоби́льный заво́д)** are built. Farther down the Volga is the smaller port and old Russian city, Syzran **Сы́зрань**.

In Samara oblast **Сама́рская о́бласть** the capital is the old Russian city Samara **Сама́ра** (formerly Kuibyshev **Ку́йбышев**), a major industrial city and port on the Volga. The capital of the whole USSR was moved here during the war. Farther up the Volga is the new city of Togliatti **Толья́тти**, whose major claim to fame is the Zhiguli **Жигули́** car factory. The sanatorium **«Во́лжский утёс»** is a favorite summer resting place of former President Yeltsin.

In Penza **Пе́нза**, the capital of Penza oblast **Пе́нзенская о́бласть**, live the Penzites **пензяки́**. It, too, is an old Russian town, a port, and a center of the grain industry.

Saratov **Сара́тов** is distinguished as a large city on the Volga but quite far removed from the center (that is, Moscow).[32] **«В дере́вню, к тётке, в глушь, в Сара́тов!» (Грибое́дов**, see Chapter 6.)

Farther south is Volgograd **Волгогра́д** (before that **Сталингра́д**, and before that **Цари́цын**); it was essentially demolished in the battle **(Сталинград)** that was a major turning point in World War II. Each Victory Day **День Побе́ды** the monument on Mamayev Hill **Мама́ев курга́н** of the Motherland **Ро́дина-Мать** is shown on television. The city is noted for major agricultural 📷 **10-223** machinery production.

Farthest south on the delta of the Volga, where it falls into the Caspian sea, is Astrakhan **А́страхань**, a major city associated with fish in general, caviar **икра́** in particular, and watermelon **арбу́з**. Between Volgograd and Astrakhan another river, Akhtuba **А́хтуба**, parallels the Volga: this is a lowland rich in wildlife and a famous hunting ground.

Southernmost but not actually touching the Volga itself is the republic of Kalmykia **Калмы́кия** (or the Kalmyk name **Хальмг Тангч**), where the markedly Mongol-featured Kalmyks **калмы́ки** have their capital at Elista **Элиста́**. The Kalmyks are Mongols who came in the 16th and 17th century. They are associated with the steppes, horses, Buddhism, and the nomadic life. The area is a semi-desert.

---

[32] A song:

Огне́й так мно́го золоты́х	So many golden lights
На у́лицах Сара́това.	On Saratov's streets.
Парне́й так мно́го холосты́х,	So many single young men
А я люблю́ жена́того!	And I love a married one!

Пе́сня:

The Urals · (Средний и Нижний) Ура́л

This region includes the republics Bashkortostan **Башкортоста́н**, Udmurtia **Удму́ртская респу́блика**, and the Kurgan **Курга́нская**, Orenburg **Оренбу́ргская**, Perm **Пе́рмская**, Sverdlovsk **Свердло́вская** and Chelyabinsk **Челя́бинская** oblasts о́бласти.

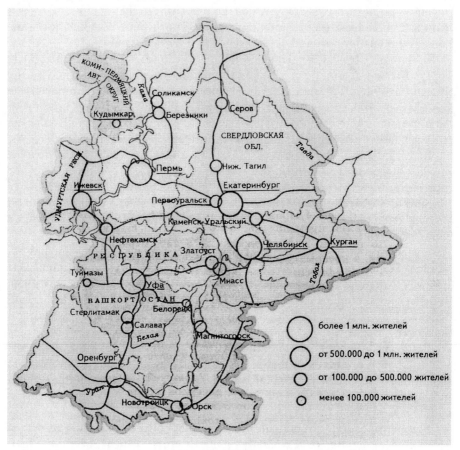

Fig. 10-14. Ural economic zone

West of these unimposing mountains, **Ура́л**, is **Предура́лье** (literally, the pre-Urals); east of them is **Заура́лье** (literally, behind the Urals). The major river in the region is the Kama **Ка́ма**, a significant tributary to the Volga. The Ural mountains **Ура́л** divide the continents, Europe **Евро́па** and Asia **А́зия** (especially along the Ural River[33]), but what comes to the Russian mind when the name is mentioned is minerals **поле́зные ископа́емые**, mines **ша́хты**, ore **руда́**, and many semi-precious stones **самоцве́ты** and precious stones **драго-це́нные ка́мни**. These mountains and their stones are the vivid background for tales by P. Bazhov about remarkable jewelers and stonecutters **го́рные масте-ра́**, for example, *Малахи́товая шкату́лка, Ка́менный цвето́к*. The mines make the Urals a major industrial region and the industry makes it a likely location of air pollution **загрязне́ние атмосфе́ры**. History brings associations with Pugachev **Пугачёв** and the peasant uprisings **крестья́нские восста́ния**. The major cities are listed here beginning in the south and proceeding northward.

Orenburg **Оренбу́рг (оренбу́ржцы)**, capital of this southernmost oblast, which bears the same name, first brings to mind the Orenburg shawl **Оренбу́ргский плато́к** which is so lightweight that it can be pulled through a ring despite its seeming bulk. (It is made from the undercoat **пух** of a particular kind of goat.) The city originated as a fort and is associated with the Ural cossacks **ура́льское каза́чество**. It is the background for Pushkin's *Captain's Daughter* **Капита́нская до́чка**.

Ufa **Уфа́ (уфи́мцы)** is the capital of the Bashkir Republic or Bashkortostan **Башки́рия** or **Башкортоста́н** and is a cultural as well as industrial center. This republic is the place to look for kumiss **кумы́с** (fermented mare's milk), and the eastern areas are particularly popular among hikers **тури́сты**.

Magnitogorsk **Магнитого́рск** was put on the language map by the first five-year plan **пятиле́тка** (1928–33), when the city was built to take advantage of a huge iron mountain **магни́тная гора́**. **«Прокля́тые рудники́»** is an expression one might use to explain a heavy coughing fit. ("I've been working in the mines too long.")

Миа́сс is an industrial city infamous for pollution.

Chelyabinsk **Челя́бинск** is the capital of the oblast of the same name and is known for its size, its major industry (metallurgy, machine-building) and the resultant pollution.

Kurgan **Курга́н**, an oblast capital in Eastern central Urals.

Yekaterinburg **Екатеринбу́рг** (formerly Sverdlovsk **Свердло́вск**) capital of Sverdlovsk oblast **Свердло́вская область**, and perhaps the spiritual capital of the Urals, is a major industrial city and cultural center. The last tsar, Nicolas II, and his family were executed here in 1918. **Уралма́ш (Ура́льский заво́д тяжёлого машинострое́ния** Ural Heavy Machinery Plant) is located here.

---

[33] The writer Vladimir Makanin tells of growing up on one side of the Ural River, crossing a bridge, and attending school on the other continent every day.

Izhevsk **Ижéвск** is the capital of the Udmurt Republic **Удмýртия** and the location of a motorcycle factory in central western Urals. The motorcycle "**Иж-46**" would have been made there.

Perm′ **Пермь (пермякú)** is the capital of Perm oblast **Пéрмская область**, a large industrial city in central Urals, and notably polluted.

Nizhniy Tagil **Нúжний Тагúл** is known as a polluted industrial city in the Urals.

Kudymkar **Кудымкáр** is the capital of the Komi-Permyatskiy Autonomous Okrug **Кóми-Пермяцкий АО**.

Solikamsk **Соликáмск** is a small, very old city, the site of a major potassium **калий** deposit.

Siberia   Сибúрь

Siberia has immense size, forests without end, swamps in the north, and a long, very cold winter. Vast rivers, much larger than the Volga or the Mississippi, pour over the frozen northland in the spring. Major population centers hover mainly along the Trans-Siberian railway **Транссибúрская магистрáль** *или* **Транссибúрская желéзная дорóга** in the south. Major gas and oil field discoveries plus the need to re-establish industry in the East during World War II **Велúкая Отéчественная войнá** have spread some population beyond the traditional areas of penal servitude in exile **кáторга** of tsarist times, and prison camps **лагеря́** of Soviet times. Elsewhere remote tribes of natives hunt, fish, and poach for a living.

Siberians **сибирякú** are famous for their sturdiness, independence, reliability, and perhaps the use of almost 100 percent alcohol (homemade) **самогóн**. They also supplied the world with Siberian ravioli **сибúрские пельмéни**.[34]

The economic geographers and politicians who made up the region system have divided Siberia in two: West and East Siberia while including Yakutia in the Far East.

West Siberia (Economic Zone)   *Зáпадная Сибúрь*

Includes the Altay Republic **Респýблика Алтáй**, the Altay Kray **Алтáйский край**, and the Kemerovo **Кéмеровская**, Novosibirsk **Новосибúрская**, Omsk **Óмская**, Tomsk **Тóмская**, and Tyumen′ **Тюмéнская** oblasts **óбласти**.

West Siberia centers on the Ob River **Обь**,[35] and apart from the mountainous south it is one giant flatland swamp in the center of which are vast gas and oil fields that now supply most of Russia's needs. Those lines disrupt fish and wildlife, a major concern at least to the native inhabitants who live off them. The southern third of the area contains the cultural and industrial centers of the region.

---

[34] See *Russian's World, 2/e*, p 138.

[35] Note the stress: **Он живёт на Обú**.

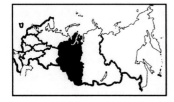

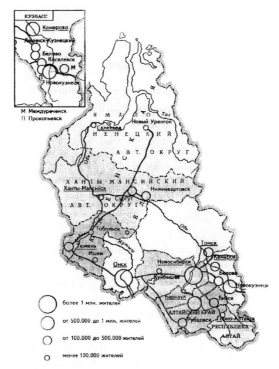

10-15. Map of West Siberia

Our description starts in the North:

Salekhard **Салеха́рд** is the capital of the Yamalo-Nenetskiy Autonomous Okrug **Яма́ло-Не́нецкий АО**, where the Ob River and the Arctic Circle intersect; it has strong associations with the gulags, and now, with its proximity to the immense natural gas fields at Urengoy **Уренго́й**.

Khanty-Mansiysk **Ха́нты-Манси́йск** is the capital of the autonomous okrug of the same name. Nearby is Surgut **Сургу́т**, a Siberian oil capital.

Tyumen′ **Тюме́нь** is the capital of Tyumen oblast **Тюме́нская область** (which contains the two preceding autonomous okrugs) and is the administrative center for much of the oil and gas business and a major transportation and industrial center. Not too far away, on the Irtysh River **Ирты́ш**, is the former and historical capital of Siberia, Tobol′sk **Тобо́льск**, the possessor of Siberia's only stone kremlin and other ancient and honorable cultural monuments. Many of the Decembrists **декабри́сты** were sent to or through Tobol′sk as were many other undesirables.

Tomsk **Томск** (on the river Tom′ **Томь**) is the capital of the oblast and a major old city noted for its culture and its university. Many old buildings remain.

Omsk **Омск (омичи́)**, at the mouth of the Om river **Омь**, is the capital of the oblast **О́мская область** and is located directly on the Trans-Siberian railway so that it has had the advantages of age, transportation links, and industry. It shares with Tobol'sk and Tomsk the association with exiles.

Novosibirsk **Новосибúрск** is capital of the oblast and also a major city, one large enough for its own subway system. Much industry transferred here during World War II. It has a major university, one especially renowned for its science, and some 20 kilometers away is "Academy City" **Академгородóк**, which under the Soviets had pleasant living and meeting quarters for academic scientists; they lived under much better conditions before unfettered capitalism.

Kemerovo **Кéмерово** is the capital of its oblast, but the largest city therein is Novokuznetsk **Новокузнéцк** whose major product is coal: this is the center of the so-called Kuzbass **Кузбáсс** (Kuznetsk Coal Basin **Кузнéцкий ýгольный бассéйн**). Where there is coal there is industry and where there is industry there is pollution, a major problem in the area.

Barnaul **Барнаýл** is the capital of Altay Kray **Алтáйский край** which is one of the major food producing areas of Russia. Barnaul itself is in the Altay mountains, and has a landing **прúстань** on the Ob **Обь** river.

Gorno-Altaysk **Гóрно-Алтáйск** is the capital of the mountainous Altay Republic **Респýблика Алтáй**. (The nearest railway station is 96 km away!)

Eastern Siberia (Economic Zone)   *Востóчная Сибúрь*

Includes the republics of Buryatia **Респýблика Бурятия**, Tyva **Респýблика Тывá/Тувá**, Khakasia **Респýблика Хакáсия**, Krasnoyarsk Kray **Красноя`рский край**, and the oblasts of Irkutsk **Иркýтская** and Chita **Читúнская óбласти**.

About a quarter of Eastern Siberia is located on the wrong side of the Arctic Circle, and winter lasts for more than 8 months at these latitudes. For much of Eastern Siberia the January average temperature is -40 Celsius or Fahrenheit (at this temperature the two scales intersect). The cold pole of the Northern hemisphere is at Verkhoyansk **Верхоянск** or Oymyakon **Оймякóн**, where the January average is -50 C. The Northern two-thirds is a relatively high flatland as far as the Lena river **Лéна**, and the rest is mountainous. Lake Baikal **óзеро Байкáл** seems to have its back to a range of mountains that doesn't stop until it comes to the Arctic Sea. If the pivotal river for Western Siberia is the Ob, then the Yenisey **Енисéй** and its tributaries is the anchor for Eastern Siberia.

When you think Eastern Siberia, think Krasnoyarsk Kray **Красноя`рский край**. It includes Taymyrskiy AO **Таймы`рский АО** at the farthest North and Evenkiyskiy AO **Эвенкúйский АО** just south of it. Those two okrugs are immense and almost empty with the exception of subsistence level natives who hunt for food and furs, or raise reindeer. In the farthest north, Norilsk **Норúльск** is a city of some size whose reason for existence is associated with mining, especially nickel. The city was founded in 1935 and built with prison labor. Igarka **Игáрка** is not far away and is a port on the Yenisey **Енисéй**. However, any major population centers will be in the south.

Fig. 10-16. Eastern Siberia (here including Yakutia/Sakha)

Krasnoyarsk **Красноя́рск**, the capital and an old city with a full complement of heavy industry and energy resources, can be found where the Lena River and the Trans-Siberian railway intersect. Some 15 kilometers from Krasnoyarsk is a state park **госуда́рственный запове́дник** along the Yenisey **Енисе́й** called Krasnoyarsk Columns **Красноя́рские столбы́** where igneous rocks, large picturesque columns, have been put in relief by the elements. (The middle reaches of the Lena River also have these columns **Ле́нские столбы́**.) **10-231** On the map you can find: **Абака́н и Респу́блика Хака́сия**; **Кызы́л и Респу́блика Тува́ (Тыва́)**, **Минуси́нск**, **А́чинск**. (Russians know them to be out there, somewhere, in Siberia.)

Eastern Siberia has one star that outshines all else: Lake Baikal **о́зеро Байка́л**. Russians who know only that Siberia exists will also know of Lake Baikal; it is the deepest freshwater lake in the world, and its length exceeds the distance from Moscow to St. Petersburg; it has its own unique species of seal, fish, and other wildlife; and it is invariably described by Russians as beautiful. It is the source of the Angara River **Ангара́**, a major tributary of the giant Yenisey. Poetically speaking, this Lake is referred to as a sea **мо́ре**, as in a well-known song:[36]

---

[36] The words are those of an escaping prisoner during tsarist times.

♪ 10-232 | Сла́вное мо́ре — свяще́нный Байка́л, | Glorious Sea, Holy Baikal,
| Сла́вный кора́бль — омулёвая бо́чка. | A marvelous ship is this whitefish barrel.
| Эй, баргузи́н, пошеве́ливай вал, | Hey, *barguzin*,[37] push the wave on,
| Мо́лодцу плыть недале́чко. | This brave boy has not far to float.

| До́лго я тя́жкие це́пи носи́л, | I wore heavy chains a long time,
| До́лго броди́л я в гора́х Акату́я. | Long I wandered in the mountains of Akatuy.

| Ста́рый това́рищ бежа́ть пособи́л — | An old friend helped me escape —
| О́жил я, во́лю почу́я. | I've come to life, sensing freedom.

Irkutsk **Ирку́тск**, capital of its own oblast, lies toward the southwest end of Lake Baikal and is an old city and a major cultural center for all of Siberia and especially Eastern Siberia. It is associated with the Decembrists (see Chapter 1), and is a major stop for the Trans-Siberian railway. Not far away is Ust'-Ordynskiy Autonomous Okrug **Усть-Орды́нский АО**.

To the north of Irkutsk, Bratsk **Братск** lies where the Angara **Ангара́** River is dammed (for the Bratskaya Hydroelectric Station **Бра́тская ГЭС**[38]) and where the **БАМ** (Baikal-Amur railway **Байка́ло-Аму́рская магистра́ль**) crosses its path.

Ulan-Ude **Ула́н-Удэ́** lies along the Trans-Siberian railway, has some manufacturing, and is the capital of the Buryat republic **Буря́тия**, which is notable for its Buddhism, and its former identity as the land of Mongols/Tartars and perhaps Huns before that. (Actually more than half the population is now ethnically Russian.).

Chita **Чита́** is also an old city with some manufacturing farther east and on the Trans-Siberian railway. Used in the last century to house Decembrists in exile. Capital of the oblast **Чити́нская область** which also contains the Agin-Buryat AO **Аги́нский Буря́тский АО**.

The Republic of Yakutiya or Sakha used to be considered part of Eastern Siberia. But the government has found it politic to include it as part of the Far East, which in the popular mind is a strip along the Pacific Coast.

The Far East (Economic Zone)   Да́льний Восто́к

The Far East (Economic Zone) includes: the Sakha Republic (Yakutia) **Респу́блика Саха́ (Яку́тия)**, Primorskiy Kray **Примо́рский край**, Khabarovskiy Kray **Хаба́ровский край**, and Amur **Аму́рская**, Kamchatka **Камча́тская**, Magadan **Магада́нская** and Sakhalin **Сахали́нская** oblasts.

---

[37] Name of a local wind on Lake Baikal.

[38] **ГЭС гидравли́ческая эле́ктроста́нция; ТЭС Те́плоэле́ктроста́нция; АЭС а́томная электростанция.**

Fig. 10-17.   The Far East without Sakha

Sakha/Yakutia   Яку́тия/Саха́

The inclusion of Sakha/
Yakutia in the Far East
Economic Zone would
seem to be inspired by political as well as economic
considerations. It was not
too long ago that Sakha was
threatening to take its diamonds and leave. This as-
sociation with the Far East
zone would seem to reduce
the separateness of Sakha.
When asked, a Russian will
usually make Sakha/Yaku-
tia part of Siberia, rather
than the Far East.

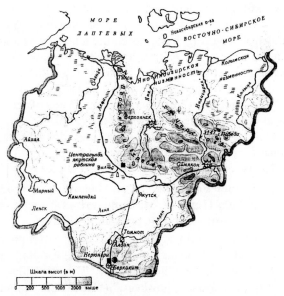

Fig. 10-18.   Sakha/Yakutia

10-233   The climate surely makes Yakutia one of the more difficult places to live. Winter temperatures are colder than at the poles; permafrost **вечная мерзлота** is everywhere and goes as far as 1.5 km deep—a fine storehouse for extinct mammoths and other prehistoric relics. The river-axis for this republic is the Lena **Лена**, with its huge delta in the north near the port of **Тикси**. On the Lena but much further south is the capital, Yakutsk **Якутск**. Industry is mostly

10-234   hunting, but gold production and the fairly recent discovery of diamonds near Mirnyy **Мирный** and Aykhal **Айхал** in West central Yakutia have made a lucrative industry possible and have strengthened the hand of local powers vis-à-vis Moscow, enough to claim their own identity and even threaten to leave the Mother Country.

In the common language, the Far East **Дальний Восток** means the remaining strip of land east of Yakutia/Sakha. Russia's easternmost point is Cape Dezhnev **Мыс Дежнёва** (one side of the Bering Straights **Берингов пролив**), a fact which may come in handy for solving Russian crossword puzzles. West and South of it extends Russia's Far East, a land of desolate mountains with a coastline in the North, and somewhat less desolation, mountains and hills and a coastline in the South. It is a land of volcanoes **вулканы**, Chukchi, forests, fishing, some mining, and many former labor camps. Its distance from the center (Moscow) and its proximity to other Pacific nations work to its benefit and detriment in both cases. Sometimes this was as far away as someone could be sent, at other times the distance made one unreachable. These days fishing, lumbering, and mining are sometimes partly foreign affairs, a matter that swings between affliction and blessing. (Investment is needed, but when it is foreign, there is a suspicion that the foreigners will take more than their due.) We will start in the North and work southward.

At the extreme north is Magadan oblast **Магаданская область** which, as much as anything, has entered the language as a house of prison camp horrors. In the oblast is the Kolyma river **Колыма** whose name has come to mean the same thing (prison camps). Gold is mined there.

Part of Magadan oblast is occupied by the Chukotskiy Autonomous Okrug **Чукотский АО (Чукотка)** on a peninsula of the same name. Its major outpost is at Anadyr′ **Анадырь**, where a river of the same name meets the ocean. The Chukchi **чукчи**, hunt or raise reindeer for a living, but their name has become such a caricature of unspoiled ignorance and the butt of many jokes that the name is sometimes euphemized to "Peoples of the Far North."

Плывёт на лодке чукча. Навстречу другой чукча с женой. Жена гребёт. Первый спрашивает: «Ты куда торопишься?» —Другой отвечает: «Жену рожать везу, однако».

A Chukcha floats along in his boat. From the opposite direction comes another Chukcha and his wife. She is doing the rowing. The first asks, "Where are you hurrying to?" The other answers, "I'm taking my wife to have a baby, however." ("However" **однако** is a traditional part of Chukcha jokes.)

Just south is the Koryak AO **Коря́кский АО** which itself is part of Kamchatka oblast **Камча́тская о́бласть** on the Kamchatka Peninsula **Камча́тка**. The peninsula has the Bering Sea **Бе́рингово мо́ре** on one side and the Sea of Okhotsk **Охо́тское мо́ре** on the other, so that the climate is not so severe. But where the climate leaves off, nature begins again: the peninsula is a volcanic ridge that supplies fireworks for tourists and sometimes devastation for the residents. (The word **со́пка** means "rounded hill or mountain" in most of Russia, but "volcano" on Kamchatka; **вулка́н** is also used.) The major city is the port of Petropavlovsk-Kamchatskiy **Петропа́вловск-Камча́тский.**

The Kurile islands **Кури́льские острова́**, **Кури́лы** are a fine source of fish, red caviar, and Japanese ill-will, since the Japanese consider the three southernmost islands to be theirs. (They were seized during the very short period at the end of World War II when the USSR was formally at war with Japan.) The islands are part of Sakhalin oblast **Сахали́нская о́бласть** whose major city is Yuzhno-Sakhalinsk **Южно-Сахали́нск** on the long, long island of Sakhalin **Сахали́н**.

Khabarovskiy Kray **Хаба́ровский край** extends all the way from Magadan oblast to China, and includes the sole autonomous oblast: the Jewish Autonomous Oblast **Евре́йская автоно́мная о́бласть** (with very few Jews therein; and notice **о́бласть**, not **о́круг**) with its capital at Birobidzhan **Биробиджа́н**. (Some sources give the English title of this entire area as "Birobidzhan.") The capital for the Kray is of course at Khabarovsk **Хаба́ровск**, a medium-sized city and transportation hub built where the Amur river **Аму́р** and the Trans-Siberian railway meet.

The Amur River **Аму́р** and the valley through which it flows is formally called **Приаму́рье**. This is a major, long river extending from East Siberia all the way to the Pacific Ocean. For much of the time the river forms the border with China, and adjacent to the river valley is the major arable land of the Far East.

Blagoveshchensk **Благове́щенск** is an old city, the capital of Amur Oblast **Аму́рская о́бласть**, the center of a major agricultural region, and a headquarters for local trade with China. Farther downriver is the aforementioned Khabarovsk and still farther is Komsomol'sk-na-Amure **Комсомо́льск-на-Аму́ре**, a Soviet city remarkable for having been built by Komsomol members.

The area south of the Amur river and east to the Sea of Japan is called **Примо́рье**; much of it is taken up by land along the Ussuri River **Уссу́ри**, a tributary of the Amur. Lumber is the major industry. 🔲 **10-235**

Vladivostok **Владивосто́к** is the southernmost major city of Primorskiy Kray **Примо́рский край**, a major headquarters of the fishing industry (a major business in the Far East), and a scientific maritime center of the Academy of Sciences. Nearby Nakhodka **Нахо́дка** is the site of the major naval base of the Far East.

FORMER RELATIVES　　　　　**БЫ́ВШИЙ СОВÉТСКИЙ СОЮ́З (БЕЗ РОССИ́И)**

Страны СНГ.Основные показатели				
Страны СНГ	Площадь, тыс. км²	Население, млн человек (1992)	Валовой внутренний продукт, млрд руб. (1992)	Столица
Россия	17075,4	148,7	19 992	Москва
Европейские страны:	844,6	66,9	5745	
Украина	603,7	52,3	4580	Киев
Белоруссия	207,6	10,3	950	Минск
Молдавия	33,7	4,3	215	Кишинев
Азиатские страны:	4182	69,5	1934	
Казахстан	2717,3	17	1120	Алма-Ата
Узбекистан	447,4	21,7	417	Ташкент
Киргизия	198,5	4,5	106	Бишкек
Таджикистан	143,1	5,5	50	Душанбе
Туркмения	488,1	4,2	...	Ашхабад
Азербайджан	86,6	7,4	182	Баку
Армения	29,8	3,7	59	Ереван
Грузия	69,7	5,5	св. нет	Тбилиси
Всего по СНГ	22222,8¹	285,2	**около 28 000**	

¹ Общая площадь включает акватории внутренних морей, Белого и Азовского.

Fig. 10-19.　Table of SNG, with titles, capitals, production, population, acreage. Notice the absence of the Baltic republics in the SNG.

▣ 10-236
▣ 10-237
▣ 10-238

Russia's relations with the other republics of the former Soviet Union (called the "near abroad" **бли́жнее зарубе́жье**, or "new abroad" **но́вое зарубе́жье**) were and are confusing to the Russians, including those formerly in the government, who were fooled by their very own propaganda. The teaching was that we Soviets were one big happy family. Pictures of varicolored small children waving a flag and dancing around a Soviet emblem were legion. Russians actually felt the republics to be part of themselves, and not a separate entity. School maps, for example, reinforced this idea, only distinguishing the various republics on a Political-Administrative Map. (Recall that Khrushchev could give the Crimea to Ukraine and few complained. Though some Crimean Tartars have returned, the Crimea is populated mostly by Russians.) The Russian tends to think of the Crimea **Крым** and the Black Sea **Чёрное мо́ре**, **Оде́сса**,[39] and Kharkov **Ха́рьков** as his land with some Ukrainians living there too. The Russian state started out in Kiev, after all, and the Battle of Poltava

---

[39] Pronounced "**Одэ́сса**" in Russia and "**Оде́сса**" in Ukraine.

took place in the Ukraine. Was Gogol talking about Russians or Ukrainians? And so forth.

Not all nationalities or parts of the country were equally acceptable or desirable. (Generally, peoples of the Baltic countries were looked up to by the Russians; Belorusians and Ukrainians were accepted as family if not necessarily admired; the Georgians and Armenians were interesting but sometimes a little too clever; the remaining Caucasians were sometimes untrustworthy; and Central Asians needed enlightenment, as did most of the peoples of the Far East.)

The fall of the Soviet Union has seen an outpouring of rejection (and sometimes overt hatred) from people in the Baltic republics, major dislike from western Ukrainians, derision from Georgians, and so forth. The strength of this reaction has been surprising to many Russians who react with hurt resentment and wonder why they were made poorer so that those other republics could live better. The change has done nothing to improve attitudes towards the outside world. If xenophobia was a problem before, it is now even larger; there are now more foreigners, and they are closer.

In the paragraphs that follow the percentage of Russians in the population of each state is given. The reader should assume that these percentages are now somewhat lower; many Russians have returned to Russia.

The Baltic Countries   Приба́лтика

Throughout the Baltic the German influence is notable. Living conditions here are visibly better than in the other former republics. From southwest to northeast, Kaliningrad **Калинингра́д**, mostly a military port with some adjacent land **Калинингра́дская о́бласть**, is still part of Russia though separated from it by the Baltic countries that follow.

Then Lithuania **Литва́ (лито́вцы)**, originally a mostly Catholic country whose capital is Vil'nyus **Ви́льнюс** (with another major city at Kaunas **Ка́унас**), whose language is Lithuanian **лито́вский язы́к** (a Balto-Slavic language), and whose major industry is agriculture with some light industry. Less than a tenth of the population is Russian.

Then comes mostly Lutheran Latvia **Ла́твия (латыши́)**, with its capital at Riga **Ри́га**. The country is associated with major light industry, especially electrical manufacturing. It also has a shoreline at **Ю́рмала** that was very popular with Russians as a resort area. About one-third of the population is Russian.

Estonia **Эсто́ния (эсто́нцы)** is mostly Lutheran in faith, and about one-quarter Russian in people. Its capital is recorded as Tallinn **Та́ллинн** by the Estonians (and often **Та́ллин** by Russians); other cities that figure for Russians are Narva **На́рва** and Tartu **Та́рту**. Particularly remarkable is the language, which is so like Finnish that Estonians watch Finnish television. (Estonian is Finno-Ugric, distantly related to Hungarian, and thus not Indo-European.) Estonia also supplies a good marketplace for Finns looking for a bargain. The Estonian dislike of Russians is almost palpable.

The Other Slavs   Другие славя́не

Belarus **Белару́сь, Белору́ссия**: the first term is used by the people who live there and seems to be gaining in Russia; the second term is preferred by Russians who have decided that the Russian term is not demeaning, after all. The capital is Minsk and the language is the closest to Russian which serves as a *lingua franca* there. A major association triggered by the country is tractors: Belarus is the name of the major tractor and its factory in the former Soviet Union. Another strong association is with incredible losses during World War II: the figure commonly cited is 25 percent of the population lost.

Ukraine **Украи́на** is a country divided against itself: its western parts with a major city at L'vov **Льво́в** (Ukr. **Льві́в**, German name is Lemberg) and mostly Ukrainian population are the most nationalistic and anti-Russian, while the eastern, more industrialized regions have a large Russian population, especially in the area of Khar'kov **Ха́рьков**. Religious backgrounds are Catholic, Uniate Catholic[40] and some Russian Orthodox. Ukraine had the reputation of being a breadbasket **жи́тница** to Russian (before 1917) as well as the rest of Europe, though it has not yet adapted to new economic arrangements. The capital of the country is at Kiev **Ки́ев**, which the Russians see as where Russia began; it was here that Prince Vladimir **князь Влади́мир** accepted Christianity for Russia **на Руси́**. The remaining major city is Odessa **Оде́сса** on the Black Sea **Чёрное мо́ре**: it is famous for lively, sociable people (especially Jews) who are particularly good at telling jokes. In the language of thieves **блатно́й язы́к: Оде́сса—ма́ма, а Росто́в—па́па.** The loss of the Crimea has been difficult for Russians; they still vacation there, but now they must carry a passport and pay an entrance fee at the border (though they do not need a visa, which *is* required in the Baltic countries).

Moldova   Молда́вия, Молдо́ва

Russian ties with Moldova (**Молда́вия** in Russia) are neither strong nor long. The Russian population is not large, 14 percent in 1989, but most live in one part of the country and the concentration has been a source of internal conflict. The country speaks a dialect of Romanian, which is a Romance, not Slavic language. The country's name is synonymous with major supplies of fruit, vegetables and wine. The capital is Kishinev **Кишинёв** for Russians and was changed to Chisinau for the rest of the world when independence was attained.

The Real Caucasians   Кавка́з

The Russian's most common association with Caucasians, of any specific ethnicity, is most likely at the food market **на ры́нке**, which is often dominated by

---

[40] A Catholic group, mostly in western Ukraine, who recognize the authority of the Pope but who use the Slavonic liturgy and discipline.

Caucasians (not in a legally accepted manner). In this case, the Russians do not distinguish one from the other, and none can expect respect from the average Russian. "Caucasian" **«кавка́зец»** is generally a term of opprobrium, and relates to the markets where Russians expect to be cheated, robbed, or both. People with dark complexions will often be stopped on the street by the police who will assiduously check their identity papers.

Georgia **Гру́зия** is an ancient civilization located among magnificent mountains and enhanced by beautiful frontage on the Black Sea. The capital at Tbilisi **Тбили́си** could be described as old New Orleans set in the mountains. The people have their own branch of Eastern Orthodox Christianity and speak a Caucasian language. Russians associate Georgians **грузи́ны** with wines, beautiful scenery **приро́да**, and Pushkin **Пу́шкин**, who described the beauty in lyrical terms. Russians are commonly aware of the Georgian poet Shota Rustaveli **Шота́ Руставе́ли** who wrote *The Knight in Tiger Skin* **«Ви́тязь в тигро́вой шку́ре»**. Georgia contains two republics, both mostly Muslim and both bordering on the Black Sea. Abkhazia **Респу́блика Абха́зия** has its capital at the ancient seaside resort of Sukhumi **Суху́ми** and was supported by the Russians against the Georgians. An Abkhazian writer, Fazil Iskander **Фази́ль Исканде́р** (pronounced ... **дэр**) has long delighted Russian audiences, especially with the autobiographical series **«Са́ндро из Чеге́ма»**. The Adzhar Republic **Респу́блика Аджа́рия** is right on the border with Turkey whose cultural influence is very apparent. The capital is Batumi **Бату́ми** on the Black Sea.

Armenia **Арме́ния** also is an ancient and mountainous Christian civilization, the capital is at Yerevan **Ерева́н**, the language is Indo-European, and there seems to be a closer cultural affinity with the Russians. Education is valued in both societies, and the Armenians bear some gratitude to the Russians for rescuing them from the Turks. They are also famous for their cognac **конья́к**, their war with Azerbaijan over ownership of Nagorno-Karabakh **Наго́рно-Караба́х** (a region populated by Armenians but totally within Azeri borders), and the famous Armenian radio jokes **армя́нское ра́дио** that were characterized by off-the-wall answers to tricky questions.

> **Армя́нское ра́дио спра́шивают: «Что лу́чше, мара́зм или склеро́з?»**
> **Армянское радио отвеча́ет: «Склеро́з, потому́ что тогда́ забыва́ешь о мара́зме!»**

(Armenian radio is asked: "What is better, senility or forgetfulness?" Armenian radio answers: "Forgetfulness is better because then you forget you're senile.")

Azerbaijan **Азербайджа́н** has a Turkic culture and language and so is much less accessible to the Russian. Its capital is on the Caspian Sea **Каспи́йское мо́ре** at Baku **Баку́** which itself is synonymous with oil **нефть**.

Central Asia   Сре́дняя А́зия

The countries of Central Asia,[41] Kazakhstan **Казахста́н**, Turkmenistan **Туркме́ния/Туркмениста́н**, Uzbekistan **Узбекиста́н**, Kyrgyzstan **Кирги́зия/Кыргызста́н**, Tajikistan **Таджикиста́н** have not left a heavy mark on Russian culture. All are Muslim and all speak a Turkic language except in Tajikistan where the language is related to Iranian (and is therefore Indo-European). When the time for separation came there was often a feeling of relief that these underdeveloped countries **недора́звитые**[42] **стра́ны** no longer had to be supported. (Note that the information in this chapter is not meant to be politically correct. It is meant to describe someone else's point of view.)

Kazakhstan **Казахста́н** is perhaps both physically and spiritually the closest of these countries. After all, it was here that the virgin soil **целина́** was introduced to the world of production. And later, when space had to be conquered, machines were launched from Baykonur **Байкону́р** and its space vehicle launching site **космодро́м**. The capital was recently removed to Akmola **Акмо́ла** from Alma-Ata **Алматы́**. In 1989, 38 percent of the population was Russian.

Uzbekistan **Узбекиста́н** may mean "cotton" to the residents but to Russians it also means melons **ды́ни** and fruits in abundance. The famous ancient architecture of Samarkand **Самарка́нд** and Bukhara **Бухара́** did not escape notice. What did escape notice, or at least attention, was the effects of deflecting water from the rivers (**Амударья́**, **Сырдарья́**) leading to the Aral Sea **Ара́льское мо́ре** for the purpose of irrigating the cotton fields. The result has been an environmental disaster for the now very salty and receding Aral Sea. In 1989, about 8 percent of the population was Russian. The capital is Tashkent **Ташке́нт**.

Turkmenistan **Туркме́ния** is known as a Central Asian republic and not much else. The capital is at Ashkhabad **Ашхаба́д**, and in 1989 almost ten percent of the population was Russian.

Tajikistan **Таджикиста́н** is very mountainous. Recently Russian troops were used to prevent one faction of Islamic fundamentalists from prevailing over the other. The capital is at Dushanbe **Душанбе́** [pronounced **Душанбэ**]. In 1989, about 8 percent of the population was Russian.

Kyrgyzstan **Кирги́зия** (**Кыргызста́н** for the residents) has the advantage of Chingiz Aitmatov **Чинги́з Айтма́тов** to speak for it. His descriptions of life high in the mountains have brought considerable acceptance of the land and its people to the Russians. In 1989, about 21 percent of the population was Russian. The capital is at Bishkek **Бишке́к**, or Frunze **Фру́нзе** [pronounced **Фру́нзэ**] in Soviet times.

---

[41] **Сре́дняя А́зия** used also to be called Turkestan **Туркеста́н**, a term now associated with the pre-revolutionary era in Russian.

[42] "Poorly developed" **слабора́звитый** would be more formal and less offensive.

FAMOUS EXPLORERS   **ВЕЛИ́КИЕ ПУТЕШЕ́СТВЕННИКИ**

A Russian would probably know of the following explorers. First names and initials in parentheses are those not closely associated with the last names. Dates are not common knowledge.

Геродо́т (~490–425 до н.э. B.C.) — оста́вил хро́ники дре́вней Гре́ции.

Ма́рко По́ло (~1254–1324) — путеше́ствие через Индию в Кита́й.

Афана́сий Ники́тин (?–1475) — Индия («Хожде́ние за 3 моря»).

Христофо́р Колу́мб (1451–1506) — морепла́ватель, откры́вший Аме́рику.

Ва́ско да Га́ма (1469–1524) — вокру́г Африки к Индии.

(Ферна́ндо) Магелла́н (~1480–1521) — португа́лец, морепла́ватель, соверши́вший первое кругосве́тное путеше́ствие.

Амери́го Веспу́ччи (1451–1512) — италья́нский морепла́ватель и гео́граф, и́менем которого на́звана Аме́рика.

(Ви́тус) Бе́ринг (1681–1741) — датча́нин. Да́льний восто́к, Бе́рингов проли́в.

(Джеймс) Кук (1728–79) — Австра́лия, Ти́хий океа́н, Но́вая Зела́ндия, Са́ндвические (Са́ндвичевы) острова́. В пе́сне Высо́цкого: «Заче́м абориге́ны съе́ли Ку́ка? Никто́ не знает. Молчи́т нау́ка!»

(И.Ф.) Крузенште́рн (1770–1846) — ру́сский морепла́ватель, адмира́л. Руководи́тель пе́рвой ру́сской кругосве́тной экспеди́ции.

(Фритьо́ф) Н а́нсен (1861–1930) — норве́жский океано́граф и иссле́дователь Арктики.

(Дави́д) Ли́вингстон (1813–73) — англи́йский путеше́ственник, иссле́дователь Центра́льной и Южной Африки.

(Ф.Ф.) Беллинсга́узен (1778–1852) — ру́сский морепла́ватель. Антаркти́да.

(Руал) А́мундсен (1872–1928) — Норве́жский поля́рный путеше́ственник и иссле́дователь обо́их полюсо́в.

(П.П.) Семёнов-Тян-Ша́нский (1827–1914) — ру́сский гео́граф и госуда́рственный де́ятель. По́сле нау́чной экспеди́ции на Тянь-Шань измени́л свою́ фами́лию.

Fig. 10-20. Nikitin's travels

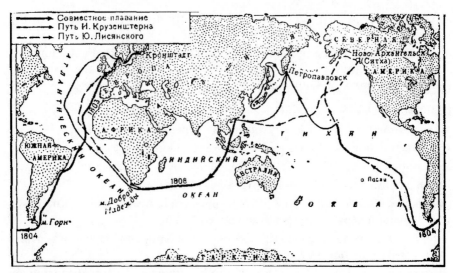

Fig. 10-21. Kruzenshtern's travels

(Н.М.) Пржева́льский (1839–88) Русский гео́граф, соверши́вший путеше́ствие через Гру́зию, Кавка́з в центра́льную А́зию (Ло́шадь Пржева́льского).

See CD[📄 **10-239**] for an explanation of using "**в**" and "**на**" in Russian with geographical place names.

See CD[📄 **10-240**] for a virtual excursion of places and people in Moscow and St. Petersburg.

<table>
<tr><td>

Government and Language

</td><td>

11

</td><td>

Полити́ческая власть и язы́к

</td></tr>
</table>

Lawrence Mansour

Fig. 11-1. The White House **Бе́лый дом.** See <http://www.pravitelstvo. gov.ru>

INTRODUCTION: FROM A RUSSIAN'S POINT OF VIEW[1]	ВВЕДЕ́НИЕ: С ТО́ЧКИ ЗРЕ́НИЯ РОССИЯ́НИНА

During the Soviet era the average Russian tended to view the machine of State as an enemy to be fought and deceived one's entire life. Calculation or concealment was an essential part of most dealings with the government; failure to think ahead was at least risky and sometimes dangerous. Yet a major fraction of the "creative intelligentsia" **тво́рческая интеллиге́нция** and the bureaucracy at all levels served the Soviet propaganda machine faithfully and received all kinds of privileges for doing so (conveniently located and larger apartments, access to special stores of all kinds, trips abroad, and the like).

When Mikhail Gorbachev **Михаи́л Горбачёв** came to power and started talking about perestroika **перестро́йка** (re-structuring society) and glasnost **гла́сность** (freedom of expression, "openness") people praised and respected him at least for a while. Pandora's box opened. He did not intend to destroy the regime, he merely wanted to make Russia more acceptable to the rest of the world. But there were several long days of silence, rather than "openness" after Chernobyl'. And when the Lithuanians in Vil'nius began to agitate "openly" for

---

[1] We are very grateful to Vera Brekhovskikh, a physicist and resident of Hawaii and Moscow, for this introduction.

their independence, and the Georgians began to riot "openly" in Tbilisi, Russians became increasingly uneasy. Gorbachev's tone seemed more and more condescending, he endlessly talked down to citizens about using "new thinking" (**нóвое мы́шление**, with the accent on the first syllable), and showing "initiative" **инициати́ва**. Meanwhile, food shortages were increasingly frequent and occasionally severe. In the end, the "democratically oriented" population disliked Gorbachev for being a communist, and the conservatives despised him for destroying the Soviet regime.

Many believed that Boris Yeltsin **Борúс Éльцин** was the right person to lead Russia to a market economy and long-desired social changes. But (by the end of 1998), his reforms **рефóрмы** had brought too few improvements for too many average citizens. Russia was importing roughly half the food she required. The gross national product **валовóй национáльный продýкт** had dropped by a greater percentage than in the United States during the Great Depression. Business people and political activists were being murdered by "hit" men **кúллеры**.

Russian society has not yet grown accustomed to the rule of law **правовóе óбщество**. Historically, the state has been no refuge in time of need, rather the state has been, for many, the tormentor. Usually it's safer and surer to turn to friends, so that who you know becomes what matters. Corruption can be found everywhere including among the highest ranking officials and the law enforcement institutions. Fraud is expected. Income is hidden. Payment in kind or barter is a common tax dodge **увёртка**. Businesses must pay substantial sums to buy protection **кры́ша** (literally, a roof) from the legal authorities or local thugs. Meanwhile, most businesses pay only a small fraction of the taxes due. (For a while a conscientious manufacturer who paid all the taxes technically required would lose 97 percent of income to that noble cause.)

So it is that teachers leave school to find better pay. Doctors demand payment for every service. And world-famous national laboratories which took years to assemble are crumbling as their personnel scatter to the corners of the world.

Three major groups of opinion about government have developed. One group is bitterly disappointed as it watches hope for real democracy and a real market economy vanish. Russia for them is moving toward some kind of dead end. This pessimism is characteristic of the intelligentsia, especially those employed by the government. A second group has an intense longing for the good old days and an active hatred for Western liberalism and all this "free thinking." This group is made up of older people, and workers and peasants, many of whom lived decently if not well in the past, and now barely have enough to keep bread on the table. The third group has a very positive attitude towards the establishment, when they pay attention to it at all. These are the "new Russians" **нóвые рýсские**—the successful businessmen whom the rest of the country does not distinguish from the mafia. The uncontrolled process of "privatization," general chaos and the lack of proper legislation and enforcement have made many opportunities for them to "catch a fish in murky water" **ло́вить ры́бу в му́тной воде́**. The devaluation of the ruble in August 1998 forced these businessmen to spend their money in Russia (rather than import goods), to Russia's advantage.

Many people have mixed attitudes. For example, the government scientist with a very low salary may think like the first group but still be glad that there's no iron curtain **желе́зный за́навес** anymore. And many people don't have any "attitude" at all: they mind their own business, struggle through life as best they can, and often don't even want to hear about politics.

THE STATE FLAG, EMBLEM, AND ANTHEM

ГОСУДА́РСТВЕННЫЙ ФЛАГ, ГЕРБ И ГИМН

The flag **флаг** of the Russian Republic is presently the "tricolor" **триколо́р** with three colors—white, (medium) blue and red—arranged from top to bottom in horizontal stripes. It was adopted in 1991 by the Supreme Soviet of the Russian Socialist Federated Soviet Republic, that is, before the present Russian Federation came into being. It is based on the background of the Russian imperial flag, which was flown from the beginning of the 18th century until the Provisional Government ousted Tsar Nicholas II in 1917. In 1923 the Bolsheviks adopted a flag with a yellow five-pointed star over a hammer and sickle **серп и мо́лот**—on a red field. The insignia were sufficiently small that a mere red rectangle was enough to indicate the national flag, or the "red banner" **кра́сное зна́мя**. In addition to flags of state there was a "yellow, black and gold" flag **жёлто-чёрно-золото́й флаг** of the Romanov monarchy, still seen today during nationalist marches.

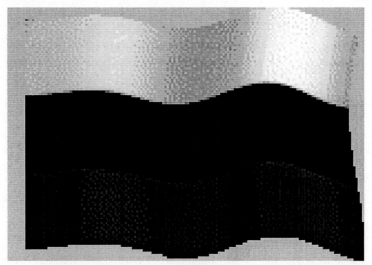

Fig. 11-2.   The flag **флаг** of the Russian Federation, or Russia

Fig. 11-3.   The national seal **герб**

The emblem **герб** of the Russian Federation also harks back to Imperial Russia. Its central device is a two-headed eagle **двуглáвый орёл**. The eagle holds an orb **держáва** and scepter **скúпетр**, across its chest is a shield with the image of St. George **Св. Геóргий («Геóргий Победонóсец»)** slaying a dragon **змей**. It was adopted in 1993.

The present Russian national anthem **национáльный гимн** finds itself in a precarious position. Many Russians still struggle to recognize it when played.[2] On the other hand, the anthem of the Soviet Union, which it has replaced, was a much-loved melody, penned by the popular composer Aleksandrov. Though citizens of the USSR were seldom sure of the lyrics to this tune, they could recognize it from the first notes and would stand at attention, often with tear-filled eyes, whenever it was played. Before the revolution the hymn "God, Protect the Tsar" **«Бóже, царя́ храни́»** was the equivalent of a national anthem.

STRUCTURES OF STATE POWER   **СТРУКТУ́РЫ ГОСУДА́РСТВЕННОЙ ВЛА́СТИ**

The Russian Federation **Росси́йская Федера́ция** (often seen as the initials **РФ**) is divided into a complex of 89 major political jurisdictions of the Federation **субъéкты федерáции**. Unlike the Soviet constitution, the Russian Constitution forbids the secession of any of these jurisdictions from the Federation and they have much the same governing structure as at the federal level (see below). Some of the names are different, indeed the constitution provides for considerable latitude in the naming and even the operations of local self-government **мéстное самоуправлéние** according to the traditions of the region. In order of descending size the political constituents[3] **субъéкты феде-**

---

[2] See Chapter 7.

[3] Notice that the transliteration system used here is that of the Library of Congress. As a result, the spelling differs somewhat from the U.S. Board of Geographic Names system used in the Geography chapter, thus: *krai* here (LC), instead of *kray* (BGN).

ра́ции are: 1. republics **респу́блики**; 2. territories or krais **края́** (*sing.*: **край**); 3. oblasts **о́бласти**; 4. autonomous areas **автоно́мные округа́** (*sing.*: **о́круг**); and 5. two cities with federal stature **города́ федера́льного значе́ния** (Moscow and Saint Petersburg).

Republics	**Респу́блики**

There are presently 21 republics, listed in Appendix 2 in Russian alphabetical order.

Krais	**Края́**

There are six "territories," or krais (see Appendix 2). The term "krai" is a holdover from Soviet days, the actual jurisdiction now is the same as for the oblasts.

Oblasts	**О́бласти**

Most oblasts/regions are named after the major city **го́род** (*pl.*: **города́**) in the respective region. The regional/oblast government in general does not have jurisdiction within the major city, which has its own governing bodies, though it does have considerable influence. In cities the top executive official is the mayor **мэр**, while a governor **губерна́тор** heads the oblast government.There are 49 regions or oblasts (see Appendix 2).

Cities with Federal Stature	**Города́ федера́льного значе́ния**

There are two cities with "federal stature" **города́ федера́льного значе́ния**: Moscow **Москва́**, the federal capital **столи́ца федера́ции**, and St. Petersburg **Санкт-Петербу́рг (СПб)**. The second of these (founded in 1703 by Tsar Peter I—"The Great"[4]) has gone through some name changes. From 1914 to 1924 it was Petrograd **Петрогра́д**, replacing the Germanic "burg" with Slavic "grad." It was renamed Leningrad **Ленингра́д** in 1924 when the Soviets' first leader died. Russians reverted to calling it by its original name in 1991. A nickname used on and off over the years is Pieter **Пи́тер**, from the Dutch form of the founder's name.

Autonomous Areas	**Автоно́мные округа́ (АО** *or* **ао)**

These 10 "autonomous areas" (see appendix) are comparable to our Indian reservations in that they are set aside for one of the less populous nationalities **малочи́сленный наро́д** (or **ма́лый наро́д**), mainly indigenous peoples of Siberia **Сиби́рь**, and Russia's Far East **Да́льний Восто́к**. As a rule they are located within an oblast or territory but are not directly subject to its laws.

---

[4] Peter the Great in English is usually Peter I, in Russian **Пётр Пе́рвый**.

A New Division of Russia   Но́вое деле́ние Росси́и

Fig. 11-4. New divisions are a way to regain some control over regional governments

In May 2000, President Putin divided the country into seven subdivisions **федера́льные округа́** and appointed his representatives, who were to make sure that administrators or governments in those areas did not countermand laws of the federal government.

CONSTITUTION   КОНСТИТУ́ЦИЯ

The most important law in Russia is ostensibly the Constitution of the Russian Federation **Конститу́ция Росси́йской Федера́ции** which begins with the following words:

"We, the multiethnic people of the Russian Federation, conjoined by a common destiny in our land, ... **Мы, многонациона́льный наро́д Росси́йской Федера́ции, соединённые о́бщей судьбо́й на свое́й земле́, ...**"
It was adopted 12 December 1993, superseding the Constitution of the RSFSR (Russian Soviet Federal Socialist Republic РСФСР **Росси́йская Сове́тская Федерати́вная Социалисти́ческая Респу́блика**), a document which had been in force since 12 April 1978, in the late years of Soviet rule. The Soviet-era constitution was also Russia's guiding law for the brief period after 12 June 1991 when Russia declared its independence **незави́симость** from the USSR СССР **Сою́з Сове́тских Социалисти́ческих Респу́блик**, and before the new constitution was drafted. As a holiday, Independence Day is still very new and is observed only in official ceremonies, if at all. In early December 1991, the

leaders of Belarus, Russia and Ukraine announced dissolution of the USSR and signed an Agreement **Беловéжское соглашéние** on the creation of the Commonwealth of Independent States (CIS) **Содрýжество Незавѝсимых Госудáрств (СНГ)**. Weeks later the other former USSR republics, except the Baltics, signed the agreement and on 25 December 1991, President Gorbachev dissolved the office of President of the USSR.

The constitution is divided into two sections **раздéлы**, the first being the basic law, and the second having to do with how the constitution will be first implemented. Each section is split into chapters **глáвы**, and the **главы** into articles **статьѝ**; on occasion these have subsections called paragraphs **чáсти**.

The new constitution was designed to secure for citizens of the Russian Federation all the rights **правá** and privileges **привилéгии** of a civil society **граждáнское óбщество**. It also designates protectors of Russia's sovereignty **суверенитéт** and territorial integrity **госудáрственная цéлостность**, two age-old preoccupations. It explicitly states that Russian is the state language **госудáрственный язы́к** of the Russian Federation. The Constitution can be changed only through a complicated system by which amendments (additions **дополнéния**, corrections **попрáвки**) may be added.

The new constitution was drafted at a constitutional convention **Конституциóнное совещáние**. Framers of that constitution were guided by principles familiar in Western democracies, especially the system of checks and balances **систéма сдéржек и противовéсов** and the doctrine of separation of powers **доктрѝна разделéния влáсти** among the three branches of government **вéтви влáсти**. At the same time it officially departs from the hyper-centralization of the Soviet Union in recognizing the rights of local self-government **мéстное самоуправлéние**.

BRANCHES OF GOVERNMENT   ВÉТВИ ГОСУДÁРСТВЕННОЙ ВЛÁСТИ

The govenmental branches (literally, **вéтви**) are often called powers **влáсти**, and their purview is similar to that of familiar American institutions: 1. legislative branch **законодáтельная власть**, 2. executive branch **исполнѝтельная власть**, and 3. judicial branch **судéбная власть**. One political institution **политѝческий институт** with features unique to Russia is that of the president **президéнт** of Russia who has broad-ranging powers **полномóчия** in dealing with the three branches.

Legislative Branch   Законодáтельная власть

The Russian legislature, or "representative" branch **представѝтельная власть** is called the Federal Assembly **Федерáльное собрáние**—journalists and others at times call it a "parliament" **парлáмент** and any member might be called a "parliamentarian" **парламентáрий**. This legislature consists of two houses **палáты**: the State Duma **Госудáрственная дýма** and the Federation Council

Fig. 11-5. The Duma **Госду́ма**

Сове́т федера́ции. A legislature that is more than just a rubber stamp for the executive branch is an essential feature of a state ruled by laws **правово́е госуда́рство**. As in many countries, the work of this body is overseen by unofficial human rights advocates **правозащи́тники**.

The State Duma is the lower house and it bears the name of a legislative body in pre-revolutionary Imperial Russia dating from 1906. Its name is often shortened to the "stump word" Gosduma **Госду́ма** and it has 450 deputies **депута́ты** from all over the Russian Federation. Deputies serve a four-year term **четырёхле́тний срок**. Candidates **кандида́ты** for the Duma must be at least 21 years old and are barred from working at any other profession (other than teaching, research or so-called "creative activities"—**тво́рческая де́ятельность**). This rule was meant to avoid the situation which arose in the Soviet Union where many deputies supposedly had "real professions"—factory worker, worker at a state farm, etc.—implying that the work of the legislature was not conducted on a professional basis **профессиона́льная осно́ва**. Other members of the Soviet legislature were directors of large state enterprises **госуда́рственные предприя́тия**, and so their participation in law-making was a clear conflict of interest. This system of vertically integrated power, where all responsible positions were filled on orders from the ruling party, was called "nomenklatura" **номенклату́ра**, and formed the basis of Soviet power **сове́тская власть**. A related article of the constitution forbids members of the upper house or any other governing body, federal or local, from being a deputy and *vice versa*. Elections **вы́боры** are held according to a schedule arranged by the president. First sittings of the Duma are opened by the eldest deputy **старе́йший депута́т**. Then they choose a chairman **председа́тель**, more commonly known by the word "speaker" **спи́кер**.

The Duma issues resolutions **постановле́ния**, and can pass laws **принима́ть зако́ны** in concert with the other house. But the right of introduction of legislation **законода́тельная инициати́ва** or to formulate a draft-legislation **законопрое́кт** is given to many others, such as, the Federation chairman, to all members of the Council, and even to high court judges. Laws in both houses are passed by a majority vote **большинство́ голосо́в**, but are subject to the president's approval.

The Duma has the power to confirm or reject the president's candidates for positions in the executive branch, such as for Chairman of the Russian Federal Government **Председа́тель Прави́тельства Росси́йской Федера́ции** (who is usually called prime minister **премье́р-мини́стр** or **премье́р**) and who is head of the government ministers **глава́ кабине́та мини́стров**.[5] But if it refuses a candidate three times, the President (of Russia) has the power to dissolve the Duma **распусти́ть Ду́му** and to call for new elections. This power to force new elections after dissolving an uncooperative legislature, exercised within certain restrictions, gives the president a very strong hand in running Russia.

The upper house or senate is the Federation Council **Сове́т федера́ции** in which every one of the political jurisdictions **субъе́кты федера́ции** (listed in Appendix 2) has a two-member representation. Presently, there are 89 delegations for a total of 178 members **чле́ны**. According to the constitution, one member in each delegation is selected for the Senate by the local representative bodies **ме́стные представи́тельные о́рганы** of the political entity where they live and one is selected by local executive bodies **ме́стные исполни́тельные органы**. Like members of the Duma, members of the Senate are chosen for four years during which time they can't hold another position **до́лжность** in the government, federal or local.

The Senate is mainly concerned with settling differences among the political constituents of the federation, but it also has the job of setting dates for presidential elections **назначе́ние вы́боров Президе́нта** and deciding, when it's justified, on the president's impeachment **отреше́ние президе́нта от до́лжности** (sometimes called "impeachment" **импи́чмент**).

Members of both houses enjoy immunity from prosecution or suits **по́льзуются пра́вом неприкоснове́нности** while in office.

---

[5] Notice that you have been supplied with three possible titles for the same person. This person is not the President of Russia **Президе́нт Росси́и** (for example, Yeltsin).

Russian Political Parties Today   *Полити́ческие па́ртии сего́дня*

In Russia there are presently about 200 national political organizations, movements and parties. Political activists are often members of more than one organization, though when elected to office they must, at least theoretically, declare for one. Some smaller parties, using the term loosely, are occasionally made "collective members" of larger parties; conversely, a party can split into contending factions **фра́кции**. In early 1999 about 40 parties had representatives in the legislative branch. Many of these parties, including the most influential, seem to follow the inspirations of a very few people (for example, the All Russia party consisting of ten governors of various regions). The parties seem to re-form or coalesce with remarkable speed (for example, the Agrarian Party in the course of a year went from Communist-leaning to merely left of Center). And even the then Prime Minister Putin **Пу́тин** and President Yeltsin **Е́льцин**, however belatedly, founded a new party, Unity **Еди́нство**, for vote-seeking purposes.

For historical reasons there is much confusion in categorizing Russian political groups. In the West, the dividing line between who is a leftist and who a rightist is quite clear to everyone: leftists are for government economic intervention and social controls that protect workers, while rightists are pro-business. In Russia, though, the very meaning of the words "left" and "right" is in a state of flux and has been for at least a decade. In the past, to be a leftist was to be against whoever was in power, while rightists supported the government. This led to a situation where both Petr Stolypin, the last tsar's top executive, assassinated by a "revolutionary" in 1913, and Lavrentii Beria, once head of Stalin's secret police, could both be called rightists. Leon Trotsky and Alexander Solzhenitsyn might be called in turn leftists.

Today's Russian politicians themselves disagree on how to characterize their movements, and some are deliberately obtuse about naming; witness the name of the Liberal-Democrats who some would say are neither. The Liberal-Democratic Party **Либера́льно-демократи́ческая па́ртия (ЛДПР)**, under Vladimir Zhirinovskii "**па́ртия Жирино́вского**" is a protest party against government as it has been recently conducted and against the Communists, while adamantly for law and order, wage payment and the like. Some people see him as ultra-nationalist and jokingly refer to "kvas-patriots" **квасны́е патрио́ты** after the traditional Russian drink **квас** made from stale rye bread).

The people who make it their business to describe Russian parties, and the Russians themselves who pay attention to such things, have indeed come to a conclusion about who is where on the left and right spectrum. The distinction is economic and is made as in the West: more government control, social programs, defense of workers is on the Left, and less government control and more pro-business is on the Right. This is crystal clear to us until we realize that this places the Young Turks, the reformers, the people we think of as liberals, on the right.

Thus, by the end of 1999, we have the following scale, starting at the extreme left and ending at the right, which seems to have no extreme:

Extreme Left:

The Stalinist bloc started with a group of Army officers but has now been joined by Working Moscow **Трудова́я Москва́** whose leader, Viktor Anpilov **Ви́ктор Анпи́лов**, now leads the Stalinist bloc. There are a number of much smaller parties in this general category.

Left:

The Communist Party of the Russian Federation **Коммунисти́ческая па́ртия Росси́йской Федера́ции (КПРФ)**, under Gennadii Ziuganov "**па́ртия Зюга́нова**"—a nationalist remake of the old Communist Party of the Soviet Union. The Communists **коммуни́сты**, at least economically speaking, are the party of Soviet socialist nostalgia, their members pining for the days of the universal social safety net from before the market reforms of late 1991; there are dozens of parties who turn out members for "red" street demonstrations. Extremists in this group sometimes join with the extremists in the preceding group to become "red-browns" **кра́сно-кори́чневые**.

Left-Center:

Fatherland is All Russia **Оте́чество вся Росси́я** is a party that now combines Moscow's Mayor Luzhkov "**па́ртия Лужко́ва**" **Оте́чество** with the All Russia **Вся Росси́я** group of ten regional governors led by Mintimir Shaimiev **Минтими́р Шайми́ев**, the astute governor of Tatarstan; and the Agrarian Party of Russia **Агра́рная па́ртия Росси́и (АПР)**, "**па́ртия Лапшина́**"—a communist-leaning party for rural Russia against individual land ownership. The coalition has been joined by the popular former Prime Minister Primakov **Примако́в** to form the most powerful centrist bloc. (In 2001 Putin's Unity **Еди́нство** party joined with **Оте́чество**.)

Right-Center:

The "Our Home is Russia" **Наш дом—Росси́я (НДР)**, under Viktor Chernomyrdin, "**па́ртия Черномы́рдина**," often called in the past the "party of power" **па́ртия вла́сти** because Chernomyrdin, who formed the party, was Prime-Minister at the time. Fedorov's Social-Political Movement "Forward, Russia" **Обще́ственно-полити́ческое движе́ние** "**Вперёд, Россия!**" "**па́ртия Б. Фёдорова**" formerly a generally reform-minded party has joined with Our Home is Russia.

The Yabloko "**Я́блоко**" (Apple) party was formed by liberal leader Yavlinskii **Григо́рий Явли́нский**, one of the best-known of the pro-reform politicians (in concert with **Бо́ндарев, Луки́н** to supply the initials **Я́БЛоко** "Apple"). Another popular and former Prime Minister, Stepashin, has joined this group.

Fig. 11-6.   Politicking on Nevsky Prospekt **Поли́тика на Не́вском**

Right:

On the right we have the Democrats **демокра́ты** (often referred to by their less delicate opponents using a vulgar pun, **дерьмокра́ты, дерьмо́** means human waste), who are interested in a free-market democracy **свободнорыночная демокра́тия**. These Young Turks are now (2001) together under the umbrella of the Union of Right-wing Forces **Сою́з пра́вых сил (СПС)**, led by Boris Nemtsov **Бори́с Немцо́в**. This party includes Irina Khakamada **Ири́на Хакама́да** and also Egor Gaidar **Его́р Гайда́р** and Anatolii Chubais **Анато́лий Чуба́йс**, who are associated with reforms of the 1990s which almost all Russians see as disastrous. However, SPS's close relationship with the Putin administration has helped them attain a relatively influential position in the Duma. Nemtsov says of his groups on the Russian Right:[6]

> "Everyone understands, even if they hate us, that we are the future of the country," he says. "The elections in Russia will not be between a Conservative and a Labour party but between the past and the future. It is Turgenev's struggle between Fathers and Sons."

---

[6] As quoted in *The Financial Times* 13 August 99, "RUSSIA: Nemtsov predicts liberal alliance" by John Thornhill.

Executive Branch   Исполни́тельная власть

The executive branch has the general name of "administration" прави́тель-ство. By law, not the President (of Russia), but the Prime minister (or Premier Премье́р) or Chairman of the Government of the Russian Federation Председа́тель Прави́тельства Росси́йской Федера́ции is the head of the government ministries. The prime-minister премье́р-мини́стр names several seconds-in-command, with divided responsibilities, called the vice-premiers ви́це-премье́ры or, rarely, замести́тель председа́теля прави́тельства, замести́тель главы́ кабине́та мини́стров. One of the vice-premiers would take over for the premier, should the latter become incapacitated. The premier also selects a minister мини́стр to each of the twenty-two ministries министе́рство that comprise the executive branch.

There are separate ministries министе́рства charged with making policy for: Fuel and Energy то́плива и энерге́тики; Economy эконо́мики; Science and Technological Policy нау́ки и техни́ческой поли́тики; Agriculture and Food се́льского хозя́йства и продово́льствия; Defense оборо́ны; Health and Medical Industry здравоохране́ния и медици́нской промы́шленности; Finance фина́нсов; Education образова́ния; Protection of the Environment and Natural Resources охра́ны окружа́ющей среды́ и приро́дных ресу́рсов; Justice юсти́ции; Public Transportation тра́нспорта; Foreign Economic Relations вне́шних экономи́ческих свя́зей; for Cooperation with States Participating in the Confederation of Independent States по сотру́дничеству с госуда́рствами-уча́стниками Содру́жества Незави́симых Госуда́рств (СНГ); Social Welfare социа́льной защи́ты населе́ния; for Nationality Questions and Regional Policy по дела́м национа́льностей и региона́льной поли́тике; Foreign Affairs иностра́нных дел; Highways and Railroads путе́й сообще́ния; Labor труда́; for Civil Defense по дела́м гражда́нской оборо́ны, Emergencies and Disaster Relief по чрезвыча́йным ситуа́циям и ликвида́ции после́дствий стихи́йных бе́дствий (МЧС); for Atomic Energy по а́томной энерге́тике; Construction строи́тельства; and a Committee for the Management of Government Property Комите́т по управле́нию госуда́рственным иму́ществом.

The prime minister and his cabinet determines policy for the executive branch with the help of the Council of Ministers Сове́т Мини́стров. Members of this body include the prime minister, vice-premiers and the ministers from the important ministries. Each ministry has its own managing organ, a collegium колле́гия on which sit the minister and the vice-minister (sometimes shortened to заммини́стра), and official persons должностны́е ли́ца. This body helps the minister to set policy разраба́тывать поли́тику through a series of executive orders прика́зы.

Fig. 11-7.   Ministry of Foreign Affairs **Министе́рство иностра́нных дел**

Under each **министе́рство** there may be a number of agencies **ве́домства**, dealing with specific problems. For example, the Committee for State Security, that is, the KGB — **Комите́т госуда́рственной безопа́сности (КГБ)** was one of the most powerful agencies in its day. Each republic of the Federation **Федера́ция** also has its system of ministries, ministers and agencies. Certain ministers, such as the finance minister **мини́стр фина́нсов**, and top officials in the Council of Ministers are charged with drafting a state budget **госуда́рственный бюдже́т (госбюдже́т)**, which is then approved **одо́брен** by the State Duma. An attempt is made each year to match expenses **расхо́ды** with revenue **дохо́ды**. If all these sources aren't enough to let the government pay off its debts **расплати́ться по долга́м**, the minister of finance can declare an emergency budget cut **секве́стр**, and then try to collect more taxes **нало́ги**.

Yes, Russian citizens are now full-fledged taxpayers **налогоплате́льщики**, like citizens of all the civilized world **цивилизо́ванный мир**, a term used without irony to refer to Western Europe, "Anglo-Saxon" countries and Japan. Unfortunately, the tax collection system is still uncivilized. Fraud is suspected everywhere yet is rarely proven by officials charged to do so. When tax evasion **уклоне́ние от нало́гов** charges are made public, the public understands that someone was not adequately reimbursed for not telling the truth. Thus it was that in the late 1990s some 20 high ranking officials in the State Statistics Committee **Госкомста́т** were arrested. Their job had been to collect statistics on assets, revenues and the like for tax collecting agencies. The public assumes they were paid to record the wrong figures, only not enough. And every business records its own, much lower, figures for employees' salaries so that income, on paper, is below the level required to file annual tax declarations. (This number, in the late 1990s, was $2000 a year.) Of course, actual salaries were paid in cash, with no receipts to trace the fraud.

Income is also collected in the form of tariffs **тари́фы** that are levied at customs **тамо́жня** by customs officials **тамо́женники** who conduct all border inspections **пограни́чный контро́ль**. The government also grants monopoly rights **монопо́лия** to exploitation of natural resources **приро́дные ресу́рсы**. With the end of Soviet rule **сове́тская власть**, the Russian government has turned to privatization **приватиза́ция**,[7] whereby government property **госуда́рственное иму́щество** (**госиму́щество, госсо́бственность**) is sold off to entrepreneurs **предпринима́тели** or businessmen **бизнесме́ны**. These rich "new Russians" **но́вые ру́сские** are joined by former members of the Soviet-era bosses **номенклату́ра**, sometimes known by the name of "functionaries"— **аппара́тчики**, a term that can be pejorative for people who work for the state **рабо́тники госаппара́та**.

One ingenious Russian, Egor Gaidar had the generous idea of distributing part of the proceeds of this sale to the people of Russia in the form of a voucher **ва́учер**. Theoretically, this government bond **госуда́рственная це́нная бума́га** could be cashed in at any time in the future. Many Russians sold their vouchers for relatively little money, though they are now being traded on the stock market **би́ржа** for substantial sums.

Another transfer of wealth did work well: people who lawfully occupied their apartments (that is, they had official permission **пропи́ска** to live there) became the true owners, without having to pay much for them, after which they could dispose of the property any way they liked.

Many industries are still under government control, for example: large sectors of the military-industrial complex **вое́нно-промы́шленный ко́мплекс** (**ВПК вэ-пэ-ка́**); the health industry **систе́ма здравоохране́ния**; education **образова́ние**; many miners **шахтёры** and energy sector workers **энерге́тики** are also government workers; these government businesses employ hundreds of thousands in Russia's work force **рабо́чая си́ла**. Such workers are known as budget based **бюдже́тники** and are often not given their wages **за́работная пла́та, зарпла́та** on time since budgeted taxes are not collected and the government tries to hold down inflation **инфля́ция**.

According to the constitution, members of the government's administration are selected when a new president is elected and must tender their resignation when that president is replaced. A Duma at odds with the administration can force resignations by issuing a vote of no-confidence **во́тум**

---

[7] A term that quickly converted to **прихватиза́ция** formed from the verb **хвата́ть** "to grab," here referring to the thieving ways of former government officials working in collusion with unscrupulous businessmen.

недове́рия. The president must then decide either that the government should resign **уйти́ в отста́вку** or, if there is a disagreement, the president may wait till a second vote of no-confidence is issued, and then dissolve the Duma **распусти́ть Госду́му**. This dissolution of the Duma **ро́спуск ду́мы** brings with it a requirement for the government to set new elections **назна́чить но́вые вы́боры**.

Russians can refer to official persons **должностны́е ли́ца** of the ministries using the neutral term "high official" **высокопоста́вленное лицо́**, or a historical term, meaning the same, "official" **сано́вник**. Or they may use the ironic term for "clerk" **чино́вник**, a name dating from the 18th century which conjures images of petty self-interest. You will also hear the international word, "bureaucrat" **бюрокра́т**. A word left over from Soviet times, since become a word in English, is apparatchik **аппара́тчик**, by which Russians referred to those who ran all the big government enterprises, offices and institutions after securing their positions through acquaintance or patronage. The word is still used today for someone who has parlayed personal ties **блат** into a lucrative job or cushy sinecure. At the other end of the spectrum is the technocrat **хозя́йственник**, a positive term from the word meaning economy **хозя́йство**. An officer in professional military service is a "man in epaulets" **«челове́к в пого́нах»**, something like "the green-suiters" in our own Army. Formally, he would be in the military **вое́нный, военнослу́жащий**.

Trying to gain the ear of a bureaucrat or deputy of the legislature by lobbying **лобби́рование** is the lobbyist **лобби́ст**, who is not a government employee though may recently have been one.

With the rise of an ostensibly free press **свобо́да печа́ти** or **свобо́да сло́ва**, Russians have witnessed a distressing increase in manipulation of the mass media **сре́дство ма́ссовой информа́ции**. Using the influence of Russia's wealthiest businessmen, the so-called "oligarchs" **олига́рхи**, politicians have begun various smear campaigns **во́йны компрома́тов** whereby they put in an "order" **зака́з** with, for example, one of TV's well-known political commentators **телеведу́щие**, who then proceed to uncover heretofore undisclosed secrets about political rivals.

Russian Federal President　　　*Президе́нт Росси́йской Федера́ции*

Russians tend to think of the president as the most powerful member of the executive branch **исполни́тельная власть**, yet the post is seldom mentioned in articles of the constitution concerning this branch, indeed the constitution treats this position **пост** or office **до́лжность** in a chapter separate from the other branches. The Russian presidency appears to be separate from and above the three branches and is endowed with considerable power to mold their behavior, thus fulfilling what seems to be a function necessary in any successful Russian government, that of the centralized or unitary power **центра́льная, еди́ная власть**. The president is head of state **глава́ госуда́рства**, and, like the French president, his office possesses the practical power to issue decrees ука́зы and executive orders **распоряже́ния**, that carry the force of administrative law **указно́е пра́во**. The powers granted to the president allow the use of a "carrot and stick" method **ме́тод кнута́ и пря́ника**, especially when dealing with the Duma.

The president is assisted by an administration **администра́ция** and by the Federal Security Council **Сове́т безопа́сности РФ**. The president helps formulate the other branches of government, for example, offering candidates for the post of federal justice **судья́**, for the federal Solicitor-General **Генера́льный прокуро́р РФ**, and others to be approved by the Senate. The president also has the power to name **назнача́ть на до́лжность** and to dismiss **освобожда́ть от до́лжности** members of the High Command of the Armed Forces **Вы́сшее кома́ндование вооружённых сил**. This abundance of positions, dozens filled by the presidential candidates, has some calling this new group around the president the new "nomenclatura" **но́вая номенклату́ра**, a reference to the old nomenclatura of party officials who were appointed by their patrons higher up in the communist party to significant posts throughout the Soviet government.

Once a year the president must read an address to the legislature **посла́ние Федера́льному собра́нию** on the state of the union **положе́ние в стране́**. The president has the power of veto (**наложи́ть**) **ве́то** over acts by the legislature but these are subject to override **преодоле́ние ве́то** if a legislative majority of two thirds agrees to do so.

Judicial Branch   Суде́бная власть

At the federal level there are three kinds of court **суд**: the Constitutional Court **Конституцио́нный суд**, Federal Supreme Court **Верхо́вный суд РФ**, Supreme Court of Arbitration **Вы́сший арбитра́жный суд РФ**. Judges on those three benches are chosen by the president, and confirmed by the Senate. There are four different kinds of law in the Russian Federation: constitutional **конституцио́нное**, civil **гражда́нское**, administrative **администрати́вное** or **указно́е** and criminal **уголо́вное** proceedings **судопроизво́дство**. Several legal codes **ко́дексы** in Russian jurisprudence **юриспруде́нция** apply to work of these courts: the civil code **гражда́нский ко́декс**, the labor code **трудово́й ко́декс**, the family code **семе́йный ко́декс**, the criminal code **уголо́вный кодекс** and others. The reliance on legislated legal codes is typical for the legal systems of continental Europe **континента́льная систе́ма** as opposed to the Anglo-American system of legal precedents **а́нгло-америка́нская систе́ма прецеде́нтов**.

The range of work that is done by the American Supreme Court is divided between two bodies in the Russian federal system. The Constitutional Court may receive a inquiry **запро́с** from virtually any organ of government in Russia on the constitutionality of official acts. It must also issue an interpretation **дава́ть толкова́ние** of the constitution regarding relations among the various provinces of the Federation and the federal government itself or regarding relations with foreign governments. To do its work the court has 19 justices **су́дьи**.

The Supreme Court **Верхóвный суд** issues final decisions in civil, criminal and administrative cases **делá**, and directs the workings of lower courts.

The Supreme Court of Arbitration **Вы́сший арбитрáжный суд** decides cases involving business and other economic disputes.

Judges **сýдьи** and prosecutors **прокурóры** are in the same branch of government. The general prosecutor's office **Генерáльная прокуратýра** represents the government in court or selects prosecutors for that purpose in all the provinces. Positions are filled at the top by presidential appointment as approved by the legislative branch.

"Power" Agencies	Силовы́е вéдомства

The agencies that seem most often to make the news are the power agencies **силовы́е вéдомства**. The ministers of these agencies are called **силовики́**. They include the armed forces **вооружённые си́лы (ВС)**, the agencies of the interior ministry **Министéрство внýтренних дел (МВД)**, the Federal Counterintelligence Service **Федерáльная слýжба контрразвéдки (ФСК)**, and the Federal Security Service **Федерáльная слýжба безопáсности (ФСБ)**, Russian Defense Procurement Agency **Росвооружéние**, and others concerned with security **безопáсность**.

Armed Forces	Вооружённые си́лы

The armed forces are the most important and the largest of the power agencies. In the Russian Federation they are under the direct control of the minister of defense **мини́стр оборóны**. The minister is advised by members of the general staff **Генерáльный штаб (генштáб)**, as well as his civilian assistants. The president of the Russian Federation is the commander-in-chief **главнокомáндующий**.

All Russian young men must spend one to two years performing either military service **воéнная слýжба** or alternative service **альтернати́вная слýжба**. Military service is notoriously dangerous and often deadly. Unfortunately, it is very difficult to get permission for alternative service so that avoiding the draft becomes a family affair: the family emigrates, or pays a large bribe; thousands of young men hide from the authorities, becoming deserters **дезерти́ры**.

At sixteen all young men in Russia have to register **станови́ться/стать на учёт**. At seventeen, the regional draft board **райóнный военкомáт** sends a registration form **присылáть повéстку** informing them that they are subject to the draft and must show up at the local draft board office. They are then subject to a biannual draft **призы́в** which takes place from 1 April to 30 June and again from 1 October to 31 December, depending on how many draftees **призывники́** are needed for full manning **комплектовáние** of the various branches. Starting in December 1992, young men and women have had the right to join as volunteers **добровóльцы**, but women generally serve only as nurses **мед-**

сёстры, telephone operators **телефони́стки**, interpreters **перево́дчицы** and the like.

You can put off service only if you get a deferment **отсро́чка**, usually for obtaining a college degree **получе́ние вы́сшего образова́ния**. Those with an advanced degree are not called up. Some major universities have an obligatory course for men only on military skills **вое́нная подгото́вка**. Completing this course exempts one from the draft. Young men can also get an exemption from the draft altogether for family reasons **по семе́йным обстоя́тельствам**, for example, if a brother has been killed in service, or if the draftee is judged unfit for military service **не го́ден к вое́нной слу́жбе** after the obligatory medical exam **медици́нское обсле́дование, медобсле́дование**.

Recruits **новобра́нцы** serve eighteen months if they are sent to the land-based units **сухопу́тные войска́**, two years if sent to the navy **вое́нно-морско́й флот (ВМФ)**, but only one year if drafted after receiving a college degree. If they like it they may stay on for another hitch **оста́ться на сверхуро́чную (слу́жбу)**.

Basic military training **нача́льная вое́нная подгото́вка (НВП)** for recruits is led by professional military men **профессиона́льные военнослу́жащие**, the officers **офице́ры** and noncommissioned officers **старшина́**. Each is generally a graduate of a military academy **выпускни́к вое́нного учи́лища**. Training takes place at a training ground **полиго́н**.[8] There new conscripts live in barracks **в каза́рмах** with about 100 soldiers to a building and eat what is jokingly called chow **похлёбка** (potato or grain soup) served up by the kitchen "police" **дежу́рные по ку́хне**, and at night sleep on a cot **ко́йка**. At around six in the morning soldiers rise to reveille **подъём**, stand for roll call **пове́рка**, do their calisthentics **физзаря́дка**, go through ordering quarters **запра́вка** to get ready for inspection **осмо́тр** (which is different from a military review **торже́ственный смотр**). Breakfast and supper offer the same food, usually tea, about one pound of bread and a bowl of hot cereal with butter. Lunch is the main meal: soup, 100 grams of meat (about a quarter pound), black bread and potatoes. Day is not done till evening roll call **вече́рняя пове́рка** and taps **отбо́й** at around 10 pm.

The recruit learns how properly to put on a uniform **фо́рма**, which consists of a forage cap **фура́жка**, a service blouse **гимнастёрка**, perhaps a jacket **мунди́р, ки́тель**[9] and, if it's cold, a hat with ear-flaps **уша́нка** and a quilted work coat **ва́тник**; there's a waist-belt **реме́нь**, and, usually, canvas-topped boots **ки́рзовые сапоги́**; sometimes foot-wrappings **портя́нки**[10] are worn instead of socks **носки́**. Whatever the boots **боти́нки** used, they must be spit-shined **до бле́ска** (literally, till they sparkle). A soldier must know not only how to march **марширова́ть** in a formation **коло́нна**, he must also take part in field-

---

[8] Also the word for an (e.g., artillery) testing range.

[9] See *Russian's World*, 2/e, 74, for army and navy uniforms.

[10] See *Russian's World*, 2/e, 77.

training exercises **полевы́е уче́ния**. During down time he can bone up on the regulations **уста́в**.

He also needs to learn marching commands:

11-1

Attention!	**Сми́рно!**
At ease!	**Во́льно!**
Form columns!	**В коло́нну (по́ 2, по 4) станови́сь!**
Fall in—single file!	**В коло́нну по одному́ станови́сь!**
Take up arms!	**В ружьё!**
Sling arms! (weapons are borne diagonally across the back)	**За́ спину!**
Order arms!	**К ноге́!**
Present arms!	**На́ карау́л!**
Mark time!	**На ме́сте ша́гом марш!**
March!	**Ша́гом марш!**
To the right!	**Напра́во!**
To the left!	**Нале́во!**
Eyes right/left!	**Равне́ние напра́во/нале́во!**
Fall out!	**Разойди́сь!**
Close on center/flanks!	**Сомкни́сь!**

11-2 He'll want to know battle commands, too: Yes, sir! or Aye-aye! **Есть!**; On the double! **Бего́м!**; Take cover **В укры́тие!**; Throw grenades! **Грана́тами огонь!**; Follow me! **За мно́й!**; Load weapons! **Заряжа́й!**; On guard! **К бо́ю гото́вься!**; Take aim! **Це́лься!**; Fire! **Ого́нь!**[11]; Fix bayonets! **Примкну́ть штыки́!**, and the ever-popular "Hands up!" **Ру́ки вверх!** and "Halt! Who goes there?" **Сто́й! Кто идёт?**

Fig. 11-8.   Soldiers sometimes have policing duties.

---

[11] A fire in the house is announced with **пожа́р!** or **гори́м!**

The first-year in the life of a private soldier **рядово́й** is made miserable by a vicious form of hazing called **дедовщи́на** where soldiers in the last half of their service **деды́** are allowed mercilessly to abuse or "haze" him **издева́ться над ним**. There is little chance of getting much leave **о́тпуск**. If he can't stand it he may want to go AWOL **уйти́ в самово́лку** and become a "deserter" **дезерти́р** for which he is likely to get punished **попа́сть на гауптва́хту, ("на губу́")**. Young men know what is coming, as do their parents, and so many do anything they can to avoid service. As a result all branches have difficulty filling units **комплектова́ние**. Upon completion of service, a soldier goes back to being a civilian.

Humor makes it possible to comment without actually saying something, so the jokes **анекдо́ты** about one's superiors are legion:

Сейча́с я разберу́сь, как сле́дует, и накажу́ кого попа́ло.	Now I'll to get to the bottom of this, and then punish anyone.
Всех отсу́тствующих постро́ить в одну́ шере́нгу!	Line up all the missing men in one column!
И не де́лайте у́мное лицо́, не забыва́йте, что вы бу́дете офице́ры.	Don't try to look intelligent. Don't forget that you are future officers.
Курса́нт, е́сли вы хоти́те что́-нибудь сказа́ть, то лу́чше молчи́те.	Cadet, if you want to say something, you'd better keep quiet.
Все в око́пы, остальны́е за мной!	Everyone into the trenches! The rest follow me!

The post-Soviet world has many "hot spots" **горя́чие то́чки** where these conscripts will have to serve and where many may be killed or wounded. Disabled veterans **инвали́ды а́рмии** are rated in three ranks: first, second and third group **инвали́д пе́рвой, второ́й, тре́тьей гру́ппы** with the worst cases in the first group. The war veteran **ветера́н войны́** has long enjoyed certain privileges in Russia: getting a phone before others, receiving certain goods without waiting in line **получа́ть проду́кты и предме́ты обихо́да вне о́череди**, and others. But these are rather less significant today than in the past. (Similarly, a worker can become a labor veteran **ветера́н труда́** by receiving some national award and also completing twenty five years at the same government enterprise.)

The Suvorovsky Academy **Суво́ровское учи́лище** for the army and the Nakhimovsky Academy **Нахи́мовское учи́лище** for the navy are essentially military boarding schools that prepare pupils, often sons of officers, for higher education as officers (see Fig. 11-9).

Officers are trained at numerous military academies **вы́сшие вое́нные учи́лища** where the training focuses on the military applications of academic truths, and on military and physical training **вое́нная и физи́ческая подгото́вка**. Cadets **курса́нты** train in one of a number of institutions which are very specific in their focus.

Fig. 11-9.   Two pupils from the
Suvorov School

There are seven branches of armed forces **ча́сти** or **ви́ды войск** in the Russian Federation; four are under the control of the Ministry of Defense **Министе́рство оборо́ны Минобро́ны:** (1) Land army **Сухопу́тные войска́** (literally: "dry-land forces"—the singular means a force or unnumbered group of soldiers and so is not used in this context); (2) Strategic Rocket Forces **Раке́тные войска́ стратеги́ческого назначе́ния**; (3) Navy **Вое́нно-морско́й флот (ВМФ)**; (5) Air Force **Вое́нно-возду́шные си́лы (ВВС)**. **ПВО (Войска́ противовозду́шной оборо́ны)** Air Defense is no longer a separate branch, but rather is under the control of the **ВВС** (Air Force).

The Interior Ministry Armed Forces **Вну́тренние войска́ (ВВ) Министе́рства вну́тренних дел**; and the border patrol **Пограни́чные войска́ (ПВ)** are also considered part of the Russian armed forces.

The Land Army   *Сухопу́тные войска́*

A soldier **солда́т** or officer **офице́р** in the armed forces serves in various types **ви́ды** of the military: he may be in the infantry **пехо́та** and called a infantryman **пехоти́нец**. Or he may be part of the elite airborne forces **Возду́шно-деса́нтные войска́ (ВДВ)** and be an airborne trooper **деса́нтник**. He may be a tanker **танки́ст** or in the mechanized forces **мотострелко́вые войска́**. He could be an artilleryman **артиллери́ст** as were the writers Lev Tolstoy and Alexander Solzhenitsyn, where he will serve not the "king of battle" as Americans would, but the god of war **бог войны́** as the Russian soldier does. He may become a combat engineer **сапёр**, or a communications personnel **связи́ст** (a woman can serve in this branch as **связи́стка**).

Ranks are mostly the same in all branches other than the navy (**ВМФ**).

A soldier **солда́т** can be a private **рядово́й**, or a lance-corporal **ефре́йтор**.

Non-commissioned officers **сержа́нты и старши́ны** include the corporal **мла́дший сержа́нт**, the sergeant **сержа́нт**, the staff sergeant **ста́рший сержант**, the sergeant major **старшина́**. (And a duty officer is **днева́льный**.)

Warrant officers **пра́порщики** include the chief warrant officer **ста́рший пра́порщик**.

Junior grade officers **мла́дшие офице́ры** include the junior lieutenant **мла́дший лейтена́нт**, the lieutenant **лейтена́нт**, the senior lieutenant **ста́рший лейтена́нт**, and the captain **капита́н**.

Field grade officers **ста́ршие офице́ры** include major **майо́р**, lieutenant colonel **подполко́вник**, and full colonel **полко́вник**.

Senior grade officers **вы́сшие офице́ры** include major general **генера́л-майо́р**, lieutenant general **генера́л-лейтена́нт**, colonel general **генерал-полко́вник**, and general of the army **генера́л а́рмии**.

Marshal of the Russian Republic **Ма́ршал Росси́йской Федера́ции** is the highest Russian military rank, equivalent to the American five-star general, and is seldom conferred, although former First Secretary of the Communist Party Leonid Brezhnev made himself a Marshal of the Soviet Union **Ма́ршал Сове́тского Сою́за** after an undistinguished military career. He did not approach, however, Generalissimo Stalin **Генерали́ссимус Ста́лин**.

Russian armed forces are organized into the following units, from largest to smallest:

Strategic units **объедине́ния**: front **фронт** when at war, or military region **вое́нный о́круг** when at peace; army **а́рмия** comes next though it also stands for "military service," "My son is in the army now" **Мой сын сейча́с слу́жит в а́рмии**. At mid-levels there are tactical groups **такти́ческое соедине́ние** called divisions **диви́зии**. Finally there are fighting units **во́инские подразделе́ния**: regiment **полк**; battalion **батальо́н**, company **ро́та**; platoon **взвод**; and squad **отделе́ние**.

Strategic Rocket Forces

Раке́тные войска́ стратеги́ческого назначе́ния

Strategic rocket forces in Russia have two branches: those armed with intercontinental ballistic missiles **межконтинента́льные баллисти́ческие раке́ты (МБР)**; and those with intermediate range missiles **раке́ты сре́дней да́льности (РСД)**. Soldiers who serve in these units are called missileers **раке́тчики**.

Air Force

Вое́нно-возду́шные си́лы

The Air Force **Вое́нно-возду́шные силы (ВВС)** has the same ranks as does the army.

Air Defense **Войска́ противовозду́шной оборо́ны (ПВО)** is now part of **ВВС**. Air Defense has two basic means of doing its job: fighter-interceptor planes **истреби́тели-перехва́тчики** and anti-aircraft rocket batteries **зени́тные раке́тные ко́мплексы**. Unlike the USA and many other western countries, Russians have a separate National Air Defense **ПВО страны́** for defense of civilian installations, and a Military Air Defense **войсковы́е ПВО**.

The Navy   *Военно-морской флот*

The Navy **Военно-морской флот (ВМФ)** has its own military ranks **воинские звания**. (And its own cooks; a chef in the Navy is **кок**, from the Dutch.)

Enlisted ranks **матросы** are seaman **матрос**, and senior seaman **старший матрос**.

Non-commissioned officers are **старшины**.

Warrant officers **мичманы** can be warrant officer **мичман**, or chief warrant officer **старший мичман**.

Junior grade officers **младшие офицеры** include ensign **младший лейтенант**, lieutenant junior grade **лейтенант**, lieutenant senior grade **старший лейтенант**, also lieutenant senior grade **капитан-лейтенант**.

Senior grade officers **старшие офицеры** include lieutenant commander **капитан третьего ранга**, commander **капитан второго ранга**, commodore **капитан первого ранга**.

Admirals **высшие офицеры** are ranked as rear-admiral **контр-адмирал**, vice-admiral **вице-адмирал**, admiral **адмирал**, and admiral of the fleet **адмирал флота**.

The Russian Navy has been in business for a long time, having celebrated its tricentennial anniversary in 1996. It is organized into four fleets: Baltic, Northern-White Sea, Pacific and Black Sea Fleets **Балтийский флот**, **Северный флот**, **Тихоокеанский флот** and **Черноморский флот**. The Russian navy has five separate divisions: its most important ships are submarines **подводные лодки (подлодки)**. There are also surface forces **надводные силы**: naval air force **морская авиация**, and shore-based rocket batteries **береговые ракетно-артиллерийские войска**. The fleet also has a marine corps **морская пехота**. There is no separate Coast Guard. Such duties are assigned to a series of local flotillas **флотилии**.

Interior Ministry   Министерство внутренних дел

Internal policing is run by the Interior Ministry **Министерство внутренних дел (МВД)**, whose minister is a member of the president's Security Council **Совет безопасности**. Ordinary citizens most often have dealings with the local security bodies **местные правоохранительные органы**. These include the police **милиция**, and the traffic police **ГАИ** (pronounced **га-и**) **Государственная автоинспекция** (now, formally, **ГИБДД**). The police detachment for special assignments **отряд милиции особого назначения (ОМОН)** is called up for especially sticky situations: civil disturbances **уличные беспорядки**, or controlling outbursts of criminal activity by armed criminal groups **вооружённые преступные группировки** which are sometimes given the more emotional name, bandit gangs **бандитские шайки**.

There is a ministry of internal affairs **Министе́рство вну́тренних дел** for each republic, and each provincial and regional jurisdiction has its Directorate of the Interior **Управле́ние вну́тренних дел: Областно́е (ОблУВД), Райо́нное (РУВД, ру-вэ-дэ́), Городско́е (ГУВД, гу-вэ-дэ́)** under which come the police. Policemen **милиционе́ры** find criminals (literally: transgressors) **престу́пники**, whom they must arrest **арестова́ть** or detain **задержа́ть**. There are a number of different "operatives" **операти́вники** among the militia, detectives **инспе́кторы** (not to be confused with **детекти́в**, usually the name for a crime novel) and there are investigators **сле́дователи**. There are also various ranks **чины́**. In fact, they are precisely the same as in the army, from private **рядово́й** to general **генера́л**.

Police and criminals have their own names for each other. The police (formally **мили́ция**) are called "cop" **мент** (also "garbage" **му́сор**). Among members of the criminal element **престу́пный элеме́нт**, one may be a thief **вор**, whose crime is theft **воровство́** (something the political opposition regularly charges incumbents with). There is an indigenous Russian cult of professional crooks, known by the adjective "**блатно́й**" or the term "thief by law" **вор в зако́не**. The "law" in this case means the rules of the thieves who make up the gang. Such a crook is not a mere gangster **га́нгстер**. A member of a gang **ша́йка** or **братва́** of such criminals, swears off the everyday life of work and family as unworthy of a true outlaw and at the same time pledges allegiance to a gangleader **паха́н** (slang for "father"). At a lower level of commitment to such a life is the "wanna-be" crook **приблатнённый**. You can meet them all when they put you under arrest **взять под аре́ст**, frisk you **обыска́ть** and put you in the holding tank **изоля́тор** or **СИЗО́—сле́дственный изоля́тор** at the jail house **тюрьма́**.

A murderer **уби́йца** is guilty of murder **уби́йство** which he has committed **соверши́ть**, and even worse is aggravated murder **уби́йство при отягча́ющих вину́ обстоя́тельствах**; but worst of all, is the professional killer **ки́ллер**, that is, one who commits murder on contract **по контра́кту**. Other crimes include disorderly conduct **хулига́нство** committed by hooligans **хулига́ны**, who, when they are recidivists **рециди́висты**, are charged with habitual disorderly conduct **зло́стное хулига́нство**; banditry **бандити́зм**—crimes of, as you might guess, bandits **банди́ты** who get involved in all sorts of trouble including theft **кра́жа** or for the more ingenious, burglary **кра́жа со взло́мом**. The desperate try robbery **грабёж**, which makes them robbers **граби́тели**. The same crime can be called armed attack **разбо́йное нападе́ние**, the work of armed bandits **банди́ты, престу́пники**. Rape **изнаси́лование** is another all too common offense. Extortion **вымога́тельство**, a crime committed by extortionists **вымога́тели**, is a favorite among racketeers **рэкети́ры**; hostage-taking **захва́т зало́жников** became more common in Russia after the 1996 end of the first Chechen War **война́ в Чечне́**, which was originally billed as a war "to bring order" **навести́ поря́док**. It's an avaricious form of kidnapping **похище́ние**, where criminals demand that friends or relatives of the hostages **зало́жники** pay a ransom **выкуп**. The most lucrative crimes of all are in the narcotics trade **наркобизнес** and pimping **сутенёрство**, where one controls trade in a business known by the international term, prostitution **проституция**. Practitioners of this trade have perhaps one hundred different names in Russian (as in many other languages) ranging from "priestess (or priest) of love" **жрица любви** to the pejorative and highly offensive "whore" **блядь** (a word *never* to be repeated by a foreigner).

Special Services   *Специáльные слýжбы*

What was once known as the KGB (**КГБ — Комитéт государственной безопáсности**; the Committee for State Security), was broken into two main parts and some less significant fragments. The Federal Security Service **Федерáльная слýжба безопáсности (ФСБ**, akin to our FBI), and the Federal Counterintelligence Service **Федерáльная слýжба контрразвéдки (ФСК**, like our CIA) are the two main parts of today's security services **спецслýжбы**. When talking about anyone in the security organs, Russians sometimes make ironic use of the word **чекист** which originally denoted someone working in the **ЧК (че-кá) — Чрезвычáйная комиссия** — the fearsome Special Committee of the post-revolutionary period, charged with opposing the enemies of the Revolution **прóтив врагóв Револю́ции**, and later in the 1930s with liquidation of enemies of the people **ликвидáция врагóв нарóда**. That office was replaced by the State Political Directorate **Государственное политическое управлéние (ГПУ**). But these are new times; each of today's agencies even has a public relations center **центр по свя́зям с общéственностью**.

The police **милиция** and the prosecutor **прокурóр** are often helped in the fight against crooks by the **ФСК** which provides information about their activities collected from devices like electronic bugs **жучки** or from informers **стукачи**. While they used to be called "GB boys" **гэбéшники**, security operatives are now called just intelligence officers **развéдчики**.

Russia's Highway Patrol   *(ГИБДД), ГАЙ*

Any violation **нарушéние прáвил вождéния** committed while driving is duly noted by the operatives of the State Auto-Inspection **Государственная áвтоинспéкция (ГАЙ**), who stand at posts **посты́ ГАЙ** waving in guilty drivers with a little black and white striped baton **пáлочка**. (State Inspectorate of Traffic Safety **Государственная инспéкция по безопáсности дорóжного движéния (ГИБДД**) is the formal new 1998 version of **ГАЙ**, but the latter is more familiar and shorter and therefore likely to remain in use.) The car-policeman (**гаишник** in Russian slang) is armed only with a pistol **пистолéт**, but drivers are generally careful not to antagonize him and so do still pull over with regularity. Drivers are fined for infractions such as driving too fast **превышéние скóрости**. For worse offenses they may suffer the loss of their

Fig. 11-10.

driver's license **лише́ние води́тельских прав**. Later they'll tell their friends, "He threw the book at me." **Он меня здо́рово штрафану́л!** (the last word is a slang version of neutral **штрафова́ть**—to fine.) It is standard practice to pay the fine to the officer immediately, and this is often cheaper than if he has to write you up. If your offense is serious, you can try to pay the operative off **дать ему́ взя́тку (на ла́пу)**. (Cars are stopped for "minor" infractions as a means of supporting the police. This will continue at least until the policeman is paid a living wage.) But paying a bribe **взя́тка** does not always work. Like as not, he will still want to write you up **вы́писать квита́нцию** which you pay to the official account at the local government-run savings bank **сберега́тельный банк, сберба́нк**. If you have done something really awful with your car, your licence plate **но́мер** will be unscrewed and you will not be allowed, temporarily at least, to drive at all.

There are two other institutions in Russian life that are presently run by the government: fire protection and ambulance services. The Directorate of Fire Security **Управле́ние пожа́рной охра́ны (УПО)** directs the activities of firemen **пожа́рники**. Ambulance services are called "emergency help" **ско́рая по́мощь**.

BEFORE THE COURT В СУДЕ́

Legally speaking, a defendant **обвиня́емый**, needs a lawyer **адвока́т** in court **в суде́**. First, there is an interrogation **допро́с** at the police station **мили́ция**. In court, there will be witnesses **свиде́тели**, evidence **ули́ки** and proof **доказа́тельства** which the prosecutor **прокуро́р** will assemble. The judge **судья́** hands down a sentence **пригово́р** which may result in jail **тюрьма́**. The worst criminals are sent for a prison term **срок** to a camp **ла́герь** in a penal colony **зо́на**. During the Soviet period these camps were organized as a kind of separate economy under the State Directorate of Camps, the acronym for which—GULag—has come to denote the sum of repressive measures taken at that time (**ГУЛáг**, a stump word for **Госудáрственное управлéние лагерéй**). Upon release from jail or prison altogether one is free **на вóле**; a soldier, upon release from the army is "in the civilian world" **на граждáнке**.

LOCAL GOVERNMENTAL SERVICES   О́РГАНЫ МÉСТНОГО УПРАВЛÉНИЯ

The nation **госудáрство** builds spaceships, issues currency, conducts foreign policy, goes to war and makes History. It's at home that everything else gets done: marriage **бракосочетáние**, bearing children **рождéние детéй**, work **рабóта**, homemaking **домáшнее хозя́йство**, divorce **развóд**. It is at the local level that government activities mean the most to the individual **индиви́дуум**.

Cities, other localities and rural areas all have their local government. In Moscow and other cities, the head of the local government is the mayor **мэр** and his offices **мэ́рия**. Moscow, for example, is divided into okrugs **округá: Центрáльный, Сéверный, Сéверо-Запáдный, Зáпадный, Юго-Зáпадный óкруг** and so forth. Each okrug has its own local administration office called the Prefecture **префектýра**, for example, **Префектýра Ю́жного óкруга**, and its chief in charge is the prefect **префéкт**.

Kinds of Identification   Удостоверéния ли́чности

You start with your birth certificate **свидéтельство о рождéнии** *or* **мéтрика** issued to your parents by the Civil Records Office, known to most by its acronym **ЗАГС—зáпись áктов граждáнского состоя́ния**. When it's all over, your heirs will receive a death certificate **свидéтельство о смéрти** from the same office. Students at the college level might require student identification **студéнческий билéт**. If you go to the library you'll need a library card **читáтельский билéт** (literally: reader's ticket, though it's actually a little booklet) with a photo of yourself pasted in. Other than that you won't need much more than your birth certificate till your fourteenth birthday when you receive your passport **пáспорт** issued by a local office of the MVD (Interior Ministry).

Fig. 11-11.   The Lubyanka, MVD offices in Moscow

The passport, and not a driver's license **водительские права́**, is the main means by which Russians establish their legal identity, which is why everyone is required to have one. If, for example, upon getting married you change your name, you'll need a new passport reflecting any changes in status and name. Your children's names are listed therein, and whether marrying or not, you'll need a new photo at 14, 25 and 45 years of age. If you want to travel abroad, you must apply for an "out-of-country" passport **заграни́чный па́спорт**; **ОПС — о́бщезаграни́чный па́спорт**.

Upon marrying you receive a marriage license **свиде́тельство о бра́ке** from the **ЗАГС**. If it doesn't work out, and there are no children, and no dispute over property, then a couple can simply register their divorce **разво́д** at the Civil Records Office. Otherwise divorce proceedings **бракоразво́дный проце́сс** are initiated with the People's Court **Наро́дный суд**. It's generally conceded that after divorce children should live with the mother; up to 98 percent of custody determinations are in the mother's favor. The father gets to play his part, though, too. He'll participate in the division of common property **разде́л иму́щества**. Then he'll be told to pay alimony **алиме́нты** of about 25 percent of his salary for one child, 33 percent for two. The ex-wife gets no alimony. The mother receives notification **извеще́ние** in the mail indicating that she may pick up the latest payment at the local bank **сберба́нк**. All that's needed is a passport for identification. Couples that stay together but do not wish to have children **безде́тный брак** pay a tax after age 25 called "tax for no children" **нало́г на безде́тность**.

Fig. 11-12. "The Big House" **Большо́й дом** was to St. Petersburg what the Lubyanka was to Moscow

Living Arrangements   Жильё

In the past, if you wanted to live in a given city, you would need to petition officially for residency. Once accepted you would be **прописан** (*fem.*: **прописана**).
That system has since been ruled unconstitutional. (Now, one must be
"registered" **зарегистрирован** instead. This permission is reportedly even
more difficult to obtain than the former **прописка**.) Upon buying a house
особняк or an apartment **квартира** in an apartment house **жилой дом**,[12] you'll
receive a deed **свидетельство купли-продажи**. State-run, and even some
privately-owned housing retains many of the housing offices **органы
жилищно-коммунального хозяйства** from the Soviet era, such as the Housing
Maintenance Office **РЭУ**. (Some Russians call it by the acronym **ЖЭК**;
Жилищно-эксплуатационная контора but the newer acronym is **РЭУ
Ремонтно-эксплуатационное управление**). This office assists in the issuance
of a residency permit **предоставлять прописку** (mainly under the jurisdiction
of the local police), sends the draft board a prospective conscript's personal information **высылать данные призывника**, or carries on repairs **вести ремонт
в жилых домах**. It also sees to building maintenance **уборка**. The monthly
"housing payment" for renters **квартплата, плата за жильё** is made to the
Community Economic Directorate **Районное экономическое управление
РЭУ**or the **ЖЭК** and includes the water. But the bills for other utilities
коммунальные услуги go to a corresponding city office, for example, in
Moscow, it is **Мосгаз** for gas **за газ**, or **Мосэнерго** for electricity **за электри-
чество**. Traditionally, those offices rarely check on how much energy you have
consumed, and never send any bills. Instead each family has to look at the
kilowatt counter **счётчик** every month, write down the number of kilowatts
used, multiply by the unit price and pay the resulting amount via the savings
bank **сбербанк**. (As a result, some people have not paid their electric bills for
years.) These same bills may be routed through the Directorate for Building
Utilization **Дирекция по эксплуатации зданий** (**ДЭЗ**), another office in the
housing block **блок корпусов** where you live.

Help for Parents   Помощь родителям

Daycare is no longer a government monopoly in Russia, but many parents use
essentially the same services today that their parents did when they were growing up. To get a child into a daycare center **детский сад, детсад**, or **садик** for
children from three to six (nursery **ясли** for children up to three), parents first
send in a personal admissions application **заявление на приём в детсад**. Then
they need a certificate of good health **справка о здоровье** for their child. They
may now send their child to nursery school or day care center **отдавать
ребёнка в ясли/в детсад**. Each month they will receive a bill **квитанция** which

---

[12] There are about 35,000 of these buildings in Moscow.

they must pay to the individual account **лицево́й счёт** of the kindergarten at a local branch of the savings bank.

Local authorities oversee operation of nurseries, daycare centers and schools, inspecting everything from ledgers to lunch rooms. The Local Education Board **Райо́нный отде́л наро́дного образова́ния (РОНО́)** holds the purse strings for government-run learning centers of all kinds. Each government-owned daycare is run by a director **заве́дующий** who may or may not have an assistant in charge of premises **заве́дующий хозя́йством (завхо́з)**. Among directors' duties **обя́занности** are setting work schedules **гра́фик рабо́т**, ordering food **выпи́сывать проду́кты пита́ния**, hiring and firing **приём на рабо́ту и увольне́ние** of day-care teachers **воспита́тельницы**, and directing the work of the bookkeeper **бухга́лтер** who has to get clearance **безнали́чный расчёт** for any expenses **расхо́ды** from the **РОНО́** people who then release funds for transfers from the supply office **конто́ра снабже́ния**. They may also want to have a look at the account book **бухга́лтерская кни́га** and regularly require an inventory **инвентариза́ция** be taken during which all government property **госуда́рственное иму́щество (госиму́щество)** is counted. The buildings undergo a periodic fire inspection **пожа́рная инспе́кция** and kitchens are checked. If there are violations, a "health hazard condition" is declared by the health inspection office **санита́рно-эпидемиологи́ческая ста́нция (СЭС)**. Trouble for everyone. Even using the same knife for both meat and vegetables is a punishable infraction **наруше́ние**.

Olga T. Yokoyama

Words have a life: they are born or adopted into a language, they live, work
and give birth to new words, and they die—fall out of use—and are eventually
forgotten and disappear. Most eighty-year-olds today wouldn't understand you
if you said that you "clicked the hypertext for *Kremlin*" because the word
"hypertext" and this usage of the word "click" might both be new to them.
These words or usages were born into English after the person learned the language. Conversely, you may have heard a seventy-year-old say "He's a swell
guy," but a twenty-year-old would never use the word "swell" in that meaning,
though it would probably be understood. (The young one might instead use
"cool," or any number of other terms that will surely sound strange to grandmother.) The most obvious change in vocabulary probably involves slang, that
is, words like "swell" and "cool."

But in fact about 90 percent of the new words born into a modern language
actually belong to science and technology. They enter the language through
many unrelated fields. Most of them name objects, however inaccessible they
may be to the naked eye, and phenomena, however abstractly they may be described. They are often coined artificially or following some field-internal conventions: -*cillins* like *penicillin* or *amoxicillin* and -*mycins* like *streptomycin,*
erythromycin, and so forth. They have clear and precise definitions within particular disciplines, although it is not unusual for the same word to refer to different things in different fields: thus in linguistics **лингви́стика**, the word *mor-*
phology **морфоло́гия** means something entirely different from what it means
in biology **биоло́гия**.

The exact definitions of scientific words do not concern lay people. When
lay people use such words, they are usually unable to provide definitions that
would satisfy a specialist. This doesn't bother non-specialists and never pre-
vents them from using these words as they see fit. When a scientific idea acquires reasonable currency among the general public, it usually begins to be
used metaphorically; an imprecise understanding of the term is sufficient for
that purpose. When a non-mathematician, for example, says **Его́ настрое́ние
коле́блется по синусо́иде** (His mood fluctuates according to a sinusoid [sine
curve]), it hardly matters that the person may not be able to explain what a sine
curve is in mathematical terms—the regular up-and-down motion is all that
needs to be conveyed.

After a while, some of these words become part of the stable lexicon of educated non-specialist speakers of the language. Ordinary educated people eventually stop feeling that these were originally scientific terms which were only occasionally used in non-scientific spheres of language for special effects. At this point these words become equal citizens of the standard literary language and they begin a life of their own. Meanwhile, of course, the process continues: other scientific terms enter their respective fields, some of them filter into non-specialist language as metaphors, and so on.

Science and technology not only give words to the language: they also take them. In Russian, just as in English, ordinary old non-scientific words often secondarily develop a more recent specialized scientific meaning. In English, for example, the word "cell" means a "small room" (as in "prison cell"), but later it also began to be used as the name for an important microscopic unit of plant and animal tissue. In Russian, too, the word **клéтка** has two senses: it means both a "cage" (from **клéть**, a "small room"), as well as the biological term. This extension of an ordinary meaning into a secondary scientific meaning happens particularly often with verbs, as in the case of resist **сопротивля́ться**, or distribute **распределя́ть**, and with deverbal nouns such as resistance **сопротивлéние** or amplifier **усили́тель**.

In Russian, one encounters a surprising number of words and expressions that sound scientific—noticeably more than in English. One of the reasons for this lies in the kind of education Russians have been receiving in schools. Generally, Russian primary and secondary education (pre-college education now totals 11 years) is fairly heavy on mathematics and science. This sort of education produces people with a relatively high level of familiarity with natural sciences. Weekly subject distribution of a fifth grader in a humanistically-oriented public gymnasium in Moscow in 1996–97 was 60 percent in humanities and social sciences and 40 percent in mathematics and natural sciences. An eighth grader attending a Moscow public school with a more general orientation in 1996–97 had a reverse proportion of mathematics and natural sciences (60 percent) as compared to humanities and social sciences (40 percent). Since even the normal, that is non-science-oriented, school curriculum gravitates towards mathematics **матема́тика** and natural sciences **есте́ственные нау́ки** (physics **фи́зика**, chemistry **хи́мия**, botany **бота́ника**, zoology **зооло́гия**, astronomy **астроно́мия**, geology **геоло́гия**, and so forth), a high school graduate—with an educated family background—is comfortable with words like:

хромосо́ма	chromosome	**арте́рия**	artery
конденса́ция	condensation	**окисле́ние**	oxidizing
моллю́ск	mollusk	**о́смос**	osmosis
метаморфо́за	metamorphosis	**гидросфе́ра**	hydrosphere
зени́т	zenith	**аксио́ма**	axiom
эмбрио́н	embryo	**молекуля́рный**	molecular
перпендикуля́рный	perpendicular		

ENGLISH-RUSSIAN CORRESPONDENCES

ПРЯ́МО С АНГЛИ́ЙСКОГО НА РУ́ССКИЙ

Most words on the short list above resemble English. Many scientific words in Russian in fact do look like English, particularly among the highly specialized vocabulary. This is a very useful thing to keep in mind. In practical terms, it helps to know that even if you don't know how to say a scientific word in Russian, chances are good that if you just learn how to transpose English scientific vocabulary into Russian your partner will understand you. It is worth remembering some correspondence patterns that frequently operate in Russian scientific vocabulary.

English prefixes

Russian prefixes приста́вки

a- (arrhythmia)
anti- (antigen, antibiotic)
ex-/ec- (excretion, eccentric)
hyper- (hypertension)
de-/dis- (deodorant, disinfection)
proto- (protoplasm)
pseudo- (pseudo-tuberculosis)
re- (reanimation)
sub- (sublimation)
super- (superphosphate)
ultra- (ultraviolet)

а- (аритми́я)
анти- (антиге́н, антибио́тик)
экс- (экскре́ция, эксцентри́ческий)
гипер- (гипертони́я)
де-/дез- (дезодора́нт, дезинфе́кция)
прото- (протопла́зма)
псевдо- (псевдотуберкулёз)
ре- (реанима́ция)
суб- (сублима́ция)
супер- (суперфосфа́т)
ультра- (ультрафиоле́товый)

English suffixes

Russian suffixes су́ффиксы

-age (voltage)
-ant/-ent (mutant, patient)
-ate (sulfate)
-er/-or (computer, regulator)
-ia (diphtheria, schizophrenia)
-ic (diabetic, lunatic)
-ing (turning, swelling)
-ion (inversion)
-y (apathy)
-ist (chemist, catalyst, therapist)

-itis (bronchitis)
-ize (organize)
-ment (enlargement, development)
-tion (evolution, equation, perception)
-osis (dermatosis, osmosis)
-um (factum, calcium)

-аж (вольта́ж)
-ант/-ент (мута́нт, пацие́нт)
-ат (сульфа́т)
-ор/-ер (компью́тер, регуля́тор)
-ит/-ия (дифтери́т, шизофрени́я)
-ик (диабе́тик, луна́тик)
-(н/т)ие (враще́ние, взду́тие)
-ия (инве́рсия)
-ия (апа́тия)
-ик/-изатор/-евт (хи́мик, катализа́тор, терапе́вт)
-ит (бронхи́т)
-из(ир)овать (организова́ть)
-(н/т)ие (увеличе́ние, разви́тие)
-ция (эволю́ция, уравне́ние, восприя́тие)
-оз (дермато́з, but о́смос)
no suffix; often end in *-ий* (фа́кт, ка́льций)

In words that use the prefixes and suffixes just listed, roots tend to be very similar to English and many are easily recognizable. Individual sounds in the roots may have the following correspondences between the English and the Russian spelling, besides the obvious ones:

English		Russian	
ci/cy/ce	(cirrhosis, cycle, cellulose)	ци/це	(цирро́з, цикл, целлюло́за)
ch	(chemistry)	х	(хи́мия)
e	(eczema, nerve)	э/е	(экзе́ма, нерв)
u	(lunatic)	у	(луна́тик)
but: eu	(eugenics)	ев	(евге́ника)
h	(hypnosis)	г	(гипно́з)
or nothing	(rhythm)	—	(ритм)
ph	(physics)	ф	(фи́зика)
th	(thermometer)	т	(термо́метр)
y	(physics)	и	(фи́зика)

Just as people migrate from one country to another, so do words and the ideas behind them. When a language community comes across a new concept, it has two basic choices. It can form a new word in its own language that would render the idea in a sort of natural translation (this method of adapting alien words part for part is called "calquing"). **Водоро́д** for "hydrogen" would be a typical example of calquing: **вод-** stands for "hydr-" and **род-** stands for "gen-." The other option is plain "borrowing." Taking "hydrogen" and calling it **гидроге́н** (which does not exist) in Russian would be a "borrowing" solution. A borrowed word is of course pronounced in a way that fits best with Russian sounds. Languages of the world tend to differ in their preferences for either calquing or borrowing. Russian has historically used both methods, although at some times it gave preference to one or the other. Most of the words using the prefixes and suffixes given above are borrowed rather than calqued. Calqued words, on the other hand, are made of native parts, and the scientific meaning is often the secondary one, as in the case of words like **сопротивле́ние** resistance, **кле́тка** cell, or **усили́тель** amplifier.

It helps to keep this calquing/borrowing distinction in mind, because borrowings from Greek and Latin account for most of the similarities between Russian and English scientific words. It's also useful to keep calquing in mind and to try to take apart lengthy Russian words like **водоро́д** or **сопротивле́ние** while looking for similarly lengthy and complex English correspondences. It's actually worth the trouble developing an eye for this procedure (linguists call it "morphological analysis," which is part of the field of "word-formation" **словообразова́ние**). After a while you will start doing it faster than it takes you to look the word up in a dictionary, and with some imagination and practice your success rate will be surprisingly good.

An Economic Approach To Scientific Vocabulary

Экономный подход к научной лексике

So there are ways to use your imagination and analytical power instead of rote memorization of vocabulary. But here is more help: linguists have found that there are about one thousand words that occur with high frequency in six major scientific fields: mathematics, physics, chemistry, biology, medicine, and geology. These words in text samples totalling 400,000 words occur more often than 10 times[1]. It should obviously be efficient to learn these most frequent words first and foremost, and that is good to know. But actually, the news is even better. Of these thousand some words, more than 10 percent are not native Russian, which means that they should be rather transparent to you if you mobilize your knowledge of the correspondences just explained in section A. Just about 10 percent of the remaining words are short simple words such as **он, из, три, опять** that every student knows by the second month of Russian. What is left are words that were borrowed into science and technology from regular language, or that were calqued from Latin or Greek using Russian roots and pre-/suffixes. Many of them you already may know in their first meaning, from which they have developed a secondary scientific meaning. Now, the best of news is that about 650 native words most frequently used in science are built from only 80 some roots! This means that if you learn one high-frequency root, you have a good chance of figuring out 8 words formed from it. Here's how it works.

Take the root *след-*, which means "trace, track, follow" and corresponds to the Latin root *sequ-/secu-*. With the help of prefixes and suffixes, this root gives birth to a number of words that are among the highest frequency words in scientific contexts:

Prefix	Root	Suffix	Suffix	Suffix	Suffix	Ending	Gloss
ис-	след-	-ова				-ть	to research
ис-	след-	-ова	-ни			-е	research
ис-	след-	-ова	-тель				researcher
по-	след-	-ова	-тель	-н		-ый	consistent
по-	след-	-ова	-тель	-н	-ость		consistency
по-	след-	-ова	-тель	-н		-о	consistently
	след-	-ова	-тель	-н		-о	consequently
	след-	-ств	-и			-е	consequence
	след-	-й				-ть	to watch, follow

Among less frequent words with scientific meaning made from the same root are:

---

[1] The discussion about frequency is based on L.G. Heien's 1980 "Root Frequency in Scientific Russian," *Russian Language Journal* 34 (117): 57–81.

Prefix	Root	Suffix	Suffix	Suffix	Suffix	Ending	Gloss
на-	след-	ств-	енн-	-ость			heredity
по-	след-	ств-	и-			-е	consequence
ис-	след-	ова-	тель-	ск-		-ий	research *adj.*

These words enter longer sequences like **научно-исследовательский/ экспериментáльно-исследовательский (институ́т)** scientific research/experimental research (institute). They also form words that occur in scientific and non-scientific contexts with the same meaning: **след** track, **после́дний** last, **сле́дующий** next, **сле́дует** it follows, **впосле́дствии** later, **сле́довать** to follow, and so forth. This one root supplies 124 words in Russian!

The root *след-* is the 9th most frequent root in scientific contexts. Here are the highest frequency 25 roots occurring in scientific contexts for your reference (the variants are given in parentheses). These 25 roots form about 40 percent of all the high-frequency native words in science[2].

1. **стой- (став-, стан-, стат-)** — stand, -*sist*
2. **ход- (шед-, хожд-, шеств-)** — go, come, pass, -*gress*, -*cede*
3. **лаг- (лёг-, лог-, лож-, леж-)** — lay, -*pose*
4. **дел- (дол-)** — divide, share
5. **им- (ним-, ём-, я-, ня-)** — have, possess, hold, take
6. **вед- (вод-, вес-)** — lead, -*fer*, -*late*, -*duce*, -*duct*
7. **раз- (образ-, рез-, раж-)** — strike, -*press*, -*flect*
8. **каз- (каж-)** — show, indicate
9. **след-** — track, trace, follow, heir, -*sequ*, -*secu*
10. **дай- (дач-, дан-, дат-, дар-)** — give
11. **знай- (знак-, знач-, знам-)** — know, sign, -*cogn*
12. **чит- (чт-, числ-, чёт-)** — count, consider, read

---

[2] The next highest frequency 60 roots in scientific vocabulary are: **полн-, ров- (рав-), серед- (сред-), яв-, верх- (верш-), выс- (выш-), вяз- (яз-), ид- (йд-), ключ-, лёг- (лез-, льз-), мест- (мещ-), мог- (моч-, мож-, мощ-), пад- (пас-), прав-, част-, вел-, вес- (вис-), вет- (веч-), верт- (ворот-, врат-, верет-, вращ-), кол- (колик-, колич-), работ- (раб-, рабоч-), сторон- (стран-), ясн-, бав- (быв-, бый-), близ- (ближ-), бий- (би-), вс- (вес), втор-, двиг- (движ-), зв- (зыв-, зов-), луч- (по-луч-, с-луч-), мет- (меч-), низ- (ниж-), основ-, пис-, род-, ряд- (руд-), сил-, слов-, смотр-, степ- (ступ-), строй-, ток-, треб-, врем(ен)-, рет- (обрет-, встрет-), зд- (зод-), как- (кач-), крой- (крый-, кров-), мен-, ник-, нов-, плоск- (пласт-), пуск- (пуст-), пыт-, рос- (раст-, рост-, рас-), свой-, стриг- (стриж-), цел-, блюд- (буд-)**. If you want to pursue this route further, a list of high-frequency general scientific vocabulary was edited by **Е.М. Степáнова**, in *Частóтный слова́рь общенау́чной лéксики,* 1970. More generally, several root lists are available, including Charles E. Gribble's *Russian Root List,* 1973, on which the form of the roots given above is based; D.S. Worth, A.S. Kozak, and D.B. Johnson, *Russian Derivational Dictionary,* 1970; and **Л.Н. Засóрина**, *Частóтный слова́рь ру́сского языка́,* 1977. The logic of Russian word-formation is explained in Charles Townsend, *Russian Word Formation,* 1975.

13.	вид-	see, view, form, -*spect*
14.	дал- (далёк-, дл-, дол-, долг-, долж-, длин-)	far, long
15.	мен-	change, alter
16.	сут- (сущ-)	being, existence, nature, -*sence, -sent*
17.	ук- (вык-, обыч-, вуч-, уч-)	accustom, learn, habit
18.	дей- (дел-)	do, make, deed, business
19.	мер-	measure
20.	соб- (себ-)	self, own, special
21.	кон- (конц-, конч-)	end, final, limit
22.	один- (един-)	one, single, lone, *uni-, mono-*
23.	ток- (тёк-, теч-, точ-)	flow, current
24.	лич- (лик-, лиц-)	person, face
25.	нос- (нёс-, нош-)	carry, bear, -*pose, -er, -port, -late*

WHERE RUSSIAN SCIENTIFIC VOCABULARY HAS COME FROM

ОТКУ́ДА ПРИШЛИ́ В РУ́ССКИЙ ЯЗЫ́К НАУ́ЧНЫЕ СЛОВА́

The oldest stratum of the most basic scientific vocabulary in any language is native. These are mostly simple words for basic substances (water **вода́**), animals (bear **медве́дь**), anatomical terms (head **голова́**), heavenly bodies (star **звезда́**) or plants (oak **дуб**). In fact, these words don't even strike us as particularly scientific: they are usually considered part of our general "encyclopedic" knowledge, rather than our scientific knowledge. At the dawn of linguistic activity, every linguistic community came up with these words on its own because people encountered these objects in their daily experience and needed to refer to them.

Mankind's conceptualization of the physical world began to go beyond the obvious at different rates in different cultures. So when the ancient Greeks came up with the idea of the smallest indivisible bits of substance of which the physical world consists, using terms like ἄ-τομος "indivisible" (ἀ = non, τομος = cutting), all other cultures on the European continent, including the Slavs, were still busy doing less speculative things. They had all the words they needed for hunting bears and making clay pots, and didn't bother with atoms. Only eventually, when the idea of atoms traveled to these other cultures and began to seem relevant, did they begin to need a word for this concept that originated with the Greeks. These languages were then faced with the choice of calquing or borrowing. For the Greek ἄτομος, both Russian and English chose borrowing. They simply took the Greek word and pronounced it in a way that fit in with the rest of their respective languages. (Naturally, they also wrote the word using their own alphabets, rather than the Greek alphabet.) Since the ancient Greeks came up with many scientific concepts much earlier than most other peoples in Europe, other European languages ended up calquing or borrowing these concepts from Greek, either directly, or via their neighbors (who may have taken them from *their* neighbors) who in turn took them directly from the Greeks. When the choice was borrowing (rather than calquing), the words were rather similar in all these languages, and this is why the words **хромосóма** and *chromosome* are so similar in Russian and English.

The Greeks were not pioneers in every scientific field, and in any case they passed on a great deal of their culture to the Romans, who developed some areas still further. During the Renaissance—that is, the time when ancient Greek and Latin writings were rediscovered, studied, and translated—European scholarly tradition developed the habit of using the classical vocabulary of both Greek and Latin. This tradition is so well established that even computer hackers today speak of "cyberspace," a term based on the Greek sequence *cyber-* and the Latin word *spatium*. I have heard Russians in Moscow call it **киберпрострáнство**. This word is probably a calque straight from English, but it has not escaped the influence of Greek and Latin: its first part **кибер-** is Greek-based, and its second part **про-стрáн-ств-о**, although it looks Russian, is actually a calque from the Latin-based word *ex-panse*.

The earliest scientific words came into Old Russian directly from Greek, and most of them were calqued. But since the need for scientific vocabulary was not too great through the middle ages, the impact of such words on the language was minimal. It was in the 18th century that a dramatic influx of scientific vocabulary into Russian began. In the early part of that century, the influence of German—some of it via Polish—was considerable. Many of these words originally came into German from Latin. Germans tended to use the calquing method, and until the mid-19th century Russians did, too. For example, the German medical and psychological term *Selbstgefühl (selbst + Gefühl)* was calqued into Russian as **самочýвствие (сам + чувств-)** "general physical and mental state as felt by the person involved." Similarly, the German word *feuerfest (feuer + fest)* "fire-resistant" came out in Russian as **огнеупóрный (огóнь + упорн-)**, part for part corresponding to the German adjective.

The earliest record of the word **огнеупóрный** appears in a Russian chemistry textbook of 1788. This textbook, which was actually translated from French, also contained many calques from Latin, such as **насы́щенный** saturated, **перегóнка** distillation and **возгóнка** sublimation. Chemistry was introduced into Russia by the 18th century Russian "Renaissance man" **Ломонóсов**, who himself calqued many terms. Because calquing was the preferred method of introducing scientific words into Russian at this time, early modern scientific concepts like hydrogen **водорóд** or oxygen **кислорóд** usually sound like authentic Russian words. The situation is very different with most "younger" elements in the periodic table **периоди́ческая систéма хими́ческих элемéнтов** (or, informally, **табли́ца Менделéева**): for example, plutonium or radon come out in Russian as **плутóний** and **радóн**.

Importing words into Russian without calquing them also took place to some extent in the 18th century, and by the 1830s this method took over. The actual sequence of events behind the incorporation of scientific vocabulary could, of course, sometimes be quite complicated. The Latin-based word **фа́ктор** "factor," for example, was imported twice. First, it entered Russian in the early 18th century from Polish, which got it from Latin via German. At that time the word was not a scientific concept: it meant something like "doer," and was used to refer to merchants, attorneys and other professional "doers." By the mid-19th century, the word had re-entered as a mathematical term, this time from France, where it was used as such (*facteur*). By the 1880s, the mathematical meaning of **фа́ктор** had established itself in Russian in the non-scientific abstract meaning it has today, roughly "something that contributes to a result." This sort of detective work about word histories, performed by historical linguists, has unearthed many complex stories like this one.

With the popularization of the natural sciences in Europe, scientific concepts belonging to "hot" fields of scientific inquiry no longer remained within strictly scientific borders. By the middle of the 19th century, a notable change in the vocabulary of Russian intelligentsia had taken place. Words from mathematics, mechanics **меха́ника**, astronomy, and chemistry, and later from physics **фи́зика**, biology **биоло́гия** and medicine **медици́на**, first entered Russian journalistic prose, and from there they crossed over in significant numbers into the spoken and written language of educated people, and finally into literature. A gentleman in Anna Karenina complains about a takeover by journals, which replaced classical humanistic education for people of a relatively underprivileged background who wanted to obtain an education. These journals, he says, tell the reader that society is simply determined by Darwinian principles: *ничего́ нет, évolution, подбо́р, борьба́ за существова́ние—и всё* (there is nothing, just "évolution," selection, struggle for existence, and that's that). Notice that this gentleman must have pronounced the word for "évolution" with a French accent, suggesting that—never mind Darwin—the word came to Russia via France. By the end of the 19th century, familiarity with scientific words meant being an educated person. Among the scientific words that had become common by that time were:

фа́ктор	factor	**аго́ния**	agony
и́мпульс	impulse	**акклиматиза́ция**	acclimatization
зени́т	zenith	**баци́лла**	bacillus
сфе́ра	sphere	**атрофи́я**	atrophy
ине́рция	inertia	**органи́зм**	organism
апоге́й	apogee	**кристаллиза́ция**	crystallization
при́зма	prism	**эмбрио́н**	embryo
до́за	dose	**симпто́м**	symptom

Besides separate words, whole phrases migrated from science into the literary language at this time, such as:

Fig. 12-1.   "Unnatural selection"

безвозду́шное простра́нство	vacuum
це́нтр тя́жести	center of gravity
звезда́ пе́рвой величины́	a star of the first magnitude
уравне́ние со мно́гими неизве́стными	an equation with many unknowns
есте́ственный отбо́р	natural selection

After the October Revolution, the emphasis shifted. Among the sciences, physics, biology, chemistry, space science **космона́втика** and, more recently, information science **информа́тика** and technology **техноло́гия** have been the "hot" fields (not counting social sciences, in particular, **нау́чный коммуни́зм** scientific communism, which enjoyed official support through the 1980s). Here are some examples of words assimilated from these fields:

запрограмми́рованный	pre-programmed	**амортиза́ция**	amortization
ва́куум	vacuum	**цепна́я реа́кция**	chain reaction
алгори́тм	algorithm	**нака́л**	incandescence
выводи́ть на орби́ту	to put into orbit	**эпице́нтр**	epicenter
ви́рус	virus		

The most recent imports, including many words belonging to technology rather than science *per se*, are from English. (The English source words, like the French ones, are in turn largely based on Greek and Latin.) Words like **байт, банк да́нных, ба́за да́нных, файл, интерфе́йс, дисппле́й, дигита́йзер, пло́ттер** or **при́нтер** were imported more or less as is, that is without calquing. In the last decade of the 20th century, after the disintegration of the Soviet

Union, this English-based computer terminology represents perhaps the most rapidly spreading scientific vocabulary. These words are no less frequent among young Russian users **ю́зеры** than are their transparent equivalents in America. (The calquing option for "user" **по́льзователь** is standard and used by those over 30.) Some scientific concepts that previously were narrowly specialized have also been gaining in currency, because of the recent availability of household technology, such as microwave ovens **микроволно́вые пе́чи**,[3] and the accessibility of health and body care products, among other results of a market economy. Liberalization also opened up certain previously unmentionable topics, increasing the usage of Latin-/Greek-based medical terms like **эвтана́зия**, **орга́зм**, **генита́лии**, or **ко́итус,** which are all easily mappable back into English using the correspondences listed in Section B above.

How Scientific Words Changed Their Role in Russian	Как меня́лась роль нау́чных слов в ру́сском языке́

The scientific words that came into the language before the October Revolution now have a different flavor from those that came in after 1917. For this reason, scientific vocabulary in Russian at the end of the 20th century is a complex mixture of different implications and effects. Educated native speakers sense the nuances of these words and expressions without necessarily knowing their actual history the way a historical linguist would. To compensate for the absence of this intuition, it may be helpful for non-native speakers explicitly to examine the changing role of scientific vocabulary in the linguistic and cultural history of the last two centuries.

In the second half of the 19th century, when scientific concepts were still something of a novelty for the intelligentsia, using a scientific metaphor was an elegant thing to do. Among educated people, familiarity with scientific ideas fashionable at the time made it possible to achieve efficient and eloquent formulations of non-scientific matters. This is how another gentleman in *Anna Karenina* «**А́нна Каре́нина**», when asked to explain what the local electoral system was all about, defined it: **Упа́вшее учрежде́ние, продолжа́ющее своё движе́ние то́лько по си́ле ине́рции** (A fallen institution continuing its motion solely due to inertia). The part after "institution" could have been lifted straight from a physics textbook. In fact, Tolstoy himself seems to have had a weak spot for scientific concepts when philosophizing about history, as he does in his epilogue to *War and Peace* «**Война́ и мир**», or about art and humanistic values, as in *What is Art?* «**Что тако́е иску́сство?**» These pages are full of terms from mathematics, biology, physics, and other natural sciences.

Ivan Karamazov, one of the brothers in Dostoevsky's famous novel, uses imagery and metaphors from natural science when he talks about a moral and highly emotional issue—the suffering of children—in his famous revolt against God:

---

[3] Often abbreviated to **микроволно́вка** but formally, **свч-печи**.

🔊 12-1 **Слу́шай меня́: я взял одни́х де́ток, для того́, что́бы вы́шло оче-
ви́днее. Об остальны́х слеза́х челове́ческих, кото́рыми пропи́тана
вся земля́ от коры́ до це́нтра,—я уж ни сло́ва не говорю́, и те́му
мою́ наро́чно су́зил. Я клоп и признаю́ со всем приниже́нием, что
ничего́ не могу́ поня́ть, для чего́ всё так устро́ено. Лю́ди са́ми,
зна́чит, винова́ты: им был дан рай, они́ захоте́ли свобо́ды и
похи́тили ого́нь с небеси́, са́ми зна́я, что ста́нут несча́стны, зна́чит
не́чего их жале́ть. О, по моему́, по жа́лкому, земно́му эвкли́дов-
скому уму́ моему́, я зна́ю лишь то, что страда́ние есть, что вино́в-
ных нет, что всё одно́ из друго́го выхо́дит пря́мо и про́сто, что всё
течёт и уравнове́шивается, но ведь это лишь эвкли́довская дичь,
ведь я зна́ю же э́то, ведь жить по ней я не могу́ же согласи́ться!**

Listen to me: I took only little children, to make it more evident.
About the rest of human tears, which soak Earth from its cortex to its
center, I don't say a word, I narrowed my topic on purpose. I am a
bedbug and I admit in all humility that I can't understand anything,
why all this is set up the way it is. So it's people's own fault: they were
given paradise, they wanted freedom and they stole fire from heaven
knowing perfectly well that they'd become miserable, so there's no
being sorry for them. Oh, I know, my miserable, earthly Euclidean
mind knows that, simply, suffering *is*, that no one is at fault, that all
things come out of one another plain and simple, that everything flows
and evens out, but this is all Euclidean nonsense, I know that, don't I?
And I can't accept life on these terms, can I?!

Give Ivan's agitated speech another reading to see where his words come from.
Do you see the linguistic "strings" attaching his cognitive universe to non-
Euclidean geometry, to the Bible, to the ancient Greeks? Members of the intelligentsia of Ivan's time had control over all this heterogeneous vocabulary and
loved using it.

After the October Revolution, the influx of scientific terms took a different
route. Instead of spreading through the intelligentsia and acquiring an intellectual ring, the language of science and—increasingly—technology became an
ideological tool and was forcibly spread into the masses. Lenin's famous motto
Коммуни́зм есть сове́тская власть плюс электрифика́ция всей страны́
(Communism means Soviet power plus the electrification of the entire country)
is a typical case in point. This eight-word sentence contains three scientific
words, if we count "communism," a scientific term from Marxist economics; the
other two are **плюс** and **электрифика́ция**, a term from mathematics and one
from industrial technology. The phrase became a national slogan, and the un-
wieldy foreign word **электрифика́ция** was so fashionable for a while that some
baby girls in the 1920s and 1930s were named **Электрифика́ция**. Equally
striking is the presence of the verb **есть** "is" which is used in the present tense

Fig. 12-2.

only in scientific definitions; it makes this political statement sound scientifically indisputable, in fact, axiomatic.

As the new post-revolutionary priorities became established in the language, the cult of ideology, science and technology was systematically enforced so as to replace traditional humanistic values and religion. A 1930 poster from the cover of the Leningrad magazine **Ревизо́р** is telling: the new Soviet man, a worker solidly planted in the soil with his thick legs, holds an industrial vacuum cleaner **пылесо́с** which sucks in all the dust of the centuries **пыль веко́в**: icons, petit bourgeois canary cages, books, records, flowers, and so forth. The picture is entitled **Электрифика́ция бы́та** The Electrification of Daily Life.

Forced to go along with the tide, but partly also genuinely enthusiastic about the new order and its linguistic possibilities, some poets and writers of the early Soviet era began to incorporate the language of science into their artistic creations. The poet **Блок** wrote in 1918, three years before his death, in his poem **«Ски́фы»** "Scythians":

Иди́те все, иди́те на Ура́л!
Мы очища́ем ме́сто бо́ю
Стальны́х маши́н, где ды́шит интегра́л,
С монго́льской ди́кою ордо́ю!

🔊 12-2

Everybody go, go to the Urals!
We are clearing the space for the battle.
Between steel machines, in which the integral breathes,
And the wild Mongolian hordes.

Despite—or rather because of—its rather obscure semantics, the word **интегра́л** was apparently fashionable among poets and writers. The writer (and engineer) Evgenii Zamiatin **Евге́ний Замя́тин** used it, too, as the name of the futuristic space ship in his 1920 science fiction anti-utopian novel **«Мы»** *We*. This is how the first chapter of the novel starts:

🔊)) **12-3**   Я про́сто спи́сываю — сло́во в сло́во — то, что сего́дня напеча́тано в Госуда́рственной Газе́те:

"Че́рез 120 дней зака́нчивается постро́йка ИНТЕГРА́ЛА. Бли́зок вели́кий, истори́ческий час, когда́ пе́рвый ИНТЕГРА́Л взовьётся в мирово́е простра́нство. Ты́сячу лет тому́ наза́д ва́ши герои́ческие пре́дки покори́ли вла́сти Еди́ного Госуда́рства весь земно́й шар. Вам предстои́т ещё бо́лее сла́вный по́двиг: стекля́н-ным, электри́ческим, огнеды́шащим ИНТЕГРА́ЛОМ проинте-гри́ровать бесконе́чное уравне́ние вселе́нной."

In 120 days the construction of INTEGRÁL is scheduled to be finished. The great, historic moment when the first INTEGRÁL shoots up into space is approaching. A thousand years ago your heroic ancestors conquered the whole globe and put it under the rule of the One State. You are about to accomplish a feat no less glorious: the integration of the infinite equation of the universe with the help of this glass, electric and fire-spitting INTEGRÁL.

The people referred to as "We," that is the citizens of an Orwellian anti-utopian state, continue to build the **ИНТЕГРА́Л** throughout the novel.

It is typical for science fiction to mention fancy scientific and technological words. In fact, science fiction was one of the reasons why scientific and even technological vocabulary retained an intellectual ring and literary potential even in 20th century Russian. Quality science fiction by authors like the Strugatsky Brothers **Бра́тья Струга́цкие** through the 20th century has served to raise the status of scientific vocabulary as literary material. The tendency to use science and technology in literature was obvious, however, in all literary genres of the post-revolutionary period. A short story by **Замя́тин**, **«Наводне́ние»** "Flood" (1930), starts like this:

🔊)) **12-4**   Круго́м Васи́льевского О́строва далёким мо́рем лежа́л мир: там была́ война́, пото́м револю́ция. А в коте́льной у Трофи́ма Ива́ныча котёл гуде́л всё так же, мано́метр пока́зывал все те же де́вять атмосфе́р.

Beyond Vasilevsky Island, across the far sea, was the world. That's where there was a war, then a revolution. But in the boiler room where Trofim Ivanych worked, the boiler hummed as usual, and the manometer showed the same nine atmospheres.

A major force in the effort to put scientific and technological vocabulary into poetry—the most "literary" form of literature—was Mayakovsky **Маяко́вский**, arguably the most visible poet of the post-revolutionary decade.

Wildly innovative, he militantly demanded that poetry renew itself so as to fit the new era. To write poetry, he said, a poet must be at home, among other things, with the history of science. In his theoretical articles, he drew parallels between poetry and mathematics, and compared the process of book publishing and distribution to electric stations, transmitting stations, and electric light bulbs. He attacked the old rules of versification and the old, well-established meters of poetry, like iambic meter. As he said in his 1923 poem «О поэтах» "About Poets," one problem with iambic meter was that its "ta TA ta TA …" alternation of stressed and unstressed syllables could not accommodate many long words, like the 8-syllable word **млекопита́ющееся**:

А попро́буй
в ямб
пойди́ и запихни́
како́е-нибудь сло́во,
наприме́р, "млекопита́ющееся".

◀))) 12-5

But try / and stick / into iambic meter / some word / like "mammal."

It is characteristic that Mayakovsky picked this rather unpoetic word as a word that needs to be accommodated by poetry. (Actually, he used a substandard form for "mammal": the correct word does not have the reflexive suffix -**ся**.) Here are excerpts from two more of his poems in which he theorizes about poetry and poets, and uses images, metaphors and a simile that would have been inconceivable only a decade earlier.

Огро́мный труд—горе́ть над го́рном,
желе́за шипя́щие класть в зака́л.
Но кто же
в безде́льи бро́сит уко́р нам?
Мозги́ шлифу́ем ра́шпилем языка́.
Кто вы́ше—поэ́т
и́ли те́хник,
кото́рый
ведёт люде́й к веще́ственной вы́годе?
О́ба.
Сердца́—таки́е ж мото́ры.
Душа́—тако́й же хи́трый дви́гатель.
    (from "The Worker-Poet" «Поэ́т рабо́чий», 1918)

◀))) 12-6

Gigantic labor it is to burn over the furnace, / to put hissing irons to be tempered. / But who is there / to accuse us of idleness? / We polish brains with the rasp of language. / Who is higher, the poet / or the technician / who leads people to material profit? / Both are. / Hearts are just the same as motors. / A soul is just the same as an intricate engine.

Note that the plural form **желе́за** "irons" is a usage that actually belongs to industrial jargon: in the literary language, the word is not used in the plural in this meaning.

🔊 **12-7**   **Поэ́зия—та же добы́ча ра́дия.**
В грамм добы́ча,
                    в год труды́.
Изво́дишь
           еди́ного сло́ва ра́ди
ты́сячи тонн
           слове́сной руды́.
(from **«Разгово́р с фининспе́ктором о поэ́зии»** "A Conversation with a Tax Collector about Poetry," 1926)

Poetry is just the same as radium mining. / To extract a gram of it / takes years of labor. / You waste / for one word / thousands of tons / of verbal ore.

Mayakovsky was very well-published during the Soviet era, and his influence in promoting scientific and especially technological vocabulary as the "verbal ore" from which poetry was "manufactured" extended far beyond poetry. Scientific and technological jargon flooded the works of pedestrian authors who cranked out hefty volumes of so-called "industrial novels" **произ-во́дственные рома́ны**, published in the millions of copies for consumption by those who only recently had learned how to read and write. The massive liquidation of illiteracy in post-revolutionary Russia went hand in hand with this new vocabulary. Without mastering the Russian literary language of the 19th century classics, millions of newly-literate Russians felt that their being able to use scientific and technological vocabulary (whether they understood it or not) was a sign of being educated, and it gave them a new sense of dignity. In the 1924 story **«Пацие́нтка»** "The Patient" by Zoshchenko **Зо́щенко**, a former peasant returns home from the capital and tells his wife Pelageia that he is now a deputy of the Soviet government. This is how Pelageia recounts his words:

🔊 **12-8**   **Ох, говори́т, Пелаге́я, така́я-то ты есть. Тёмная, говори́т, ты у меня́, Пелаге́я Макси́мовна. Про что, говори́т, я с тобо́й тепе́рь разгова́ривать бу́ду? Я, говори́т, челове́к просвещённый и депута́т сове́тский. Я, говори́т, мо́жет, четы́ре пра́вила арифме́тики наскво́зь зна́ю. Дробь, говори́т, уме́ю … А ты, говори́т, вон кака́я! Небо́сь, говори́т, и фами́лию не мо́жешь подпи́сывать на бума́ге?**

Oh, Pelageia, he says, so this is what you're like. You are ignorant, my dear lady Pelageia, he says. What would I now talk with you about? I, he says, am an enlightened man and a Soviet deputy. For me, he says, the four rules of arithmetic are practically a snap. I can do fractions, he says … And you, look at what you're like! I bet you can't even sign your name on paper, can you?

When later in 1932 Stalin called writers the "engineers of human souls" **инженéры человéческих душ**, this was a command from on high to continue shaping the minds of people like Pelageia and her husband.

Becoming literate and knowing how to do fractions and arithmetic is of course not the same as becoming educated in science. But the thinning ranks of intelligentsia survivors from before the revolution were gradually supplemented by a new class of broadly educated science students, who read the classics of Russian literature, learned foreign languages, and valued humanistic experience. Theoretically-oriented, difficult, and especially foreign scientific terms or phrases like **ортогонáльный** orthogonal, **герметѝчный** hermetic, **энтропѝя** entropy, **протоплáзма** protoplasm, or **вторóй закóн термодинáмики** the second law of thermodynamics naturally came to be perceived as intellectual, and entered the literary language of the new intelligentsia. Technological and industrial terms from applied science or vocational training, especially those based on native roots using native suffixes and prefixes (such as **отдáча** recoil/kick, **накáл** incandescence, or **вáлка** felling), came to be perceived as slangy and low style, as a result of their association with the language of the lower-ranking work force. Nevertheless, the continuous mixing of social classes, both through compulsory military service for all males and through the massive gulag experience of the totalitarian era, has served as a lasting route for introducing industrial vocabulary into the lexicon of the intelligentsia, and especially the language of men.

В дерéвнях наблюдáется мáссовое стремлéние жéнщин к грáмоте. "There is a mass movement toward literacy among women in the countryside."

Пахóм (в тщéтном ожидáнии обéда): —Ну што, Пелагéя ... Как щи-то?

Пелагéя (в просветлённом самозабвéнии): —Как? Очéнно дáже прóсто. «Ща» да «и» —тóлько и всегó. Постóй, сейчáс напишý ...

Pakhom (anxiously awating dinner) says: Well, Pelageia, how's the soup?

Pelageia (lost in thought): How? Very simple. "Shcha" and "I," and that's all there is. Just a minute, I'll write it down for you."

Fig. 12-3.   N. Radlov. From the news paper "New Life" (1923) **Нóвый бы̀т**

How Educated Non-specialist Russians Use Scientific Words Now

Как образо́ванные ру́сские неспециали́сты испо́льзуют сейча́с нау́чную ле́ксику

When two specialists "talk shop" about their job, an outsider can hardly follow them. This is true in any language, and Russian is no exception. When non-specialists talk or write about topics related to potentially scientific issues, they naturally use some scientific vocabulary that is called for by the topic. A lot of this usage occurs when talking about the weather, pets, children, health problems, vacation travel, the household, the job environment, or news events. There is no easy way to arm oneself against all possible occasions of this sort, except by developing skill in morphological analysis and memorizing roots and pre-/suffixes. Scientific words that one is likely to encounter in non-specialist usage are given in the Appendix.

Scientific and technological words and expressions have several functions and effects, depending on the words themselves, on the kind of context, and on the people using them and their relationship to each other. At the threshold of the 21st century, the language of the intelligentsia reflects all the historical pushes and pulls against and towards scientific and technological vocabulary discussed in the preceding sections. Words assimilated before the October Revolution are used in distant, formal and polite discourse to raise the level of speech style. Some of them are no longer perceived to be particularly scientific, but just intellectual.

More recently imported and relatively unassimilated scientific words (mostly of foreign origin) carry a connotation of scientific reliability about them. They imply that the speaker is broadly educated and sufficiently informed to be conversant with scientific concepts. These words are used in their first scientific meaning in formal settings or when talking to someone to whom one does not feel close. That the exact meaning of these words may be obscure to the users or to the addressees, makes them more prestigious. These words may also be used metaphorically. A member of a new profession "personality designer" **диза́йнер челове́ка** (a counselor who gives advice on philosophical and psychological problems of lifestyle), in her interview on a television talk show in 1995, used phrases like **эсте́то-терапи́я—выра́внивание психи́ческого состоя́ния** (esthetotherapy means balancing of psychological condition), **всё прохо́дит че́рез медитати́вное простра́нство** (everything passes through a meditative space), **прохо́д че́рез анализа́тор** (passage through an organ of sense perception), **напра́вить ве́ктор движе́ния к зри́телю** (to direct the vector of motion towards the viewer).

The speaker who feels that the word is unclear might even provide explanations to make the point. For example, the speaker may say **Са́ша—челове́к жёсткой фокусиро́вки, это, зна́ешь, когда́ электро́ны мча́тся в ускори́теле с большо́й ско́ростью, но не уклоня́ясь. Вот он то́же всегда́ по́лон э́той стра́шной эне́ргии, всегда́ мчи́тся к це́ли.** (Sasha is a man of hard focus. You know, when electrons spin in the accelerator with high speed but stay on course. So he is also always full of this awesome energy, always running towards his goal).

The most recently naturalized words, such as the technological concepts involved in the language of computer users and in consumer culture, have so far been limited to corresponding topics—they have not yet been used metaphorically. Similarly, Latin-/Greek-based medical terms used to discuss formerly unmentionable topics are so far used only in their original definitions. It will be interesting to see when, if ever, Russians begin to feel uninhibited enough about such words to follow more relaxed practices, such as naming a super-rich chocolate brownie a **шоколáдный оргáзм** (as do some gourmet bakeries in America). The new discipline of ecology **экология**, on the other hand, has become very fashionable during the past few years, and the word is used metaphorically in many combinations, including some that seem rather inappropriate from the point of view of the original scientific definition of the term: **экология жúзни** ecology of life; **душú** of the soul; **лúчности** of a/the person; **дýха** of spirit; **мýзыки** of music; **языкá** of language. There is even a new houseware store in Moscow named **Экология быта**.[4]

Choosing the non-scientific word over the scientific one in cases where there are doublets also usually shows that the speaker feels close to the addressee and that the conversation is casual. For example, when the speaker chooses to say the words in the left column below rather than those in the right column, the effect is comparable to that in English:

укóл	shot	**инъéкция**	injection
скрýтый	hidden	**латéнтный**	latent
сáмый лýчший	best	**оптимáльный**	optimal
óпухоль	swelling	**отёчность**	edema
вшúвость	being full of lice	**педикулёз**	lice-infestation

Scientific words may be used for fun, something which is typical of colloquial Russian **рýсская разговóрная речь**.[5] Because they are in principle out of place in a relaxed atmosphere among friends, such words are effective in introducing humor. A mildly humorous usage of the mathematical idiom **что и трéбовалось доказáть** "Q.E.D." is a way to conclude a heated discussion **спор** after producing what was meant to be an irrefutable argument. The fun is usually magnified if scientific words are used in the same sentence along with

---

[4] I am grateful to Vera Khokhlova for bringing this store name to my attention.

[5] The actual vernacular used by the Russian intelligentsia began to be recorded and described only in the 1960s. Since then, the work has been carried out by a group of Russian linguists **Зéмская**, **Капанáдзе**, **Китайгорóдская**, **Крýсин**, **Панóв**, and **Рóзанова**, among others, who have produced a huge body of data, as well as analyzed it. I draw on their recordings in several instances in this chapter. For more details, see E.A. Zemskaia, **«Русская разговорная речь»**, 1973.

solemn archaisms or other elements unusual for relaxed conversation. Sentences like the following, actually recorded in Moscow by the linguists cited in footnote 13, deserve special appreciation:

Го́лос у него́ гро́мкий, потому́ что дециба́лов у него́ хвата́ет.

His voice is loud, because he's got enough decibels.

Я с шизофрени́ей от млады́х ногте́й канту́юсь.

I've been fooling around with schizophrenia since my salad days.

The first of these sentences is moderately funny because referring to decibels in such a trivial context is somewhat inappropriate, and the whole second clause is really tautological. The second sentence is even more creative because the clash is more drastic, and actually involves a triple contrast: in this single short sentence we find the medical Greek-based term **шизофрени́я**, the Old Church Slavonic-based idiom **от млады́х ногте́й** (literally meaning "since the days when (my) nails were young," and first attested in Old Russian in the 12th century), and the 20th century slang **кантова́ться**. It is not surprising that from the point of view of many Americans "Russian humor" is notoriously unfunny: a good deal of it involves untranslatable linguostylistic play of the sort just seen, deeply rooted in cultural and historical associations carried by Russian vocabulary.

Some technical jargon based on Russian roots is often used in the speech of the intelligentsia precisely because such words lend a connotation of roughness. They can add a somewhat macho colloquial flavor, and in this usage they occur in informal speech between people who feel close to each other, as in the case of the following phrase about the Russian Parliament[6]: **Éсли они́ э́тот зако́н при́мут, они́ вру́бят спусково́й механи́зм стра́шной си́лы** (If they pass this law, they will mortise in/turn on a trigger mechanism of awesome power). The industrial term **вруби́ть** "to push something into a space that has been cut out for it," which further gave rise to the slangy meaning of "turning on," in combination with the military technological expression **спусково́й механи́зм стра́шной си́лы** make the statement both macho and informal. The speaker was male. (More below on male/female speech distinctions.)

Word play may be based not only on whole words but also on parts of them (that is, on morphemes). Scientific vocabulary plays a special role here as well. Adding the archaic and elevated suffix **-иня** (as in **княги́ня** princess or **боги́ня** goddess) to foreign-born names of scholarly disciplines provides a humorous but slighting way to refer to a woman specialist in that discipline: **геологи́ня** female geologist, **метеорологи́ня** female meteorologist, **филологи́ня** female philologist. Such words are typically used in colloquial Russian, and almost exclusively by men. Following the productive scientific word-formation pattern of **микроцефа́л** microcephalic person, **микроко́см** microcosm, **микрово́льт** microvolt, and **античасти́ца** antiparticle, **антивещество́** antimatter, **антипрото́н**

---

[6] This phrase was recorded by **Зе́мская**, **Китайгоро́дская**, and **Ро́занова**.

antiproton, **антителá** antibodies, high-frequency prefixes like **микро-** a n d **анти-** serve to make many spontaneous and humorous new words, such as **микропáльчики** microfingers, **микроплéчики** microshoulders/microhangers, **антидóм** antihouse, and even **анти-Кóля** anti-Kolya. If someone says **Я егó не люблю́, он анти-Кóля** (I don't like him—he's an anti-Kolya), this means that the person in question does not have all the wonderful qualities Kolya has, or in other words, "He's the opposite of Kolya." These prefixes are also used to form plain non-scientific and not particularly funny words like **антигерóй** antihero, **антирекá** anti-river (a river that is artificially made to flow against its original direction), **микрофи́льм** microfilm, **микроройль** baby grand piano, and so forth.

One of the funnier uses of scholarly suffixes in colloquial Russian involves the creation of spontaneous neologisms for the names of diseases. Here is a conversation between two friends recorded in Moscow:

—У тебя́ нет остеохондрóза?   🔊)) 12-9
—И хандрóз, и хандри́т, и всё на свéте.

"Maybe you have osteochondrosis?"
  "I have chandrosis, and chandritis, and everything else in the world."

Because according to Russian sound rules the third unstressed "o" in **остеохондрóза** must be pronounced as if it were an "a," the ailing friend chooses to jocularly interpret the second half of the disease name as if it were spelled with "a" rather than with "o," that is, as **-хандрóз**. The word **хандрá**, however, means something completely different from the meaning of the root **хондр-**. **Хандрá** is a slangy Russian word that means "the blues," while the **хондр-** that appears in the friend's question is from the Greek root *chondr-*, meaning "cartilage." After intentionally misinterpreting **хондр-** cartilage as **хандр-** blues, the ailing friend adds to **хандр-** first one and then another of the two suffixes that are generally recognized to form disease names in medical vocabulary, **-оз** -osis and **-ит** -itis. The result is a self-ironic, evasive, and quite funny statement about being depressed on account of suffering from a host of unspecified ailments.

This particular kind of word-play has produced a funny fixed phrase **хи́триус симуля́нтиус**, an untranslatable 20th century fake-Latin formation which means "taking a sick leave/day when one is not sick." The first word is based on the Russian root **хитр-** cunning, and the second one on the noun **симуля́нт** simulator, formed from a foreign-born (in fact, ultimately Latin-based) verb **симули́ровать** to simulate. The Latin-looking suffixes are of course the main ingredients responsible for imparting the pseudo-medical flavor that makes the phrase particularly funny, given its meaning.

The Marxist canon also gets parodied in colloquial speech. When something is lost, stolen, or otherwise unlawfully appropriated, one might solemnly say, tongue in cheek: **Вéщи не исчезáют, они́ тóлько перехóдят из одни́х рук** в другие (Things do not disappear, they only get transferred from some hands to others). This is a mock version of one of the tenets of dialectic materialism: Материя не исчезает, она переходит из одного состояния в другое (Matter does not disappear, it only changes from one state into another). The original idea of permanency of physical entities goes back to the Greeks, and the modern concept of the conservation of mass goes back to Lavoisier and Lomonosov before him. Engels and Marx adopted the idea as one of the bases of dialectal materialism.

In the media today, the treatment of scientific and technical terms in articles that deal with specialized topics has been inconsistent, ranging from the indiscriminate and unapologetic overloading of a story with specialized terms, to the use of parenthetical explanations of technical material provided for lay readers. In articles that deal with non-scientific topics, figurative usages are common. In the context of complaining about a failure on the part of the authorities to provide information about an accident, a 1995 *Izvestia* «Известия» article says, for example: Информационный вакуум мог заполнить только один человек в области—губернатор (The informational vacuum could be filled in only by one man in the region, the governor). In another article on the same page of Izvestia, entitled «Постчеченский синдром аукается на наших улицах» (Post-Chechen Syndrome Echoes in Our Streets; note the non-medical use of the term "syndrome"), the author talks about the suppression of information by the military authorities: Сами свидетельства солдат, не профильтрованные в армейских штабах, мягко говоря, не стыкуются с официальными рапортами высших армейских чинов (The soldiers' testimony that has not been filtered by army headquarters, to put it mildly, does not agree with the official reports by the senior army officials). Note here the non-chemical usage of профильтрованные filtered.

Science-based expressions like these are not unusual even in articles about art or literature. In an issue of «Сегодня» from 1994, the Russian Association of Filmmakers is called абсолютно консервативная и термоядерная сила an absolutely conservative and thermonuclear power; pre-Perestroika literary criticism is described as размышления по отработанным алгоритмам ideas that follow well-established algorithms; and an ideologically prejudicial interpretation of a poet is criticized as leading к вивисекции организма поэта to a vivisection of the poet's organism.

Open any Russian newspaper today and you will find many similar examples of the figurative usage of scientific words and concepts; you will also find them in fiction, although the death of the industrial novel has led to a decrease in the frequency of technological jargon in literary prose. Scientific words are basically used in literature now in the same way they are used in real life: literally in suitable contexts, metaphorically between adults who are not close, and playfully between those who are close. They no longer appear, for the most part, in poetry.

In both direct and figurative usages of scientific concepts, Russian men and women operate differently, which makes cross-gender generalizations about this sort of Russian speech behavior somewhat inaccurate. When talking about matters potentially technical or scientific, men use relatively more precise technical terms, while women express the same ideas in a more pre-scientific, encyclopedic way. Here are some typical examples:[7]

Wife:	**Там тако́е тёмное пя́тнышко. Ну там элеме́нты каки́е-то потекли́.**	◀)) 12-10
Husband:	**Да, жи́дкие криста́ллы.**	

"There is a small dark spot here. Ugh, some elements ran."
   "Yeah, liquid crystals."

Wife:	**Ну вот, я перо́ (для поду́шек) всё вы́сушила на бал-ко́не. Тепе́рь бы прожа́рить его́ хороше́нько. Мо́жет, над плито́й пове́сить?**	◀)) 12-10
Husband:	**Ты зна́ешь, не сове́тую. Там же оста́тки са́жевых час-ти́ц, углеводоро́ды. Они́ же возгоня́ются, испаря́ются, попада́ют на хо́лод, всё там бу́дет.**	

"Well, here, I've dried all the feathers [for pillows] on the balcony. It'd be good now to heat them through well. Maybe I should hang them over the stove?"
   "You know, I don't advise it. There are remnants of soot particles there, after all, carbohydrates. They sublimate, evaporate, then get exposed to the cold. All sorts of things will be there."

Male-female differences regarding scientific terms show up in the use of metaphors as well. Russian men's, but not women's minds seem to work in such a way that even things that are not particularly scientific apparently evoke scientific or technological associations. Interestingly, this difference does not depend on the education or the occupation of the speakers, but first and foremost on their sex. Whether a literary critic or an engineer, a female is not likely to use technical metaphors. On the contrary, men, even literary men, regularly use them. The sentence given above in which debates in the Russian Parliament were compared to "mortising in" (or "turning on") a trigger mechanism was actually uttered by a man with a background in humanities. The following exchange between a technician father and his daughter (who happens to be a technology student, following in her dad's footsteps!) shows the male-female contrast in the use of scientific concepts quite well:

---

[7] These and the remaining examples in this chapter were recorded by **Зе́мская**, **Китайгоро́дская** and **Ро́занова**.

🔊 **12-11**   Daughter: **Ну вот—как на экза́мен уходи́ть, и голова́ зарабо́тала.**
             Father: **Прогре́лся дви́гатель.**

"Oh well, just now that it's time to go take my exam, my brain started working."
  "The engine got warmed up."

And here is what a female humanist and a female technician say (these are examples from conversations recorded by the same linguists):

🔊 **12-12**   Female humanist: **Мне вчера́ ху́до совсе́м бы́ло. Зна́ешь, как бе́лым медве́дям на ю́ге.**
             Female technician: **Я присоса́лась к вам, как пия́вка. Ну ещё немно́го попия́влю и уйду́.**

"I felt really sick yesterday. You know, like polar bears feel sick in the south."
  "I got stuck to you like a leech. Oh well, I'll leech a bit longer and go."

Even though the second woman is a technician by training, she still uses a pre-scientific simile, a leech. Note that this woman is also creative in a different way. She has spontaneously created a verb from the noun **пия́вка** leech: you can be sure that you will not find the verb **попия́вить** "to leech" in any Russian dictionary.

Scientific vocabulary in non-scientific modern Russian is, as you see, a very complex matter, sensitive to the sex, educational level, and creativity of the speaker, to the relationship between the speaker and the hearer, and to the setting of the conversation or the context of the writing. Its usage in scientifically appropriate contexts and among specialists, on the other hand, is fairly straightforward.

DICTIONARIES FOR SPECIALISTS

General Science

Callahan, Ludmilla I. *Russian-English Dictionary of Science and Technology*. New York: Wiley, 1996.

Chalakov, G. *Elsevier's Russian-English Dictionary*. Amsterdam: Elsevier, 1993.

Macura, P. *Elsevier's Russian-English Dictionary*. Amsterdam: Elsevier, 1990.

Biology

Anglo-russkii biologicheskii slovar'. 1976. Moskva: Russkii iazyk.

Smirnov, N.N. *Elsevier's Dictionary of Fundamental and Applied Biology*. [Russian-English and English-Russian] Amsterdam: Elsevier, 1996.

Botany

Macura, P., comp. *Elsevier's Dictionary of Botany*. [Russian-English] Amsterdam: Elsevier Scientific Pub., 1982.

Schroter, A.I. *Dictionary of Plant Names*. [Russian, Latin, Chinese] Koenigstein, Germany: Koeltz Scientific Books, 1999.

Chemistry

Callaham, Ludmilla Ignatiev. *Russian-English Chemical and Polytechnical Dictionary*. New York: Wiley, 1975.

Carpovich, Eugene A. and Vera V. Carpovich. *Russian-English Chemical Dictionary: Chemistry, Physical Chemistry, Chemical Engineering, Materials, Minerals, Fuels, Petroleum, Food Industry, Pharmacology*. New York: Technical Dictionaries Co., 1961.

Macura, Paul. *Elsevier's Dictionary of Chemistry*. [Russian-English] Amsterdam: Elsevier, 1993.

Civil Engineering

Bhattacharya, S.K. *Elsevier's Dictionary of Civil Engineering*. [Russian-English] Amsterdam: Elsevier, 1988.

Ecology

Ekologia: russko-angliiskii terminologicheskii slovar'. Moskva: VNIIKI, 1993.

Electronics

Macura, Paul. *Russian-English Dictionary of Electrotechnology and Allied Science*. Malabar, FL: Krieger, 1986.

Mirimanov, R.G., comp. *Dictionary of Electronics: English, German, French, Dutch, Russian.* [English-Russian] Deventer, Netherlands: Kluwer Technische Boeken, 1985.

Prokhorov, K. Ia. *Anglo-russkii slovar' po mikroèlektronike.* Moskva: Russkii iazyk, 1985.

Geology

Alekseev, M.N. *Russko-angliiskii geologicheskii slovar'.* Moskva: Russo, 1998.

Bhattacharya, S.K., ed. *Elsevier's Dictionary of Geosciences.* [Russian-English] Amsterdam: Elsevier, 1991.

Korzhinskii, D.S, ed. *Anglo-russkii geologicheskii slovar'* Moskva: Glavnaia red. inostrannykh nauchno-tekhn. slovarei Fizmatgiza, 1961.

Zhylka, Romuald. *Geological Dictionary.* [English-Russian] Warszawa: Wydawnictwa Geologiczne, 1970.

Medicine

Akzhigitov, G.N. *Anglo-russkii meditsinskii slovar'.* Moskva: Russkii iazyk, 1992.

Bolotina, A.Iu. *Anglo-russkii i russko-angliiskii meditsinskii slovar'.* Moskva: Russo, 1998.

Eliseenkov, Iu.B. *Russko-angliiskii meditsinskii slovar'.* Moskva: Russo, 1997.

Physics

Emin, Irving. *Russian-English Physics Dictionary.* New York: John Wiley & Sons, Inc., 1963.

Tolstoi, D.M., ed. *English-Russian Physics Dictionary.* Oxford: Pergamon Press, 1978.

Appendix: Terminology for Non-Specialists

Приложе́ние: Нау́чные те́рмины в ненау́чном употребле́нии

Alexander Prokhorov

Astronomy[8]

Астроно́мия

Russian children study astronomy in the 11th grade (the last one), where they learn about the structure of the solar system **строе́ние со́лнечной систе́мы**, the sun and stars **со́лнце и звёзды**, the structure and evolution of the universe **строе́ние и эволю́ция вселе́нной**. The course includes the constellations 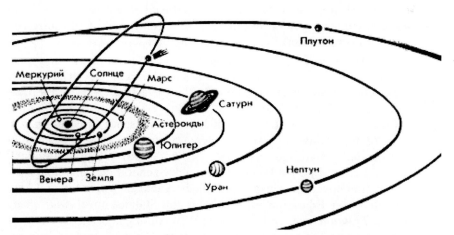 12-13 **созве́здия** that can be seen in Russia. The North Star **Поля́рная звезда́** is probably the best-known. Many Russians like to locate it in the night sky. The Milky Way **Мле́чный Путь** is the best-known galaxy **гала́ктика**. Some people remember that our solar system is part of the Milky Way. And an educated Russian can list the planets **плане́ты** of the solar system: Mercury **Мерку́рий**, Venus **Вене́ра**, Earth **Земля́**, Mars **Марс**, Jupiter **Юпи́тер**, Saturn **Сату́рн**, Uranus **Ура́н**, Neptune **Непту́н**, and Pluto **Плуто́н**. Many people remember the distance from the Earth to the Moon **расстоя́ние от Земли́ до Луны́** (approximately 380,000 km) and from the Earth to the Sun **и до Со́лнца** (approximately 150 million km).

Fig. 12-4.   Structure of the Solar System **строе́ние со́лнечной систе́мы**

[8] The information included in this section is based primarily upon **Е.П. Левита́н, Астроно́мия (Москва́: Просвеще́ние**, 1994).

The astronomy course usually recounts the controversy around the geocentric and heliocentric systems **геоцентри́ческая и гелиоцентри́ческая систе́мы ми́ра**. The latter was first described by the Polish astronomer Nicholas Copernicus **Никола́й Копе́рник** whose work was posthumously condemned: **Уче́ние Копе́рника бы́ло при́знано не сра́зу. Вы зна́ете, наприме́р, что по пригово́ру инквизи́ции в 1600 г. был сожжён в Ри́ме выдаю́щийся италья́нский фило́соф, после́дователь Копе́рника, Джорда́но Бру́но.** The introduction to the history of astronomy ends with an examination of Kepler's Laws **Зако́ны Ке́плера.**

⌗ 12-14 Russian students now also learn about both the Russian and American space programs: that the space era originated with the launching of Russian satellite **спу́тник**, that the first male and female astronauts **космона́вты** were the Russians Yuri Gagarin **Ю́рий Гага́рин** and Valentina Tereshkova **Вален-**
⌗ 12-15 **ти́на Терешко́ва.** The American expedition to the moon **пе́рвая экспеди́ция**
⌗ 12-16 **на Луну́** is also mentioned (in general, the textbook is less Russocentric than it
⌗ 12-17 used to be). Along with pictures of the Russian Space Station *Mir*
⌗ 12-18 **орбита́льная ста́нция** *Мир* and the space telescope **Грана́т**, one can see the
⌗ 12-19 American space probe Voyager 2 **Во́яджер 2** and the Hubble Space Telescope
⌗ 12-20 **Телеско́п и́мени Ха́ббла.**

Knowledge and Belief   Зна́ния и пове́рья

- ❖ Black Hole **чёрная дыра́**. Even though very few know the physical nature of this phenomenon, the expression is used in colloquial language to mean a costly and useless project.

- ❖ Sputnik **спу́тник**. This Russian word means satellite. Russian scientific discourse distinguishes between the artificial satellites of the Earth **иску́сственный спу́тник Земли́** and the natural satellite of the Earth, the Moon **есте́ственный спу́тник Земли́—Луна́**.

- ❖ UFO **НЛО (неопо́знанный лета́ющий объе́кт).** Russians like to discuss, and especially to watch TV shows about, extraterrestrial visitors **гумано́иды** or Martians **марсиа́не**. In the 1980s there was even a rock-group named **НЛО.** Many Russians enjoy reading science fiction **нау́чная фанта́стика**, some of which deals with space exploration, and some of which involves flying saucers **лета́ющие таре́лки.** Popular Russian authors are the Strugatsky Brothers **бра́тья Струга́цкие** and Eremei Parnov **Ереме́й Парно́в.** The older generation remembers science fiction novels of Alexander Beliaev **Алекса́ндр Беля́ев** and Ivan Efremov **Ива́н Ефре́мов**, especially his anti-Stalinist novel *Andromeda Nebula* **Тума́нность Андроме́ды** (1957). Among non-Russian science fiction writers the most popular are Isaac Asimov **А́йзек Ази́мов**, Arthur Clark **Арту́р Кларк**, and Stanislaw Lem **Станисла́в Лем**. Andrei Tarkovskii's film *Solaris* **Соля́рис** (1972) is based on one of Lem's novels.

BIOLOGY[9]   Биология

In school the biology course is the last in a sequence of life science courses which include botany **ботáника**, zoology **зоолóгия**, anatomy **анатóмия**, and finally general biology **óбщая биолóгия**. Some schools specialize in the biological sciences; students can transfer to them in the eighth or ninth grade.

A biology textbook describes six levels in the organization of living matter **ýровни организáции живóй матéрии**: the molecule **молéкула**, the cell **клéтка**, the organism **органúзм**, populations and species **популя́ции и вúды**, the biological community **биоценóз**, and the biosphere **биосфéра**, or the sum total of all biological communities together **совокýпность всех биоценóзов**.

In school, Russian children also learn about the major properties of living matter **живáя матéрия**:

1. All matter consists of the same basic chemical elements **едúнство химúческого состáва живóй и неживóй матéрии**. Many educated Russians remember that four of these chemical elements—carbon **углерóд**, oxygen **кислорóд**, hydrogen **водорóд**, and nitrogen **азóт**—make up 98 percent of living matter.

2. Metabolism **обмéн вещéств и энéргии** is another generally known property of living matter.

3. Reproduction of one's own kind **самовоспроизведéние**. Post-Soviet textbooks, as opposed to earlier editions, especially emphasize the dependence of life on heritable information **наслéдственность** encoded in DNA **ДНК (дэ-эн-кá)**. 🔲 **12-21**
🔲 **12-22**

4. Growth and development **спосóбность к рóсту и развúтию**.

5. Response to the environment (irritability) **раздражúмость**.

One section in the chapter on human origins discusses the evolutionary 🔲 **12-23** origins of races and emphasizes that representatives of all races belong to the 🔲 **12-24** species of *Homo sapiens*. A chapter is usually devoted to the discussion of human origins (see Fig. 12-5 on the following page). Ecology **Экóлогия** is another major topic in school as is the mathematic modeling of biological processes and phenomena **математúческое изучéние биологúческих процéссов и явлéний**.

History of Biology   История биолóгии

Post-Soviet textbooks offer a more balanced view of the role of Russian and Soviet biologists in world science, and also contain pictures and small articles about American and British biologists. The most striking example is the section on genetics. In the Stalin era it was pronounced a bourgeois pseudo-science, and even after Stalin's death in 1953 genetics was always minimally represented

---

[9] The information included in this section is based primarily upon **В.К. Шумный**, **Óбщая биолóгия (Москвá: Просвещéние**, 1995).

Время, млн. лет	Эра	Период	Событие
0	Кайно-зойская	Четвертичный	Эволюция человека
50		Третичный	Дивергенция млекопитающих
100	Мезо-зойская	Меловой	Последние динозавры Первые приматы Первые цветковые растения
		Юрский	Динозавры Первые птицы
200		Триасовый	Первые млекопитающие Господство рептилий
250	Палео-зойская	Пермский	Великое вымирание морских организмов
300		Каменноуголь-ный (карбон)	Первые рептилии Семенные папоротники
350		Девонский	Первые амфибии Увеличение разнообразия рыб
400		Силурийский	Первые наземные сосудистые растения
450		Ордовикский	Взрыв разнообразия в семействах многоклеточных животных
500 550		Кембрийский	Первые рыбы Первые хордовые

Fig. 12-5. A Time Line on the History of Life

in Soviet school textbooks. The 1995 textbook, however, devotes 90 pages out of 540 to the discussion of the gene **ген** and inheritance **насле́дственность**. In addition, there are also pictures and descriptions of Western scientists such as Gregor Mendel **Гре́гор Ме́ндель**, Maurice Wilkins **Мори́с Уи́лкинс**, James Watson **Джеймс Уо́тсон**, and Francis Crick **Фре́нсис Крик**. The book also mentions Nikolai Vavilov **Никола́й Вави́лов**, a prominent Russian geneticist and president of the International Congress of Genetics (1939), who was killed on Stalin's orders and whose name was avoided in Soviet-era school textbooks.

12-25
12-26
12-27
12-28
12-29

Knowledge and Belief   Зна́ния и пове́рья

Since the mid-19th century, the intelligentsia's fascination with positivism and Darwin's Theory of Evolution, various concepts from the biological sciences found their way into popular usage as linguistic metaphors.

❖ Cell **кле́тка**. The idea of the cell as the structural unit of a living organism is in everyday usage: "She was aware of his presence with every fiber (cell) of her being." **Она́ чу́вствовала его́ прису́тствие ка́ждой кле́ткой своего́ те́ла.**

❖ Poor metabolism **обме́н веще́ств** is a general popular explanation of why one does not look well:

— Why does she look so bad today?

— I think she does not feel good today (literally: I think she has problems with her metabolism).

— **Почему́ она́ так пло́хо вы́глядит сего́дня?**

— **По-мо́ему, у неё пробле́мы с обме́ном веще́ств.**

❖ Chernobyl **Черно́быль.** After the 1986 disaster at the nuclear power plant people ironically call large vegetables or fruit "Chernobyl harvest." Why are your apples so big? Are they from Chernobyl? **Почему́ ва́ши я́блоки таки́е больши́е? Черно́быльские, что ли?**

❖ Fetus **заро́дыш.** The word is used as a pejorative form of address: Hey you, fetus, come over here! **Эй ты, заро́дыш,[10] поди́ сюда́!**

❖ Genetic resource **генети́ческий фонд (генофо́нд).** This concept is used to describe figuratively, and inevitably in somewhat mystical terms, the Russian national identity: Alcoholism destroys the genetic resource of the nation **Алкоголи́зм разруша́ет генофо́нд на́ции.**

❖ Inheritance **насле́дственность.** This popular concept explains differences in achievements of children and parents, for example. One speaker explains to the other why the son of a famous composer is a mediocre musician: "Well, you cannot go against the laws of inheritance: As they say, nature rests while (working) on the children of talented people." **Ну что поде́лаешь, про́тив зако́нов насле́дственности не попрёшь. Как говори́тся, приро́да отдыха́ет на де́тях тала́нтливых люде́й.**

❖ Nerd **бота́н. Бота́н** is slang derived from "botanist" **бота́ник.**

❖ Organism **органи́зм.** The promotion of sports and physical health was the object of many Soviet-era slogans. For example: "Sun, fresh air, and hiking make you stronger!" **Со́лнце, во́здух и тури́зм укрепля́ют органи́зм!** Late Soviet urban folklore slightly changed the health-giving incantations: Sun, fresh air, and onanism make your organism stronger! **Со́лнце, во́здух, онани́зм укрепля́ют органи́зм!**

❖ Species **вид.** The concept of species is often used to describe social groups: "With the advent of a market economy the intelligentsia will become extinct as a species." **С прихо́дом ры́ночной эконо́мики интеллиге́нция вы́мрет как вид.**

❖ Unicellular **однокле́точный.** The word is used to describe a dumb primitive person: "He is dumb." **Он однокле́точный.**

---

[10] Pre-publication readers suggested some additional examples: **эмбрио́н, крети́н, уро́д** (freak), **ублю́док, недоно́сок.**

CHEMISTRY[11]   ХИ́МИЯ

Most Russian children study chemistry for four years: in the 8th and 9th grades they take general chemistry, in 10th and 11th grades—organic chemistry. Universities run special programs for students interested in learning more about chemistry. For example, Moscow State University has classes for high school students **Шко́ла ю́ного хи́мика**, where they cannot earn college credits, but can learn about their favorite subject far beyond the high school program.

Russian chemistry textbooks and the *Children's Encyclopedia* «**Де́тская энциклопе́дия**» include material on the history of chemistry. As opposed to Soviet era textbooks which emphasized Russian discoveries of chemical laws and technological processes, post-Soviet books give a more balanced picture of world science history. However, in comparing Russian and Western scientific discoveries, who did what first still remains an issue. For example, Russian children learn that Mikhail Lomonosov **Михаи́л Ломоно́сов** founded modern chemistry in the middle of the 18th century by developing molecular and atomic theory: «**Уче́ние о моле́кулах и а́томах в основно́м бы́ло разрабо́тано в середи́не XVIII в. вели́ким ру́сским учёным Михаи́лом Васи́льевичем Ломоно́совым**». According to the school text, Lomonosov's experiments also demonstrated the law of conservation of mass **зако́н сохране́ния ма́ссы веще́ств** long before Antoine Lavoisier made similar discovery in the West.

All Russians know the table of the elements as the Mendeleev Periodic Table of the Elements **периоди́ческая табли́ца хими́ческих элеме́нтов Д.И. Менделе́ева**, or simply **табли́ца Менделе́ева**. For many Russians Mendeleev is not only a scientist, but also a promoter of modern technology in late Imperial Russia.

Early in their studies school students learn about elements **просты́е вещества́** and compounds **сло́жные вещества́**. They also learn about chemical formulas **хими́ческая фо́рмула вещества́** and chemical equations **хими́ческие уравне́ния**.

Reading Chemical Formulas   Чте́ние хими́ческих фо́рмул

(The following material is in addition to indications given in the appendices of *Russian's World* on reading chemical formulas.) The following list shows the familiar chemical abbreviations, the pronunciation of that abbreviation in Russian, the chemical being referred to in Russian, and then in English.

H_2O, **аш два о, вода́**, water
H_2S, **аш два эс, сероводоро́д**, hydrogen sulphide
CO, **цэ о, уга́рный газ**, carbon monoxide
CO_2 **цэ о два, углеки́слый газ**, carbon dioxide
H_2O_2, **аш два о два, пе́рекись водоро́да**, hydrogen peroxide

---

[11] The information included in this section was based primarily upon **Г.Е. Рудзитис**, **Хи́мия** (**Москва́**: **Просвеще́ние**, 1997).

H$_2$SO$_4$, **аш два эс о четы́ре, се́рная кислота́**, sulfuric acid

HCl, **аш хлор, соля́ная кислота́**, hydrochloric acid

NaCl, **на́трий хлор, пова́ренная соль**, table salt

CaCO$_3$, **ка́льций цэ о три, карбона́т ка́льция (мел, мра́мор, известня́к)**, calcium carbonate

CH$_3$OH, **цэ аш три о аш, метано́л (мети́ловый спирт)**, methyl (wood) alcohol

C$_2$H$_5$OH, **цэ два аш пять о аш, этано́л (эти́ловый спирт)**, ethyl alcohol

Knowledge and Belief   Зна́ния и пове́рья

As a nation Russians share certain beliefs about the qualities and uses of certain elements and compounds. The contradictory nature of some of these facts usually does not puzzle the native users of Russian. One set of beliefs is that everything linked with chemistry as a science or technology is dangerous for the health or environment. Closely related to this belief is the colloquial meaning of the word chemist **хи́мик**, which means a person who was released on parole with mandatory employment at a chemical plant **«Его́ посла́ли на хи́мию»**. A "chemist" **химик** is also slang for a clever and resourceful cheat. **«Что ты там хими́чишь?»** What are you up to? (With only the worst expectations.)

The other set of beliefs share one common fact: practical information about the usefulness of certain elements or compounds for human health and nutrition. Some of these beliefs exist as an alternative to mainstream medicine. Many Russian physicians, however, do not reject these beliefs and even use some of them in their practice. Popular myths about chemical elements and practices based on these myths include the following:

❖ Aluminum **алюми́ний**. Many Russians remember from their Soviet-era literature classes Nikolai Chernyshevskii's novel *What is To Be Done?* (1863). The protagonist, Vera Pavlovna, experiences utopian dreams of a communist future when all people will live in the buildings made out of aluminum and glass. Russian native speakers often use this imagery ironically referring to unreasonable utopianism of a project: **Пра́вильно, и всё вокру́г бу́дет из стекла́ и алюми́ния.**

❖ Bromine **бром**. Many men who have served in the Russian army claim that compounds of bromine were added to their food to control their libido. The Russian conceptualist poet Timur Kibirov **Тиму́р Киби́ров** incorporated this popular motif in his poem, "Èleonora" **«Элеоно́ра»** (**«Сантименты»**, 1988):

🔊 12-32

Вот говоря́т, что добавля́ют бром
В солда́тский чай. Не зна́ю, дорога́я.
Не зна́ю, сомнева́юсь. По́тным лбом
Казённую поду́шку увлажня́я,
Я, засыпа́я, ду́мал об одно́м.

So they say that they add bromine
To soldiers' tea. I don't know, my dear.
I don't know, but I doubt it. Pressing my sweaty forehead
Against my state-issued pillow,
I thought about only one thing while trying to go to sleep.

❖ Copper **медь**. Copper is believed to heal bruises and back pain. One needs to attach a piece of copper to the aching part of the body. For the bruises one usually uses a cold copper coin. American pennies **пе́нсы**, **однопе́нсовые моне́тки**, tsarist-era five copeck coins **ме́дные пятаки́**, and Soviet-era copper coins issued before 1961 monetary reform are greatly valued for those purposes. Supposedly they have pure copper in them as opposed to Brezhnev-era one, three, or five copeck coins.

❖ Ethanol **этано́л, эти́ловый спирт**. Also known as drinking alcohol **питьево́й спирт**. Many people believe that vodka is made by adding water to ethanol, and people who have access to ethanol at work often drink it. See, for example, the recasting of the last supper in Mikhail Kalatozov's film *Cranes are Flying* «**Летя́т журавли́**» (1957). The doctor's family prefers ethanol over red wine at the last meal before the older son goes to war. Ethanol (*or* vodka) is often used as surrogate money to pay contractors, plumbers, movers, etc.

❖ Iodine **йод**. After the Chernobyl accident some Russians share a belief that some salts containing iodine assist thyroid and can be taken as a medication in the areas contaminated by radioactive elements. A similar curative power is also attributed to vodka and red wine.

❖ Iron **желе́зо**. Women who experience excessive bleeding during menstruation lose a lot of iron. In addition to medication, they eat buckwheat kasha **гре́чневая ка́ша**, meat, and pomegranates to replenish the iron.

❖ Methanol **метано́л, мети́ловый спирт**. This kind of alcohol is known to cause blindness, impotence, and even death if imbibed. In many Russian labs it is prohibited to keep methanol and ethanol together.

❖ Silicon **кре́мний**. In the 1980s Russians stopped using the Russian word for silicon **кре́мний** and replaced it by English-sounding **силико́н** to describe certain Western silicon-based products or locations where these products are produced. For example, **силико́новый импла́нт, сили-ко́новый чип, Силико́новая доли́на. Зеленогра́д—это на́ша Сили-ко́новая доли́на. Силико́новая доли́на** in crude maletalk also means a woman with large breasts.

❖ Silver **серебро́**. Russians often put silver objects in drinking water (coins, spoons, etc.) in the conviction that silver disinfects water.

PHYSICS[12]   ФИ́ЗИКА

In Russian secondary schools students study mechanics **меха́ника**, thermal physics **фи́зика тепловы́х явле́ний**, electricity and magnetism **электри́ческие и магни́тные явле́ния**, light and optics **световы́е и опти́ческие явле́ния**, quantum physics **ква́нтовая фи́зика**. During the five years of their studies, students go over the main parts of the physics curriculum twice: the first time, in the seventh and eighth grades and, the second time, in the remaining grades.

In the third through fifth grades, children take a nature studies course **природове́дение**. This course introduces them to elementary concepts of astronomy, geography, biology, chemistry, and physics. In some high schools mathematics and physics are the major subjects **шко́лы с углублённым изуче́нием фи́зики и матема́тики** also known as **физма́т шко́лы**. Students can transfer to these physics- and math schools after eighth or ninth grades.

Secondary school textbooks include materials on the history of physics, mostly biographical facts from the lives of great physicists and information about remarkable machines and physical instruments. Among Russian scholars, the textbooks always include Mikhail Lomonosov **Михаи́л Ломоно́сов** (1711–65) and Dmitri Mendeleev **Дми́трий Менделе́ев** (1834–1907) for their contribution to molecular and kinetic theory **молекуля́рно-кинети́ческая тео́рия**. Russian texts often mention Petr Lebedev **Петр Ле́бедев** (1866–1912), 🔲 **12-33** a Russian scientist who studied electromagnetic properties of light and founded the first Russian physics research center.

The 11th grade physics text has material on the invention of radio by Alexander S. Popov **изобре́тение ра́дио А.С. Попо́вым**. According to the 🔲 **12-34** book, Popov demonstrated his radio on May 7th 1895 at the meeting of Russian Physics and Chemistry Association **Ру́сское фи́зико-хими́ческое о́бщество**. The textbook also includes an illustration from the Journal of Russian Physics and Chemistry Association. As opposed to the Soviet-era film *Alexander Popov* (Eisymont and Rappaport, 1949), textbooks, and histories of science, post-Soviet textbooks do not now juxtapose the Russian inventor and his Western "impostor," Marconi. Rather, at the end of the chapter Marconi is mentioned as an engineer, who developed a similar device abroad: **За грани́цей усоверше́нствование подо́бных прибо́ров проводи́лось фи́рмой, организо́ванной италья́нским инжене́ром Г. Марко́ни.**

The section on modern physics is especially generous with facts about the history of science. There are portraits and biographical information on Albert 🔲 **12-35** Einstein **Альбе́рт Эйнште́йн** (1879–1955), Enrico Fermi **Энри́ко Фе́рми** 🔲 **12-36** (1901–54), Igor′ Kurchatov **И́горь Курча́тов** (1901–60), Marie Sklodowska- 🔲 **12-37** Curie **Мари́я Склодо́вская-Кюри́** (1867–1934), and others. 🔲 **12-38**

---

[12] The information included in this section is based primarily upon **Г.Я. Мя́кишев и Б.Б. Бухо́вцев, Фи́зика: уче́бник для 11 кла́сса** (Москва́: Просвеще́ние, 1997).

Knowledge and Belief   Зна́ния и пове́рья

- ❖ Acceleration **ускоре́ние**. This physical concept is also remembered as part of perestroika political discourse. Acceleration of economic development was one of Gorbachev's buzz-words in the early period of his rule.

- ❖ Atom **а́том**. That all matter is composed of atoms is the key theme of all science courses in Russian schools.

- ❖ Center of gravity **центр тя́жести**. This concept is often used figuratively to refer to social and economic issues: "The excessive military expenses shifted our economics' center of gravity." **Непоме́рные вое́нные расхо́ды смести́ли центр тя́жести на́шей эконо́мики.**

- ❖ Chain reaction **цепна́я реа́кция**. If nothing else, high school students usually remember that chain reactions can be controlled **управля́емые** and uncontrolled **неуправля́емые**: the former are used in nuclear reactors **я́дерные реа́кторы**, the latter—in nuclear weaponry **я́дерное ору́жие**. "Chain reaction" is also widely used as a figurative expression.

- ❖ Hologram **гологра́мма**. Holograms came into everyday life of Russians with the introduction of plastic money: hologram logos appear on many debit and credit cards.

- ❖ Laser **ла́зер**. The most well-known application of lasers is in ophthalmology developed in Russia by Sviatoslav Fedorov **Святосла́в Фёдоров**. In Russian science fiction laser guns and canons are the weapon of choice.

- ❖ Measures **ме́ры**. Russian children learn basic information about units of measurement in their science classes. The physics course introduces the students to two systems of units *SI* **СИ**[13] and CGS **СГС**.[14] (*Neither* system uses *our* everyday measures, please note!)

- ❖ Newton's Laws of Motion **зако́ны движе́ния Нью́тона**.[15] Out of the three famous laws only the third one **тре́тий зако́н Нью́тона** became part of common idiom. It is usually cited as: For every action there is an equal and opposite reaction **Де́йствие равно́ противоде́йствию**.

- ❖ Centrifugal force **центробе́жная си́ла** is also part of language, if not science.

- ❖ Photon **фото́н**. The formula for energy of a photon is on the cover of the physics textbook for 11th grade. The word is also widely known from numerous science fiction works in which space ships are equipped with photon engines **фото́нные дви́гатели**.

🔲 **12-39**

---

[13] "Systeme internationale"—kilograms/meters/seconds.

[14] CGS—centimeters/grams/seconds.

[15] The stress dictionary says **Нью́то́н** is traditional while **Нью́тон** is correct.

❖ Radioactivity **радиоакти́вность**. Most people believe that radioactivity is dangerous to their health. Since the Chernobyl accident concern with the effects of radioactivity on human health is a regular topic in the news and popular reading.

❖ Speed of light **ско́рость све́та**. Many Russians remember from school that the speed of light in a vacuum is 300,000 km/s.

❖ Speed of sound **ско́рость зву́ка**. Some Russians, especially those who are interested in aviation history, know that the speed of sound is approximately 1200 km/h, and that some modern jets can fly at supersonic speeds **сверхзвукова́я ско́рость**.

❖ Temperature **температу́ра**. In everyday temperature measurements Russians use the Celsius scale **шкала́ Це́льсия** where water freezes at 🔲 **12-40** 0° and boils at 100°. In high school children also learn about the Kelvin temperature scale **шкала́ Ке́львина** or **абсолю́тная ш к а ла́ температу́р**. Things start at absolute zero **абсолю́тный ноль**.

❖ The total energy of an object **связь ме́жду ма́ссой и э не́ргией**. For many Russians $E = mc^2$ is not only part of Einstein's theory of special relativity **специа́льная тео́рия относи́тельности**, but also common knowledge.

❖ Transistor **транзи́стор**. The word has two meanings: (1) transistor, (2) portable radio. The second meaning appeared with the introduction of portable radios in Russia in the 1960s. It is not used often anymore because most of portable radio-receivers are combined with either tape-recorders **магнитофо́н**, **кассе́тник** or CD-players **прои́грыватель компа́кт-ди́сков, си ди пле́йер**. Most Russians use the words designating tape-recorders or CD-players for the whole appliance.

❖ X-rays **рентге́новские лучи́**. In Russia the medical profession widely uses X-ray images **рентге́новские сни́мки** for diagnostic purposes. In the 1950s, black marketeers used the photographic plates for X-ray images to make records of Western jazz music. The slang term for that kind of home-made records, alternative to the official vinyl records, was: music on the ribs (that is, on the X-ray images of someone's ribs) **му́зыка на рёбрах**.

❖ Wave **волна́**. The wave nature of electro-magnetic phenomena is the key theme of the sections on electrodynamics and optics. The Russian textbook for 11th grade includes on the inside of its cover the electro-magnetic spectrum **шкала́ электромагни́тных излуче́ний**. 🔲 **12-41**

❖ Pseudo-waves (vibrations) are also part of everyday language: "I cannot sit next to him—he generates unpleasant waves." **Я не могу́ сиде́ть о́коло него́ —от него́ исхо́дят каки́е-то неприя́тные во́лны**. The other variant is: "He emits negative (or positive) energy." **Он излуча́ет негати́вную (позити́вную) эне́ргию**. Especially since late 1980s, when television psychics, such as Alexander Kashpirovskii, became part of popular entertainment, Russians started emitting positive and negative energy and generating pleasant and unpleasant waves.

❖ Weight **вес**. The difference between weight and mass **мácca** of an object is a widely-known fact. Many children learn about the relativity of weight from Nikolai Nosov's book *Neznaika on the Moon* **Незнáйка на Лунé**, in which the protagonist, Neznaika[16], travels to the Moon and discovers that he weighs six times less than on the Earth.

---

[16] "Not+know"

Appendixes

Appendix 1. Transliteration Systems

It is sad but true that at least three Russian and English transliteration systems are *commonly* in use. One would think that intelligent professionals could agree on a single system so as to alleviate editors' headaches and researchers' frustrations, not to mention writers' normal sloppiness.

The first thing to realize is that there is no such thing as a better, or even good transliteration system. They all have their weaknesses. So do not even dream of making up your own. Second, the names of places and people that have become part of English (as shown in a biographical or geographical dictionary) are usually allowed to remain that way, for example, *Moscow*, *Tchaikovsky*. Third, the choice of systems to be used is crystal clear: (1) use the system your editorial offices insist you use; or (2) use the system most appropriate to the *audience* for whom you are writing.

(a) Most academic writing calls for the Library of Congress (LC) system. Learn it very well, so that you can make points when others fail to do so. Do not believe anybody who says it doesn't matter. Formally, in library catalogs, for example, this system uses diacritical marks which are elsewhere ignored.

(b) If you are writing for an audience outside the university, the (US) Board of Geographic Names (BGN) system is used. It is the one you are most likely to have come across already in newspapers and magazines. It is usually required in US government work. The Board of Geographic Names has recently tried to anglicize some Russian names for larger areas, calling these names "conventional" names, such as Mordovia or even Mordvinia for **Мордва́** Mordva (the "native" name). This effort has been only partially successful since the result has been another layer of confusion about names for places in an already confused public mind. It is interesting that the Library of Congress itself specifies the use of a BGN system for maps (see <http://www. nima.mil>).

(c) If you are writing to a Russian using Latin letters (for example, in e-mail) then the Russian system is standard. They, however, will probably not complain if you get it wrong. What we show here is the system they are using.

(d) In the effort to assure a one-to-one correspondence between letters or their combinations (for example, ts = ц), linguists employ both diacritical marks and any of several transliteration systems, one of which is shown here. Since linguists are by nature picky, it would behoove writers in linguistics carefully to follow the requirements of the publisher or the professor involved.

Cyrillic	Board of Geographic Names	Library of Congress	Russian	Linguistic
А а	a	a	a	a
Б б	b	b	b	b
В в	v	v	v	v
Г г	g	g	g	g
Д д	d	d	d	d
Е е	ye,[1] e	e	e	e
Ё[2] ё	ye,[1] e	ё	e	e, ё
Ж ж	zh	zh	zh	ž
З з	z	z	z	z
И и	i	i	i	i
Й й	y	ĭ	j	j
К к	k	k	k	k
Л л	l	l	l	l
М м	m	m	m	m
Н н	n	n	n	n
О о	o	o	o	o
П п	p	p	p	p
Р р	r	r	r	r
С с	s	s	s	s
Т т	t	t	t	t
У у	u	u	u	u
Ф ф	f	f	f	f
Х х	kh	kh	h	x, ch
Ц ц	ts	t͡s	ts	c
Ч ч	ch	ch	ch	č
Ш ш	sh	sh	sh	š
Щ щ	shch	shch	shch	šč
Ъ ъ	″, ″[3]	″, ″	*none*	″, ″
Ы ы	y	y	y	y
Ь ь	′, ′	′, ′	*none*	′, ′
Э э	e	ė	e	è
Ю ю	yu	i͡u	yu	ju
Я я	ya	i͡a	ya	ja

Apostrophes, quotes, and diacritical marks are commonly ignored in the popular press as acknowledged in the Russian system. Stress marks are not customarily indicated in authentic Russian printing, but have been added in this book as an aid to the non-native reader.

---

[1] At the beginning of a word and after a vowel or ъ or ь.

[2] Not considered a separate letter; in transliteration the diaeresis may be ignored.

[3] Straight marks are typographically correct, but ordinary apostrophes and quotation marks are commonly used as well.

Appendix 2. Geographical Designations

Republics   Респу́блики

There are presently 21 republics. They are followed by their Library of Congress (LC) transliteration, the conventional spelling from Webster's *Dictionary of Geographic Names*, 1998, and then the US Board on Geographic Names (BGN) listing in March 1999.[1] (See the discussion of transliteration systems in Appendix 1.) The shorter alternative titles shown in the first column (for example, **Адыге́я** instead of **Респу́блика Адыге́я**) are less formal, though standard. **Респ.** = **Респу́блика**. Capitals follow in parentheses.

Formal title (Capital)	Informal title	Using LC System	1. Conventional 2. BGN "Native"	Titular nationality
Респ. Адыге́я (Майко́п)	Адыге́я	Adygeia	1. Adygea, Adegeya 2. Respublika Adygeya	адыге́йцы
Алта́йская Респ. (Го́рно-Алта́йск)	Алта́й[2]	Altai	1. Altay or Altai Republic 2. Altayskaya respublika	алта́йцы
Респ. Башкорто-ста́н[3] * (Уфа́)	Башкорто-ста́н	Bashkorto-stan	Bashkortostan	башки́ры
Респ. Буря́тия (Ула́н-Удэ́)	Буря́тия	Buriatiia	1. Buryatia, Buryat Rep. 2. Buryatskaya respublika	буря́ты
Респ. Дагеста́н* (Махачкала́)	Дагеста́н	Dagestan	Dagestan	дагеста́нцы
Ингу́шская Респ. (Назра́нь)	Ингуше́тия	Ingushetia	1. Ingushetia, Ingush Rep. 2. Ingushskaya respublika	ингуши́
Кабарди́но-Балка́рская Респ.* (На́льчик)	Кабарди́но-Балка́рия	Kabardino-Balkariia	1. Kabardino-Balkaria 2. Kabardino-Balkarskaya respublika	кабарди́нцы, балка́рцы
Респ. Калмы́кия-Хальмг Тангч* ** (Элиста́)	Калмы́кия	Kalmykiia	1. Kalmykia 2. Kalmykiya (Khal'mg-Tangch)	калмы́ки
Карача́ево-Черке́сская Респ.* (Черке́сск)	Карача́ево-Черке́сия	Karachaevo-Cherkessia	1. Karachay-Cherkessia 2. Karachayevo-Cherkesskaya respublika	карача́евцы, черке́сы
Респ. Каре́лия (Петрозаво́дск)	Каре́лия	Kareliia	1. Karelia 2. Kareliya	каре́лы

---

[1] This is the form (that is, "native" BGN) used by U.S. government offices.

[2] There were (in 1999) both an Altai Republic *and* an Altai Krai and they were adjacent. Before 1992, Altay Republic was Gorno-Altayskaya Avtonomnaya Oblast.

[3] Formerly **Башки́рская АССР**.

Респ. Ко́ми (Сыктывка́р)	Коми	Komi Republic	1. Komi 2. Respublika Komi	ко́ми
Formal title (Capital)	**Informal title**	**Using LC System**	**1. Conventional** **2. BGN "Native"**	**Titular nationality**
Мари́йская респу́-блика, Респ. Ма́рий Эл* (Йошка́р-Ола́)	Ма́рий Эл	Marii El	1. Mari El, Mariy El 2. Mariy El	мари́йцы, ма́ри
Респ. Мордо́вия (Сара́нск)	Мордва́	Mordoviia	1. Mordovia 2. Mordva, Mordovskaya respublika	мордва́
Респ. Саха́/ Яку́тия[4] (Яку́тск)	Саха́/Яку́тия	Yakutiia (Sakha)	1. Yakutia *or* Sakha 2. Yakutiya, Sakha, Yakutskaya respublika	яку́ты
Респ. Се́верная Осе́тия* (Владикавка́з)	Северная Осетия	Severnaia Osetiia	1. North Ossetia, Alania 2. Severnaya Osetiya	осети́ны
Респ. Татарста́н* (Каза́нь)	Тата́рия	Tatarstan	Tatarstan	тата́ры
Респ. Тыва́**, Тува́* (Кызы́л)	Тыва́, Тува́	Tuva	1. Tuva, Tyva 2. Respublika Tuva, Tyva	туви́нцы (тывинцы)
Удму́ртская Респ. (Иже́вск)	Удму́ртия	Udmurtiia	1. Udmurtia, Udmurtiya 2. Udmurtskaya respublika	удму́рты
Респ. Хака́сия (Абака́н)	Хакасия	Khakasiia	1. Khakassia 2. Khakasskaya respublika	хака́сы
Чече́нская Респ.* (Гро́зный)	Чечня́, Ичке́рия**	Chechnia	1. Chechnya 2. Chechenskaya respublika	чече́нцы
Чува́шская Респ.* (Чебокса́ры)	Чува́шия	Chuvashiia	1. Chuvashia, Chuvash Rep. 2. Chuvashskaya respublika	чува́ши

*Less than one-half the population in these republics was Russian in 1993.
**The name preferred by the native inhabitants.

Krais   Края́

There are six "territories," or krais. The term "krai" is a holdover from Soviet days; the actual jurisdiction now is the same as for the oblasts.

Russian	**Library of Congress**	**Conventional**
Алта́йский край (Барнау́л)	Altaiskii krai	Altay Kray
Краснода́рский край	Krasnodarskii krai	Krasnodar Kray
Красноя́рский край	Krasnoiarskii krai	Krasnoyarsk Kray
Примо́рский край (Владивосто́к)	Primorskii krai	Primorskiy Kray, Primorski Krai, Primorye Territory

---

[4] The natives have successfully insisted on Sakha officially, while the standard Russian refers to Yakutia.

| Ставропо́льский край (Ста́врополь) | Stavropol'skii krai | Stavropol' Kray |
| Хаба́ровский край | Khabarovskii krai | Khabarovsk Kray |

Oblasts   **О́бласти**

Most oblasts/regions are named after the major city **го́род** (*pl.*: **города́**) in the respective region (and therefore most capital names will be found in the third column). The regional/oblast government in general does not have jurisdiction within the major city, which has its own governing bodies, though it does have considerable influence. In cities the top executive official is the mayor **мэр**, while a governor **губерна́тор** heads the oblast government.

There are 49 regions or oblasts (obl.):

Russian	Library of Congress	Conventional, then BGN
Аму́рская область (Благове́щенск)	Amurskaia oblast	Amur Oblast, Amurskaya obl.
Арха́нгельская область	Arkhangel'skaia obl.	Arkhangelsk Obl., Arkhangel'skaya obl.
Астраха́нская область (А́страхань)	Astrakhanskaia obl.	Astrakhan Obl., Astrakhanskaya obl.
Белгоро́дская область	Belgorodskaia obl.	Belgorod Obl., Belgorodskaya obl.
Бря́нская область	Bryanskaia obl.	Bryansk Obl., Bryanskaya obl.
Влади́мирская область	Vladimirskaia obl.	Vladimir Obl., Vladimirskaya obl.
Волгогра́дская область	Volgogradskaia obl.	Volgograd Obl., Volgogradskaya obl.
Волого́дская область (Во́логда)	Vologodskaia obl.	Vologda Obl., Vologodskaya obl.
Воро́нежская область	Voronezhskaia obl.	Voronezh Obl., Voronezhskaya obl.
Ива́новская область	Ivanovskaia obl.	Ivanovo Obl., Ivanovskaya obl.
Ирку́тская область	Irkutskaia obl.	Irkutsk Obl., Irkutskaya obl.
Калинингра́дская область	Kaliningradskaia obl.	Kaliningrad Obl., Kaliningradskaya obl.
Калу́жская область (Калу́га)	Kaluzhskaia obl.	Kaluga Obl., Kaluzhskaya obl.
Камча́тская область (Петропа́вловск-Камча́тский)	Kamchatskaia obl.	Kamchatka Obl., Kamchatskaya obl.
Ке́меровская область	Kemerovskaia obl.	Kemerovo Obl., Kemerovskaya obl.

Кировская область (Вятка)	Kirovskaia obl.	Kirov Obl., Kirovskaya obl.

Russian	Library of Congress	Conventional, then BGN
Костромская область	Kostromskaia obl.	Kostroma Obl., Kostromskaya obl.
Курганская область	Kurganskaia obl.	Kurgan Obl., Kurganskaya obl.
Курская область	Kurskaia obl.	Kursk Obl., Kurskaya obl.
Ленинградская область (Санкт-Петербург)	Leningradskaia obl.	Leningrad Obl., Leningrad skaya obl.
Липецкая область	Lipetskaia obl.	Lipetsk Obl., Lipetskaya obl.
Магаданская область	Magadanskaia obl.	Magadan Obl., Magadanskaya obl.
Московская область	Moskovskaia obl.	Moscow Obl., Moskovskaya obl.
Мурманская область	Murmanskaia obl.	Murmansk Obl.
Нижегородская область (Нижний Новгород)	Nizhegorodskaia obl.	Nizhniy Novgorod Obl., Nizhegorodskaya obl.
Новгородская область	Novgorodskaia obl.	Novgorod Obl., Novgorodskaya obl.
Новосибирская область	Novosibirskaia obl.	Novosibirsk Obl., Novosibirskaya obl.
Омская область	Omskaia obl.	Omsk Obl., Omskaya obl.
Оренбургская область	Orenburgskaia obl.	Orenburg Obl., Orenburgskaya obl.
Орловская область (Орёл)	Orlovskaia obl.	Orel Obl., Orlovskaya obl.
Пензенская область	Penzenskaia obl.	Penza Obl., Penzenskaya obl.
Пермская область	Permskaia obl.	Perm' Obl., Permskaya obl.
Псковская область	Pskovskaia obl.	Pskov Obl., Pskovskaya obl.
Ростовская область	Rostovskaia obl.	Rostov Obl., Rostovskaya obl.
Рязанская область	Riazanskaia obl.	Ryazan' Obl., Ryazanskaya obl.
Самарская область	Samarskaia obl.	Samara Obl., Samarskaya obl.
Саратовская область	Saratovskaia obl.	Saratov Obl., Saratovskaya obl.

Сахали́нская область (Ю́жно-Сахали́нск)	Sakhalinskaia obl.	Sakhalin Obl., Sakhalinskaya obl.

Russian	Library of Congress	Conventional, then BGN
Свердло́вская область (Екатеринбу́рг)	Sverdlovskaia obl.	Sverdlovsk Obl., Sverdlovskaya obl.
Смоле́нская область	Smolenskaia obl.	Smolensk Obl., Smolenskaya obl.
Тамбо́вская область	Tambovskaia obl.	Tambov Obl., Tambovskaya obl.
Тверска́я область	Tverskaia obl.	Tver′ Obl., Tverskaya obl.
То́мская область	Tomskaia obl.	Tomsk Obl., Tomskaya obl.
Ту́льская область	Tul′skaia obl.	Tula Obl., Tul′skaya obl.
Тюме́нская область	Tiumenskaia obl.	Tyumen′ Obl., Tyumenskaya obl.
Улья́новская область	Ul′ianovskaia obl.	Ul′yanovsk Obl., Ul′yanovskaya obl.
Челя́бинская область	Chelyabinskaia obl.	Chelyabinsk Obl., Chelyabinskaya obl.
Чити́нская область (Чита́)	Chitinskaia obl.	Chita Obl., Chitinskaya obl.
Яросла́вская область (Яросла́вль)	Iaroslavskaia obl.	Yaroslavl′ Obl., Yaroslavskaya obl.

There is also a curious political entity among the oblasts in the Far East: the Jewish Autonomous Oblast **Евре́йская автоно́мная область**, where the capital city is Birobidzhan (*or* Birobijan) **Биробиджа́н**. (The US Board of Geographic Names decided to call the oblast simply "Birobijan" after the major city rather than translate the official title.)

Autonomous Areas   **Автоно́мные округа́ (АО *or* ao)**

These ten "autonomous areas" are comparable to our Indian reservations in that they are set aside for one of the less populous nationalities **малочи́сленный наро́д** (or **ма́лый наро́д**), mainly indigenous peoples of Siberia **Сиби́рь**, and Russia's Far East **да́льний восто́к**. As a rule they are located within an oblast or territory but are not directly subject to its laws. They are in Russian alphabetical order and capitals are in parentheses.

Russian	Library of Congress	BGN	Located in	Nationality of natives
Аги́нский Буря́т-ский ао (Аги́нское)	Aginskii Buriatskii ao	Aginskiy Buryatskiy ao	Чити́нская о́бласть	буря́ты
Ко́ми-Пермя́цкий ао (Кудымка́р)	Komi-Permiatskii ao	Komi-Per-myatskiy ao	Пе́рмская область	ко́ми-пермяки́
Коря́кский ао (Пала́на)	Koriaskii ao	Koryakskiy ao	Камча́тская область	коря́ки
Нене́цкий ао (Нарья́н-Ма́р)	Nenetskii ao	Nenetskiy ao	Арха́нгельская область	не́нцы
Таймы́рский (Долга́но-Нене́ц-кий) ао (Дуди́нка)	Taimyrskii (Dolgano-Nenetskii) ao	Taymyrskiy (Dolgano-Nenetskiy) ao	Красноя́рский край	долга́ны, не́нцы, нганаса́ны
Усть-Орды́нский Буря́тский ао (Усть-Орды́нский)	Ust′-Ordynskii Buriatskii ao	Ust′-Ordynskiy Buryatskiy ao	Ирку́тская область	буря́ты
Ха́нты-Манси́йский ао (Ха́нты-Манси́йск)	Khanty-Mansiiskii ao	Khanty-Mansiyskiy ao	Тюме́нская область	ха́нты, ма́нси
Чуко́тский ао (Ана́дырь)	Chukotskii ao	Chukotskiy ao	Магада́нская область	чу́кчи, эскимо́сы
Эвенки́йский ао (Тура́)	Evenkiiskii ao	Evenkiyskiy ao	Красноя́рский край	эве́нки, яку́ты
Яма́ло-Нене́цкий ао (Салеха́рд)	Iamalo-Nenetskii ao	Yamalo-Nenetskiy ao	Тюме́нская область	тата́ры, не́нцы, ханты́

Appendix 3. List of Periodicals

Throughout the book *The Russian Context* reference is made to many newspapers and magazines. Below is a list of the titles in English.

Аргуме́нты и фа́кты	Arguments and Facts
База́р	Bazaar
За́втра	Tomorrow
Изве́стия	Izvestiya
Ито́ги	Summary
Коммерса́нтъ	Kommersant
Комсомо́льская пра́вда	Komsomolskaya Pravda
Крестья́нка	The Peasant Woman
Ку́клы	(TV show) Puppets
Кура́нты	The Chimes
Литерату́рнся газе́та	The Literary Gazette
Моско́вский комсомо́лец	Moscow Komsomol
Незави́симая газе́та	Independent Newspaper
Но́вое Вре́мя	New Times
О́бщая газе́та	General News
Огонёк	The Little Flame
Пра́вда	Pravda (Truth)
Росси́йская газе́та	Russian Newspaper
Сего́дня	Today
Собесе́дник	Companion
Сове́тская Росси́я	Soviet Russia
Социа́льная защи́та	Social Defense
Труд	Labor
Черномо́рская здра́вница	The Black Sea Sanatorium

Appendix 4. Finding Russian Content on the Internet

Lindsay Johnston

There are several web directories that are very useful for finding information on Russian cities, towns, and cultural institutions on the internet:

- For resources on a wide variety of subjects, *Sher's Russian Index* is an amazing, constantly updated collection of links divided by subject: www.websher.net/inx/icdefault1.htm
- *Worldskip.com*: http://www.worldskip.com—choose "Europe," then "Russia." The site is divided into 3 areas: "News, Information and Radio," "Business, Economy, and Government," "Travel, People, and Culture." If you are looking for information about cities, there are useful links under "Travel, People, and Culture."
- Russian Cities on the Web: http://www.city.ru
- Looksmart Travel Destinations: http://www.looksmart.com/eus1/ eus62920/eus328057/eus135212/eus76116/r?1&iaci&—choose "Europe" then "Russia."
- NIS City and Regional Sites: http://users.aimnet.com/~ksyrah/ekskurs/ ruscity.html

There are also specialized Russian Search Engines:

- weblist.ru – search in English or in Russian
- www.rambler.ru – search in English or in Russian
  - ➢ If you want to search in Cyrillic, you will have to download or enable Russian fonts on your computer. Go to Sher's Computer Index (http://www.websher.net/inx/icdefault1.htm) and look for the heading "Computers—Software—Russify" for help.

General search engines will work as well:

- www.google.com—the most effective search engine in my opinion. Includes an option to search only for sites in Russian. Click on "Preferences," then select Russian.
- www.altavista.com - Includes and option to search exclusively for images. Click on "Media/Topic Search" and select Images.
- http://www.hotbot.lycos.com - Includes and option to search exclusively for images. Select "Image" on the left hand side of the screen.

Things to look for:

- Each search engine works slightly differently, so look for "Search Tips" to find out the best way to search.
- Instead of web addresses that end in ".com" or ".org," look for ones that end in ".ru."
- If you are looking for sites with permanence, look for web addresses that don't have a ~ in them. Sites with ~ are personal sites, and are less likely to remain on the web for a long time.
- University sites often have useful pages of links
- English dominates on the Internet, and many webmasters will make a Russian *and* an English version of their sites. Different language options are often indicated by flags (a Union Jack or the Stars and Stripes for English; a Russian flag for Russian; a Ukrainian flag for Ukrainian, etc.)
- **Evaluate the sites you choose!!** Look for:
  - ➤ AUTHORITY—who is responsible for the site? Look for logos and/or contact information.
  - ➤ CURRENCY—how old is the site?
  - ➤ ACCURACY—compare the information given in the site to authoritative publications
  - ➤ USEABILITY—Is the site well organized and easy to use? Does it download relatively quickly? (Images may take some time to download)

Viewing Cyrillic Fonts on the Web:

Sometimes your browser will adapt immediately and properly display Cyrillic. However, sometimes the writing on the screen will look like gibberish. If that is the case, go to "View" and select "Encoding", then select one of the Cyrillic encodings. Some pages will tell you what encoding you need to select. If it isn't indicated, guess until you get it right. For Russian, the standard fonts are:

- ➤ Cyrillic (Windows)
- ➤ Cyrillic (KOI8-R)
- ➤ Cyrillic (ISO)
- ➤ Cyrillic (DOS)

Счастливого пути!

Appendix 5. Using the CD-ROM

This book is accompanied by a CD-ROM disk which contains the full text of the book, together with approximately 1,700 illustrations (most in full color), sound files, and supplementary texts which we were unable to present in the book. The CD is compatible with any Pentium-class PC, PPC-class Macintosh, or any other computer which can read ISO 9660-format CDs. Detailed instructions for use of the CD materials are provided on the CD itself, but we provide a brief introduction in this appendix.

When you insert the CD in your CD or DVD drive, you see the following files: *Instructions.pdf*, *Instructions.htm*, *Front_Matter.pdf*, and *The_Russian_Context.pdf*. (Depending on how your system is configured, you may not see the three-letter extensions identifying the file type.) First-time users should probably read the instructions, but you may also go straight to *The_Russian_Context*. The two *Instructions* files are identical; *Instructions.htm* may be opened in your web browser; *Instructions.pdf* should be opened in Adobe Acrobat Reader. It provides detailed instructions for getting the most out of the CD, and it also provides links via which you may download any additional software necessary to use the CD, if it is not already installed on your system. All the software you need is free, generally pre-installed on newer computer systems, and easy to use. You need Adobe Acrobat Reader 4.0 or higher plus software to play the included sound files in MP3 format, such as QuickTime 4.0 or higher (for both Macintosh and Windows), Windows Media Player 6.0 or higher (Windows), or other suitable utility. The *Instructions* page also provides a link to the publisher's web site, where additional links are provided to internet sites which complement *The Russian Context*. This page will be updated regularly, so you may want to bookmark it.

To go straight to the book, simply open *The_Russian_Context* in Acrobat Reader. In the frame at the left are expandable bookmarks for easy navigation through the text. When you want to view a picture on the CD, click on any picture icon 🖾 in the margin (or on any black and white picture inside the text) and it will pop up in a separate window. Close this window to return to the main text. When you want to play a sound file, click on the marginal icons (🎵 for musical excerpts, ◀)) for spoken word files), and your system will play them automatically. Pop-up text files are flagged with the icon 🗐 .

If you need technical support, please email the publisher at slavica@indiana.edu. We regret that telephone support for *The Russian Context* cannot be guaranteed. The publisher also welcomes corrections to any errors in the book or CD, as well as suggestions for improving eventual revisions of both. Each purchaser of the book/CD package is entitled to one free upgrade to a later version of the CD, and subsequent upgrades will be available at a nominal cost.

Appendix 6. Bibliography

Please note: Bibliographies and lists of recommended reading were included (or not) at the author's discretion. They are listed here in the order in which the chapters appear in the book.

CHAPTER 1. RUSSIA'S HISTORY

A Note about Sources

To start this project, I assembled a list of Russian historical terms that I had encountered in tours of historical places in Russia, in classes on Russian history, and in conversations with educated Russians. I circulated that list among a number of native speakers and colleagues and collected additional terms to fill out my outline. Using that list, I wrote a narrative that would connect the ideas represented in these terms. To assure accuracy in dates, definitions and other details at this stage of writing, I consulted many current Russian, Soviet and American texts on Russian history. Since the way that national history is taught in school exerts a strong influence on the common base of historical knowledge that native speakers share, I relied heavily on secondary school textbooks of Russian history (both newly published texts and those from Soviet times). Once the narrative was written, the whole chapter was reviewed once again by native speakers, some known to me, others anonymously selected by the editors of this volume. I thank them all for their many comments, recognizing that any mistakes in the text remain my own.

Readers

Irina Prokhorova, Galina Griffiths, David Shengold, Professor Tatiana Spektor of Iowa State University, Professor Maia Kipp and Dr. Yaroslava Tsiovkh, both of the University of Kansas

Russian and Soviet History Textbooks Consulted

Ostrovskii, V.P. and A.I. Utkin. *Istoriia Rossii: XX vek*. 2nd ed. Moscow: Drofa, 1996. [11th Grade Textbook]

Zuev, M.N. *Istoriia Rossii: Khronika*. Moscow: Drofa, 1995. [6–11th Grades Textbook]

Fedotov, I.A. *Istoriia SSSR*. Moscow: Prosveshchenie, 1967. [8th Grade Textbook]

Sakharov, A.N. and V.I. Buganov. *Istoriia Rossii: S drevneishikh vremen do kontsa XVIII veka.* 2nd ed. Moscow: Prosveshchenie, 1996. [10th Grade Textbook].

Rybakov, B.A., et al. *Istoriia Otechestva.* 6th ed. Moscow: Antikva, 1996. [8th Grade Textbook].

Anisimov, E.V. and A.B. Kamenskii. *Rossiia v XVIII–pervoi polovine XIX veka: Istoriia, Istorik, Dokument.* Moscow: Miros, 1994.

Pashuto, V.T., et al. *Illiustrirovannaia istoriia SSSR.* Moscow: Mysl', 1980.

Skazkin, S.D., et al. *Detskaia entsiklopediia. Vol. 8: Iz istorii chelovecheskogo obshchestva.* 2nd ed. Moscow: Prosveshchenie, 1967.

Shestov, A.V. *Istoriia SSSR: Kratkii kurs.* Moscow: Gos. Uzhebno-Pedagogicheskoe izdatel'stvo, 1945. [4th Grade Textbook]

For Russians who want to refresh their historical knowledge, the classic works of 19th century historians have become quite popular. Their works have been published in many editions, so I list only the most representative titles here.

Nikolai Mikhailovich Karamzin (1766–1826), *Istoriia gosudarstva rossiiskogo*

Nikolai Ivanovich Kostomarov (1817–85), *Russkaia istoriia v zhizneopisaniiakh ee glavneishikh deiatelei*

Sergei Mikhailovich Solovev (1820–79), *Istoriia Rossii s drevneishikh vremen*

Vasilii Osipovich Kliuchevskii (1841–1911), *Russkaia istoriia*

Although no authors seem to have become "classics" for twentieth century Russian history, the reader might want to consider the following authors and texts.

Geller, Mikhail and Aleksandr M. Nekrich. *Utopiia u vlasti: Istoriia Sovetskogo Soiuza s 1917 goda do nashikh dnei.* London: Overseas Publication Interchange, Ltd., 1989.

Govorukhin, Stanislav. *Strana vorov na doroge v svetloe budushchee.* Narva: Firma "Shans," 1994.

Medvedev, Roy Aleksandrovich. *Oni okruzhali Stalina.* Benson, Vt.: Chalidze Publications, 1984.

Volkogonov, Dmitrii Antonovich. *Triumf i tragediia: politicheskii portret I.V. Stalina v 2-kh knigakh.* Moscow: Izd-vo Agenstva pechati Novosti, 1989.

My personal (and somewhat eclectic) suggestions for further reading in English

Billington, James H. *The Icon and the Axe: an Interpretive History of Russian Culture.* New York: Random House, 1970.

Crummey, Robert. *The Formation of Muscovy 1304–1613.* London and New York, 1987.

Figes, Orlando. *A People's Tragedy: the Russian Revolution, 1891–1924.* London: Jonathan Cape, 1996.

Gaddis, John Lewis. *We Now Know: Rethinking Cold War History.* Oxford: Clarendon Press, 1997.

Pipes, Richard. *Russia under the Old Regime.* New York, 1974.

Pospielovsky, Dimitry. *The Russian Church under the Soviet Regime 1917–1982.* 2 vols. Crestwood, NY: St. Vladimir's Seminary Press, 1984.

Riasanovsky, Nicholas V. *A History of Russia.* 5th ed. New York: Oxford University Press, 1993.

Stites, Richard. *The Women's Liberation Movement in Russia: Feminism, Nihilism, and Bolshevism, 1860-1930.* Princeton, N.J.: Princeton University Press, c1978.

Venturi, Franco. *Roots of Revolution: A History of the Populist and Socialist Movements in Nineteenth Century Russia.* New York: Grosset and Dunlap, 1966.

Walicki, Andrzej. *A History of Russian Thought from the Enlightenment to Marxism.* Stanford, CA: Stanford UP, 1979.

CHAPTERS 2 AND 3. QUOTING POETRY AND QUOTING PROSE

Ashukin, N.S. and M.G. Ashukina. *Krylatye slova. Literaturnye tsitaty, obraznye vyrazheniia.* Moscow: Pravda, 1986.

Berdiaev, Nikolai. *Istoki i smysl russkogo kommunizma.* Paris: YMCA-PRESS, 1937/1955. (Especially recomended: chapters "Obrazovanie russkoi intelligentsii i ee kharakter. Slavianofil'stvo i zapadnichestvo" and "Russkaia literatura XIX veka i ee prorochestva.")

Berdyaev, Nicholas. *Dostoevsky.* Trans. Donald Attwater. New York: Meridian Books, 1957.

Chukovskaia, Lidia Korneevna. *Zapiski ob Anne Akhmatovoi.* (In English: *The Akhmatova Journals*, by Lydia Chukovskaya. Trans. Milena Michalski and Sylva Rubashova; poetry trans. Peter Norman. New York: Farrar, Straus & Giroux, 1994.)

Lotman, Iu. M. *Besedy o russkoi kul'ture. Byt i traditsii russkogo dvorianstva (XVIII–nachalo XIX veka).* St. Petersburg: Iskusstvo-SPB, 1994.

————. *O poetax i poezii. Analiz poeticheskogo teksta. Stat'i, issledovaniia, zametki.* St. Petersburg: Iskusstvo-SPB, 1996.

Lotman, Iu. M. *Pushkin. Biografiia pisatelia. Stat'i i zametki 1960–1990. "Evgenii Onegin" Kommentarii.* St. Petersburg: Iskusstvo-SPB, 1997.

Mandelshtam, Nadezhda Iakovlevna. *Vospominaiia.* (In English: *Hope against Hope: A Memoir,* Nadezhda Mandelstam. Trans. Max Hayward. With an introduction by Clarence Brown and an obituary, "Nadezhda Mandelstam 1899–1980," by Joseph Brodsky. New York: Modern Library. 1999.)

Pasternak, Boris Leonidovich. *Safe Conduct: An Autobiography, and Other Writings.* New York: New Directions Books, 1958.

Slonim, Marc. *An Outline of Russian Literature.* New York: New American Library, 1958.

Terras, Victor, ed. *Handbook of Russian Literature.* New Haven & London: Yale University Press, 1985.

Terts, Abram (Andrei Siniavsky). *Progulki s Pushkinym.* (In English: Trans. Catherine Theimer Nepomnyashy and Slava I. Yastremsky. New Haven & London Yale University Press, 1993.

Zemskaia, E.A. "Tsitatsiia i vidy ee transformatsii v zagolovkakh sovremennykh gazet." In N.N. Rozonova, ed. *Poetika, stilistika, iazyk i kul'tura. Pamiati T.G. Vinokur.* Moscow: Nauka, 1996.

CHAPTER 4. CHILDREN'S LITERATURE

Brandis, E.P. *Ot Ezopa do Dzhanni Rodari. Zarubezhnaia literatura v detskom i iunosheskom chtenii.* Moscow: Detskaia literatura, 1980.

Dushenko, K.V. *Slovar' sovremennykh tsitat.* Moscow: Agraf, 1997.

Cherniavskaia, Ia. A. *Sovetskaia detskaia literatura.* Minsk: Vysheishaia shkola, 1971.

Petrovskii, M.S. K*nigi nashego detstva.* Moscow: Knigi, 1986.

Russkaia poeziia detiam. Ed. E.O. Putilova. St. Petersburg: Akademicheskii proekt, 1997.

Russkie destkie pisateli XX veka: Bibliograficheskii slovar'. Moscow: Flinta/Nauka, 1997.

Zarubezhnaia detskaia literatura. Ed. I.S. Cherniavskaia. Moscow: Prosveshchenie, 1974.

CHAPTER 6. THEATER IN LANGUAGE

Anisimov, A.V. *Teatry Moskvy*. Moscow: Moskovskii rabochii, 1984.

Ashukin, N.S., M.G. Ashukina. *Krylatye slova. Literaturnye tsitaty, obraznye vyrazheniia*. 2nd ed. Moscow: Khudozhestvennaia literatura, 1960.

Ashukin, N.S., S.I. Ozhegov, V.A. Fillipov. *Slovar' k p'esam A. N. Ostrovskogo*. Moscow: Vesta, 1993.

Bushueva, S.K., ed. *Russkoe akterskoe iskusstvo XX veka*. St. Petersburg: Ministry of Culture, 1992.

Dmitriev, Iu. A., ed. *Istoriia russkogo sovetskogo dramaticheskogo teatra v dvukh knigakh. Kniga vtoraia: 1946–1980e gody*. Moscow: Prosveshchenie, 1987.

Griboedov, Aleksandr. *Gore ot uma*. Moscow, 1963.

Markov, P.A. *Teatral'naia entsiklopediia, tt. 1–5*. Moscow, 1963.

Stenberg, Douglas Graham. *From Stanislavsky to Gorbachev: The Theater-Studios of Leningrad*. New York: Peter Lang, 1995.

CHAPTER 8. ART AND THE LANGUAGE OF RUSSIAN CULTURE

Valkenier, Elizabeth. *Russian Realistic Art: the State and Society: The Peredvizhniki and Their Tradition*. New York: Columbia University Press, 1989.

CHAPTER 9. POPULAR ENTERTAINMENT

Elistratov, V.S. *Slovar' krylatykh slov (russkii kinematograf)*. Moscow: Russkie slovari, 1999.

Khaniutin, A. "Paremiologiia kino." *Kinovedcheskie zapiski* 19 (1993): 49–55.

Kino: entsiklopedicheskii slovar'. Ed. S. Iutkevich, et al. Moscow: Sovetskaia entsiklopediia, 1987.

Kinomaniia 97: Entsiklopediia Rossiiskogo kinoiskusstva. Windows CD-Rom. Moscow: Cominfo CD-Rom Publisher, 1997.

Leyda, J. *Kino, A History of Russian and Soviet Film*. 2nd ed. New York:Collier Books, 1973.

Sovetskie khudozhestvennye filmy, Annotirovannyi katalog 1966–67. Ed. M. Pavlova and V. Borovkov. Moscow: Izdatelstvo vserossiiskoi gazety, 1995.

Stites, Richard. *Soviet Popular Culture*. New York: Cambridge University Press, 1992.

von Geldern, James and Richard Stites. *Mass Culture in Soviet Russia 1917–53.*
Bloomington: Indiana University Press, 1995.

Zemlianukhin, S. and M. Segida. *Katalog: Filmy Rossii 1991–94.* Moscow: Dubl.
D, 1995.

Zemlianukhin, S. and M. Segida. *Domashniaia kinomateka: Otechestvennoe
kino 1918–96.* Moscow: Dubl. D, 1996.

CHAPTER 10. GEOGRAPHY

In addition to informants listed in Acknowledgements, major sources of
information have been school texts which, by their very nature, reduce
information and expectations to the essentials:

Geografiya Rossii. Uchebnik dlya 8–9 klassov sredney shkoly. Ed. A.V.
Darinskii. Moscow: Prosveshcheniye, 1993.

Alekseyev, A.I. and V.V. Nikolina. *Geografiya: Naseleniye i khozyaystvo
Rossii. Uchebnik dlya 9 klassa.* Moscow: Prosveshcheniye, 1996.

Barinova, I.I. *Geografiya Rossii. Priroda. 8 klass, uchebnik.* Moscow:
Izdatel'skiy dom Drofa, 1997.

Rom, V. Ya. and V.P. Dronov. *Geografiya Rossii. Naseleniye i khozyaystvo,
Uchebnik, 9 klass.* Moscow: Drofa, 1995.

Sukhov, V.P. *Fizicheskaya geografiya, 6, nachal'nyy kurs.* Moscow:
Prosveshcheniye, 1995.

Bulatov, V.E., S.S. Karinskiy, and A.V. Novikov. *Obshchaya geografiya:
eksperimental'nyy uchebnik dlya VI klassa.* Moscow: MIROS, 1994.

Sukhov, V.P. *Geografiya. Uchebnik dlya 8 klassa.* Moscow: Prosveshcheniya,
1991.

Solov'yev, Dik, Karpov, and Matrusov. *Fizicheskaya Geografiya SSSR.
Uchebnik dlya 7 klassa.* Moscow: Prosveshcheniya, 1977.

Gladkiy, Yu. I. and S.B. Lavrov. *Ekonomicheskaya i sotsial'naya geografiya
Mira.* Moscow: Prosveshcheniye, 1995.

The following are useful for the non-native speaker of Russian:

Ageyenko, F.L. and M.V. Zarva. *Slovar' udareniy dlya rabotnikov radio i
televideniya. Stress Dictionary for People in Radio and Television.* 5th
edition. Moscow: Russkiy yazyk, 1984.

Slovar' nazvaniy zhiteley (RSFSR). A Dictionary of RSFSR Resident Names.
Ed. A.M. Babkin. Moscow: Sovetskaya Entsiklopediya, 1964.

Entsiklopedicheskiy slovar' geograficheskikh nazvaniy. An Encyclopedic Dictionary of Geographic Names. Ed. S.V. Kalesnik. Moscow: Sovetskaya Entsiklopediya, 1973.

CHAPTER 11. GOVERNMENT AND LANGUAGE

Carpovich, Vera. *Solzhenitsyn's Peculiar Vocabulary.* New York: Technical Dictionaries, 1976.

Flegon, A. *Za predelami russkikh slovarei.* London: Flegon Press, 1973.

Konstitutsiia Rossiiskoi Federatsii. Moscow: Izdatel'skaia gruppa "Infra-M-Norma," 1996.

Russian-English Military Dictionary. London: Joint Technical Language Service, 1979.

Semeinyi kodeks RF. Novosibirsk: IUkza, 1996.

Slovar' sovremennykh russkikh sokrashchenii i abbreviatur. Moscow: Infoglob, 1995.

About the Authors   Об áвторах

ELOISE M. BOYLE (M.A., Ph.D. Ohio State University), who began her study of Russian in the German and Russian Department at the University of Vermont, is a Lecturer in Russian language and language program coordinator for the Department of Slavic and East European Languages and Literature at the University of Washington, Seattle. She has taught at the Ohio State University, the Defense Language Institute, and Ohio University. She has published in the areas of Russian literature and culture, and pedagogy.

WILLIAM J. COMER is Associate Professor of Slavic Languages and Director of the Ermal Garinger Academic Resource Center at the University of Kansas. Receiving a BA degree in Russian from Middlebury College in 1984, he was awarded the doctoral degree from University of California, Berkeley in 1992. Between 1982–96 he spent five extensive periods of study and research in Russia. At Kansas he regularly teaches courses in Russian language, Russian culture, and the methods of teaching Russian, and his research interests include the use of computer technology in language teaching, content-based instruction, and the interactions of Russian religious and literary cultures at the turn of the twentieth century. His articles "How do Dzhon and Dzhein Read Russian? On-Line Vocabulary and its Place in the Reading Process" (with Leann Keefe) and "Making Our Way toward Teacher Education Programs in the Slavic Languages" have appeared in the recent volume *The Learning and Teaching of Slavic Languages and Cultures: Towards the 21st Century* (Slavica, 2000).

THOMAS J. GARZA is Associate Professor of Slavic Languages and Literatures and Russian Language Coordinator at the University of Texas at Austin. His primary research interests are in foreign language teaching and pedagogy, and contemporary Russian popular culture. He teaches a course on the history of Russian rock music and its impact on the politics and society in the major cities. He is currently co-authoring two textbooks with Russian writing teams, one for advanced Russian language and culture, the other an intermediate level follow up to *Breakthrough! American English for Speakers of Russian*, which he co-authored in 1995.

GENEVRA GERHART writes: Some people are so intrigued by Russian, the people and the language, that they find it difficult to occupy themselves with something at least more lucrative if not more reasonable. I am one of those beleaguered who has not stopped struggling since the first Russian class in the summer of '48. Canwell committee and all. Ever since my first teaching job was relegated to graduate students, I have amused myself by collecting information all Russians seemed to have and most language students didn't. I am very grateful to the writers who contributed to the job, and eternally grateful to Eloise Boyle, the co-editor, for keeping us on an even keel despite over-heated winds of fate. My participation in this effort and the supplies it required were totally financed by my husband, James B. Gerhart, a now retired professor of physics at the University of Washington. He deserves considerable gratitude from the profession for his contribution.

LAWRENCE MANSOUR is an assistant professor of Russian language and culture at the US Military Academy, West Point, where in any one year, citizens will be happy to know, there are still upwards of a hundred cadets studying Russian. He has taught Russian literature and language at Dickinson College, Old Dominion University and University of Maryland-College Park. Among his interests: current events in Russia and Kazakhstan; nineteenth century Russian letters, literary criticism and intellectual culture; English and Polish poetry; language pedagogy; and wood lore.

ALEXANDER PROKHOROV is a Ph.D. candidate in the Department of Slavic Languages and Literatures at the University of Pittsburgh. His dissertation is entitled "Tropes of Soviet Culture in Literature and Film of the Thaw." His interests are 20th and 21st century Russian film, literature and culture.

LUDMILA A. PRUNER, Ph.D. (University of Pittsburgh, 1983) Russian Literature. Native Speaker of Russian completed her M.A. in Russian Philology and Spanish Language at Moscow Friendship University, Russia. Taught Russian Language and Literature in Paris, France and Santo Domingo, Dominican Republic. Taught Russian and Spanish Languages and Russian Literature and Civilization at University of Pittsburgh, Vanderbilt University and the U.S. Naval Academy in Annapolis. Conducted Seminars on Russian Cinema of the 1960s through 1990s at the Summer Research Lab at the University of Illinois at Champaign-Urbana. Author of numerous Computer Assisted Programs in Spanish and Russian based on Authentic Television Programs, at USNA Interactive Video Project (1992 National Award). Author of numerous articles on contemporary Russian cinema of the 1960s through 1990s published in the U.S. and abroad. Currently lives in New England and continues her research on Russian Cinema and Civilization.

ROBERT A. ROTHSTEIN is professor of Slavic and Judaic Studies and of Comparative Literature and adjunct professor of Linguistics at the University of Massachusetts, Amherst, where he directs the program in Slavic and East European Studies. He has published widely in the areas of Slavic and Yiddish linguistics, folklore, cultural history and music.

HALINA WEISS, an independent scholar living in Amherst, Massachusetts, has written about Russian and Polish literature (including children's literature), folklore and culinary history.

JAMES WEST is Associate Professor of Slavic Languages and Literatures at the University of Washington. He studied Russian at London University during national service in the Royal Air Force, then Russian, French and German at Cambridge University, and his doctoral studies included a period at Leningrad State University, where his adviser was D.E. Maksimov. His publications are on the culture and philosophy of the late nineteenth and early twentieth centuries (particularly Viacheslav Ivanov and Andrei Bely) and the early nineteenth century in Russia. His research interests focus on the interactions of different realms of discourse—literature, philosophy, the visual arts, and music—in Russia and Europe, including some of Russia's non-Russian cultures. He is currently completing books on the origin and persistence of visual images in Russian culture, and the "Russian Idea," the national component of Russian philosophy between the 1880s and 1930s. Besides courses on modern Russian culture, he teaches advanced written comprehension and translation courses for fourth-year and graduate students, for whom an understanding of the cultural context of the Russian language is crucial.

OLGA T. YOKOYAMA (Ph.D. 1979, Harvard University) teaches in the Department of Slavic Languages and Literatures at UCLA. Her publications are primarily in the field of Russian linguistics. Her interest in Russian proverbs goes back to her childhood: her mother used many Russian proverbs in her own speech, and her father, who learned Russian as an adult, became a connoisseur of Russian proverbs. (His ambition to write a book comparing Japanese, Chinese, and Russian proverbs was unfortunately never realized, although he took extensive notes on the subject.) Yokoyama's interest in science is related to her earlier training in natural sciences. For publications and other professional details, see: <http://www.humnet.ucla.edu/humnet/slavic/ html/f-yokoyama.html>.

VALENTINA ZAITSEVA, Ph.D. in Slavic Linguistics, Harvard University Born in Sochi, a popular resort town in the sub-tropical part of Russia near the Black Sea. Presently lives in New York City with her two bilingual teenage children (Maria and Yuri Gitin) and her third husband, a historian. Zaitseva studied Russian literature and language first in Leningrad at Herzen Pedagogical University, then after emigrating to the USA, at Norwich University Russian Summer School and at Harvard. For many years taught Russian language, literature and culture at Harvard, SUNY Albany, Norwich, and presently works at New York University. Research interests: interaction between language, culture and communication; national identity and cultural stereotypes; gender linguistics and foreign language acquisition. Zaitseva is the author of the book *The Speaker's Point of View in Grammar and Lexicon* and a number of articles published in professional journals and monographs.

Indexes

Index of First or Famous Lines

HISTORY

Пролета́рии всех стран, соединя́йтесь!
Workers of the world, unite!

При́зрак бро́дит по Евро́пе, при́зрак коммуни́зма.
A spectre is haunting Europe, the spectre of Communism.

Сла́ва октябрю́!
Glory to October!

POETRY

The following lines of poetry are among the most commonly known by Russians of all ages:

Беле́ет па́рус одино́кой
В тума́не мо́ря голубо́м! ... (Lermontov)
There is a lonely white sail in the blue mist of the sea.

Бессо́нница. Гоме́р. Туги́е паруса́. (Mandelshtam)
Insomnia. Homer. Tight sails.

Бу́ря мгло́ю не́бо кро́ет ... (Pushkin)
A blizzard covers the sky with gloom ...

В ду́шном во́здуха молча́нье ... (Tiutchev)
In the sultry silence of the air ...

В по́лном разга́ре страда́ дереве́нская ... (Nekrasov)
The hard work of harvest time is at its full height ...

Во глубине́ сиби́рских руд ... (Pushkin)
In the depth of Siberian mines ...

В одну́ теле́гу впрячь не мо́жно
Коня́ и тре́петную лань. (Pushkin)
It is impossible to harness to one cart a horse and a trembling fallow deer.

Во всём мне хо́чется дойти́
До са́мой су́ти. (Pasternak)
In everything I wish to reach the very essence.
Воро́не где-то Бог посла́л кусо́чек сы́ру. (Krylov)
Once a crow happened upon a piece of cheese.

Вот опя́ть окно́ … (Tsvetaeva)
Here again is a window …

Вчера́ ещё в глаза́ гляде́л … (Tsvetaeva)
Only yesterday he looked into my eyes …

Вы́пьем, до́брая подру́жка … (Pushkin)
Let's drink, O dear friend of my poor youth …

Выхожу́ оди́н я на доро́гу …(Lermontov)
I go out alone on the road …

Глаго́л времён; <…> мета́лла звон! (Derzhavin)
The voice of the ages! [Lit.: A word of the times!] The ring of metal!

Го́рные верши́ны
Спят во тьме ночно́й … (Lermontov)
Mountain summits slumber in the night darkness …

Гул зати́х. Я вы́шел на подмо́стки. (Pasternak)
The hum quieted down. I came out onto the stage.

Де́вушка пе́ла в церко́вном хо́ре … (Blok)
A young girl sang in the church choir …

До свида́нья друг мой, без руки́ и сло́ва … (Esenin)
Goodbye, my friend, without a handshake or a word …

Друзья́ мои, прекра́сен наш сою́з! (Pushkin)
My friends, how beautiful is our union!

Духо́вной жа́ждою томи́м … (Pushkin)
Tormented by a spiritual thirst …

Есть же́нщины в ру́сских селе́ньях … (Nekrasov)
There are women in Russian villages …

Есть не́кий час—как сбро́шенная кла́жа … (Tsvetaeva)
There is a certain hour like a discarded load …

Есть ре́чи—значе́нье
Темно́ или ничто́жно … (Lermontov)
There are words [lit.: speeches] whose meaning is either dark or insignificant …

Есть це́нностей незы́блемая ска́ла
Над ску́чными оши́бками веко́в. (Mandelshtam)
There is an unshakeable scale of values above the tedious mistakes of the centuries.

Ещё в поля́х беле́ет снег … (Tiutchev)
There is still snow whitening the fields …

Ешь анана́сы, ря́бчиков жуй … (Mayakovsky)
Eat pineapples, munch on grouse …

Жди меня́ и я верну́сь … (Simonov)
Wait for me and I'll come back …

За что же, не боя́сь греха́,
куку́шка хва́лит петуха́? (Krylov)
Why does the cuckoo praise the rooster so shamelessly (lit.: without being afraid of
falling into sin [lying])?

И ску́чно и гру́стно, и не́кому ру́ку пода́ть … (Lermontov)
I am bored and lonely …

Испо́лнились мои́ жела́ния. (Pushkin)
My wishes are fulfilled.

Как усыпи́тельна жизнь! (Pasternak)
How somnolent is life!

Клён ты мой опа́вший, клён заледене́лый … (Esenin)
O you, my maple tree with fallen leaves …

Когда́ я но́чью жду её прихо́да … (Akhmatova)
When at night I am waiting for her to come …

Кра́сною ки́стью
Ряби́на зажгла́сь. (Tsvetaeva)
A rowan-tree was set afire by clusters of berries.

Кто со́здан из ка́мня, кто со́здан из гли́ны … (Tsvetaeva)
Some are created of stone, some are created of clay …

Любви́, наде́жды, ти́хой сла́вы
Недо́лго не́жил нас обма́н … (Pushkin)
We did not revel in the illusions of love, of hope, and of peaceful fame for long …

Люби́ть ины́х тяжёлый крест … (Pasternak)
To love some people is a heavy cross …

Люблю́ грозу́ в нача́ле ма́я … (Tiutchev)
I love a thunderstorm in the beginning of May …

Люблю́ тебя́, Петра́ творе́нье,
Люблю́ твой стро́гий, стро́йный вид … (Pushkin)
I love you so, Peter's creation, I love your stern, elegant appearance …

Мело́, мело́ по всей земле́ … (Pasternak)
The blizzard swept and swept all over the earth …

Мильо́ны—вас. Нас—тьмы́ и тьмы́ и тьмы́. (Blok)
There are millions of you. There are billions and billions of us!

Мне нра́вится, что вы больны́ не мной ... (Tsvetaeva)
I like it that you are [love-]sick not over me ...

Мои́м стиха́м, напи́санным так ра́но ... (Tsvetaeva)
My poems, written so early ...

Мой дар убо́г, и го́лос мой не гро́мок ... (Baratynsky)
My gift is meager and my voice is not loud ...

Мой дя́дя са́мых че́стных пра́вил,
Когда́ не в шу́тку занемо́г,
Он уважа́ть себя́ заста́вил,
И лу́чше вы́думать не мог ... (Pushkin)
My uncle was a man of the strictest morals; when he got seriously sick, he suddenly made everyone appreciate him, and could not have invented a better trick ...

Моро́з и со́лнце; день чуде́сный! (Pushkin)
The frost and the sun. The day is wonderful!

Москва́! Како́й огро́мный
Странноприи́мный дом! (Tsvetaeva)
Moscow! What a huge homeless shelter!

Нам не дано́ предугада́ть ... (Tiutchev)
We are not destined to foretell...

Настоя́щую не́жность не спу́таешь ... (Akhmatova)
Real tenderness can't be confused with anything ...

Не жале́ю, не зову́, не пла́чу ... (Esenin)
I do not regret, do not call out, do not cry ...

Не искуша́й меня́ без ну́жды
Возвра́том не́жности твое́й ... (Baratynsky)
Don't tempt me needlessly by showing me your tenderness again [Lit.: by returning your tenderness] ...

Не ослеплён я му́зою мое́ю ... (Baratynsky)
I am not dazzled by my muse ...

Не продаётся вдохнове́нье ...(Pushkin)
The inspiration is not for sale ...

Не самозва́нка—я пришла́ домо́й ... (Tsvetaeva)
Not an imposter—I came home ...

Не спи, не спи, худо́жник ... (Pasternak)
Don't sleep, don't sleep, artist ...

Никто́ ничего́ не о́тнял … (Tsvetaeva)
Nobody took away anything …

**Ни страны́, ни пого́ста
не хочу́ выбира́ть.** (Brodsky)
I don't want to choose either country or cemetery.

**Но я
            себя́
                    смиря́л,
                            становя́сь
на го́рло
            со́бственной пе́сне.** (Mayakovsky)
But I constrained myself, stepping on the throat of my own song.

Ночь, у́лица, фона́рь, апте́ка … (Blok)
Night, the street, a streetlamp, the drugstore …

О му́за пла́ча, прекра́снейшая из муз! (Tsvetaeva)
O Muse of lament, the most beautiful of Muses!

Облака́—вокру́г … (Tsvetaeva)
Clouds are all around …

О́браз твой, мучи́тельный и зы́бкий … (Mandelshtam)
Your image, tormenting and vacillating …

**Одна́жды, в студёную зи́мнюю по́ру,
Я и́з лесу вы́шел; был си́льный моро́з.** (Nekrasov)
Once in the cold winter, I came out of the forest; it was freezing.

**Одна́жды Ле́бедь, Рак да Щу́ка
Везти́ с покла́жей воз взяли́сь** … (Krylov)
Once, a swan, a crayfish and a pike agreed to draw a cart loaded with freight …

**Октя́брь уж наступи́л—уж ро́ща отряха́ет
После́дние листы́ с наги́х свои́х ветвей** … (Pushkin)
October is here already: the grove shakes off the last leaves from its naked limbs …

Отвори́те мне темни́цу … (Lermontov)
Open up my prison …

Отговори́ла ро́ща золота́я … (Esenin)
The golden grove has ceased talking …

**Печа́льно я гляжу́ на на́ше поколе́нье!
Его́ гряду́щее, иль пу́сто, иль темно́** … (Lermontov)
I look sadly at our generation: its future is either empty or dark …

Печа́льный де́мон, дух изгна́нья ... (Lermontov)
A sad Demon, the spirit of exile ...

**По вечера́м над рестора́нами
Горя́чий во́здух дик и глух** ... (Blok)
In the evenings, over the restaurants the hot air is wild and muffled ...

Поги́б Поэ́т! —нево́льник че́сти ... (Lermontov)
The Poet perished! —the slave of honor ...

Пора́, мой друг, пора́! Поко́я се́рдце про́сит ... (Pushkin)
Tis time, my friend, tis time! My heart is begging for rest ...

Послу́шайте! (Mayakovsky)
Listen!

Поэ́т—издалека́ заво́дит речь. (Tsvetaeva)
A poet takes his speech from afar.

**Поэ́том мо́жешь ты не быть,
Но граждани́ном быть обя́зан. (**Nekrasov)
You may not be a poet, but a citizen you must be.

**Проща́й, немы́тая Росси́я,
Страна́ рабо́в, страна́ госпо́д** ... (Lermontov)
Farewell, unwashed Russia, the country of slaves and masters ...

**Пусто́е *вы* серде́чным *ты*
Она, обмо́лвясь, замени́ла** ... (Pushkin)
The empty *you are* by the heartfelt *thou art* she substituted through a slip of the tongue ...

Пью го́речь туберо́з ... (Pasternak)
I drink the raw bitterness of tuberoses ...

Рождённые в года́ глухи́е ... (Blok)
Those born in godforsaken years ...

Ро́слый стрело́к, осторо́жный охо́тник ... (Pasternak)
Tall shooter, careful hunter ...

Росси́я, ни́щая Росси́я ... (Blok)
Russia, poverty-ridden Russia ...

Сестра́ моя—жизнь ... (Pasternak)
Life is my sister ...

**Сижу́ за решёткой в темни́це сыро́й,
Вскормлённый в нево́ле орёл молодо́й.** (Pushkin)
A young eagle brought up in captivity, I am behind bars in a damp dungeon.

Смея́ться, пра́во, не грешно́
Над все́м, что ка́жется смешно́. (Karamzin)
It is really not a sin to laugh at anything that seems funny.

Ты жива́ ещё, моя́ стару́шка? (Esenin)
Are you still alive, my old dear?

Ты запроки́дываешь го́лову … (Tsvetaeva)
You throw back your head …

Ты, меня́ люби́вший фа́льшью … (Tsvetaeva)
You, who loved me with the falseness of truth …

Ты со́лнце в вы́си мне за́стишь … (Tsvetaeva)
You obstruct the sun in the sky for me …

У лукомо́рья дуб зелёный;
Злата́я цепь на ду́бе том:
И днём и но́чью кот учёный
Всё хо́дит по́ цепи круго́м …(Pushkin)
By the curving shore of the sea there grows a green oak, and on that oak there is a
golden chain. Day and night, a learned [trained] cat paces that chain …

Улица провали́лась, как нос сифили́тика …(Mayakovsky)
The street caved in, like the nose of a syphilitic …

Умо́м Росси́ю не поня́ть … (Tiutchev)
One cannot comprehend Russia rationally …

Февра́ль. Доста́ть черни́л и пла́кать! (Pasternak)
February. Get the ink and sob!

Цыга́ны шу́мною толпо́й
По Бессара́бии кочу́ют. (Pushkin)
A noisy crowd of gypsies roams through Bessarabia.

Что ж де́лать? (Lermontov)
What shall I do?

Что мо́жет со́бственных Плато́нов
И бы́стрых ра́зумом Невто́нов
Росси́йская земля́ рожда́ть. (Lomonosov)
The Russian land can give birth to its own Platos and quick-minded Newtons.

Шёпот, ро́бкое дыха́нье … (Fet)
A whisper, the faintest breath …

Я вас люби́л. Любо́вь ещё, быть мо́жет,
В душе́ мое́й уга́сла не совсе́м … (Pushkin)
I loved you once. This love might not yet be extinguished in my heart …

Я встре́тил вас—и всё было́е
В отжи́вшем се́рдце ожило́ … (Tiutchev)
I met you—and all the past came alive in my tired heart …

Я па́мятник себе́ воздви́г нерукотво́рный. (Pushkin)
I have erected a monument to myself not built by hands.

Я по́мню чу́дное мгнове́нье … (Pushkin)
I remember a wonderful moment …

Я пришёл к тебе с приве́том,
Рассказа́ть, что со́лнце вста́ло … (Fet)
I came to you with a greeting, to tell you that the sun is risen …

Я пришла́ к поэ́ту в го́сти. (Akhmatova)
I came to visit the poet.

Я сиде́л у окна́ в перепо́лненном за́ле. (Blok)
I sat in a crowded room near the window.

Я сло́во позабы́л, что я хоте́л сказа́ть … (Mandelshtam)
I forgot something that I wanted to say …

Я царь—я раб, я червь—я бог. (Derzhavin)
I am a king, and I am a slave, I am a worm, and I am a god.

English Index   Указатель

Russian Index

Указатель